ROY HATTERSLEY

Roy Hattersley was elected to Parliament in 1964. He served in Harold Wilson's government and in Jim Callaghan's Cabinet. In 1983 he became deputy leader of the Labour Party. As well as contributing to a host of national newspapers, he has written twenty-five books, including *The Edwardians*; *Borrowed Time: The Story of Britain Between the Wars*; *In Search of England*; acclaimed biographies of John Wesley and Lloyd George, and most recently, *The Devonshires*. Roy Hattersley has been visiting Fellow of Harvard's Institute of Politics and of Nuffield College, Oxford. In 2003 he was elected a Fellow of the Royal Society of Literature.

ALSO BY ROY HATTERSLEY

Non-fiction

Nelson

Goodbye to Yorkshire

Politics Apart

Endpiece Revisited

Press Gang

A Yorkshire Boyhood

Choose Freedom

Between Ourselves

Who Goes Home?

Fifty Years On

Buster's Diaries

Blood and Fire

A Brand from the Burning

The Edwardians

Campbell Bannerman

Buster's Secret Diaries

Borrowed Time

In Search of England

David Lloyd George

The Devonshires

The Socialist Way (editor)

Fiction

The Maker's Mark

In That Quiet Earth

Skylark's Song

ROY HATTERSLEY

The Catholics

The Church and its People in Britain and
Ireland, from the Reformation to the
Present Day

VINTAGE

1 3 5 7 9 10 8 6 4 2

Vintage
20 Vauxhall Bridge Road,
London SW1V 2SA

Vintage is part of the Penguin Random House group of companies
whose addresses can be found at global.penguinrandomhouse.com.

Penguin
Random House
UK

Copyright © Roy Hattersley 2017

Roy Hattersley has asserted his right to be identified as the author
of this Work in accordance with the Copyright, Designs and
Patents Act 1988

First published by Vintage in 2018
First published by Chatto & Windus in 2017

penguin.co.uk/vintage

A CIP catalogue record for this book is available from the British Library

ISBN 9780099587545

Printed and bound by Clays Ltd, St Ives plc

Penguin Random House is committed to a sustainable future for
our business, our readers and our planet. This book is made
from Forest Stewardship Council® certified paper.

In memory of my father, Frederick Roy Hattersley
Born, July 24th 1902
Ordained priest, April 24th 1927
Said last Mass, January 17th 1932
Died, December 10th 1972

Contents

Author's Notes

A number of terms need early definition:

Lay priest: a priest living in the community – now more often called a secular
Oblate: a person dedicated to monastic life
Recusant: a person who refuses submission to an authority or compliance with a regulation
Regular or regular priest: belonging to a religious or monastic Order
Secular or secular priest: not bound by the rules of a religious Order
Ultramontane: advocating supreme papal authority in matters of faith and discipline.

Quotations always appear in their original, neither corrected nor modernised, form. I have not followed strange usages with the explanation '*sic*'.

Introduction

The history of the Catholic Church in Great Britain and Ireland is an anthology of adventure stories. Not all of them have happy endings. But each one is a triumph of faith and a victory for the moral certainty that provides the confidence that reasonable doubt cannot guarantee. Catholics gain both courage and comfort from the knowledge that, no matter how much pressure is put on a principle, it will not break. They survived the long years of persecution, proscription and prejudice that began with the Reformation because their faith allowed no compromise. Men and women do not willingly die in defence of common sense and sweet reason. The Catholics who were executed at Tyburn were sustained in their sacrifice by convictions that were unclouded by doubt.

Religion in general – the belief in the unbelievable – fascinates me. That is one of the reasons why I wrote biographies of John Wesley and William Booth, the founder of the Salvation Army. Their faith was attractive because of its brash vitality. It is the gospel of certainty that attracts me to Catholicism – though as an observer rather than as a participant. With the exception of sanctity of life and the need to create a more equal society, I am riddled with doubt about every philosophical precept and can find exceptions to every moral rule. So I can only envy men and women who – thanks to the received truth of scripture, the writings of the early Fathers and the judgement of St Peter's successors – *know*, more often than not, what is right and what is wrong.

I began to feel a detached admiration for Catholics and Catholicism during my early teens. It was the result, I now realise, of stories told to me by my father during apparently unreligious conversations. I learned that St Damien had sacrificed his life to serve a leper colony and that a priest, whose name I no longer remember, had neglected saying his offices in order to succour a sick pauper and had been rewarded by a vision of Christ which was an endorsement of his priorities. I never wondered why my father – a lowly local-government officer who went, with my mother, to Church of England evensong – knew that Bonnie Prince Charlie's brother had been made the Cardinal Archbishop of Frascati and that Nicholas Breakspear, the only English Pope, had given Henry II dominion over Ireland. Nor was I in the least surprised when – during the visits to historic churches that we often made together – he translated the Latin tombstone inscriptions on sight.

The conundrum, which I had not recognised in youth, was unravelled a month before my fortieth birthday and ten days after my father's death. One of the accumulated condolence letters, which I opened at my mother's request, began, 'as you will know ...' and continued, 'we were at the English College in Rome together and were young priests in the diocese of which I became bishop'. The Right Reverend William Ellis left me to find out for myself that my father – parish priest of St Joseph's church in Shirebrook, Nottingham – had met my mother after he agreed to 'instruct' her for admission to the Catholic Church in anticipation of her marriage to a young collier. Father Hattersley had performed the wedding ceremony. Two weeks later the priest and the bride ran away together. For the next forty-five years they lived in bliss – married after my mother's first husband died in 1951.

The last episode of the story was recounted to me by an ancient Catholic priest – Monsignor 'Frick' Wilson – who ventured out from his Blackpool retirement home to meet me during a lull in the Labour Party Conference. He spoke of my father with great affection, before weeping at the memory of their last meeting. He and William Ellis had been deputed to persuade the miscreant to return to the Church. 'We were,' he said, 'far too censorious. Had we been more forgiving he would have recognised his error.' I chose to disagree. 'By then he and my mother had a son ...' Monsignor Wilson responded with what he clearly regarded as reassurance: 'We would have found someone to look after the lad.' He had apparently forgotten that the lad was me.

Wilson's single-minded concern with bringing the sinner to repentance illustrated the inhumanity that sometimes characterises the absolutist view of the Roman Catholic obligation. Worse examples than Wilson's insensitivity are scrupulously recorded in *The Catholics*. So are the acts of murderous brutality that were committed in the Church's name. But during the six centuries from the Reformation to the present day, the Catholics of Great Britain and Ireland were far more sinned against that sinning. The faith survived because of the courage of the faithful and the certainty with which their convictions were held. Courage and certainty are qualities to be admired. And they make the history of the Catholic Church and its people a series of adventure stories, some of which have happy endings.

PART ONE

The Making of a Minority

CHAPTER 1

As Far as the Law of God Allows

The Reformation was an idea, not an event. Ideas mature slowly. So it is impossible to ascribe its origin to any one date. But the time and place at which the challenge to the Church of Rome gained irresistible momentum can be identified. On October 31st 1517, Martin Luther nailed a copy of his Ninety-Five Theses to the door of the castle church in the German city of Wittenberg, and what came to be called Protestantism – already a force in northern Europe – had a hero and a text around which its sympathisers could rally. The Theses were best known, and became most resented by the Church, because of their attack on the sale of indulgences. But they amounted to a comprehensive assault on Roman Catholic theology as well as on the conduct of the Roman Church. The two complaints were indivisible. The sale of indulgences – the exploitation of simple laymen by a corrupt priesthood – could not be separated from the belief that tormented souls languished in purgatory until enough of their friends and relations had bought their redemption. The idea that one man's redemption was dependent on another's generosity was too absurd to escape Luther's excoriation. And he examined the whole body of Catholic doctrine with the same calm logic and in the same explosive language. The Ninety-Five Theses challenged the whole dogma, authority and conduct of the Roman Catholic Church. It was the arguments they raised, not disagreement over the validity of a marriage, which sustained the long years of the English Reformation.

At the time of the Theses' publication, Henry VIII of England rejected, without very much thought, the concepts on which they were based. He accepted the authority of the Pope and the dogma of the Church of Rome. He believed that the Virgin Mary interceded on behalf of sinners and that, during the Eucharist, the wine and the wafer were transubstantiated into the body and blood of Christ. The idea that men of humble origin were capable of understanding the Bible for themselves he regarded as both dangerous and absurd. So, in his opinion, was the contention that, because Christ had been sacrificed to redeem the world, men could be saved by faith alone. The priesthood he knew to be, in part, corrupt. But he regarded corruption as endemic throughout society. Henry was not a good man, but he was, at the time, a good Catholic – more out of habit than conviction. When he was eventually persuaded to denounce Martin Luther (or arranged for others to denounce the apostate in his name), the polemic that he published represented his genuine, if recently dormant, views.

Luther's early work had been sold in England, without its sale being suppressed or denounced as the propagation of heresy. Its free circulation did not survive a sequence of events that began on June 15th 1520, when their author was formally excommunicated. Luther retaliated by publicly burning the Papal Bull by which he had been anathematised and publishing three tracts – *On the Liberty of a Christian Man*, *An Address to the Nobility of the German Nation* and *On the Babylonian Capture of the Church of God*. They were all direct attacks on the Pope and the papacy and, in consequence, made the campaign to proscribe Luther's work – burning his books and prosecuting those who read them – irresistible throughout the Holy Roman Empire. England (notorious, then as now, for its semi-detachment from continental Europe) did not immediately join in the required destruction. The Vatican sent a stern message which demanded compliance.

Thomas Wolsey – a cardinal since 1515, Papal Legate, holder of numerous other honours and offices, both Roman and English, and a defeated candidate for the papacy – received a letter from an exasperated Pope Leo X, which asked, ironically, if he possessed enough power to take the necessary action.[1] William Warham, both Chancellor of Oxford University and Archbishop of Canterbury, reinforced the demand for suppression of the offending tracts with the warning that Luther's writing was growing increasingly popular within the university. Cambridge, he added in resentful embarrassment, had already ordered its proctors to confiscate and burn Protestant work.

Wolsey responded in a manner which was consistent with his character. He commanded the organisation of a book-burning extravaganza. It was held at St Paul's Cross on May 12th 1521 and was preceded by a service in the cathedral. The Cardinal approached the Cross under a golden canopy which was held above him by four doctors of divinity. The Archbishop of Canterbury was in attendance but John Fisher, the Bishop of Rochester, preached the sermon. Being a man of generous disposition, as well as a scholar, he commended Luther's personal purity, but condemned the arrogance with which he disputed papal authority. The pieties being complete, Wolsey read the full text of the bull of excommunication to a crowd which was estimated to be 30,000 strong. The offending books were ceremoniously burned. Wolsey then, reverentially, displayed the manuscript of a book which he said had been written by the King himself. It was entitled *Assertio Septem Sacramentorum*.

Wolsey was, at best, exaggerating. *The Defence of the Seven Sacraments* was based on the work of a number of scholars, which – after Thomas More had acted as a 'sorter-out and placer of the principal matters contained therein'[2] – Henry, in effect, edited. It is not clear who – the King or More – should take credit for the literary style. Luther was dismissed as 'a venomous serpent ... infernal wolf ... detestable trumpeter of pride'.[3] The vulgar abuse proved popular, and translations were made as gifts for the German Protestant princes. A special copy – its binding decorated with gold and jewels and with poetry written by the King himself in the form of a dedication – was presented to the Pope in October 1521. Shortly afterwards its 'author' received the title that he and his successors were to retain, with doubtful legitimacy, for the next five hundred years.

Henry was not made Defender of the Faith, as is popularly supposed, as a reward for the publication of the *Assertio Septem Sacramentorum* in his name. As early as 1512 the King's emissaries had petitioned Julius II to grant him a title which was comparable to those in which the Most Christian King of France and the Most Catholic King of Spain rejoiced. Their suggestions included King Apostolic and Protector of the Holy See. Despite the petition being presented time after time for nine years, Julius had not responded. Then Leo X succeeded to the papal throne and, in May 1521, the English emissaries petitioned again, adding the publication of the *Assertio* to the arguments in support of a the claim to a papal honour. The new Pope did not think that the pleasure of frustrating Henry's wishes was worth the tedium of arguing with his petitioners. So the King of England became *Fidei Defensor*. The title was granted to Henry for a lifetime of loyalty and was meant to be a personal award. It was an Act of Parliament, passed in the reign of Elizabeth I, which bestowed it on English monarchs in perpetuity. By then 'the faith' was no longer the faith of Rome.

Martin Luther read a German translation of *Assertio* in the year that followed its presentation to the Pope. His published reply was as notable for its vituperation as for its theology. So – although others, who should have known better, followed suit – he must share with King Henry much of the blame for the degeneration of the argument into an exchange of insults. Luther described the King as a 'deaf adder', a 'miserable scribbler' and a 'fool'.[4] Henry did not condescend to respond in public, though he wrote, in private, to the Duke of Saxony to remind him of the vicissitudes that Catholic princes had to endure.

Instead, John Fisher contested Luther's theological argument, point by point, in an erudite disquisition on the indisputable power of Rome. Its title, *The Defence of the King's Assertion Against Babylonian Captivity*, was an image stolen from the unauthorised, and therefore schismatic, translation of the Bible by William Tyndale. But even the scrupulous Bishop of Rochester felt no obligation to acknowledge his debt to a known dissident and heretic. Thomas More – undoubtedly at the King's request – replied to Luther with a short volume of abuse, which he composed in 1522 but held back from publication until King Henry had completed and sent the more measured letter to the Duke of Saxony.

Although Wolsey arranged a series of book-burnings in outlying parishes, he must have realised that it was impossible to destroy or confiscate every copy of all the books named on the continually expanding 'index' of forbidden works. The best that could be done was a public show of moral outrage. So a second ceremonial book-burning was arranged. A thunderstorm – so violent that the burning had to take place inside the church rather than at St Paul's Cross – did nothing to convince the organisers that God did not approve of their decision. Once again Wolsey was supported by the princes of the English Church, and once again John Fisher preached the sermon. An added feature of the service was the parade of convicted heretics. Among them were Robert Barnes, an Augustinian friar who had been under arrest since he was interrogated by Wolsey; Henry Pickles, the vicar of All Hallows in London (who had replied to the charge of reading Luther with the defence that, since it was in Latin, he could not have understood it); and three merchants from the Hanseatic League (of German traders) who had been found guilty of importing heretical literature. They all had faggots – the badge of heresy and the symbol of the heretic's fate – tied round their necks and, throughout the service, knelt in supplication. Each of them recanted, but Robert Barnes was returned to the Fleet prison. He escaped before he could face his trial by bishops. Pickles and the Hansa merchants were released after they had promised to be of good behaviour and were warned that, if they lapsed again into heresy, there would be no second chance of their escaping death by burning.

Man's ingenuity and his insatiable desire for knowledge – especially knowledge that he has been forbidden to acquire – made it impossible for the book-burners even to reduce the number of forbidden volumes in circulation. And they were attempting to extinguish a fire which had burned for two hundred years. Making 'knowledge' freely available, rather than 'secret' to the priesthood, had been an essential element of the Protestant faith ever since 1378 when John Wyclif had contended – in his treatise *On Truth and the Holy Writ* – that an English translation of the testaments was essential to the belief that Christians could commune with God without the intercession of saints or priest. The Lollards, who followed Wyclif's teaching, had done their best to find and distribute vernacular testaments. The numbers had been so small that – although the reading of unauthorised versions of the Bible had been illegal in England since 1410 – the Church had done little more than disapprove. When, in or about 1525, William Tyndale – a West Country school master – started to make a new English translation, the threat of unregulated knowledge began to be taken seriously.

The rise of Protestantism, and Luther's intellectual aggression, made Tyndale a greater threat than Wyclif had ever been. Anticipating arrest, he fled to Germany, where his work was finished and published. Not only was his bible more easily available than any earlier unauthorised version, but it had become one of the texts of an international theological revolution. Tyndale had visited Luther to pledge his support for the Protestant cause and his treatise, *The Obedience of the Christian Man*, proclaimed that 'the pope's doctrine is not of God'. But the offence of which he was convicted, condemned and eventually burned was not the dissemination of heretical ideas. It was the sin of making it possible for the laity to read the Bible themselves – a prospect so vile that Wolsey instructed the whole Church to rise up in defence of the clergy's exclusive right to receive, directly, the Word of God.

Most of the episcopate responded to the call to arms with undisguised enthusiasm. Cuthbert Tunstall, Bishop of London, instructed – on pain of excommunication – every archdeacon in his diocese to demand that all copies of the Tyndale Bible be handed to Church authorities within thirty days of the announcement. In the parishes, the edict – which was unenforced and unenforceable – was greeted with some defiance and much weary cynicism. Father John Parkyns of St Andrew's, Eastcheap, told a friend, 'If I had twenty books of the Holy Scriptures translated into English, I would bring none of them in for my Lord of London, curse he or bless he, for he does it so that we should have no knowledge but keeps it secret to himself.'[5]

The enemies of Protestantism had still to learn that men may be executed, but ideas do not die. The suppression of Luther's theology was as impossible as the suppression of his books. It had already taken root. In Cambridge, the White Horse Tavern had become so notorious for harbouring men who would not have their thoughts circumscribed that it was known as 'Little Germany'. The leaders of the group – including Robert Barnes and Thomas Bilney, a Cambridge divinity graduate – were certainly attracted by Luther's theology. But some of its members were true to Rome and attended because they were interested in ideas. From time to time Stephen Gardiner – the Bishop of Winchester, one-time private secretary to King Henry and a sufficiently reliable Roman Catholic eventually to become Mary Tudor's Lord Chancellor – joined the discussions. It was because of its ecumenical membership that the King and Court – still violently opposed to Luther and all his work – were willing, for a time, to tolerate what they believed to be harmlessly academic activities. They did not remain harmlessly academic for long.

The first offence was impudence. Two regular visitors to 'Little Germany' – William Roy and Simon Fish – wrote and produced within the Tavern a play which mocked the pride and pomp of the episcopacy. Roy himself played the main character in a way which left no doubt that Wolsey was the target of his scorn. That notwithstanding, the two men were allowed to slip, discreetly, away to the Netherlands, but on Christmas Eve 1525, Barnes – back in England – abandoned comedy and preached a sermon which denounced the celebration of holy days. That could not be overlooked or brushed aside. He was summoned to appear before Wolsey who, at first, passed lightly over questions of faith, but then asked for Barnes' opinion about satire on extravagance in high places. Much to his credit, Barnes replied – with courage if not relevance – that Wolsey would be a better Christian if he gave all his wealth to the poor. The Cardinal changed tack again and said that the assault on feast days would have to be referred to a tribunal of bishops – and then, surprisingly if not sincerely, wished Barnes well.[6] The Cardinal had more important things on his mind.

Books disputing the truth and wisdom of the Roman Catholic religion were coming into England in increasing numbers. In 1526 – after several members of 'Little Germany' moved from Cambridge to Oxford to teach in Wolsey's new Cardinal's College – banned books were found buried in a field near the university. Twenty-two suspects were interrogated. Half of them admitted their offence and were imprisoned. In 1529 a change of tactics followed the appointment of Thomas More as Chancellor. Wrongful reading was to be suppressed by the burning both of books and of the men who were found to possess them.

Execution of one sort or another – burning, beheading or hanging with attendant butchery – was already the usual punishment for spreading the ideas which the prohibited books contained. But there was still an army of willing martyrs who were prepared to risk – indeed, to embrace – the flames. In 1525 Thomas Bilney, one of the regular visitors to 'Little Germany', had been granted a preaching licence by the Bishop of Ely. Although he had promised, on oath, not to spread the Lutheran heresies, his sermons reflected, if they did not advocate, Luther's criticisms of Catholicism. He condemned the worship of saints, denounced lighting candles before statues and argued that the Church required the observations of so many regulations that failure to comply was unavoidable. He was arraigned before two archbishops and eight bishops, who took it in turn to examine him about twenty-four 'errors' which they had discovered in his sermons. Some of his answers satisfied his interrogators. Others did not. It was clear that he was not a Lutheran but, almost as bad, a man of independent thought and judgement.

Cuthbert Tunstall, the Bishop of London, pressed Bilney to recant. He refused, with the claim that nothing he had said offended against the teaching of the Church. His defence guaranteed that he was condemned as a 'contumacious heretic'. Tunstall, still hopeful of recantation, did not pronounce sentence and was rewarded when Bilney eventually agreed that in seven of the twenty-four 'errors' of which he had been accused, the case against him had been proved. He agreed only to preach when given explicit permission to do so, and carried a faggot in procession to St Paul's Cross, where he stood, head bent in shame, throughout the subsequent service. His reward was imprisonment for life, rather than death, the usual fate of heretics.

Bilney had served a year of his prison sentence when he was allowed to return to Cambridge. His promise to preach only when given permission, was kept for as long as his conscience allowed. Then, after announcing that he was 'going up to Jerusalem',[7] he set off for Norwich where – often in fields, since no church was open to him – he preached, as before, against the veneration of saints and the worship of statues. Only one result was possible. Thomas Bilney was convicted as a lapsed heretic and burned at the stake. The epoch of religious martyrdom had begun. The charges became more numerous and the offences more widely defined. In 1532, Thomas Bennet in Exeter, Thomas Harding in Chesham and James Bainham in Bristol were executed for doing no more than expressing sympathy with unspecified Protestant dogma.[8]

In Norwich, Thomas Bilney's execution had been followed by half-hearted demonstrations of sympathy and support. But England was still a Catholic country and most of the Protestant martyrs went to their deaths unmourned. Some of them went to their place of execution accompanied by the excoriation of the mob. In Exeter, Thomas Bennet was stopped on his way to the stake by citizens who threatened to carry out the execution themselves and told him, 'Whoresome heretic. Pray to Our Lady and say *Sancta Maria ora pro nobis*, or by God's wounds I will make thee do it.'[9] In Chesham, a hotbed of Lollardry, the fire that consumed Thomas Harding was fed by wood carried to the pyre by local children.[10] The people's ardour was encouraged by carefully contrived miracles. When a fire almost destroyed the parish church in Rickmansworth, John Longland, the Bishop of Lincoln, announced that it had been the work of heretics and, despite an equal lack of evidence, attributed the preservation of the host and rood screen to divine intervention.

The time was fast approaching when all of England would be required to change its religious allegiance. In the year that Thomas Bilney was executed, Sir Thomas Boleyn of Kent – the father of Anne – told the Papal Nuncio that England 'cared neither for pope or popes'. Henry was 'both pope and emperor in his own kingdom'.[11] The King was about to end the burning of men because they rejected the Pope's doctrine, and start burning them because they upheld the Pope's authority. The Henrician Reformation was under way.

It is understandable that Cardinal Reginald Pole, the most powerful statesman and one of the most distinguished theologians of Mary Tudor's reign, should have chosen to attribute the whole English Reformation to 'fleshy will, full of carnal concupiscence'.[12] But Pole must have known that Henry's rage to marry Anne Boleyn swiftly turned into a passion to rule – supreme and unlimited – in his own kingdom, and that England accepted the rejection of Rome for far more complicated reasons than solidarity with the King in his determination to have a new wife and a male heir. The Pope's refusal to make way for the new union, by endorsing the annulment of Henry's marriage to Catherine of Aragon, was the occasion, not the fundamental cause, of a schism that was bound to have happened sooner or later. The King's temperament made the break from Rome likely. The disposition of the English people – pragmatic, insular and religiously indolent – made it inevitable.

At first, Henry was determined to dispose of his old wife with the blessing and approval of the Pope, and he worked hard and waited long to convince Rome that he could be lawfully married to Anne. His motives were more complicated than simply respect for the Holy Father or sympathy for the discarded queen. He was fearful of offending powerful foreign princes and did not anticipate that most of the 'devout Catholics' at Court – far from opposing him – would lamely accept and articulate views on papal supremacy which, before the great schism, they had denounced as heresy. Romantic fiction paints a portrait of a briefly infatuated king and a beautiful young woman who withheld her favours from him until they were married. Authors disagree about the lady's motives. Some say that she was chaste. Others insist that she was merely ambitious. Of one thing we can be sure: whether or not Henry was deeply in love with Anne Boleyn, he was certainly out of love with Catherine and profoundly – and, by the standards of the time, legitimately – concerned by her apparent inability to produce a male heir, guarantee the succession and ensure that England was not, once again, rent by dynastic wars.

After much agonising about the future of the kingdom – and a little agonising about the future of his soul – Henry came to the convenient conclusion that he was, or should be, free to marry Anne. He had, he decided, offended Providence by entering into an unlawful union with Catherine. The offence had been committed when he was a boy of fifteen, acting under his father's instructions. But that in no way reduced his guilt. Catherine had been married to Prince Arthur, Henry's elder brother. On his death she had, for reasons of state, become the wife of the new heir apparent. Marriage to the widow of a deceased brother was against the law, but there had been some argument about whether or not Catherine's first marriage had been consummated. Young Arthur's boast that he had spent 'all his wedding night in Aragon' was generally attributed to youthful wishful thinking. But, back in 1509, Julius II had agreed to avoid all possible embarrassment to Prince Henry and his family by granting a dispensation which said, in effect, that if the marriage between Arthur and Catherine had ever been lawful, the law was overruled.

When, in 1527, the 1509 dispensation had become an obstacle rather than a convenience, Henry responded by showing a laudable respect for the Old Testament as well as a remarkable knowledge of its contents. He quoted Leviticus, Chapter 20, Verse 21: 'If a man marries his brother's wife, it is an act of impurity.' Reliance on the scriptures rather than on their interpretation by Rome was a Protestant way to behave. But it was realpolitik, not dogma, that made the Pope, Clement VII, unsympathetic to Henry's cause. Queen Catherine was the aunt of Charles V of Spain and, while Henry was deciding how to pursue his claim that she had never been his legal wife, the Holy Roman Emperor had invaded Italy and taken the Pope prisoner. Clement was neither in the position nor the mood to rule that Charles' aunt had lived in sin with Henry for twenty years. There was a moment of fantasy when Wolsey suggested setting up a rival papacy in Avignon, forging a new alliance with France and declaring, *ex cathedra*, that Henry was free to marry. No one else found merit in the proposal.

What little hope there was of the Pope acting against the interests of the Emperor's family depended on his agreement to send an emissary to London with the instruction to prepare, with Wolsey, an opinion on Henry's claim. Before he left, the Pope and the Emperor were reconciled. Clement had no intention of risking a renewal of hostilities. And, thanks to the return of confidence which followed the rapprochement, the Pope was explicit that if Henry had a request to make, he – or his representative – must travel to Rome to make it. The message was accompanied by rumours from Rome that Henry's submission had indeed offended, by implying that biblical texts were superior to papal pronouncements. Henry's emissaries, nevertheless, made the journey. Their claim was rejected.

Wolsey appealed to Clement to establish a 'decretal commission' which would first set out the law in principle and then decide how it applied in Henry's case. The idea, he argued, should be attractive to both Pope and King. No appeal against its findings would be possible. So there would be no question of the Pope coming under pressure to offend the Emperor by supporting Henry's claim. The Pope's agreement to the proposal was unrelated to either its merits or its ingenuity. Wolsey was Rome's only true friend at the English court and needed some sort of victory to guarantee the continuation of the King's favours. Henry agreed to the scheme because he foolishly assumed that, with Wolsey a member, he could rely on the commission's findings being in his favour.

Pope Clement announced his agreement in April 1528. Six months later, Cardinal Campeggio arrived in London to chair the commission. The wheels of Rome ground slowly. The commission opened its proceedings in June 1529 – by which time its purpose had already been undermined. Knowing that the conclusions could not be the subject of an appeal to Rome, Catherine had petitioned the Pope before the proceedings began. John Fisher, the Bishop of Rochester, who bravely acted as counsel for the Queen, was addressing the court with a vigorous defence of Pope Julius' dispensation when Charles V – in a sudden change of allegiance – turned on the French army that was besieging the Pope in his own capital. The rescue confirmed the Pope's dependence on the all-powerful Emperor's goodwill. Clement announced, 'I have quite made up my mind to become an imperialist'[13] and disbanded the decretal commission.

Henry had lost all hope of immediate papal support and endorsement of his divorce – or, as he would have it, annulment. Wolsey's enemies announced that the collapse of the commission was conclusive proof that the Cardinal had failed in his duty to the King. An indictment was drawn up. It included 'the abomination, ruin and seditious and erroneous violations used at the pulling down of the abbeys'[14] – the dissolution of the monasteries for which Henry had been directly responsible. Wolsey fell, although – by the standards of the time – he was treated with a leniency that amounted to indulgence.

All hope of legitimising the King's divorce depended on the King's advisers finding, or inventing, proof that two Popes were wrong – Julius II for issuing the dispensation that declared Prince Arthur's marriage invalid, and Clement VII for upholding that decision. The newest recruit to the group of scholars who had prepared his case for the aborted decretal commission was Thomas Cranmer, sometime Fellow of Jesus College, Cambridge, habitué of 'Little Germany' and public opponent of papal power. He suggested that the legitimacy of Julius' dispensation should be examined by academic authorities on canon law – itself an implication that the Pope could be wrong. Emissaries with the mandate to prove that Henry was free to marry were despatched to all the universities and libraries of Europe. Among them was Reginald Pole, a descendant of the Plantagenet Duke of Clarence and a temporary royal favourite. Pole was a devout believer in papal authority – a theological view that was to qualify him to become Mary Tudor's First Minister. His agreement to participate in what he must have known to be a sham, designed to provide spurious proof of a legal opinion which he knew to be false, illustrates one of the shameful truths about the Reformation. In England, few men in high places remained true either to Rome or to the Reformation. Constancy was the prerogative of the humble and the meek.

Pole – whose studies in Padua had been financed by the King – had returned to England faithful to the Church of Rome, but a humanist who, under the influence of Erasmus, believed that its teaching should reflect the realities of earthly existence as well as the hope of heaven. He had taken up residence in the Carthusian monastery at Sheen and was appointed Dean of Exeter *in absentia*. After the fall of Wolsey, when it became clear to even the most preoccupied scholar that Henry was going to marry Anne, he had applied to the King for permission to continue his studies in the University of Paris. It was then that Henry had the idea of making him his Paris advocate. So Pole's wish was granted. He left for Paris with the King's blessing and a gift of £100, in return for his promise to argue the merits of a case in which he did not believe.

Pole was doubly unsuited to the task before him. As well as respecting the authority of the Pope, he had personal reasons for opposing Henry's plans. His mother, the Countess of Salisbury, was a close friend of Queen Catherine and governess to the Princess Mary, whose status would be changed, by an annulment, from heir presumptive to bastard. Yet he agreed. Not only did he accept the King's commission, but he set about his task with such determination that Henry awarded him an additional £70 and he received, from the King himself, a letter which expressed royal approval in the most fulsome terms: 'To your dexterity and faithfulness we ascribe the furtherance of our cause.'[15] Unfortunately for Henry, the exercise of those qualities did not have the desired result. Paris found against the King. Pole was recalled and, despite the failure of his mission, was showered with gratitude.

Cardinal Wolsey died in November 1530. Pole – just thirty and yet to be ordained priest – was offered the vacant Archbishopric of York, on condition that he confirmed his support for the royal annulment. His reply was both craven and bold. He opposed the annulment in the King's own interest. Were it to be ruled that the marriage to Catherine was invalid, Henry would have lived in sin for twenty years. The King stood 'on the brink of the water and may yet save all his honour. But if he put forth his foot one step forward, all his honour is gone.'[16] His warning to Henry might have cost a less-favoured man his head. But Pole persisted. Henry – dissatisfied but, for once, not vengeful – agreed that Pole should leave England for ever. He was to return in righteous glory when the Princess became the Catholic Queen of England.

Throughout Europe, independent scholars were near to unanimous in their judgement that Henry's marriage to Catherine had been lawful. A majority of university faculties – some of them bribed – favoured the King's contention that it was not. The findings which supported the King's case were based on the supposed evidence that, since ancient times, a king had been absolutely sovereign in his own country. They were collected in a volume entitled *Collectanea Satis Copiosa* and the King, having decreed that there was enough evidence to support his cause, prepared for the battle by leaving the episcopate in no doubt that they had to choose between giving him their support and incurring his profound animosity. At the Convocation that met at Canterbury in January 1531, Henry threatened to issue a writ of *Praemunire* (unlawfully asserting or upholding papal jurisdiction) against the entire clergy – citing, as reason for the prosecution, the whole episcopate's complicity in what he chose to misrepresent as the treachery of the late Cardinal Wolsey. The bishops knew they had not 'applied the laws of an alien jurisdiction against the sovereignty of the monarch'. But they had no doubt that Henry was prepared to charge them with the offence and find them guilty. So when, in his benevolence, the King was prepared to grant a general pardon if Convocation was sufficiently contrite, they gladly agreed. Contrition, Henry estimated, cost £100,000 (£35 million in today's prices). That, Henry calculated, would compensate him for the expense he had incurred by pursuing, on the bishops' advice, the divorce suit which, they should have known, Rome would dismiss out of hand. After some half-hearted haggling, Convocation paid the full amount.

Henry announced his intention to prepare (or to have prepared) a document which defined his own and the episcopate's role within the Church. Although they expected that their powers would be drastically reduced, many of the bishops were grateful that they would, at least, have rules to guide their conduct which, if they were observed, would protect them from arbitrary assault. But the time had not yet come when Henry's opponents bowed to his wishes without a fight. And, before the breach with Rome was too wide to bridge, the King was not ready to brush all opposition aside. So there was much haggling about the text in which the definition would appear. It ended in a defeat for the King. The notion of royal supremacy, which Henry had wished to establish, was not fully accepted by either Church or Parliament.

The King had wanted the text to declare him 'Supreme Head' of the Church in England. Bishop Fisher suggested adding the caveat 'as far as the law of God allows', and Archbishop Warham persuaded Henry to agree. The compromise left the Church compliant but resentful. The final wording – 'singular protector, supreme lord and even, as far as the law of Christ allows, supreme head of the English church and clergy' – was endorsed by the bishops only because Archbishop Warham ruled that silence meant consent. The first step had been taken towards the Church's acceptance that the sovereign possessed both spiritual and temporal authority in England. The inevitable consequence was the separation of the Church of Rome and the Church in (and eventually of) England.

To most of Henry's subjects, the Reformation – assuming they had even heard of the dispute between King and Pope – meant nothing. Neither the liturgy nor the dogma of their Church had changed. The notion that John Calvin and Huldrych Zwingli were heretics because they did not believe in transubstantiation and that Luther was a heretic, even though he did, passed them by. Their King knew a theological debate was raging in Europe. But – until he was persuaded that there was a relationship between the denial of his sovereignty and the whole body of Catholic doctrine – Henry never thought of disturbing the workings of the Church. So most of England worshipped unmoved by, or oblivious of, the religious revolution that was about to engulf them.

The Church's acceptance – reluctant and partial – of the King's enhanced authority had been supported by the publication of new, though corrupt, academic opinions. They were in Latin. Henry, breaking all established precedent, ordered their immediate translation into English and wide circulation of the judgement that 'it is so unlawful for a man to marry his brother's wife that the pope hath no power to dispose therewith'.[17] That limitation on the power of the Pope was another assertion of Henry's power and a justification for a view of national sovereignty – a matter of high principle which often required the diversion of money from the Church to the King's coffers. In 1532 he instructed the House of Lords to demonstrate England's independence by withholding the payment on annates or first fruits: taxes paid to Rome after the inauguration of every new bishop. A year later he claimed that the decision was justified by the cost of subduing the Catholic-inspired uprising in Ireland. Resistance in both Houses of Parliament – less the result of respect for Rome than of fear that the Holy Roman Empire would combine to retaliate by imposing a trade embargo – was peremptorily swept aside. Henry decided that the time had come to put Parliament in its place. Help in that endeavour was at hand.

In 1528, Thomas Cromwell – a former soldier of fortune, and by then only a virtually unknown Member of Parliament – had drafted a *Supplication of the Commons Against the Ordinaries*. It was a bitter complaint that ecclesiastical courts were usurping the powers of the civil judiciary. The *Supplication* had lain fallow for two years. But by 1531 Cromwell had become Master of the Jewels and Wards and was about to take Wolsey's place as Henry's most trusted minister. Motivated by the belief that an independent England could become the most powerful state in Europe, and untroubled by theological arguments, he was to drive the Reformation on, long after Henry had begun to lose his enthusiasm and his nerve. But at the time of the *Supplication*'s emergence, Cromwell was the King's enforcer, the man who made sure that neither malice nor incompetence prevented the royal wishes being obeyed. His role and character are both exemplified by a letter which he sent to an emissary who was to negotiate with the King of France. It is authoritative, precise in its language and menacing in tone – characteristics that leave little doubt about why Cromwell was not greatly loved by the rest of King Henry's court:

> You will receive letters from His Highness concerning matters of great importance. Just as he has no doubt that you will, with utter

dexterity, shed light on these matters for the accomplishment of his desire, so too is it his desire that you should elaborate on the delivery of ships with such great zeal and strength that you should not only obtain the thing itself but that you should also explain and expound how unworthily he has behaved with His Highness in this matter.[18]

The original version of the *Supplication* – even though it contained the justified allegation that ecclesiastical courts were imposing secular laws – was robustly challenged by the bishops. Indeed, Convocation's response, the *Answer of the Ordinaries,* was so aggressive in its affirmation of their rights and powers that Henry – who had previously been preoccupied – thought it necessary to intervene and secure a result that was consistent with his view of the relationship between Church and state. The King – at a meeting with Members of Parliament – encouraged the Commons to repeat, in a stronger form, its assault on the bishops' power. Their response was so enthusiastic that when he was sent by the Speaker of the House of Commons to the Archbishop of Canterbury, William Warham composed a reply which was less a defence of the Church's rights than a plea for mercy and protection against the anti-clericalism of the Commons. The clergy, he claimed, were even subject to Commons-inspired physical violence, 'so injured in their own persons, thrown down in the kennel in the open streets in mid-day even here within your own city'.[19]

Warham seems not to have realised that the King had encouraged the Commons in its assault on the Church's assumption of powers, but Henry's response to the Church's cry of anguish must have convinced him that he could expect royal assault rather than regal protection. He ignored what the bishops had actually said and addressed the Commons as if the episcopacy was in open revolt. 'We thought that the clergy of our realm had been our subjects wholly but we have now well perceived that they are only half our subjects . . . For all the prelates at their consecration make an oath clear contrary to the oath they made to us.'[20] It was the bridging passage that united Henry's assault on the Church in England for the usurpation of royal powers and his assault on the Church of Rome for the denial of his sovereign authority. It was also the beginning of the obsession with oaths that was to be a feature of the debate on divided loyalty – Rome versus England – for the next three hundred years.

Only seven bishops had the courage to attend the meeting of the Canterbury Convocation at which the King's message was considered. One of them, John Clerk of Bath and Wells, anticipating a decision to which he could not subscribe, left before the response was agreed. The rest eventually acquiesced, with varying degrees of reluctance, to the formal *Answer of the Ordinaries*. It was called, with no intention of irony, the *Submission of the Clergy* – it was fulsome in its acceptance of the King's authority, but demanded that Parliament respected the 'liberty and privileges of the Church'. Henry – unwilling to accept anything except capitulation – determined not to give ground on any aspect of his supremacy.

Confident of the Commons' support, the King laid down his terms of surrender. They were very near to unconditional. All future Church legislation could be negated by royal veto. Existing canon law was to be examined, and when necessary revised, by a committee that included laymen. All the canon law which then remained was to be acknowledged as only possessing legislative force because it had been endorsed by the King's authority. Henry announced the immediate prorogation of Parliament – meaning that the Church must either meet the King's demands or face uncertain consequences. The bishops capitulated and accepted, virtually word-for-word, Henry's redraft of their *Submission*. Thomas More – who was bitterly opposed to the bishops' surrender to the temporal power – had wanted, for over a year, to relinquish the office of Lord Chancellor. In his last act of friendship to a man he had once claimed to love, Henry allowed him to resign. His successor, Thomas Audley, immediately released all the heretics who had been imprisoned by More. Denigrating the Pope was no longer a crime.

There followed an annual reduction in the Pope's power in England. In 1533 the Act of Appeals decreed that all matrimonial dispute and disagreements over tithes (once decided under consistory jurisdiction) must be settled in English courts. The preamble referred to England as an empire, to emphasise its status as a sovereign state. Then, in 1534, a swathe of Acts confirmed Henry's authority over the English Church. The Act in Restraint of Annates abolished completely the previously suspended payments to the Pope, and the Act of Praemunire made it illegal to refuse to consecrate a bishop who had been nominated by the King. The Submission of Clergy Act enforced by law the erosion of power to which the bishops had already agreed. The Heresy Act declared that it was no longer illegal to deny the Pope's authority and, during a second session of Parliament in 1534, the process of rejecting all papal power was completed by passage of the Acts of Supremacy and Succession, which established Henry's overriding authority and made the issue of his union with Anne heirs to the throne of England. A Treason Act followed. Under its provisions, a Syon monk, three Carthusian priors and the vicar of Isleworth were executed at Tyburn on the same day for denying that the King was head of the Church.[21]

From then on, prosecution (or persecution) of heretics took second place to the persecution (or prosecution) of 'traitors' who refused to subscribe to the principles laid down in the Acts of Supremacy and Succession. Most of the population knew neither that the laws had once been administered by the Church nor that they had become the responsibility of the secular authority. The few who did realise that they lived in turbulent times accepted the change with supine resignation. The Oath, swearing to uphold the new laws, was signed by every member of both Houses of Parliament who were present on the prescribed day. Citizens of London who were members of guilds were instructed – worshipful company by worshipful company – to affirm their agreement. There is no record of any guildsman refusing to sign. Even after the Pope had struck back, by declaring that Henry and Catherine were still married, there was little resistance to the demand that every citizen, when required to do so, should take the Oaths of Succession and Supremacy. The two glorious exceptions were John Fisher and Thomas More.

There was a moment when the high drama of the Reformation briefly turned into tragic farce. Elizabeth Barton, a Kentish servant girl, had first heard voices when she was nineteen. An examination by Church authorities concluded that they were genuine and responded to her wishes that she be found a place in a nunnery by admitting her to St Sepulchre's Convent in Canterbury, where she became an object of veneration – a status confirmed by her acquisition of the sobriquet 'Maid of Kent'. The voices followed Elizabeth into her cloisters, but in 1534 they began to express recklessly controversial opinions. It was, they said, Elizabeth's duty to tell the King that he must accept the supremacy of the Pope and warn him that, if he married Anne Boleyn, a great plague would destroy the nation. Somehow Elizabeth Barton gained access to the royal presence and repeated the warnings. The King was moved neither to heed nor punish her. But some members of the Privy Council thought it right to examine her further. Thomas More neither rejected nor supported her views, but urged her to be cautious in expressing them. It was a severe tactical error. Henry saw The Barton Affair as an opportunity to dispose of More who continued publicly to oppose the King's refusal to accept the Pope's judgement on the validity of his marriage to Catherine of Aragon. When Elizabeth Barton was named in a Bill of Attainder (an indictment for treason which allowed conviction without due legal process), More was accused of being party to her treachery.

The name of John Fisher, Bishop of Rochester, was also added to the bill. He had certainly met Elizabeth Barton and – even after she had called for the King to abandon Anne Boleyn – had expressed direct sympathy for her honesty and implied sympathy for her views. That was wholly consistent with Fisher's conduct and character. From the earliest indication that the King was contemplating a divorce, he had been Catherine's man. At first he had done no more than provide scholarly evidence that Henry's first marriage, having been validated by a papal dispensation, was 'indissoluble'. Then he had argued the Queen's case before the decretal commission and had gone on to oppose, in the House of Lords, the King's claim to be Supreme Head of the Church in England. All in all, it was amazing that he had survived for so long with only one brief period of house arrest, one shooting (narrowly avoided) and one attempted poisoning, as the price of his independence. He escaped the poisoning – probably contrived by the Boleyn family rather than the King – because of his habit of fasting and giving what he would have eaten to the poor. Two beggars died and Fisher's cook was executed, as the law required. He was boiled to death.

Thomas More and John Fisher – each of them major players in the drama of the Reformation – both chose death rather than commit apostasy. In other ways their lives could hardly have been more different. Fisher, the son of a Beverley merchant, was a scholar whose worldly success was due to his single-minded devotion to learning and the greater glory of Cambridge, which university rewarded him for his scholarship – and the new colleges that he had founded – by electing him Chancellor for Life. His academic distinction had attracted the attention of Lady Margaret Beaufort, Henry VII's elderly mother, and it was through her that he briefly became a figure in society. He preached the sermon at Henry VII's funeral in 1509 and remained sufficiently in favour, even in the new reign, to accompany the Court to the Field of the Cloth of Gold in 1520. But he found high life uncongenial. So he declined all offers of promotion from the poor and unfashionable See of Rochester and spent his time writing learned treatises on the errors of Protestantism. Fisher, untypically of his times, never resorted to the brutality that was endemic in society. The story of him using hot coals to burn the feet of John Browne, a Lollard, was invented by John Foxe – later famous for his *Book of Martyrs*.

Fisher suffered from the inability – literally fatal at the Court of Henry VIII – to hide his feelings or disguise his beliefs. When Henry turned on the monasteries and convents (more to raise revenue than because of their loyalty to Rome), it became fashionable to attack the extravagance and debauchery that were said to be a feature of cloistered life. But Fisher had been an early public critic of the clergy's shortcomings. 'They were wont, and indeed ought still, like lights of the world to shine in virtue and godliness [but] now there cometh from them no light but rather an horrible misty cloud or dark ignorance.'[22] The expression of such sentiments offended complacent bishops as well as indolent and sinful priests – even though, like Thomas More, Fisher moderated his criticism in order to avoid contributing to a process which he feared might end, as in Germany, with the total alienation of the people from the priesthood.

In 1529, the House of Commons had debated the financial exploitation of parishioners by their priests. There was particular resentment at the fortunes made from the mortuary fees – levies collected when a corpse lay overnight in church – charged during the previous year's epidemic of the sweating sickness. The condemnation was unanimous and a bill, limiting mortuary fees, was sent up from the Commons to the Lords, where John Fisher chose to say what he believed about clerical greed: 'If the truth were known, ye shall find that they rather hunger and thirst after the riches and possessions of the clergy, than the amendment of their faults and abuses.'[23] That was bad enough, but when he went on to warn the Lords about the dangers of following in Germany's footsteps, he ended with the expression of his forebodings: 'All these mischiefs among them riseth from a lack of faith.'[24] It was clear enough that his complaints were being made against the Germans. But his critics believed, or pretended to believe, that he referred to the English clergy. The uproar that followed illustrated the penalties incurred by those who speak their minds. It was a habit that Fisher could not break.

When Henry told Convocation that it would no longer possess an independent right to pass Church legislation, Fisher – although already suffering from the illness which would have killed him, had Henry not ended his life on Tower Hill – drafted a declaration. It was entitled 'That the bishops have immediate authority of Christ to make such laws as they shall think expedient for the weal of men's souls'.[25] From then on, a head-to-head collision, with only one possible result, was inevitable. And Fisher did nothing to avoid it. In May 1533, after Cranmer had pronounced the legality of Henry's annulment in the Upper House of the Canterbury Convocation, John Stokesley, the Bishop of London, and Stephen Gardiner, Bishop of Winchester, argued the King's case. Fisher spoke against. When the Convocation capitulated and denied that the 'Bishop of Rome' possessed either authority in or over England, Fisher was too ill to attend. Nobody doubted that the sickness was genuine. Had he been fit, he would have been there to argue his case.

Most often consistency is a virtue, but it can become a dangerous liability, especially when it is combined with an inability to temporise or prevaricate. Working from the first principle that God wanted England to return to the Catholic faith, and judging, on the basis of empirical evidence, that Henry's stranglehold could not be broken without outside help, Fisher concluded that salvation lay in invasion. For ten years he urged the Catholic powers of Europe to do their duty. He was the most distinguished example of a condition which was common in King Henry's England – high-minded high treason.

Obsessive consistency was not one of Thomas More's failings. The son of a Lincoln's Inn lawyer, he was of equal intellectual standing to Fisher. But his metropolitan background combined with his cultivated tastes to make him a much more sophisticated figure. The temperamental differences that distinguished More from Fisher were exemplified by the conflicting ways in which they responded to the Maid of Kent indictment. More pleaded his innocence in letters to Thomas Cromwell and the King and – after an examination by Cromwell, which dealt less with the relationship to the Maid of Kent than with his attitude towards the royal divorce and marriage – confirmed his evidence in writing. In a passage which the hagiologies omit, he repudiated the suggestion that he had ever opposed the annulment of Henry's marriage to Catherine. 'I neither murmured at it, nor dispute upon it, nor never did nor will.'[26] Then he reinforced his repudiation of Elizabeth Barton with an equivocation that was so blatant it could only have been the result of desperation. He was, he wrote, unable to respond to questions about the King's supremacy until he had read *Assertio Septem Sacramentorum* – Henry's own treatise on the subject, to which More had himself contributed. Then he confirmed his claim to the King's affection by sending an obsequious letter to Thomas Cromwell, which he clearly hoped Henry would read. More was found not guilty.

John Fisher's response to his inclusion in the Bill of Attainder was clearly also calculated to secure an acquittal, but it was the sort of demonstration of intellectual superiority that is more likely to cause offence than to encourage sympathy. Fisher, no doubt to the King's irritation, argued points of logic. He admitted to knowing that Elizabeth Barton had warned the King that he would die within a month of marrying Anne Boleyn, but had no reason to believe that she had made the same prophecy to anyone else. If she had only told Henry of the danger he faced, she could hardly be guilty of treason. If she was innocent, so was he. It was not an argument Henry was disposed to accept.

More was cleared of all charges. Fisher was sentenced to life imprisonment, but was pardoned and required to pay a crippling fine. It was clear from the accompanying reproof which he received from Thomas Cromwell that he was punished not for the single offence, but for his unremitting opposition to Henry's rejection of papal authority: 'I believe that I know the king's goodness and natural gentleness so well, that his grace would not so unkindly handle you, as you unkindly write of him, unless you gave him other causes.'[27] From then on, the only doubt about Fisher's downfall and execution was the date on which the formal processes of indictment would begin. The Maid of Kent's fate was not so long delayed. She admitted, under torture, that her voices had been an invention. Together with her alleged accomplices, she was sentenced to death.

Barely a decade earlier, both John Fisher and Thomas More, acting on the King's behalf, had denounced Martin Luther and all his works in tracts that, in their differences of approach, had illustrated the temperamental gulf which separated the two men. Fisher had contested Luther's theological argument point by point, in an erudite disquisition on the indisputable power of Rome. More had composed a short volume of abuse, which illustrated both the violence of his nature and the vulgarity of his mind. He later defended his descent into crude vituperation with an explanation that was as perverse as was his choice of language. The object of his hatred would, he claimed, be most likely to abandon his heresy if he were 'overwhelmed in filth'. So he wrote that Luther was a 'lousy little friar' who was 'filthier than a pig and more foolish than an ass ... Father Toss pot', who had been a pimp and allowed 'nothing in his mouth but privies, shit and dung'. He was only fit 'to lick with his anterior the very posterior of a shitting she mule' and should be required to 'swallow down his filth and lick up the dung'.[28] More's scatological language – he accused Luther of celebrating Mass while defecating[29] – was extreme, even by the standards of the age. Sometimes he was vicious and absurd in equal measure. He claimed that Luther's marriage to a woman who had once been a nun made him an 'open, incestuous lecher, a limb of the Devil and a manifest missionary from Hell'.[30]

It is always said, in More's defence, that his failings – the brutality of his prose, the suppression (rather than refutation) of inconvenient ideas and the enjoyment of gratuitous brutality – were simply a reflection of the habits of his age. But More is, to his many devotees, a man who rose above the barbarity of his times. One of his claims to progressive admiration is the publication of *Utopia*, which, as well as adding a new word to the English language, set out his vision of the ideal state. In 'Nowhereland', education is universally available, religious tolerance accepted as normal as well as necessary, and freedom of expression regarded as a mark of the civilised state. Yet when high office required it, More became – as well as a heretic hunter – an enthusiastic book-burner. Worse still, for a man with intellectual pretensions, devotion to truth seemed to baffle him. In an admission of complete incomprehension, which suggests that he did not even understand the true nature of faith, he was open in his astonishment that so many men were prepared to risk so much in order to bring bibles into England: 'Though they cannot there be printed without great cost [nor] non there sold without great adventure and peril, yet they cease not, with money sent from thence, to print them thither by whole vats full at once and in some places, looking for no lucre, cast them abroad at night.'[31]

More did not just acquiesce in the errors of the time. He exhibited a positive enthusiasm for compounding them. Despite his high office, he personally led a company of men-at-arms in a raid on the Hansa headquarters and, himself, arrested the Scandinavian merchants who had brought 'the most horrible plague' of banned books into England. He then pursued the culprits through the courts. For him, the suppression of dangerous ideas was a matter of absolute principle. 'Our Lord,' he wrote, 'send us now some years as plenteous of good corn as we have had of late years of plenteous evil books.'[32] He then went on to argue that evil books are more deadly than famine and that the 'years as plenteous of good corn' would be ended by divine retribution for the growing habit of reading heresy. That is not what they believed in *Utopia*.

Cardinal Wolsey, for all his many faults, was not an enthusiastic burner of men. He sent men to their death when it was politically expedient to do so. Thomas More – Wolsey's successor as Lord Chancellor of England and a late convert to outright opposition to the King's rejection of the Pope's authority – burned with a passion which came from the conviction that he was doing God's will. Catholics, who believe that some truths transcend time and place, must defend his gratuitous barbarity with the claim that he was a man of his time. But there were men of pity and compassion even in Tudor England. In contrast to them, More's view on burning combined respect for the division between ecclesiastical and temporal law with a positive relish for the thought of the victim's suffering and a fine disregard for God's infinite mercy: 'The clergy doth denounce them ... the temporality doth burn them. Then, after the fires of Smithfield, hell doth receive them where the wretches burn for ever.'[33] Even in an age when death was the punishment for petty theft, that must have sounded very like a symptom of dementia.

More's appointment as Chancellor was followed by an incident which raises more doubts about his sanity than are provoked by his addiction to self-flagellation – as well as posing more questions about his saintly disposition. Ten days after Wolsey's fall, More spoke in Parliament in support of a petition which demanded that his deposed predecessor should be more severely punished. That was, in itself, bad enough. He knew that Wolsey's only crime was failure to deliver the divorce to which, Henry should have known, the Pope would never agree. The debate provided an opportunity for More's grotesque imagination to allege a new offence for which Wolsey had to answer: breathing in the King's face with the intention of infecting him with syphilis.

Most saints are less than saintly in their early lives. Some of them are sanctified because of the courage with which they turned their backs on sin. But More's place in Catholic history is the result of an unusual indulgence. The early years – more gross than gracious – are not forgiven. They are ignored. More's reputation, within the Catholic Church and beyond, is largely dependent on his choice of death and his conduct between his arrest, on or about April 13th 1534 and his execution on July 6th 1535. Until then he was a scholar of some merit and a statesman of some distinction. But without that final year he would not have become the moral paragon against whose behaviour generations of Catholics were judged. The apparent sudden change of character is not easily explained. Perhaps the prospect of death concentrated his mind on the need to rise above his baser instincts. Catholics – who admit his early failings – will attribute the conversion to Divine Grace. All of which we can be sure is that More changed.

The days of glory began with Thomas More receiving a summons to appear at Lambeth Palace and answer for his conduct. The King already knew that his fallen favourite contested the legality of the royal divorce and was opposed, in principle, to the consequent rejection of the Pope's authority. But the tribunal before which he appeared – Cranmer, Cromwell, Audley (the Chancellor) and the Abbot of Westminster – politely invited him to sign the Oath of Allegiance. After requesting, and receiving, permission to study the Oath's wording and the text of the Act of Parliament which gave it statutory force – the first indication of the legalistic battle that More intended to fight – the invitation was rejected. Audley showed More a list of signatures as

proof that everybody else of consequence supported the King's pretension. He misjudged his man. More's resolution was strengthened by
the knowledge that he stood alone.

On April 17th More was taken to the Tower – in time to see Elizabeth Barton, Maid of Kent, and the five priests who had supported
her, strapped to boards and dragged behind horses through the city
of London before they were hanged, drawn and quartered. A year of
butchery had begun. In the first month of More's imprisonment, the
London regular clergy were called to take the Oath. Only one, Nicholas
Wilson, refused. He was executed. May was the month of the religious houses. On the 4th the priors of Charterhouse, Beauvale and
Axeholme and a Carthusian monk, who had ignored the injunction,
were butchered at Tyburn. On June 19th, the vicar of Isleworth and
three more Carthusians went to their deaths. The Catholic Church in
England was beginning to accumulate its most precious asset, a heavenly host of martyrs.

During his early weeks in the Tower, More refused visits from his
family. So Margaret Roper, his daughter, wrote to him. It may be that
dark days in prison – as well as the thought of impending death –
softened both More's heart and his language. Much of what is known
of his last days – both the conditions in which he lived and his thoughts
on the word, the flesh and the devil – was obtained from letters that
he wrote in reply. They were addressed to his family, but clearly intended
for posterity. Some of them were written with what was described as
'a coal'. Although More was housed in one of the 'apartments' which
were kept for the occasional use of the rich and famous, he was at
first denied the use of a pen. All his letters display a certainty of salvation and a serenity in the face of death. He feared torture, but
composed himself sufficiently to assure Margaret that he was 'in good
health of body and in good quiet of mind'.[34] The best service she could
render him was to 'make you all merry in the hope of heaven'.[35] Her
pleas for him to recant, sign and save his life were gently rejected. 'I
neuer haue prayed God to bring me to hence nor deliuer me from
death, but referring all things whole vnto his onely pleasure.'[36] When
he was allowed books, pen and paper, he read devotional works, by
and about the saints and the early Fathers, and he wrote about the
victory of faith.

On the day before his execution Thomas More wrote to his
daughter, 'I cumber you, good Margaret, much, but I would be sorry
if it should be longer than tomorrow ... I never liked your manner
to me better than when you kissed me last; for I love it when daugh-
terly love and clear charity has no leisure to love worldly courtesy.

Farewell my dear child and pray for me, and I shall for you and all our friends that we may merrily meet in Heaven.'[37] That last message contributed to the picture of More which the early biographers – conscious of its importance to the Catholic cause – chose to paint. Many of the letters that they, understandably, chose not to publicise reveal a character that was deeply disturbed. Attempts 'perversely [to] change the world ... into a joyful haven of rest' could only result in the denial of 'true happiness' in heaven.[38] Christ had shown the way by using his divine power to increase his suffering to a level never experienced by a mortal. More lived up to that desperate view of salvation by wearing a hair shirt and regularly mortifying the flesh with self-flagellation. Severity was all. The expulsion from the Garden of Eden was, More believed, the result of Eve answering God's questions rather than referring them to her husband.

More's conduct during the long wait for certain execution would, in itself, have been enough to guarantee his place in Catholic history, but his posthumous reputation was further enhanced by what he said, or is believed to have said, during his trial and imprisonment and on the scaffold. Nicholas Harpsfield, a Catholic scholar writing about More's trial fifty years after his death, reported the most famous of all the defendant's rebukes to his accusers: 'I have, for every Bishop of yours above one hundred; And for one Councell or Parliament of yours (God knows what manner of one) I have the Councells made these thousand years. And for this one kingdome, I have all other Christian Realms.'[39] There is disagreement about whether or not More joked that his beard should not be severed as it had done no wrong; and he may, or may not, have warned the executioner that, because he had a short neck, a clean cut would need much skill. William Roper, his son-in-law and devoted follower who was close by, wrote that More asked the watching crowd 'to bear witness with him that he should now there suffer death in and for the Holy Catholic Church', and then protested that he was always 'the King's good servant, but God's first'.[40]

John Fisher's last words were not immortalised in the lexicon of martyrs' valedictions. Created Cardinal by the Pope, in the unaccountable belief that Catholic eminence would save him from execution, he was beheaded, quietly, on Tower Hill on June 22nd 1535. More followed him to the block on July 6th. Both men were canonised on the same day in 1936. More is remembered – in the words of Erasmus, the humanist theologian – as 'the man for all seasons'. Fisher, although not accorded such historical renown, was, according to Erasmus, 'the one man of his time who was incomparable for uprightness of life, for learning and for greatness of soul'. He was also venerated by his repentant contemporaries. On his deathbed, John Stokesley, sometime Bishop of London and flagrant apostate, cried out, 'Oh that I had holden still with my brother Fisher and not left him when time was.'[41]

Integrity, constancy and learning do not count for as much as glamour, when history makes heroes. Fisher suffered the fate of a self-effacing martyr. More enjoyed the benefit of celebrity status. He possessed all the glamour of the sinner come late to repentance – despite having more to repent than Fisher. In the years that immediately followed their deaths, there were hundreds of martyrs for the faith who – although humble and inarticulate – equally deserve our admiration. Their sacrifice kept the Catholic Church alive in what is now the United Kingdom. During the dark days which followed the Acts of Supremacy, many thousands of men and women – torn between faith and fear – were inspired to hold fast to truth by the example of those who had gone before. And More, despite his faults, became the most famous martyr of them all. Without his example, thousands more Catholics would have fallen by the way.

CHAPTER 2

The Cause Thereof

Among the educated classes – mostly priests active or prospective – new philosophies, represented within the Church itself by 'humanists', were encouraging the spirit of enquiry. And enquiry encouraged scepticism. What, in *St Joan*, Bernard Shaw called 'the heresy of nationalism' was growing more quickly in Britain than in much of continental Europe. It was the one heresy to which Henry remained true all his life. He wanted to accept the Pope's faith, but – perhaps irrationally – rejected the notion that, to do so, he must accept the Pope's orders. If, at the conclave of 1524, Cardinal Wolsey had been elected Pope and had opened up the possibility of Henry becoming Holy Roman Emperor, the King of England would have remained passionate in his defence of papal authority. However, Henry's instinctive nationalism does not explain why so many English men and women followed – or at least passively accepted – his rejection of their religion in the name of an idea which meant nothing to them. The state of the Catholic Church itself provides at least part of the explanation.

Loud and persistent voices were complaining that the Catholic Church was failing its followers, and the dissatisfaction – which they reflected – prepared the way for the Reformation. When the assault on rules and rites began, the resentment dulled the instinct to resist the schism. Although there were many places in which priest and people lived in harmony, in some parishes the alienation was complete, deep-rooted and long-standing. John Wyclif and his Lollard followers had anticipated Luther's denunciations of a corrupt and indolent clergy a hundred and fifty years before the Wittenberg declaration. But – after a little flourish of aristocratic support and an unexpected brief second coming in Scotland – the movement had been suppressed. Wyclif's Christianity – like Luther's – was built around the dogma that 'each man that shall be damned by his own guilt and each man that shall be saved shall be saved by his own merit'. The belief that *Sola Fide* (Faith Alone) was the only path to justification (redemption and life eternal) was the assertion that man could, and must, have a direct relationship with the Maker on whom his salvation depends. Wyclif made classic Roman Catholic doctrine – the necessity of interpretation of the scriptures by priests and the importance of intercession by saints – an offence against God and an insult to man. And he denied the supreme authority of the Pope as St Peter's heir in the Apostolic Succession.

Wyclifism also had a social dimension. The Lollards, who followed his teaching, rejected belief in transubstantiation and regarded every word in the Bible as divinely inspired. They also spoke for the poor and claimed that the Church – as represented by both its regular clergy (who belonged to a monastic Order) and its secular clergy (who did not) – was just as likely to exploit as succour its flock. Luther echoed that accusation. His denunciation of indulgences combined his social and theological condemnation of the Roman Catholic faith. Indulgences robbed the poor by misinterpreting the will of God. Long before the publication of the Wittenberg Articles, English voices had been raised against the allegedly corrupt and venal conduct of the priesthood.

The denigration of the clergy was a feature of early English literature. The second Vision in William Langland's *Piers Plowman* – published sometime between 1377 and 1379 – includes an argument between Truth and a priest about the validity of a pardon. Ten years later – in or about 1387, when Wyclif had retired to his rectory in Lutterworth – Geoffrey Chaucer caricatured the contemporary view of the priesthood in *The Canterbury Tales*. The Pardoner speaks of his greed, gluttony and gambling with more pride than regret. Many of the pilgrims, who were making their way to the shrine of St Thomas à Becket would have added lechery to that litany of misconduct.

The sins of the priesthood were certainly exaggerated by the outriders of the Reformation. But, at a crucial moment in its history, the Catholic Church in England was undoubtedly damaged by the conduct of the minority of miscreant and incompetent clergy. Evidence about their sins and misdemeanours was lovingly collected – much of it by men who never even considered either rejecting the authority of the Pope or denying much of Rome's teaching. It proved a potent weapon in the hands of men who wanted England's Church to stand alone.

They had many examples of misconduct from which to choose. During Cardinal Morton's visitation to Suffolk in 1499 he examined eight allegations of sexual misconduct. In 1511, William Warham, the Archbishop of Canterbury, suspended six priests who had been found guilty of debauchery. Between 1514 and 1521 there were twenty-five accusations of similar wrongdoing in parishes of the Lincoln diocese alone. Moral misconduct was matched in some dioceses by incompetence and corruption. In 1530, John Stokesley, the Bishop of London, examined forty-eight curates and found only eight of them 'adequate'. Twenty-one priests were banned from service, sixteen were suspended and four were ordered to take further instruction. Ten years later, in the diocese of Gloucester, three hundred priests were examined. One hundred and seventy were unable to repeat the Decalogue. Twenty-seven did not know who wrote the Lord's Prayer.[1] We know, from recent experience, that great institutions – especially those that have a moral purpose – are inclined to hide the wrongdoings of their members rather than expose, in order to eradicate them. That is how the pre-Reformation Church behaved, when confronted with complaints against priests. So the incidence of inadequacy, of every sort, was almost certainly greater than the record shows.

In 1528, one Simon Fish – the violently Protestant polemicist and habitué of 'Little Germany' – published a tract entitled *The Supplication for the Beggars*. Its most combustible claim was that a woman earned only three pence a day for working in the fields and a man earned four, but that a woman could earn twenty pence for sleeping with a priest for an hour and a man could earn twelve for acting as her pimp.[2] That indictment was given popular credence by a couplet which appeared in *Rede Me and Be Not Wrothe*, a scurrilous pamphlet which was probably written by William Royce, a lapsed friar. It claimed that the priesthood existed for 'Worshipful matrons to beguile / Honourable virgins to defile'.[3]

Fish was far less exercised by the priesthood's sexual morality than by its alleged indifference to the conditions of the poor and its exploitation of the gullible. He alleged that purgatory was 'invented for the covetousness of the spirituality'. That is to say, the idea was put into the minds of simple laymen in order to enable priests to reap a harvest of bought and sold indulgences.[4] *The Supplication* went on to claim that church ritual was no more than a device for extracting money from the poor. Masses for the dead were said to be a form of extortion. The refusal to allow vernacular translations of the Bible was denounced as no more than a crude device to surround the clergy with an aura of the mystery which reinforced their authority.

In truth, most priests lived amongst their parishioners at or about the same level of prosperity or poverty. Their income, no less than the incomes of their congregations, depended on the quality of the year's harvest, the debasement of the currency and the disruptive effects of the epidemics which were a feature of life in both town and country.

And there were times when the Church establishment stepped in to right the wrong done by errant priests. Henry Tankerd lost his benefice after the Archbishop of Canterbury discovered that parishioners in Barfreston, Kent, were denied Communion if, in the opinion of their rector, they were late with or refused payment of tithes. But it was the news of injustices, condoned by the Church establishment, which travelled fastest and furthest. Robert Pele of Chilham in Kent – who claimed a payment for every cart and plough in his parish and levied a tithe on wood sold, as well as crops sent to market – survived in office, despite his parishioners raising a fund to finance their legal challenge against his demands.[5]

Death was accepted in Tudor England with an equanimity that was bred by the marriage of faith and familiarity. But special offence was caused by the insensitive levying of 'mortuary charges'. Long before John Fisher denounced the whole system, its operation caused outrage in the parish of St Mary Matfelon. In March 1511, the parish priest expropriated – in lieu of the charge – the christening gown which had been used as a shroud for the corpse of a one-year-old boy. The child's father, Richard Hune, applied for its return to the Consistory Court. It found in the priest's favour. Hune protested against the verdict with such fervour that he was said to have offended against the dignity of the Church itself. So he appeared before the court a second time – charged with maleficence. He was excluded from church and, as a result, was denied confession, absolution and the consequent hope of redemption.[6] Such incidents rarely led to open rebellion. But they nurtured the feeling that the word of the Church was not beyond question and it was time for a change.

Sentimentalists always claim that, whatever the shortcomings of the lay clergy, their brethren in the monasteries enjoyed and deserved the affection of the common people. Monks, they say, were notable for their devotion to the welfare of the poor and sick and for their provision of food and shelter for travellers. That was certainly sometimes the case. But it was easy enough for malcontents to find cause for complaint about the monasteries. Critics claimed that the monks of northern England – who had originally gone out into the inhospitable wilderness in order to work and pray in the sanctity that comes from solitude – had suffered from the sin of pride, which was reflected in the mighty abbeys they created. The charge was that they had gone on building when no more building was necessary. At Rievaulx, the twenty-two monks employed 122 servants and augmented their income from the land by letting out rooms to 'corrodians', rich locals who paid for comfort and care.[7] Fish's condemnation of bad landlords included the denunciation of monasteries which enclosed common land and of monks who were notoriously harsh employers. On average, monasteries discharged their obligation to the destitute by spending no more than 5 per cent of their total income on charitable enterprises. Even that caused as much resentment as admiration. The working poor complained about the exploitation of a system which, they claimed, encouraged what we would now call welfare dependency.[8]

Abbeys and monasteries certainly offered accommodation to weary travellers, but only a very small proportion of the Tudor population travelled. Monks claimed the special grace of devoting at least part of their lives to praying for the delivery of souls from purgatory. Few of the men and women who bought prayers for the dead would have considered the irrationality of the notion that the speed of ascent into heaven was determined by the number of friends and relations who paid to implore God to grant a swift passage. But charges for prayers on behalf of the dead – like chantry bequests, the endowment of post-mortem Masses – stimulated one of the controversies that united theological doubts and social unrest. Were they acts of faith or commercial transactions? Dissatisfaction with the clergy was not confined to troublemakers, malcontents and men and women who would later be called Protestants. Thomas More used the preface to a disquisition on God's influence on secular events to list some clerical shortcomings. Priests, he wrote, misled 'the common herd' by inventing stories about saints and miracles. Their 'horrendous tales of hell . . . drove some old women to tears' and 'although acting with pious intent', they used 'inventions and lies'[9] to intimidate their followers into sobriety and orderly behaviour.

On his return to Queen Mary's Catholic England in 1553/4 – as Cardinal and Papal Legate – Reginald Pole made more substantial accusations against the priesthood. He called together the priests and clergy of both York and Canterbury, with the express purpose of accusing them of the sins which he had identified, during his enforced stay in Rome, as infecting the worldwide Church. Chief among them were sloth, greed, ignorance and envy. Those were the shortcomings which, according to Pole, caused Catholics 'of the weaker sort' to lose faith as soon as heretics 'put before their eyes the abuses, and especially the covetousness of priests'.[10]

For half a century before the Reformation there were men who boldly demanded that the Church reform itself. In 1510, John Colet, Dean of St Paul's, had told the Convocation of Canterbury that the time had come for the 'reformation of ecclesiastical affairs and never was it more necessary'.[11] Loyalty, rather than respect for historical evidence, made him careful to absolve the Church itself from any responsibility for the 'pride of life ... covetousness, lusts of the flesh [and] worldly occupations' which stained many clerical reputations. 'The need ... is not for the enactment of new laws and constitutions but the observance of those already enacted.' Nor did he suggest that clerical corruption was a new phenomenon. But the need to find a cure for the 'diseases' was more urgent than ever before. The 'sickness' was worldwide. Reginald Pole spent four studious years in Padua before he visited the Vatican. He stayed in the Eternal City for less than a week. 'Having seen the abomination of the cardinals, bishops and other offices of that city, he could no wise tarry there any longer.'[12] Resentment at the 'abominations' of some English clergy certainly did not turn the whole, or even the majority, of the Catholic Communion against Rome, but it smoothed the path to the schism of the apostate king.

Men about to die for their faith cannot be relied on to give an accurate estimate of the support that their particular brand of religion commands. But Reynolds of Syon – under cross-examination in the Tower in April 1535 – was surely right to claim that only 'the smaller part' of the kingdom sided with the King and that 'the larger part is at heart of our opinion, although outwardly, partly from fear and partly from hope, they profess to be yours'.[13] John Hales, the vicar of Isleworth, who was burned with Reynolds at Tyburn, judged that 'three parts of England is against the King'.[14] But the opposition was, in general, strangely passive. One of the causes of the indolence was the low esteem in which parts of the Church were held.

In one particular, the allegations of bad conduct – justified or not – had a direct influence on the progress of the Reformation. The Dissolution of the monasteries was employed as a way of diminishing the power and influence of the Church of Rome. It was begun as early as the fifteenth century with the closure of 'alien priories' and was continued, with increasing enthusiasm, by Henry VII and his son. As the title of the first dissolution declaration made clear, the desecration was always justified with the claim that the monks or nuns had offended against the law of God and man. In fact the closures were an easy way to raise money, for monarchs who were both short of capital and of respect for the Church. But it was accelerated when the dispute about the Pope's authority was at its height, often with the claim that it was the essential result of the monks' indolent and dissolute lifestyles and with the assurance that the sequestered income would be diverted to worthy purposes. Local attitudes towards monasteries were usually determined by the behaviour of the specific monks who inhabited them – not by a general theory about the propriety of the monastic life. So was the reaction to closures. Unpopular monasteries were more likely to be dissolved than those which, because of good works and pious living, were popular in the surrounding country. Small monasteries – with little connection with their localities – were particularly vulnerable.

As early as 1497, the Bishop of Ely had expelled the St Radegund nuns from their convent and used the money, raised by its sale, to found Jesus College in Cambridge. Doubts about the bishop's motives were removed by public denunciation of the nuns as salacious and dissolute. With the encouragement of John Fisher, her chaplain and confessor, Margaret, Countess of Richmond and Derby, had obtained a papal dispensation which allowed her to dissolve several small houses and use the revenue so obtained to build St John's College in the same city. In 1518, Thomas Wolsey – not always altruistic in his use of the Church's funds – obtained papal permission to close the St Frideswide monastery in Oxford, and built Cardinal College (now Christ Church) on the site, with revenue raised from the seizure of its assets and the closure of twenty-one other monasteries in nine counties.

When, in 1535, Henry VIII assumed the title of Supreme Head of the English Church, there were 563 religious houses in England[15] – a figure about which it is possible to be exact because Thomas Cromwell, when he was appointed the King's Vicar General, set up a series of commissions to establish the value and income of every abbey and monastery in the land. The results of their examinations were published in *Valor Ecclesiasticus*. A companion volume, *Liber Valorum*, was, in effect, a working handbook which recorded the donation that each benefice would be expected to make to the King as a result of 'tenths' and 'first fruits' being denied the Pope and diverted to Henry's coffers. It estimated that the total addition to his income would be £50,000 a year – almost half of the revenue he collected from taxation. But Henry – defending the border with Scotland, suppressing revolt in Ireland and fortifying Calais and the Channel ports – was still in desperate need of funds. Cromwell's solution was the expropriation of monastic property which, on some estimates, included one-third of all the land in England.

The bill of 1536, which legitimised more general dissolution, made clear in its long title that the King's object was to eliminate the smaller, and theoretically most likely to be corrupt, houses and transfer their residents to the 'great and solemn monasteries of the realm'.[16] The bill – which became law within fourteen days of its introduction into Parliament – proposed the closure of all houses with an annual income of less than £200. But both Lords and Commons must have realised that it was no more than the first stage of a plan to close every religious house in England. Indeed, Cromwell could not have been more frank about his determination to cleanse the realm of the 'abomination of religious persons'.[17]

His chosen method was a series of visitations which, in form, were not unlike those carried out by inspecting bishops in earlier years. The difference in fact lay in the character of the visitors. Cromwell's 'Commissioners' were looking for reasons to justify closure and therefore worked on the assumption that each abbey and monastery had something to hide. Dr Richard Layton, Commissioner in the north, was proud to boast that he and Dr Thomas Leigh, his colleague, were so familiar with the counties which they inspected that 'no knavery can be hid from us in that country'.[18] The fact that only one major revolt disturbed Henry's peace can be attributed to many causes. One of them was Cromwell's decision to make it known that a change of ownership would leave most of the tenancies undisturbed. Another was the determination – present in all classes – to benefit from the closures, when benefit was possible.

Even before the Act of 1536 was passed, rumours about Cromwell's intentions caused Viscount Lisle to make enquiries about the future of the abbey at Bewley, now spelt Beaulieu. He was told that its future was uncertain but if, after an enforced change of ownership, it came on the market, his interest would be protected by his 'own poor servant [keeping a] vigilant and diligent ear thereunto'.[19] A month after the bill became law, Sir Simon Harcourt, writing to Cromwell direct, managed simultaneously to defend the Church's, and his own, financial interests. He was willing to pay the king £100 and the same sum to Cromwell, with a further £20 to follow, so that the 'little house of canons in Staffordshire, called Routon ... may continue'. But if, on the other hand, the King was 'determined to dissolve', Harcourt was in the market for the sale of land which followed. 'I desire to have it as it adjoins such small lands as I have in that country.'[20]

It was not only the landed and prosperous laymen who sought to take advantage of the closures. 'The poor people,' wrote one disillusioned commentator, 'thoroughly and in every place be so greedy upon these houses when they are suppressed that by night and day, not only in the towns but in the country, they do continually resort as long as any door, window, iron or glass or loose lead remaineth in any of them.'[21] And the holy men often joined in the hunt for spoils. 'I well perceive that diverse precious stones, emeralds and others of great value, taken out of the jewels of the house here privily by the prior and four or five monks of his affinity.'[22] Inertia, fear, the hope of gain and dissatisfaction with the Church were more of a barrier to revolt than honest belief in the righteousness of the Reformation. Even so, it is extraordinary that, from start to finish of King Henry's reign – including, first, the rejection of the power of the Pope and, then, an assault on the Church itself – there was only one uprising that was anything like a national revolt.

The revolt was neither a sudden national explosion of determination to defend the Church of Rome nor a carefully planned plot either to re-establish a Roman Catholic monarchy or change the monarch. Its underlying causes included the condition of England. Thanks to a series of bad harvests, wheat prices had risen by 80 per cent in a year. Taxes had been increased and there were rumours that they were about to rise again. The coinage had been intentionally debased. The north of England – then as now – believed that its interests were sacrificed in favour of the soft and prosperous south.

That suspicion seemed to be confirmed by Thomas Cranmer, the new Archbishop of Canterbury – a Nottinghamshire man who should have known better. The north, he wrote, was inhabited by a 'barbarous and savage people who were ignorant and turned away from farming and the good arts of peace and who were so utterly unacquainted with knowledge of sacred matters that they could not bear to hear anything of culture and a more gentle civilisation'.[23]

At the height of the rebellion, all of the north of England was in arms. But the one great uprising against the Reformation began as a town rising. It was the product of local factors – jealousies, rivalries and loyalties – combined with economic grievances and the northern temperament. Its immediate cause was an incident which was replicated, time after time, all over England. The King's Commissioner proposed to sequestrate treasure which belonged to a parish church. The spark might have lit the fire of revolt anywhere in the country. It happened to ignite the profusion of combustible material which, in the autumn of 1536, burst into flame in Louth, a Lincolnshire market town.

Thomas Kendall, the vicar of St James', was a profound opponent of the Reformation. In the days before the split with Rome he had been employed by the Bishop of London to root out old-style heresy in Colchester. Had he confined his passion for Catholic orthodoxy to the expression of views on the intercession of saints, the veneration of the Virgin Mary and the processes by which the penalties of purgatory could be avoided, all would have been well. But he was explicit in his public rejection of the rights and powers of the three

Commissioners who were simultaneously examining the parishes of Lincolnshire – one to assess the viability of smaller monasteries, one to determine how much each parish owed in taxes, and one (acting on behalf of the bishop) to assess both the moral standing and the assiduity of the county's clergy. Rejection of the rights of the Commissioners was a rejection of the rights of the King.

Two religious houses near Louth – the Cistercian abbey at Louth Park and the nunnery at Legbourne – had been closed before the general visitation began. Anger about the dissolutions, which had already happened, combined with the fear that there were more closures to come. On the morning of October 1st 1536, Thomas Kendall announced, at the end of Mass, that the St James' treasures were in imminent danger of confiscation. He justified his claim by reporting that one of Cromwell's Commissioners – probably for no other reason than to provoke the rebellious parishioners – had announced, whilst examining parish plate, that 'a silver dish with which they went about to beg for their church was more meter for the king than for them'.[24] If provocation was his purpose, his plan succeeded. One 'parishioner fashioned to draw his dagger, saying that Louth and Louthesk would make the king and his masters a breakfast such as they never had'.[25] The vicar's warning, combined with the Commissioner's apparent threat, was enough to make all the parish take up arms. Rumours of imposed indignities multiplied. The idea that the number of feast days was to be limited by law caused particular offence.

Among the treasures was a large silver-gilt cross which, together with other crosses, was borne at the front of processions on feast days. Thomas Foster (a yeoman farmer who sang in the church choir) called out, 'Let us follow the cross this day. God knows whether ever we shall follow the crosses again.'[26] A hundred men appointed themselves guardians of the treasures, took possession of the church keys and agreed to stand watch all night, with the intention of ringing the bells if the church was attacked.

It was a day of unfortunate coincidences. Two days earlier the town had celebrated Michaelmas, both an important feast day in the Church's calendar and a quarter day on which rents were paid. The town was, therefore, unusually busy and many of the men who filled the streets were pious Catholics who were particularly sensitive to the King's threat to reduce the number of feast days. John Hennage, a member of the Bishop of Lincoln's staff, was still in Louth after supervising the election of town officials which had taken place two days earlier. The Bishop was deeply disliked in Louth because he was close to the King and was therefore associated with the confiscation of

Church property. So the townspeople were not in a mood to welcome his representative. He was taken by force to the church, which the vigilantes – by then under the command of Nicholas Melton, a shoe-maker of dubious character, who had assumed the title 'Captain Cobbler' – had occupied. Hennage was forced, on pain of death, to swear that he would be 'true to Almighty God, to Christ's Christian Church, Our Sovereign Lord the King and the Commons of this realm'.

The mob next turned on John Frankishe, the Bishop's registrar, who was in Louth to examine the competence of the clergy. His books and papers were burned and he too was forced to take the oath, as were the twenty priests he was to examine. The Commons of Louth were – by any definition of the condition – now in open rebellion. But its members could not shake off the inbred instincts of feudalism. From start to finish of the biggest insurrection in English history, the rebel oath always included a vow of loyalty to the King – an obligation deeply embedded in the national psyche by a thousand years of serfdom. The rebels' chosen enemies were (first) Thomas Cromwell, who plundered the churches, and (later) Thomas Cranmer, who chal-lenged the Pope's doctrine as well as his authority.

There was a rumour that revolt was imminent across the Humber in the East Riding of Yorkshire, but Captain Cobbler – determined that Louth should act alone – led 'the Commons of Louth' to nearby Caistor, where the King's Commissioners were meeting. They marched behind the banner of the Dymoke family, which they had taken from the parish church: their chosen standard because they wanted, and believed they needed, the support of the gentry. The notion that noble support would encourage the King's representatives to parley with them proved to be wishful thinking. The Commissioners, either because of fear or disdain, refused to meet them and made to ride away. One was caught and beaten so savagely that he died. The other the Commissioners were taken back to Louth and forced to help in the composition of a message to the King, which described grievances rather than made demands. The letter repeated the request that Crom-well, and those who served him, be handed over to the Commons of England and that there should be no more closures of religious houses. The letter ended with an assurance which, because of its effrontery, must have offended the King far more than the demands they described as requests. The Commons of Louth had no objection to Henry remaining head of the Church in England.

The rebels could not agree about how they should spend their time before they received the King's reply. Some urged the occupation of other sympathetic towns. Others proposed temporary disbandment, either because there were crops to harvest or in order emphasise the essential moderation of their campaign. In their uncertainty, they mustered – almost 10,000 strong – on Hambledon Hill, outside Market Rasen in Lincolnshire, to await their leaders' decision. They were united by a rumour that Lord Burgh, one of the Commissioners who had been driven out, had recruited mercenaries and was about to attack them, and – in a show of bravado – all agreed to march on Lincoln.

Sir William Fairfax, a grandee from the north bank of the Humber, blamed the uprising on local monks: 'The houses of religion not suppressed make friends and wag the poor to stick hard to this opinion and the monks who were suppressed inhabit the villages round the houses and daily wag the people to put them in again.'[27] As the rebellion spread, there was much evidence to support his claim. The abbeys at Bolton, Byland, Guisborough, Rievaulx and Whitby all contributed to rebel funds. But Richard Hooker, scholar and Master of the Temple church in London, was nearer the mark. In *Laws of Ecclesiastical Polity* he dismissed objections to the theft of church plate as no more than a symptom of the real reason for rebellion. 'The cause thereof . . . was only respecting religion.'[28] The Commons of Louth would certainly not have been unanimous in their explanation of why their little town had been the first aggressively to resist the humiliation of the Church and the theft of its property. But they all must have agreed – with different degrees of enthusiasm and apprehension – on one fact about their rising. What had begun as a local protest was, irresistibly, becoming a revolution.

CHAPTER 3

Forth, Pilgrims! Forth!

Henry did not reply to the rebels' letter. So they wrote to him again. If they had managed to convince the King that their first list of grievances was no more than a respectful request, there was no hope of disguising the nature of the second. It was clearly a series of demands. No additional taxes except in time of war. The restoration of the Church's ancient rights. The crown to renounce all rights to tenths and first fruits. Cromwell to be surrendered to the Commons of England. A full pardon for all the Commons – no more than was their due since they were not, and never had been, in rebellion.

The northern nobles who were loyal to the King had been slow to react to the uprising. But eventually Lord Burgh wrote to the Earl of Shrewsbury in Sheffield Park and to Lord Thomas Darcy in Selby urging them to march against the Louth men. By then the news had already reached the King at Windsor. His first reaction had been to send an army north under the command of the Duke of Norfolk. Then he had second thoughts and announced that the punitive exhibition had been postponed. The Duke shared the rebels' hatred of Cromwell. Indeed, according to Eustace Chapuys, the French Ambassador, Norfolk hoped and believed that the rebellion would 'ultimately work the ruin and destruction of his competitor and enemy'.[1]

After a week or so of indecision, the march north was abandoned altogether. Tales of potential risings in the south amounted to little more than a London priest describing the Louth dissidents as 'God's people who did fight to defend God's cause'[2] and rumours that the Lincolnshire host was 40,000 strong and expected reinforcements from Yorkshire. However, they convinced the King that his interest lay in defending the south and waiting for the insurgents to run out of supplies, enthusiasm and courage. An army was mustered and stationed at Ampthill on the road to the capital. At one point Henry even thought of moving his court to the little Bedfordshire town and taking command of the army himself. But he changed his mind again and ordered Henry Brandon, Duke of Suffolk – supported by Richard, nephew of Thomas Cromwell, and Henry Howard, son of the Duke of Norfolk – to reclaim Lincoln in the name of the King.

Brandon marched north at the head of 3,000 men of dubious conviction and low morale. But the message he sent before him claimed that he was 100,000 strong and warned the insurgents that they faced the choice between surrender and annihilation. His ultimatum reflected the King's contempt for what he had described as no more than the 'rude commons of one shire and that one of the most brute and beastly in the realm'. He too sent a message north. 'You like traitors and rebels have behaved and not like the true subjects as you have named yourselves.' They had a clear choice: 'deliver unto the hands of one of our lieutenants one hundred persons' for exemplary punishment or 'put yourselves, lives, wives, children, lands, goods and chattels . . . in utter adventure of destruction and utter ruin by force of violence and the sword.'[3] There is no doubt that Henry meant what he said. Catholic or not, Tudor monarchs still relied on the Homily on Obedience to justify taking terrible revenge on rebels. Indeed, it required them to impose savage penalties on recalcitrants. 'Where there is no right order their reigneth all abuse, carnal liberty, enormity, sin and Babylonical disorder.'[4]

The threat worked. Brandon entered Lincoln unopposed. Captive royalists were released. The draconian punishments were not, for the time being, carried out, and what appeared to be clemency won over waverers to the King's cause. The stratagem was so successful that Thomas Cromwell felt able to describe the uprising as 'the late rebellion attempted in the north parties of the realm'. Though in the same letter he made clear that while it had been briefly necessary 'to appease' the rebels, the King's vengeance would not be long delayed. 'And now my lord of Norfolk shall go thither and lie there as the king's lieutenant for the administration of justice.'[5] Cromwell, prudently, had no intention of going thither himself.

Cromwell's assessment of the situation was based on wishful thinking by the barons of the north. Far from dying out, the rebellion was about to assume the full form which would guarantee its place in history. The Dymoke family banner, behind which the protestors had marched from Louth, had been returned to the parish church and replaced, at the head of the column, by a white sheet to which had been attached a hand-painted representation of the Trinity. It amounted to an assertion of the righteousness of their cause. Complaints about taxes were almost forgotten. They marched for Jesus Christ and the Church of Rome. They were pilgrims and, in October 1536, they found a man of principle and purpose to lead their pilgrimage.

Robert Aske, of Aughton in Yorkshire, was accounted a gentleman. After a brief period in the employment of the Earl of Northumberland, a distant kinsman, he had been admitted to Gray's Inn. It seems likely that he rode south, in the autumn of the revolt, with the intention of following his profession in London. He was stopped by the pilgrims shortly after he crossed the Trent and taken, against his will, to join a muster on Hambledon Hill. It was convenience rather than conviction that made him reluctant to join the rally. In Aughton he was already a wanted man, accused – almost certainly correctly – of encouraging unrest in the East Riding. Having been forcibly delayed on his travels, he felt enough sympathy for the cause of those who delayed him to remain freely in their company. He first joined and then led what became a holy war.

Most of the men who were to become Aske's followers saw the revolt in purely local terms – a refusal to accept the pillage of their parish churches and the degradation of the saints to which they were dedicated. Aske, the provincial lawyer, fought against the Act of Supremacy, a 'mean division from the unity of the Catholic Church'.[6] But he too was a champion of local causes. The Beverley disturbances, in which it was thought Aske had been implicated, were – like the rising in Louth – provoked by a variety of grievances. Chief among them was the demand that tithes must be paid in cash, not kind. But it was the imposition of the new religious order which pushed the people over the line that separated unrest from uprising. The revolt began in earnest when it became known that Robert Holgate, Prior of Watton Abbey, intended to obey the King's injunction to ignore all but the officially recognised holy days and neglect the celebration of the Feast of St Wilfrid, the man who had argued for the Church of Rome at the Synod of Whitby in 663 and prepared the way for the whole Christian Church in England to accept the spiritual sovereignty of the Pope. Although the revolt was slow to spread throughout the West Riding, Edward Lee, Archbishop of York, had written to London warning against what he described as hotheads and reporting that beacons were being lit along the north bank of the Humber. If Aske was, as supposed, involved in the Yorkshire unrest, there is no wonder that the Commons of Louth came to believe that his fateful journey south was arranged by Providence.

In the same month that Aske first met the Lincolnshire dissidents, Pope Paul III decided that Rome should do all it could to encourage what might become an irresistible English uprising. After some cautious deliberation he concluded, not very decisively, that Reginald Pole – still in exile in the Vatican – 'could do service to God by going to England whenever an insurrection should arise'.[7] He had, for some time, wanted to make Pole a cardinal but he had respected, if not understood, Pole's reluctance to join the college. He had, therefore, let the matter rest. The news from England changed his attitude. On December 22nd 1536 he sent his Chamberlain to Pole's apartment with the message that his scruples were no longer of any account. Like it or not, Pole was to become a cardinal. To emphasise his determination, the Pope sent a barber with his Chamberlain. Pole was tonsured – the sign of a monk, though not of a priest – on the spot[8] and made Papal Legate to England, with the instruction to have his writing disseminated there while he made slow progress across Germany and France. The brave original intention was that Pole would be ready to land in England and reclaim the nation for Rome when the insurgents were on the point of victory. But the Pope – discouraged by the cautious reaction to his gesture in Catholic Europe – did not give Pole permission to set out until February 1537. By then it was too late. The rebels had, as the Pope hoped, made spectacular progress south but – although they did not know it – by the time the march on London began, their cause was already lost.

The processes by which Aske became the rebels' leader remain unknown and it must be assumed that he was chosen largely because of the strength of his character and the depth of his conviction. It was his decision that on St Wilfrid's Day 1536 there would be a general muster on Skipworth Moor in Yorkshire, and it was Aske who read out a proclamation which confirmed the pilgrims' loyalty to the crown. Every man was to swear to be 'true to the king's issue and the noble blood and preserve the Church of God from spoiling and to be true to the Commons and their wealth'. Formally Aske remained no more than the Chief Captain of Marshland in the Isle of Howdenshire. Other chief captains were elected during the muster. But there was no doubt where the real authority lay. Aske was the captain of the captains. During the day on which the muster ended he summoned a conference of representatives from each of the contingents which had gathered on Skipworth Moor and addressed them as a general would address his army on the eve of battle. God would be with them in their endeavours. They were 'pilgrims and had a pilgrims gate to go through'. That was the moment when the idea of a pilgrimage took hold and ensured that the great enterprise would go down in history not as a revolution, but as the Pilgrimage of Grace.

The knowledge that they did God's bidding was not enough to eradicate what amounted to the pilgrims' social insecurity. The Pilgrims of Grace – mostly respectable men who claimed, with pride, to speak for the loyal Commons of England – grew increasingly desperate to make recruits from the gentry and nobility. As support spread (first from East to West Riding and then to Lancashire and Northumberland), the hopes were first concentrated on Lord Darcy of Templehurst, a soldier who had fought for both King Henry VIII and his father. Darcy had signed the petition for an annulment which Henry had sent to Clement VII. But it was said that, when the plea was rejected and the Pope's authority ignored, Darcy had told the Emperor's ambassador in London that he would welcome an invasion by the Catholic powers. When the request to join the Pilgrims was made, Darcy was holding Pontefract Castle as a refuge for men loyal to the King. He dismissed the idea out of hand.

Attempts to recruit the Earl of Northumberland also failed. There were nobles who had expressed private sympathy for the Pilgrims' cause but, fearing for the safety of their wives and children, had refused openly to announce their support. It was decided to press them to make their views public. Lord Latimer of Snape yielded to the pressure. So did Sir Christopher Danby of Masham who – once he was incriminated by the oath – followed the dictates of his true faith, changed status from conscript to volunteer and became a noble captain. Other nobles fled before the Pilgrims arrived. Lord Scrope left in such haste that he left his wife and infant son behind.

With or without the nobility, the Pilgrimage was irresistible in the north. Suppressed abbeys and priories – Cartmel and Conishead in the Furness peninsula and Coverham and Eastby in North Yorkshire among them – were reopened. Encouraged by their success, some of the new northern recruits wanted to extend the objects of the Pilgrimage. A 'Captain Poverty' joined the ranks at Richmond with the intention of widening the Pilgrims' purpose. But even he – and the Brother Poverty, Master Poverty and Lord Poverty who followed his lead – called for the restoration of Church privileges and the reopening of dissolved monasteries, as well as a redistribution of wealth. The Pilgrims began to think of themselves as crusaders, freeing English Christendom from the tyranny of the heathen.

Despite their noble declaration of purpose, it had become clear to the Pilgrims' captains that the achievement of their aims would only be possible if they could convince the King and his council that they were strong enough to seize power. Sporadic uprisings, no matter how numerous and well supported, were not enough – even if they came together from time to time in great demonstrations of solidarity. The north of England had to be occupied and effectively governed by the Pilgrims. Robert Aske and William Stapleton, the original captain of the Lincolnshire Pilgrims, decided that York and Hull should be the Pilgrims' first strategic objective. Stapleton met the aldermen of Hull in Holy Trinity – the biggest, and first brick, parish church in England – who told him that they remained true to the King, but offered to relay the Pilgrims' grievances to London. They also offered to allow any local rebels, who so chose, to leave the town unhindered as long as they did not attempt to take with them the weapons and provisions that might be needed in the town if it was besieged. As it was the Pilgrims who were likely to besiege them, it was a strange offer to make. It was duly rejected and the siege began. Hull held out for five days.

William Harrington, the Mayor of York – caught between Pilgrim armies marching south from Richmond and north from Beverley – sent the city treasure to the royal castle in Tickhill and surrendered. Aske and his lieutenants were greeted at the great west door of the Minster by the Bishop's Treasurer and, together with the diocesan clergy, went in procession to the high altar to celebrate Mass. As Aske waited, in triumph, for news from Hull, he composed what he called 'The Oath of the Honourable Men'. It reaffirmed love of God, Church and King and required Pilgrims to swear that they did not join the 'Pilgrimage of Grace' in the hope of 'particular gain' for themselves and did not intend 'to do any displeasure to any private person ... nor slay or envy for profit'.[9] A proclamation, drafted at the same time, was less uplifting. It accused the Privy Council of a conspiracy to 'spoil and rob the realm'. Both documents were signed by 'Robert Aske, Chief Captain'. Formalising his status by giving it a name caused no controversy. Exercising his seniority by taking strategic decisions did. Aske ignored the complaints and announced, without consultation, that the Pilgrimage would march on Pontefract.

Pontefract fell without a fight and the Pilgrims celebrated their bloodless victory by adding Princess Mary's legitimisation to their list of demands.[10] Lord Thomas Darcy, who had commanded the garrison, and Edward Lee, the Archbishop of York, both swore the Pilgrims' oath. Later, when he was accused of treachery, Lee explained that 'if we refused, [Aske] had ways to constrain us and we should find them people without mercy'.[11] But Darcy found himself attracted to the Pilgrims' cause by more than fear of death. True to the King but faithful to the Church of Rome, he was persuaded by the wording of the oath that the Pilgrims shared both loyalties. It was an early manifestation of the question that dominated much of the later Reformation. Was it possible to be both a good subject and a good Catholic? When Thomas Miller, Lancaster Herald, arrived in Pontefract with a message from the King, he found that 'Aske sits in state with the Archbishop of York and Lord Darcy on either side of him.'[12] Miller was refused

48

permission to read the King's message from the market cross. It contained an announcement that the Lincolnshire revolt had collapsed and that the King expected the Yorkshire rebels to send him their list of grievances and then, like loyal citizens, retire to their homes.

Miller reported to London that the Pilgrims were unyielding and had been joined by various nobles. He might have added, as confirmation of Darcy's complicity, that the Pilgrims had adopted, as their badge, the banner which the noble recruit had followed when he led the English expedition against the Moors in Spain: 'The Five Wounds of Christ, centred upon the Eucharist and surmounted by the crown of thorns above the name of Christ: IHS'.[13] The news of Darcy's recruitment confirmed Henry's conviction that the rebellion must be crushed, not conciliated. Even as he offered to consider the Pilgrims' grievances, he was ordering a brutal response to the news that the Pilgrims had restored the dispossessed monks to Sawley Abbey in Lancashire. Edward Stanley, Earl of Derby, was instructed to 'repress the insurrection immediately, apprehend its captains and have them immediately executed as traitors or sent up to us ... You are to take the abbots and monks without violence and have them hanged without delay in their monks' apparel.'[14]

It was raining hard and not, in Stanley's view, suitable weather for a long march. Henry would not countenance delay. 'You shall at once cause the abbot and chief monks to be hanged on long pieces of timber or otherwise out of the steeple and the rest to be executed in places you think fit ... Let non escape.'[15] Stanley attempted to obey the King's instructions even though he knew that, when battle was joined, he would be heavily outnumbered. The armies never met. Henry changed his mind again. Yet another message from the King told Stanley to take his weary soldiers home and prepare to reinforce the royal forces in Yorkshire.

The stalemate in the north-east continued with both sides preparing for battles that did not take place. The Earl of Shrewsbury initially intended to press on to a decisive confrontation. But after he discovered that Doncaster was lost to the Pilgrims, he offered an immediate discussion of the grievances. The offer was rejected. The problem was not the idea but the proposal that both sides of the threatened conflict should nominate four emissaries to examine the prospects of an agreement. The Pilgrims suffered from an excess of democracy. They did not believe that four men could, adequately, represent thousands.

The next approach came from Thomas Howard, Duke of Norfolk and commander of His Majesty's forces at Ampthill. It was more an ultimatum than an offer. Again the Pilgrims were told to choose between annihilation and negotiation. Annihilation was no more within the power of the King's army that it had been when the Pilgrims were first threatened with destruction. The earlier bluff had been intended to intimidate. The second was meant to buy time until the army was strong enough to carry out the threat. Norfolk sent a message to Henry which assured the King, 'Whatever promise I shall make to the rebels . . . I shall observe no part thereof.'[16]

Lancaster Herald – still in Yorkshire – perhaps innocently led the Pilgrims to believe that if they accepted Howard's offer, Cromwell would be deposed. So, after one of the innumerable conferences which confirmed their democratic instincts but undermined their negotiating strength, the Pilgrims agreed to a meeting on Doncaster Bridge. Howard, Talbot and the Earls of Rutland and Huntington led the delegation which represented the King. Aske – anxious to demonstrate the support he enjoyed among the northern nobility – nominated Darcy to lead the Pilgrims, while he remained with the host that was assembled, 30,000 strong, in view of the bridge. The morning meeting was adjourned while the two delegations considered if there was a realistic prospect of agreement. Both sides concurred that a peaceful settlement was possible – the Pilgrims because of their gullibility, and Howard because of his guile. It was the only way of avoiding an early battle, which he knew he could not win.

Howard wrote to the King, 'The pestilence is in our army. We want victuals and money. The country is theirs. They have made it desolate.'[17] As he rode south from Doncaster he sent Henry an even more sobering message. His knights had behaved valiantly, but there were 'right few of the soldiers but thought [the Pilgrims'] quarrels to be good and godly'.[18] Had he been defeated in battle, half Howard's army would have joined the rebellion. Failure made Henry think less about peace and more about vengeance – particularly against Darcy, 'the most arrant traitor that ever was living'.[19]

Henry feared that the rebellion was spreading. A combination of superstition and panic induced the Court to believe improbable stories about impending insurrections, including the accounts of a new revolt in East Anglia which was said to be led by a Norfolk woman who, in May 1537, had declared, 'We shall never have a good world till we [come] together and with clubs and clouted shoon [hobnailed boots] shall the deed be done for we had never a good word since this king reigned.'[20] The King was again haunted by the spectre of invasion by the armies of the Holy Roman Empire. Cardinal Pole had sent a message to the Emperor, Charles V of Spain: 'I humbly entreat Your Majesty to try peaceful means first . . . before having recourse to arms.'²¹ The plea anticipated an invasion which the Catholic powers of Europe were too timid and too unprepared even to contemplate. But Henry felt less secure than at any time in his reign.

Hugh Latimer, Bishop of Worcester, preached a sermon at St Paul's Cross which called the Pilgrims 'poor ignorant people' and justified the brutal suppression of the uprising. Its logic was perversely impeccable. 'The foundation of the monasteries argued purgatory to be. So putting them down argues it not to be.'²² Thomas Cranmer, who thought it tactically wise to counterfeit conciliation, instructed Latimer to preach a second sermon which commended 'unity without special note of any man's folly'.²³ He described the Reformation as 'not new learning but old truths'.²⁴ Extreme advocates of a breach with Rome and the suppression of the monasteries were told to moderate their language and, in some cases, were put under house arrest. Henry himself composed a message to the Pilgrims in what he believed to be conciliatory language. The Church, he wrote, should be grateful for his small mercies. 'We have not done so much prejudice as many of our predecessors have done upon lesser grounds.' So the people should give thanks that he had closed the monasteries and thus ended the 'vicious and abominable life' that they supported. He suggested that the north misunderstood the purpose of his policy because it was inhabited by people who had never 'heard [his bishops] preach nor yet knoweth any part of their conversation'. The big lie followed:

> Ye shall know that our princely heart rather embraceth [of his own disposition] pity and compassion of his offending subjects than will to be revenged of their naughty deeds. We are content if we may see and perceive in you all sorrowfulness for your offences and will henceforth do no more so, nor to believe so lewd and naughty tales or reports of your most kind and loving prince and his council to grant unto you all our letters patent of pardon for this rebellion: so that ye will deliver unto us ten such of the ringleaders and provokers of you in this rebellion, as we shall assign to you and appoint.²⁵

The letter did not concede the justice of one of the Pilgrims' grievances. But despite that, and the demand that the Pilgrims sacrifice ten of their leaders, it would – by the standards of the time – have been a monarch's merciful response to open rebellion, had it not been for the fact that Henry had no intention of granting an amnesty under letters patent or in any other way. But time was on his side. So he agreed to yet another meeting between rebels and loyalists in Doncaster. During the truce that followed, the Pilgrims replenished their funds with (usually voluntary) donations from the restored monasteries, and the King – as well as bidding his commanders to recruit and regroup – plotted his special revenge on his principal enemies. A messenger passed though the Pilgrims' lines and handed Darcy a letter from Howard. It contained a complaint that the Pilgrims were breaking the truce (which was true) and the assurance (which was false) that the King believed that Darcy was held by the rebels, under duress. Darcy's loyalty could easily be confirmed. All he had to do was deliver Aske 'dead or alive, but alive if possible' to the King and thus 'raise [himself] in the favour of his Highness.'[26] Darcy immediately showed the letter to Aske, but did not consult him about his reply. 'Alas my good lord that ye, being a man of so much honour and great experience should advise or choose me to be a man of any such sort of fashion to betray or disserve any living man ... to get or to win me four of the best duke's lands in France or to be king there. I would not do it to no living person.'[27] Allowing for the stress of the moment and the nobility of the message, the double negative is forgivable.

The brief peace provided the Pilgrims with an ideal opportunity to indulge their passion for discussion. A conference at Pontefract – called to decide their agenda for Doncaster – considered the need for a revised Act of Succession. Pilgrims were fearful that Henry would nominate Cromwell to succeed him. They were also, with more reason, concerned about the promised pardon and demanded that it should be guaranteed in an Act of Parliament. Their more spiritual proposals were, as an indication of their moderation, offered in the form of an opinion rather than a demand. 'We think that preaching against purgatory, worshipping of saints, pilgrimages and images [and] all books set forth against the same or sacraments'[28] should be condemned. They added a note in favour of the old feast days – one cause of the first rising.

Aske – although distracted by a visit from his brother Christopher, thought by some Pilgrims to be a spy for the King – occupied himself in providing a strategic plan for an advance south. The whole Pilgrim army should be divided into three separate units, which would cross the Trent separately and rendezvous in Nottingham. At the same time he wrote to ask Mary of Hungary – the Emperor's regent in the Netherlands – to supply the Pilgrims with arms, ammunition and, more improbably, cavalry. Mary was also asked to intercede with Pope Paul III on their behalf. In Rome, Reginald Pole was beginning to look with more sympathy on proposals for an imperial invasion of England and was openly supporting the Pilgrims in their insurrection.

The Pontefract Conference came to a conciliatory, but obviously unacceptable, conclusion about the revision of the Supremacy Act. The

Church's temporal powers should be exercised by the King, but the Pope should remain supreme over matters affecting 'the care of souls'. Other new demands (still called grievances) were even less realistic. Princess Mary should be Henry's successor, and the Annates (payments to the Pope on the appointment of bishops, which the King had misappropriated) were to be collected less frequently and, like first fruits, returned to their rightful recipient. Old 'grievances' were repeated. The Pilgrims' negotiating position was set out in Twenty-Four Articles, which concluded with the demand that 'heretics, bishops and temporals and their sects ... or such other or else try their quarrel with us and our partaker in battle' suffer 'condign punishment by fire'.[29] The list of miscreants included – as well as Cromwell, Cranmer and Latimer – Leigh and Layton, the King's northern Commissioners.

The Pilgrims chose a delegation, three hundred strong, to represent their case on Doncaster Bridge, half a dozen of whom would take part in the actual negotiations and report back to their colleagues. The negotiators were armed with written advice. It included what modern Civil Service briefing papers call 'line to take'. The first three points were an assurance of the Pilgrims' good faith, the expectation of safe conduct and the call for a general pardon. The fourth was a demand that 'Thomas Cromwell nor none of his band nor sort be at our meeting in Doncaster'.[30]

A preliminary meeting, held on December 6th 1536, was adjourned until the Earl of Shrewsbury arrived with new orders from Henry to the Duke of Norfolk. They were, in substance, very like the old ones. The objective was total submission (as signified by individual oaths of allegiance) in return for a general pardon for all except the ringleaders. He added a secret codicil. If the rebels refused to accept his terms, Norfolk would return to London and put their case to the King, on the pretext of seeing which, if any, of their demands could be met. Norfolk was in strong support of the proposal. As a soldier, he realised the advantages of delay. As a Christian, he felt some sympathy for the Pilgrims. As a courtier, he was determined not to do anything which strengthened the position of his rival, Thomas Cromwell.

When the discussion finally got under way, Norfolk's fraudulent promise of concessions was so convincing that Darcy could proclaim that 'all true Catholics may joy'.[31] The Duke played for time by speculating about coming to an agreement which he knew the King would not allow him to make. Some monasteries could be reopened if the abbots discussed their future with the Commissioners. Cromwell might be impeached. The pardon might be extended to cover all the leaders of the revolt. Aske reported back, first to the three hundred Pilgrims who had been chosen to support the negotiators, and then to the host in Pontefract. He adjudged his followers well satisfied. Then other members of the negotiating team, who saw the outcome differently, returned. They argued that there should be no agreement until the form of the general pardon was made known, and some proposed an immediate resumption of hostilities to convince the King that they were in earnest.

Aske, virtually repudiated by his followers in Pontefract, was persuaded to return to Doncaster and argue for a better deal. Despite hours of wrangling, he achieved nothing except increasing pessimism that a deal of any sort could be achieved. Lancaster Herald, back in Pontefract, took advantage of the stalemate to read the proclamation of the King's pardon. Aske – whose gullibility belied his reputation – accepted the offer at its face value and announced that he was resigning the leadership of the Pilgrimage. Tearing the badge of Christ's Five Wounds from his tunic, he swore 'to wear no badge nor sign but the badge of our sovereign lord'. There was much rejoicing that the Pilgrimage of Grace had ended without a bloody confrontation. It took some time for the rank-and-file of the Pilgrim host to realise that virtually none of their demands had been accepted by the King.

Although Norfolk had ended the nascent revolution without making any significant concession, Henry was profoundly dissatisfied with the outcome of the Pontefract peace talks. The half promises could be, and were, repudiated. But his enemies had remained unpunished. The wording of a proclamation addressed to the dissident counties – which followed the reoccupation of Yorkshire by the royal forces – made clear that they would not remain unpunished for long.

There were too many Pilgrims to allow the King to wreak his vengeance on the entire host. So he justified selective retribution with the explanation that, because most of Aske's followers had 'proceeded out of ignorance and by occasion of sundry false tales ... set abroad among you by sundry malicious persons', he was inclined to 'extend his most gracious pity and mercy towards you'. The implication that mercy would be denied to the 'sundry malicious persons' was clearly understood by those members of the nobility who had, with varying degrees of reluctance, joined the Pilgrims. Darcy stood firm, but less resolute characters wrote to their friends at Court to secure confirmation of their pardons. Edward Lee, Archbishop of York – fearful that his vows of loyalty to the King would be forgotten and his oath to support the pilgrimage remembered – told Thomas Cromwell, 'If I could have foreseen that such an office would fall upon my head, I had rather been your priest than a bishop.'[32]

The behaviour of the fearful nobles was predictable. Robert Aske's conduct was not. When he received the message that the King had 'conceived a great desire to speak with him and therefore commands him to come with great diligence ... And trusts that Aske at his access will, by plain speaking, deserve reward', he accepted at once. Even the warning that he must travel to London 'making no man privy thereto'[33] was not enough to convince him that he was being lured into some sort of trap. After his death, it was claimed that he posted associates along the road south so that – if he were arrested – a swift message to the north could renew the uprising. But abduction was not what the King had in mind. Henry wanted to destroy Aske's reputation in the north and, as a result, the unity of the Pilgrims.

There is no doubt that Aske was well received at court. Stories of Henry greeting him with a warm embrace, making him presents of a scarlet silk coat and a gold chain and appointing him to the Privy Council were, almost certainly, rumours maliciously spread by Pilgrims who were dissatisfied with the Doncaster agreement and suspected Aske of being in secret alliance with the King. In his absence the dissatisfaction increased, as the Pilgrims' rank and file gradually realised how little they had gained. Protests against the King escalated into violence against his representatives. The monks of Sawley Abbey – no doubt conscious that their continued residence depended on the Pilgrims' grievances being remedied – produced a document that demanded that the Pilgrims take up arms again. It was nailed to the door of parish churches. Leaseholders of monastery lands refused to pay rent to the crown. In Richmond and Barnard Castle no taxes were collected. Militancy was encouraged by stories – none of them true – of new risings in Cambridgeshire, Suffolk, Kent, Worcester and Oxford. Serious plans were made to reoccupy Hull and Scarborough and hold the cities ransom until Parliament met in York and addressed the grievances.

Aske was back in Yorkshire on January 8th 1537 and began, at once, to argue in favour of the Pilgrims respecting the agreement they had made on Doncaster Bridge. His choice of words convinced the sceptics that he had become the King's agent. 'The King's Highness is a good and gracious Lord unto us ... He has granted all our desires and petitions and will keep a parliament shortly in York.'[34] In the inexplicable belief that it would provide some sort of reassurance, Aske told the Pilgrims that the Duke of Norfolk would soon come north. About that, at least, he was right.

Despite Aske's call for the Doncaster deal to be respected, there was a new rising in Beverley and a great rally, reminiscent of the Pilgrims' early days, was held in the grounds of Fountains Abbey. A rumour that Aske had been assassinated persuaded some of his friends to join the sporadic uprisings. So he travelled to Ripon to prove that he was still alive, and to Beverley to persuade its citizens to be patient. After a traveller from Boston told the local Pilgrims that the supposed amnesty, agreed in Doncaster, was not being respected in Lincolnshire, there was nothing he could do to prevent new risings in Lancashire. The tales were true. The hostages, demanded by the King before the local revolts had ended, had been captured and were already in prison – among them Captain Cobbler.

The King called Darcy to Court. Wisely he chose not to go. His official explanation was that he thought it his duty to remain in the north and work with Aske to prevent an uprising which was more powerful, but less principled, than the Pilgrimage of Grace. Whether or not the desire to broker peace was the real reason for his rejection of the King's invitation, there was certainly the need for a moderating influence among what was left of the Pilgrims. Impatient and suspicious, they had found a new leader: Sir Francis Bigod of Mulgrave Castle near Whitby. Thanks to him, the Pilgrimage of Grace ended in disorder and despair.

Bigod had been a Protestant zealot. He had emerged from East Riding obscurity as a protégé of Cardinal Wolsey, was appointed one of the King's Commissioners for Yorkshire and had contributed mightily to the completion of *Valor Ecclesiasticus* – the inventory of the wealth owned by English churches and monasteries. During the performance of his duties, he had happened to be in the congregation in Jervaulx Abbey when a monk, George Lazenby, had preached against the Act of Supremacy. Bigod had the monk arrested and, in consequence, became anathema to the Pilgrims. When they approached Whitby, where he had taken refuge, he tried to escape their wrath by sea, but his boat was blown north to Hartlepool. Captured by the Pilgrims, he underwent what seems to have been a genuine conversion. From then on, he was a zealot for the Pope and Rome.

Shortly after his conversion, Bigod met, by chance, John Hallam – a militant among the original Pilgrims and one of the men behind the move to occupy Hull and Scarborough, which Aske had frustrated. Bigod regarded the meeting as an Act of God which the Almighty had arranged to initiate another rising, and announced that Hallam had convinced him that a fresh pilgrimage must begin. The Yorkshire militants had found a new leader. Bigod's eloquence moved his audiences to religious rapture. 'Also here is that the king should have cure of your body and soul, which is plain false for it is Gospel of Christ and that I will justify to my death.'[35] His strategic thinking was not of the same quality as his oratory. Short of men, the new rebels failed to take Hull, where the citizens had grown weary of religious wars. Bigod retired in disorder, leaving behind to their fate many of the men to whom he had promised a victorious pilgrimage.

The failure of the second uprising – sometimes regarded as independent of the first – convinced all but the most passionate Pilgrims that their best hope lay in Aske's assurance of the King's mercy. But Bigod's behaviour had changed the prospect of even that. Henry knew that his belatedly recruited army could easily crush what little resistance remained. And he had been provided with a pretext for doing so. During his flight from Beverley, Bigod had dropped a number of papers. One of them denounced the Act of Supremacy in the most extreme terms. Discovery of the polemic made plausible the spurious charge that an armed rising had been mounted to defeat the will of King and Parliament. That was a breach of the agreement negotiated on Doncaster Bridge. The King was no longer required to keep his side of the bargain.

Bigod, still at large, continued to encourage revolt and did manage to incite one or two ineffectual risings. But, north of the Humber, all was confusion. Some Pilgrims feared that the Duke of Norfolk would treat Yorkshire as Lincolnshire had been treated. Others hoped that he would come, with no more than his personal household, to give pardons and administer oaths of loyalty. The spirit of righteous obligation which had once inspired the Pilgrims was dead. When Norfolk eventually arrived – at Candlemas 1537 – he proceeded with caution that was mistaken for leniency. One by one, Pilgrims confessed that they had 'Offended the King in this rebellion', swore that they repented and would not transgress again, handed over their arms and named the captains who had led the Pilgrimage.

It became clear, even to the most naive Pilgrim, that anyone who had taken part in a rebellion, after the Doncaster amnesty, would not be included in its provisions and would die. Hallam and Bigod had already been executed. There was to be one last spark of rebellion before the fire of faith was finally extinguished. Six thousand rebels mustered outside Carlisle and opened fire, with longbows, on the garrison. They were slaughtered by mercenaries recruited on the Scottish border, whom the rebels – in their simplicity – believed God would give them the power to vanquish. In town after town across Lancashire, Cumberland, Durham and Northumberland, hostages were taken and executed alongside men who were casually nominated, and often wrongly identified, as instigators of the new rebellion.

The carnage spread across all of England north of the River Trent. Two hundred and sixteen men and women were executed on Norfolk's orders. Most of them were hanged, cut down before death, disembowelled and then beheaded. As many others died in his prison, were summarily executed or were murdered by his rapacious looting troops. The leaders of the Pilgrimage, and its most prominent supporters, were sent to London for prosecution in show trials. Among them were Lord Darcy and Robert Aske.

Darcy exercised his right to be tried by his peers. At the hearing which preceded his trial he set out, bravely and convincingly, who he believed the true miscreant to be: 'Cromwell, it is thou that art the very original and chief cause of this rebellion and mischief.'[36] There was no doubt that Darcy had been in rebellion against the crown. But it was equally certain that, after the Doncaster amnesty, he had kept the oath of loyalty and done his best to persuade others to do the same. Since it was necessary to charge him with an offence committed after the Doncaster agreement was signed, he was charged with the treasonable attempt to capture Hull and was convicted on perjured evidence. On the King's instruction, Darcy's execution was planned to take place in the north, so that the men and women who were still tempted to support the cause for which he died were reminded that the penalty for treason was death. Henry was persuaded that a whole army would be needed to prevent his prisoner being rescued. Death was, for Darcy, an insufficient penalty. He was posthumously expelled from the Order of the Garter; and a recent addition to the chivalrous company, Thomas Cromwell, was given his stall in Windsor Chapel.

Robert Aske was taken to the Tower for what can only be described as a show trial. The prosecution had prepared 107 questions for him to answer. They ranged from dates and details of meetings with Darcy, to his opinion on the general behaviour of the King. There was no mention of his attempts, after Doncaster, to convince his followers that Henry was their rightful sovereign. Christopher Aske confirmed the Pilgrims' earlier suspicions that he was one of Henry's agents by giving evidence at his brother's trial that he had tried to persuade Robert to be loyal to the King and that his pleas had been rejected. The conviction was a formality and the sentence mandatory. Aske was to be hanged, drawn and quartered.

It was decided to risk carrying out the execution in York and that it should take place on market day – so as to attract the largest possible crowd – at the top of the hill by Clifford's Tower. The proceedings could not begin until the Duke of Norfolk arrived, and Aske spent some of the time making the customary speech. He described the resentment he felt on hearing that Cromwell had described all northern men as traitors and called on God to witness that the King had granted him a pardon. Then he made his last wish. 'Let me be full dead ere I be dismembered.' The wish was granted. So it was a corpse that the hangman butchered, before draping the torso in chains and hanging it from the arm of the scaffold.

CHAPTER 4

The Necessity of Doctrine

During the three years in which the Pilgrimage of Grace fought the good, if hopelessly naive, fight, the Reformation moved on from its political phase and became no longer principally concerned with Henry's unfettered authority – spiritual as well as temporal. Henry was agreeable, though not passionately committed, to the critical examination of the profound questions about the liturgy, ceremonials and theology in what was to become the Church of England. The pace and extent of the Reformation's second phase increased because the King's two closest advisers – Cromwell and Cranmer – encouraged him to make greater and swifter changes than he, left to himself, would even have contemplated. Some of the changes, when he had the time and inclination to think about them, he came to regret and reverse. Whatever he had believed in the early years of the Reformation, the only passionate commitment to 'reform' which survived to the end of his reign was the determination that the Pope no longer had dominion in England.

Henry's inconstancy complicated the lives of his two principal councillors. Their motives were, at least in part, different. Each wanted to prove himself the man in whom the King could most trust. Both believed that establishing a Protestant Church and state guaranteed security and stability. But Cromwell – who had become Vicar General as well as Master of the Rolls – hoped to see England, freed from the shackles of Rome, form an indomitable alliance with the Protestant states of northern Europe. Cranmer – a scholar before he became Archbishop of Canterbury in 1533 – simply and sincerely believed that the Protestant religion was the true faith.

For a time both men were prepared to compromise with the conservative – that is to say, Roman Catholic-inclined – bishops. In Easter week 1534, Cranmer agreed a concordat with John Longland of Lincoln, John Stokesley of London and Stephen Gardiner of Winchester. For a year there would be no contentious preaching. The Pope's claims to authority over the English Church were to be denied and denounced. But sermons were to be 'neythr with nor against purgatory, honouring of saynts, that priests may have wives, that faith only justifieth, to go on pilgrimages, to forge miracles'.[1] The list of forbidden topics amounted to an agenda of issues which, sooner or later, would have to be resolved.

In April 1535, Thomas Cromwell shattered the final weeks of the truce on the pretext of enforcing it. He wrote, in the King's name, to every bishop, Lord Lieutenant, noble and Justice of the Peace in every county. His letter contained a stark instruction. It was their duty to imprison every priest who had been 'seduced with filthy and corrupt abominations of the Bishop of Rome or his disciples or his adherents'.[2] Cromwell was the man the clergy feared. Cranmer excited only contempt; he was a priest and a scholar who must, his critics argued, recognise that the Reformation was pure evil. Yet to rise in this world he had sacrificed the hope of eternal life in the next. In fact Cranmer was a convinced and sincere Protestant. But even that qualified him, in many priests' opinion, for the proper fate of heretics. The chaplain to John Clerk, Bishop of Bath and Wells, expressed publicly what many other priests were thinking. He 'trusted to see the day when my Lord of Canterbury should be burned'.[3]

Cromwell's beliefs were expressed in the crude language of a soldier. His hatred of the Eucharist – 'that visible thing which the people saw with their eyes and took for the very God'[4] – was passionate and personal. And he openly objected to the compromise which allowed images to remain in churches as long as they were used as 'laymen's books' rather than as objects of veneration – a concession which he claimed, with much justification, was being abused. The echoes of the Pilgrimage of Grace, which set out to protect pictures and statues, were still reverberating around Canterbury. There was much alarm in London, when Cromwell discovered that the parish of St Keverne in Cornwall had commissioned a banner which depicted the Five Wounds of Christ together with a representation of 'the commonality kneeling . . . making a petition . . . that they might have their holy days restored'.[5] The Five Wounds were the badge of the Pilgrimage of Grace. Cromwell's agent in the south-west urged him to defuse what might become a second rising by granting the parishioners' wish. He refused. There were to be no concessions to Popery. However, concessions were on their way, and opposition to them would lead to Cromwell's destruction.

Back in 1530, the Protestant Princes of northern Europe had met at Augsburg to agree a common theological position, and in 1535 – believing that an uncertain England was in need of friends – they proposed that Henry should endorse the Lutheran text, which they had agreed five years earlier, and give his support to a new alliance. British ambassadors discussed the proposal with the Princes' emissaries (including Luther himself) and in 1536 produced the seventeen compromises that were known as the Wittenberg Articles. Neither side was satisfied with the outcome. The English delegates were not so much opposed themselves as cautious about the King's reaction. The Lutherans wanted the proscription of 'four abuses': clerical celibacy, the Catholic form of Communion, private Masses and monastic vows. Cranmer saw the Articles as providing an opportunity to make progress towards a statement of belief which would confirm the Church of England as a distinct and independent Protestant Church. He had no reason to think the King would disagree. It is unlikely that, at the time, Henry realised that – when turned to serious thoughts of death and damnation – there would be elements of Catholicism which he could not bring himself to reject.

In an attempt to make a pre-emptive strike against acceptance of the Wittenberg Articles, a group of conservative clergy arranged for the Lower House of Convocation to complain to the bishops about seventy-six heresies which, they claimed, were being practised without punishment or rebuke. But they were outmanoeuvred. Attention was deflected from their complaint by the publication of Ten Articles, the work of a hundred senior churchmen. They had modified the Wittenberg agreement and produced what amounted to a compromise that it was thought would satisfy the King. Their submission set out three orders of religious obligation. The first order – which included the sacraments – declared that baptism, the Eucharist and penance were *essential* to salvation. The second order – confession and absolution – were described as *necessities*. The third – works of charity – were no more than *required*. The language had been carefully chosen. The term 'transubstantiation' was never used. The alternative description of the most sacred moment in the Mass asserted that the 'very substance' of Christ's body and blood were present at the Eucharist. Disagreement over the path to redemption – grace or good works – was avoided by describing justification as brought about by 'contrition and faith joined with charity'.

Initially Henry found it convenient to give the Ten Articles his support – even though it implied belief in justification by faith alone, one of Luther's 'heresies' by which the King had been genuinely outraged, at the time of the Wittenberg declaration, and had, in consequence, honestly condemned. He wanted to maintain the prospect of an alliance with the Protestant Princes and the Ten Articles' general tone created the impression of reform, without revolution. There was some continued doubt about his endorsing the recommendation to limit the number of holy days. But Convocation supported the proposed restriction. Cromwell issued another of his injunctions to the

clergy. They were instructed to publicise the Ten Articles and implement the decision to limit holy days without delay. Then Henry decided
that, although he wanted a more substantial statement of Protestant
theology, it should not be as sympathetic to Lutheran ideas as Cranmer
and Cromwell intended.

Henry's uncertainty and the differences which divided members of the
nascent Church of England were tragically illustrated by the arrest, in
Antwerp, and execution of William Tyndale – betrayed by 'procurement
out of England'.[6] It is not clear who the English agent was and who was
his paymaster. But the King, who had refused to allow Cromwell to write
to the Dutch Court with a plea for clemency made in his name, must
be the chief suspect. Tyndale was convicted – with at least Henry's passive
acquiescence – of publishing an English version of the Bible. Cromwell
(with Henry's agreement) was about to require a colloquial version of
the scriptures to be made available in every English parish.

The King's revised position resulted in more months of discussion
before the new text of required belief was available for royal scrutiny.
It reflected much of the dogma which had been set out in the Ten
Articles, though there were new statements – inevitably the result of
further compromise – on the power of extreme unction to redeem sins,
and Confirmation that was said to be desirable but not essential. Henry
still refused to endorse the document but, entirely out of character,
agreed that it should be published. He then read the text more
carefully and reacted by proposing two hundred and fifty amendments,
including his own versions of the Lord's Prayer and the Ten
Commandments. The revision took so long that, by the time that it
was completed, it was too late for incorporation in the printed document. So what was officially known as *The Institution of a Christian
Man* never received the royal imprimatur. Twenty-five bishops had
signed the preface. So it came to be called *The Bishops' Book*.

Some of the King's objections to *The Bishops' Book*'s conclusion
were so fundamental that it is hard to understand how a man of so
autocratic a disposition allowed its publication. He rejected out of
hand the doctrine of justification by faith alone – an absolute corner-
stone of Protestant theology. He diametrically altered the meaning of
the passages on forgiveness by adding two words to one sentence.
Henry's revised version read, 'The penitent must conceive certain hope
and faith that God will forgive him his sins and repute him justified . . .
not only for the merit and worthiness of any work done by the penitent but chiefly for the only merits for the blood and passion of our
Saviour Christ.'[7] By adding the words 'only' and 'chiefly' to the original
text, Henry had stood the whole idea on its head.

The original text had explicitly reaffirmed the doctrine of transub-stantiation. Henry proposed to strengthen the reaffirmation by adding that, after the consecration of the host, there remained no element of the bread and wine which had gone before, but 'none other substance but the substance of His body and blood'.[8] But the King was just as determined to establish his distinctive convictions on the issue that had alienated him from the Church of Rome as he was to confirm and clarify his position on issues on which he remained a quasi-Catholic. The reason for the schism was disagreement over his own status within and above the Church in England. The first draft of *The Bishops' Book* called him 'Supreme Head of the Church of England'. Henry proposed an amendment which drove the point home. It described him as 'by God's law supreme Head of this whole Church and congregation of England'.[9]

It seems that Henry enjoyed his excursion into theology, decided that he was an expert on doctrine and dogma, and looked about him for more errors to correct. So, with enviable if unjustified confidence in his own judgement, he rejected the findings of a paper, written by Hugh Latimer, on the subject of purgatory and insisted that sinners escaped from that unhappy state – or at least reduced the period of their stay – not only by God's grace but also by meritorious behaviour. It was not, nor ever has been, clear if the King simply insisted on items of dogma which took his fancy or if he made a calculated decision to edge closer to Catholicism.

Cranmer's respect for serious scholarship, as much as his devout beliefs, made him deeply distressed by the King's initiative. Bravely, though brutally, he decided to organise a demonstration of militant Protestantism in order to demonstrate – to the King as well as other doubters – that the creation of an independent English Church had only just begun. So he launched a campaign of carnage. What he claimed to be 'fraudulent relics' were burned at St Paul's Cross and they were followed to the flames by a friar who – having claimed the Pope was head of the Church and John Fisher a true martyr – was convicted of heresy. Images of the Virgin were burned on the pretext that they had been worshipped rather than respected as symbols of faith. Lighting of candles at the foot of statues or before holy pictures was forbidden. Cromwell joined in with gusto by issuing an injunction which initiated an orgy of declaratory destruction. In order to demon-strate the rejection of the ways of Rome, rood screens and statues were to be removed from churches and either destroyed on the spot or stored in a repository in Chelsea to await public burning.

There was plenty of support for the officially sanctioned vandalism.

John Hilsey, Cardinal Fisher's successor at Rochester, welcomed the burning of the rood screen which had been taken from Boxley parish church, and accompanied the sacrilege with a prediction that 'the idolatrie will never be left till the said images be taken away'.[10] Hugh Latimer wrote from Worcester to urge the destruction of statues of the Virgin Mary, which he described with an intentionally offensive flippancy. He told Cromwell that the Worcester Virgin, 'our great Sybyll', should burn, alongside 'her older sister of Walsingham, her younger sister at Ipswich with their other two sisters of Doncaster and Penrice'.[11] Latimer added gratuitously that opposition to the removal of the Worcester Virgin came not from pious Christians, but from avaricious shopkeepers who feared a loss of trade if the number of pilgrims to the city significantly decreased.

The King's new-found sympathy with the traditional mode of worship did not, it seems, impel him to defend its physical manifest-ations. Nor did it dispose him to forbid or prevent the repetition of the previous year's highly un-Catholic attempts to make bibles available to the common people. Carrying out the instruction was made possible by another of Cromwell's initiatives. In 1537 he had commissioned the publication of what he claimed was a new translation of the Bible by Thomas Mathew. It was a disguised version of the Bible which the murdered Tyndale had produced. That was only the beginning. Miles Coverdale was employed to produce a genuine original translation. Copies were sent to every parish in England.

As the theological weathervane spun round and round, new attempts were made to come to some agreement with the northern European Lutherans. The talks broke down after the delegates from the German principalities decided, rightly, that Henry was more inter-ested in securing power than in finding the theological truth and that he only took a periodic interest in dogma and doctrine. Cromwell – once exalted for having helped the King to dispose of Anne Boleyn – was, like all of the royal favourites, vulnerable to Henry's capricious changes of mood. He attempted to reclaim lost political influence by an attack on what he chose to describe as the two extreme positions – uncompromising in their support for, and opposition to, Rome – which threatened the unity of the realm. Henry became increasingly strident in the defence of his own authority, fearful of invasion by the Catholic powers and determined to root out and eradicate his enemies. One enemy, who had caused particular offence, was an old friend.

For years Cardinal Reginald Pole – probably still feeling gratitude for Henry's earlier favours – had been guarded in his criticisms of the English Reformation and had echoed More's view that 'Our evils, the evils of England, are not really ours; they are the evils of the whole church.'[12] Reforms in the Vatican, and the executions of More and Fisher, had convinced him that England was unique in its degeneracy. His initial response had been *De Unitate (pro ecclesiasticae unitatis defensione)*, a letter to Henry which became a book, 280 folio pages long. The first part was an open attack on Henry and the schism that he had brought about. The second was a resolute defence of the Pope as head of the Church. Both parts were intentionally offensive about the King. Passages were written as if the accusations were made to Henry in person. One direct assault described Henry's sins: 'You have squandered huge treasures. You have made a laughing stock of the nobility. You have never loved the people. You have pestered and robbed the clergy in every conceivable way. And lately you have destroyed the best men in the kingdom, not like human beings, but wild beasts.'[13]

Richard Sampson, Bishop of Chichester, had suggested that the moral depravity of past Popes could not be reconciled with the notion of Apostolic Succession. *De Unitate* refuted the Bishop's assertion with a rhetorical question which was intended as an insult to Henry. Who would hand the leadership of the Church to a depraved king? To avoid the slightest doubt about the strength of Pole's feelings, *De Unitate* ended with the demand that the Pope publish the bull of excommunication that was already prepared. The Imperial Ambassador in London convinced himself – without any evidence to support his wishful thinking – that Pole had been made a cardinal and nominated as Papal Legate to England not as a provocative act but as a prelude to invasion by the Catholic powers, the execution of Henry and the restoration of England to the true faith.[14]

Henry probably never saw *De Unitate*, but he was told of its contents and his reaction confirmed all that Pole had written about him. A reward of 100,000 pieces of gold was offered to anyone who would 'by some means, have [the traitor] trussed up and conveyed to Calais'.[15] In anticipation of Pole's journey across Europe assassins were hired to foment revolution in England. When the mission was postponed, Henry made Pole's family pay the price for their kinsman's incitement to rebellion. The Cardinal's two brothers and his cousin were indicted for treason, found guilty and executed. At Henry's invitation, Parliament passed a Bill of Attainder against the whole Pole family. Pole's mother, the sixty-eight-year-old Margaret Plantagenet, Countess of Salisbury, was beheaded on Tower Green. Her crime was the possession of a coat of arms, decorated on one side by the symbols adopted by the Pilgrimage of Grace. Henry, confused about his true beliefs and fearful of a successful insurrection, struck out blindly.

More humble heretics – enemies of the King's quasi-Roman theology as well as of his sovereign status – were pursued and prosecuted. Henry's formal links with Rome had been severed by his excommunication in December 1538. But he still drew a sharp distinction between Papism, which must be extinguished, and Catholicism, which must be protected. A commission was appointed to identify and punish evangelicals who denied and disobeyed those elements of the old religion which Henry accepted. His often-conflicting views on true Christianity – changing from time to time and from authority to authority – were, cynics would say, no more than early indications of the Church of England's doctrinal uncertainty. The rival view – that acceptance of diversity is a strength, not a weakness – still provides the justification of the 'broad church'.

There is no reason to suppose that Henry shared the Roman Catholic conviction that certainty is an essential element in the preservation of faith. It is more likely that he took it for granted that, having worked out his own body of dogma and doctrine, his theological conclusions – no matter how confused and contradictory – must be accepted and respected by all his subjects. So on May 16th 1539, the Duke of Norfolk – at the King's instigation – told the House of Lords that it was necessary to re-examine six crucial issues: transubstantiation, Communion in its traditional form, chastity, votive Masses, celibacy and confessions. When the subjects were debated in the (still predominantly Catholic) Upper House, the discussion was led by the King himself who, loyal subjects said, 'confounded them all with God's learning'.[16] He also made sure that the peers reinstated, as essential elements of faith, the celibacy of the clergy, traditional Communion and transubstantiation – the denial of which would lead to certain burning and forfeiture of all property. Hugh Latimer, the most evangelical of the bishops, resigned from the See of Worcester. Cranmer and Cromwell tenaciously hung on to office. But the tide of Reformation had not simply halted. It had begun to recede.

On June 16th 1539, Parliament passed into law the Bill of the Six Articles. The Act received Royal Assent twelve days later. It stipulated that the laity was only to receive bread during Communion, that priests must remain celibate and that confession to a priest was a vital element in the forgiveness of sins. It was rumoured that Cromwell would not implement such obviously 'Catholic' legislation. He was never given the opportunity. Convicted of high treason, he was executed on July 28th 1540. His fall, like every fall in Henry's court, was partly the work of jealous rivals – in Cromwell's case, Stephen Gardiner, the Bishop of Winchester. But there was a perverse logic in including heresy in his indictment. Henry was increasing the speed at which England reflected his determination to move back towards Rome. Cromwell would not travel in that direction. He thus became, though he is rarely recognised as, a Protestant martyr.

Henry, who never felt as secure as his hold on power justified, still thought it necessary to demonstrate that he was not in thrall to Rome. In London, sixteen priests and two hundred laymen were arrested and imprisoned on suspicion of being, or sympathising with, 'Papists' – a noun which reflected Henry's antagonism to an institution rather than to faith. To maintain a balance of brutality, three prominent Protestants were burned for heresy, despite their justified claim that they had done nothing except ridicule the Pope's claim to supremacy. Then, to confirm that he remained impartial in his inhumanity, three well-known Papists followed the trio of Protestants to the stake. To avoid pains and penalties in England of the late 1530s it was necessary either to say nothing or to subscribe to the form of mongrel Catholicism which Henry happened to support at the time.

Despite the risks, there were men and women who were brave enough to remain true to their beliefs. After the fall of Cromwell and the end of the oppressive Protestant regime, Catholics – who had remained true but cautious – took advantage of the King's ambivalence to proclaim again their support for the articles of Catholicism, if not their continued affection for the head of the Catholic Church. The reaction was particularly swift in Cranmer's own archdiocese, where cathedral staff collected evidence that the Archbishop had tolerated heresy. The Mayor of Sandwich prohibited, within his town, reading of the Bible by laymen and imprisoned protestors. The vicar of Faversham removed the Bible which had been placed in his church for public scrutiny. The great Canterbury Easter Pageant and Procession – once condemned and abandoned as superstitious – was revived. The King intervened to save Cranmer, after telling him in a joke, which the Archbishop could not have enjoyed, 'I know now who is the greatest heretic in Kent.'[17]

The Six Articles – although they included all the essential elements of Henry's religious belief – did not satisfy the King's need for a text by which he and his people should live. The necessary document was written as a revision of *The Bishops' Book* after long and sometimes acrimonious discussion between Thomas Cranmer and three bishops (two of whom were of a Roman inclination). The result of their labours – published under the title of *A Necessary Doctrine and Erudition for Any Christian Man* in the summer of 1543 – was again revised by Henry himself and, because the revision was completed in time for incorporation, he pronounced himself satisfied with the result. So the text came to be called *The King's Book*. It proclaimed that Jesus Christ was the only universal governor of the Church, with Christian kings and princes 'governing under him in particular Churches'. But that dismissal of papal authority did not, as is sometimes claimed, make *The King's Book* a statement of 'Catholicism without the Pope'. It was more a statement of 'Catholicism *à la carte*'. That, in itself, made it a Protestant document. For Catholics cannot pick and choose. But it endorsed central items of Catholic belief and therefore stands both as proof of Henry's capricious intellect and as a milepost on his journey back to the public acceptance of most Catholic doctrine.

The Protestant objection to the doctrine of purgatory (and the consequent importance of prayers for the dead) was reiterated and emphasised and the demand for regular Communion was dismissed as 'pestiferous and devilish'.[18] But there was a reduced emphasis on the importance of the Bible, the acceptance of images (as long as they were not objects of worship) and the restoration of much traditional ceremonial. One of the basic principles of the Reformation was formally rebutted. Belief in justification by faith was replaced by redemption and salvation by good works. Two of the fundamental beliefs of Catholicism – transubstantiation and the importance of confession – were re-emphasised. The inclusion of 'consecrating and offering the blessed body and blood of Christ in the sacrament of the altar'[19] in the definition of the priests' duty was confirmation that, at the time of *The King's Book*'s publication, Henry was in one of his pro-Mass phases. When he was in favour, he was strongly in favour. For months he attended Mass several times in one day (sometimes acting as server) and, on the death of Jane Seymour in 1537, he had several thousand Masses said for the repose of her soul. When he was against, he was strongly against. In 1540, he had told the French Ambassador that he was considering abolishing the Mass completely and that France should do the same.[20]

When *A Necessary Doctrine* was considered by Convocation, the genuinely Protestant bishops fought a determined rearguard action. Thomas Cranmer tried to restore several of the items of dogma which had been deleted by the King. They included the assurance that anointing the sick was 'an assured promise of recovery'.[21] Irritated by Cranmer's persistence, Stephen Gardiner, the Bishop of Winchester, had him arrested and charged with heresy. The King, after the intervention of the 'reforming' bishops, ordered his release. *A Necessary Doctrine* passed through Parliament after several new obligations had been added to its list of duties which were required of Christian men. One of them – inspired by fear of widespread learning – required that 'no woman nor artificers, prentices, journeymen, serving men of the degree of yeomen or under, husbandmen or labourers' were to read the scriptures.[22] Henry marked its passage, as well as revealing his fear of purgatory and revolution, by giving a demonstration of his belief in transubstantiation. He presided – dressed in the white of purity – at the trial of John Lambert, an Anabaptist, who confessed to denying the 'real presence' during the Eucharist. Lambert confessed. He was convicted and burned with more than usual barbarity. After his legs had been burned away, the fire was allowed to die down and two soldiers held what was left of him above the embers on their pikes, like an ox on a spit. He was roasted to death.

During the years that lay ahead, theological differences within the Protestant faith multiplied and, as a result, schism followed schism and old denominations divided into new sects. The Roman Catholic Church attempted, with mixed success, to hold the doctrinal and liturgical line. A succession of Popes were steadfast in their insistence that the Catholic Church could not compromise with heretics, but after the formal breach with Rome, many of its followers in England felt it was better to compromise with the state than accept the penalties of rejecting the new religion. But compromise is not capitulation. Some Catholics certainly did capitulate, just as some chose death rather than apostasy. More (perhaps most) kept as true to the old faith as they dared, hoping both to save their lives on earth and their souls in heaven. Measuring the extent to which they achieved those two ambitions is complicated by the absence of a contemporary definition of Catholicism itself.

Most of the sixteenth-century definitions were tautological. In 1531, John Fisher, Bishop of Rochester, said that the true Church was 'catholica, that is to saye unyversall ... because it is not lymyt to any certain natcyons, but is common to all'.[23] That did not provide much guidance for Catholics who were struggling to reconcile imminent death and eternal life. Nor did More, in his Response to Martin Luther. He defined Catholicism as 'the common and perceptible multitude of men professing the name and faith of Christ's Church by whose teaching the scripture is determined and the faith is learned and recognised with certainty'.[24] That definition includes the implication that the determination might change with a change in the body of men.

The view that Catholicism is whatever the Pope chooses to make it was, despite the authority conferred on him by the Apostolic Succession, usually only advanced by sworn enemies of Rome. But in 1531 that definition had been good enough to free Nicholas Shaxton from the suspicion of heresy. The inquiry dismissed all charges when he agreed to uphold 'all articles and points as the Catholic Church of Rome believeth, holdeth or maintaineth at this time'[25] – without thinking it necessary to set out what they were. The qualification 'at this time' was important, for there were regular changes, usually reflecting political necessity, in the 'articles and points'.

To accommodate those necessities, even the most distinguished and devout Catholic leaders equivocated from time to time. In 1530, Reginald Pole condemned Henry's assumption of royal supremacy as 'satanic'. Four years later, he congratulated 'Henrician schismatics' – men who accepted Henry's supremacy, but held fast to the liturgy and dogma of Rome – for resisting heresy.[26] In voluntary exile he claimed that it was the executions of More and Fisher that convinced him that Henry was evil. If so, he was slow to come to that conclusion. On October 28th 1535 – more than three months after More's death – he had written to Cromwell with the request that the King be informed of his readiness to do him service at all times.[27] It was not until 1536 – and the publication of De Unitate – that he expressed, in admirably trenchant language, his opinion of the King. Self-serving vacillation knew no religious boundaries.

The King himself was the most unreliable and inconsistent theologian in England. He claimed to support the views put forward by William Tyndale in The Obedience of the Christian Man and he told the Imperial Ambassador, with every justification, that there was much in the writing of Martin Luther with which he agreed.[28] Yet he proscribed their work and allowed More and the bishops to burn their supporters as heretics. In the light of the King's inconsistent apostasy, it is not surprising that so many humble men and women, in fear of their lives, sought to remain Catholics, but hide their Catholicism.

Some received both Anglican and Catholic Communion. Others, at Church of England services, only responded to those parts of the liturgy which reflected the Mass. Recusants refused to attend Church of England services – even when the law required them to do so. Only the hard core called themselves, or were called, Papists. Most men and women accepted that Henry was head of their Church, but rejoiced when he moved its theology closer to that of Rome. There is no serious way of calculating the size of the English Catholic population or of the various groups, inclinations and tendencies of which it was composed, But one thing is clear beyond doubt. Unless Catholicism is narrowly defined as belief in papal supremacy, at the end of Henry VIII's reign, in terms of belief, England was still a Catholic nation.

CHAPTER 5

Sufficient Sacrifice

The Reformation came to Scotland long before Henry championed it in England, and north of the border it was attributable to more reputable – that is to say, theological rather than political – origins. The Lollards, fleeing persecution in England, and Hansa merchants, carrying goods to Leith and Dundee, spread the Protestant word. One self-confessed Lollard, James Resby, was executed as early as 1407, and Paul Crawar, a Hussite, was burned in 1433, but there was no coordinated attempt to purge Scotland of heresy. In 1494 thirty men were arraigned before the Archbishop of Glasgow and questioned about their deviant beliefs. They must have given convincing answers, for they were dismissed with a warning, not about their future conduct, but about the dangers of false dogma. The concerted, but by no means fanatical, campaign against heresy began in 1525 when the Scottish Parliament passed an Act which prohibited the importation of Lutheran books and pamphlets and the dissemination of Lutheran doctrine.

The first martyr to stir the Scottish conscience was Patrick Hamilton, Abbot of Ferne – a title he bore, despite not being in Holy Orders, because his father was the head of a noble house and his mother was a direct descendant of James II of Scotland. Hamilton was, by the standards of the time, an undoubted heretic, who was said by his critics to have been corrupted by too much learning. He studied in Paris and Louvain, before returning to the University of St Andrews where he began, at once, to spread Luther's gospel. Warned that he faced arrest, Hamilton fled from Scotland. He spent six months in Germany, including a visit to Luther in Wittenberg, before returning home. James Beaton – Archbishop of St Andrews – was waiting for him. Because of Hamilton's noble connections, Beaton chose not to arrest and charge him in the way that he would have arrested and charged a commoner. Instead, he invited Hamilton to take part in a public disputation at St Andrews University. Hamilton's performance made a formal indictment unnecessary. He condemned himself. He was convicted of heresy and executed on the same day.

Hamilton died a particularly brutal death. And whichever version of his final minutes is true, he went bravely to meet his Maker. The fire beneath the condemned man burned slowly. So it took him six hours to die and the gunpowder, which should have exploded and ended his torment, only blew away one hand and the left side of his face. One account of his last minutes claimed that he roared defiance in the face of the Blackfriars prior who persisted in asking him to repent. Another tells a very different story. 'The martyr never gave any sign of impatience nor anger, nor ever called upon heaven for vengeance' upon his persecutors.[1] The description of Hamilton dying in a paroxysm of fury was supplied by John Knox, who believed that Hamilton's death had a profound effect on Scottish opinion. 'When the cruel wolves had, as they supposed, clean devoured their pray, they find themselves in worse case than they were before ... Almost throughout the whole realm (who had heard of the fact) there was not found one who began not to inquire: Wherefore was Master Patrick Hamilton burned?'[2] It certainly had a profound effect on Knox, though he attributed his conversion to Protestantism to sermons preached by Thomas Gwilliam (a Blackfriars prior) in Edinburgh.

Gwilliam was a moderate, and so was Knox until he met George Wishart – a preacher with a long and chequered history of antagonism to Rome. Wishart, while a student in Louvain, had fled to England to escape prosecution for heresy. A sermon preached in Bristol resulted in him being charged again with the same offence. Examined by Cranmer, Cromwell and a selection of bishops, he had recanted, escaped the fire and returned to Scotland – where he immediately began to preach defiance of Rome and the Pope. Knox became his friend, disciple and protector. Together – Wishart carrying a Bible and Knox armed with the broadsword which his statues always feature – they visited town after town and contributed more to the turbulence of the times than to religious enlightenment. After their visit to Dundee, a mob sacked the local monasteries.

David Beaton – who had inherited the See of St Andrews from his uncle, James, and been appointed Cardinal – led the Catholic Church in Scotland during a bizarre episode in the story of the Scottish Reformation. Half of the Scottish nobility had become temporary converts to Protestantism. They demonstrated the zeal with which they held their new beliefs by imprisoning the Cardinal as punishment for crimes that he had committed with their approval. It was a brief incarceration. As soon as it was over, Beaton embarked on a campaign of trial and execution which cast the avenging net widely. In 1544, he had burned seven Protestants for offences which ranged from insulting the Virgin Mary to eating goose on a Friday, and it seemed likely that he would resume his hunt for heretics with equal fervour. Wishart, if caught, was doomed. His friends urged him to lie low. But he refused to 'lurk as a man that wee shamed and durst not show himself before men'.[3] Inevitably – after a month of peripatetic preaching – it became obvious that he could not escape the Cardinal's wrath for much longer. According to his own account, Knox did not want to leave him, but Wishart insisted: 'Nay, return to your bairns. One is sufficient for sacrifice.'[4]

Wishart surrendered after receiving assurances that he and his party would not be handed over to Cardinal David Beaton. The promise was not kept. Wishart recanted, as he had recanted in England. Two apostasies were more than his conscience could bear for long. So he recanted his recantation and was charged with heresy. However Wishart had behaved, the public trial that followed could have had only one possible outcome. The defendant made certainty more certain by denouncing the sacrament of confession and rejecting the belief (as he described transubstantiation) that God 'could be comprehended [between] the priest's hands'. On March 1st 1546, George Wishart was hanged and his body was ceremoniously burned. David Beaton became a hero to Scottish Catholics of a nationalist disposition. The Scottish historian Compton Mackenzie wrote that he 'stands with Bruce and Wallace ... among the great patriots' of Scotland and excused his brutality with an argument which was more ingenious than convincing. 'Of the people who suffered death under his administration ... none was tortured and even his personal enemy Wishart suffered less on the scaffold than the Jacobite martyrs.'[5]

Wishart, like his mentor Martin Luther, denounced the corruption of the Church with as much venom as he employed in his denunciation of its doctrine. There were many good Scottish Catholics who knew the evidence that supported his complaints to be irrefutable and deeply regretted the damage that was done to the Catholic cause by conduct that was indisputably disreputable. One of them was Mary of Guise – widow of James V, and Regent of Scotland during the minority of her daughter. The Dowager Queen Mary complained to Pope Pius IV about the debauchery which she said was rife in Scottish religious houses and cited, in support of her accusation, Cardinal Niccolo Caetani di Sermoneta, who confirmed that Scottish nuns gave birth to children, Scottish monks lived in luxury and Scottish bishops misappropriated Church lands. It is not clear how the Cardinal, who was Archbishop of Capua, became an authority on the Scottish clergy. Nor is it obvious how Mary's proposed remedy, a clerical tax, would have improved the situation. When the Vatican did not even respond to the idea of a fiscal corrective, the Queen Dowager announced that 'the only hope lies in the Holy Father' and begged Pius to set up an episcopal commission to root out the offenders That 'solution' was also ignored by Rome.

Cardinal David Beaton bears some responsibility for the low esteem in which the Catholic Church in Scotland was held. He had, and was publicly known to have, a permanent mistress or partner, one Marion Ogilvy. They lived together openly and produced eight children in what would have been an irreproachable union, had the eleventh-century Gregorian reforms not reaffirmed that the clergy must remain celibate. Legally the Cardinal was guilty of concubinage – an offence so common within the Church that the consistory courts could not possibly have acted against each case. The relationship between David Beaton and Marion Ogilvy is put into proper domestic perspective by a poignant fact about his death. When the assassins arrived at St Andrews Castle – where the couple were lodging – she was out shopping.

Beaton's death was the consequence of a combination of factors. Norman Leslie – the Sheriff of Fife with whom Beaton had been in legal dispute – struck the first, and probably fatal, blow. As Beaton died, one of Leslie's accomplices preached a little sermon which described the victim as a 'vile papist'.[6] But the main motive was greed, jealousy and the wish – for good reasons or bad – to eliminate a friend of France and, in consequence, an enemy of England. Beaton was too rich and too powerful both for his Scottish rivals and for the English agents who were preparing for the union of the two nations. His assassins were paid by the English Ambassador to Edinburgh.[7]

After Beaton was dead, one of his killers – a man called Guthrie – urinated into the corpse's mouth.[8] The naked body was first hung from the castle battlements. Then it was taken to the castle dungeon, where it was left as a memorial to the men who had been imprisoned there. Knox was later to describe the Cardinal's death with a concluding comment that confirmed the brutal character of the Man of God who became the most famous figure in the Scottish Reformation: 'These things we write merrily'.[9] It was not the only proof of his bestial nature which Knox provided. When Mary of Guise called for the capture and execution of the assassins, he attributed her demands to personal grief. The Cardinal, he said, had been the 'comfort to all gentlewomen and especially to wanton widows'.

It was not only the death of Cardinal David Beaton which confirmed the savagery of the sixteen Protestants who took and held St Andrews Castle. They were reinforced by men of similar disposition, held their ground against half-hearted attempts at recapture and made occasional forays into the town. According to a contemporary observer, they 'used their bodies in lechering with fair women, serving their appetites as they thought fit'.[10] That, naturally enough, alienated the local inhabitants, both Catholic and Protestant, and made the recapture of the castle only a matter of time – unless English troops came to the rescue of the Protestant and anti-French garrison.

Henry's campaign against the Scots had, itself, strange religious overtones. It had begun as the 'Rough Wooing' – a bitter epitaph on the causes of the English invasion. The Lords of Congregation (Protestant nobility) had concluded a treaty with Henry which included the promise to marry the infant Queen Mary Stewart to the adolescent Prince Edward, the heir to the throne of England. The promise had been broken and Henry had decided that conquest was the next best thing to matrimony. At one point Henry's generals in Darlington suggested that the morale of the Earl Arran's regiments could be undermined by sending English translations of the Bible to Edinburgh. The King rejected the idea because he feared that the extremism which Bible-reading promoted would spread south of the border. The campaign ended on September 10th 1547, nine months after King Edward's accession, when the Duke of Somerset – Lord Protector of England and of its boy king – routed the Scots at the Battle of Pinkie, a village outside Musselburgh, north of Edinburgh. It was – Flodden notwithstanding – the greatest disaster in the history of Scottish arms. The English army, 16,000 strong, had defeated 25,000 Scots. Scotland lost 14,000 dead, England a few hundred. But, despite the size of the victory, Somerset was unwilling or unable to push on and relieve the siege of St Andrews.

There had been brief truces during the year-long siege and strange negotiated agreements – typical of the Scottish Reformation – during which Protestant and Roman Catholics preached in the parish church on alternate Sundays. During one lull in the fighting, John Knox had taken refuge in the castle and there he remained for several months. Three years earlier he had been appointed religious tutor to the son of a local laird, Brounefield of Greenlaw, and immediately on his arrival he prepared a new catechism on which he examined the young man and his friends when he met them each Sunday in the St Andrews parish kirk in South Street. After a week or two he began to preach in the castle chapel during the daily services.

Knox had affected some doubt about his right to preach. But the apostate friar, who was the chapel's incumbent, told him that the only necessary qualification was to have 'espied the gifts of God'. And that convinced him that preaching was his 'holy vocation'. The castle garrison – despite being largely composed of men who were crude of thought and brutal of habit – began to attend Sunday services. That may well have been because Knox's sermons were crude and brutal, too. He described the Catholic Church as 'the synagogue of Satan, the last beast and the Hoore of Babylon' and 'that horrible harlot in her filthiness'. The Pope was 'the man of sin' and the Mass was the manifestation of all that was wrong with the Church of Rome. His calculated abuse of the sacraments must have offended many Protestants. The wafer was 'a god of water and meal'. It could be destroyed by 'a bold and puissant mouse' which could 'desire no better dinner'. Knox preached with the self-confidence of a man who knew and respected God's will. His sermons – abuse of Catholic dogma and liturgy aside – reasserted the principles of Protestantism one by one and (as was the habit of the populists among Protestant preachers) associated the demands for Church reform with the remedying of social grievances. The violence of his pulpit language more than matched his reaction to the Beaton murder and revealed his belief in an unforgiving Providence. 'These are the works of God, whereby he would admonish the tyrants of the earth, that in the end He will be revenged of their cruelty, what strength so ever they made to the contrary.'[11]

Knox was still at St Andrews when the French – encouraged by Mary of Guise – intervened. Taking advantage of Somerset's slow progress north, they first renewed the siege and then bombarded the castle from the sea. The garrison surrendered and the men who survived – Knox among them – were made galley slaves. According to his own account of his two years in chains, the prisoners were treated with exceptional brutality at the request of the Scottish Catholic establishment. By agreeing to the request that the prisoners be 'sharply handled', the French captors provoked Knox into a rare moment of introspection:

> I know how hard the battle is between the spirit and the flesh, under the heavy cross of affliction, where no worldly defence except present death does appear ... Rests only Faith, provoking us to call earnestly and call for the assistance of God's spirit, wherein, if we continue, our most desperate calamities shall turn to gladness and to prosperity.[12]

During his enslavement in the galleys, Knox refused to attend Mass and rallied his fellow prisoners to the Protestant cause. But although his spirit was strong, his body began to weaken and his health deteriorated to a point at which he was of no further use to the French navy. When he was released he made his way to England – there to add an abrasive voice to the liturgical and doctrinal changes for which young King Edward is given credit. A Reformation, more comprehensive and complete than Henry had thought either possible or right, was about to begin.

CHAPTER 6

Come to Redeem His People

John Hooper was a man of firm and inconvenient convictions. Created Bishop of Gloucester and Worcester, during the slow purge of the conservative episcopate, he chose – rather than accepting his promotion with gratitude and grace – to argue about the 'popish' nature of the enthronement ceremony. He declined to take the established oath or wear the traditional vestments. The Privy Council yielded to his first demand and the oath was reworded. But his objection to the ceremonial cope and mitre was more difficult to accommodate. Eight months of argument followed – most of which Hooper spent in the Fleet prison – before a compromise was reached. Hooper would conform during the enthronement. Thereafter he would wear what he chose in his own cathedral. The dispute established Hooper's position – alongside Nicholas Ridley, who became Bishop of London after Edmund Bonner was deposed – in the leadership of those Protestant reformers who believed that Thomas Cranmer, the Archbishop of Canterbury, moved against Rome with too much tolerance and too little haste. It also gave special force to his judgement that the King whom he served was 'The most faithful and intrepid soldier of Christ'.[1]

The object of Hooper's admiration was Edward VI, a sickly boy who inherited Henry VIII's crown in January 1547 when he was ten years old and was, either by mistake or design, prepared for the throne by tutors of a distinctly Protestant inclination. There is no doubt that the Reformation acquired a new impetus during his six-year reign and that Edward was in sympathy with the increased pace of change. Perhaps he was – as Martin Bucer, the newly appointed Regius Professor of Divinity at Cambridge, claimed – also 'a youth of such godliness as to be the wonder of the whole world'.[2] Edward's piety is not in doubt. Nor is the assiduity with which it was pursued. He was said to read ten chapters of the Bible every day and he took notes, while listening to sermons, and studied them at the end of the service. There were certainly moments of spontaneous and independent action. Believing that the numerous references to St George were in conflict with Protestant practice, he revised the litany used in the annual service that celebrated the Order of the Garter and, during the dispute over

the Gloucester enthronement, he noticed – no doubt to the embarrassment of the new Bishop – a 'popish' sentence in the revised oath: 'So
help me God, all saints and evangelists.' Striking it out with his own
hand, Edward asked, 'What wickedness is here, Hooper? Are these
offices ordained in the name of saints or God?'[3] But, his many virtues
notwithstanding, it is unlikely that a youth of his age could – despite
his undoubted ability – have been the new Josiah and could have
initiated a purge of idols which justified his admirers comparing him
to the iconoclastic eight-year-old King of Judah.

Because of his age and religious inclinations, Edward's reign was
welcomed as a gift from a Protestant deity and greeted with language
which was extreme even by the standards of the age. During the coronation service, Archbishop Cranmer told the young King, 'Your majesty
is God's vice-regent and Christ's vicar within your own dominions,
and to see with your predecessor, Josiah, God truly worshipped and
idolatry destroyed, the tyranny of bishops banished from your subjects
and images removed.'[4]

From the age of ten, Edward kept a diary. As well as proof that he
was a prodigy, it confirms that he retained the character of a Tudor
youth. It records a burning; the acceptance, by the Bishop of
Winchester, of the new theology; and the rebuke which he administered
to his sister, Mary, for allowing Mass to be celebrated in her apartment: 'She was called with my Council into a chamber where it was
declared how long I had suffered her mass in the hope of her reconciliation but that now, there being no hope which I perceived from
her letters, unless I saw amendment I could not bear it. She answered
that her soul was God's and she would not change her faith nor hide
her opinion through contrary doing. It was said that I constrained not
her faith but willed her as a subject to obey.'[5] That little revelation of
the tension at Court is not typical of the diary. Far less space is devoted
to theology and the organisation of the Church than is occupied by
accounts of bull- and bear-baiting and competitions of strength and
chivalry arranged between gentlemen of the Court.

What has come to be called 'the Edwardian Reformation' was the
work of sincere theologians, who recognised a change in the spiritual
weather; and of cynical courtiers, who exploited the breach with Rome
for their own ends. Cranmer was, as he had been for twenty years, a
genuine believer who was ready to change the Church at the fastest
speed compatible with the general acquiescence – genuine enthusiasm
being out of the question – of the common people. Edward Seymour
(Duke of Somerset and Lord Protector after Edward's accession to the
throne) and John Dudley (the Duke of Northumberland, who seized

Seymour's powers in 1550) regarded the rejection of the Pope as a way of enhancing their prestige and consolidating their power. They represented, if they represented anything theological, the peculiarly English form of Protestantism that they had inherited from King Henry: rejection of the Pope's authority rather than his doctrine. But they regarded the campaign to subdue Rome as far less important than the campaign to subdue the Scots, which was the preoccupation of Edward's ministers during the boy king's final years.

The risings against Rome in Scotland were, in themselves, of little consequence to the Pope. But they were a replication of much larger revolts all over Europe, which it had become impossible to ignore. Ever since the excommunication of Martin Luther in 1520, influential figures within the Roman Catholic Church – both traditionalists and reformers – had argued in favour of an Ecumenical Council which would certainly reaffirm, and perhaps in some ways refine, the doctrine of the True Church. Pope Clement VII, fearful that it would result in a renewed attack on established doctrine, had resisted the idea. Paul III, his successor, was daring in his determination to stimulate a debate about the place of the Church in the sixteenth century. He first sponsored the Ratisbon Colloquy, at which Roman Catholics and Protestants had attempted to find common ground on which they could reunite. It collapsed after the expression of fundamental disagreement over every issue they discussed, apart from papal supremacy and justification by faith alone. A head-on collision over the status of the Pope had only been avoided by the unsatisfactory expedient of agreement not to discuss the subject. The still-exiled Cardinal Pole had hoped to agree a compromise on justification – the assertion that neither faith nor good works was its exclusive ingredient. The formula was still being discussed when the Colloquy broke up. The gulf which divided the communions was too wide to bridge.

Encouraged by the emergence of progressive cardinals, Pope Paul III tried again to redefine the Church's place and role in the world. He convened an Ecumenical Council. It first met at Trento on December 13th 1545 and was not officially dissolved until December 4th 1563. In all it held twenty-five sessions during 'periods of deliberation': 1545-7, 1551-2, 1562-3. Because of wars and revolutions, it was forced to move from Trento to Bologna, but it retained its name and purpose. The Council of Trent was set the task of agreeing a united response to the challenge of the Reformation – which, by conviction as well as necessity, it began by condemning outright as 'heretical'.

The Council's eventual conclusions confirmed traditional doctrine.

The Latin Vulgate of St Jerome remained the one true text, and vernacular versions of the scriptures were declared unlawful. A possible compromise on the doctrine of justification was not even discussed. Instead there was the simple rejection of the Lutheran doctrine of justification by faith alone. The doctrines of purgatory, the intercession of the Virgin Mary, the invocation of saints and the veneration of holy relics were all reasserted. Christ was said to be 'really, truly and substantially present' during celebrations of the Eucharist – a definition which gave rise to the terms 'real presence' and 'transubstantiation'. Although the Council was unyielding on doctrine, it was admirably flexible on those aspects of the Church's conduct and administration which had contributed to Protestant rejections of Rome. Indulgences were still to be sought and given, but they were not to be bought and sold. Bishops were to reside in their diocese and would, therefore, be unable to accept pluralities. Convents were to observe strict rules of moral conduct and those that refused to do so were to be closed. Programmes of education were to be put in place in order to guarantee a more knowledgeable and responsive priesthood.

The first session reached its conclusion just as Edward VI came to the throne. Although it dealt with the scandal of absentee bishops, most of its time was devoted to the reassertion of dogma, so its conclusions were sufficiently unbending to enable the English enemies of Rome to warn the young King Edward that compromise with, and tolerance of, the Trent conclusions would be both sinful and unsafe. 'We are,' the bishops asserted, 'desirous of setting forth in all churches the true doctrine of God and have no wish to adapt it to all tastes or deal in ambiguities.' The certainty was magnificent. The Protestant extremists, who had been held back by King Henry's equivocation over everything except papal supremacy, realised that their hour had come.

John Hooper – admittedly a prejudiced witness – concluded that Henry VIII had 'destroyed the Pope but not popery'. Although the monasteries had been 'pulled down' and the 'possessions of monks and nuns ... transferred to his exchequer ... the invocation of saints, auricular confessions, superstitious abstinence from meats and belief in purgatory, were never before held by the people in greater esteem than at the present moment'.[6] Hooper was not alone in wanting to quicken the pace of reform. After Henry's death, Cranmer – who had found the old king an inconstant ally in life – paid tribute to him as indispensable to the Reformation. But, in private, he regretted that during his last years Henry had been more inclined to row back than to press forward. Edward's succession seemed to sound the call at least to cautious advance. The new King had confirmed in office and favour the men who had supported his father during Henry's dying days. 'In consideration of faithful, diligent and painefull service', the 'severall rewards and advancements[s]' which they had received from 'the most excellent and mighty Pryncce ... late Kynge of this our realm' were renewed.[7] But it was to be a continuity of men, not measures. King Edward wanted, or was persuaded to support, changes in the Church which his father would never have tolerated.

While Somerset was in Scotland – inflicting a defeat on the Old Enemy, which should have boosted both his popularity and his self-confidence – Thomas Cranmer and Nicholas Ridley preached sermons before King Edward. Cranmer believed in steady change that attempted to accommodate popular feeling. Ridley's idea of progress was far less measured. But they both chose to denounce the iniquity of erecting and worshipping images – the Protestant description of church statues and paintings – irrespective of whether they were objects of veneration or merely decoration. There followed a period of unofficial iconoclasm. It was less a demonstration of the two bishops' influence than proof that they realised the direction in which their followers were determined to be led.

Images were smashed in Southampton, Hull and St Neots. In Portsmouth the rood screen was 'contemptuously pulld down and spitefully handled'.[8] Undergraduates from Magdalen College, Oxford, toured the university city, burning or breaking every religious artefact they could find. At St Neots, a riotous assembly successfully demanded the restoration of the images. The Privy Council, more sympathetic to Protestantism than in King Henry's day, decided that discretion required them to support the iconoclasts. When the image-breakers who had desecrated the church of St Martin Pomeroy were brought before them, the unavoidable conviction was followed by dismissal with a caution.

Cranmer seized the moment to make the sort of cautious progress which was the central feature of his strategy for ensuring that the Reformation endured. In July 1547, he issued a series of royal injunctions. They were intended to clarify Church policy on the still-contentious subject of idolatry. Injunction Two forbade 'wandering to pilgrimage', kissing relics and 'other such-like superstition'. Injunction Three required the clergy to destroy all images which encouraged the abuse of worship and prayers for intercession. Injunction Twenty-Eight went further than Injunction Three and required the removal of all artefacts which it described as 'monuments of feigned miracles, pilgrimage and superstition'. When parishes complained that the apparent contradiction had become an excuse for inaction, they were told that the two conflicting injunctions could be reconciled if it was assumed that Injunction Twenty-Eight called for destruction *only* when idols, pictures and relics were used for disreputable purposes. The Injunctions on parish processions (forbidden), altar candles (limited in number) and bell-ringing (to be 'utterly forborne' during services) were clear enough, though it is doubtful if they achieved their claimed objective of eliminating 'all contention and strife'.[9] They did, however, succeed in making church services – and in consequence religion itself – more drab than it had been in the high days of Roman Catholicism. The Edwardian Reformation took the colour out of worship and painted it grey.

The promulgation of the Injunctions was followed, in June 1553, by the publication of Forty-Two Articles of Faith – again the work of Thomas Cranmer. The assiduous Archbishop had also prepared Forty-Four Articles for Uniformity of Rites. They were never issued. The Forty-Two Articles confirmed the political settlement. Article Thirty-Six asserted that the King of England was 'the Supreme head on earth, next under Christ, of the Church of England and Ireland'. It also confirmed that the Pope was no more than the Bishop of Rome. There was a point at which canon and temporal law overlapped. Obedience to the civil power had always been an implied requirement of the Reformation. The Forty-Two Articles were explicit: 'The Civil Magistrate is ordained and allowed of God. Wherefor we must obey him not only for fear of punishment but for conscience sake.' As well as suppressing endowed prayers (a blow struck against the chantries), the Forty-Two Articles authorised communicants to take both bread and wine. The assault on images was legally sanctioned the following year by relating the Injunction to an edict of 1538. Thomas Cromwell continued to influence the Reformation from the grave.

The zealots were not satisfied. Legitimising the destruction of images was not enough. They wanted the law to require it. So did the London Commissioners who, under the terms of the Cromwell legislation, had been given the task of ensuring the conformity of priests and churches. Somerset chose to support what he judged to be the increasingly influential Protestant iconoclasts. So he issued an edict requiring all images to be removed immediately from London churches. In November 1547, the Commissioners supervised the removal of St Paul's rood screen and what remained of the cathedral's statues. In 1548 the edict was extended to the whole of England. It was received with different degrees of acceptance and defiance from parish to parish. More often than not it was obeyed, although some churches hid away the venerated statues in the hope that they would be restored in more pious days to come. Others smashed and burned with such enthusiasm that a restraining order had to be issued, stipulating that the destruction 'shall not extend to any image . . . of any king'.[10] Even in the parishes which were totally 'cleansed', the militant Protestants were neither grateful nor satiated. They simply focused their attention on the next objective in the path of their reforming zeal.

Despite having acquired the evangelical views which suited the mood of the time, Somerset, the Lord Protector, was too busy fighting the Scots and fighting off his enemies at Court to spend much time or effort on strengthening or extending the Reformation. The changes for which he deserves praise or blame were driven by necessity rather than conviction. The final destruction of the chantries (endowments to finance priests saying prayers for the founder's soul) was entirely consistent with the Protestant rejection of indeterminate purgatory. But, although it was not mentioned in the preamble, the Chantries Act of 1547 was the result of penury rather than principle. Somerset had run out of money to finance the war in Scotland. In the bill's 'long title' its purpose was described as the suppression of 'vain opinions of purgatory and masses' and the diversion of assets, released by the closures, to such 'good and godly uses as erecting grammar schools to educate youth in virtue and godliness'. There was to be a special emphasis on 'better provision for the poor and needy'.[11]

A previous Chantries Act, two years earlier, had only been passed after fierce opposition in the House of Commons and the conflicting explanations that King Henry was in urgent need of money and that he proposed to embark on a programme of reform rather than of wholesale closures. The Act of 1547 authorised seizure without any explanation about its necessity and was, in consequence, initially rejected by the Commons. The addition of the undertaking to create new grammar schools, subsequently included in the preamble but not in the body of the bill, helped to ease a second version through Parliament. So did the promise of pensions to deposed priests. The priests were paid, but the schools were never founded. The £610,000 raised from the sale of chantry property and land went straight into Somerset's war chest. Schools which had been financed by chantry bequests were forced to close. So – its preamble notwithstanding – the Chantries Act destroyed more schools than it created. Most of them were reopened during the following decades' enthusiasm for education, which saw the number of grammar schools in England rise from 217 to 271. Many of the King Edward schools remain. But they are the enduring achievement of individual benevolence, neither a by-product of the Reformation nor a memorial to the benevolence of the boy king.

Commissioners – as always, since the reign of Henry VIII – were the instrument of what they understood to be the government's real, if unstated, policy. They set out to expropriate 4,000 chantries and an unknown number of associated memorials and foundations. The extent of their success is uncertain and, like the strength of opposition to their intentions, differed from parish to parish. There was open rebellion in Lancashire and the West Country where a mob, estimated to number 3,000, murdered the official who was charged with both tearing down images and dissolving the chantry. But – as at almost every stage of the Reformation – the opposition to what amounted to a religious revolution was strangely muted. Only the Pilgrimage of Grace had threatened to halt the Protestant tide. More, in London, and Pole, in Rome, had been right to argue that the Catholic Church in England, without reform, would slide into slow decline.

During the years between the passing of the two Chantry Acts, the pace of reform quickened. In 1549, yet another of Cranmer's injunctions permitted priests to marry. Heresy laws were repealed and burnings ended – though, as always, exceptions were made for Anabaptists, an umbrella term of abuse which was applied to all manner of radical Protestants who were stigmatised as threats to stable government and executed under the provisions of the civil law. All restrictions on Bible-reading were abolished and – as a contribution to understanding the new faith – Thomas Cranmer published the *Book of Homilies* on which he had been working for five years. The homilies dealt with twelve subjects, ranging from 'universal usefulness' to 'whoredom and uncleanliness'. Belief in the intercession by saints was brushed aside as a Roman heresy. The book strongly recommended that the habit of concluding wills with the hope that 'the Blessed Mary and all the Saints' would pray for the soul of the departed be replaced by the assurance that the author 'trusted only in the merits of Christ the Saviour'.[12] As always with Cranmer, the *Homilies* drew a clear theological distinction between his reasonable Reformation and the wild revolution of the dangerous continentals. 'Antinomianism'– justification by faith alone – was explicitly rejected.

Far away in Edinburgh, the emergence of the Lords of Congregation – firmly in control of Scotland's destiny, though not of Mary Stuart – removed all restrictions from the printing, sale and circulation of English translations of the Bible and made it an offence, punishable by death, to prevent or deter the vernacular texts being read. Scotland had become an increasingly Protestant country with a staunchly Catholic queen. In England, the King himself decided that respect for his father's memory no longer required him to endorse Henry's drift back to popish practices.

So the prodigious Edward initiated the repeal of the Act of Six Articles. Political action was accompanied by intellectual speculation. He wrote a commentary on the work of Bernardino Ochino – an Italian refugee living in England – in which he digressed from academic analysis to call the Pope 'a true son of the devil, a bad man, an Antichrist and abominable tyrant'.[13] He had also excoriated those items of English law which required the observance of popish practices. 'In my father's day, when [the Pope's] name was struck out of books, he stopped the mouths of Christians with six articles like six fists'.[14]

Despite his iron will and steely determination, Thomas Cranmer still chose to approach his objective in stages. In 1548 he drafted a new Order of Communion. It provided for English prayers and exhortations to be included in a still-Latin Mass. St Paul's and some other London churches followed that lead by holding whole services in English, in the belief that the ground was being prepared for the introduction of a vernacular liturgy. So – happy to be led in the direction of his choice – Cranmer began to compose a whole new English form of service. A committee of bishops, packed with Protestant sympathisers, approved the draft.

The Act of Uniformity – which abolished Latin services and replaced them with an English order of service set out in the Book of Common Prayer – came into force on Sunday June 9th 1549. Eight bishops and three peers of the realm had opposed the bill's passage, but in the House of Commons there had been virtually no objection. Princess Mary had made a last desperate and doomed attempt to save the Mass. Her plea that the form of service should remain untouched until Edward reached his majority was rejected out of hand. Contrary to the evidence of her brother's diary, she insisted that she had been given licence to worship as she chose in her own apartment and blamed on the King's advisers the demand that she support the new orthodoxy. Then she made a solemn promise: 'Have patience till I have more years. Then I will remedy all.'[15]

Cranmer had tried to find a compromise which accommodated the wide spectrum of views, even within the Church of England, on the nature of the Eucharist. It was not an easy task. He needed to satisfy sympathisers with the Roman Catholic view of complete transubstantiation, Lutherans who believed that there was a 'real presence' after the consecration of the bread and wine, and the followers of Huldrych Zwingli who believed the whole Communion service to be no more than a metaphor. The result pleased virtually nobody. One exception was Stephen Gardiner, the Bishop of Winchester, who thought that he could revive the technique which had enabled him to survive – whatever the creed of the King – and earned him the sobriquet 'Wily Winchester'. Although he accepted the new Prayer Book, he did so with the proviso that it was not 'what I would have made myself'.[16]

Gardiner's endorsement alienated Protestants, without reconciling Catholics. Discontent was general and grew large and serious enough in Buckinghamshire, Oxfordshire, Cornwall, Devon, Hampshire and Yorkshire for the consequent disturbances to be called riots. One passage of the revised scriptures caused particular offence. The new Prayer Book required 'The Supper of the Lord and Holy Communion, commonly called the Mass' to be celebrated in English. Elevation of the bread and wine was forbidden as Communion was a sacrament in which the congregation was to share. The logical extension of those new edicts was the removal of altars – the presence of which confirmed worship of the sacraments upon them and the notion that the Eucharist was a repetition of Christ's sacrifice. They were to be replaced by the altogether more prosaic Communion tables. The process began in London where Nicholas Ridley – never a man to spare feelings – said that his intention was to 'move from the simple superstitions of the popish mass to the right use of the Lord's Supper'.[17] His decision was so unpopular that St Paul's altars had to be dismantled and removed at dead of night to prevent an uprising. Ridley was undeterred. He extended the instruction to the rest of his diocese.

During the debate that preceded the Act of Uniformity's passage through the House of Lords, Bishop Tunstall of Durham had rightly described it, and the service that it endorsed, as *implying* the denial of transubstantiation. Cranmer had responded by asserting his belief in the 'spiritual presence' – a phrase open to several interpretations. That helped to convince Protestant opinion that Cranmer had paid too high a price for what he hoped would be Roman Catholic acquiescence. Roman Catholics, on the other hand, shared Bishop Tunstall's view that the way was being prepared for the outright denial of transubstantiation. Amid the doubts and denials, contradictions and confusion, the Reformation moved irresistibly on.

The introduction of the new Prayer Book was hotly opposed in parish after parish. Sometimes the priest simply ignored the royal injunction and said Mass in Latin. Sometimes a priest who had – either willingly or reluctantly – accepted the edict was forced by a rebellious congregation to return to the Roman liturgy. More often priests and people combined to make the new services sound as like the old Mass as possible. Frequently, English prayers were chanted as if they were

Latin. The West Country was particularly wedded to old ways and the Latin Bible, which men in Cornwall said they must retain because they could not speak English. At Bodmin, churchgoers chanted, 'Kill the gentlemen and we will have the Six Articles up again and ceremonies as there were in King Henry's time.'[18] In Exeter the mood was even more aggressive. 'Come out those heretics and two-penny book men! Where are they? By God's wounds and blood we will not be pinned to serve their turn ... We will have the mass in Latin as before.'[19]

The Prayer Book riots coincided with – and were, perhaps, encouraged by – economic hard times. Opponents of Somerset, who had long been plotting to depose him, attributed the discontent to the cost of his Scottish war. Somerset himself blamed (or pretended to blame) the sporadic uprisings on the wilful failure of the priesthood to explain the purpose and necessity of change. 'We believe your complaints about the blindness and unwillingness of your curates to set forth our proceedings and think that much of the dangerous stir comes from them.'[20] Two uprisings were too substantial to be put down by the local gentry. In Devon the revolt was so extensive that troops had to be diverted from reinforcing the campaign against the Scots and, together with mercenaries, deployed to defeat the insurgents in pitched battle. In some parts of England, Catholics rioted in defence of the Mass and Protestants rioted in protest at Catholic attempts to keep it. Kett's Rebellion – second only in size and success to the Pilgrimage of Grace – was largely a response to poverty and deprivation. But many of the Norfolk rebels added religious upheaval – the constant imposition of new rituals and regulations – to their list of grievances.

Kett – a forty-seven-year-old tanner and farmer whose temperament was not altogether suited to the role of rebel leader – was motivated by moral outrage. Norwich, the second city of England, was home to the nation's largest concentration of the homeless, unemployed and destitute. Although Kett claimed that his rebellion was also mounted in the name of the true faith, his supporters' chief grievance was economic. And many of them were not sure what the true faith was. Kett issued orders to his followers and dispensed justice from the shade of what he called the Tree of Reformation and demanded that 'priests and vicars that be not able to preach and set forth the word of God to his parishioner, may be thereby put from his benefice and the parishioners there to choose another, or else the patron lord of the town'.[21] His complaints against the local priesthood were amply justified. When, in 1551, John Hooper made a general visitation in Norfolk, he found that, of the 311 priests examined, 170 could not recite the Commandments and ten could not repeat the Lord's Prayer.[22]

In the second week of July 1549, 16,000 men, under Kett's leadership, assembled on Mousehold Heath in Norfolk. Edward's tutor denounced them in a poem called 'The Hurt of Sedition' and the Archbishop of Canterbury advised 'if they will be true gospellers, let them be obedient, meek and patient in adversity and long suffering and in no way rebel against the laws and magistrates'.[23] The Duke of Northumberland reacted with the more practical approach of a soldier. The first foray resulted in the rout of the token force, which he had thought was enough to restore the King's Peace. Then his army of hardened soldiers mounted a full assault and 2,500 rebels were slaughtered. Several hundred more, including Kett, were executed. At Court, Sir William Paget, the King's secretary, identified the malaise that had caused the rebellion and was affecting all England. 'Society is maintained by religion and laws: you have neither. The old religion is forbidden and the new not generally implanted.'[24] The Reformation – having been imposed from above – had left the generality of men and women bewildered about Church, faith and virtue. And it had destroyed the often-corrupt institutions which governed their lives.

In Rome, the Catholic Church was going through one of its periodic upheavals – crises which never quite turned into catastrophes, because a thousand years of spiritual certainty had made it able to survive the strains that would have destroyed a less deeply rooted institution. Pope Paul III died on November 10th 1549. The progress of the conclave, which met to elect his successor, should have been kept secret. Each day's deliberations became public within hours of the session closing. Partly because of the fear of contagion in an overcrowded Vatican and partly because of their wish to maintain their luxurious lifestyles, the cardinals spent much of their time in the city. They gossiped and, acting on their information, bookmakers quoted odds on the election of the rival candidates. It was assumed that the election would reflect the power struggle between France and Spain. As a result, Pole was the early favourite. He had – or seemed to have – the support of the Emperor who, being King of Spain, was naturally sympathetic to a man who had, so bravely, defended Catherine of Aragon. But a substantial number of cardinals were bitterly opposed to the election of a 'reformer', particularly one who wished to reform their conduct as well as their Church.

In the absence of the French cardinals, delayed en route, the successful candidate needed twenty-eight votes – two-thirds of the total cast. The first ballot was held on December 3rd. Pole received twenty-one votes. The second ballot was held on the next day. Pole's vote rose to twenty-four. The cardinals from the Empire proposed to elect him by acclamation – an offer which he refused. However, Pole had received enough promises of support to make his election, on the third ballot, seem certain. The promises were not kept. Pole's vote only increased to twenty-five. The announcement of the result coincided with receipt of the news that the French cardinals' ship had reached Corsica. The conclave was suspended to await their arrival. Pole's prospect of election – and of becoming the first English Pope since Nicholas Breakspear in the mid-twelfth century – disappeared. Cardinal del Monte, a compromise candidate, was elected Pope Julius III. From then on, Pole rarely attended the Curia. He resigned the governorship of *Patrimonium Petri* (the Vatican's property in Rome) and eventually entered, as a guest rather than a brother, the Benedictine monastery on the shore of Lake Garda. Pious Catholics came to believe that Providence had saved him for England.

In October 1549 the Duke of Somerset was replaced as the King's favourite, confidant and effective chief minister by the Earl of Southampton. He did not last long. In 1550 John Dudley, Earl of Warwick was appointed Lord President of the Council. The Duke of Northumberland, as he soon became, obtained his high place by allying himself with the religious conservatives at Court and on the Council, but it soon became clear that, if he was to maintain his place at the King's right hand, he would have to change sides and become the Protestants' champion. King Edward was complaining that the clergy, papist at heart, were ignoring the changes that he had caused to be made to the liturgy and ceremonial of the Church of England. He was right, but help was at hand. John Knox was on his way south.

By the time of Knox's arrival in England, Somerset had become Lord Protector and, in partnership with Cranmer, was modulating the speed at which the Reformation took hold. They were responding to the fear – felt by an increasing number of moderate Protestants – that the whole movement would be taken over by extremists who were as much the enemies of the state as of the Roman Catholic Church. Gardiner, who had opposed Cranmer's policy on the principle that 'once the door is open, you cannot withstand the attack of those bursting in',[25] had been deposed and imprisoned as an enemy of reform. But Cranmer was in such sympathy with his view that, for some time, he required licensed clergy – rather than preaching sermons of their own invention – to read to their congregations from his *Homilies*. It was not an outbreak of Catholicism that Cranmer feared. Freed from Roman discipline, the Church of England had spawned cults which orthodox Protestants barely recognised as Christian.

Somerset had attacked the extremists in the name of the state Church. The pronouncement that 'it is the part of the Godly man not to think himself wiser than the King's Majesty and his Council but patiently to expect and conform'[26] at least implied that the temporal authority was also the arbiter in spiritual disputes. What he believed to be a statement of moderation was about to be challenged by a man from the wilder shores of Scottish Protestantism. John Knox had no hesitation in contesting the judgement of kings and princes, if it was in conflict with his simultaneously rigid and idiosyncratic conscience. The Church of England had made Knox a grant of £5 and promised him employment as a preacher. He was to repay the patronage by denouncing as heresy a feature of the Protestant service which Cranmer and the bishops had regarded as too inconsequential to warrant reform.

Initially Knox was sent to Berwick-on-Tweed, a border town in the diocese of Durham with a garrison of ill-disciplined soldiers. There were three possible reasons for his appointment. The Privy Council may have wanted to keep him well clear of London or it may have thought that a preacher who carried a two-handed sword would not be intimidated by a rough congregation. The most cynical explanation was that Knox was appointed to the Durham diocese in order to be a thorn in the side of Cuthbert Tunstall, a brave enemy of the Reformation, who remained Bishop – although imprisoned – until 1552. For three years, the House of Commons – backed by Cranmer, a usually honest and often dispassionate zealot – had rejected the bill that proposed to deprive him of his see. Tunstall had kept his bishopric but lost his influence. The Reformation was moving on and the views of Knox, a man who was once thought to be an extremist, were swirling along in the mainstream of Protestant theology. As a result, Knox was able to exploit to the advantage of his notoriety an issue which, while a matter of principle to devout Protestants, was little more than an appendage to changes in doctrine and liturgy that had been going on for years.

In 1548, when Cranmer published *The Order of Communion*, the notion of the Real Presence had been orthodox doctrine, even though there were a variety of explanations about what the term actually meant. A year later in Oxford, Peter Martyr Vermigli defended Zwingli's rejection of the whole notion and, in Cambridge, Martin Bucer taught that the 'presence' was purely symbolic. The shift in academic opinion – significantly under the influence of scholar refugees – proved remarkably influential. The Council forbade the teaching of out-and-out transubstantiation and arranged a disputation between two dissidents, who had been released from prison for the occasion and were advocates of what had become the new orthodoxy. The sceptics won. The scene had been set for the construction of yet another Prayer Book. The new text would be designed to set out an order for the Communion service that was indisputably free from all taint of 'Popery'.

Cranmer's first Book of Common Prayer had been published simultaneously with the passage, by the House of Lords, of the Act of Uniformity and was first used on the Whit Sunday that followed the Act becoming law in January 1549. It reflected the decision to abolish the Latin Mass. But parts of the Sarum, York and Hereford litanies of rites were retained. So the changes in observances were not as radical as the changes in the language. The text was written in the hope of reconciling some Roman Catholics to the new order. Like many attempts at compromise, it pleased neither of the competing factions.

The second Book of Common Prayer, published in 1552, was much more acceptable to most Protestant ultras. The text, which again emerged from Cranmer's deliberations, reflected the Forty-Two Articles. It contained far more of a Protestant liturgy. Cranmer was creating a coherent Protestant theology which was designed to separate the Church in England from Anabaptists as well as Roman Catholics. So the heresy of adult and limited baptism was condemned as roundly as the doctrines of transubstantiation, purgatory, the intercession by saints and justification by faith alone. The ceremonies – baptism, confirmation and burial – were rewritten. Ordinary bread (not the mystical wafer) was to be given to communicants. The new Prayer Book was first to be used on All Saints' Day – November 1st – 1552 and the Forty-Two Articles were incorporated into English law, in the same year, by the Second Act of Uniformity.

Neither the existence of a new Prayer Book nor the incorporation of the Forty-Two Articles meant much to the mostly illiterate laity. But one clause in the Second Act of Uniformity had an immediate and intimate effect on their lives. It obliged them to attend a Church of England service on every Sunday of the year. Although Rome had been formally excluded from all influence over English affairs – civil as well as spiritual – the Protestant ultras were not satisfied. Ultras never are. They made an issue out of the importance of kneeling: whether or not it was allowed and what it signified. Knox was just the man to transform a disagreement over posture into an issue of absolute principle.

John Knox became the most vocal and violent opponent of kneeling.

But he was not alone in his intransigence. It was during the early months of his Berwick ministry that John Hooper's refusal to wear vestments at his consecration had established him as the spokesman for the Protestants who would tolerate no compromise with the Pope and Rome. Hooper's show of independent zeal drew renewed attention to a Lenten sermon which he had preached before the King in March 1550. His denunciation of altars and vestments was no more than what had become conventional Protestant thinking. But he also argued that kneeling was an act of adoration and, in consequence, implied the Real Presence. Kneeling must be prohibited.

It was not Knox's style to philosophise about the nature of the Communion or any other service and he rarely troubled to consult academic authorities on the scriptures. He was guided by instinct – which he believed to be divinely inspired. Nor was it his way openly to challenge authority and thereby risk imprisonment and the consequent silence of a voice which spoke the word of God. But the Book of Common Prayer – as authorised by the 1549 Act of Uniformity – was silent on the subject of communicants' posture. And that was the law until the second Uniformity Act was passed in 1552. So Knox's congregation could follow the Hooper prescription and remain seated during prayers without breaking the law.

Neither Hooper's theorising nor Knox's direct action had convinced Cranmer that a prohibition on kneeling should be included in the new Prayer Book. It seems unlikely that he regarded the matter as a question of principle. Perhaps, having gone through a long process of consultation and revision, he was simply unwilling to disturb the careful balance of his proposals. The Prayer Book was to go ahead unchanged. And so it might well have done, had not the Council of the North – exercising, north of the Trent, the power of the Privy Council – called Knox before it to explain his conduct. They interpreted the old Act of Uniformity differently. The Prayer Book, which it authorised, accommodated the idea of a Real Presence. The new Prayer Book had yet to replace it. According to the Council of the North (much under Tunstall's influence), refusing to kneel whilst taking Communion was sacrilege. Knox, by encouraging such behaviour, was guilty of heresy.

Knox was not a man to accommodate his critics – unless they were likely, and able, to burn him. His speech to the Council of the North lived up to the title it was given when it was published as a pamphlet, *A Vindication of the Doctrine that the Sacrifice of the Mass is Idolatry*. Knox's argument owed nothing to learned texts or scholarly conclusions. It was no more than the rough and raw assertion that 'the mass' – he never referred to the sacraments or the doctrine of transubstantiation – was intrinsically ungodly:

> If in your mass ye offer Jesus Christ for sin, then necessarily in your mass ye needs to kill Jesus Christ ... And so Papists, if ye offer Christ as sacrifice fir sin ye slay His blood and thus newly slay Him ... Ye have deceived the people, causing them to believe that ye offered Jesus Christ as sacrifice for sin; which is frivole and false for Jesus Christ may not be offered because he did not die.[27]

Knox was arrested, but released, without charge. For the moment he abandoned the argument that kneeling was the affirmation of the belief that Christ was sacrificed again at every Mass. But there is no doubt that he intended to return to it, since it symbolised the mysteries which were essential to Catholicism but which were treated with growing scepticism, perhaps even contempt, by the increasing – though probably still minority – Protestant population.

Knox was ideally suited to become a hero of the essentially coarse Edwardian Reformation. There was never anything original in his arguments. It was the force with which they were employed that caught the Protestant imagination. Passion, not intellect, had made Knox the most famous preacher in Scotland, where the Reformation – its natural leaders having died in the English war – depended on the faith and wisdom of the humble and meek. A German Protestant refugee, normally resident in England but taken on a visit to Scotland, wrote home that he could 'see little else than cruelty and ignorance'; 'as for the common people, however, it is generally thought that more of them are rightly persuaded to the true religion than here in England'.[28] He was speaking of a nation which, as late as July 1550, had confirmed its reputation for cruelty and ignorance by condemning a man to death for reading the Bible and burning him in Edinburgh's Grassmarket. It was the same brutal spirit, but another faith, which Knox took to the Durham diocese.

In the north of England the progress of the Reformation was slower than in the south and had to be hurried along. The Duke of Northumberland – having convinced a lay tribunal to convict Cuthbert Tunstall of offences which the House of Commons had found not proven – proposed to replace him with Nicholas Ridley and expropriate most of the See of Durham's land for himself and the crown. In August, he made a visit to the north-east and attended several services at which John Knox preached. Knox had become the most famous preacher in England.

A forceful style and uncompromising opinions – combined with his distaste for 'frivole' – had made him the standard-bearer of the Protestant extremists, who even regarded Hooper (who, in the end, had worn vestments at his consecration) as willing to tolerate the heresies of Rome. Association with Knox would, Northumberland believed, encourage support from the ultras and protect him from the moderates who had surrounded the Duke of Somerset and still hoped to avenge his deposition and death. When, in August 1552, Northumberland returned to London, Knox travelled with him, carrying an invitation to preach at Court before the King.

Although the politics of the Reformation required the Church to support the authority of the state, the Church was expected to render unto Caesar what was Caesar's. So when Cranmer tried to resurrect *Reformatio Legum Ecclesiasticarum* – with the undoubted intention of recovering some of the power the Church had lost – Northumberland left him in no doubt that the Reformation had not just diminished the Church of Rome. It had made every Church subservient to civil power. 'You bishops look to it at your peril that the like happen not again or you and your preachers shall suffer for it together.'[29] It was another example of the problem caused by the leaders of the Reformation disagreeing about its objects and the speed of its progress. Those problems were exacerbated – not reduced, as Cranmer hoped – by the constant changes in dogma and liturgy. Gradualism was not always taken to be a mark of moderation. And there was always something new about which to complain. And Protestants, by their nature, were inclined to protest.

Knox first preached at Court in September, about six weeks before the second Act of Uniformity was to come into force and, with it, the revised Prayer Book. The theme of his sermon was, as expected, the iniquity of a statute that authorised an Order of Service which endorsed the heresy that, during Communion, Christ was sacrificed again. That, he argued, was the significance and symbolism of requirement that the congregation kneel before they accepted the bread. The King, sympathetic to the idea that the Reformation was losing momentum, took up the cause and the Court followed his lead. Knox became fashionable. The Imperial Ambassador reported that Northumberland 'hath brought forth a new Scottish apostle who has already begun to pick holes in the new and universal reformation'.[30]

Northumberland, recognising the mood of the moment, grasped the opportunity to diminish Cranmer's influence. At his suggestion, the Privy Council wrote to the Archbishop of Canterbury asking for his opinion on the significance of kneeling. He replied that it was no more than a gesture of respect. The Privy Council deliberated and decided that although Cranmer was right, simple people would believe kneeling to be a sign of adoration. So – five days before the new Prayer Book was to be in general circulation – they decreed that it must include the explanation of kneeling's insignificance. The paragraph which sought to achieve that end was known to Catholics – overt and covert – as the 'black rubric'.

Cranmer had won the theological argument and prevailed over Hooper and the extremists, leaving Knox to decide which conscientious route to follow: obedience to the law (as expected of the godly man) or rejection of every vestige of 'Popery'. His decision was conveyed to his Berwick parishioners in a long letter which began with his account of his willingness to die rather than yield to Rome. It ended with an explanation of why he proposed to make an exception to that general principle, in the case of kneeling. 'Remembering always, beloved brethren, that due obedience be given to magistrates, rulers and princes, without tumult, grudge or sedition ... Except in chief points of religion.'[31] Knox must have known that, as well as endorsing Cranmer's insistence that the 'godly man' must respect the civil law, he was diminishing the importance of the campaign against kneeling, which he had carried with such apparent conviction. However, his temporising did nothing to diminish his popularity among those Protestants who had grown tired of Cranmer's cautious advance and the politicians who found it expedient to support them.

On the day after the Privy Council decided to publish the 'black rubric', Northumberland had written to William Cecil, the Secretary of State, 'I would to God it might please the King's Majesty to appoint Mr Knox to the office of Rochester Bishopric.'[32] And he was admirably frank about the reasons for his recommendation. Knox would be 'a whetstone to sharp the Bishop of Canterbury whereof he hath need'. Cecil agreed. So did King Edward. The offer of Rochester was made – and refused. Knox's reputation had survived the kneeling apostasy. It would have been totally destroyed by a decision to join the English episcopacy. He chose the power that comes from the support of the people rather than from the patronage of princes.

That Knox was held in especial esteem by King Edward is not in doubt, but the offer of Rochester was part of a general policy of appointing bishops who were sympathetic to the King's aims – if necessary, by the arbitrary dismissal of Catholic-inclined incumbents. Edmund Bonner had been deprived of the See of London as early as 1549 and replaced by Nicholas Ridley. Stephen Gardiner – already a prisoner in the Tower of London – was replaced as Bishop of

Winchester in February 1551 by John Ponet, the author of *In Defence of Married Priests*. In the same year, John Voysey was forced to resign Exeter in favour of Miles Coverdale; George Day of Chichester was succeeded by John Scory; and John Hooper became Bishop of Gloucester as well as Worcester, after the dismissal of Nicholas Heath. In 1552, a sufficiently corrupt lay commission was eventually assembled and Cuthbert Tunstall – already in prison and spending his time writing a book on transubstantiation – was deprived of the See of Durham.

It was easier to change the prelates than to convert the people. After years of suppression and the several forms of bogus conversions that they spawned, the true size of the Catholic population was difficult even to estimate. But Protestant laymen certainly remained a minority in England. John Hooper conceded that 'the people, that many headed monster is still wincing, partly through ignorance and partly fascinated by the inveiglements of the bishops and malice and impiety of the mass priests'.[33] The malice and impiety of the Mass priests was only one of the factors which held back the march of the Reformation. Men and women were alienated from the new faith by the combination of ignorance of, and sympathy with, the Roman faith which was displayed by Protestant clergy. And there was a problem with a shortage of preachers who were willing and able to instruct the people in the new practices – and even less the new beliefs – of the Reformation. Peter Martyr wrote that although there were plenty of preachers in London, 'throughout the kingdom there are very few'.[34] In Lincolnshire, for a whole year – after the death of Bishop John Longland, who had attempted to license only good Catholics – there were no sermons preached in ten of the sixty-one county's parishes, and in Buckinghamshire none in twenty-five out of forty-nine. Hugh Latimer despaired. 'How shall they hear without a preacher?'[35] The problem was not only a shortage of preachers. Catholicism was beautiful in its simplicity. Protestantism – with all it provisos, exceptions and constant adjustments – was a difficult religion for the common people to understand and accept.

Protestantism still had to be imposed from above on a people who had to be convinced that change was necessary, as well as taught what the necessary changes were. Robbed of the authority which came from an infallible Pope, Protestantism lacked the certainty of dogma and liturgy that made it easy for simple people to accept and understand what seemed to be eternal truths. Then as now, there were arguments within the Protestant community and each communion held its exclusive view with uncompromising passion. In 1550, George van Parris, a Dutch physician living in London, was burned for denying Christ's divinity. A year earlier, Joan Bocher, the wife of a tailor, had suffered the same fate for denying His humanity.[36] Mrs Bocher was a woman of spirit. Before her execution several attempts were made to persuade her to recant and be saved from the fires of hell and Smithfield. She had rebutted her inquisitors' arguments, item by item. She had dealt particularly severely with the Protestant change of belief about Communion. 'It was not so long ago,' she told Cranmer 'that you burned Anne Ayscough for a piece of bread, yet came yourself to believe the doctrine for which you burned her.'[37] It is easy to understand why people who had been brought up on certainty found it hard to accept the variable tenets of an evolving Reformation. Some of them never did. In 1553, the rector of Radnage in Buckinghamshire told his parishioners 'to keep a good portion of their church plate, saying that the time would come that they should have need of it and the old ceremonies be restored to the church again'.[38] He did not have long to wait.

King Edward VI died on July 6th 1553. According to rumours spread by enemies of his sister, Mary, he had been poisoned by Papists. In fact, after sixteen sickly years, he died of tuberculosis. He had reigned, in name alone, for barely six years. His death was not unexpected. Indeed John Dudley, the Duke of Northumberland, Great Master of the Household and Lord Great Chamberlain, had prepared for it with meticulous care. The enfeebled King had been persuaded to nominate, as his successor, Lady Jane Grey – his seventeen-year-old cousin – who, thanks to the distinction of being Henry VIII's great-niece, occupied a remote place in the table of precedence. Lady Jane was Northumberland's daughter-in-law and it was taken for granted that, once crowned, she would yield all power and authority to her husband. The claim, which the conspirators imagined would have irresistible appeal to the common people, was that only Queen Jane could save England from the succession of Mary Tudor, re-enslavement by Rome and the cruel tyranny of a Catholic monarch. A document – excluding both the Princesses Mary and Elizabeth from the succession – was secretly drawn up and signed by, among other dignitaries, Thomas Cranmer, Archbishop of Canterbury. It was his last, and most desperate, effort to preserve and extend the Reformation to which he had dedicated – and for which he would soon sacrifice – his life.

The plan to usurp the throne failed for many reasons. The people were not as afraid of Rome as the nobles who governed them imagined. And much of the population was content to observe whichever religious practices could be followed without fear of prosecution. But there were also more noble reasons for the failure of the plot. A minority of the people possessed an enduring faith that could be suppressed but not eliminated. Catholicism could be outlawed and Catholics penalised, but the belief was too strong to be destroyed.

CHAPTER 7

The Unquenchable Fyre

Mary Tudor, Henry VIII's oldest surviving child, was second in the line of succession which her father had set out before he died. That was a tacit admission that his marriage to Catherine of Aragon had been lawful. But opposition to Mary succeeding to the throne was less concerned with her legitimacy than with her upbringing. Like her mother, she was a devout Roman Catholic and was, therefore, anathema to both genuine and counterfeit Protestants who – for reasons both religious and political – lived in dread of a Counter-Reformation. But Mary had inherited her father's iron will, as well as her mother's piety. She did not intend to be denied her destiny.

Northumberland's preparations for the coup, which he had planned would follow Edward's death, had included the fortification of the Tower of London and Windsor Castle. So Mary had no doubt that her throne, and possibly her life, were in danger. The suggestion that she should keep a vigil by her brother's deathbed was rejected as a ruse to ensure that she could be kept under surveillance. Most of her entourage thought that the best for which she could hope would be a life under the suspicious supervision of Queen Jane's henchmen. And even that would require Mary to make an early act of submission and take an oath of fidelity. Mary remained – despite the auguries of doom – convinced that she would become Queen. It was God's will.

Edward's death had been kept secret for three days, but on July 10th 1553, Lady Jane Grey was brought, in majesty, to the capital. Thousands of Protestants lined the street to welcome her – a small proportion of London's population, but enough to make her seem to be the people's choice. On the following day, Mary Tudor wrote to the Privy Council belatedly asserting her claim to the throne. The Council's reply was almost apologetic in its implication that it was too late to prevent Jane's succession because a challenge to her authority had been overtaken by events. Queen Jane had been 'invested and possessed the just right and title to the imperial crown of the realm ... We must therefore assent to the said queen ... except which we fall into grievous and unspeakable enormities.'[1] Northumberland's message to the Lord Lieutenants, sent at the same time, combined brutality towards Mary with a show of respect for the House of Tudor. He rejected the claim of 'the bastard daughter of our dearest cousin and progenitor uncle, Henry VIII of famous memory'.[2] Mary's determination to inherit what was rightfully hers was in no way diminished. The throne was not only hers by right. It was her divine destiny to lead England back to the true faith. Who could prevail against her?

Mary fled from London and made for East Anglia. Her entourage was stoned in Cambridge and she was refused entry into Norwich. But when she reached Framlingham the tide began to turn. An army of supporters – according to a Spanish adherent, 'few of them persons of distinction' – began to rally to her cause. In London, Northumberland – normally a decisive soldier – was torn between reinforcing his stronghold and challenging Mary in the field. His indecision was regarded by Mary as more evidence that God was on her side. He eventually decided to march north with only 3,000 soldiers, and guns from the Tower of London, at his back. From the start of the forced march it was clear that the boroughs through which he passed supported Mary and that Cambridge and Norwich did not speak for England. Then he received news that Oxfordshire, Middlesex and Berkshire had declared against Jane.

Mary eventually recruited a force of almost 30,000 men – many of them volunteer civilians who had enlisted to fight for the 'old religion'. The nine-day reign of Queen Jane was over. Among the nobles who rapidly changed sides was the Duke of Suffolk, Jane's father. He went to Tower Hill to proclaim Mary queen and then abandoned his daughter to the Tower itself, there to await whatever punishment the new Queen thought appropriate. Northumberland – retreating from East Anglia – issued a similar proclamation in Cambridge. All that was left for Mary to do was make a victorious entry into London through the cheering throng.

Support for Mary's return owed as much to fear and hatred of Northumberland – who was held responsible for the arbitrary imposition of the new Prayer Book – as to the popularity of the rightful Queen. But Mary had her own explanation of the rejoicing. The defeat of the would-be usurpers had been so swift, and her own victory so complete, because God wanted her to send a sign to the people. Let them have no doubt that Divine Providence had chosen her to return England to the Church of Rome. The Pope agreed and struck a medal to commemorate not Mary's, but God's, victory.

The Catholics of England greeted Mary's return with open rejoicing – and an immediate return to the old ways. At Melton Mowbray they rebuilt the altar, and in York chalices were brought out of hiding. Even while the Act of Uniformity was still in force, and the celebration of the Roman Mass remained illegal, recusant Catholic priests returned to the Roman forms of celebration and worship – much to the delight of their faithful parishioners who were angrily described by Knox as marking the restoration with 'fires of joy and riotous banqueting'.[3] He so forgot his duty to respect the civil power that he openly boasted about preaching incitement to rebellion, a claim which was substantiated by the Emperor's ambassador who wrote that 'several preachers, certain Scotsmen in particular, have preached scandalous things to rouse up the people, going as far as to say that men should see Antichrist come again to life'.[4]

The Antichrist began God's work with admirable moderation. Edward's prisoners were released. Among them were Edmund Bonner, who was restored to the See of London, and Stephen Gardiner, the deposed Bishop of Winchester, who was to become Lord Chancellor of England. Neither men had been unequivocally opposed to every aspect of Henry's Reformation. But both had been unwilling to endorse the excesses which followed during Edward's reign. Mary's willingness to reprieve and reappoint two agents of her father's attenuated schism reflected the policy of her first Parliament. The validity of Henry's marriage to Catherine was confirmed and the ceremonies of worship – particularly those which were traditional parts of the Mass – were restored. But the rule of caution and respect prevented the repeal of her father's declaration of independence. So the Pope remained no more than Bishop of Rome without authority over the Catholic Church in England.

Initially Mary seemed, by the standards of Tudor England, to be unreasonably merciful. Only three of the conspirators were immediately executed. Northumberland was the first, despite announcing from the scaffold that he was a true Catholic who had been led into error by the hope of reward from the Protestant kings and by the arguments of 'seditious preachers and teachers of new doctrine'. Jane and her immediate family were imprisoned and condemned to death, but the sentences were not carried out. Cranmer – who had signed the letter which denied Mary's claim to the throne – could not have expected to be spared for long. He was, according to any definition of the term, guilty of high treason as well as continual heresy. So he was a candidate both for burning and beheading, fates it seemed that he still might escape. For Mary began her reign with proclamations which were as benign as they were unexpected and appeared to demonstrate a degree of religious tolerance that was wholly untypical of the age.

Queen Mary's Declaration to Council on August 12th 1553 was emphatic. 'She meaneth graciously not to compel or constreyne other mennes consciences otherwise than God shall [as she trusteth] put in their hearts a persuasion of the truth.'[5] Her First Proclamation, made on August 15th, began equally emolliently. Despite her devotion to 'that religion which she had professed from her infancy' and the hope that the 'same was of all her subjects, quietly and charitably embraced' she 'mindeth not to compel any [of] her said subjects thereunto'. But there was a caveat. As well as denouncing 'evil-disposed' preachers, forbidding the preaching of sermons without permission and proscribing biblical analysis, she warned that the promise of tolerance would only hold good until a 'further order by common consent' was made. England was on probation.

The first official, Roman Catholic sermon of Mary's reign was preached at St Paul's Cross on August 13th – three days after King Edward's funeral – by Gilbert Bourne, chaplain to Queen Mary and future Bishop of Bath and Wells. There were mutterings of disagreement when he reasserted the obligation to 'pray for souls departed'; and when he criticised the late King, not yet cold in his grave, for imprisoning the recently released Edmund Bonner, the dissent was so great that his safety was in doubt. 'There was a great uproar and shouting . . . as it were like mad people, what young people and women had ever heard, as hurly burley and casting up of caps.'[6] Two Protestant clergymen – John Bradford and John Rogers – rescued Bourne from the mob and were then accused of inciting the violence and of going to the chaplain's aid only to cover their complicity in a riot that got out of hand. The Mayor and Aldermen of London were instructed to keep better order and a week later, when Bourne preached a second time, two hundred pike-men were in attendance to ensure that his sermon was received in silence.

The violence was either the cause of or pretext for action to prevent a general uprising. Hooper, Latimer and Cranmer were arrested and all foreign nationals expelled from England. Knox therefore had to choose between the risk of imprisonment and leaving the country. After some public agonising about the pain of abandoning his wife and his followers, he fled to Dieppe, from where he wrote (the unconsciously ironically entitled letter) 'A Comfortable Epistle to the Afflicted Church of Christ', exhorting them to bear His Cross with Patience. It included a warning against attempts to assassinate Queen Mary.

During the autumn of 1553 the Lower House of Convocation reaffirmed the English Church's belief in transubstantiation. The Mass was reinstated as the central and crucial act of worship – required by law in all churches – and the Book of Common Prayer was proscribed. In February 1554 the obligation to hear and make auricular confessions was renewed, in preparation for Lent. It was clear that the religion of Rome, if not Roman supremacy, had returned to England. Yet there were only occasional and sporadic demonstrations of Protestant protest. The most violent was a shot fired at a preacher at St Paul's Cross. The most sacrilegious was the theft of the host from St Mary's in Hull. The most significant was the unsuccessful opposition of eighty Members of Parliament to the repeal of Edward's Protestant legislations. There were disturbances in some churches when priests criticised Protestant habits and practices which, within a quarter of a century, had become familiar and therefore indispensable, but the agitation was certainly no more than Queen Mary should have expected. It is now estimated that about eight hundred devout Protestants chose to emigrate to countries where they could openly follow their faith. The Wyatt Rebellion, in 1557, hoped to rally support in the name of Queen Jane and the need to protect England from Spanish domination. It achieved only the execution of its heroine and her family. Sir Thomas Wyatt recruited to his cause less than one-tenth of the number of rebels who had followed the Pilgrimage of Grace. Not even his own tenants rallied behind him.

Priests had been allowed to marry since the Act of 1549. A Royal Injunction of March 1554 allowed married priests to choose between their incumbencies and their wives. In May 1554 Thomas Martin, a pamphleteer, wrote in support of a return to celibacy on the spurious grounds that the sins of a lecherous king were somehow connected to the laxity of a married priesthood. Some priests resisted, but more acquiesced. A few simply abandoned their wives to lives of poverty as well as shame. A parish priest in the City of London sold his wife to a butcher – an act so heartless that his parishioners dragged him through the streets in a dung cart. Being in obedience to the recently amended law of God, he was rescued by the Church and a parish was found for him in rural Kent.[7] At the other extreme of uxorious devotion, a priest in St Keye, in the West Country, simply ignored the injunction. He and his wife were taken from their beds by scandalised parishioners and set in the stocks.[8]

Mary believed that the reception of her Catholic edicts confirmed that her subjects had never, in their hearts, rejected the true faith. In fact it was proof of many less clear-cut characteristics. One of them was the religious complacency of most English men and women. Another was England's natural instinct to conform. The Reformation had been accepted by many Catholics because it became enshrined in the law of the land and the chosen faith of their sovereign. Most Protestants had accepted the Counter-Reformation for much the same reason. Some were bewildered by the sudden change in the injunctions they received from on high. In an essentially deferential society, simple men and women followed the lead of their betters – hence the pockets of Catholicism which survived every stage of the Reformation under the patronage of great families in great houses. Most men and women did what they were told and, when a change came about, were punished, sometimes by death, for earlier obedience or for being slow to change their allegiance. The leaders of both the Reformation and the Counter-Reformation were constantly misled, by the devotion of their hard core of support, into the belief that they spoke for all of England.

The seven heretics burned at Smithfield on January 27th 1556 were executed for doing what they thought was expected of them. 'During the time of King Edward VI, hearing the gospel preached and the truth opened, [we] followed the order of the religion and doctrine as then set forth.'[9] Isobel Foster, the fifty-five-year-old wife of a cutler, was a Catholic, 'as other common people [were] ... till the reign of King Edward, at which time, hearing the gospel truly preached ... received thereupon the faith and religion as we were taught it'.[10] The unrepentant Henry Aldington had been 'truly taught in the days of that good king Edward of the goodly preachers sent by God'.[11] Their sin was constancy.

The Heresy Laws had been revived by a bill which was promoted in the House of Lords by Stephen Gardiner. Initially their Lordships refused to discuss it. They were not overcome by a sudden passion for tolerance, but by a determination not to stir up unnecessary trouble before the Queen embarked on a highly unpopular marriage with Philip of Spain. The pretext, by which they sort to justify their timidity, was the claim that no new legislation should be introduced until the crown and Rome had come to an agreement about the restoration of Church property. The bill was passed in a week, at the second attempt, in the same year and came into force on January 20th 1555.

Mary – who was so sure that she lived in God's grace that she felt no need to dissemble – was probably honest in her insistence that she wanted converts, not martyrs, and therefore proposed to use her providential powers lightly, 'sparing punishment for heretics'. But – confident that she was now sufficiently secure on the throne to follow her uncompromising instincts – she was determined that the false prophets would not escape so lightly. The reconversion of England was to be 'done without rashness, not leaving in the meantime to do justice to such as learning would seek to deceive the simple'.[12] However, the pace was still set by a minority of zealots. Thinking that their hour had come, they were not satisfied with merely rooting out the false prophets. Those who were seduced by the heretics had also sinned. The righteous anger was infective. Mary decided that it was God's will that Protestants be burned at the stake.

On January 28th 1555, a week after the bill became an Act, a panel of bishops – under the instruction of the rehabilitated Stephen Gardiner – began to examine the imprisoned Protestants. The first victim to die was Bishop John Hooper. He was sent to Gloucester, his own diocese, for burning, in the mistaken belief that the people who had followed him would be chastened by the sight of their hero at the stake. It was a major miscalculation. When he was led out from prison on the morning of February 4th, a crowd of 7,000 sympathisers greeted him and escorted him to the pyre. During the forty-six months between the reinstatement of the heresy laws and Mary's death in 1558, at least 280 Protestants were burned. The burnings went on until the last two weeks of the Queen's life. Among the victims were five Suffolk farm labourers; Joan Waste, a young and blind Derby woman; and Agnes Prest, an Exeter widow.[13]

During the years which followed, and in history, the burnings did both Mary and her Catholic cause immense harm. An anonymous letter to the restored Edmund Bonner – Bishop of London and a committed burner – warned him, no doubt correctly, that in death John Philpot, a Protestant evangelist, had done more damage to the Catholic cause than the martyr had achieved in life.[14] But at the time the public reaction to the Marian burnings was much the same as it had been to the burnings which had taken place during the previous two reigns. Crowds assembled to watch. Among them, men and women who either supported or opposed the execution were far outnumbered by sensation-seekers who were attracted by the excitement of public death. There were executions to which spectators brought fruit and pastries to sustain them while they enjoyed the spectacle. And there were executions at which, in an excess of righteous brutality, the victim's last words were shouted down while the dying man was pelted with stones and clods of earth.

To the modern mind, the uninhibited brutality of the burnings seems to illustrate some terrible psychological disorder in those who perpetrated then. William Fowler was said to have struck a priest. He was condemned to death by burning. But 'first, his hand, having been held up against the stake, was struck off'.[15] The heroic stoicism of some victims is equally incomprehensible. John Rodgers was told that a recantation would be followed by a reprieve. 'His wife and children, being eleven in number (one suckling at the breast) met him on the way to Smithfield. The sight of his own flesh and blood could not move him, but that he constantly and cheerfully took his death with wonderful patience.'[16] Some persecutions were as bizarre as they were brutal. John Warne, an upholsterer, was already under suspicion when he was accused of having his 'great rough water spaniel'[17] tonsured like a priest. It was later discovered that Warne had not cut the dog's hair himself but, almost as bad, 'did laugh at it and like it.'[18] That was enough to begin a course of events that ended, for Warne and his wife, at the stake.

There were occasional acts of Christian charity. The people of Laxfield in Suffolk provided a rare example of opposition to the burnings by civil disobedience. John Noyes, a shoemaker, was condemned for responding to a question about transubstantiation with an answer which was bound, because of its dismissive style as well as its Protestant content, to secure his conviction of heresy: 'I thought the natural body of Christ to be in heaven not in the sacrament.'[19] On the day of his burning – April 19th 1557 – his neighbours, knowing that the executioner would need glowing coals for kindling, doused the fires in their cottage grates. But 'smoke [was] espied from the top of a chimney'. The executioner 'went and broke down the door'.[20] Hot coals were carried from the cottage. The fire was lit. John Noyes burned.

Demonstrations in support of the martyrs were denounced by officiating priests. John Day, a curate in Maidstone, was shouted down as he preached before the pyre that was to burn seven Kentish men and their wives. He told the angry crowd, 'Good people, ye ought not in any way to pray for these obstinate heretykes, for loke how ye shall see their bodies burn here with material fyre. So shall ther damnable soules burne in the unquenchable fyre of hell everlasting.'[21] Despite the righteous joy with which some priests sent heretics to eternity, the claim was and remains that the interrogators – who examined the suspects before sending them on to Consistory Court – did all they could to persuade them to repent and be saved. Thomas Tomkins, the first layman to be burned, had his hand held over a candle in order to illustrate the pain he would suffer in the fire. He nevertheless chose burning rather than apostasy. John Williams, the Chancellor of Gloucester Cathedral, asked Thomas Drowry, a blind boy whom he was cross-examining, where he had learned to be a heretic. Drowry replied that his teacher was Williams himself. Unabashed, the Chancellor replied. 'Then do as I have done and thou shalt lyve as I do and escape burning.'[22] Drowry refused and Williams pronounced him guilty and sentenced him to death.

The enthusiasm for burning, which some restored priests displayed, was not shared with equal indiscrimination by the Queen. Her reservation was tactical rather than conscientious. Martyrdom was a display of faith which encouraged the fearful to be brave and the weak to be strong. Mary and her ministers wanted public recantations, which could be exploited to reduce the morale and undermine the faith of other heretics. They were obtained by a mixture of argument, entreaty and torture, which was known by the official euphemism 'examination'. John Philpot endured fourteen examinations before he swore that he had never spoken against 'the sacrifice of the mass and the sacrament of the altar', but he would not recant his denunciation of 'the usurped power of the Bishop of Rome'. So he burned.[23] Richard Woodman underwent six examinations, 'wearing sometimes bolts, sometimes shackles, sometimes lying on the bare ground, sometimes sitting in the stocks, sometimes bound with cords and all my body be swollen much like to be overcome by the pain that has been in these things.' He too burned.[24]

Thomas Cranmer – theologian of the English Reformation, architect of its Edwardian consolidation and traitorous supporter of Jane Grey – could not be allowed to escape the fire, however complete, obsequious and even sincere his recantation. But he might be persuaded to repent before he died. In the spring of 1554, Cranmer, Nicholas Ridley and Hugh Latimer were moved from their London prisons to Oxford where, for several weeks, they endured continual cross-examination by a team of scholars. The exercise ended with the examiners announcing that they had won the theological argument, but their adversaries had refused to accept God's law. They were returned to prison and remained there for over a year. On October 26, 1555, Hugh Latimer and Nicholas Ridley – being of no further use alive – were burned with more ceremonial than usually accompanied executions. Richard Smith, Regius Professor of Divinity, preached a sermon – more to the attendant crowd than to the condemned men. It compared the defrocked bishops to Judas and warned against showing sympathy towards anyone who chose to die outside the Church. They were prevented from making a statement to the crowd, but repeated the last words of Jesus. According to the 1570 edition of Foxe's *Book of Martyrs* – a catalogue of Mary's crimes, real and fictitious – Latimer then cried out, 'Be of good comfort Master Ridley and play the man. We shall, by God's Grace, light such a candle as shall never be put out.' The story is an invention, based on the dying valediction of Polycarp, a martyred Greek bishop.

Thomas Cranmer was forced to sit in the window of a house that overlooked the pyre and watch Latimer and Ridley burn. The whole event was thought to have passed off sufficiently peacefully to suggest that, even in Oxford, there was no great opposition to the burnings or great enthusiasm for them, despite the mob oratory of Thomas Martin, the prosecutor, at Cranmer's trial. He had compared Cranmer's conduct with the devil's temptation of Christ in the wilderness, and his final remarks – both threat and warning – had been addressed to the public gallery. 'Do you se how he looketh about for help? . . . If any of you bid God strengthen him, or take him by the hand or embrace him, or show him a cheerful countenance you shall be excommunicated.'[25] That stern injunction could not have encouraged the defendant's expectation of mercy. But his continued imprisonment after the execution of the two bishops may have given him a flicker of hope. By then he had been driven half-crazy by the continual interrogation, which was suddenly abandoned. It was renewed after two months and Cranmer at last recanted. But there was to be no reprieve. On February 14th 1556 the reason for delay was revealed. The prisoner had been created Bishop by the Pope. So the ritual of removal of all his clerical orders had to await receipt of permission from Rome. During the twelve days after it was received, Cranmer signed his four further recantations. Although each one was more comprehensive than its predecessor, the sentence remained death by burning.

The execution took place on March 21st 1556. The proceedings began with a public service conducted on a platform which had been erected in the nave of St Mary's church. The scene was set by James Brooks, Bishop of Gloucester. 'Remember from whence you have fallen. You have fallen from the universal and Catholic Church of Christ, from the very true and received faith of Christianity and that by open heresy. You have fallen from your promise to God, from your fidelity and your allegiance by openly preaching marriage and adultery. You have fallen from your sovereign prince and queen by open treason.'[26] Dr Brooks continued to identify the depths to which Cranmer had descended for another ten minutes. His address ended in bathos: '. . . and after that you fell lower and lower'. Henry Cole, Provost of Eton College, preached the sermon. Then came the planned grand climax – a carefully constructed confession of guilt read out by the condemned man. It was not the confession which Cranmer had agreed with his captors. Nor was the guilt to which he confessed the guilt for which he was to be executed. Cranmer recanted his recantation.

The first few words of his valediction were the opening lines of the agreed text. He believed in 'every article of faith of the Catholic faith, every word and sentence taught by our Saviour Jesus Christ, his

apostles and prophets in the Old and New Testaments'. That made
the deviation which followed all the more dramatic. He was expected
to beg for forgiveness for the sins of supporting false doctrine and
promoting the Reformation. Instead he renounced:

> all such bills and papers which I have written or signed with my
> hand since my degradation, wherein I have written many things
> untrue. And forasmuch as my hand offended, writing contrary to
> my heart, my hand shall be the first punished thereafter; for may I
> come to the fire it shall be first burned.[27]

The final flourish – a denunciation of the sacraments, as recently
redefined by Stephen Gardiner – was lost in the explosion of noise,
some triumphant, some horrified, but all astounded, which followed.
Cranmer was hustled off the platform and out of the church, but he
brushed his captors aside and ran ahead of them to the waiting pyre.
He was as good as his word. 'When the wood was kindled and the fire
began to burn near him, he stretched out his right hand which had
signed the recantation into the flames and there held it steadfast that
all the people might see it burned to a coal before his body was touched.'[28]

Cranmer's valedictory coup was not the only example of the inevitable failure of Mary's policy for cleansing England of heretics. Her
strategy – conversion and recantation whenever possible, with burning
as the last resort – was based on the mistaken belief that England was
still a Catholic country in which a minority of men and women had
been persuaded to become little more than Protestants in name alone.
But even the Catholics whose Catholicism had survived King Edward's
reign were reluctant to be caught up in another upheaval and, whatever their doctrinal position, had developed a sturdy belief in English
independence from foreign influence. Mary was wise – not a characteristic with which she is usually associated – to move slowly towards
her undoubted intention of restoring relations with the Pope and
Rome.

Immediately that he heard of Edward's death, Cardinal Reginald
Pole – Mary's constant and true, but exiled, adviser – wrote to the
Pope, Julius III, to assure him that England would soon restore 'the
justice, piety and true religion which have hitherto been utterly
crushed'.[29] The Pope replied in the most fulsome language. But it was
clear, from the tentative verbs, that the rehabilitation had only begun:

> If ever at any time it were permissible, certainly now most appro-
> priately it may now be said that 'the right hand of the Lord has

wrought strength' . . . the most flourishing Realm of England, having been led away into separation and secession by Henry the Eighth and thereafter by the succession of Edward his son strengthened and confirmed in that hereditary error should now be suddenly brought back again into that state whereby it seems that it may most easily be recalled to the holy flock and to the fold of the Catholic Church, indeed this is nothing other than the change of the right hand of the Most High.[30]

Reginald Pole, 'appointed as Legate *a latere* of Ourselves and the Holy See', was intended by the Pope to assist in the work of national redemption. Mary Tudor, a woman with a mind of her own, was not so ready to receive the Pope's emissary. She welcomed Pole's advice. But at the start of her reign she preferred to receive it in writing rather than in person. It would, in all probability, have been difficult for Pole to reach England. The forces of the Holy Roman Empire may well have barred his way. The Emperor Charles was planning for his son Philip to marry Mary and feared that Pole – whose ordination as priest had been inexplicably delayed – might be a rival for the Queen's hand. The notion was not as fanciful as it now seems. There had been a time, in Mary's girlhood, when a match with Pole – a Plantagenet – was seriously contemplated. But by 1553 the Emperor's suspicions were groundless. Mary, on the other hand, had serious reasons for wanting Pole's visitation to be delayed.

The day after Pole had sent the good news of Edward's death to the Pope, he had written to Mary a letter which concluded with a quotation from the Magnificat: 'He hath put down the mighty from their seats and hath exalted the humble and meek.' The identity of the humble and meek he had in mind for exaltation was not clear. But there was no doubt about the mighty whom he wanted to put down from their seats. The list included the sovereigns who had challenged the authority of the Pope. Mary had no doubt about the Pope's supremacy. But she did not intend to acknowledge it until she felt more secure. It was her view that England would gladly accept the theology and liturgy of Rome but not the elevation of its bishop to head of the worldwide Church. And Pole's immediate arrival would have been regarded as a sign that the Pope was once more to have authority in England.

Pole was deeply offended by Mary's suggestion that he should postpone his arrival in England, and sent her a rebuke which a less pious monarch would have regarded as near treason: 'I do not know if your councillors who urge you to set your kingdom's affairs in order first and then restore religion believe the words of the gospel, saying that God watches over and governs even the smallest things and that without him no good can be accomplished ... The establishment of Kingdoms is not founded on mighty armies or even on human foresight. Their strength lies in God.'[31] Mary was unmoved. She knew that the reconversion of England had already begun – in the way, and at the speed, she judged to be right.

The Imperial Ambassador and Pole both underestimated Mary's cunning. The Ambassador described Mary's policy as the determination to 'return to the conditions as they were at the time of King Henry's death',[32] and Pole – who also believed that the Queen's reluctance to acknowledge the Pope's authority was prompted by respect for her father's memory – regarded her reluctance to renounce Henry's policy as misplaced loyalty. Even the decision of Mary's first Parliament to recognise as valid Henry's marriage to Catherine of Aragon was seen by Pole as the daughter doing her duty, not a Queen edging her way towards the repeal of the Act of Uniformity. Having denounced Henry in life, Pole felt no obligation to treat him more gently in death. Henry was 'knoweth of all men as the author of the holy schism'. Defending him and his heresy was, in itself, an 'impietie'.[33] He added that it was Mary's duty to welcome him to England as an ally in the holy war.

Mary's response was affectionate and frank. She would gladly give half her kingdom to have Pole by her side.[34] However, she must proceed at a pace which did not give comfort to heretics. At the beginning of her reign she would rather correct errors of doctrine than reassert her duty to obey Rome. She began that process in March 1554. A Royal Injunction required 'the suppression of corrupt and naughty opinions, unlawful books and other unlawful devices'.[35] It was followed, a year later, by an edict that forbade 'seditious and unlawful publications' and what amounted to an index of proscribed writing. Protestant printers were put out of business and their presses handed over to reliable Catholics.

The paradox of Pole's position was that although (unlike Mary) he did not understand England's antagonism towards the Pope, he did (again unlike the Queen) recognise that England would be violently opposed to her marriage to Philip of Spain. Mary was not prepared to take advice or, on the subject of marriage, proceed with caution. In her Catholic piety, she was determined to do her duty as a woman as well as a queen. That required her to marry and have children.

Mary and Philip were married in July 1554. In September Pole wrote to the Holy Roman Emperor – the Queen's new father-in-law – comparing his exclusion from England to St Peter's imprisonment in

Herod's gaol. The quotation from the Acts of the Apostles probably did less to influence the old man's judgement than the fact that, Mary's marriage being contracted and consummated, there was nothing Pole could do to prevent it. Another year passed before Pole was able to fulfil his destiny. In a letter of August 13th 1555 he reminded Mary that she had ascended the throne of England without the help of any human agency and had triumphed because her victory was God's will. It was now her duty to respond to that benevolence by recognising and re-establishing, in England, the authority of the Pope, God's Vicar on earth – a return to grace which should have been accomplished in her first Parliament. Mary still feared that some of Pole's views would provoke rebellion.

The argument over the status of property which had been confiscated from the Church had still to be resolved. The dispute was so bitter that one suggestion for its solution was a ruling that its confiscation had been God's vengeance on the unworthy clergy and therefore there could be no recompense or return. The need to resolve the disagreement before Pole's return was used, for several months, as justification for the Legate's continued exclusion. But Mary either relented or felt the need of one counsellor at court whom she could trust. Whatever the reason, she agreed that Pole should make his way to England, and on November 13th Pole began his journey across Europe. On November 19th 1555, he arrived in Calais – before Mary's reckless involvement in the ruinous war with the French, still English territory. At Dover he was welcomed by a personal letter from the Queen. It heralded a triumphant progress to London which – like Mary's own reception in the capital two years earlier – was interpreted, by easily convinced Catholics, as proof that all England was impatient for a return to the old faith.

From the start to the finish of the journey to Gravesend, Pole was accompanied by five hundred horsemen. At Gravesend he was officially notified that the Act of Attainder, initiated by Henry VIII as a preliminary to his trial and execution, had been formally revoked by Parliament. In anticipation of his arrival, it had been in session since November 12th. The rest of the journey to London was made along the Thames in a boat which bore the silver cross of a Papal Legate on its prow. Pole landed at Westminster pier on November 24th and went at once to Whitehall, where he was greeted by Philip and Mary. According to a broadsheet, published in Milan, the Queen 'embraced him with the affection of a son who she had long given up for lost'.[36] Pole presented his credentials and hurried away to Lambeth Palace. He had work to do.

The following day he refused an invitation to a banquet designed to celebrate his arrival, but could not avoid a discussion with Philip about the restoration of papal property. The agreement was reached, subject only to papal endorsement, that Pole would issue a blanket absolution for all of England's schismatic sins, save for the continued retention of property held as a result of the assault on the monasteries. That problem was overcome by a combination of expediency and corruption. First Philip accepted that, with the passage of time, all land that could not be held 'in good conscience' would be returned to its rightful owners. Then the Pope issued a Dispensation which absolved from blame or restitution the great families who lived in what once were monasteries and owned what once was monastic land. The stage was set for Pole to address Parliament on November 28th.

Pole's speech, though apparently delivered extempore, was based on *De Unitate*, his treatise written to denounce Henry VIII's apostasy after the executions of More and Fisher. He thanked Parliament for ending his exile, but said that he was not able to end a far worse forced separation – 'you being cutt of from the Church through your own wilful defection and schismatical revolting from the unity of the same … All holy rites and observances neglected and held for superstition and abomination.'[37] It was then that he attributed the whole of the English Reformation to Henry's 'fleshy will, full of carnal concupiscence', although he must have known that the royal divorce was the occasion rather than the cause of the breach with Rome. It was not the moment to remind England that it had once asserted its independent sovereignty.

Pole then added a passage on a subject that was to become a major theme of the texts which supported the English Counter-Reformation – the civil upheaval which inevitably followed schism. 'Neither was any man so sure of his goods and possessions, but he stood in abject danger and hazard of his life too.'[38] Praise for Philip, Mary and the Emperor was followed by an assurance – calculated to appeal more to Parliament than to historians – that England enjoyed a special place in God's affection. Because it was the first kingdom to accept Christianity, it possessed 'a great prerogative of nobility'.[39]

On St Andrew's Day, forty-eight hours later, Parliament reassembled to hear Pole's response to a petition, presented to him by Philip and Mary, asking that the nation be absolved from the sins of heresy and schism. The whole assembly, including the royal couple, knelt while absolution was pronounced. Fortunately, on the previous day, the document setting out general terms for the restoration of Church property had been agreed. So the absolution was complete. As is so often the case with agreements arrived at in haste, the various signatories had different interpretations of its meaning. The issue remained contentious during five hundred years of argument about the extent of the restitution. In the spring of 1912, David Lloyd George – the Chancellor of the Exchequer and an active Nonconformist – responded to attacks on the Welsh Disestablishment Bill with his analysis of how two dukes, who had been particularly critical of the proposal, and their noble ancestors, had acquired the foundations of their family fortunes. 'They robbed the Catholic Church. They robbed the monasteries. They robbed the altars. They robbed the poor. They robbed the dead. Then they come here ... hands dripping with the fat of sacrilege.'[40]

Despite their long association and protestations of affection, Pole's and the Queen's hopes for the future of Catholicism in England were incompatible. The problem was not the status of the Pope. When she felt secure on her Catholic throne, Mary was happy, indeed enthusiastic, to abandon her claim to be head of the English Church and gradually, despite the respect she owed her father, she agreed to restore the Pope's authority over the English Church. But her long-term objective was the restoration of the Church to the state it had enjoyed before the Reformation. Her instinct was to look back. Pole's intellect convinced him of the need to look forward. He was the advocate of institutional change – the obligation of bishops to live within their dioceses, the establishment of seminaries and an improvement in the quality and conduct of the priesthood. Absentee clergy with no knowledge of the scriptures had been one of the pre-Reformation complaints against the Catholic Church. Mary was gradually persuaded at least to attempt the reforms which Pole – although under pressure from Rome to return – was determined to impose on the dormant Catholic Church in England.

Pope Julius III had died in March 1555 and his successor, Marcellus II, died three weeks later. For the second time in his life, Pole himself might have been a realistic contender for the papal throne. But he had turned his back on personal ambition, a sin to which he claimed 'God has granted me the grace to show myself very averse during the whole course of my life'.[41] God had given him to England.

The new Pontiff was seventy-nine-year-old Pietro Carafa, Paul IV, a Neapolitan who, true to his origins, hated the Spanish Hapsburgs. A year after his enthronement, Charles V abdicated, and Philip – husband to Mary Tudor – became the King of Spain, the Netherlands and Naples. The Pope withdrew all his legates from Philip's dominions and ordered Pole home. Queen Mary asked for a revocation of the order and, so as to avoid open defiance of the Pope, refused permission for the messenger – who carried the rejection of her request – to land in England. Pole simply ignored the papal injunction. Disobedience was heresy. The Pope denounced 'the whole apostate household of the Cardinal of England'.[42] Pole wrote, but did not send, a letter which was both an apology and a justification. His obligation, he made clear, was to the country of his birth.

Pole's work of reforming the English Church had begun before Pope Paul deprived him of the status of Legate. In November 1555 he had issued notice of a joint synod of both English archdioceses. When it met a month later, Pole resumed his assault on the English clergy who, he claimed, were ignorant and covetous. The instructions which he issued, in the name of the Pope, were a replication of the rules of conduct which he, and a group of reformers, had unsuccessfully proposed to the Council of Trent, in *Consilium de Emendanda Ecclesia*.

The Council of Trent, which had begun before Mary's accession, continued for so long that it was still in session after her death. It was convened by Pope Paul III and continued by Julius III and Pius IV – none of whom attended – with a basic purpose of providing a response to the Reformation. Because it chose to advocate retrenchment rather than reform, its conclusions were more to Mary's way of thinking than to Pole's. The leadership of the Catholic Church concluded that the only way to confound the Protestant threat was by a reaffirmation of all the basic dogma which had sustained it since its creation. The Church faced the same dilemma – compromise with the demand for change or resist it – time after time during the next five hundred years. At Trento the balance between conservatives and reformers changed from session to session. Sometimes there were as many as seven hundred bishops present. Sometimes there were as few as thirty. The conservatives won most of the votes, though two institutional reforms were agreed. The sale of indulgences was forbidden and schemes for improved clerical education were put in place.

Pole revived, in the English synod, the reforms which Trent had rejected. All priests were obliged to preach as well as pray, avoid ostentation, give part of their earnings to charity and remain celibate. Seminaries must be set up to train the clergy. The Church's property must be restored. The synod reaffirmed that simony – selling indulgences – was designated a mortal sin; prepared a new book of homilies; composed a new catechism; and, in a remarkable volte-face, agreed to promote an English translation of the New Testament to complement the English Prayer Book, which had been used for private devotions since 1555. It was silent on the subject of papal authority. Even allowing for that omission, it moved appreciably closer to the position at which Catholic reformers and moderate Protestants met. Pole placated Rome by persuading Mary – without much difficulty – to surrender her rights to tithes and first fruits. But he was developing an essentially English brand of Catholicism. Offers from the Jesuits to help in the work of reconversion were declined. England would save itself.

Before the synod's work was finished, the Pope had stripped Pole of his legatine powers. Pole responded with a rebuke which was majestic in its disdain. He was particularly offended to hear rumours of his dismissal before he had received official notification from the Pope and was sceptical about the notion that it was the result of the hostilities between the Pope and Mary's father-in-law:

> You said not just once, but first to the Ambassador of England and then to my messenger ... that whatever you did in this cause you did not do on account of the fact that something in me gave offence but on account of the fact, there being a state of war between Your Holiness and King Philip, you did not deem it appropriate that whilst you had recalled from other kingdoms and jurisdictions all your nuncios and legates, you should have a legate in the kingdom of England ... Yet shortly thereafter, although Your Holiness being reconciled with the King has restored your nuncios to the rest of his dominions ... you had been besought concerning the restitution of the legation to me you have still deferred doing so [and] have allowed the rumour to go forth that a legal process has been taken against me.[43]

The Pope was unmoved, but Pole's authority in England was restored by the device of arranging for his ordination as priest and, two days later, his appointment as Archbishop of Canterbury. The principles of reform were reiterated at a specially assembled convocation and Pole set out – in a series of visitations – to reinvigorate and educate the slothful and often ignorant clergy. The *Reformatio Angliae* had begun. It was Pole's intention to carry out God's work in the spirit that he had described to Parliament when he absolved England of the sin of heresy: 'I am come not to destroy but to build: to reconcile not to condemn.'[44]

Pole's apologists absolve him from responsibility for the persecutions, which gradually took the place of attempts to bring sheep and shepherds closer together. The burnings, they claim, were the eventual result of decisions taken before Pole returned to England. As early as 1553, the Lower House of Convocation had asserted that the doctrine of transubstantiation was part of the true faith and called for action against the heretics who refused to accept it. The Wyatt Rebellion had convinced some – and allowed others to claim – that Protestants were a threat to the security of the realm. The idea had been encouraged by the speech from the scaffold by the Duke of Northumberland, a convicted traitor who combined sins spiritual and temporal by denouncing the 'seditious preachers and teachers of the new doctrine' who had persuaded him to deny the authority of both the Pope and the Queen.[45]

Pole was not as opposed to the new severity as his apologists claim. In 1554, the heresy laws had been re-enacted to become a weapon against supposed treason as well as the denial of the true faith. That was wholly consistent with Pole's prescription for purifying England. It was Pole, in correspondence with the Queen during the years of exile, who had advised Mary that God had restored her to the throne of England 'for no other reason than that ribaldry and disobedience to the holy laws may be punished and the seditious receive their reward'. Having accepted the relationship between Protestantism and rebellion, he had left no doubt about Mary's obligation to suppress the twin evils. She had a duty both to follow the true faith and to 'compel her subjects to do likewise'.[46] Foxe, uncharacteristically, gave a balanced description of Pole's position. 'Although it cannot be denied by his acts and writings, that he was a professed enemy [of Protestants and Protestantism] and not otherwise to be reputed but for a Papist: yet again it is to be supposed that he was non of the bloody and cruel sort of Papist.'[47] He regarded burnings as an occasional necessity, not a continual obligation.

Initially Pole was more interested in preaching than in burning. For the two years beginning in March 1556 he gave sermons with three constant themes: the authority of the Church, the bodily presence of Christ during the Eucharist, and England as the land of which Jacob dreamed. The ladder, which stretched back though St Augustine to Peter himself, had only one rotten rung, Thomas Cranmer. The importance of the sermons lay less in their content than in the fact that they were given. Pole's new Catholicism required priests to teach their followers rather than expect them to accept – without understanding – the authority of the priesthood. He expected the sermons to be more than 'shallow entertainment' – a difficult task for those priests who could barely understand the scriptures themselves.

Pole's sermons challenged, head-on, the precepts of the Reformation and were supported by innumerable other publications which, over the next half-dozen years, sought to compete with the volume of

Protestant tracts and broadsheets that were being printed in continental Europe. Bishop Edmund Bonner explained their purpose in the introduction to *A Profitable and Necessarye Doctryne* – a statement of Catholic theology. The new enthusiasm for the dissemination of Christian knowledge was the result of a determination 'both that errors, heresies and naughty opinions may be weeded, purged and expelled ... and also that a very pure, sincere and true doctrine of the faith and religion of Christ ... may faithfully, plainly and profitably be set forth'.[48] In July 1555, Bonner's London diocese published *An Honest Godly Instruction for the Bringing up of Children*. It included both the letters of the alphabet and a simplified statement of faith. It was not the only publication that was designed to reach out to the poor and dispossessed. A companion volume, *Homilies Set Forth*, was a collection of thirteen sermons which were said to be suitable for reading to congregations of the uneducated. In 1556, Pole authorised its use in parishes throughout England. The most important of the homilies, *A Plaine and Godlye Treatise Concerning the Masse for Instructyon of the Simple and Unlearned*, advocated the burning of heretics. Nicholas Harpsfield, the Archdeacon of Canterbury and a More memorialist, wrote the *Treatise on the Pretended Divorce* in a style that echoed language which the subject of his panegyric would have found familiar. Henry's life of sin had transformed him into a 'monstrous shape', and mad dogs drank the diseased blood which dripped from his split coffin.[49]

It would be wrong to attribute the acceleration in burnings, which characterised the later years of Mary's reign, to the *Plaine and Godlye Treatise*. They began before its publication and varied from diocese to diocese, according to the assiduity of the presiding bishop and the severity thought appropriate. And as early as February 1554, Bishop Bonner – 'Bloody Bonner' as he came to be called – had begun to seek out heretics by requiring every adult within his London diocese to make a confession in preparation for Lent, and every parish priest to report those who failed to do so. But at first, public prosecution was largely limited to the publicly obdurate figures whose Protestant beliefs might plausibly be associated with treason. In the end, the burnings were greater in number than the total of heretics burned during roughly the same period in the Spanish Netherlands. Marian England even out-burned the Spanish Inquisition. Indeed, the Emperor Charles II abandoned religious executions completely, and Philip II warned Mary that her burnings were harming, not promoting, her cause. His judgement was endorsed by two anonymous laymen who wrote to Bonner demanding to know 'where prove you that Christ and his Apostles killed any man for his faith?'[50] There is no record of his reply, but it seems that – despite his reputation – in early 1555, Bonner slowed down the pace of examinations, convictions and executions.

On May 24th 1554, Queen Mary complained to Bonner and his fellow bishops that heretics were being allowed 'to continue in their errors, to the dishonor of Almighty God and a dangerous example to others'.[51] The reproof was the result of her discovery that only one martyr had been burned in the London diocese during April. Bonner reacted sufficiently swiftly to guarantee his place at the top of the year's burnings' league table: 113 in London as compared with 52 in Canterbury. His performance might have been even better, had it not been for his initial habit of burning heretics one at a time rather than exploiting the economies of scale. In 1555, after the rebuke, he changed his ways. Thirteen men were martyred together at Stratford-le-Bow in June 1556. Other dioceses were less diligent. There were no burnings in the Durham diocese. Archdeacon Bernard Gilpin reported that he could find no one who did not believe in the Real Presence. His uncle, Bishop Cuthbert Tunstall, had not lived, and died, in vain.

In Canterbury where – Pole having been made Archbishop – activity should have been particularly intense, the Archdeacon, the assiduous Nicholas Harpsfield, devised a system that would encompass every man and woman in the diocese. Churchwardens were to identify everyone who did not take Easter Communion. Absentees were to be cross-examined about their beliefs and – assuming the answers did not suggest heresy – required to give assurances of future good conduct. Canterbury (having in its care fewer souls than London) could claim to be the more diligent in rooting out heresy. Canon Dixon, in 1557, described it as 'the hottest diocese in England'. He did not mean the description as a compliment. He also claimed that Pole was vicariously responsible for the burnings. Concerned with reforms to the whole Catholic Church, he left the management of his diocese to 'reckless subalterns, shutting his eyes to their rigours, willingly not knowing what was done by them, though feeling himself bound not to forbid it'.[52]

In February 1557 a National Heresy Commission was established to 'enquyre and search out all such persons as obstinately do refuse to receive the blessed sacrament'.[53] The powers that were intended to allow it to perform those duties were draconian, even by the standards of the sixteenth century. They included the power to 'inquire into all singular and heretical opinions, Lollardies, heretical and seditious books, concealments, contempts, conspiracies and all false rumours' and the right to 'search out such persons as obstinately do refuse to receive the blessed sacrament of the altar, to hear mass or come to their parish churches'.[54] Mary was attempting by force to make England a unified Catholic country in which no other faiths were tolerated. The attempt failed.

Mary decided to demonstrate her determination to convert even the most hardened heretic by making an example of Sir John Cheke, the one-time tutor to Edward VI, who had left the country under a dispensation that allowed notable Protestants to escape the fires of home. He was lured from Strasbourg to Brussels by a bogus invitation to meet members of the Privy Council in order to discuss his return, was kidnapped and subjected to the torture which was regularly employed on recalcitrant heretics. Cheke cracked and recanted. The deception and brutality caused no great outrage. Such behaviour was common in Tudor England. But now, if not at the time, the pointless attempt to catch and condemn a Protestant who could do no harm seems like the conduct of a queen who, knowing her cause was lost, struck out blindly at any adversary, no matter how unthreatening.

Mary's error was the mirror-image of the mistake her brother had made. He thought that the genuine Catholics in his kingdom were a perverse and recalcitrant minority who were wholly unrepresentative of a nation of people who were natural Protestants and longed for the suppression or expulsion of all things Roman. Mary believed England to be a Catholic country which had, temporarily, endured the tyranny of a Protestant dictatorship that was only supported by a morally and spiritually corrupt minority. They were both justified in claiming that the faith they despised was not the overwhelming choice of the English people. But that was because most of their subjects chose to float along with the religious tide. It was an attitude which zealots, like Edward and Mary, could not understand. But their other misjudgement was less explicable. They should have realised that, in both cases, devout followers of the faiths they abhorred – although minorities – were too strong in their convictions for their beliefs to be consumed by fire or washed away in blood.

Mary Tudor died on November 17th 1558. Cardinal Pole, her friend, adviser and confidant, died twelve hours later. Pole knew that his life's work – the reconversion of England – was left unfinished. Mary, who retained hope that her reign had killed the virus of the Reformation, nevertheless ended her days a broken woman – crushed not by the burdens of state and the demands of religion, but by the disappoint- ments of her private life. Philip, who had always regarded their marriage as a political convenience, had returned to Spain. The much-wanted and long-awaited baby had not been born. That meant she had not done her duty as a Catholic wife and she had failed in her duty as a queen, by lending England's support to Philip in wars from which England had nothing to gain. Mary was not to know that her personal life was to have a greater influence than her edicts and proclamation on the future pattern of English religion. It was not an influence of which she would have been proud. Her conduct associated Catholicism, in the public mind, with Spanish aspirations to dominate, perhaps even annex, England. The association awoke England's sleeping patriotism. For the next three hundred years Catholicism was regarded as an agent of foreign interference. The English Catholic Church, and its members, paid a far heavier price for Mary's multiple follies – religious, political and matrimonial – than for the fires of Smithfield.

Ten years after her death, Francis Godwin of Hereford, a Protestant bishop, composed a requiem for Mary Tudor which provides a moving example of Christian charity. She was, he wrote, 'a lady very godly, full of mercy, chaste and in every way praiseworthy'. The encomium falters when its author deals with her zealotry. But Bishop Godwin did his best. 'And what wonder is it for a heretic to condemn her for matters of religion who ever remained zealous in the profession of the Catholic faith? They contradict themselves and profanely enter into God's judgement who dare pronounce that, for her cruelty, God cut off half her days.'[55] Perhaps. But the sobriquet remains. She will always be 'Bloody Mary'.

CHAPTER 8

God Gave Us Elizabeth

Elizabeth I ascended the throne of England a Protestant, but a Protestant who, during the reign of her Catholic sister, Mary, had thought it wise to affect a sympathy for Rome. During those turbulent and terrible five years she had been under constant suspicion of conspiring with the nobles who had never been reconciled to rule by a Catholic queen. She had been arrested, charged with treason and imprisoned in the Tower, where she had daily expected to follow in the innocent footsteps of Lady Jane Grey. After much pleading, many interrogations, the agreement to attend Roman Mass and the transportation to and from almost every royal palace in the Home Counties, she was at last allowed to meet her sister and swear her loyalty to the crown (which was genuine) and her adherence to the Church of Rome (which was not). So she survived to complete the Reformation that her father had begun.

Mary, although she received a rapturous reception, had chosen to begin the conversion of England cautiously. Elizabeth, whose accession was greeted with far less enthusiasm, ignored the warnings of her closest advisers and began the work of reconversion at once. She appointed Protestants as her most trusted councillors, invited only Protestants to preach at Court and spontaneously demonstrated her true feelings by telling Westminster monks – who proceeded her in procession with candles – 'Away with those torches. We see very well.'[1] On Christmas Day 1558, two months after her succession, the Queen issued a proclamation which required the use of English prayers in all services. As an earnest of her intentions, she instructed that, when Parliament began in the New Year, the service of thanksgiving in the Chapel Royal at Westminster should not include the elevation of the host. It was the first step in the eventually successful campaign to restore the 1547 Royal Injunctions, the 1552 Book of Common Prayer and what amounted to a revision of the 1553 Forty-Two Articles of Religion, which Queen Mary had revoked. But there was more objection to the changes that she proposed than Elizabeth had anticipated. Some came from Catholics and Catholic sympathisers. The most vehement came from Protestants ultras who – despite the new Queen's clear sympathy for the Protestant cause – thought that the reversion to the extreme form of Edwardian Protestantism was coming too slowly and feared that it might never come.

In February 1559, the legislation which was necessary to effect the second reconversion was introduced into the House of Commons. The new Supremacy Bill, which made the Queen 'Governor' rather than 'Head' of the Church of England, was passed without facing much opposition. But antagonism to the legislation which proscribed dogma and liturgy was so strong that the separate bills that dealt with individual items of doctrine and procedure were withdrawn and replaced with a single bill. The strongest opposition was to changes in the words, spoken by the priest, during the administration of Communion. The version that appeared in the first 1552 Prayer Book had been drafted with the intention of placating traditionalists, but Edward – who had no time for compromise – had insisted that a second edition be published with all concessions to Popery removed. Elizabeth proposed to reintroduce the original version. That was unacceptable to rabid Protestants. They claimed that to give thanks for 'the blood of our Lord Jesus Christ which was shed for thee, preserve thy body and soul unto everlasting life' implied the possibility of transubstantiation. Other changes were found almost equally objectionable. The litany had been purged of offensive references to the Pope. The words of the Communion service had been altered to allow (though not, of course, to require) belief in a 'real presence'. Vestments and ornaments were no longer prohibited. Ministers were to conduct services from the place at which priests had stood when performing the Mass. The bill was passed in the House of Lords with a majority of three votes. Had it not been for the arbitrary exclusion of hard-line Protestant peers, and the imprisonment of Protestant bishops, it would have been overwhelmingly defeated.

Once again the typical Catholic (or ex-Catholic) family – whatever its response to the dogmatic disputes and doctrinal changes – was forced to recognise the primacy of the Church of England and acknowledge it as part of its daily life. A Third Act of Uniformity (composed to placate Protestant extremists) imposed a fine of twelve pence on persons who failed to attend Sunday services for a month. It also prohibited, by law, all forms of Catholic worship. The substance of the Act became the Thirty-Nine Articles, as drafted by the Convocation of Canterbury in 1563, revised – largely by the Queen herself – and finally endorsed by Convocation in 1571. From then on, until the present day, they stand – together with the Book of Common Prayer – as the statement of Church of England litany and doctrine.

Some Englishmen took pride in what they believed to be Elizabeth's moderation. Sir Thomas Smith in *De Republica Anglorum* boasted that 'Torment ... which is used by the order of civil law and custom of other countries ... is not used in England.'[2] Whether he knew it or not, he was wrong. But unlike its incidence in Mary's reign, torture was used in moderation as compared with its use in France and Spain. And the advent of a new queen would, it was hoped, herald an era of stability in which such cruel expedients were rarely necessary. Elizabeth was expected to be, and was welcomed as, the harbinger of tranquillity. In 1570, John Jewel, the Bishop of Salisbury, looked back on twelve years of her reign and rejoiced, not at the suppression of Catholicism, but at a decade largely untroubled by civil strife and theological commotion. 'God gave us Elizabeth and with her gave us peace and so long a peace as England has seldom seen before.'[3] The first twelve years did not pass in complete tranquillity. But, after the bloody turbulence of Mary's reign, it seemed that England was in repose. Not even the appearance of tolerance and calm was to survive long into Elizabeth's second decade.

Elizabeth's Catholic subjects were concerned less with theological argument than with liturgical practice. They wanted their lives to be undisturbed by change. To the illiterate parishioner, a chalice – as used in the Mass – was hard to distinguish from a cup which was used in the Protestant Communion service. Some men and women of simple faith were still comforted by their preacher's habit – developed in King Edward's reign - of reading the English liturgy in such a way and at such a speed that it was indistinguishable, in its incomprehensibility, from the Latin it had replaced. Ingenious priests told their parishioners to attend Church of England services, as the law required, but not to regard them as genuine acts of worship and then, later that Sunday, secretly distributed the host, which had been consecrated at an authentic celebration of the Mass. Often relics of Catholicism were retained long after they should have been removed or destroyed. In one Lancaster parish church the taper, in front of the image of St Nicholas, burned on for most of Elizabeth's reign.[4] At Sedgefield, in County Durham, the Bishop's instruction to remove the altar and replace it with a Communion table was ignored for five years. The blurring of the boundaries that separated the two faiths – although in part cosmetic – helped to reconcile most Catholics to the end of the Marian dream. But Elizabeth's concessions and the clergy's contrivances did little or nothing to appease the dedicated minority.

Elizabeth was more conciliatory towards idols than she was towards men. Bishops who refused to swear that they accepted the royal supremacy were deposed. The most intransigent were the first to go. So the list was headed by Edmund Bonner, Bishop of London. The work of seeking out Papists was done by Commissioners – appointed for each diocese – who, being almost always unyielding Protestants, rooted out Catholics and Catholic sympathisers with a rigour that went beyond the Queen's early inclinations. Working on the principles first laid down by Cranmer in 1548, they were particularly severe in their attitude towards images – one of the aspects of Catholic worship which Elizabeth would have been prepared to tolerate. In London they ordered public burnings to which churchwardens were required to bring their statues. Lincolnshire followed suit. In parts of the country their attitude was applauded – sometimes after a little encouragement. In Ashburton the churchwardens were paid ten pence each 'for their labour that carried the images to be burned and their drinking'.[5]

The iconoclasm was so indiscriminate that at Bures in Suffolk family tombs were destroyed during the demolition of the canopy above the Easter sepulchre. In October 1559 – perhaps as a sign of disapproval – Elizabeth first announced that a crucifix and candles were to be placed on the Communion table in the Chapel Royal. And then decreed that rood screens were to be erected in parish churches. The Protestant bishops who had been appointed to complete the Reformation rose up in condemnation, and the Queen capitulated in face of their insistence that she was proposing to defy God's will.

During the first two years of Elizabeth's reign three hundred priests were formally deprived of their benefices because of their 'popish' inclinations. Rather more conducted secret Catholic services for recusants, performed their daily offices in the great houses where noble families felt powerful enough to ignore the law, or simply worshipped their chosen God as laymen. The shortage of Protestant priests was exacerbated by the flu epidemic of 1558, which, killing a disproportionate number of recently converted clergy, was regarded by Catholics as God's vengeance on apostates. Elizabeth, who took a more prosaic view of the situation, wholly unreasonably blamed the crisis on the bishops. When they told her that there were 13,000 parishes in England and that it was not possible for each one to be served by a suitably qualified incumbent, she replied with the exasperation that was her invariable response to inconvenient reality. 'Jesus! Thirteen thousand is not to be looked for ... my meaning is not that you should make a choice of learned preachers only for they are not to be found, but of honest and wise men such as can read from the Scriptures and the Homilies, well to the people.'[6] Unfortunately even that reduced ambition was beyond achievement and, throughout the country, shortage of Church of England ministers intensified.

The Church of England Hierarchy first responded by allowing an increase in pluralities – one of the causes of parish dissatisfaction before Henry VIII's Reformation. Then some churchmen experimented with a reduction in the quality and qualifications of candidates for ordination, despite the inadequacy of parish priests already contributing to thousands of Protestants returning to the Church of Rome. Edmund Grindal, the new Bishop of London, ordained 107 priests during his first seven months in office. Others were more cautious. Matthew Parker, Elizabeth's Archbishop of Canterbury, emphasised the need 'to be very circumspect in admitting to the ministry' and, remembering the resentment of thirty years earlier, warned that ministers 'not brought up in learning . . . are very offensive to the people'.[7] His advice either did not reach or was ignored in the Chester diocese where William Downham's 176 ordinations did not include one graduate, but admitted into Holy Orders fifty-six men who, on examination, had been found inadequate. Even intellectual dilution did not solve the problem. In 1554 there were 172 working Protestant ministers in south Lancashire. By 1563 there were only ninety-eight. Twenty-one of them had died and were not replaced. The rest had just drifted away. In 1563 one-third of all Suffolk benefices were vacant.[8] The experience of the two counties, north and south, was typical of the country as a whole.

Concerns about the number and quality of men admitted to the ministry were moderated by the belief that the clandestine Catholic communion was suffering from an even more grievous shortage of priests and that, combined with the apparently effective proscriptions and prohibitions, the result would be a gradual, but irreversible, decline into eventual oblivion. In 1563, Elizabeth attempted to accelerate the process by prescribing the death penalty as the punishment for saying Mass. The defence of papal supremacy was, on conviction, to be followed by confiscation of the offender's property.

The Protestant establishment – underestimating the strength of Catholic conviction – believed that time was on its side. So it was prepared to tolerate the minor manifestations of the old faith: the representations of crosses and the crucifixion, scrawled on parish church walls in place of the burned images, and the Corpus Christi plays, most notably at York, depicting transubstantiation as an essential part of Christian dogma. Children of Catholics, who were brought up on Protestant imitations of the Mass, would – optimistic Protestants insisted – eventually lapse from the faith of their fathers. And it was taken for granted that neither they nor their parents would support the Pope or the invasion of England by a Catholic king or emperor. Catholicism, being no threat to the crown or state, could be left to die of natural causes. All the Queen and her councillors had to do was wait. But in the autumn of 1568 they were given cause to revise their complacent judgement about the safety of the realm. The north of England rose up in revolt.

The Rising of the Northern Earls had many causes. The Duke of Norfolk – humiliated by Elizabeth reneging on her promise to arrange his marriage to Mary, Queen of Scots – had given the dissatisfied Earls of Westmorland and Northumberland to believe that, in London, the Queen had lost support and popularity. When a real rising was about to begin, he changed his story and lost his nerve, but by then it was too late. The march south could neither be postponed nor abandoned. The revolt had begun. The real reason for the rising was hubris – the earls' resentment that they did not number among the Queen's favourites and the belief that they would receive their proper reward in a Court over which Mary Stewart presided. Both their flagging spirits and their self-delusion were encouraged by Mary, Queen of Scots' message to the Spanish Ambassador: 'Tell your master that if he will help me, I shall be Queen of England in three months.'[9]

The earls, expecting Spanish reinforcements, determined that their first strategic objective would be a port on the north-eastern coast. Hartlepool was chosen as the beachhead for the promised Duke of Avila's invasion. The Spaniards did not come. And, since it lacked a cause, the revolt had little popular support. A quarter of the soldiers who marched south were pressed men – tenants of the earls who led them. No doubt there were rebels who genuinely supported the Catholic cause, and their leaders certainly saw the call to defend Catholicism as the best way to keep morale high and desertion low. When they reached Durham Cathedral, they issued a proclamation – not so much to increase Catholic support of the enterprise as to assert it: 'Your duty doth bind you for the setting forth of His true religion.'[10]

Whatever effect the call to service had on recruitment, it certainly inspired an orgy of destruction. The Church of England Prayer Books were torn apart and their pages scattered in the nave of the cathedral. The practice was repeated in eight churches in the county and seventy churches in Yorkshire. The Mass was restored in at least fifteen churches. In Durham Cathedral a vast congregation was absolved en masse from any involvement in England's rejection of Rome.

The rebels advanced as far south as Leeds before they had to face

Elizabeth's generals. A hastily prepared and badly thought-out plan to rescue Mary was abandoned after they heard that the Queen of Scots had been moved from Tutbury to Coventry. Hopes of support from a Catholic rising in the East Riding of Yorkshire and south Lancashire were not realised. The earls – with only self-interest to guide them – decided that they were doomed, gave up the struggle and fled to Scotland, leaving their followers to face the wrath of both the English troops and the local inhabitants who had decided, on second thoughts, that they were loyal to the Queen and the Church of which she was Supreme Governor. The Northern Earls' Revolt was not a second Pilgrimage of Grace.

Elizabeth responded even more savagely than her father had reacted to the only genuine threat to his throne. Eight hundred rebels were executed. All of them were peasants, farm labourers or vagrants. Like all the Tudor monarchs, Elizabeth was chronically short of revenue. Rebels who could buy their freedom were reprieved on a payment of £5. Elizabeth's orders were brazenly explicit: 'You may not execute any that have freeholdings or noted wealth, for to do so is the Queen Majesty's pleasure.'[11] So the poor died and the well-to-do and wealthy took refuge in Scotland, where the Reformation was following a confused course of theological scholarship and tribal loyalty.

Mary Stuart, although crowned Queen of Scotland when she was six days old, lived in France from her sixth to her nineteenth year. In 1561 – after the death of her first husband, Francis II – the double queen reluctantly returned to Edinburgh, where she was almost certainly party to the death of her second husband, before marrying his murderer. Scotland was under the governance of the Protestant Lords of Congregation, but before her flight to England (and, as it turned out, to captivity), Mary's presence in Edinburgh protected and sustained Catholicism in what was an increasingly Protestant country. Her private chapel at Holyrood was described as 'nothing less than a Catholic parish church'[12] and when, one Palm Sunday, she heard that the Protestants of Edinburgh had tied a priest to the market cross and pelted him with refuse until he was dead, she called on the Catholics 'of Fife, Lothian, Tiverdale and Liddesdale to rise up and avenge him'[13] – only to discover that the priest was alive and well.

Mary's matrimonial record made her a less-than-ideal champion of Scottish Catholicism and her turbulent emotional life contributed to her rejection by the Lords of Congregation and the consequent loss of Scottish Catholicism's most potent icon. But, in Scotland, the enemy was England. So, despite her close connection with French ambitions, the Queen of Scots' religion helped Scottish Catholics to escape the accusation that bedevilled Catholics south of the border. They were, or claimed to be, patriots rather that potential traitors. In 1564, John Scott, a priest found saying Mass, successfully defended himself against the charge of Popery by claiming that he was 'of the Queen's religion'.[14] But Mary was a straw in the theological wind. Scotland had become Protestant by nature.

The Scottish Reformation was partly the result of theological conversion and partly – the one feature it shared with England – the result of a contempt for the Scottish priesthood. In the border counties the people had fallen under the spell of Knox's anti-clerical Calvinism. Further north they thought less about Calvin's doctrine and more about the failure of the Church to meet their needs. In both Highlands and Lowlands the rejection of things past took on a particularly violent form. Churches, as well as monasteries, were attacked and their physical fabric desecrated. In Glasgow the Collegiate Church of Our Lady and St Anne was in part demolished, and the cathedral church of St Mungo's was so badly damaged that services had to be cancelled and it was left to rot for so long there were fears that 'this greit monument will allturlie fall doun and dekey'.[15] The physical destruction that occurred throughout lowland Scotland was accepted, by most Catholics, with the resignation that follows recognition of the inevitable. Few attempts were made at rebuilding. The churches were left in ruins, like the relics of a lost civilisation, adding to the impression that Scottish Catholicism was dead and incapable of resurrection.

The brutality of the assaults on consecrated buildings matched the uncompromising nature of the laws passed by the Scottish Parliament. As early as 1560, it had legislated to prohibit 'Idolatry and all acts contrary to the Confession of Faith published in its Parliament', and to secure the 'abolition of the mass'.[16] The laws were to be enforced by a series of penalties which escalated from confiscation of property to death. For years they were ignored by Scotland's wayward sovereign. In 1562, a year after Mary's return to Scotland, a pyre was prepared in Dunblane for a Catholic priest, but it was used to burn his vestments while a jeering crowd pelted him with rotten eggs. It was a rare example of leniency. Resentful Protestant elders attributed the aberration to the influence of the Queen.

Scotland became more and more Protestant. The Kirk was part of the community and offences against it were tantamount to the rejection of generally agreed conventions and beliefs. So exclusion from the Presbyterian Church incurred social as well as civil penalties – ostracism, in addition to fines and the threat of imprisonment. It was the Kirk, rather than the civil authorities, which attempted to purge Scotland of

Roman practices and influence. And it enforced conformity with a thoroughness that was not a feature of the English Protestant offence against Rome. Instead of imposing a negative obligation – possible dissidents being required to abandon Catholic practices and deny the Catholic faith – it demanded a positive assertion of Protestantism, the 'confession of Calvinistic faith' at 'Kirk Sessions'. That did not mean that popish practices were overlooked. After Mary Stuart left Scotland in 1568, persecution, prosecution and simple mob violence were as great as they were in England. By the 1570s covert priests were being hanged in Edinburgh for saying the Mass.

Catholic life was very different in Ireland, where the Church benefited from continued supervision by the Vatican, and its English colonial masters' habit of thinking about it as only a plantation, with cheap crops to export, until it was in actual rebellion. A Jesuit, David Wolfe, supervised Trent-inspired reforms which included the creation of Mass centres, the imposition of strict rules of conduct on the priest-hood and the prohibition of simony. The Irish Catholic Church had reasserted its faith in all things Roman, while swearing loyalty to 'the natural crown and queen of England whom the Lord God maintain now and forever'. That position was impossible to sustain and the leadership of the Irish Church split.

In 1569, Philip II of Spain received a manifesto signed by four Irish Catholic archbishops, eight bishops and thirteen nobles. It reaffirmed the Irish people's determination 'to remain firm, constant and unshak-able in the faith of the Catholic Church [and] also persevere even to their last breath in their immemorial obedience and attachment to the Roman Pontiffs and the Apostolic see'. It also asked for Spain's assis-tance in freeing Ireland from the 'infection and ruin of the accursed and contagious heresy raging in England'.[17] The manifesto suggested that the release be brought about by the nomination of a Spanish Hapsburg as King of Ireland. Pope Gregory was so moved by the Irish manifesto that he, briefly, thought of compensating for King Philip's inaction by mounting an invasion of Ireland from the Papal States. Nothing came of it. But Ireland remained a predominantly Catholic nation for the rest of time.

The collapse of the Northern Earls' Rebellion might have been followed in England by a period of relative tranquillity. The Queen announced that she did not intend her subjects to 'be molested either by inquisition or examination in any matter ... of faith ... for as long as they shall, in their outward conversation ... shew themselves quiet and comfortable and not manifestly repugnant and obstinate to the laws of the land which are established for frequentation of divine service'. She was, in fact, asserting her support of freedom of conscience rather than freedom of worship, but even that limited degree of tolerance did not survive the folly of February 2nd 1570.

On that day Pope Pius V, apparently still under the impression that England was ripe for revolution, tried to accelerate the process by issuing the Papal Bull *Regnans in Excelsis* – 'The Sentence Declaratory of the Holy Father against the Pretended Queen of England and those heretics adhering to her'. It excommunicated Elizabeth and made treason against her the obligation of all good Catholics. 'Peers, subjects and people of the said kingdom, and all others on whatever terms bound to her, are freed from their oath and all manner of duty, fidelity and obedience . . . They shall not once dare to obey her or any of her laws, directions or commands, binding under the same curse those who do anything to the contrary.' Encompassing Elizabeth's murder became a moral duty. 'The guilty woman of England . . . is the cause of so much injury to the Catholic faith and loss of so many souls [that] there is no doubt that who ever sends her out of this world with pious intention of doing service, not only does not sin but gains merit.' From then on, every Catholic was thought to be Elizabeth's enemy and the friend of Spain. And an enemy of Elizabeth was an enemy of England. The process which Mary Tudor had begun was complete. Protestants could claim, on the authority of the Pope, that every Catholic was a traitor and potential regicide.

Neither King Philip of Spain nor the Emperor Maximilian was told of Pius' intention to excommunicate Elizabeth. Neither approved of a decision which required them either to disobey the Pope or increase – possibly to the point of war – their antagonism towards England. Both monarchs prohibited the bull from being publicised or published within their kingdoms, which may account for the extraordinary fact that – despite her notorious network of spies – neither the Queen nor her Court knew of its existence until a copy was nailed to the Bishop of London's garden gate. Thirty-seven years after that act of calculated effrontery, Mrs Frances Salisbury, daughter of the perpetrator of the daring deed, described to George Farrar, her priest, how and why it had come about and what, for her father, the consequences were:

When Pius V, his Bull concerning the Excommunication of Queen Elizabeth was to be sent into England, Mr Felton, being known to be a gentleman of approved resolution and virtue, was dealt withal to undertake the business of publishing it, one way or another, about the City of London. The danger of such an employment, which he took to be an act of virtue, daunted him not a whit. Whereupon, promising his best endeavours on that behalf, he had the Bull delivered to him in Calais and, after the receipt thereof, came presently to London, where being assisted by one Laurence Webb, Doctor of Canon and Civil Law, he set it upon the gate of the Bishop of London, his Palace but stayed not by it.

He had given a copy of the Bull to a gentleman of Lincoln's Inn, a special friend of his. Now the houses and lodgings of all Catholics about London being narrowly searched upon the publication of the aforesaid Bull, the closet of this Inns of Court gentleman (for he was a known Catholic) was in his absence broken up and the afore mentioned copy found therein. The gentleman, being hereupon apprehended and put to the wrack, confessed of whom he had it. Upon this were sent next day the Mayor of London with men and halberts to the number of five hundred to apprehend him, whom, as soon as from the window Mr Felton saw the knocking at the gate and ready to break in, he desired them to have patience, saying he knew why they came for him and would come down unto them.

From his house he was carried by the Mayor and the Lord Chief Justice to the Tower where he remained prisoner almost three months, having been thrice in that space put upon the wrack not withstanding that at his apprehension he had confessed he was the man who put the Bull on the Bishop's gate. Being condemned he was brought on the eighth day of August 1570 from the Tower to St Paul's Church yard near to the bishop's Palace, drawn on a hurdle to the place of execution. He hanged but a while and was cut down and bowelled while still alive insomuch as the hangman, having his heart in his hand, he said once or twice, Jesus.[18]

By declaring that the murder of Elizabeth had ceased to be a crime and become a duty, *Regnans in Excelsis* brought to an end what little tolerance had preceded its publication. During 1571 new laws were passed with the stated intention of preventing revolution – encouraged by the 'false, usurped and alien authority of Rome' – and the practical effect of penalising Catholics. The assertion that Elizabeth was not, or should not be, Queen of England, or that she was a heretic or infidel, became high treason. So did the circulation and dissemination of Papal Bulls, acceptance of absolution from the sin of schisms and attempts to promote a reconciliation with Rome.

It may have been pride, or perhaps it was genuine fear of assassination, that made Elizabeth respond to *Regnans in Excelsis* with twenty years of unremitting violence. Whatever the reason, the campaign against Catholicism was extended, to the trivial extent of prohibiting the importation of crosses, beads and holy pictures. In 1581 an Act with the avowed purpose of 'reconciling' Papists to the authority of their 'lawful sovereign' made recusancy an indictable offence to be tried at quarter sessions, and the fine for failure to attend Church of England Sunday services for a month was increased from twelve pence to £20. Catholic education was prohibited. Attendance at Mass incurred a penalty of one hundred marks or a year's imprisonment. Converting to Catholicism, or attempting to make converts, was punishable by death. Inevitably some Justices felt the need to demonstrate their unequivocal loyalty to the Queen and her Church. They did so by asking suspects what became known as 'The Bloody Question'. In the event of invasion, would they fight for the Queen or the Pope?

Then the murderous assault on the priesthood began. Priests who had trained abroad were forbidden to return to England. Those who did so were said to be guilty of high treason and were executed. Those already in the country were required to leave within forty days or face the same penalty. During the reign of Good Queen Bess – unlike her sister, Mary, spared the prefix 'Bloody' – 126 priests were executed.

After the death of Mary Tudor, many Catholic scholars had chosen to live and study abroad. The most notable among them – though by no means the most distinguished – was William Allen, a graduate of Oriel College and Principal of St Mary's Hall in Oxford. Allen was to become one of the Catholic Church's great evangelists. But initially he shared the view that the reclamation of England would come in 'God's good time' and that it was therefore impious – as well as uncongenial – to attempt an acceleration of the process by proselytising among the godless English. While they waited for God to do His duty, the exiled English scholars had, they believed, an obligation to continue their examination and clarification of Catholic theology – 'nothing more being proper to men of their profession, or possible as long as a heretical government held sway in their country'.[19]

During 1567 Allen – then a virtual refugee in the University of Louvain – had travelled to Rome with Jean Vendeville, Professor of Law at Douai University, and Vendeville had suggested that some sort of Catholic institution should be founded in the Netherlands. With funds supplied by Vendeville, Allen set out to attract 'the best wittes out of England' to a college which was devoted to Catholic scholarship. The college closed as the result of pressure – and some violence – from the Calvinist minority in Douai. Allen, who was better at urging others to face danger than at facing it himself, became rector of a college in Rheims. Most of the Douai seminarians went with him, but a handful chose Rome, where the college in Via di Monserrato – once a hospice for pilgrims – had greatly increased in size after Pope Gregory had agreed, despite initial doubts, to provide a grant to finance its expansion. At first the money was not well spent. The head of what had become the English College in Rome, Dr Morys Clynnog, had been inherited from the hospice, and the supervision of an institution that was both academic and missionary was beyond him. The favouritism he showed towards the handful of Welshmen under his supervision led to disturbances which almost caused the college to be closed. But in October 1578, two Italian Jesuits were added to the staff and a new rector was appointed. He, too – Father Agazzari – was a Jesuit. The Jesuits had launched their own mission to England in 1572 and Allen, who was appointed to the staff, complained bitterly that, as a consequence of the new rector's influence, the best English seminarians were being persuaded to abandon the notion of becoming lay priests and join the Society.

Allen's instinct that it was his duty to encourage study rather than missionary zeal was rejected by many of the young men he recruited. Their passion to save English souls convinced him that God's wishes had been misinterpreted or that He had changed His mind. Allen announced that 'God himself decided otherwise than we had foreseen.'[20] The Vatican was not sure that God was so capricious. It had never been enthusiastic about the English College usurping a task which the Jesuits were founded to perform, and openly wondered if sending good priests to almost certain death was the best use of its resources. Yet, notwithstanding all the regrets and reservations, the seminarians became Soldiers of God on the model of the Society of Jesus. Despite the rejection of cooperation with the Jesuits, the curriculum included the Jesuits' Spiritual Exercises. But there remained a fundamental disagreement about the purpose of the mission. Most of the English priests thought of England as a Catholic country which was waiting for liberation from the Protestant minority who had seized power. The Jesuits, and those who followed them, thought of England as Francis Xavier thought of Goa: a heathen country, many years away from salvation.

But there was also a more material reason for the change in role. It soon became clear that the original intention – the recruitment, for seven years of study, of young men between the ages of fourteen and twenty-five from good families – was economically unsustainable. So the college became a missionary seminary, financed in part by the crowned Catholic heads of Europe, and its members swore 'to Almighty God that I am ready and shall always be ready to receive holy orders, in His good time and I shall return to England for the salvation of souls, whenever it seems good to the superior of the college to order me to do so'.

Even before the new wave of priests had time to save many souls, the Protestant establishment – apart from Elizabeth herself – panicked and began groundlessly to fear that, despite its best efforts, England was being overrun by Papists. In 1577 the Bishop of London had complained that 'the Papists grew marvellously both in numbers and in the obstinate withdrawing of themselves from the Church and the service of God'.[21] Despite Elizabeth's agreement to (and in some cases the initiation of) an increasingly draconian penal regime, he still feared that 'Her Majesty is slow to believe that the great increase in Papists is a danger to the realm.'[22] Whether or not his fears about the Queen's complacency were justified, he was right about numbers. Many Catholics shared his opinion about the changing pattern of religious allegiance. Although they accepted they could never regain the old supremacy, they believed that persecution was strengthening their ranks and their cause. What they most feared was tolerance. One exile went as far as to claim that 'the rigour of the law and the severe execution thereof . . . has been the foundation of our credit . . . the only thing to be feared is a report about liberty of conscience at home'.

A year later, Don Bernardino Mendoza, the Spanish Ambassador, rejoiced in reporting to Madrid that 'The numbers of Catholics are increasing daily so abundantly that even Lord Burghley [Elizabeth's first minister] . . . is looking decidedly askance at the wonderful and constant growth [and] has confessed . . . That for every one staunch and constant Catholic at the beginning of Elizabeth's reign there were now ten.'[23] Mendoza attributed the growth to the 'college and seminary for Englishmen which your Majesty ordered to be supported . . . Of the old ones [Marian priests] very few remain . . . This was the cause of great decay in religion as there was no one to teach it . . . This cause is being remedied.'[24]

The Pope was more realistic. He knew that the English Catholic Church remained beleaguered and that its members were being subjected to pressures which many of them found difficult to withstand. Catholics in England were being forced to choose between heresy and treason and, although the punishment for heresy was more drastic, the penalty for treason was more immediate. English Catholics needed help and encouragement. The first missionary priest had landed in England from France in 1574. But in 1580 the campaign to save the heretic nation for a Catholic God acquired a new dimension. What amounted to a Jesuit expeditionary force landed on the south coast.

England was so desperately short of priests that there were fierce arguments about the proper employment of the few clergy who were available. The fundamental disagreements over the purpose of the English mission had not been resolved. But Allen, having been convinced that England could and must be reconverted, became the most passionate exponent of spreading the missionaries' net as widely as the number of priests allowed. The Pope agreed that reconversion was the vocation of Allen's seminarians. Allen's letter of gratitude – sent to Gregory XIII from what had become the English College in Rome – is too sycophantic in tone to sound genuine to the modern reader. But there is no doubt that he meant every word of it:

> I give the greatest and most humble thanks, as great as spirit and affection are able to compass acts towards us, especially for the two seminaries ... For there is nothing more distinguished, Most Holy Father and Lord, of all your great services towards our Country, non more salutary among all your wise counsels received for the restoration of the collapsed religion, nothing more glorious in all the works for eternal commemoration for God and men, nothing which either now earns more souls for the Lord or from which greater hope exists of reconciling the whole people into the future.[25]

Allen, although now associated with the English College in Rome – where he is buried – secured his place in Catholic history at Douai. Not only did he make it a model for other English seminaries abroad, but he supervised the preparation of the Douai–Rheims translation of the Bible, which remained the authorised Catholic text for five hundred years. However, he is best remembered for the part that he played – always in the rearguard rather than the front line – in the campaign for the reconversion of England. He equivocated about the purpose of the mission. The determination to 'earn' rather than 'preserve' souls for God was, like the hope of reconciling the whole people, indistinguishable from the aspiration to reconvert the entire nation, but whatever Allen thought about the religious future of England, he had no doubt that the Jesuits must play a part in it. That was a view shared by Robert Parsons (or Person, as he is sometimes called), a disenchanted Fellow of Balliol (then a Puritan college) who, during travels in Europe, had decided that his future lay with the Society.

Parsons had taken Jesuit vows before the notably demanding Society had agreed to admit him and had spent his novitiate undergoing the six exacting *experimenta* which were designed to test his courage, his stamina and his determination, as well as his faith. During two years of what amounted to probation, he had completed the Spiritual Exercises, spent months in retreat, lived as a mendicant begging alms from door to door, and taught the catechism to the children of the poor. He had performed all the menial tasks of a servant and demonstrated his humility by obeying the rule that required all Jesuits 'to hide no temptation, but to disclose it to their confessor or Superior, nay more, to take pleasure in thoroughly manifesting their whole soul to them, not only discussing their defects . . .'[26] Despite, or perhaps because of, the obligation to 'yield himself to perfect obedience' to his superior and to 'acquire perfect resignation and resignation of his own will and judgement',[27] Parsons exuded the self-confidence and belief that typifies the Jesuit. Armed with those indispensable assets, he joined with Allen in arguing that the Society had a duty to contribute towards the salvation of England and the English.

During December 1579, William Allen and Robert Parsons discussed the proposals with Father Everard Mercurianus, the General of the Society, and Father Claude Aquaviva, his deputy. Neither man was attracted by the idea. One objection transcended all others. Sending a missionary to England was sending a missionary to death. Jesuits had proved, time after time, that they were not afraid to die, but to approve a mission which they knew would end in almost immediate capture and death was knowingly to waste scarce resources. But there were other reasons why they were opposed to the idea. Jesuits were careful to avoid involvement in domestic politics and – partly because of their Spanish connection – they would be (wrongly) seen in England as agents of King Philip, not of God. A handful of Jesuits would be in 'everlasting hurly-burly', with 'no time to renew their fervour in retreats'.[28] The arguments against sending Jesuits to England were so strong that Parsons and Allen must have begun to think that all was lost. But Parsons, in one last desperate attempt to save the day, offered a reason for setting aside all the objections. The Benedictines were honoured as the society that converted England to Christianity. The Jesuits could outshine them with the glory of reclaiming it for Rome.

Jesuits will argue that the explanation for their mind change was invented by their enemies. But the widespread belief that it was true – right or wrong – illustrates the (often irrational) unpopularity of the Society and its members, even among Catholics. The association with the Inquisition was, and remains, far less damaging than the Society's reputation for regarding itself as superior to other societies. Jesuits do what other Orders dare not do, go where other Orders dare not go, think and say what other Orders dare not think and say. They obey a rigid code and accept an iron discipline that only men of indomitable will could survive. Jesuits are feared and disliked because they are so shamelessly admirable.

On Low Sunday, April 18th 1580, the Pope pronounced his blessing on the expedition to England. Parsons was accompanied to the valedictory audience by Edmund Campion, an English Jesuit with whom he was already well acquainted, and Ralph Emerson, a Jesuit lay brother. During their long and torturous journey to the Channel coast – turning back on themselves time after time to cover their tracks – they were joined by other priests from the seminary, including Ralph Sherwin, Edmund Rishton and Luke Kirby. It was agreed that secrecy and safety demanded that they should make the crossing separately. Parsons landed on June 16th, Campion nine days later.

Parsons 'went disguised as a soldier of choleric disposition, and he would have eyes, indeed, who discern beneath that costume, face and gate the goodness and modesty that lay in hiding'.[29] Campion claimed to be an Irish travelling salesman from Dublin. It was a role that itinerant priests were to assume many times during the perilous days that lay ahead. A 'pedlar's chest', found hidden in a wall at Samlesbury Hall near Preston in Lancashire, was a relic of the subterfuge. The ponyskin-covered wooden box looked as though it contained tools. In a sense it did. It held all that a priest might need to discharge his duties – including a portable altar stone. The likelihood is that it was the property of St Edmund Arrowsmith, a priest who was hanged, drawn and quartered in Lancaster in 1628.[30] Missionaries gambled their lives on the travelling-salesman disguise for at least fifty years.

Rome once more – but not for the last time – changed its position on the purpose of the mission to England. Jesuits who landed in Kent during the summer of 1580 were under strict instructions. They were forbidden to waste their time on heretics. Their task was 'the preservation and augmentation of the faith of the Catholics of England', not to make converts.[31] They were also bound by 'new and particular laws' which they were to obey 'besides the common and ancient laws of religious orders and the institute of the Society'.[32] Some of the new regulations appear to have been designed to help the missionaries merge into the local landscape. They were required 'to live without choir and chant' – the obligation of coming together in church for prayers several times during the course of the day. It was their duty 'to have and wear no [distinctive] habit or kind of clothing'. The severest strictures of the institute were repeated, – reminding the missionaries that, legally, they were wholly in the hands of the Society. 'The contract entered into between the Society and the subject is not equal for both parties.' The 'defects of subjects' were to be 'punished without judicial process'. The missionaries were enjoined to remember the principle – 'the union of obedience' – on which the Society's cohesion was built. 'The whole governance depends on one head, namely the Superior General.'

Informers warned the Privy Council that Jesuits were coming, and presumably in part as a response to the Society's reputation, the government reacted by introducing new punitive legislation. The statute of 1581 was designed to frustrate the work of itinerant priests and their avowed intention to encourage those Catholics who remained true to the faith to regularise their relationship with the Church by fulfilling the obligation to attend regular acts of worship. Between 1580 and 1585 – when it was made high treason for a priest who had been trained abroad to enter England – most of the missionaries were not Jesuits. They were 'seminary priests' from colleges run by other Orders. Their numbers grew rapidly – more than a hundred by 1589, and more than six hundred by the end of Queen Elizabeth's reign. It was, however, the Jesuits who made their mark on the history of the time – partly because they were so tirelessly reckless; and partly because, when they went to the stake, they left behind testaments of their work and faith. The most famous testament was written by Edmund Campion.

CHAPTER 9

Touching Our Society

Like most English Jesuits, Edmund Campion initially intended to become a seminary priest. He could, had he chosen to remain a Protestant, have risen to great heights of fame and distinction. While still at Oxford, his reputation as a theologian and man of letters made him a favourite of the Queen – probably on account of his blank verse, which is more to be admired for its metaphysics than for its metre:

> Dearest son, choose a cube, for a slippery form
> Is the ball, and in unsightly manner at every slight breeze
> It moves about. It never stands still or performs well.
> A cube is stable, wherever it be impelled by a stroke
> Wherever you move it, balanced by the correct weight,
> It holds firm and whatever way it is thrown, it rights itself.
> Do not cast down your spirit to me in sudden tempest.
> Bear it and be firm, thus one may live, put on
> A peaceful mind and, unmoved by whatever bitterness may
>   come against you
> Stand with straight feet. Never forsake good works, once you
>   have begun.[1]

Campion, who had been ordained Deacon of the Church of England, intended to take Holy Orders but, after travels – Dublin, Prague, Douai and Rome – and a conscience troubled by doubts about the schism, he was received into the Catholic Church. He became a Jesuit in 1573 and was ordained five years later. On December 5th 1578, he was notified that God and the Society of Jesus had called him to England. He obeyed with resignation and misgivings. 'It is a venture which only the wisdom of God can bring to good and to His wisdom we lovingly resign ourselves.'[2]

Robert Parsons, not Campion, was the pathfinder for the first party of Jesuits to land in England. Twenty years later, he published *The Memorial for the Reformation of England*. It revealed what had motivated the missionaries during the desperate days at the end of the sixteenth century. Jesuits or not, they rejected the notion that England was a heathen nation, to be treated as the Jesuits treated India and China. It was a Catholic country beset with doubts as well as enforced apostasy. It would not return to the true faith unless the Church remedied some of its past mistakes rather than hoped and worked for a return to the formal ritualism that had preceded King Henry's Reformation. Parsons wanted a totally new Church, organised under three archbishops and supported by three universities. Its most welcome members would be those who were Catholics by conviction. But where conviction failed, the law would guarantee compliance with the tenets of faith. It was to be a universal Church at which attendance would be compulsory. In Parsons' judgement, religious liberty promoted heresy. *The Memorial* did not say, though the implication was clear, that the vision could only become reality if a foreign power imposed its brand of Catholicism on England. Parsons spent the last years of his life attempting to persuade Spain to become that nation. And there is no doubt that, from the very beginning of his mission, he was dedicated to the complete reconversion of England by whatever means could achieve that end. His colleagues – Campion in particular – took a softer approach to the business of conversion. But total conversion (as well as reassurance) was their aim. That put them at odds with the leadership of their Order – a severe fault in so disciplined a society. In his reverential biography of Campion, Evelyn Waugh rightly asserts that Campion and his companions were instructed not even to speak to heretics.[3]

The *Records of the English Province of the Society of Jesus* suggests that, when the missionaries arrived in England, the Pope – whatever the Jesuit Society believed – intended that they should save the souls of Protestant apostates as well as providing comfort and grace to the steadfast and secure. The record is precise and explicit: 'After the persuasion of the Most Reverend William Allen, His Holiness sent to England for the conversion of heretics and the assistance of Catholics.'[4] There was certainly some ambiguity in the instructions that the Vatican issued. They included the order 'to preach and teach, though not openly but in private houses, after the old example of the Apostles in their day, the Catholic faith and administer the sacraments to such as have need and were capable of that heavenly benefit'.[5] It is difficult to imagine how, from the security of 'private houses' they would have been able to achieve 'the conversion of heretics'. The contradiction may well be that – neither for the first nor last time – the Jesuits thought they knew better than the Pope and followed their own conscientious judgement rather than his orders.

Campion's own description of his duties was sufficiently comprehensive to cover either or both definitions of his task. 'My charge is, of free cost, to preach the Gospel, to minister the Sacraments, to instruct the simple, to reform sinners, to confute errors, and in brief to cry alarm spiritual against foul vice and proud ignorance, wherever my countrymen are abused.'[6] With that mandate to inspire him, he set out on his mission – first by boat from Dover to Hythe and from there along the Thames to London. In Chancery Lane – at the home of George Gilbert, a wealthy Catholic layman who was to become one of the expedition's patrons – he was reunited with the other missionaries. Together they spent the first few days in conclave with half a dozen old Marist priests in what they chose to call the Synod of Southwark. It was there that they composed a *Brief Discourse on Why Catholics Refuse to Go to Church*. Their didactic duty done, they left London in some style, thanks to the generosity of George Gilbert. Each seminary priest and Jesuit was given a pair of horses, a travelling servant, a suit of gentleman's riding clothes and the immense sum of £60 in cash. The splendour of their departure – though justified as both a disguise and as the assurance that the mission could afford to spread out from the Home Counties – was to become a cause of both criticism and regret.

Campion went north, noting with some embarrassment that he had been sent to one of the safer parts of the country. However, he seemed to enjoy the months he spent in Lancashire. 'I ride about some piece of the country every day. The harvest is wonderful great. On horseback I meditate my sermon. When I come to the house I polish. Then I talk with such as come to talk with me or hear their confessions. In the morning, after Mass, I preach; they hear with exceeding greediness and often receive the sacrament.'[7]

Every account of the missionaries' daily lives confirms that they lived in constant danger of capture and death. 'Sometimes when we are sitting at table quite cheerfully conversing familiarly about matters of faith and piety ... if it happens that someone rings at the front door a little insistently, so that it can be put down as an official, immediately, like deer that have heard the voice of hunters and prick their ears and stand alert, all stop eating, stand to attention and commend themselves to God'.[8] It was faith combined with the certainty that was, and still is, Catholicism's hallmark which made them strong.

The Pope, having realised the folly of *Regnans in Excelsis* and the encouragement of Elizabeth's assassination, had warned the missionaries to avoid any involvement in politics – a difficult task, but one that Campion accepted with the assurance that matters of state were 'things which appertain not to my vocation and from which I gladly restrain and sequester myself'. England was not in the mood to distinguish between religion and politics – both, when practised by Catholics, seemed committed to the overthrow of England's lawful government. The confusion was compounded by hotheads who insisted that 'The state of Christendom depends on the stout assailing of England.'[9]

Knowing that it could only be a matter of time before they were arrested, the missionaries prepared for the day of reckoning. Campion was warned by messages smuggled out from Catholic priests imprisoned in the Marshalsea prison that, if he were caught, he would be given neither time nor opportunity to state his case. So, in anticipation of inevitable capture, he wrote a message to the Right Honourable Lords of the Privy Council. It came to be called either 'Campion's Challenge' or 'Campion's Brag'. It acquired those pejorative descriptions because Campion – having explicitly denied, in the text, the intention to commit either bombastic offence – went on, in the same paragraph, to make both errors of taste and judgement:

> I am loathe to speak anything that might sound of a prank or an insolent brag or challenge – especially now, being as a dead man to this world . . . Yet have I such courage in the advancing of the majesty of Jesus Christ, my king . . . and such assurance in my quarrel and my evidence is so impregnable because I know perfectly that non of the protestants of England, nor all the protestants living, nor any sect our adversaries (however they may . . . overrule us in the kingdom of grammarians and of unlearned ears) can maintain their doctrine in disputation.[10]

Right or wrong, it was a foolish claim to make and diminished the majesty of the rest of the document.

The 'brag' included a necessary and genuine assurance of political neutrality. 'I never had in mind, and am strictly forbidden by the father who sent me, to deal in any respect with matters of estate, or policy or the realm', and there was a (no doubt sincere) obeisance to Elizabeth, 'my Sovereign Ladye' whom 'God had been pleased to enrich with notable gifts of nature, learning and princely education'. Then, after a defiant mention of the 'English students . . . beyond the sea' who were 'determined to win you to heaven or die upon your torments', came the passage that ennobled the whole document. It was a brag. But it was about something that was worth bragging about: Jesuit indomitability.

And touching our society, let it be known to you that we have made a league – all the Jesuits of the world whose succession and multitude must overreach all the practices of England – cheerfully to carry the cross you shall lay upon us, and never to despair your recovery while we have a man left to enjoy your Tyburn or be wracked with your tortures or consumed in your prisons. The expense is reckoned, the enterprise is begun; it is of God, it cannot be withstood. So the faith was planted: so it must be restored.[11]

Campion ended with a farewell that was, in truth, addressed not to the Privy Council, but to all England. 'I have no more to say but to recommend your case and mine to Almighty God, the Searcher of Hearts, who send[s] us His grace and set[s] us to accord before the day of payment, to the end we may at last be friends in heaven, where all shall be forgotten.'

The 'brag' was intended to be Campion's dying testimony, the statement he would not be allowed to make at the stake. But he showed it to several of his colleagues, one of whom – when he was arrested – took a copy with him to the Marshalsea. From there the 'brag' found its way into the world of besieged and bewildered Catholics. The Bishop of Winchester told the Privy Council that copies were circulating in his diocese, and the Sheriff of Wiltshire complained that it was being openly read in his shire. What had been written as a personal valediction became a public proclamation of invincible faith and the manifesto of the missionary zeal. A treatise intended for publication – *Ten Reasons* why Catholicism was the one true faith – added to Campion's reputation as Rome's most successful advocate in England. Without either seeking or expecting the role, he had become the most famous of the Jesuits who risked their lives in the hope of keeping English Catholicism alive. He had also become the 'most wanted' of the missionaries.

For a while the missionaries' efforts were a gratifying success. In Parsons' words, they 'passed through most part of the shires of England, preaching and administering the sacraments in almost every gentleman's house we passed by, whether he was a Catholic or not, providing that he had any Catholics in his house to hear us'.[12] Although they took what precautions they could, often moving about the country in disguise – Campion 'in apparel to myself very ridiculous.'[13] – all the Jesuits knew they could 'not long escape the hands of the heretics. The enemy has so many eyes, so many scouts and crafts.'[14]

Campion was not the first of the Jesuits to be arrested. Between Advent 1580 and Easter 1581, eight missionaries were captured, indicted and tortured on the rack. After failing to name any of their (as yet free) associates, they were left to rot in gaol. The persecution was extended to include the Catholic laity as well as the priesthood. Parsons wrote to Alfonso Agazzari, the Rector of the English College in Rome, with the ominous news that 'the violence is now extreme and unheard of since England first became Christian. Everywhere gentlemen and commoners, men, women and even children are being dragged off to gaol. They are bound in chains, despoiled of their goods, deprived of light.'[15]

Despite the mounting risk of capture, for three months Campion continued preaching without apparent fear of arrest. Overconfidence was his undoing. In mid-July, against the strong advice of Parsons, he spent a night at Lyford Grange in Berkshire – a well-known centre of Catholic activity and a refuge for fugitive priests and nuns. He left after a day of discreet private prayer, but was prevailed upon to return a couple of days later. By then his fame had attracted Catholics from all over the county and beyond. On the second day of Campion's visit, George Eliot – a professional priest-hunter – arrived at the Grange. He had heard that Mass was to be said there, but had no idea of the celebrant's identity until he attended the service and listened to Campion preach on the text 'Jerusalem thou killest the prophets'. Eliot left to return later in the day with enough men to surround the house. They searched the Grange throughout the evening and into the night, but found nothing. Then, as dawn broke, they noticed early sunlight shining through a narrow cavity between the stones of the stairwell. They broke down the wall and found Campion in the 'priest's hole' that had been constructed behind it.

Before formal proceedings against him were begun, Campion – once one of Elizabeth's favourites – was taken to Leicester House in the Strand for cross-examination by the Earl of Leicester and the Queen herself. His answers to their questions must have exasperated his inquisitors and might well be described by the Society's critics as 'Jesuitical'. Could the Pope lawfully depose the Queen? It was not for him to judge. If Catholic Spain invaded England, what would he do? He would do 'as God shall give me grace'. He was still offered a pardon if he would agree to attend a Protestant service – just once. Campion could recite *Ten Reasons* why he must reject the offer. The law was left to take its course.

The series of examinations that followed included a number of 'conferences' at which the prisoner was required to argue theology with various Protestant scholars, including the Regius Professor of Divinity at the University of Cambridge. Often Campion answered questions in the obtuse language that has come to be associated with Jesuit disputation. But on the crucial issue of transubstantiation his reply was simple and passionate. Told that belief in the Real Presence denied the truth of the Bodily Resurrection, he came near to losing his temper. 'What? Will you make Him a prisoner now in Heaven? Must He be bound to those properties of a natural body? Heaven is His palace and you will make it His prison.'[16]

After four conferences, the Privy Council decided that there was enough evidence to indict Campion for offences against the English Church. The charge was then changed to conspiracy to murder the Queen. The trial – of Campion and seven other priests – began on November 20th 1581. On December 23rd, Parsons wrote again to Alfonso Agazzari. All the defendants had been accused of plotting with 'the Pope, the Catholic King [of Spain] and the Duke of Florence to invade England . . .' Their principal accusers were 'three young men who had been one time in Rome . . . Who, if only on account of their age and insignificance could never have known anything of such a matter had it been mooted.'[17] Parsons did not think it necessary to add that such a matter had been, or was about to be, mooted by him.

The result was a foregone conclusion. Campion's final address to the jury included the affirmation for which he is best remembered: 'If our religion do make us traitors we are worthy to be condemned; but otherwise we are and have been as good subjects as the queen ever had.' He was condemned 'to be hanged and let down alive and your privy parts cut off and your entrails be taken out and burnt in your sight and your head be cut off and your body divided into four parts and disposed of at her Majesty's pleasure'. The execution took place at Tyburn on December 1st 1581. More by chance than intention, he was left hanging until he was dead. It was the only indulgence he received on the day of execution. His final prayers and last words were interrupted by abuse, which was shouted at him by the courtiers and councillors who had been deputed to watch the execution. The following day, having sensed the mood of the people, Sir Francis Walsingham expressed his bitter regret at the executions. He was not moved by moral outrage, but by expediency. He belatedly concluded that 'it would have been better for the Queen to have spent 40,000 gold pieces than to have put these priests to death in public'.[18] Martyrdom was Rome's recruiting agent.

Among the silent Catholics, who were emboldened by the execution of Edmund Campion, was the wife of William Byrd, the composer and organist in the Elizabethan Chapel Royal. She, at least according to folklore, was in the crowd that witnessed the disembowelling, and dipped her handkerchief in the martyr's blood. Byrd and his fellow composer and Chapel Royal organist, Thomas Tallis, were remarkably open about their Catholic sympathies. That they escaped censure was probably more the result of their numerous aristocratic patrons than the consequence of Burghley's belief that loyalty must take second place to artistic genius.

Initially, Robert Parsons' reaction to the deaths seemed as brave as, if less dramatic than, Juliana Byrd's demonstration at Tyburn. He published a rebuke – *Confessio Fidei* – which was addressed to the London magistrates: 'You are persecuting a corporation which will never die, and sooner will your hearts and hands satiated with blood fail you than there will be lacking men eminent for virtue and learning who will be sent by this Society to allow their blood to be shed by you for this cause.'[19] However, instead of allowing his own blood to be shed for the cause, Parsons left England for France, never to return.

There is no doubt that a number of good Catholics urged him to go. Their concern was less his safety than the security of their community as a whole. While Parsons remained, the persecution would continue. Some of the seminary priests – whose mission had preceded his – claimed that, far from furthering God's work, his presence had become the excuse for a reign of terror which the Church could not survive. They threatened to expose him if he did not go. Whatever the true reason for Parsons' flight, his subsequent explanation reeks of guilt that is felt, but not acknowledged. 'I returned into Sussex . . . and finding the commodity of passage to go to France, I resolved to go to confer with Dr Allen . . . With full intention to return presently . . . One cause was also to print some books which I had written In England or was in writing . . . Another reason of my coming over was to make a mission of Scotch fathers into Scotland.'[20] Although Parsons explained why he left, he offered no reason for why he failed to return.

Initially Parsons settled in Rouen, from where he wrote to the Vicar General of the Jesuits to say that he experienced 'a slight feeling of sadness' when he recalled how many of the comrades who set out together for England had 'attained their reward' in heaven.[21] He consoled himself with the explanation that he had fled not to avoid martyrdom, but to be in a position to carry on the work which God had set him. That included telling the Duke of Guise, Philip II of Spain and any other Catholic king or prince who would listen that it was a Christian sovereign's duty to invade England and return its citizens to the true faith by force of arms.

Other Jesuit missionaries thought that the redemption of England lay in the hands of priests rather than soldiers. The suffering that their presence might cause to their followers was nothing as compared with the horrors that awaited them. Robert Southwell, a fugitive priest, described conditions inside the Bridewell gaol. Prisoners, he wrote, welcomed the release of death, 'even though as full of pangs as hanging, drawing and embowelling quick can make them ... Some are hanged by their hands 8 or 9 or 12 hours together till not only their wits but their senses fail them ... some have been watched and kept without sleep until they were passed the use of reason and then examined when they could barely give an account of their own names ... What insufferable agonies we have been put to on the rack, it is not possible to express, the feeling so far exceedeth speech.'[22]

Robert Southwell, knowing the fate that awaited him, had continued his mission in the north of England until the day of his arrest, and, in London, Henry Garnett had enjoyed almost equal success. Three months before Campion's death, Sir Francis Knollys told the Queen, 'The Jesuits are going from house to house to draw men from allegiance to Her Majesty into the false politics of the church of Rome hath and will endanger Her Majesty's person and state more than all the sects in the world, if no executions shall follow upon their traitorous practices that are for the same apprehended.'[23]

There was still an army of the faithful who shared Campion's certainty that since the 'enterprise is of God, it cannot be withstood'. But the prevailing spirit had changed. Time and persecution had undermined Catholic convictions. So had a shortage of priests and the consequent break in the habit of worship. Most corrosive of all was the increasing belief – encouraged by the calls for invasion made by expatriate and exiled ultras – that Rome was the agent of Spain. As well as unnerving patriotic Catholics, it hardened Protestant resistance to Catholicism. An onlooker at Edmund Campion's execution had echoed the fears and feelings that were felt by much of England: 'In your Catholicism, all treason is contained.'[24]

News of the programmes and the persecutions had reached Rome back in April 1580, and Pope Gregory – partly because of concern for beleaguered Catholics, partly on account of his long-standing doubts about its justification, but mostly out of expediency – retreated from the claim that the death of Queen Elizabeth was the hope, and should be the aspiration, of all true believers. His *Explanatio* was intended to absolve the faithful from having to make a choice between fidelity to Church and loyalty to the state, without either relinquishing his claim to spiritual domain over England or moderating Pope Pius' condemnation of Elizabeth and all her works. *Regnans in Excelsis* was reaffirmed as the statement of intention. But Catholics were not obliged to follow its instructions until the objective that it sought became a practical possibility. That might have seemed a step away from support for assassination and revolution, had it not been for the way in which the doctrine was interpreted.

Six months after it was promulgated, Cardinal Como, the Vatican Secretary, was obliged to provide a clarification of what the Pope regarded as a practical possibility. The Papal Nuncio in Madrid had been approached by two English nobles who wanted to know if the murder of Elizabeth would be a sin. They were assured that, to the contrary, it would be a sin not to take whatever opportunity for assassination Providence provided. 'Since the guilty woman of England is the cause of so much injury to the Catholic faith and the loss of so many million souls, there is no doubt that whosoever sends her out of this world with pious intention does God a service.'[25] In the following year the English Parliament passed the Act of Persuasion, which made it a capital offence to alienate English subjects from their lawful sovereign. A little over a year later, Pope Gregory retaliated by offering a plenary indulgence to all new converts to Catholicism, and the English College in Rome changed its mandate from preparing candidates for Holy Orders to sending missionaries to England 'for the help of souls there led astray'.[26]

Whatever effect *Explanatio* – and its interpretation and associated activities – had on the English Catholics, it certainly did nothing to diminish the determination of those councillors who wanted Elizabeth to purge England of the seminary priests. Their anxieties were increased by the indomitability of the Catholic minority and by the success of its martyrs in bearing public witness to their undying faith. Arthur Pitts, a priest awaiting execution in the Tower of London, described the death of Thomas Cottam, a fellow priest, whose execution by burning at Tyburn he was taken to witness:

He came to his window over against my door, saying with joy of heart and voice 'Give God thanks with me for tomorrow is my day and I now hope that I shall not escape the happy hour which I have so earnestly desired, because I find my name first on the roll of the Tower assigned to die tomorrow.' The next day he departed joyfully, but arriving at the place of his martyrdom he was quailed again. For albeit he was the first to be taken up, yet the officers fearing that his example might draw many to be of his religion, because he was well known and beloved in the City having been before a Schoolmaster there. They, desirous to save his life, solicited him earnestly to recant his religion in which, he persisting, they take him down to see if the death and torments of the other of his brethren could move him. But when they perceived that his courage, by their blood increased, he had his desired crown of martyrdom.[27]

The constancy of most English Catholics had certainly unnerved some of Elizabeth's councillors. In 1577, just as the Protestant hegemony was becoming unassailable, the Bishop of London had complained that 'the Papists marvellously increase in both numbers and in obstinate withdrawing of themselves from the Church and the service of God'. Obviously unimpressed by the penal legislation of 1559, 1563 and 1570, he had gone on to argue, 'Her Majesty must herein be made to be *animo abfirmato* or else nothing will be done and all our travail turned into a mockery.'[28] A year later, the Earl of Leicester had written to warn Lord Burghley that 'since Queen Mary's time, the Papists were never in that jollity they be in at this present time in this country'.[29] Burghley shared the Bishop of London's view that the Queen was too lenient. 'Her Majesty hath, from the beginning, showed her natural disposition to be such towards her subjects in the cause of religion that those who have ben repugnant or mislikeous of her religion have not lacked her favour.'[30]

The danger to Elizabeth came not from numbers, which were diminishing, but from the possible action of individual fanatics, encouraged to treason and murder by men of learning and virtue who, from the safety and comfort of the Vatican, lectured their followers in England on the importance of killing and being killed. The conduct of the English émigrés increased the Privy Council's determination to root out 'Papist traitors' and reduced what little chance there was of Elizabeth making some sort of accommodation with the 'loyal Catholics' who genuinely wished her no harm.

William Allen, safe in Rome, kept anxious (and probably spurious) count of the number of English missionaries who risked torture and death. In the autumn of 1585 he told the Pope, 'We have now ... almost 300 priests in the households of noblemen and men of substance and are daily sending others who will direct the consciences and actions of others when the time comes.'[31] The coming time of which he spoke was the day of the invasion of England. He had completely changed his view on the proper role of seminarians and had come to see them as agents of a Catholic revolution which, exclusively in his imagination, would be ignited by a Spanish invasion. Being a scholar, he thought it necessary to support his belligerence with the learned opinion that the Pope, 'being the first and chief prelate of all Christendom', was entitled to give 'his consent that anything be done or attempted by arms or violence against any lawful or anointed prince whatever'.[32] Allen had become the Catholic that Elizabeth's councillors warned against.

Allen, made a cardinal in 1587, expanded his justification of a Spanish invasion in his *Admonitions to the People of England*. It was not written in the grave and measured language which might have been expected of his elevated status. The condition of England had reached the point at which the rule of Elizabeth 'cannot be tolerated without the eternal infamy of our whole country, the whole world deriding our effeminate bastardy, that have suffered such a creature almost thirty years together to reign over our bodies and souls'. Neither the *Admonitions*' style nor its substance chimed with Campion's heroically gentle view of the priestly vocation. But most of Elizabeth's councillors saw all missionaries – indeed, all Catholics – as threats to the stability of the state. Their error was encouraged by the mindless extremism of men like Nicholas Sanders, an émigré priest. Sanders told the Duke of Alba that 'the State of Christendom depends on the stout assailing of England'.[33]

There was plenty of evidence to confirm that they meant what they said. All the major plots of Elizabeth's reign – the Northern Earls in 1569, Ridolfi in 1571, Throckmorton in 1583, Parry in 1585, Babbington in 1586 and Essex in 1601 – were either Catholic-inspired or attracted Catholic support. The three Armadas were sent by Catholic Spain to invade England and overthrow Protestant Elizabeth – 1588 being the first and therefore the most famous – and numerous other expeditions were all mounted in the name of the True Church. The constant rumours of often-imaginary plots in England were usually associated with Mary Stewart, not because she was a Scot, but because she was a Catholic who still, it was assumed, attracted the treasonable allegiance of the apparently irrepressible legions of other Papists in England. She survived for so long, in an unmerciful country during an unmerciful age, not because of Elizabeth's confidence or compassion, but because the Queen was reluctant to remove a crowned head.

The contemporary notion that Elizabeth was, by contemporary standards, lenient – even indulgent – towards her Catholic subjects reveals much about the brutality of the age. The Queen of England was obsessive in her determination to rule a country that was totally Protestant in form, if not in genuine belief. She could not convert every one of her Catholic subjects. But she could suppress, or perhaps even eliminate, all manifestations of the forbidden faith – a process which, in 1587, she attempted to accelerate first by instructing Justices of the

Peace to confiscate the land and property of recusants who failed to pay their fines, and then by prohibiting recusants from buying or selling land. In 1593, ten years before her death, Elizabeth signed into law the last of the punitive statutes which were as much a defining feature of her reign as the more popular notion of the all-conquering Gloriana. Catholics were obliged to obtain permission before travelling more than five miles from their homes, and those who were absent from their usual place of residence for more than three months were sent into exile. Persistent recusants, above sixteen years of age, were to be imprisoned.

The case for even more repressive action was, in the Privy Council's judgement, obviously strengthened by the apparent increase in open recusancy. Catholics rejoiced at what they attributed to a brave rejection of intimidation. Protestants were bewildered by what seemed to be the failure of their penal policies to drive Catholics to Church of England services. In fact what looked like an upsurge of rebellion – as measured by the number of prosecutions – was less the result of an increase in defiance of the penal code than the statistical consequence of anxious Justices taking the identification of recusants more seriously. In the Archdiocese of York, commissioners began to search out and fine recusant gentry – a class of Catholics previously thought to be beyond pursuit.[34]

Francis Ingleby of Ripley Castle, close to Fountains Abbey, had returned to Yorkshire from Rheims an ordained priest. He had – by his departure, ordination and return – defied three ordinances. He followed his vocation, disguised 'as a poor man without a cloak', until, one day in March 1586, he made the mistake of engaging a known Catholic in conversation 'on an open spot called Bishopsfield . . . which was overlooked by a window of the Archbishop's palace of Bishopthorpe. It happened that chaplains of the Archbishop espied them and that the Catholic took off his hat to Ingleby and showed him greater marks of respect that were fitting towards a common person meanly dressed.'[35] Ingleby was arrested, convicted at York Assizes and executed on June 3rd 1586. Though the history is too dazzled by Elizabeth's brilliance to say so, for ten years there was a Reign of Terror in England.

The penal legislation of 1581, and its extension in 1585, certainly reduced the numbers of prosperous and established families that were willing to employ domestic priests as they employed lawyers and bailiffs – often the only celebrants of Mass in the county. A meeting of Catholic gentry in Kent decided that the dangers of residence were so great that 'all priests should shift for themselves'; and when John

Brushford arrived in England from Rheims, he 'found everybody so fearful that none would receive [him] into their house' and, after some weeks in hiding in London and the West Country, he went home to France.[36]

Ten years or so after the disastrous interpretation and reinterpretation of *Regnans in Excelsis* had provoked an increase in the butchery and burning, the Catholic gentry regained their nerve and resumed the patronage that sustained the Church for much of the seventeenth century. In the absence of parish structures, they alone could afford a priest's upkeep, and the great houses of the south-east and East Anglia were convenient stopping places for missionary priests entering England from Calais or Dieppe and landing in Dover and Rye. So, at the end of the sixteenth century, the labouring poor – particularly in the north – suffered from acute spiritual neglect. In some parts of England – notably Lancashire – the ancient Catholicism of the local aristocracy held sway even after the old Marian priests had died. The same was true of Wales. Despite the patronage of the (mostly English in origin) nobility, the Welsh Catholics were chronically short of priests and in consequence fell 'into considerable ignorance'.[37]

Elizabeth never contemplated even the grudging tolerance of Catholics who worshipped in private and made no attempt to proselytise for their faith, and even the few moderate voices that were sometimes heard at court were silenced by a series of aggressive Jesuit initiatives – the most provocative of which was a conference on the succession to the English throne. Under the guidance of Robert Parsons, it concluded that Elizabeth's successor should be neither James VI of Scotland, the rightful heir, nor Arbella Stuart, the next in line. In an act of calculated *lèse-majesté*, it concluded that the next English sovereign should be the Infanta of Spain. Outrage combined with incredulity – two emotions that were intensified, among the seminary priests, by their increasing animosity towards the Jesuits.

At the heart of the antagonism was a fundamental disagreement about the nature of the Catholic Church in England. Many of the seminarians, who wanted a national Church with its own hierarchy and episcopate, felt an instinctive loyalty to England and its sovereign. The division between the militants and the moderates had been increasingly a reflection of the protagonists' age and experience. William Allen still hoped that England would be invaded by Spain and published his *Declaration of the sentence and deposition of Elizabeth the Usurper.*[38] Father Thomas Wryght, a young secular priest, publicly posed the question 'Is it lawful for Catholics in England to take up arms. And in other ways, defend the queen and the realm against Spain?'[39] He bravely concluded that it was.

It was not only disagreement about the nature of the mission to England that divided the men who were ordained to carry it out. The lay priests deeply resented the Jesuits' presumption. There was, they complained, 'nothing holy except that which they had sanctified'. Some seminarians in the English College in Rome demanded that their rivals for the souls of England be put in their place. In the castle at Wisbech – a community of captured and imprisoned priests – the seminarians refused to accept Jesuit leadership and rebelled against the seating arrangement at meals as a reflection of their discontent. At the height of the controversy, two items of news about William Allen reached England. The first, which was greeted with incredulity, was that he had so mellowed that he was offering his protection to English Protestants who were travelling through Rome. The second, which was accepted as more authoritative, was that he was dead. The Catholic Church in England needed a new titular head.

Richard Bancroft, the Bishop of London, saw Allen's death as an opportunity to widen the division between intransigent Catholics and Catholics who wanted to live in loyal peace. With the enthusiastic approval of Cecil and the acquiescence of the Queen herself, he invited Father Thomas Bluet, the leader of the secular priests, to Fulham Palace to discuss the possibility of reconciling the moderate Catholic clergy and the crown. After five months of talks it was agreed that a petition, *The Protestation of Allegiance*, be presented to the Queen in the name of all Catholic clergy and laymen. It did not go so far as to demand, or even request, freedom of expression, but promised complete and perpetual fidelity and asked, in return, for the right privately to exercise freedom of conscience. Bancroft and Bluet made a brave, but fruitless, attempt to ensure its success by including a clause which was welcomed as much by the Catholic seminary priests as the Protestant bishop. It proposed the suppression of all Jesuit publications. Elizabeth was unmoved. 'If I grant this liberty to the Catholics, by this very fact I lay at their feet my honour, my crown and my life.'[40] Bancroft was disappointed but not dismayed. With the Queen's knowledge, if not her actual approval, he endorsed Bluet's decision to present to Rome a petition which called for the Catholic Church fully to recognise Elizabeth's right to the throne of England. Without her knowledge, he relaxed the censorship regulations so as to allow the publication and circulation of material produced by the seminary priests. He was motivated less by a belief in liberty of expression than by the hope of tactical advantage. The Pope had appointed George Blackwell, a Jesuit sympathiser, to lead the Catholic Church in England. Both Bancroft, as a Protestant, and Bluet, as a Catholic, wanted to diminish the influence of the Society by increasing the visibility of its rivals. In 1602, Elizabeth made their tactical manoeuvring pointless. She confirmed the order for the expulsion from England of all Jesuits and secular priests.

Clement VIII had given George Blackwell the title 'Archpriest' – a rank previously unknown to the Church – and instructed him to work closely with the Jesuits. The lay priests and seminarians had been severely affronted. They had no doubt about what, though not whom, their titular head should be. They wanted the independent status of the Catholic Church in England to be confirmed by the appointment of a bishop. Their appeal to Rome – which won them the title of 'Appellants' – was precise. England should be provided with 'a hierarchy approved by a free vote of the seminary priests and by them alone'.[41] There was no hope of their solution being adopted. Robert Parsons, who had become Rector of the English College in Rome as a consolation prize after failing to inherit Allen's red hat, opposed it. So did many influential English lay Catholics, who feared that a hierarchy would challenge their position as leaders of their local communities. And, most important of all, the Vatican was not in a mood to antagonise the Society of Jesus. The delegation that the Appellants sent to Rome, in the hope of preventing endorsement of the appointment, was not even granted an audience by the Pope, and Blackwell was confirmed in office. Inevitably the Appellants rejected the archpriest's authority – without, since it was a recently invented office, being sure what it was. Four uneasy years passed before the Pope revised his instructions, ordered the Archpriest to work independently of the Jesuits and decreed that lay priests and regulars were to be segregated and limited to the performance of their separate and distinct functions. The post-Reformation Catholic Church in England was beginning to take shape.

Most Catholics who thought about the future of their Church aspired to no more than creating little enclaves of belief among the heathens. But there was still a movement to treat English Catholicism as the depleted, but still viable, continuation of the Church that Augustine founded. The conflict between the two groups was exacerbated by Parsons' *Memorial for the Reformation of England*. It disturbed moderates by being wholly realistic about the prospects of concessions from the government and excited extremists by being wholly fanciful about the hopes of relief by invasion. But the desire for a settlement – still a minority position – was growing irresistibly in both Protestant and Catholic Churches.

Attempts to accommodate Pope and Queen had always foundered on what even the most moderate of the priests invariably regarded as both reasonable and non-negotiable: the assertions of loyalty to the crown, balanced with the acceptance that Rome's spiritual authority should be respected in England. In the autumn of 1602, John Popham, the Lord Chief Justice, made the last attempt of Elizabeth's reign to broker an uneasy peace. He had become convinced – during various cross-examinations of secular priests – that the offer to reject *Regnans in Excelsis*, the bull of excommunication, was sincere and he had persuaded Robert Cecil that the genuine revision of the Church's animosity was enough to justify the gradual and informal relaxation of restrictions on freedom of worship. Priests who believed that a formal reconciliation was right and necessary responded and made their last attempt to live in peace with the old Queen. In January 1603, thirteen priests signed a Protestation which acknowledged that Queen Elizabeth had 'as full authority, power and sovereignty over us and over all the subjects of the realm as her highnesses predecessors ever had'.[42] The difficulty caused by slight ambiguity of the Protestation's wording was compounded by the addition of the proviso that England and Elizabeth were exceptions and that, in other instances, the Pope might be entitled to depose a secular ruler. That contradicted the general rejection of the Pope's authority which had become an essential part of Protestant theology. So the approach was rebuffed.

Attempts at reconciliation – never made by more than a tiny minority in either community – were invariably prejudiced, and sometimes prevented, by fears of a Spanish-inspired *coup d'état*. Sometimes the fears of an attempt to depose Elizabeth – as distinct from fears of the coup succeeding – were justified. But often they were the result of what amounted to neurosis. The most bizarre fears of a Catholic uprising were spread over two reigns and were associated with Arbella Stuart, a young woman who – while fractious by nature – wanted only to live as normal a life as was possible in the courts of Queen Elizabeth and King James. She was denied the opportunity because she was a Tudor by birth and a Catholic by religion.

Arbella Stuart – descended from Queen Margaret of Scotland, Henry VII's older daughter and therefore niece, at least by marriage, to Mary, Queen of Scots – was, at various times, third, second and fourth in line to a throne to which she never aspired. In consequence she was the constant victim of rumours, which usually predicted marriage to a Catholic prince as a preliminary to seizing the crown. The list of supposed suitors was said to include two princes of the House of Savoy, the eldest son of Alexander Farnese, Duke of Parma, and a cardinal brother of the Pope, who was to be unfrocked in preparation for becoming a husband and a king. The perpetrators of the Main Plot against James I – a serious but doomed attempt on his life – claimed that they acted in Arbella's interest. The claim was probably an afterthought and certainly made without the authority of the supposed beneficiary. Other alleged conspiracies were examples of how neurosis can give credence to the most unlikely stories.

The story that 'two Scotch Catholics [were to] convey Arbella by stealth out of England'[43] seemed to be confirmed by the discovery that Sir William Stanley, an exiled zealot, had given the Spanish court notice of the proposed flight. It was then revealed that Rome's 'greatest fear' was that 'her Majesty should die and that Arbella should be proclaimed Queen'.[44] In Stanley's version of events, Arbella was seen by the Vatican as a possible obstacle on the path to the throne of a genuine Catholic pretender. Whatever the young woman's prospects and whoever her supporters might be, Elizabeth was not prepared to take any risks. Arbella, like Mary Stuart before her, was kept in the genteel custody of Bess, Countess of Shrewsbury in Sheffield Castle and Hardwick Hall in Derbyshire. It was a county of willing martyrs. The Earl of Shrewsbury had arrested two fugitive priests, Nicholas Garlick and Robert Ludlam, in Padley Manor at nearby Hathersage. Local outrage at their conviction and sentence to death turned into mass hysteria when they converted a convicted murderer on their way to the scaffold. An informer named Barnes offered his opinion on the real cause of the 'agitation. All platforms fell to the ground on the death of the Queen of Scots ... They harp much on Lady Arbella, despairing of the King of Scots.'[45]

Arbella was briefly infatuated with the Earl of Essex, who reciprocated her affection by claiming, after the failure of his plot in 1601, that he had intended to see her crowned Queen. Her enthusiasm for acting as the banner around which Catholics rallied can be judged by her response to the arrival in Mansfield – ten miles away from Arbella's enforced home at Hardwick Hall – of Henry Stapleton, 'a very wilful Papist'. Stapleton was accompanied by forty armed men, one of whom – in what was regarded as proof of his intention – had a pillion attached to his saddle. Arbella's page visited Stapleton on the night of his arrival in Nottingham. It seemed that a Catholic pretender was Rome's for the taking.

Next morning two of the armed men stationed themselves outside Hardwick's gate while Stapleton asked, and was refused, permission to ascend the tower of Ault Hucknall parish church, from which he could have watched events outside the Hall. He would have witnessed the humiliating anticlimax of his plot. First, 'Arbella did come forth from her chamber, went towards the gates, as she said intending to walk, but being persuaded that it was dinner time did stay.'[46] Then a servant came to the gate with a simple message. 'She cannot come out this day.'[47] Stapleton made one last effort to salvage the expedition by formally requesting an audience with Arbella. It was denied. So ended in fact – though not in fervid imaginations – Arbella Stuart's involvement with Popish plots to seize the throne, leaving the unhappy lady to years of suspicion and the denial of her modest hope to marry for love and live happily ever after. The Privy Council reacted to accounts of 'the Hardwick Plot' with commendable calm. The Shrewsbury family was admonished and, much to their relief, Arbella was removed from their custody and a warrant was issued requiring Derbyshire magistrates to prohibit 'unlawful assemblies and disorderly attempts'. It may be that they were less calm than preoccupied with more important events. Stapleton's men attempted the rescue (or abduction) of Arbella Stuart on March 8th 1603. On March 24th Queen Elizabeth died.

After the accession of James VI and I, Arbella's life alternated between periods of exaltation at court and virtual imprisonment in Derbyshire. Both were equally unwelcome. She wanted marriage, children and peace. At the age of thirty-five she married twenty-two-year-old William Seymour – without the king's permission. Husband and wife were sent to the Marshalsea to await James' pleasure. Arbella was sentenced to be held, indefinitely, in the custody of the Bishop of Durham. During the journey north she escaped. The plan to flee to France with Seymour was botched. He got away. She did not. During the next four years she slipped gradually into madness. In early 1615 she began to refuse food. On September 25th she died and was pronounced to have committed suicide by starvation.

CHAPTER 10

More an Antique Roman?

No period in English history has been more tumultuous and tyrannical than the last ten years in the reign of Elizabeth I and the first ten years of James I's succession. Those two decades were also the golden age of English drama. It was the era of Thomas Kyd, Christopher Marlowe, Ben Jonson and William Shakespeare – four playwrights who navigated the tempestuous waters of purge and persecution with different degrees of success. Kyd and Marlowe were accused of 'holding monstrous opinions' – the definition of which differed from accuser to accuser and included out-and-out atheism, libels against Jesus Christ and the Virgin Mary and the blasphemous suggestion that the English sovereign was not head of the English Church. Jonson was certainly a Catholic from time to time – usually at moments of great stress or danger. Three of the playwrights clearly reflect their religious beliefs in their work. But Shakespeare's faith is not so transparently revealed. After discovering how Kyd, Marlowe and Jonson chose (or chose not) to worship, the intriguing question remains: was William Shakespeare a Catholic?

Marlowe – author of *Dr Faustus*, *Tamburlaine* and *The Jew of Malta* – was a rumbustious atheist whose religious views were a combination of progressive thinking about the literal truth of the Old Testament and a desire to outrage conventional society. After his death in 1593, Richard Baines – like Marlowe, an associate of Francis Walsingham, Elizabeth's spy-master – published what he claimed to be the playwright's views on the Bible. Baines was hardly a reliable witness. He had, among his other accomplishments, spent some time 'under cover' as a seminarian in Rheims and, after his ordination, had planned to murder the whole community by poisoning the seminary's well. The plan came to nothing and, in consequence, Baines' infamy was never discovered. He was sent to England in the belief that he would say secret Masses for fugitive Catholics. Once he was free of his disguise, he resumed his old trade. He was an informer by instinct.

Baines reported – almost certainly correctly – that Marlowe rejected the Old Testament's timeframe. His 'damnable lies' included doubts about the very existence of Adam, 'proved to have lived within six thousand years' while 'the Indians have assuredly written of above sixteen thousand years ago'.[1] Moses he regarded as a charlatan who 'made the Jews travel forty years in the wilderness – which journey might have been done in one year'. His views on the New Testament were even more inflammatory. 'Christ was a bastard and his mother dishonest ... All the New Testament is filthily written ... The sacrament would have been much better administered in a tobacco pipe.'[2] Most offensive of all, Marlowe insisted that there was an erotic implication in the description of St John as 'the disciple whom Jesus loved'.

The allegations against Marlowe were substantiated by Thomas Kyd, author of the *Spanish Tragedy*. The two men had shared the same lodgings and worked in the same room. So when Kyd was accused of publishing a 'lewd and malicious libel', it was easy for him to claim that incriminating documents, found in his possession, had been left behind by Marlowe. The 'libel' was included in material which he was said to have produced as a contribution to a campaign designed to encourage riots in protests against immigration. One of the leaflets produced in evidence was a doggerel verse, signed 'Tamburlaine'. The quality of the work – 'We'll cut your throats in your temple praying / Not Paris Massacre so much blood did spill'[3] – confirmed that Marlowe was not the author. But Kyd, under torture, repeated the charge and added that Marlowe was the proposed leader of an atheist uprising. Marlowe was arrested but, probably because of his association with Walsingham, was treated far better than Kyd had been. He was actually released to await trial. Shortly after his parole he was killed in a tavern brawl. There is still no certainty about the true author of the undoubtedly combustible attack on immigration – a feature of Tudor life that was welcomed by the Protestant leadership because most of the newcomers were, or were said to be, refugees from Catholic tyranny – material which Kyd disowned. But Kyd shared Marlowe's atheism and shared the joke when he made a 'jest of the Scriptures with these horrible vile, heretical words, denying the eternal deity of Christ' – less out of an intellectual conviction than in a spirit of reckless bravado.

Ben Jonson equivocated. But at least he took religion seriously and his Catholicism was reflected in his plays. He was converted to Catholicism in 1598 – a dangerous year to acknowledge the authority of the Pope – while he was in prison awaiting trial for causing the death of one Gabriel Spencer, a fellow actor. Jonson's claim that Spencer was killed in a duel was dismissed, but he pleaded 'benefit of clergy' – the reduction of punishment in cases where the criminal is in Holy Orders – and the sentence of execution was reduced to branding.

During the weeks when his plea was being considered, it seemed that Jonson was destined for the gallows. The old adage proved correct. His mind, wonderfully concentrated, turned to the idea of writing a religious play. The result was *Sejanus*, written and first performed in 1603, the year of Queen Elizabeth's death, and printed in 1605, the year of the Gunpowder Plot.

Sejanus is a Roman courtier who ingratiates himself with the Emperor Tiberius, exploits the imperial patronage by obtaining positions of power and influence for his supporters and aspires to lead the empire. The parallel with the rise of Cecil and Bacon is less than exact. But both men – like Sejanus – strengthened their position by exaggerating the threat to the established order posed by the followers of a different faith. The enemy, according to Sejanus, were the Catiline family. Catholics were represented in the same way to Elizabeth by Bacon and Cecil.

It is easy to overstate the extent to which *Sejanus* was meant to be a covert attack on the corruption, cruelty and conspiracies (real and imaginary) in Elizabethan England. Some Jonson scholars have identified representations of every prominent figure of the period – including Mary, Queen of Scots – among the dramatis personae.[4] But, although the parallels have been exaggerated, they were close enough for the Earl of Northampton to cite the play as evidence to support his claim that the Privy Council should indict Jonson for 'Popery'.[5] Whether or not Elizabethan audiences appreciated the political nuances of the play must remain in doubt. So must the attitude of the King's Players who performed it. But we do know that one of them was William Shakespeare.

Much of Shakespeare's life is a mystery, and virtually nothing is known of his religious inclination. There is no record of him attending Mass or associating with recusants. Nor did he ostentatiously proclaim his Protestantism, although – as a member of, and playwright to, a company of Elizabethan Court players – he lived among men and women who would expect him to exhibit loyalty to the Queen and the Church of which she was head. There are, however, two areas in which evidence of his faith can be found. One is family background, friends and neighbours. The other is the texts of his plays.

The notion that Shakespeare was an unrepentant Catholic first gained serious credence with a discovery that was made, in 1757, by workmen who were retiling the roof of a house in Stratford-upon-Avon. Concealed in the rafters, they found what came to be called *John Shakespeare's Spiritual Testament*. John was the given name of William Shakespeare's father. Before 1757 there had been some casual and unverified suggestions that Shakespeare was inclined towards Catholicism. Fifty years after his death, Richard Davies, chaplain of Corpus Christi College, Oxford, wrote in the margin of notes on the tragedies, 'He dyed a Papist'[6] – leaving whoever read his observation to decide whether he meant that Shakespeare had remained true to Rome to the end or that he had a deathbed conversion.

During Shakespeare's lifetime, the cartographer John Speed denounced Shakespeare in a polemic entitled *The Theatre of the Empire of Great Britaine*. Without providing much evidence to support his claim, he alleged that 'This Papist and his Poet, of like conscience, the one ever feigning, the other ever falsifying the truth',[7] were guilty of treason. The attack was thought, at the time, to be the result of jealousy combined with prejudice. But after the discovery of the *Testament*, it was not so lightly dismissed. John Shakespeare could sign his name, but he could not read. So the claim that the document was connected to him was only plausible if it is assumed that he was handed it, ready-made, and then added his signature.

The document included an oath of allegiance to the 'Romaine and Apostolic Church', described the Virgin Mary as 'my Angell guardian' and venerated 'the holy sacrifice of the Mass'.[8] Those expressions – like much else in the *Testament* – are word-for-word translations of the call to live and die for the old faith, from a spiritual that was composed by Carlo Borromeo, Archbishop of Milan. Four thousand copies were brought to England by Edmund Campion, who certainly visited villages five miles outside Stratford. The *Testament* ends with the invocation of St Winifred, which was not in the Borromeo document and can be explained – say subscribers to the Campion-connection theory – by John Shakespeare's anxiety to make the *Testament* appear his own work. St Winifred was the patron saint of Holywell, a favourite place of pilgrimage for Warwickshire. So far, so plausible. But one passage that was added to the Borromeo text is too good to be true.

John Shakespeare allegedly stated that the *Testament* was written as a precaution: 'I may be cut off in the blossome of my sins.'[9] Those words – or words much like them – are spoken by the ghost of Hamlet's father, who lamented that he had been 'Cut off euen in blossom of my sinne' (1:5:76). There are two possible explanations for the similarity. William Shakespeare could have remembered his father's agonies for thirty years and incorporated them in his most celebrated play. Or the *Testament* could have been written sometime later than 1599 (and long after John Shakespeare's death) and the line from *Hamlet* included to give it bogus authenticity. The second explanation seems by far the more likely.

It is, however, certain that John Shakespeare – a glover by trade – was, at one time, a recusant. His name appears on a list of Stratford citizens who were 'presented [before the magistrates] for not coming monthlie to the Church according to Her Majesty's laws'.[10] However, when refusal to conform would have disqualified him from holding local office, he turned apostate. John's appointment, in 1558, as a town constable required him to take the Oath of Allegiance. He agreed, but the evidence suggests that he was reluctant to accept the obligations of Protestantism and that when they could not be avoided, he forswore his true faith as little as possible. His attitude was illustrated by the way in which he interpreted the injunction to 'utterly extinct and destroy' the symbols of Catholicism in Stratford's parish church. The edict had been in force for five years before he obeyed it. Then he limewashed the church wall – making restoration possible – and removed the rood screen in one piece, thus allowing it to be re-erected when the true faith was restored to England. Despite his clear reluctance to conform, by 1568 John's Protestant orthodoxy was sufficiently established for him to be elected bailiff (mayor) of Stratford. In 1576 he retired from all municipal office, for no apparent reason. That was the year in which the Privy Council set up a commission more generally to enforce the obligation of public servants to take the Oath of Supremacy. John Shakespeare may have wanted to avoid close scrutiny of his record. Or perhaps there was only so much heresy that he could stomach.

William Shakespeare was four at the time when his father was made mayor of Stratford. We have no way of knowing what he was taught, at his mother's knee, though it is certain that the Ardens – his maternal grandparents – were strong and consistent recusants. In 1583 the head of the family was executed for involvement in the Summerville Plot, and Mary Arden's father, a gentleman landowner, had been notable for the expression of public pleasure at the succession of Mary Tudor and the deposition of Lady Jane Grey. But whatever family prayers were said each evening, by the time William Shakespeare was old enough to notice such things, his father represented the Catholic compromise with Protestantism that was common among men who wanted to get on in this world and were too busy to worry about the next.

Despite his father's acceptance of the outward signs of the Protestant faith, William Shakespeare grew up surrounded by Catholics. Hugh Latimer – the Bishop of Worcester who, during the Counter-Reformation, was burned at the stake for his Protestant zeal – located Stratford 'at the blind end' of his diocese. His Archdeacon reported that in Warwickshire 'great Parishes and Market towns [were] utterly destitute of the word of God'. And John Whitgift (one of Latimer's successors in Worcester) complained that Stratford was a closely knit community that shielded Papists and refused to provide the names and numbers of either recusant or yet-to-be converted and redeemed Catholics in the town. The Worcester clergy estimated that there were one hundred Papists, of one sort or another, in Stratford. A dozen or more were the Shakespeares' neighbours.

Known Catholics who – like the Shakespeares – lived in Henley Street included George Whateley, a woollen draper, who was rich enough to endow a small school outside the town. Two of his brothers were fugitive priests. John Cawdrey, the landlord of the Angel Inn, was the father of a Jesuit. George Badger, another woollen draper, was forced to resign from the aldermanic bench when it was discovered that he too was a recusant. And the Shakespeares had Catholic connections in other parts of Stratford. Thomas Nash, who bought the Bear Inn from Thomas Barber, was a distant Shakespeare relation. Both landlords were Catholics. William's parents were close enough to the practising Papists of Stratford to convince young William that Papists were not the treacherous heretics depicted in Protestant propaganda. And he was to learn more about the Roman faith at school.

Stratford Grammar School employed a succession of Catholic masters. Some of them forswore their faith – as John Shakespeare had forsworn his – in order to secure their appointment, but their continued (if secret) adherence to the old religion was not in doubt. Simon Hunt left the school for the seminary at Douai and became a Jesuit priest. Thomas Jenkins' long association with Edmund Campion had begun at St John's College, Oxford. John Cottom was certainly a Catholic and was believed to be the brother of Thomas Cottam, a Jesuit who was tried alongside Campion and subsequently executed. It may be that it was because of connections made at school, and the influence of his masters, that William Shakespeare left Stratford at the beginning of the ten 'lost years'.

There are many theories about how the decade was spent, and the suggestion that he passed most of the time in Lancashire is no more capable of verification than any of the others. But the proposition that Shakespeare was the Shakeshaft who was employed by the Houghtons of Lancashire is as plausible as the rest of the theories, and it provides a suitable bridge between schooldays in Stratford and life as an actor and playwright-actor in London. The transmutation from Shakespeare into Shakeshaft can be explained by the variations in name and spelling that were common in Tudor England. William's paternal grandfather signed himself 'Shakestaff'.[11] Or it may have been the result of the need to hide his true identity.

The Houghtons knew the Cottoms of Preston whose kinsman, John Cottom, had taught young William Shakespeare in Stratford. He was named in John Houghton's will as a one-time 'servant' – an omnibus description that could easily encompass resident schoolmaster. It does not require a great leap of imagination to assume that, having moved on to Stratford Grammar School, he recommended his brightest pupil to fill the post he had once held. Lancashire, the most Catholic county in the realm, was notorious for ignoring the edicts of its Protestant sovereign. Nine of the twenty-one Popish schoolteachers who were executed in the reign of Queen Elizabeth taught in Lancashire. William Shakespeare, or Shakeshaft, may have been one of those who escaped. His survival may have been the result of his employer's friendship with the Stanley family. The Stanleys had played an ignoble part in the suppression of the Pilgrimage of Grace, but Lord Strange – the eldest son of the family, and future Earl of Derby – was a Catholic sympathiser who, in the years before he succeeded to the title and the estate, was patron of a group of travelling players. Was it in Lancashire that Shakespeare joined Lord Strange's Men and became first an actor and then a playwright? It may have been gratitude that made him, in later life, go out of his way to please and flatter the Stanleys.

In *The Tragedy of Richard III* (5:4:17) it is Stanley who seizes the crown from the dead tyrant's head, presents it to the Earl of Richmond and symbolically crowns him Henry VII, King of England:

> Lo! Here, this long-usurped royalty
> From the dead temples of this bloody wretch
> Have I plucked off to grace thy brows withal:
> Wear it, enjoy it and make much of it.

Richmond – gracious in victory – enquires, 'is young George Stanley living?' and is gratified to discover that he is 'safe in Leicester town'. The story establishes the Stanleys as crucial to the emergence of the whole Tudor dynasty and is, of course, pure invention.

The works of William Shakespeare are so complete and comprehensive that it is possible to use the evidence of his plays and poetry to prove that he was whatever the reader wants him to be. In *The Heart of His Mystery,* John Waterfield devotes six hundred pages of careful textual analysis to the Catholic references, images and coded messages in the plays and poetry. He dedicates the book to Clare Asquith, the author of *Shadowplay*, and endorses her belief that the plays have a hidden message, which had to be deciphered by the recognition of a 'breathtakingly simple' code: 'High and fair stand for Catholic, Low and dark stand for Protestant.'[12] That is not the only reason why Waterfield's work should be treated with caution. The evidence for his confidence that the collected works are Catholic tracts includes the assertions that 'when Capulet threatens to drag Juliet "on a hurdle" to her wedding with Paris, it reminds us that this was the way in which priests were conveyed to the place of execution', and 'the mutilated figure of Lavinia in *Titus Andronicus*, with hands cut off and tongue torn out, acquires additional poignancy when we see her as standing for the powerless, persecuted and gagged Catholic Community'.[13] That may or may not be true. The connection is in the eye of the beholder. But neither quotation tells us anything about Shakespeare's religion.

Only once – in all his works – did Shakespeare quote directly from the Bible. *Measure for Measure* takes its title from Chapter 7 of Matthew's Gospel, 'Judge not, that ye be not judged. For with what judgement ye judge, ye shall be judged: and with what measure ye mete, it shall be measured unto you again.' The play begins with the imprisonment of Claudio for the crime of fathering a child with Julietta, to whom he is betrothed. Any claims it has to being a stern rejection of sexual licence are undermined by what follows – the offer of repeal in return for sexual favours (provided by a surrogate), and the final speech of the play in which the Duke of Vienna proposes marriage to a nun. *Measure for Measure* teaches us very little about Shakespeare's attitude towards religion and nothing about his attitude towards Rome.

We do know that Shakespeare never wrote a word that openly commended Catholicism. He did, however, heartily support, from time to time, the idea that temporal monarchs enjoyed an authority which the Pope could not subvert. The supremacy of kings is most trenchantly expressed in *King John* (3:1:147–54) – a play set in England three hundred years before the Reformation:

> What earthly name to interrogatories
> Can task the free breath of a sacred king?
> Thou canst not, Cardinal, devise a name
> So slight, unworthy and ridiculous,
> To charge me to an answer, as the Pope.
> Tell him this tale; and from the mouth of England
> Add thus much more: that no Italian priest
> Shall tithe or toll in our dominions.

But Shakespeare's religious inclinations should not be judged by the great set speeches, which he must have thought – as a Court player – needed to meet the mood of the time. It is more rewarding to look for indications of belief in less bravura passages.

In *Romeo and Juliet*, Juliet asks Friar Lawrence, 'Are you at leisure, holy father now / Or shall I come to you at evening mass?' Evening Mass had been prohibited by the Council of Trent in 1566. But it would be wrong to assume that the question was put in Juliet's mouth to indicate that Rome's writ did not run in the Globe Theatre. It may have been an obeisance to historical accuracy. The action of the play is set before 1556 and Verona was slow to implement the Tridentine obligations. Shakespeare's genius included a general and proper willingness to require fact and truth to take second place behind the needs of rhythm and rhyme. The likelihood is that he wrote of evening Mass without a thought about its religious implications.

There is no doubt that Shakespeare was a patriot. And it is easy to believe that he was a Protestant patriot. Professor A D Nuttall wrote in *Shakespeare the Thinker* of commentators who regard the absence from his plays of 'Protestant ferocity' as an indication of his 'not so crypto Catholicism'[14] and dismiss his rare excursions into verbal violence against Rome as a 'young dramatist ... temporarily toeing the party line'. The example he cites comes from *Henry VI Part 1*. It is 1429 and the English army is besieging Orleans. Talbot announces, 'our English troops retire, I cannot stay them', (2:1:17) and then confronts the cause of all the panic, St Joan:

> Devil or devil's dam, I'll conjure thee
> Blood will I draw on thee, thou art a witch.

Subsequently, Bedford describes the French king as 'Coward of France', who, 'wrongs his fame, despairing of his own arm's fortitude, to join with witches and the help of hell' (2:5:5).

It is perfectly true that the authorised Protestant version of Henry VI's defeat was that English arms were beaten by witchcraft and that St Joan was the chief witch. But the story was not invented in Tudor England. It was the excuse for defeat offered by Henry VI's army. Shakespeare recorded it because the English soldiers said it. He also wrote (1:6:4–7) – given a little poetic licence – what the French said about her:

> Divinest creature, Astraea's daughter.
> How shall I honour thee for this success?

> Thy promises are like Adonis' gardens,
> That one day bloom'd and fruitful were the next.

In the play, Joan does not make constant references to the Virgin Mary in order to make plain that she is no ordinary witch, but a Catholic witch. She does it onstage because that is what she did in life.

Interpreting Shakespeare's words as vehicles for ideas beyond the narrow scope of the play is an amusing pastime which, over the years, has got out of hand. *Macbeth* – first performed at the Globe in 1606 – is said to be a response to the discovery of the Gunpowder Plot, the year before. The idea was said to be made credible by Macbeth's decision 'to doubt the equivocation of the fiend' that promised him immunity until Birnam Wood came to Dunsinane (5:5:43). That is said, by those who have a vivid imagination, to echo the indictment against Father Henry Garnett, an executed Jesuit, who was accused of equivocation during his trial.[15] *Pericles* – the same authorities explain – is, in form and content, like a mystery play of the sort performed in Coventry which, during his boyhood, Shakespeare may or may not have seen. The sudden appearance of Diana was thought to be so evocative of visitations by the Virgin Mary that the play was performed in recusant households and became required reading at the English Jesuit College at Saint-Omer.[16]

There is only one of Shakespeare's plays which we can be sure provoked a violent religious-cum-political reaction from its first-night audience. In June 1613 the Globe Theatre was set on fire during the performance of *Henry VIII*. It is by no means certain what made the audience so angry. Wolsey – whose fall and death the play portrays – is a tragic character: 'I charge thee Cromwell, put away ambition.' Cranmer triumphs over his enemies, and Anne Boleyn – after a sumptuous coronation, which is re-enacted on stage – gives triumphant birth to Princess Elizabeth. A spectator at the coronation procession actually speaks of the King's 'scruples' about the validity of his divorce from Catherine being extinguished by 'learned and reverend fathers' who confirmed that the 'late marriage [was] made of non effect'. But the impeccably Protestant nature of the play is undermined by the character of Queen Catherine herself. Her speeches make clear that her courage and regal dignity survived her humiliation. She tells Wolsey (2:4:74):

> I do believe,
> Induc'd by potent circumstance, that
> You are mine enemy; and make my challenge

> You shall not be my judge; for it is you
> Have blown this coal betwixt my lord and me
> Which God's dews quench. Therefore I say again
> I utterly abhor, yea, from my soul
> Refuse you for my judge.

Whatever message Shakespeare intended to convey, he certainly expected trouble. The epilogue begins, 'Tis ten to one this play can never please.'

All this amounts to is the glorious truth that William Shakespeare, as well as being 'not for an age but for all time' was also not for one denomination, but for many. Only by a prodigious leap of the imagination can we conclude that Sonnet 73 – 'bare ruin'd choirs, where late the sweet birds sang'[17] – is a criticism of the Dissolution of the monasteries or that the constant occurrence of shipwrecks and storms is 'meant to suggest the dire upheaval and destruction of traditional values that had been the Catholic experience of the Reformation'.[18] Yet there is evidence to suggest that William Shakespeare was of a Catholic inclination. It is revealed by lines in his plays which contain ideas that came naturally into his mind.

Shakespeare created a number of notable ghosts – unquiet souls who wander through the purgatory that Protestants dismissed as a Catholic invention. They appear most notably in *Hamlet*, *Julius Caesar* and *Macbeth*, but they are also, at least, mentioned in plays that do not need them to move the action along. The ghost of Hamlet's father deserves particular attention. Even though he is in the half world between heaven and hell while he is waiting for the sins against him to be purged, he is allowed to return to the land of the living.

During his (or its) early manifestations, the ghost is visible to Horatio. 'Look, my lord, it comes' (1:4:39). When, after his real or feigned madness, it appears to him again, no one else sees it. Gertrude says to him, 'you do bend your eye on vacancy' (3:4:116). It is clear that the ghost which (or who) materialises on the platform before the castle at Elsinore is meant to be taken seriously. That does not necessarily mean that Shakespeare himself believed in ghosts and, in consequence, purgatory. But there is no doubt that he expected his audiences to do so.

There is, among Shakespeare's minor characters, an undoubted bias in favour of the Catholic clergy. Friar Lawrence, who is – as a result of his foolish advice – criminally responsible for the tragic deaths of Romeo and Juliet, is portrayed as a fireside philosopher who takes refuge from the wickedness of the world in 'the powerful grace that lies in plants, herbs, stones and their true qualities' (2:3:15). The priests in *Two Gentlemen of Verona*, *Twelfth Night* and *Much Ado About Nothing* are similarly benign. Friar Patrick, in *Two Gentlemen of Verona*, hears Silva's confession – an act of grace which must have been denied to the (presumably Protestant) actor who played the part. The plays are set in the years before the Reformation, and the appearance of a Protestant clergyman would have been as much of an anachronism as Caesar's clock. But although a true enemy of the Pope and Papists would have made the agents of Rome wicked, sinister or ridiculous, it is the incumbents of Queen Elizabeth's Church who are treated with little respect. Sir Nathaniel, a 'curate' in *Love's Labour's Lost*, is a sycophant. Sir Oliver Martext, a 'vicar' in *As You Like It*, has doubts about the legality of the marriage between Audrey and Touchstone, but lives by the adage, ''Tis no matter; ne'er a fantastical knave of them all shall flout me out of my calling' (3:3:114).

By portraying Martext as more interested in his living than his principles, Shakespeare was reflecting the common criticism – sometimes justified, sometimes not – levelled by unreconciled Catholics against the Protestant clergy. But Shakespeare was not of an extreme Catholic disposition. He was not an extreme anything. His upbringing and instinct inclined him towards Rome. But the inclination was not so strong that he was prepared to risk his life and livelihood to observe its rites and respect its rituals. And that made the most extraordinary of men typical of the age in which he lived.

PART TWO

Love God, Honour the King

CHAPTER 11

Defiled with Some Infirmities

By the beginning of James I's aggressively Protestant reign, the Catholics of England amounted to little more than a besieged community of devout believers, which could never again dominate the life of their country or influence its alliances. The Church's ranks had been substantially depleted by Elizabethan savagery, which had been far more severe than her father's punitive polices and had lasted far longer. Numbers were never clear and are still in doubt, but rough estimates are possible. In 1603, the calculation, which was required in every Church of England diocese, identified a total of 85,000 recusants and 2.5 million regular Anglican communicants in England and Wales. Bishops were reluctant to admit the extent of dissent that flourished within their diocese. So the recusant figure is probably an underestimate. Ten years later Guido Bentivoglio, the Papal Nuncio to the Spanish Netherlands, reported to Rome that there were six hundred priests in England and that, on average, each one served thirty families.[1] The typical family had six or seven members. So, on the Bentivoglio calculation, the English Catholic population totalled something approaching 120,000. Whatever its true size, 1603 was not to be the year of its release from bondage. The son of Mary, Queen of Scots – regarded by Catholics as the rightful Queen of England and martyr to their faith – was no less the enemy of Rome than Elizabeth, his mother's nemesis.

James I of England was a strange man whose peculiarities would, today, be attributed to his disturbed upbringing. He was born on June 19th 1566 and seven months later baptised with the full rites of the Roman Catholic Church. He was not destined to keep the vows which were made on his behalf. When he was less than a year old he was put in the care of the Protestant Lords of Congregation and on July 22nd 1567 – the day on which Mary reluctantly abdicated the throne of Scotland – he saw his mother for the last time. James was crowned in her place during a service which respected the liturgy of the Scottish Presbyterian Church. John Knox preached the sermon. From then on, he was the Protestant king of a Protestant kingdom. It was his faith – rather than the fact that he was the legitimate heir – which encouraged Robert Cecil to ensure that he inherited the English throne.

At the time of James' accession, very few Catholics believed that a full restoration of their faith was possible. But many of them still hoped that greater tolerance would follow their continued protestations of loyalty to the crown. In the north, the sentimental assumption that the accession of Mary Stewart's son would herald a new era of understanding was particularly strong. Although they had failed in their vain attempts to win the throne for the sovereign of their choice, they had lived to witness the accession of the dynasty which they certainly preferred to the Tudors. James – although a Protestant and Mary's bitter rival for the succession to the throne of England – was sanctified by her martyrdom. Catholics of a more practical turn of mind saw James' arrival as a new opportunity to broker the sort of peace deal which Elizabeth had always rejected. As an apparent sign of the changing times, the ruling dynasty changed the spelling of its family name: Stewart became Stuart.

The Catholic aristocracy led the way – not least because they hoped to avoid the sequestration of their property. During the first year of James' reign, Sir Thomas Tresham – who had become so disenchanted with the Jesuits that he denounced them with a vehemence that they claimed was proof of his atheism – revived an idea which had been considered, and rejected, fifty years earlier. His *Petition Apologetical* proposed that, in return for the promise of toleration, the number of Catholic priests in England would be reduced to the number that was necessary to meet the needs of those country gentlemen who kept a family confessor. The suggestion was built on the assumption that, if the landowning classes asserted their loyalty, they could be relied upon to keep their word. Priests, on the other hand, needed to be treated with caution. So, the proposal went, they should be required to swear allegiance to King and country 'before they shall be admitted to our houses, otherwise they shall not have release from us'.[2] Their employers would then take responsibility for their conduct.

The idea came to nothing. It was probably not even presented to the King. But had it been put into operation, it would have helped to create the sort of Church of which the Catholic gentry wanted to be members. Before the beginning of the Reformation, English Catholicism belonged, under God, to the bishops and, through them, to the Pope. During the Reformation it survived, at least in part, because priests could live and work – sometimes in secret and sometimes with the tacit acquiescence of the authorities – in country houses. That gave the Catholic gentry a power over the Catholic Church in England which, throughout the seventeenth century, they struggled to keep and increase. The *Petition Apologetical*, had it been accepted, would have tightened the grip. It would also have put English Catholicism in danger of becoming a country-house religion.

Hopes that some sort of arrangement would be possible were encouraged by the King's conduct during the months immediately before and after his accession. He was an enemy of the Jesuits. But so were many Catholics, and his enmity towards priests in general was more a reaction to their arrogance than to their piety. In December 1602 he told Cecil, 'I greatly wonder ... that not only so great flocks of Jesuits and priests dare both resort and remain in England but do so proudly use their function.'[3] Three months later he wrote to Cecil again. 'I will never allow in my conscience that the blood of any man shall be shed for diversity of opinion in religion.'[4] His first speech to Parliament was even more encouraging. It promised an end to the execution of priests and 'incorrigible Catholics', and went on to emphasise his personal moderation. He was, he said, a Protestant by conviction as well as upbringing, but he 'was never violent or unreasonable in the profession [of that faith]. I acknowledge the Romane Church to be our Mother Church, although defiled with some infirmities and corruptions ... And, as I am non enemie to the life of a sicke man because I would have his body purged of all ill humours, no more am I an enemie of their Church because I want them to reform their errors.'[5]

All thought of compromise and reconciliation might have been destroyed by two inevitably abortive conspiracies which were exposed during James' first year on the throne. The Main Plot, although it rallied support by promising to make Arbella Stuart a Catholic queen, was really no more than the product of resentful courtiers (including Walter Raleigh) who were out of fashion and favour. The Bye Plot – which aspired to do no more than hold the King prisoner until he agreed to a relaxation of the penal laws – was obviously doomed from the start. However, both futile conspiracies were used – perhaps even promoted – by the more extreme Protestants as evidence that some Catholics were still active regicides and that even the sullenly submissive supported them in their hearts.

The two plots undid most of the good that had been done by the open enthusiasm with which Catholics welcomed the new King. They were enough to convince Parliament that England could not risk a sudden outbreak of toleration. The House of Commons urged the King to be more vigilant in the face of the (wholly imaginary) threat of invasion and to accept the need to introduce 'all manner of persecution, banishing priests and re-imposing recusancy fines'.[6] James exceeded their expectations. The laws against recusancy were reinforced and reimposed with such severity that one Jesuit, Henry Garnet, described the persecution as 'worse than in Bess's time'.[7] Another, Richard Blount, told a story which at least gives some credence to the notion that James' instincts were not as accommodating as his apologists suggest. 'His Majesty has gone this last day to Newmarket to hunt. As he passed Tyburn, being a little past it, he returned back to the gibbet, rode under it, looked upon it and struck it with his rod, saying scoffingly, 'all you Jesuits and priests that have been hanged here, pray for me'.[8]

The Gunpowder Plot of 1605 made relaxation of the penal laws impossible. The most ambitious conspiracy in British history very nearly achieved its object – the murder of the whole British establishment in one explosion. Its instigator was Robert Catesby, a staunch Catholic and already convicted recusant, whose father had been imprisoned during the reign of Queen Elizabeth. His plan was to blow up Parliament on the day when both Houses, and attendant dignitaries, assembled to witness the formal opening by the King. Six months before the planned date of the explosion, Catesby and his co-conspirators rented a house in Westminster with a cellar that stretched under the Parliament building, and filled the cellar with twenty barrels of gunpowder. All that prevented the gunpowder being ignited was an indiscretion by one of the plotters. Francis Tresham warned his brother-in-law, Lord Monteagle, not to attend Parliament on November 5th, and Monteagle – himself a Catholic – warned the government that some sort of outrage had been planned. A search of local premises revealed the twenty barrels of gunpowder and Guy Fawkes, who was keeping guard over them.

King James told his closest advisers that he was determined that the madness of a small group of regicides should not stigmatise all Catholics and be used as an excuse for another assault on their liberties, but in May 1606, Parliament passed two bills which were designed 'for the better discouraging and repressing of popish recusants'. The first bill empowered a bishop, or two Justices sitting together, to require recusants to take an oath of loyalty to the crown and extended the definition of religious disobedience to anyone who had not taken Communion, in a service of the Established Church, at least twice during the previous year. The Oath of Allegiance could also be demanded of travellers. The second bill was a ragbag of deterrents. Anyone who left England to serve a foreign government, without swearing oaths of loyalty, automatically became a convicted felon. Informers were to be paid £50 for exposing either a priest who said Mass or a layman who attended. Protestants who married Catholics were to be subject to the same restrictions and penalties as their spouses. Recidivists were to be subject to harsher punishment – arbitrary imprisonment at the King's pleasure.

The oath, around which the first bill was built, was comprehensive and explicit. It required those who took it to swear allegiance to James I as the rightful and lawful King of England, promise to support him against rebellion and – more difficult for Catholics to accept – repudiate the Pope's claim to possess the power to depose secular monarchs whom he had judged to be heretics. The idea of swearing allegiance had been included in the 1603 Protestation of the Thirteen Appellant Priests. But the oath of three years later was a far stronger rejection of papal authority than the draft prepared by Bishop Bancroft in his attempt to reconcile loyal Catholics to Queen Elizabeth. It was composed in language which even the most reckless and desperate Catholic would not contemplate using in a description of papal conduct, and began with a denunciation of the dormant, if not defunct, *Regnans in Excelsis*, which it described as the 'impious and heretical damnable doctrine' that 'princes which be excommunicated or deprived by the Pope may be deposed or murthered by their subjects or any whatsoever'.[9] The oath was concerned not with the safety of James alone and in particular it denied, at least by implication, that the Pope possessed any secular authority beyond the bounds of the Papal States. The initiative was, therefore, doomed from the start.

Some Members of Parliament wanted the oath to go even further in dismissing papal powers. James claimed that the Commons proposed that the oath should assert that 'the Pope had no power to excommunicate' and that he had forced them to accept the more moderate version.[10] Even in its more modest form, it was anathema to many Catholics. Most of the thirty martyrs who were executed in the reign of James I went to the scaffold because of their refusal to take an oath which only required them to deny temporal power to the Pope. They could not accept any limit on the authority – secular no less than theological – or the behaviour of God's Vicar on earth.

Robert Parsons attributed the idea of the oath, and the principles on which it was based, to the Appellant priests' hopes of creating a 'National Catholicism' – a development that would inevitably result in limitations of the Pope's spiritual authority. Even Archpriest George Blackwell – the leader of the secular priests – originally declared the Oath to be unlawful. Later, remembering that he must speak for England, he slightly revised his position. When he realised the Pope had issued a condemnation of the oath, he reverted to his old position, leaving behind him a trail of Catholics who had followed his apparent advice and signed. Then, after much pressure from the Privy Council, he changed his mind again and, as well as declaring the oath lawful, urged Catholics to swear, as required. The Pope issued a statement describing Blackwell as 'in error'. On September 18th 1607, Cardinal Roberto Bellarmine, theologian and controversialist, declared that God had granted the Pope secular as well as spiritual authority. James retaliated. On February 21st 1608, he published *Triplici nodo, triplex cuneus, An Apology for the Oath of Allegiance*. Anyone who refused to endorse his sovereign rights committed treason.

That notwithstanding, for a while it seemed that circumstances conspired to promote a compromise. Popes Sixtus V and Clement VIII – elected in quick succession – had not endorsed the militant evangelism of Gregory XIII, as embodied in *Regnans in Excelsis*, and many Protestants had begun to accept Catholicism as a religion rather than a subversive political movement. Sympathetic Justices – not all of them Catholics – ignored minor breaches in the religious laws. Often offenders who had been convicted were released from prison after demonstrations in their support. In many areas riots followed the arrest of recusants. The Protestant establishment began to recognise the advantages of living in peace with those Catholics who were loyal to King and country.

In 1611, Catholics were encouraged to demonstrate their fidelity by buying baronetcies[11] and, from time to time, Cecil himself exhibited sufficient open-mindedness to arrange for Catholics of his class and acquaintance to be excused the pains and penalties imposed on less exalted miscreants. Lady Elizabeth Lovell – a distant relative of Thomas More – was granted permission to leave the country, despite admitting having entertained Catesby and Digby, two of the Catholic Gunpowder Plot conspirators. Cecil first released her from house arrest and then excused her from taking the loyalty oath that was required of travelling Catholics. She entered the English Benedictine convent in Brussels.[12]

As well as being England's only (openly) bisexual sovereign, James was, and remains, the only (either openly or secretly) intellectual monarch to occupy the English throne. It was his respect for the English language, rather than his support of the English Church, which made him endorse the proposal, made by the President of Corpus Christi, Oxford, that there should be a new translation of the Bible to replace the texts that were in common use – the 'official' Bishops' Bible (which James thought was a poor translation) and the Geneva Bible, which he thought was even worse.

James' interest in ideas prevented him from seeing the Reformation in the simple terms which had given the strength of certainty to his predecessors. He was, by upbringing, a Calvinist and never lost his belief in a divinely ordained predestination, which divided the world into the elect, who were destined for heaven, and the damned, who could not even hope for salvation. But he promoted Arminians, who believed in the absolute opposite, because he admired their scholarship and shared their even more inconvenient insistence that the post-Reformation Church of England had roots buried deep in the Church of Rome. Indeed, in the public theological argument with the Vatican, which preoccupied him for two years of his life, he called upon an Anabaptist, Lancelot Andrewes, to help him confound his opponents and then – despite the contest, at best, ending in a draw – promoted Andrewes from the See of Ely to the See of Chichester.

It was James' genuine intellectualism which prompted him to turn from the sonnets of his youth to the composition of theological treatises and participation in rhetorical tourneys. During his twenty-first year he had publicly contested the doctrine of justification as set out by Father James Gordon, a distinguished Jesuit; and, after his accession, he sought to engage in public disputations with Catholic theologians – which he was certain he would win. Some of James' closest associates were not so sure. The Earl of Salisbury, believing that James was no match for his adversaries, did his best to persuade the King to abandon intellectual controversy.[13] James would not listen. Challenges were issued in bellicose language. One, 'with a preface to all the princes of Christendom', was a call to arms which was intended to convince the Vatican that, 'The Pope's bulls should pull in their horns and himself wish that he had never meddled in this matter.'[14]

Robert Parsons lowered the tone of the debate by publishing the *Judgement of an Englishman*, a personalised challenge to the King of England. The deterioration continued. Cardinal Bellarmine might have been expected to deal calmly with the central issue under dispute – the source from which rulers derive their power – but, despite his eminence, he opened one disputation with a claim that was an irrel-evancy, but which was also a telling low blow. In a *Responsio*, published in the name of one of his chaplains, he revealed the contents of a letter, written in 1599, from James to Pope Clement VIII. Its purpose was to announce that James was considering becoming a Catholic. It is unlikely that the thought was any more than a moment's aberration. By the time of his succession James had certainly put all idea of conversion aside. But he had written the letter, and a scapegoat had to be found to take the blame. The King's Scottish Secretary, James

Elphinstone, the Lord Balmerino, was induced to say that he had drawn it up without consulting the King and had given it to James to sign just as he was leaving Holyrood to hunt deer. He was convicted of treason, sentenced to death, reprieved and allowed to go into honourable retirement.

James decided that, despite his intellectual strengths, he could not – with any hope of success – carry on the battle alone. So two genuine scholars were employed to rebut the reasoning of his theological adversaries. Lancelot Andrewes, Bishop of Chichester, published *Responsio ad Apologiam Cardinalis Bellarmini*, and William Barlow, the Dean of Chester, responded to Parsons with an *Answer to a Catholike Englishman (so by himself entituled)*. Both men toiled for nine months, augmented from time to time by other scholars. The final version of the Apology was heavily edited by James – hence his fury when factual errors were discovered in the text. A revision corrected some, though not all, of the mistakes. Critics concentrated on the passages in which what passed with James for humour produced comments that were perilously close to blasphemy – including his judgement on Mary's intercession on behalf of repentant sinners. James found it hard to believe that the Virgin 'hath no other things to do in heaven than to hear every idle man's suit and busy herself with their errands; whiles requesting; whiles commanding her son, whiles coming down to kiss and make love to priests and whilst disputing and brawling with the devil'.[15]

In one of his more thoughtful passages, James raised again the question that, seventy years earlier, had exercised Cardinal Pole during his first visit to Rome. If Popes possessed the power to denounce and dethrone the wicked, why had they not urged and authorised uprisings against the early Roman emperors? Bellarmine took refuge in an explanation that echoed Pope Gregory's *Explanatio*, the absolution of good Catholics from the obligation to take *Regnans in Excelsis* literally and immediately attempt to overthrow Elizabeth I. There was no virtue in attempting the impossible, especially when failure would damage the Church. The strength of the early Roman emperors meant that 'severity would have been pointless'. The Popes were right to 'exercise patience rather than authority'. Condemnation would have been 'not only unprofitable, but utterly pernicious to the Christians . . . It is not sufficient to say that the Church is bound to doe some thing because she can lawfully doe it, unless she can also doe it with prudence and profit.'[16]

The doctrine of feasibility – the obligation to act only if action is likely to have the desired result – was a side-issue in the long argument between James I and Cardinal Bellarmine. They sought to answer serious, indeed fundamental, questions – including whether or not kings and princes derive their sovereignty from the communities which they govern or from God. The conventional Catholic position – derived from Aristotle via Aquinas – was that God had invested the right in society. On that point, James and Bellarmine basically agreed. Their difference lay in conflicting views of what justified and legitimised the removal of a sovereign. The papal view was that the Oath of Allegiance was vitiated by a greater obligation. 'A Christian Commonwealth may not proceed against their Christian Prince, though he be a tyrant, without the advise and consent of the supreme Pastor of their souls'[17] – and, therefore conversely, could proceed if they obtained the Pope's approval. The Pope possessed God-given power to protect the people's spiritual welfare and, therefore, had a duty to intervene when souls were in jeopardy.

Parsons, extreme in all things and incapable of missing an opportunity to condemn godless England and its heretic King, announced that no Catholic could, 'with safety of Conscience, [deny that] in certeyne urgent cases, [the Pope had the power to act] for the universal good of God's church'.[18] Other Jesuits joined in. Anthony Hoskins wrote that the Pope could depose a 'prince when it was necessary for the salvation of souls'. Archpriest Blackwell condemned the Gunpowder Plot in language which was consistent with that theory and, therefore, of little comfort to James. 'Our divines do say that it is not lawful for private subjects, by private authority, to take arms against their lawful king, albeit he become a tyranny.' As the Earl of Salisbury pointed out, Blackwell was arguing by implication that revolution and regicide were lawful, if approved by the Pope. When the Gunpowder conspirators came to trial, the prosecution quoted Parsons' virtual exhumation of *Regnans in Excelsis*, 'If any Christian prince manifestly turns away from the Catholic faith and tries to take others with him, he at once loses all power and authority by both human and divine law. All subjects are freed from their oaths to him.'

None of the contestants in the oath controversy could be said to have won or lost. Each participant remained immovable in his initial position, tethered to the spot by principles which were not subject to rational examination. The exchange of polemics did, however, keep open the channels of theological communication between Rome and England and clearly gave James great pleasure. Indeed, he enjoyed the arguments so much that he developed a taste for public disputation with anyone who would accept his challenge. Father John Percy, SJ, recalled the King's courtesy. Just as 'fencers were wont to salute and embrace one another, so before he entered into argument, he would embrace me with a speech'.[19]

While the disputations were conducted in high places, rank-and-file Catholics, born since the beginning of the Reformation – many of whom had never even heard of the issues which their betters found so compelling – attempted to balance their wish to worship as their fathers had done with the need to avoid penalties for ignoring the proscriptions imposed by the state. A number of first-generation Protestants risked all and were converted to Rome. Among them were a number of notable priests whose desertion not only handed a propaganda victory to the Vatican, but also exacerbated doctrinal divisions within the Church of England. They included Benjamin Carier, a royal chaplain and prebendary of Canterbury Cathedral, and Theophilus Higgons, an ex-Catholic, who 'with great learning and aboundance of tears' announced his reconversion during a four-hour sermon at St Paul's Cross.[20] The congregation was scandalised, and there were whispered allegations that the promise of a 'fatt benefice' had influenced his decision. But Higgons was neither burned as a Catholic nor lynched as Protestant. Somehow he managed to avoid no more severe a punishment than the destruction of his books, and even that was brought to a premature end by the intervention of the Lord Mayor of London. Higgons felt sufficiently confident in his new status to publish two pamphlets justifying his double apostasy, *The first Motive of T. H. Maister of Arts and lately Minister to suspect the integritie of his Religion* and *The Apology of Theophilus Higgons lately Minister now Catholic*. But he still did not burn. Tolerance, although not yet breaking out, was beginning to bubble under the surface of society.

The fiery preaching of John Knox – vituperation not very well disguised as sermons – had done nothing to hurry the arrival of tolerance in Scotland. The examination of new ideas which had stimulated the Scottish Reformation had been replaced by a one-sided war of polemics, with Protestant publications dominating theological debates. Knox's public sermons and debates had led the humblest of lay Presbyterians into the consideration of theological principles. But the involvement of the whole Kirk in the government of the Scottish Church had done nothing to make its leadership more emollient. In what amounted to a declaration that Christ did not recognise class distinction, its ministers dismissed even the consideration of the concession – common in England – that the gentry should be allowed licence to worship as they wished in their own houses. There was to be no compromise with Rome. The General Assembly of the Kirk expressed its views in language that illustrated the strength of Scottish feeling, when it condemned 'the bloody decrees of the Council of Trent against all that trewlie profess the Religioun of Chryst'.[21] The Reformation was often a ruthless business. But in Scotland it exhibited an intellectual brutality that certainly had its effect on the Vatican. It also seemed to act as a deterrent to attempts at reconversion. Clement VIII's bull of foundation of the Scottish College in Rome did not impose a missionary obligation on its members. None of the first group of seminarians returned to Scotland. Nor did many of their successors.

Attempts to guarantee Ireland's loyalty by the introduction of Protestant settlers into the normally rebellious province only served to add to the confusion of beliefs and interests which disturbed the peace for the next five hundred years. There was already a class of Irish gentry who, although native-born, regarded themselves as English and interpreted their obligation to loyalty as the duty to support England's economy as well as England's monarch. Initially the 'Old English' Catholic apostates benefited from the closure of the Irish monasteries as their contemporaries in the homeland benefited from the Dissolution. But gradually, as 'New English' settlers were introduced into Ireland, the established families lost the privileged status they had traditionally enjoyed and, with it, the chance to acquire, at knockdown prices, the land and property of the dissolved religious houses. Seeking solace and support, they returned to their old religion and began to feel an increasing community of interests with Catholics, of all classes, who had not lost their Roman faith. The result was the creation of a whole class of Catholic gentry whose return to the faith of their fathers was the result of alienation rather than conviction.

Sometimes the grievances were imaginary and sometimes they amounted to no more than resentment at the loss of an inherited elite status. But sometimes they were tangible. The Stanihursts of the County Dublin Pale were one of the many families whose loyalty to the 'Old English' – values as well as people – was lost over three generations. Richard Stanihurst – although 'a devout Catholic' – had, because of his close association with the English ruling class, been a beneficiary of the monastery closures in County Dublin and County Meath. James, his son, walked the tightrope of faith and patronage so adroitly that he managed to be both Speaker of the Irish House of Commons and host to Edmund Campion during his visit to Ireland. Sometime about the end of the sixteenth century he lost both his influence and the fruits of the consequent patronage. The result was *De Rebus in Hibernia Gestis* – a treatise in 'defence of the power of the old English', as distinct from new arrivals,[22] and a prominent place among the Irish Counter-Reformation Catholics.

The alienation of the Barnwells – also part of the Anglo-Irish aristocracy inside the Dublin Pale – was the consequence of one of King James' lapses into mindless prejudice. Sir Patrick Barnwell had been a King's sergeant and, in consequence, a revered figure in the Crown Courts. His grandson, who might have been expected to follow in the legal tradition, became a leader of the Irish Counter-Reformation. He was, because of his religion, prevented from practising law. James had suppressed the entire Dublin Bar on the grounds that 'the greatest number of them are Iryshe, arrogant papysts that will neyther com to church, nor take the oath of obedience'.[23] In the rest of Ireland, Catholicism, of a sort, was eliminated from the courts more gradually – too gradually for some bigots. In 1604, Protestant vigilantes complained that 'the chief and principal places of justice in the realme are supplied by such of the Irish as are open recusants or dissembling hypocrites'.[24] However, the situation was soon rectified. In 1607, John Everard, the last Catholic Irish judge of the period, was forced, by threats of violence, to resign.

No such draconian policy was necessary in Wales. In the year of Elizabeth's death there were only 808 identified recusants in the whole Principality, as compared with almost one quarter of a million church-going Protestants. There were, however, a large number of Welsh men and women who only accepted the Church of England if, where and when it incorporated elements of the Mass into its services. Wales was also in thrall to the Tudors and, because of its affection for the family – which it thought of as blood relations of the whole country – was as reluctant to defy Elizabeth as it had been to disobey Mary.

The pattern of Welsh belief was deeply influenced by residual pagan superstitions. At Holywell, locals combined primitive Catholicism rituals with pre-Christian rights. The grove in which the well stood was dedicated to St Beuno, and bullocks were sacrificed to assuage his anger. There were reports of 'companie of people dauncing and singing of rimes about the altar in the chapel ... having pots and cups upon the said altar, drinking and making merrie'.[25] The Catholic Church – reluctant to change with the times – finds that some of its minor problems are repeated with the passing of the years. On February 20th 1833, Thomas Penswick – Vicar Apostolic of the Northern District – wrote to Rome to ask 'what hereafter must be my conduct towards secret societies, not banded together by any oath but using signs and passwords given out at a lodge. Such is the society calling itself Loyal Druids?'[26] At least Penswick was spared the rumours current in the early seventeenth century of Spanish landings on the Welsh coast – usually at Milford Haven where, on one occasion, it was said that 10,000 Welshmen waited to support the invaders, who neither came nor planned to come. Immediately after the death of Queen Elizabeth, a William Watson had attempted to raise a rebellion. His abject failure only served to show that Wales posed no real threat – even though opposition to the Reformation was associated, in some Welsh minds, with national identity. Catholicism was *'yr hen ffydd Cymru'* – the old faith of Wales. Protestantism was *'y ffydd newydd y Saesin'* – the new faith of England.[27] But in the Principality, as in the rest of Britain, the 'new faith' had become the irresistibly dominant religion.

CHAPTER 12

Let Loose to Say Masses

In the early summer of 1614, James VI and I – the first monarch to rule the dual kingdoms of England and Scotland – was at odds with both the Scottish nobles and the English Court and, following fractious discussions with the House of Commons about revenue and the royal prerogative, had dissolved the 'Addled Parliament' three months after it was elected. He felt in need of friends. The man in whose company he found comfort was Diego Sarmiento de Acuña, Count Gondomar, the new Spanish Ambassador, who assured him that King Philip of Spain believed that the two sovereigns should 'live as brothers'. The Ambassador had a better idea. They could become relations. For some time James had wondered if it was possible to forge a new alliance by arranging a marriage between Charles, Prince of Wales, and one of Europe's Catholic princesses – even though the match would require the relaxation of the penal legislation which, without amendment, would make the future Queen of England a heretic and criminal in her own country. De Acuña revived the idea with the news that Philip, who was also seeking new allies, would not be averse to Charles marrying the Infanta of Spain.

Charles, who had become heir apparent after the death of his elder brother, enjoyed a close and highly emotional relationship with James I, who – in a Court accustomed to the public show of affection between the King and his male favourites – still surprised his councillors by referring to the Prince of Wales as 'my baby'. The Prince of Wales certainly wanted to marry. Indeed, being a romantic by nature, he wanted to be in love. But, in part, it was the acceptance of filial duty which prompted him to fall in with his father's plans. James' first hopes had been for a match with Princess Christiana of France, the sister of Louis XIII. But negotiations had broken down before the unlikely match appeared to be on offer.

The Spanish Ambassador to the Court of St James's was admirably forthright about the religious settlement that must precede the betrothal. The prosecution of Catholics and Catholicism must cease at once and the formal repeal of the laws, under which the prosecutions were mounted, must begin without delay. There were also promises to be made about the treatment of the Infanta and her entourage – in their own way more difficult to accept than the demand that the laws of England be changed. The Princess of Wales, as the Infanta would become, must remain a Catholic and be allowed to observe the full rites of the Roman Church. Her priests would wear the robes and vestments of their calling. Most important to Spain, and least acceptable to England, the children of the union were to be brought up in the Catholic faith, and their Catholicism was not to be a bar to their succession to the Crown of England. James was prepared at least to negotiate.

Although the King was of a mind to consider meeting the Spanish demand, the terms on which the marriage was proposed were so objectionable to Ralph Winwood, the Secretary of State, and George Abbot, the Archbishop of Canterbury, that they proposed an alternative scheme for establishing England's position in the world. James should immediately declare war on Spain. The King revised his position. Struck down by a series of simultaneous sicknesses with symptoms ranging from vomiting to boils, he summoned the Court to hear what he told them was his 'death-bed speech'. It included the advice to his son that 'marriage to the daughter of a king' should not require him to 'marry her religion'.[1] But James had not abandoned his determination to secure new alliances by means of marriage – even though an earlier excursion into matrimonial diplomacy had caused him much pain and, worse still, considerable expense. His daughter, Elizabeth, had married the Palgrave of the Palatinate, a small Protestant state with Heidelberg as its capital. The Palatinate was under threat from the Catholic Spanish Netherlands. So James was under moral and diplomatic pressure to provide military support for his faith and daughter, while he was attempting to betroth his son to the aggressor.

Not surprisingly, much of the Protestant priesthood – purged of its Roman sympathisers – was outraged by the idea of a Catholic princess becoming the Queen of England. The Bishop of London, loyal to the King, called a diocesan synod and ordered the clergy 'not to meddle in their sermons with the Spanish match or any other matter of state'.[2] But the following Sunday, preachers at St Paul's Cross denounced the proposed match and, during the three months that followed, priest after priest described the prospective union as an offence against God and the dignity of the realm. The Reverend Matthew Clayton tried to disguise his defiance of his bishop by the use of a metaphor which was as transparent as it was offensive. He was imprisoned for calling attention to the dangers of importing a 'Spanish ewe'.[3]

James recalled Parliament and punctuated his opening address with complaints about how grievously he was treated and promises to maintain, at all cost, the Protestant religion. Nevertheless, he sent Prince Charles – accompanied by his bosom friend George Villiers – to Madrid to embark on what was to become a long and fruitless courtship. The party arrived in Madrid on March 7th 1622. When he was admitted to the Prince's presence, Count Gondomar fell on his knees in a gesture of supplication and cried out 'Nunc Dimittis'. Count de Olivares – the Chief Minister of Spain – embraced Charles round the thighs, kissed his hands and gave thanks to God in language which suggested that he imagined the object of the visit was an announcement of England's intention to return to the true faith.[4] In London bonfires were lit to celebrate the peace that matrimony would guarantee. There was, however, a growing tide of opposition to the whole idea. Dr George Hakewill, the Prince's personal chaplain, had – before he left for Madrid – given the King a memorandum opposing the match. He was dismissed within minutes of Charles discovering his perfidy.

Charles declared himself desperately in love and moped, while Villiers (soon to become the Duke of Buckingham) assumed command of what was essentially a political operation. His letters home kept the King informed about the initiative's progress. The Spaniards were sympathetic to the proposal, but the Papal Nuncio worked 'maliciously and actively' against the idea. It fell to Villiers to ask James 'how far we may engage you in the acknowledgement of the Pope's spiritual powers?' He had come to believe that, without such a major concession, the Spaniard would not agree to the marriage; and yet, if it were made, the Nuncio's outright opposition would be brushed aside. James was ahead of his emissary. He had sent two of Charles' chaplains – Leonard Mawe and Matthew Wren – to Rome with orders to judge the mood of the Holy See. His reply to Villiers' enquiry (based on their reports of the Pope's inclination) confirmed his command of the argument, if not of the situation. 'I know not what you mean by my acknowledging the Pope's spiritual supremacy. I am sure you would not have me renounce my religion for all the world. But all that I can guess at your meaning is that it be an allusion to a passage in my book where I offer that if the Pope would quit his godhead and usurping over kings, to acknowledge him as chief bishop to whom all appeals of churchmen ought to lie.'[5] That was 'as far as his conscience [would] permit him to go'.

Villiers replied that although the Spaniards had originally negotiated, 'in the hope of the conversion of us both', they had come to realise the futility of that approach. They were ready to do a deal. 'We never saw the business in a better way than now is. Therefore, we humbly beseech you, lose no time in hastening the ships.'[6] The conversion of Charles and Villiers had been a more realistic prospect than the letter admitted. Both men had spent time with Catholic scholars and had been impressed by the arguments in favour of papal supremacy. But, for reasons of convenience or conviction, they retained their Protestant faith.

The Dispensation contained so many provisos and conditions that Villiers thought it necessary to urge James to keep the Spanish requirements secret, lest public opinion be antagonised still further against the match by the sheer effrontery of the demands – the most impertinent of which was the insistence on the written confirmation of the verbal agreement. The conditions included the demand for English Catholics to be allowed to 'worship freely'. Prince Charles was happy to confirm his father's decision to suspend, if not to abolish, the laws that penalised recusants. But 'freedom of worship' implied the state's endorsement of all religions other than the Protestantism of what was becoming the Church of England – effective acceptance that another faith had merit which was equal to that of the Anglican communion. And the Stuarts – with their Scottish experience to guide them – had a second objection to unlimited freedom. They were almost as afraid of Calvinists as they were of Catholics.

Villiers renewed negotiations with an argument that was intended to replace the complexity of theological disputation with an ultimatum which, he hoped, would frighten the Spaniards into accepting that failure to reach agreement would harden the English inclination to treat Catholics as enemies of the state. 'If this marriage is not concluded, what remains of Catholicism in England will be utterly rooted out and they will proceed against the Catholics with the utmost rigour.'[7] The Spaniards – regardless of failure on the fate of English Catholics – would not budge. The marriage negotiations were deadlocked. Villiers and Prince Charles prepared to travel home.

The only way out of the impasse, Villiers decided, was an appeal over the head of the Spanish Catholic bureaucracy to the King of Spain. The marriage and its diplomatic consequences were in the interests of both countries, and Prince Charles had proved his sincerity – and England's – by travelling to Spain and waiting upon the Infanta for so long. The Spaniards presented a new draft agreement. Like its predecessor, it both guaranteed the Infanta's Catholic status and promised protection to English Catholics who still endured persecution and discrimination. As the Spaniards must have realised, the promise of protection, even if made, could not be fully kept. The true mood of England was soon to be revealed.

It may have been belated recognition of the obvious, or perhaps it was just tedium, that made the negotiations grind to an adjournment. When, in early 1623, Charles returned to England, Matthew Wren, his chaplain, arranged for him to give audience to Lancelot Andrewes, Bishop of Winchester, Richard Neale, Bishop of Durham, and William Laud, then Bishop of St David's. He prepared them for the meeting with his assessment of the Prince of Wales' theological position. It began with the admission that he 'had not his father's learning', but went on to say, 'I know his judgement to be very right and as for his affections for those particulars that your lordships have pointed at for upholding, the doctrine and discipline and the rights of the church, I have more confidence in him than in his advisors.'[8] The audience was arranged to consider 'those things in foresight whereof we conceive will soon come to pass'. King James had not long to live. Plans had to be laid to defend the faith.

Parliament – anxious about the lengths to which father and son would go to secure the related alliances – flexed its muscles. Before the King addressed a joint sitting on February 24th 1624, the Speaker thought it necessary to remind Honourable Members of the need strictly to apply the recusancy laws. The Commons then used the weapon which it always employed against recalcitrant monarchs: the threat to refuse to raise revenue or, in parliamentary jargon, to 'with-hold supply'. The Subsidy Bill – a measure to finance greater military expenditure – was only passed after a new clause relating to the Prince of Wales was agreed. 'When it shall please God to send him any lady that is a Papist, she should have no further liberty but for her family and no advantage for recusants at home.'[9]

Although the negotiations were resumed and the deal was done, the Infanta was never to enjoy even those limited freedoms. While waiting for the Papal Dispensation that would exonerate the Infanta of the sin of marrying a Protestant, both the Spanish and English royal families – confident that the Pope would oblige – prepared to celebrate a proxy wedding. The English Court already referred to the bride as the 'Princess of Wales, 'and Madrid was *en fête*, with flowers decorating the streets and a vast podium erected to ensure that the cheering multitudes could watch the ceremony. It was then that Charles discovered he was no longer in love, and his father decided that Spain was a better enemy than friend. The Dispensation was published, but the wedding was cancelled. However, the danger – as Parliament and prelates saw it – had not passed. The fears were justified. England was still to have a Catholic queen who would give birth to two Catholic kings – one a secret Papist and the other open enough about his faith to ensure his downfall.

Even before they left Spain, Charles and Villiers had begun to consider with whom the Prince of Wales should next fall deeply in love. They chose Henrietta Maria, the sixth and youngest child of Henry IV of France and Marie de Medici. The negotiations which passed for a courtship were speedily concluded. As anticipated, France – being less pious than Spain – made fewer demands about respect for the young princess's religion. And it was hoped that English public opinion would be more willing to accept an alliance with a Bourbon than a compact with a Hapsburg. Nevertheless, the terms of the engagement agreement, signed in July 1624, were kept secret. They included the promise that all Catholics imprisoned in England would be released. There were to be no more religious prosecutions. Catholics, whose land had been confiscated during the previous year, were to have it restored. The promises became public in December, when the recusancy laws were suspended and the Lord Keeper was told to release all prisoners who were held under laws that proscribed or punished Catholicism. The King explained his earlier decision to keep the terms of the agreement secret with an example of anti-logic which also revealed exactly how much respect he felt for his future daughter-in-law's religion. There was no need to make the terms of the agreement public, for he had agreed with the King of France that they were only intended to ensure a Papal Dispensation for the marriage and were never meant to be binding. When, in the year of his death, James needed to raise extra revenue, he increased his income by charging Catholics (and Nonconformists) double rates.

King James had the opportunity neither to break nor keep the rest of his promise. He was dying when the protracted nuptials began, and dead by the time they had finished. There was a proxy marriage – in full Catholic splendour – outside the Great West Door of Notre-Dame, in which the Duc de Chevreuse played the part of the bridegroom. In a more subdued ceremony in Whitehall, Charles promised that the children of the union would be brought up as Catholics and it may well be that when the besotted Prince of Wales made the promise, he meant to keep it. He certainly indulged his wife's wish to be a very public, as well as a very devout, Catholic. A chapel was built in Somerset House for her personal use. It was staffed by twelve Capuchin monks. Attendance at Mass increased wherever the news of the Queen's conduct became known. If the King permitted his wife to be a Catholic, surely he would also tolerate his subjects' Catholicism.

During the years in which King James and his son were acting out great dramas of state – confused in Charles' simple mind with affairs of the heart – the Catholic Churches of the two kingdoms over which

James ruled were arguing no less passionately about their form of governance. In 1623 William Bishop was given what amounted to episcopal authority and the courtesy title of Bishop of Chalcedon, one of the ancient sees with which senior clerics were associated, before the English hierarchy was re-established. That, in itself, was a victory for the secular clergy, the vast majority of whom wanted the Church to enjoy the status that the degree of autonomy provided. During Bishop's few months in office, before his premature and unexpected death, he introduced reforms which met many of the demands that were made by the 'Appellant' clergy who had petitioned Rome against the appointment of George Blackwell as 'Archpriest', and the consequent assumption that England was still under the control of the Vatican. He set up a network of vicars general and rural deans. The creation of what he called, without authority, a Dean and Chapter was a signal of his belief that the secular clergy must play a part in the management of the Church. The reorganisation also gave notice that, in the future, the institutions of the English Church would expect to nominate a bishop for Rome's approval. The logic of the nascent bishopric was that the regulars should also come under the bishop's supervision, if not control. The Benedictines agreed to respect his authority. The inevitable battle with the Jesuits he left for another day.

Richard Smith, who succeeded William Bishop in 1624, was not a man to tread lightly. Indeed, he seemed to possess a talent for causing offence. When he believed that Lady Montague made disorganised confessions, his criticism of her performance was so brusque that she believed he was accusing her of hiding sins.[10] And it was not just over-sensitive elderly aristocratic ladies who found his manner intolerable. During the first two years in office he lost the goodwill of the Benedictines, who seemed likely to join with the Jesuits in the rejection of the whole nascent episcopate.

Smith was too authoritarian to be tolerated even by a Church that believed, implicitly, in respect for authority. He claimed control over all missionary funds and endowments and attempted to impose a discipline that, while correct in itself, was far too arcane to be accepted in a Church which was struggling to hold on to its members. Smith was right to say that, according to the decision of the Council of Trent, only a parish priest who had been authorised by the bishop of his diocese was allowed to exercise the 'jurisdiction of confession'. In other cases, absolution was withheld. Catholic gentry – who had appointed their own confessors without reference to any authority – were left to wonder if years of sin, for which they had done penance, would go unforgiven. That was not, however, his greatest mistake. Smith's crucial blunder was an attempt to set up what amounted to Church courts in which he would exercise jurisdiction over a range of sensitive subjects. The most sensitive of all was matrimonial disputes. Unwisely, Smith took contentious decisions on his own authority. He was deposed and, overcome by the humiliation, fled to France.

The departure of Richard Smith relieved the Catholic Church in Scotland of what they, no doubt, regarded as a humiliation. Until he died in 1603, its leader had been Archbishop James Beaton of Glasgow. For much of the time he had exercised his authority from exile in Rome but he had maintained his enthusiasm for Scottish scholarship – an interest which he had confirmed by taking the Glasgow University mace with him when he fled. He also founded the Scottish College in Rome. After he died, a number of Archpriests were appointed. Then Scotland was put under the control of William Bishop – by then Vicar Apostolic. When Smith was deposed, the Scottish Catholic Church was freed from the English yoke.

In England the Catholic Church continued to agonise over what it regarded as irregular unions. Almost two hundred years later, they were still the cause of doubt and confusion. Thomas Walsh, Vicar Apostolic of the Midland District from 1826 to 1848, bombarded Nicholas Wiseman, then in Rome, for rulings on dubious cases and for general advice: 'What is to be done in the case of a proposal of marriage between a Catholic and a Quaker or any other baptised person of whom there are many in this country?' On July 11th 1868 Henry Edwards, the Archbishop of Westminster, wrote to Cardinal Barnabo at Propaganda Fide – the department in the Vatican which supervised the Church's work in missionary territories – to ask for permission to authorise marriages 'where mixed religions are concerned ... Provided that the conditions established by the Church are protected and especially those regarding the removal of danger of perversion from the Catholic spouse.' Cardinal Barnabo replied on July 23rd that Pope Pius IX 'grants the renovation of the authority'. The agonies of indecision continued for the next hundred and fifty years. The subject was discussed, inconclusively, at the 2015 Synod. In 2016 the Pope speculated on the possibility of relaxing the prohibition.

The title and status of Vicar Apostolic – ancient in origin and re-created – were part of the Vatican's plan to strengthen its worldwide control. Vicars Apostolic – who, although in bishops' orders, acted not on their own authority but on the authority of the Pope – were the agents through whom it exercised its power. After Smith's flight to

France, the Catholic Church in England struggled on for forty years without a head. Then John Leyburn was appointed quasi-bishop under the supervision of Propaganda Fide. Ronald Knox – a twentieth-century priest, intellectual and media celebrity – described Vicars General including Vicars Apostolic as 'emissaries from Rome, personally responsible to the Holy See – as if this island had been some newly discovered territory in the Pacific whose inhabitants were mere beginners in the faith'. That was to be the status of England and Wales until the restoration of the Hierarchy in 1850. Propaganda Fide remained directly in charge of Scottish Catholicism until 1908. Despite all the blood and the burnings, the Catholics of Britain had to work hard and wait long to prove themselves to Rome.

For a time after Charles' succession in 1625, it seemed to Catholic optimists – possessors of a characteristic which their faith encouraged – that England's two Churches might live in some sort of partnership. The fantasy was given some credence by the presence, in King Charles' inner circle of close advisers, of men who made no secret of their Catholicism: the Earl of Portland, Sir Francis Windebank and two courtiers who had served him since his youth, Francis Cottington and Endymion Porter. In October 1633, the King provided even stronger evidence of his wish for some sort of understanding with the Vatican. Sir Robert Douglas, a Scottish Catholic, was sent to Rome with the task of convincing the Vatican of the King of England's goodwill. The optimists were destined to be disappointed.

Charles did not possess his father's enquiring mind. He saw life in simple terms. To him, the Church of England was 'the nearest [form of religion] to the practice of the Apostles and the best for the propagation and advancement of Christian religion of any church in the world.'[11] In his opinion, it charted 'a middle way between the pomp of superstitious tyranny and the meanness of fantastic anarchy'. Yet there was much about Roman Catholicism that attracted him. He believed in the absolute necessity of confession as an assurance of moral discipline in this life, as well as of eternal peace in the next. He regarded celibacy as essential to guarantee the secrecy of the confessional, and argued that indulgences were a penalty imposed on sinners, not the encouragement of easily condoned sin.

There was also a part of Charles' character to which the practices of Catholicism, as distinct from its theology, appealed. The beauty of the Mass attracted him far more than the conscious austerity of Puritan services and he enjoyed listening to plainsong. He possessed an aesthetic enthusiasm for images, which he admired without bothering to worry if they became objects of worship as well as veneration, and he sent to Catholic Spain for a crucifix that was said to possess healing powers. A small piece of wood – found in the mud of the Thames at low tide – was presented to him in the sincere belief that it was a fragment of the True Cross and he accepted it as genuine. That was a symptom of a deeply damaging (and, in the end, fatal) weakness. Charles I believed what he wanted to believe. His view on the rival liturgies was limited to the conviction that the Roman Mass book and the Church of England service book had much in common, and his judgement on the conflicting theologies was that the Protestant Thirty-Nine Articles were barely different from the Catholic Creed.

Rome was far too theologically sophisticated to take the King's apparent sympathy at its face value. Cardinal Bagna – because of his age, thought to be an authority on human conduct – judged that 'Charles's motives, as all who know him at all will admit, are beyond guessing.'[12] However, for a while, it was thought as well to woo him. A series of emissaries was sent to London. The first, Gregorio Panzani, arrived in England in 1634 on what was represented as a semi-private mission, which had been promoted by Queen Henrietta Maria and was given the most encouraging of welcomes. The King greeted Panzani with the meaningless assurance that, had the choice been offered him, he would 'rather have lost his right hand' than been responsible for the schism[13] and added the promise that no Catholic blood would be shed during his reign. Panzani was surprised but encouraged to discover that Francis Cottington had a particular admiration for the Jesuits. The Nuncio concluded that Charles was a 'person of strict virtue and great benevolence' who attended services in his wife's chapel, where it was 'a satisfaction to him to observe the order and significance of the ceremonies'.[14] Indeed, he became so optimistic about promoting Rome's relationship with England that he had to be warned against overplaying his hand. 'The English are a mysterious people ... The sea which you passed over on your way to visit them is an emblem of their temper.' Despite its doubts about Charles' malleability, Rome continued to bombard him with the sort of gifts that kings and emperors exchange at times of great moment. Amongst them was a portrait bust of Charles I by Bernini – based on Van Dyck's triple portrait.

The bust was brought to England in 1636 by George Con, Panzani's successor. The new emissary was charged with the specific task of exploring the prospects of reconciliation. He too was impressed by Charles' apparent sincerity. 'It is well known that His Majesty is altogether innocent in his affections and aversions.'[15] His aversions, in Con's judgement, included Puritanism, and his affections embraced

Rome. At one point something like a negotiation took place. 'You must,' said the King, 'induce the Pope to meet me half way.' Wisely Con chose not to respond, but flattered Charles with the promise that 'His holiness will even come to London to receive you into the Catholic Church.' He knew that the halfway point, which the King had in mind, was an impossible distance away from any position that Rome could accept.

Despite Charles' claims to Con, there was one basic item of dogma that the King could not accept. He rejected, without hesitation, the notion that the Pope had any authority, spiritual or secular, over England. Had there been no other impediment to a concordat, that in itself would have made it impossible. But other insurmountable obstacles grew up on the road to reconciliation. The most important was growing popular feeling against the royal tolerance, about which Con rejoiced when he reported to the Vatican, 'whereas in the past, Catholics could only hear mass within the embassies and at great risk of being arrested when they came out, now the chapels of the queen and embassies are frequented with great freedom'.[16] There were further manifestations of increasing Catholic confidence. The Queen's chapel became a place of public worship, a sanctuary for Catholic trouble-makers and, it was feared, the headquarters of the campaign for the reconversion of England. Protestants came to a wholly reasonable conclusion that William Watling of Suffolk thought self-evident. 'The king has a wife and loves her and she is a papist and we must all be of her religion.'[17] After the discovery of a Jesuit meeting place in Clerkenwell, anti-Catholic feeling rose to such heights that Contarini, the Venetian envoy, reported that Catholics feared that their children would be taken from them and brought up as Protestants.

The Catholic faction at Court had overplayed its hand and the scandalised Protestant establishment, led by William Laud (by then Archbishop of Canterbury) struck back. Private Catholic worship was – in the case of the Queen and her retinue – tolerable. The public manifestation of allegiance to Rome was not. Archbishop Laud preached a sermon on the evils of freedom of worship, and the King forbade his English subjects to attend Mass in his wife's chapel. A gentleman usher of the Queen's privy chamber was posted at the door, during services, to make a note of anyone who defied the royal will. The Spanish Ambassador was summoned to court and rebuked by the King himself for making too-frequent attendances at the Somerset House chapel.

Although the trouble had been caused by the noisy Catholics at Court, action was also taken against the mostly quiet Catholics in the country. All Jesuits, and those who harboured them, were to be arrested. The sons of nobles who were in foreign seminaries were ordered home. Catholic office-holders were required to take the Oath of Allegiance. A large majority of those affected were happy to confirm their formal allegiance to the English crown, as long as the recusancy laws were operated flexibly, and sometimes not at all. Between 1625 and 1640 only three Catholics were executed for crimes related to their Catholicism. A commission on prisons joined in the fashionable pursuit by condemning the laxity of gaol housekeepers by whose folly 'priests and Jesuits are let loose to say masses ... and to seduce our people in all places to the great and just offence of both God and our laws'.[18] There were a number of exemplary prosecutions. A Captain Scott of Queensborough in Scotland was charged with organising the transport of English subjects to continental seminaries.

Charles himself feebly claimed that he 'did not approve of so much rigour ... against the papists'[19] but added that they occasionally needed 'to be curbed as they were sometimes seditious'. Whether he wished it or not, he was totally unable to curb Henrietta Maria. He agreed to the construction of a second chapel in Somerset House, designed by Inigo Jones and decorated in the lavish style of European Catholicism. There were hundreds of observers at its opening, and thousands at the papal Masses that celebrated its consecration. A number of ladies who were regulars at Court, including Lady Newport and Lady Hamilton, announced their conversion. A plan was laid to mount a procession from the Somerset House chapel through the streets of London, singing the *Te Deum* to celebrate the birth of the Dauphin.

Henrietta Maria became even more ostentatiously provocative after her mother's arrival in England. Marie de Medici had fled from France, in 1631, after a failed (one-day) coup against the government of Cardinal Richelieu. After seven years in the Spanish Netherlands she joined her daughter in London, where she never hesitated to press the merits of the Catholic Church on her son-in-law and correct his theological errors. Over dinner one evening, Con returned to the subject of Charles' possible conversion and the King – relying on the broader definition of the word – replied that his faith was already catholic. His mother-in-law immediately contradicted him. He was not, but 'must become an Apostolic Roman Catholic'.[20] Henrietta Maria's choice of friends became, at best, reckless. At worst, it was intentionally provocative and even possibly seditious – the term by which her husband had described those Catholics who had left him no option but to reintroduce modified penal policies. The principal conspirators in the Army Plot of 1641 – a doomed plan to free Thomas Wentworth,

Earl of Strafford, from prison, where he awaited execution – included Henry Jermyn, the Queen's principal adviser and Master of Horse. After the failure of the Army Plot, fearing that Parliament would turn on her, the Queen confined her intrigues to what amounted to collective wishful thinking with trusted friends. But she still came perilously close to committing treason. She told Count Rossetti, the Papal Nuncio, that in return for £150,000, Charles would guarantee more freedom for Catholics in England and Ireland and 'extirpate' the Puritans.[21]

Thanks to the behaviour of his queen, the reign of Charles I marked a great move forward in the domination of the English Catholic Church by the gentry and nobility. Henrietta Maria not only provided reassurance of safe conduct, but she made faith fashionable. As a result, the King's edict against the Jesuits had no effect. Indeed, they grew in strength. It had always been their wish to be separate from the secular clergy and free from interference from the Vicars Apostolic. Located in and around great houses, answerable only to God and their Captain General, they had prospered in their independence, even in King James' time. At the turn of the century there were eighteen Jesuit priests active in England. Six years later there were forty. By 1623 the number had increased to 123. But many of them were Frenchmen and Spaniards. In 1639, 193 Englishmen applied to join the Society.[22] They had become the elite battalion in the army of God.

Jesuits were, however, notably absent from Scotland, King Charles' other kingdom. There the Catholic Church had been deserted by the old nobility and, leaderless, had disintegrated south of the Highland line – despite the missionary attention that it sometimes received from across the border in England. Lowland Protestants found it convenient to represent all attacks on the Kirk as part of a Spanish plot to subvert Scotland in preparation for the invasion of England, even though they knew that the Spaniards had never even considered the idea. To the north, Catholicism survived amongst the remote mountain moorland where, according to a report to Rome, there was the potential for a genuine revival. 'These people are neither Catholic nor heretical, since they detest Protestantism as a new religion and listen to the preachers out of sheer necessity, straying in matters of faith out of ignorance caused by lack of priests who would be able to instruct them on those issues.'[23] Scottish seminarians who had experienced the delights of Rome and Louvain rarely found that their vocations called them home. In 1629 an attempt was made to remedy the deficit by giving Gaelic Scotland into the spiritual care of regular priests. The Vatican convinced itself that the initiative had almost instant success. Propaganda Fide claimed that in 1631 the Church in Scotland had '10,000 adherents' and that the Irish Franciscan mission to the Hebrides (which it regarded as a separate nation) 'bore consoling fruit, claiming 10,000 converts and the institution of ten or twelve parishes'.[24]

During the whole period of what Propaganda Fide called 'the Scottish revival' there were 'only five or six diocesan priests in the whole country'.[25] Rome 'twice requested Queen Henrietta Maria ... to use her good offices with her husband, Charles I, in favour' of his beleaguered Scottish Catholic subjects and 'urged the French King to come to their aid'. Nothing came of either initiative, and by 1647 even the hopes of a Highland revival were forgotten. The Dominicans were refused permission to reinforce their numbers with five Irish volunteers, on the grounds that the Highlands were already occupying the time of more trained priests than the scattered population justified. The Catholic Church became reconciled to Scotland, like rural Wales, persisting in observing rites and venerating saints who were said to be Christian but were unknown to Rome.

In Ireland – a colony in all but name – Catholic confidence and Catholic activity were both increasing, at least in part, as a result of the laws governing the punishment of recusants and the requirement of public office-holders to take the Oath of Supremacy being enforced with Gaelic flexibility. The report to Rome that 'the king of England, in order to gain the good will of the Irish through fear of Spain has declared that the Irish are free to practise whatever religion they wish and that Catholics are not to be molested'[26] was no more than wishful thinking. It reflected Irish Catholics' optimism about the ultimate triumph of their faith. During the following three hundred years weight of numbers and the indomitable piety of simple people gave Irish Catholics some protection – allowing occasional disputes between secular and lay clergy to flourish. But Ireland's strength was its piety. It was said to be 'almost impossible to find a lay person in Ireland who would wish to die without having been clothed in some sort of religious habit'.[27]

The strength of the Irish religious conviction contributed to a feeling, amongst the more spiritually casual English, that the two people had little in common. Apart from a moment when desperate King Charles – under threat from Scottish Covenanters and Parliament – was willing to recruit Irish mercenaries to his cause, the Irish were increasingly treated by the English establishment as an alien race. And it was assumed in London (not without some justification) that all native Irishmen were encouraged by both race and religion to be the enemies of England. Irish Catholicism had become synonymous with subversion.

It therefore seemed wholly plausible that a particularly grotesque plot to assassinate John Pym – at the height of his parliamentary campaign to prevent the King raising taxation without parliamentary approval – was the work of rebellious Irish Catholics. A package was delivered to Pym at the House of Commons. It contained dressings which had been recently removed from plague sores. It was immediately assumed, and soon after declared, that the attempt on Pym's life had been the first act of a popish plot. Two weeks later, seventeen Privy Councillors, who had been asked to enquire into the Outrage, reported to Parliament 'of certain intelligence that were lately come of a great Treason and general rebellion of the Irish Papists in Ireland; and a design of cutting off all the Protestants in Ireland and seizing the King's forts there'.[28]

They were right in so much as Ireland was in an even greater state of turmoil than usual. The dispossessed Catholic 'Old English' had been promised redress by what was called 'The Graces'. They amounted to the removal of some of the limitations on Catholic land ownership, and relief from some of the disabilities imposed as penalties for 'popish' practices. But Charles, who could take some credit for introducing the reforms, lost his nerve and, instead of activating them on the agreed date, prevaricated and procrastinated. He was afraid that relaxing the penal laws would so provoke Protestants that the 'New English' settlers of the 'plantation' would combine with the Calvinistic Church of Ireland in a disastrous but doomed attempt to impose a late but savage Reformation on the whole of Ireland, and that the result would be civil war. There was an uprising, but not the one that Charles feared. The Irish peasantry and the 'Old English' nobility combined, under the leadership of Sir Phelim O'Neill, to assert their rights. The revolt began on October 25th 1641, with an audacious, but hopeless, plan to take Dublin Castle. When that failed – according to O'Neill, the result of betrayal – the rebels issued a call to arms in defence of ancient liberties. The insurgents were (either out of expediency or principle) explicit in their support for the King. It was not all that they held in common with their 'oppressors'. From then on, both sides in the conflict saw the uprising as a religious war.

The inhabitants of Galway – in their declaration of independence – spoke for all Catholic Ireland when they swore they were open and explicit about their aspiration to 'shake off the heavy yoke and tyranny of England and at the same time anxious to live as Catholics with a free exercise of our holy religion'.[29] The Munster rebels were less frank about their motives, but a letter to the House of Commons – which described the atrocities of which they were said to be guilty – left no doubt about whom, according to their enemies, was their chosen victim. It was 'poor Protestants' on whom were perpetrated the alleged barbarities. They included 'cutting off of privy members, ears, fingers and hands; plucking out their eyes, boiling the heads of little children before their mothers' faces and then ripping up their mothers' bowels . . .[30] It was not the first instance of the demonisation of Catholics, but it was the most lasting and effective. Before 1641, Catholics were the enemy. After 1641, Irish Catholics were a threat.

Apprehension was increased in England by the reaction in Parliament – in truth, more concerned with the battle against royal supremacy than with the threat of Catholic insurrection, but cynically exploiting the fear of a popish plot. 'Additional Instructions' to the parliamentary Commissioners denounced but did not describe 'miseries, burdens and distempers' imposed on the people by 'cunning, false and malicious practices' carried out by men close to the King, who were 'favourers of Popery, superstition and innovation, subverters of religion, honour and justice'. They were identified as 'Jesuit Papists' and the 'corrupt part of the clergy who favour formality and superstition'.[31] Parliament had barely drawn breath before Pym tabled what has come to be called The Grand Remonstrance.

The Grand Remonstrance was intended to encourage support for strengthening the power of Parliament at the expense of the sovereign. It aimed to achieve its objective by claiming that the King was being manipulated by advisers who supported 'the insurrection of Papists within your kingdom of Ireland and the bloody massacre of your people' in Great Britain[32] and that, as a result, precautions taken in more prudent times had been ignored. Initially the Commons agreed to endorse, but not publish, what amounted to an indictment for treason. When, in December 1641, it was agreed that it should be published, the result was what its proponents should have expected and probably wanted. Anti-Catholic feeling increased to fever pitch. Hatred was again combined with panic.

It is impossible now to know how many, if any, of the fears were well founded. In his history of the Civil War, Michael Braddick listed some of the more implausible rumours. Guildford, Norwich and London expected to be burned down by Catholic incendiarists. Bands of armed Catholics were said to be roaming about Lancashire, Staffordshire, Warwickshire and the capital, waiting for the moment to strike. In Bedfordshire and Berkshire, assemblies and movements of unspecified size or nature were reported and were assumed to be the build-up to a revolution. Liverpool, Conway and Beaumaris decided to take no chances and ordered the arrest of strangers, known Catholics and men travelling at night. Newcastle, Hull and Berwick appealed for parliamentary protection. Ludlow and Bewdley spent mid-November 1641 'in very great panic'.[33]

It was the Jesuits who were most feared and suspected. Yet, thanks very largely to the continued patronage of great houses, they increased in numbers during the second half of Charles' reign. At the outbreak of the Civil War there were about twenty Jesuit missions in London, thirty in the north of England, twenty-eight in Wales and the west, and eighty in the south and Midlands.[34] Those who were not resident chaplains were sustained by the income from two funds which were established sometime shortly after 1624. William, the Second Lord Petre, donated £8,000. Mrs Eleanor Brooksby and Anne Vaux, the daughters of Lord Vaux, donated £9,000.[35]

When the real war began, not every Catholic rallied to Charles I's standard, but most did. More than one-third of the 'gentlemen' – five hundred in all – who died fighting for the King could have been prosecuted as Papists. The Eyre family of Hassop in Derbyshire was, perhaps, not typical, but it certainly espoused King and Catholicism with equal devotion. Five miles away in Chatsworth House, the 3rd Earl of Devonshire had allowed his mother, a friend of Henrietta Maria, to negotiate a deal with the Royalists by which her son's neutrality was recognised in exchange for a substantial donation. The surrounding minor aristocracy usually followed the Cavendish lead. But Colonel Thomas Eyre of Hassop raised a troop of cavalry and led it into battle at Edgehill and the Siege of Newark, where he was wounded and captured. He died in a Commonwealth prison. Thirty years later his kinsman, Rowland Eyre, cheerfully broke the laws of the King for whose father his kinsman had fought and died. The funds that were set up to finance the Jesuit missions had fallen on hard times. The Petre bequest had been depleted by fraud and the Vaux endowment had been diminished by Commonwealth sequestration. With the help of local Jesuits, Rowland Eyre of Hassop acquired the remaining capital and invested it, in his name, in an estate in Ashbourne. In 1672 it earned, for the use of Jesuits, the sum of £349.

The Great Civil War – King versus Parliament – did not deflect attention from the 'Catholic threat'. The continued fear of Rome resulted in the promotion of Oliver Cromwell, whose first position of note was the membership of a committee that was set up, during the spring of 1642, to supervise the disarmament of recusants[36] in response to an appeal from nervous Protestants. After ending the incipient resistance in Monmouth, he moved on to Cambridge, where college plate was being sent to London, in anticipation of the King needing money with which to buy arms. Cromwell, acting with exemplary speed and initiative and without waiting for orders, raided all the college plate rooms. He went on first to capture and then demolish the great fortified houses. The primary intention was to prevent them from becoming rallying points for the Royalist Army. But their destruction also often denied the Catholic Church a safe haven in which a priest could live in something like security. After the capture of the Marquess of Winchester's Basing House, Cromwell's men burned down the chapel.

O'Neill's rebellion of 1641 had made Cromwell – normally tolerant of religious denominations other than his own – profoundly intolerant of Catholics in general and of Irish Catholics in particular. In his Declaration of 1649, he warned the Irish Catholic priesthood that they would no longer be allowed to enjoy the more casual enforcement of the law which had followed the uprising of eight years earlier. The Mass had been illegal in Ireland for eighty years before O'Neill's insurrection and he was 'determined to reduce things to their former state on this behalf'.[37] Cromwell's anti-Catholic passion increased with the years. In 1651 he issued an edict which prescribed the death penalty for any Catholic priest found in Scotland. The new law was to be enforced from the day that followed its proclamation.

In Ireland, the situation was confused in a typically Irish way. James Butler, Earl of Ormond, who had commanded the English army during the 1641 O'Neill Rebellion, was confronted by a new alliance. The Catholics and 'Old English' found that they had common interests and made common cause. The partnership was strong enough – or thought itself strong enough – to call the arrangement a 'confederation' and to set up an independent Catholic government in Kilkenny. From then on, Ireland was a land of shifting alliance. Catholic troops – who had fought against Charles in Ireland – went to Scotland to fight for him against the Covenanters. Catholics and Old English combined to fight Cromwell as they had fought the King – and, towards the end of the Civil War, formed a shaky alliance with the local nobility. Cromwell swept the confederation aside, confiscated the land that was left in Catholic ownership and distributed most of it among Protestant veterans of his victorious New Model Army. What was left was sold to merchant adventurers and Scottish Covenanters. The already embittered Irish Catholics had a new reason to hate the English. The Irish peasantry had been left landless.

During his years in power, Cromwell was unyielding in his savage suppression of Catholics – whom he assumed to be subversive – in Ireland. When the Governor of Ross had the temerity to ask why the freedoms that Parliament claimed to hold dear were not respected to the west of the Irish Sea, he received an answer that embraced the whole Commonwealth. 'I meddle not with any man's conscience. But if by liberty of conscience you mean liberty to exercise the mass, I judge it best to use plain dealing and let you know that where the Parliament of England have power, that will not be allowed of.'[38] Unyielding though that statement was – and despite the determination with which its message was driven home – it was not Cromwell's prohibition of the Mass which made him anathema to Catholics in Ireland and beyond. It was his conduct during the siege and subsequent capture of Drogheda.

In August 1649 – seven months after the execution of Charles I – Oliver Cromwell led an army of 8,000 foot and 4,000 horse to Ireland, there to put down a new attempt at rebellion. It was led by the Earl of Ormonde who, for the moment, was more of a Royalist than a Protestant and was therefore prepared to command Catholics in a campaign against the Commonwealth. The first obstacle, as Cromwell marched north from Dublin, was the heavily fortified town of Drogheda. Cromwell sent a message to Sir Arthur Aston, the commander of the garrison. His offer – sympathetic treatment of the garrison in return for a quick surrender – was meant to be an act of Christian charity. It was, however, not made in charitable language. He told the city at large that he proposed 'to reduce it to obedience, to the end that an effusion of blood may be prevented'.[39] But if Aston refused to surrender, whatever happened to the garrison, its commander would 'have no cause to blame' Cromwell. Aston replied that his soldiers were 'unanimous in their resolution to perish rather than to deliver this place'. It is, therefore, possible to argue that, according to the rules of war as understood in the seventeenth century, Cromwell was entitled to wreak a terrible vengeance on the obdurate garrison, which chose to fight rather than accept the inevitable and surrender. But he was certainly not in any way justified in either ordering or allowing the massacre of civilians. Although official instruction to his troops was death to anyone who had borne arms, he knew that his soldiers were not in a mood to make careful distinctions. More than one thousand non-combatants were murdered in Drogheda – among them every Catholic priest in the town.

Most of the dead – counting soldiers as well as civilians, nearly 4,000 in all – were cut down as the parliamentary troops rampaged through the town. But the clergy at St Peter's, in the north of the town, died terrible premeditated deaths. They took refuge in the church tower. Cromwell's soldiers tore out the pews and every other combustible article of the nave of the church, built a bonfire at the foot of the tower and watched the priests roast to death. They became instant Catholic martyrs – and the reason, in Catholic mythology, why Cromwell died in terror as he listened to the thunder that accompanied his last hours. If he did repent Drogheda, it was late in life that he felt any guilt. At the time, as he reported to Parliament, he regarded the slaughter as both a military necessity and the expression of divine vengeance on sinners. 'I am persuaded that this is the righteous judgement of God upon those barbarous wretches who have inbrued their hands in so much innocent blood; that it will prevent such effusions of blood for the future, which are satisfactory grounds for such actions which otherwise cannot but work remorse and regret.'[40]

Cromwell remained in Ireland for nine months. During that time – and during the suzerainty of Ireton and Ludlow, his successors – the country was subject to a policy of calculated devastation and its people were systematically massacred. At Wexford, Cromwell's troops slaughtered every captured soldier who had fought against them, and then watched with amusement while two overloaded boats capsized in the harbour and the men who had hoped to escape drowned. The subsequent Irish peace was as savage as the war. Yet more veterans of the New Model Army and English Puritans were given title to land previously owned or occupied by native Irish families, and it was said that the deposed were given the choice of going to 'hell or Connaught' – the most barren of Irish provinces. Despite the influx of Protestant settlers to the Irish 'plantation', four years of famine and slaughter killed so many Irish Catholics that the total population of Ireland was reduced by one-third.[41]

In 1653, on Cromwell's instruction, the Act of the Long Parliament – which required English Catholic 'delinquents' to forfeit two-thirds of their estates – was repealed. Clarendon observed that 'Cromwell proceeds, with strange dexterity, towards the reconciling of all sorts of persons'.[42] It was the sort of expedient gesture which English Catholics – without much evidence to support their optimism – always used to convince themselves that their continued hope for some sort of accommodation with the Protestant state was about to be realised. Cromwell's concession to 'delinquents' encouraged new reconciliation initiatives. The most ambitious plan was formulated in 'Blacklow's Cabal' – the followers of Thomas White, also known as Blacklow, sometime Professor of Philosophy at Douai. It was made public after Charles had lost the Civil War and left English religion in unprecedented confusion. The Church of England, as it had been established by Queen Elizabeth in 1559, had been abolished by

Parliament. Attempts to impose a Presbyterian orthodoxy on the whole country had been frustrated by the leaders of other denominations, supported by the army. In what seemed to be an era of tolerant diversity, it was inevitable that a combination of ingenuity, naivety and faith in the eventual irresistibility of Rome should result in a proposal through which Catholicism could benefit from what appeared to be a belief in religious pluralism.

The Blacklow scheme – which one Catholic, Sir Kenelm Digby, described as conceived by the Holy Ghost[43] – required Parliament to draft an Oath of Allegiance that would be sworn by all Catholics. The penalty for refusal was to be banishment. The Catholic Church was to have six or eight bishops (bearing traditional geographical titles) who, although appointed by the temporal powers, would receive their authority directly from Jesus Christ rather than the Pope. Indeed, each bishop would be required to renounce the Oath of Allegiance to Rome that was normally taken on ordination – as would every priest. In consequence, the Pope, who had been bypassed, would have power neither to dismiss nor to instruct them. Henry Holden, the 'Blacklow' disciple who had worked out the details of the plan, was so enthusiastic about its attractions that he told Sir Kenelm Digby, who had friends in Catholic high places, 'You may freely give out [in Rome] that the Independents intend us an absolute toleration.'[44]

The attraction of the scheme to the Commonwealth Parliament – insomuch as such a feeling existed – lay in the duties it imposed on bishops. They were 'obliged both by the principles of their religion and by their particular interests to be watchful over the persons and the actions of the priests, who they appoint under them, to guide the conscience of the laity'.[45] In return for allowing the *form* of Catholic worship – albeit to the exclusion of the Pope – Parliament was to be provided with a mechanism by which the behaviour of potentially rebellious Catholics could certainly be observed, and possibly be contained. The initiative – and several other attempts at rapprochement – came to nothing. Rome rejected it because it denied the supreme authority of the Pope. The Commonwealth Parliament rejected it because there were easier ways of ensuring the subordination of the Catholic population. So English Catholics were left to wait and pray for the Restoration, which – it was at least rumoured – would begin with a Catholic being crowned King of England.

CHAPTER 13

Liberty to Tender Conscience

The hope that Charles II would be a Catholic king was realised late in his reign. He was received into the Church on February 6th 1685, six hours before he died. The King was in great pain – as much from the treatment he had received from his numerous doctors as from the still-undiagnosed disease they sought to alleviate or cure. So the Duke of York took some time to satisfy himself that his brother was in a fit state of mind to understand the significance of the request to be admitted to the faith which, for all of his life, Charles had claimed to reject. Those precautions left no doubt that the decision to become what he had once denounced was undoubtedly his own, although several pious Catholics took credit for putting the idea into Charles' troubled head.

During the week that followed the King's death, the Duke of York claimed that, shortly before his sudden illness prevented a steady and orderly journey to Rome, Charles had composed a statement asserting his wish to become a Catholic. A year later, James II – as the younger brother had then become – published the precis of two declarations of Catholic faith which he said had been found in the dead King's strongbox. No one was allowed sight of the original manuscripts. From time to time James told an alternative story. In exile, seven years later, he explained to the nuns of Chaillot, in France, that, on the evening of his brother's death, he had suddenly (and perhaps providentially) been inspired to send for a priest. No mention was made, in that version of events, of Charles' declaration of faith.

There were several other claimants to the title of shepherd to the royal sheep. Charles Barrillon d'Armoncourt, Marquis de Branges and Ambassador of France, boasted to King Louis that the idea of sending for a priest was his. Father Benedict Gibbon, an English priest, published a pamphlet which claimed that he had told the Duke of York that his brother was ready to become a Catholic. However, Father John Huddleston – who received Charles into the Church and performed the last rites – was a model of circumspection. He merely recorded that the bedchamber had been cleared of everyone except the King, his brother and two Anglican witnesses (the Earls of Bath and Faversham), confirmed that Charles had been conscious, that he had declared his willingness to be received and listed the rites that had been performed. But Father Huddleston was not looking for a place in history. His only intention was to protect the memory of the dead King as he had protected his life more than thirty years earlier.

During his escape from the Parliamentary army after the Battle of Worcester in 1651, Charles – as well as hiding in the famous oak tree – had taken refuge in houses that were owned by the Catholic gentry of Worcestershire, Shropshire, Warwickshire and Staffordshire. Moseley Hall, the home of Thomas Whitgreave, on the Hereford border of Worcester, had a priest-hole and a priest to go with it. His name was John Huddleston and in 1688 – shortly before James II was deposed – supporters of Catholic emancipation published a pamphlet which contained testimonies from both the priest and his employer. Charles, they said, had visited the chapel in Moseley Hall and told them that, as a boy, he had possessed 'an altar, crucifix and silver candlesticks of his own'.[1] Opponents of the campaign to confirm Charles' genuine Catholicism dismissed the feeling of peace, which the King was said to have experienced within the chapel, as an aesthetic rather than spiritual experience. The rest of the two men's testimonies was more difficult to discount. It went on to claim that, on the same evening, Charles had been read a defence of Catholicism and pronounced it unanswerable. He had also joined Father Huddleston in a recital of the catechism. Most important of all – to Catholics who were concerned about their own hopes of salvation – he had promised that Catholics would have freedom of worship after the restoration of the monarchy. It was a promise that he was to make time after time during his eventual reign – sometimes meaning it and sometimes not. But in 1651 it was enough to make Father Huddleston follow Charles Stuart into exile and return with him to England in 1660 as chaplain and confessor to his Roman Catholic queen.

It seems unlikely that the day of his death was the first occasion, during his reign, on which Charles had considered the possibility of becoming a Roman Catholic. Throughout his life he had been surrounded by Catholics who, by nature of their conviction, constantly reminded him which Christian denomination was the true faith. His mother, Henrietta Maria, accepted that, despite the marriage settlement, her children would be brought up as Protestants. But her son must have been influenced by her pious example as well as his father's open admiration for Catholic liturgy, ceremony and ritual. Charles' wife, Catherine of Braganza, was as devout as her mother-in-law, and at least two of his many mistresses were Catholic. So was his brother, the Duke of York – openly and formally after 1669, and secretly much earlier. However, the Marquess of Halifax was almost certainly wrong to claim that Charles, 'when he came to England [after the Restoration], he was certainly a Roman Catholick as he was a Man of Pleasure'.[2] Catholicism came to him gradually – almost casually.

Charles II did not think deeply about anything, and it is unlikely that he thought about theological questions at all. His attitude towards the Church of Rome was best illustrated during his exile when, on the eve of a journey to encourage German support for the Stuart cause, he left Henry – his youngest brother – in Paris with their mother. The Dowager Queen promised not to exploit the opportunity of Charles' absence to convert the boy to Catholicism. She did not keep her word. As soon as Charles left Paris, she sacked the Prince's Protestant tutor and sent him to a nearby abbey for instruction in preparation for admission to the Church. On his return, Charles was scandalised and immediately despatched his brother to the safety of Protestant Holland. Charles' anger had nothing to do with the rival theological merits of the two views of Christianity. His complaint was that making his brother a Catholic would dishonour his father's memory and ensured that his restoration to the throne remained completely unacceptable to the English Parliament. He was a gambling man and, until the day of his death – when only the kingdom of heaven was at stake – continued to see the Catholic Church as a gambling chip to be played according to the circumstances of the time. Sometimes he gambled on Catholic support keeping him on the throne of England. More often, he secured his hold on the crown by responding to Parliament's (often hysterical) calls for punitive action against imagined Papist intrigue and invented popish plots.

When the Pope learned that Henry had been sent to Holland explicitly to save him from the clutches of Rome, he was deeply offended by Charles' refusal to contemplate the conversion of his brother. The Venetian Ambassador in London echoed the Pontiff's anticipation of divine retribution. 'The House of Stuart, being expelled from the kingdom of this world will now have to submit to banishment from the Kingdoms of Heaven.'[3] Rome should have grown accustomed, if not reconciled, to Charles judging Catholicism – both his own public position and the conversion of England – as no more than an aspect of his determination 'not to go on his travels again'. A few months after his escape from England, he had written to Rome offering to return England to Catholicism if the Pope supported his attempts to regain the English throne. The Pope had replied that Charles' personal conversion must precede even discussion of the subject. So the idea was abandoned and the Restoration was achieved without papal support.

Estimates of the number of Catholics in Charles II's England vary both because of the difficulty of definition and the unreliability of seventeenth-century statistics. Claudius Agretti, the Apostolic Minister to Flanders, put the 1669 figure at 200,000, including 230 secular priests and at least 255 regulars, including 120 Jesuits and 80 Benedictines.[4] Agretti's figures were almost certainly an underestimate. But even allowing for the social composition of the Catholic population – persecution having decimated the working classes and left the gentry almost untouched – the numbers did not justify the fears of a successful domestic uprising. Something between 4.5 and 5 per cent of Charles II's subjects were Catholics. Despite continual evidence to the contrary, many of them persisted in believing that King Charles would set them free.

It had all begun so well. The 1660 Declaration of Breda – the prospectus that Charles offered England as he negotiated his return – had been explicit: 'We do declare a liberty to tender conscience and that no man shall be disquieted or called to question for differences of religion which do not disturb the peace of the kingdom.' And it seemed that the prospect of tolerance, if not civil liberty, increased with Charles' arrival in England and the confidence that his restoration engendered. In December – following the release from gaol of the Nonconformists who had been imprisoned by the Commonwealth – he issued a Declaration of Indulgence. Its good intentions were not in doubt. The Act of Uniformity of 1559 should, in effect, be repealed. So should all other penal legislation directed at Catholics. The choice of verb was important. The Declaration simply set out reforms which a cautious King proposed to consider suggesting to Parliament. It did, however, include a robust justification of the course of action he might possibly take. 'The Roman Catholic subjects of this kingdom, having deserved well from our royal father of blessed memory and from the Protestant religion itself in adhering to us with their lives and fortunes for the maintenance of our Crown',[5] should be rewarded by the gift of a measure of religious liberty. They were rewarded by the Act of Conformity, which (pointlessly) prohibited Catholics from holding Church of England Office, and by the Conventicle Act, which made acts of worship outside church premises illegal if more than four persons were gathered together – a measure primarily intended to prohibit Nonconformist open-air payer meetings, but which also added to the list of laws that were broken at Mass centres.

The 'Cavalier Parliament' indicated that it was not likely to agree that Catholic royalists should be rewarded, and the King, not a man to stand on principle, retreated before his plan could be rejected. By February 18th 1672, the day on which the House of Commons, in its fourth Restoration session, declared itself ready and willing to consider the Declaration of Indulgence, Charles had lost his nerve and amended his proposals. He still asked for both Roman Catholics and Nonconformists to be relieved of the penalties that were imposed upon them, but – in order to make the repeal more palatable to the House of Commons – he also proposed that Catholics should still be disqualified from holding office. For good measure, he also expressed the hope that their numbers should not be allowed to increase. He did not suggest any ways in which that desirable state of affairs might be achieved. The Commons was not impressed. The King's proposals were rejected without a division.

From the very beginning of his reign Charles' cynical equivocation spawned a patchwork of legislation which sometimes relaxed the penal laws, but more often extended and strengthened them. In 1661 the powers of the English ecclesiastical courts were revived, but although they recorded the names of men and women who had offended against Church laws, no attempt was made to punish them. In the same year, the Corporations Act excluded from municipal office and employment anyone who failed, within twelve months of the new law passing, to take the Oaths of Allegiance and Supremacy and refused to take the sacraments as prescribed by the Church of England.

Charles was proclaimed King of Ireland on May 14th 1660. Peace was made with the Irish lords in an agreement which included the promise that they would be free to practise their religion. The promise was repudiated by the Irish Parliament. Twelve years later, after the Restoration had been firmly established, Ormond – by then a duke – tried to broker another deal. As always in Ireland, the barrier on the road to religious reform was erected by the Protestant Parliament. Ormond attempted to overcome the objections by providing assurances about temporal sovereignty. Influential Catholics were asked to draw up a 'Remonstrance' which would be accepted as proof of good faith by King and Parliament. The Remonstrance was ingenious as well as explicit. Sovereigns, it declared, were 'God's lieutenants'[6] and disobeying them was, therefore, a denial of His dominion. In consequence, any foreign power or potentate who challenged their authority was disobeying God's law. The attempt to recruit Providence as an ally in the Pope's battle with the Irish Parliament's dispute failed. Twenty-one peers and numerous Catholic laymen signed the Remonstrance, but only seventy of Ireland's 2,000 priests. Another attempt at compromise had failed – rejected, as was so often the case, not because of differences over the status of statues, transubstantiation, the intercession to saints or prayers for the dead, but over the authority of the Pope. The dispute, like the Reformation itself, concerned theology's political dimension.

The following year, Ormond replaced the Civil War's General Monck as Lord Lieutenant of Ireland. Ormond was Irish born and bred and realised that rebellion was as likely to be provoked by land-hunger as by religious persecution. Disputes over ownership – the result of Oliver Cromwell's misappropriation – continued and Ormond's attempt to resolve them en masse was included under the provisions of the Settlement Act. It was passed by the Irish Parliament in the face of bitter hostility and only after much amendment. The result was legislation of such confused complication that its meaning had to be clarified by an Act of Explanation. The muddle was compounded by King Charles intervening to influence individual adjudications – according to Ulster Protestants, invariably on the side of Catholic claimants. If their complaints were justified, the King's involvement did little to rectify the overall injustice. At the beginning of the Civil War, Catholics owned more than two-thirds of Irish land. After the Ormond 'reforms', they owned less than a quarter.

King Charles' real attitude towards Catholicism and the religious freedom of his Catholic subjects remains a mystery. The likelihood is that he was vaguely in favour of limited tolerance, but – in that as well as in other matters – was not prepared to antagonise those on whom his continued reign depended. The French Ambassador wryly reported to King Louis that Charles 'will do nothing against our religion – except under pressure from parliament'.[7] That gave him more credit than he deserved. It would have been more true to say that he never stood up to Parliament (whether under pressure or not) and often bowed to its anticipated wishes before they were formally expressed. Occasionally he tried to frustrate its will by deception and prevarication. When he was found out, he either weakly submitted or – when religious liberty was the issue – actually added fuel to the flames of intolerance. Only in one particular did he take a firm stand: the religious freedom of his Catholic brother and, therefore, the security of the Stuart succession.

The process of protecting his own position at all costs had begun with one of the regular revisions of the Prayer Book – originally in a gesture of ecumenism. The first draft was to be drawn up by a joint committee of Episcopalians and Presbyterians, but Charles again lost his nerve and agreed to the whole job being done by the Church of England Convocation. The result was a new definition of the liturgical and theological character of Reformation in England. All clergy who had not been ordained according to the rites of the Church of England were excluded from the ministry, whether or not they had renounced their allegiance to Rome. Those who remained were required to accept the Book of Common Prayer in every detail and to subscribe to all the doctrinal articles of the Church of England. Nine hundred and sixty ministers – many of them with sympathy for 'Roman practices' – either left or were ejected from their livings. It was not only 'Anglo-Catholics' who were penalised. Four thousand Quakers were imprisoned after their refusal to accept the doctrine of the Established Church. Despite having sanctioned the Act, Charles concurred in attempts to soften its impact. Edward Hyde – First Earl of Clarendon, father-in-law to the Catholic Duke of York and Charles' principal adviser – proposed that the King should be empowered to relieve some ministers of the more onerous provisions of the new dispensation. Charles agreed, but the notion of flexibility in the face of dissent was defeated in the House of Lords.

Charles II was far less nervous about the activities of Catholics than he was about the discontent of the defeated Puritans. But legislation directed towards the discouragement of dissent and Nonconformity inevitably bore down on all religious denominations, save the Established Church of England. The Conventicle Act of 1663 was intended to prevent the 'field preaching' to which Puritans were addicted. But it was another obstacle in the way of organising 'Mass stations'. In 1665 the Five Mile Act – which prohibited dissenting ministers from living within five miles of a parish from which they had been ejected – was directed explicitly at Nonconformists. But it was used to harass priests. A year later the Catholics were found guilty of an offence that transcended in wickedness all the crimes and misdemeanours of which the Dissenters were guilty. Parliament agreed that Papists had set fire to London.

On the first day of the Great Fire, a rumour that 50,000 French troops had landed on the south coast swept through London. It was taken for granted that the Catholics in the capital had been complicit in the plan to burn down the city, in preparation for a French invasion. Men suspected of collaboration with the supposed enemy were hunted down. Clarendon wrote sympathetically of the indiscriminate arrest of known Catholics. 'Some of them, and of quality, were taken out of their houses and carried to prison.'[8] One of the Portuguese Ambassador's servants – seen fumbling in his pocket with a piece of bread – was accused of preparing a fire-bomb. The mob reacted so violently that he had to be taken into protective custody. Men of swarthy complexion and shopkeepers who were known to have foreign-sounding names were beaten in the street.

Charles reacted with commendable good sense. Troops had been sent into the city to restore order. Hysterics claimed that their deployment was proof of imminent invasion. The King ordered that they be withdrawn. On the second day of the panic he visited the smoking ruins and, speaking from the graveyard alongside what was left of St Paul's, told the anxious crowd which surrounded him, 'Many of those who have been detained upon suspicion I have myself examined and I have found no reason to suspect connivance in burning the City.'[9] For added reassurance, Charles asked the Privy Council to examine the possibility that the fire had been started maliciously. Their report was unambiguous. 'Nothing had been found to argue the Fire in London to have been caused by other than the hand of God, a great wind and a very dry season.' London was not in a mood to be reassured. So when Robert Hubert – the clearly demented son of a Rouen watchmaker – 'confessed' that he had been hired to start the fire, his ramblings were accepted as incontrovertible proof that France, no doubt as the agent of Rome, had burned down London. The magistrates who examined Hubert were sceptical about the truth of his story. But he argued his guilt with such passion that they felt an obligation to send him for trial. He was found guilty and hanged.

Within a month of Hubert's execution, Parliament had set up a Committee to inquire into the origins of the fire. Before it reported, the House of Commons asked Charles to banish all Catholic priests from England. It is only possible to guess at the spirit in which he acceded to their request. He certainly did not regard it as justified. And he could not have regarded the English Catholics (by then somewhere between 1.6 and 4 per cent of the population[10]) as a threat in themselves. But he may have been fearful that anything other than an enthusiastic response would encourage the suspicion – absurd, but common – that he, in league with his Catholic mother at the Court of King Louis and his French Catholic wife in London, conspired to suborn his own kingdom. Or he may simply have lacked the energy and courage to fight Parliament. In any event the Commons – the epicentre of prejudice – could not have complained about his response. Andrew Marvell, the Member of Parliament for Kingston upon Hull, told the Mayor of that city 'all Popish priests and Jesuits, except those attached to the queen [are to be] banished in 30 days or else the law be executed upon them'.[11] That was only the beginning. Justices of the

Peace were instructed to apply, with consistent severity, penal laws which in many parts of the country had been ignored for years.

Rumours about the origins of the fire were not confined to the ignorant and superstitious lower orders of society. Sir Thomas Crew assured Samuel Pepys that the House of Commons Committee, of which he was not a member, would 'conclude it as a thing certain that it was done by a plot ... that endeavours were made in several places to increase the fire and that it was bragged by several papists that upon such a day and in such a time we should find the hottest weather there ever was in England'.[12] And so it did. The report, published on January 22nd 1667 was, according to Andrew Marvell, 'full of manifest testimony that [the fire] was by wicked design'.[13]

The House of Commons retained the power to influence the King's conduct by refusing to 'Grant Supply'. So Charles' requests for extra funds were usually accompanied by popular initiatives – most often new proposals for the suppression of Papists. The same palliative was employed to soothe the pain of national humiliation. The Treaty of Breda in 1667, which ended the Dutch Wars and confirmed British ownership of New York and New Jersey, might have been welcomed by Parliament, had not the Dutch fleet – in the final act of hostility – sunk *The Royal Charles*, *The Royal Oak*, *The Royal James* and *The Loyal London* at anchor in the Medway. The passage through the House of Commons of the Act which ratified the treaty was smoothed by the parallel announcement that, in the new peace, all public servants would be required to take the Oaths of Allegiance and Supremacy – thus purging the military and judiciary of men with 'popish' inclinations.

Despite Charles' apparent willingness to respond to Parliament's demands to root out 'Popery', the House of Commons – and to a lesser extent the Lords – remained suspicious about his genuine inclinations. It did not fear that he was guilty of possessing deeply held convictions. Their concern was that, while he possessed little personal faith, he did want to make alliances with Catholic nations and would be prepared to swear his allegiance to Rome, if it was necessary for the achievement of that objective. The suspicions were justified. The 1670 Treaty of Dover – ostensibly designed to ensure that England would not face a Franco-Dutch alliance – contained secret clauses which promised Louis XIV that, in return for £150,000 (some reports say £200,000), Charles would declare himself a Catholic and, with the help of 6,000 French troops, ensure that the people of England followed suit. Charles wrote to Louis, 'I have a desire to enter into a rich personal friendship with you and to unite our interests.'[14]

Neither the King's intentions nor the uncharacteristically thorough way in which he prepared to achieve them are in doubt. He had, in early 1669 (the Feast of the Conversion of St Paul being thought a suitable day) met half a dozen of his closest friends – all of them Catholics or Catholic sympathisers – to plan both the approach to Louis and the best way to follow up what he hoped would be the French king's sympathetic response. The likelihood is that Charles only wanted French assistance in his pursuit of absolute power and that his claims to latent Catholicism were only a charade. His brother James offered what he regarded as evidence to the contrary. According to his – admittedly fallible – recollection, at the conspirators' meeting Charles had described the pain he felt because of his inability to declare his true faith. The statement had been made 'with tears in his eyes'.[15]

It was not a fellow feeling with Catholics that made Charles, in 1672, issue his second Declaration of Indulgence – unlike the first, not a promise to initiate future reforms, but a declaration of an imminent change of policy. The King's intention was to gain the support of Dissenters by allowing them to establish meeting houses, but the Declaration, by its nature, also made it lawful for Catholics to worship as they chose in the privacy of their own homes. Once again, King Charles was suspected of dancing to King Louis' tune. Once again, Parliament reacted with fury and threatened to 'withhold supply' necessary to sustain the army. Once again, Charles responded by initiating new laws to protect the kingdom from 'popish' intrigue.

The Test Act of 1673 reiterated the obligation of all public office-holders – civil and military – to take the Oaths of Allegiance and Supremacy, but added a requirement which no conscientious Catholic could possibly accept. Servants of the state were obliged to swear that they did not believe in transubstantiation and were required to receive Communion according to the rites of the Church of England. There was some talk of the Duke of York being excluded from the Act's provisions, but Members of Parliament – led by William Cavendish, soon to become the Earl of Devonshire – bridled at the idea of tacitly accepting that the heir presumptive was a Catholic. The Duke himself (either in order to avoid embarrassment to the King or to display his determination not to be bullied into apostasy) brought the argument to a sudden end. He resigned the post of Lord High Admiral.

For a couple of years Parliament and King made declarations to each other which were, in the case of the Lords and Commons, more warnings than greetings and, in the case of Charles, models of insincerity. The 1675 Speech from the Throne promised that the King 'would leave nothing undone that might show the world his zeal for the Protestant religion as established by the Church of England from which he would never depart'[16] and Parliament responded with a Humble Address which gave thanks for 'His Majesty's constancy towards the Protestant religion at home and abroad [but] felt bound by conscience and duty [to warn against] the dangerous growth of Popery within His Majesty's dominions and the dire consequences of which must be prevented'.[17]

The fear of treason – real and imaginary – and the consequent sudden bouts of repression reached their bizarre climax in what was called the 'Popish Plot' – a concoction of such obvious nonsense that it could only have been believed by fools and accepted by rogues for whom truth was less important than power. To Charles' credit, when Christopher Kirby – a natural scientist of his acquaintance – warned him of a Catholic assassination plot, he dismissed the idea as an invention. Even when Kirby introduced him to Israel Tonge – an Anglican clergyman who claimed to have documentary evidence of an impending uprising – he did no more than, dismissively, pass on the papers to the Earl of Danby, Treasurer of the Navy, royal confidant and politician of such sophistication that his failure to treat the supposed threat with casual disdain must have been a stratagem devised to strengthen his faction at Court.

The argument in favour of taking the warning seriously was strengthened by Tonge supplying Danby with letters written by the Duke of York's private secretary to Louis XIV's confessor. They were either forgeries or too old to be of any significance, but they were a powerful weapon in the hands of unscrupulous men who used them to provide evidence of royal duplicity. Danby agreed to meet Titus Oates, Tonge's informant. Oates was a man of such manic prejudice that he had feigned conversion to Catholicism and enrolled in the seminaries of both Valladolid and Saint-Omer in order to accumulate evidence about the Pope's plans to overthrow the government and reconvert England to Roman Catholicism. Having found no evidence to confirm his suspicions, he invented the 'Popish Plot'. His story was supported, though not substantiated, by Miles Prance, a Catholic silversmith who confessed to complicity in the plot, recanted and then, under torture, confessed again. By the end of his interrogation he had implicated three innocent men, all of whom were hanged.

Anti-Catholic hysteria grew to a point at which otherwise sensible people believed Oates' claims that the Catholic families of London would rise up and murder their Protestant neighbours, fires would be started in the hope of once more destroying the heart of the city and the King would be murdered so that the crown could be passed to his Catholic brother. A number of alternative methods of assassination were predicted – stabbing by a gang of specially recruited Irishmen, shooting (with the aid of an invincible silver bullet) while the King was walking in St James's Park and poisoning by the Queen's physician. Charles remained sceptical. He announced that he had 'been informed of designs against his person by the Jesuits' but, when asked for details and substantiation, 'forbore to give his own opinion on the matters, lest he should say too much or too little'.[18] It was a characteristic response from 'the wisest fool in Christendom'.

Oates appeared before the Privy Council on October 10th 1678. His story was too implausible to justify a formal examination. But the Council's decision to proceed with its investigation was based on prejudice, panic and the hope of political gain. So a magistrate, Sir Edmund Berry Godfrey, was asked to interrogate Oates and his associate, Israel Tonge, a man whose Oxford divinity doctorate was thought to confirm his credibility. However cynical their original decision, circumstances conspired to make the Privy Council, though not the King, genuinely fear that Oates was to be believed. On November 22nd, fourteen days after his appointment and before the formal examination had begun, Sir Edmund Berry Godfrey was found dead. His murder was almost certainly unrelated to his impending task. He appears in Samuel Pepys' diary in an entry that describes a dispute in which he offended the King by having one of the royal physicians arrested for debt.[19] So he was clearly the sort of man who was not afraid of making enemies. But his death was enough to convince the Privy Council that Oates was telling the truth and to spread panic in the streets.

The Privy Council responded – as much to restore calm as to prevent rebellion – with the Proclamation of November 20th 1678. Its most important injunction took the form of a message to magistrates. The law requiring recusants to live ten miles outside the capital and the obligations required by the Test Act of 1673 – generally ignored – were to be strictly enforced. All priests arrested for offences set out in the Act of 1585 should be tried at once rather than allowed to return home. Unsympathetic local magistrates responded by sending so many priests for trial in London – usually under the pretext that they were suspected of involvement in the Popish Plot – that a second proclamation, requiring trials to be held where the arrests were made, was necessary. Most of the trials (London and local) ended in acquittals. Francis Smith, a Nottingham Jesuit, was sent to London on suspicion of being one of Oates' associates. Interrogation led to the conclusion that he had neither met nor corresponded with the plotters. So he was sent back to Nottingham, where he was released without trial.[20]

A second Test Act – introduced 'for the more effective preserving of the King's Person and Government by disabling Papists from sitting in either House of Parliament'[21] – required peers and MPs to take the oath already required of other public servants. Again special provision was demanded for the Duke of York. An amendment proposed that 'nothing in this bill should extend to his Royal Highness'. Again there was outrage in the Commons – some from genuine friends of the Duke and some from Members who wanted to incriminate him – that the 'House should agree to have the Duke declared a Papist by Act of Parliament'. But the bill was passed as amended.

A rumour that the French had landed at Purbeck swept through London and it was taken for granted that a fire, which gutted part of the Temple, was the work of Papist arsonists. Sir William Scroggs, the Lord Chief Justice, condemned to death William Staley, a banker, for the crime of uttering treasonable words. He had been overheard to say that the King was a great heretic and he would gladly kill him. Dozens of other suspects were arrested and arraigned. Although there was no plot, twenty-four plotters (seventeen of them priests) were arrested, convicted and executed. The Jesuits – whose name was said 'to be hated above all else' – bore the brunt of Protestant fury. Seven were hanged, drawn and quartered. Twelve died in gaol.[22] Many more were killed by rough handling by the mob. One was committed to Bedlam lunatic asylum.[23]

None of the executions could be justified, even by the standards of the seventeenth century. But one stands out from the rest as an example of barbarism, corruption and sheer evil. Father Nicholas Postgate, after some years in York and briefly acting as visiting priest to the Saltmarsh and Meynell families, returned to his native East Riding, where he said Mass in houses, stables and barns all over Blackamoor, an area of 550 square miles. He also cultivated daffodils in the garden of his cottage. For thirty years he carried on his work, without persecution or prosecution, as a beneficiary of the increasingly respected convention that the penal laws would not be applied to priests in remote places who carried out their vocations without flaunting their faith. Then an accident of fate took John Reeves to Whitby. Reeves, who had been manservant to Sir Edmund Berry Godfrey, was probably employed by His Majesty's Customs to investigate smuggling into the port. Whether or not that was his employment, it was not his life's work. He was dedicated to avenging Godfrey's mysterious death, for which he blamed rebellious Catholics. When he heard that a priest in the Whitby area openly carried out his duties, he determined to make it impossible for the locals to ignore the Papist in their midst.

Reeves persuaded William Cockerill, a local constable, to join him in his campaign. Any qualms Cockerill may have felt were removed by Reeves' assurance that Postgate was a potential regicide as well as a priest and that, in consequence, there would be a £30 reward for his apprehension. The two men raided a prayer house where, they had heard, a baptism was to take place. Postgate was caught in the act of saying Mass and brought to trial in York, where the case for the prosecution was supported by a battery of perjured evidence, including a statement from Richard 'Hang Priest' Morrice.[24] The judge summed up in the defendant's favour. 'All that we have heard is that he was reputedly a priest of Rome ... What you must decide is whether or not this man is a traitor.' Nicholas Postgate was found guilty of high treason under the act of 1585, which required priests who were trained abroad to leave the country. The mandatory sentence was death.

The execution took place on the morning of Thursday August 7th 1679. The condemned man told the crowd that surrounded the gallows, 'I do not die for the plot but for my Catholic religion.' Mercifully, his neck was broken by the long drop through the trapdoor in the scaffold, so he was spared the agony of drawing and quartering. Father Nicholas Postgate was the oldest martyr in the history of the Catholic Church in England. When he died he was eighty years of age.

The Popish Plot killings ended with the execution of Oliver Plunkett, Archbishop of Armagh, Primate of Ireland and the last of the Catholic martyrs who died for their faith in England or its Irish province – men and women of such diversity that every Catholic could, and can, identify with one of them. Nicholas Postgate and Oliver Plunkett, though united by the manner of their deaths, lived in circumstances which could hardly have been more different. Plunkett was destined – by birth as well as conviction – to become a Prince of the Church. He was born in Loughcrew, County Meath, into a family which was well established, prosperous and, since it was distantly related to the Earls of Roscommon and Fingall, by the standards of the time, noble. He was educated under the supervision of the Abbot of St Mary's Monastery in Dublin and, when he heard the call to the priesthood, travelled to Rome under the care of Father Pierfrancesco Scarampi, a scholar of some merit. Plunkett entered the Irish College in 1646 and was ordained priest in 1654. Irish priests were required by their vows to return to Ireland and contribute to the work of saving their Church from the Protestant heretics, but Plunkett sought and obtained permission to remain in Rome. Despite his absence, in 1669 he was appointed Archbishop of Armagh. On March 7th 1670, after twenty-three years' absence – if it was exile, it was self-imposed – he returned home.

Dispute continues about whether or not it was coincidence that he was absent from Ireland during the years of Cromwellian persecution and returned while the post-Restoration leniency still held good. Whatever his reasons for not resuming his mission before he could say the Mass in safety, Plunkett used the years of religious peace to good effect. The dispirited Irish priesthood was reinvigorated by a combination of praise and condemnation. Typical was his assault on drunkenness, their abiding weakness: 'Let us remove this defect from an Irish priest and he will be a saint.' His establishment of a Jesuit college in Drogheda provided an example of ecumenical Christianity which was unique for the time. Forty of the one hundred and fifty students whose names appeared on its first register were Protestants.

The work of reorganisation and reconciliation might have continued in peace, had it not been for the Test Acts and the oaths of loyalty they required. Plunkett was willing neither to swear that he rejected the Pope's supreme authority nor to register as a dissenting Catholic and go into voluntary exile for a second time. The Protestant mob burned down the Drogheda college, but the Duke of Ormond, still the Lord Lieutenant of Ireland, was prepared to leave Plunkett in peace as long as he lived and worked in discreet anonymity. So he continued to perform his offices and travelled about the country, in disguise, to encourage the besieged priests in his episcopate. Plunkett became the victim of Stuart politics. The Earl of Essex – Ormond's predecessor, who still smarted from the indignity of replacement – told the Privy Council that, in Ireland, the Lord Lieutenant allowed tyranny to thrive. That, combined with the outbreak of hysteria that followed the invention of the Popish Plot, made tacit tolerance no longer possible. Peter Talbot, Archbishop of Dublin, was imprisoned. Plunkett went into hiding. He escaped capture for almost a year, but was arrested in Dublin in December 1679.

Plunkett was brought to trial in Dundalk, accused of treason and fomenting rebellion. The prosecution claimed that he had plotted an invasion of England by 20,000 French troops and had collected enough subscriptions from the Irish clergy to finance the recruitment of 70,000 Catholic irregulars. According to Ormonde, the jury at his Irish trial was made up of 'silly drunken vagabonds ... whom no schoolboy would trust to rob an orchard'.[25] Despite that, or perhaps because of it, the Privy Council concluded that there was no hope of a conviction in Ireland. Plunkett was moved to Newgate Prison and the trial to London, where it was held, as show trials always were, in Westminster Hall. Plunkett's request to be represented by qualified counsel was refused and his application to be given sufficient time to assemble witnesses was rejected. 'Look you, Mr Plunkett,' said the Lord Chief Justice. 'Don't mis-spend your own time. The more you trifle in these things, the less time you will have for your defence.'[26]

On June 21st 1681, the Westminster Hall jury took fifteen minutes to reach the decision that Archbishop Plunkett was guilty of 'promoting the Roman faith'. The sentence was death and, in passing judgement, the Lord Chief Justice told the condemned man, 'You have done as much as you could to dishonour God in this case. The bottom of your treason was your setting up your false religion, than which there is not any thing more displeasing to God or more pernicious to mankind in the world.'[27] Plunkett responded, '*Deo Gratias.*' Too late, Essex – who had provoked the purge that engulfed Plunkett – told the King that the Archbishop was innocent and should be pardoned. Charles replied, 'Then, my lord, be his blood on your own conscience. You might have saved him if you would. I cannot pardon him because I dare not.'[28] On July 1st 1681 Oliver Plunkett was taken to Tyburn and there hanged, drawn and quartered.

During the years before the Popish Plot, English Protestants had begun to exhibit a glimmering of toleration towards Roman Catholics. But the light never shone as brightly as some optimists believed. William Leslie, an alumnus of the Scots College in Rome, was wrong to claim that, during the early years of Charles II's reign, the faith prospered 'as it did when we had that happiness in Catholic times', when England was 'united and joined together under our own prince'.[29] Richard Ride of Coverdale in Yorkshire left a will which included a bequest to the Church, in anticipation of the day 'that the Catholic religion comes in'. But, by the time of Plunkett's execution, it was clear that his hopes would not be quickly realised. The notion that the King might be assassinated had alerted the English people – now Protestant, by large and genuine majority – to a new threat. Sooner or later, King Charles II would be succeeded by his Papist brother. And a Catholic king would feel obliged to impose his beliefs on a Protestant nation.

Parliament responded to the people's anxiety and the King, in turn, responded to Parliament's determination to frustrate Papist ambitions – real and counterfeit. Charles pre-empted attempts to remove his brother from the Privy Council by persuading him to withdraw on his own initiative. Then, in a message to both Houses, he gave the assurance that he was 'ready to join with them in all ways and means that might establish a firm security for the Protestant religion'.[30] A firm security for the Protestant religion could only be established by removing the Catholic heir presumptive from the succession. So Parliament's most ardent anti-Papists took the King at his word and tabled a resolution which proposed 'that a bill should be brought in to disable James, Duke of York, from inheriting the Crown of this Realm'.[31] The bill was introduced into Parliament on May 15th 1679. It included a clause which proposed that 'all acts of sovereignty which the Duke should exercise, in case of the King's death, be not only declared void but be declared High Treason and punishable as such'. Despite the inclusion of a proposal which contemplated the execution of a prince of the blood royal, and the conclusion that the succession should pass to the Duke of Monmouth, Charles' illegitimate son, the bill's early stages were endorsed by a substantial minority. It was eventually defeated by 207 votes to 128. The King dissolved Parliament.

Encouraged by Parliament's supine reaction to its dissolution, Charles recalled his brother from brief and self-imposed exile. The Commons retaliated with a second exclusion bill, which was rejected by the House of Lords. Charles, insisting that the peers' decision had legitimised his intransigence, dissolved Parliament again. Denied what they believed to be their constitutional rights, the most rabid Protestants convinced themselves – and each other – that high treason was their only, as well as a legitimate, option. Plans were made to murder both the King and his brother as they returned from Newmarket. The Rye House Plot failed because, having left the races early, the royal couple passed the spot chosen for the assassination before the assassins were assembled. The conspirators were captured. The Earl of Essex committed suicide in prison. Lord Russell was hanged.

The exposure of the Rye House Plot did more than rally support for the providentially protected King and his brother. It demonstrated that it was not only Catholics who plotted to suborn the constitution. Combined with the exposure of Titus Oates as a fraud – the previous year, after being convicted of soliciting, he had confessed that the Popish Plot was an invention – the bungled attempt on the King's life helped to reconcile the politicians around him both to his autocratic style and his Catholic sympathies. He spent his last two years in comparative peace and his last hours openly in the faith in which he had secretly long believed. The scene was set for a Roman Catholic succession.

CHAPTER 14

Disobedience, Schism and Rebellion

King James II possessed a characteristic which, although admirable in a commoner, could only bring disaster to a Catholic king who ruled a Protestant nation. He was incapable of sustaining the pretence that he believed what he did not believe. Public criticism about his commitment to Catholicism had, to a degree, been stifled by his marriage, in 1660, to Anne Hyde, daughter of the Earl of Clarendon and a Protestant. But her sudden death renewed anxieties which Samuel Pepys illustrated in a diary entry for February 1661. Pepys had welcomed the news (false, as it turned out) that Charles II was secretly married to 'the neece of the Prince of Ligne and that he already had two sons by her'. That made it impossible that 'the Duke of York and his family should come to the Crowne' – a highly undesirable prospect, 'he being a professed friend to the Catholiques'.[1]

In 1668, James married for a second time. His new wife was a Catholic – Mary Beatrice, daughter of the Duchess of Modena – and, according to Pepys, it was because of her that James began openly to observe the rituals of the Catholic Church. A few weeks after the second marriage the diarist noted that the Duke of York 'and his lady' had begun publicly to take part in the 'silly devotions'[2] required by Rome. It took four years for James completely to abandon the Church of England's rites and rituals. In 1672 he failed, for the first time, to take Easter Communion with the rest of the formally Protestant royal family. In 1685 his succession was greeted with more apprehension than joy.

Suspicions that James would be an openly Catholic king were quickly confirmed. On the first Sunday of his reign he attended High Mass in the Queen's chapel in St James's and, on his instruction, the funeral of Charles II was conducted, in John Evelyn's words, 'very obscurely'.[3] The secrecy led to the obvious assumption that Charles had been sent to meet his Maker with a Requiem Mass. The new King's instructions about the Coronation Service were disturbingly explicit. Nothing was to be said, sung or done that was contrary to Catholic doctrine. In consequence, it was assumed that James had been anointed and crowned by his confessor on the previous night and that

224

the public ceremony was not so much an act of dedication as a public show of respect for the throne he had inherited.

James' first address to the Privy Council was, at its face value, a model of moderation. 'I have often hithertofore ventured my life in defence of this nation and shall go as far as any man in preserving it in all its just rights and liberties.'[4] But to many members of the Council the endorsement of freedom and democracy sounded like the beginning of a process by which his co-religionists would gradually evolve from disadvantaged minority into a church militant that was big enough and bold enough to dominate English religious life. Catholics increased Protestant fears by responding to James' promise of tolerance with an explosion of triumphant public enthusiasm, which was interpreted as the prologue to the Catholic monarch imposing his faith on a Protestant people. Catholic newspapers and broadsheets multiplied and began to argue both for the acceptance of Roman doctrine and against the acceptance of Anglican clergy as genuine priests. Great families who had employed priests to celebrate Mass in secrecy opened their private chapels for public worship. In Baswick in Staffordshire, the Fowlers decorated their chapel with pictures of Jesus Christ, the Virgin Mary, Thomas Aquinas and St Peter and Mary Magdalen and Sts Monica, Dominic and Thomas à Becket. They also bought a cope and mitre, as well as vestments for each stage of the liturgical cycle, so that they were prepared to welcome any priest or bishop who paid them a visit on any Sunday of the year.[5] No doubt they hoped to welcome John Leyburn, who was appointed Vicar Apostolic of England and Titular Bishop of Hadrumetum in the year of James' succession.

The last Marian English bishop, Thomas Goldwell of St Asaph, had died in exile in 1585. Cardinal William Allen, the founder of the English Colleges in Douai and Rome, had possessed the title of Prefect of the English Mission, but was never able to visit England. From then on there had been a series of appointments which – for reasons ranging from bombastic temperament to poor health – had done little to further the Catholic cause. James' succession and John Leyburn's appointment made Catholics believe that God had not forgotten England.

Leyburn was, by background and instinct, a scholar – first a student in, and then the Principal of, the English College at Douai. Much of his first year in England was occupied by a tour of the north and Midlands, during which he baptised countless converts, administered the sacrament to men and women who had not received it in years and confirmed 20,857 Catholics – including 422 in Stafford, 499 in Edgbaston and 360 in Newcastle.[6] In a single month he solidified the support Rome had always enjoyed in Lancashire with the mission that confirmed 1,143 men and women in Preston, 1,182 in Tulketh and 1,252 in Wigan.[7] Leyburn's strength was the belief that the tasks of making new Catholics and sustaining old ones could be combined. In 1687, his pastoral letter to the Catholics of England included the usual exhortations to the clergy 'to labour in more than the ordinary measure' and to the gentry 'to enlarge their charity'. But it ended with an elegantly expressed admission of the limited status of the Catholic Church in England. 'Being fallen into other hands than those [it was] intended for [it was] reduced unto its prime [original] condition and accordingly may, by the rules of justice as well as piety, require to be maintained after the prime method.'[8] And it seems that his admission of the English Catholic Church's limited status – and its consequent duty to proselytise – was endorsed by King James. Leyburn had served in Rome as secretary to the Dominican Cardinal Philip Howard who, in 1679, had been made (absentee) Protector of England. But, when the time came to revive the role of resident Vicar Apostolic, the King had interceded with the Pope and, with Howard's self-sacrificial agreement, secured the appointment of John Leyburn.

Leyburn's arrival did not mark the absolute end of the parochial, rather than missionary, approach to the work of the English Catholic Church. An Association of Staffordshire Clergy – deeply suspicious of regulars in general, and Jesuits in particular – attempted to revive and perpetuate practices that were universally accepted when England was a Catholic country. Priests were to say no more than two Masses a day and provide pastoral care as well as perform their offices and grant absolution. To emphasise the parochial obligation, the Association required that once a month a pastoral message be 'read to our flocks . . . so that every penitent may know its own pastor and call on him when need requires'. Nor was a priest 'to depart any considerable distance out of the county'.[9] But the Staffordshire clergy were standing in the path of history – and probably in conflict with the view of its Catholic king. James certainly looked favourably upon the Jesuits and probably accepted that his Church was destined to remain a minority in his lifetime.

Whatever view they held of England's Catholic future, the relaxation of hostility towards their teaching made it possible for both regular and secular priests to perform their ministry with a confidence they had not previously enjoyed. They were also helped, in or about 1688, by the open publication of a new version of the catechism, the main instrument of Catholic teaching. Earlier versions had been either wordy and old-fashioned or large, complex and expensive. So the *Abstract*, prepared by John Gother 'for the use of Children and ignorant people', was particularly welcome. Gother's concern for the humble and meek was not in doubt. He had offended rich Catholics by accusing them of overworking their servants on the nights before feast days, in order to recoup time lost to labour on the holiday. And he was a severe critic of the casual irreverent attitude displayed towards the sacraments by the gentry. Some took Communion 'in such a disrespectful undress as would be an affront to the meanest Friend'. Their conduct could 'be called nothing less than stepping out of bed to the Altar'.[10] Others 'approached the Holy Table, powdered, perfumed, bare-necked or any other way set forth as seems suitable for the ball'.

John Gother also attempted to popularise ideas about the Christian vocation which echoed the Protestant ethic of redemption through hard work. His *Instructions for Particular States and Conditions of Life* asserted that 'He has expressly commanded that they shall eat their Bread by the Sweat of their Brows' – a slight misquotation of Genesis 3:19. He held the, slightly heretical, view that greater stress should be placed on redemption by grace and faith. Even more controversial were his reservations about the merits of monastic life. His ideal priests worked among the people. 'If, in Submission to this Command, they undertake their Work, it is certain that their daily lives will be as much an Act of Religion and Obedience, as what those do who live in a Cloyster.'[11]

Reservations about the virtue of rejecting the wicked world complemented – some would say compounded – Gother's rigorous view of the priest's obligations. It was the clergy's duty to protect their followers from the sins that surrounded them by 'drawing upon himself the difficulties, calumnies and insults of men by those undoubted truths of which it is his duty to speak'.[12] All in all, Gother appears to be one of the most attractive characters in the sombre drama of late-seventeenth century religion. But his importance lay not in his personality, but in his advocacy that the secular clergy accept a missionary role, side by side with their regular brothers. He had not given up hope of England's redemption. Like other plans for reform and reorganisation, all Gother's initiative was overshadowed by the controversy that diverted attention from all other religious issues – the Catholic king's relations with his Protestant Parliament.

It seems unlikely that King James spent much time considering the form that English Catholicism should take. He simply wanted to do the most he could, and the best possible to promote a faith to which he subscribed long before his accession to the throne, and there is nothing to suggest that he ever even contemplated the creation of a continental-style theocratic despotism. But the spectre of an absolute

monarchy haunted England. And in 1685 – the year of his accession –
France provided a terrible example of the tyranny that English Protestants feared. Louis XIV revoked the Edict of Nantes, which had
guaranteed freedom of worship to his Huguenot subjects. About 1,500
of their leaders were made galley slaves. 'Popery and slavery, like to
sisters, go hand in hand,' wrote the Earl of Shaftesbury.[13] Perhaps as
many as 80,000 Huguenots fled to England, bringing with them their
skills and horror stories of life under a Catholic despot.

The fear of Catholic tyranny was felt even in James' own family.
James' only surviving son had died in 1671. So Mary and Anne –
daughters by his first marriage, who had been brought up as
Protestants – were inevitably drawn into the arguments about the
succession. Mary was thought to be irrevocably Protestant. In 1677,
she had married – on Charles II's initiative – William Prince of Orange,
and life in the Netherlands had confirmed the principles of faith and
authority that she had been taught as a girl. But there was a
good deal of loose talk about Anne being converted to Catholicism
and being named as James' successor.

Paul Barrillon, the French Ambassador, speculated about the
possibility, but wisely concluded that the idea was 'chimerical and
impracticable',[14] and a visitor from Versailles asked the Danish envoy
in London – probably on his own initiative – if Prince George of
Denmark would be agreeable to Anne, his wife, converting to Catholicism. Surprisingly, Prince George sent a reply: Anne had already begun
to take instruction. The answer was a lie – no doubt prompted by
George's desire to share the crown of England. His hopes were dashed
by his father-in-law who, on being urged by the Pope to lead his
daughter to Rome, replied that she had been 'brought up by people
who inspired in her a great aversion to the Catholic Church and had
a very stubborn nature'. He added, by way of substantiating his assessment of her wilful character, that – with the deliberate intention of
demonstrating her dissent – she carried on conversation with her
neighbour at table while the priest was saying grace. He might have
added that if Anne showed the slightest sympathy for Catholics or
Catholicism, Mary always reminded her of her Protestant duty to
protect England from the fate which had befallen the Huguenots.

On the day that his brother died, James told the Privy Council that
he relied, in all that he did, on the loyalty of the Church of England.
His misplaced confidence, like his abiding fear of a rebellion that
would end with his exile, was the product of his father's reign and
death, and it caused him to act in a way which he should have realised
was certain to antagonise men whom he needed to be his friends.

Sometimes his insensitive impetuosity was justified by the reckless espousal of noble causes. Within a month of his succession he had told the Privy Council of his emollient intentions and gone on to instruct judges, on his own authority, to release from gaol all 'Popish priests', recusants who refused to attend Church of England services and would not (or could not) pay the prohibitive £20 a month fine which their refusal incurred; and, more worrying to men and women who were fearful of a Catholic *coup d'état*, prisoners who had been convicted of refusing to swear the Oaths of Allegiance and Royal Supremacy. There were many prosperous and powerful Catholics who feared that James' enthusiasm for the complete abolition of the penal laws could have only one result: an end to the partial and selective tolerance which they already enjoyed.

Their fears proved to be justified. In March 1686, Sir James Reresby, a Protestant, described how James had promoted the interests of the Catholic Church in the first year of his reign. He lacked either the power or the will to impose on Parliament the repeal of the punitive legislation. So, said Sir James, he gave all the 'encouragement he could to the increase of his own [Church] by putting more Papists into office here [but especially in Ireland]'.[15] That – as the King was foolish enough to admit – was a calculated first step towards his ultimate goal. In May 1686 he told the Papal Nuncio that the repeal of the penal legislation would ensure that 'two years later, England would become a Catholic country'.[16] That was exactly what the Protestants feared.

The idea of the, inevitably gradual, creation of a Catholic state was not universally popular among Catholics. Aristocrats among the laity sought to retain the ascendancy over the priesthood which had been achieved during the years of Elizabethan persecution when Mass was most frequently said in safe houses. The revival of a clerical establishment threatened their supremacy. And James' plans – whether they succeeded or not – were a prescription for an upheaval. The rich were already left to worship in peace. They saw no reason to jeopardise their comfortable condition. For the next three hundred years the drive towards emancipation was regularly held back, and sometimes even temporarily halted, by Catholics who were fearful of moving too fast. Usually they were persons of privilege whose souls were secured by arrangements which frustrated the punitive and proscriptive laws.

James continued to pluck ideas out of the air. In May 1686 he had written to the Archbishops of Canterbury and York ordering them to instruct all the clergy in their archdiocese not to engage in the dissemination of 'abstruse and speculative notions'[17] about theological matters – effrontery that was made more acceptable to Catholicism's bitter enemies by the additional instruction that they were also to remind the clergy of their duty to read the (quintessentially Protestant) Thirty-Nine Articles twice a year. The Primates obliged, but – inevitably – their injunction was resented to the point of disobedience by some of the clergy. Dr James Sharp was almost certainly not the first transgressor. But because he was Dean of Norwich and Rector of St Giles-in-the-Fields, his sermon – warning Protestants of the folly of sympathising with Catholics and Catholicism – could not be ignored. Proof that rebellion is contagious was provided by the Reverend George Tully – Sub-Dean of York and Canon of Ripon – who, shortly after Dr Sharp's outburst, was reported to have preached a similar sermon. James wrote to Henry Compton, the Bishop of London, ordering him to suspend Sharp for the expression of opinions that were 'unbecoming reflections and improper expressions calculated to beget evil opinion of the king and thereby encourage disobedience, schism and rebellion'. Compton refused.

James reacted by creating an Ecclesiastical Commission with authority over both the Anglican Church and the universities. Its membership included the Lord Chancellor, the Lord Chief Justice, the Lord President of the Council and the Lord Treasurer, as well as three carefully chosen bishops. The Commission's first act was the suspension of the Bishop of London. Henry Compton had agreed, on reflection, to reprove, though not suspend, Sharp. It was a provocative act which compounded the Commission's provocative creation. King James, Supreme Governor of the Church of England, was undoubtedly within his rights to create the Commission. But its mere existence offended the Church and alienated many members of its clergy who, otherwise, would have been loyal to the King. And, because it existed, the temptation to find it work to do was irresistible. The work usually served only to make James more enemies. The Commission became the instrument by which James – following the step-by-step policy that Sir John Reresby had described – attempted to impose his Catholicism on the universities.

There is no way of knowing if James would have survived as a Catholic king had he avoided the self-inflicted damage to his reputation. The King's conduct raised questions about his judgement and (far more important) his integrity, which dissipated whatever goodwill he had initially enjoyed. During the heady early days of his reign it had seemed that Providence, and perhaps even the English people, were on his side. A hundred or so of the 513 Members of the new Parliament

IGNEM VENI MITTERE IN TERRA

THE MARTYR'S PICTURE – English College in Rome

CARDINAL REGINALD POLE
Attributed the Reformation to 'carnal concupiscence'

THOMAS MORE
'The King's good servant but God's first'

JOHN FISHER
'Incomparable for uprightness of life'

FOUNTAINS ABBEY
Dissolved in 1539 and sold to raise royal revenue

THE PILGRIMAGE OF GRACE
Its banner bore the Five Wounds of Christ

THOMAS CRANMER
Claimed to preach 'not new doctrine but old truths'

THOMAS CROMWELL
Outstripped Henry in Protestant zeal

CRANMER, LATIMER AND RIDLEY
As celebrated in Foxe's *Book of Martyrs*

JOHN KNOX
Called the Catholic Church 'the Hoore of Babylon'

CARDINAL DAVID BEATON
The English ambassador paid the assassins

TITUS OATES
Invented the Popish Plot

RICHARD CHALLONER
'The advanced guard of change'

had been elected for the first time. 'Exclusionists' – who would have barred James' path to the throne – were in a minority. Even had the House of Commons chosen to 'refuse supply' – the way in which it had imposed its will on James' father and brother – the new King could have ruled, at least for a time, without the provision of extra funds. And it was ten days before Parliament assembled that Titus Oates was convicted of perjury, defrocked and, so that his perfidy be made public, ordered to be whipped through the streets from Newgate to Tyburn. The first whipping took place on the opening day of the new session. Proof that the Popish Plot had been an invention was expected to ease the King's troubled relationship with Parliament and ensure that he was secure on the throne.

James did not remain untroubled and apparently secure for long. On June 11th 1685, the Duke of Monmouth – Charles II's illegitimate son – landed at Lyme Regis in Dorset and asserted his claim to the throne. The 4,000 followers he attracted were mostly Protestant Dissenters. So his rebellion took on the form of a holy war. After capturing Taunton, Monmouth was defeated by royalist troops at the Battle of Sedgemoor. The prisoners were treated with unrestrained savagery – atrocities for which history has blamed Lord Chief Justice George Jeffreys, who presided at what came to be called 'the bloody assizes'. But King James was at least complicit. Most of the rebels were transported as indentured labour to the West Indies. On his personal instructions, any man among them who refused to acknowledge James' right to rule had an ear cut off.

The experience – behaving as his detractors had always feared that he would – bolstered James' self-confidence. The Marquess of Halifax – Lord President of the Council, but never one of the King's favourites – was asked his opinion of the Test Acts, passed in the reign of Charles II. The King left no doubt about what answer he wanted. Before Halifax could respond, he was warned that James 'would be served by none but those that would be for repeal of the Tests'.[18] Nevertheless Halifax replied that he believed the law should remain unchanged, 'since the nation trusted so much to them that public quiet was largely maintained by that means'. He was dismissed and replaced by the Earl of Sutherland, not yet a Catholic, but an open sympathiser. His appointment had been urged upon the King by Father Edward Petre, a Jesuit who had supervised the education of James' illegitimate children. In the years that lay ahead, Father Petre was to become a source of regular advice to the King and of continual of irritation to those who surrounded the throne.

Father Edward Petre might have been invented to provide

Protestants with spine-chilling stories about Rome's designs on England. He was a member of one of England's noble Catholic families and of England's least popular and most feared religious Order – the Society of Jesus. His close relationship with the King was, in consequence, interpreted as a declaration of the King's militant Catholicism. On the day of his accession James made Petre a priest at the Chapel Royal in St James's Palace and soon thereafter petitioned the Pope first to make Petre a bishop and then to create him cardinal. Both petitions were rejected. James proposed to soften the blow of the papal snub by making Petre a member of the Privy Council. Petre declined on the grounds that his admission to Court would be wildly unpopular in the country. A second offer was accepted in the belief that the passage of time had made his elevation more acceptable.

He was wrong. His conduct was not even acceptable to John Keynes, the Jesuit provincial, who was – unusually for members of his Order – following the instructions of a pastoral letter from the Vicar Apostolic and assisting in the setting up of a network of churches and schools – a more worthy occupation, in his view, than hearing the confessions of royalty. Had it been widely known that letters from Petre had been submitted in evidence at Popish Plot trials – only to be judged inadmissible because they did not relate to that day's defendant – his position at Court would have been unsustainable. Petre maintained his influence, and retained the support of the notoriously fickle James, by warning the King against invented enemies. Each Friday night he held a *camarilla* (caucus) which intrigued against supposed conspirators.

It is doubtful if Petre did any major damage, though he disrupted the smooth working of the Court and Privy Council by persuading some of the King's least perceptive advisers to work through him. His position on the great issues of the day – the speed at which the penal legislation could be repealed, and the King's relationship with the Pope – was largely determined by John Warner, a more substantial fellow Jesuit who, on Petre's recommendation, became James' confessor. But royal favourites always irritate the Court, especially when there is no obvious reason for their status. Edward Petre was probably favoured because of the care he had taken during the time when he was tutor to James' illegitimate children. He became a potent symbol of the King's lack of judgement – a characteristic that defined the reign.

James associated all Puritans with the forces which had deposed and executed his father. So he was reluctant to extend the freedom of worship to them. Ireland, he concluded, would accept the end of the

Test Acts without complaint. And he believed – wrongly, as it turned out – that Scotland would bend more readily to his will than England. In James' judgement, the relaxation of penal laws was best accomplished gradually in all his kingdoms. So, relying on his powers as Supreme Governor of the Church and the authority provided by the royal prerogative, he absolved army officers – as a first step – from the requirement to be practising members of the Protestant faith. His plan to extend freedom of worship to other professions and to public employees was interrupted by the intervention of the judges, led by William Jones, Chief Justice of Common Pleas, who denied the King's right to change or overrule the law. James exercised his right to change the judiciary. The changes did not have the desired effect. Both the Attorney and Solicitor General refused to implement the King's law. Someone (the idea was too convoluted for James' not very subtle mind) had to find a way of changing the judicial mind. A test case was contrived.

Sir Edward Hales, a Catholic of no distinction, was made Governor of Dover, and Arthur Godden, his coachman, was instructed to sue his employer for unlawfully accepting public office, despite not taking the sacraments of the Church as required by the Test Act of 1673, notwithstanding the fact that the Act had been suspended by the King. The case was heard by a bench of carefully chosen judges who, to nobody's surprise, found for Sir Edward on the grounds that the King possessed the power to change the law. The precedent having been established, James proceeded to act in accordance with its provision.

His decisions were as capricious as they were arbitrary. Four Roman Catholic peers were appointed members of the Privy Council and preparations were made to absolve them from the obligation to swear loyalty to the Church of England. The Earl of Castlemaine, a Roman Catholic, was made James' representative in the Vatican. Ferdinand, Count d'Adda, who arrived in England during November 1685 as the Pope's unofficial envoy, received such a warm welcome that, six months later, he was promoted Archbishop of Amasia *in partibus infidelium* (in heretical countries). His elevation was celebrated in the Chapel Royal, where James knelt at his feet. Within the year he was welcomed at Windsor as official Papal Nuncio. The Duke of Somerset, Lord of the Bedchamber in Waiting, refused to conduct the visitor to the presence chamber on the grounds that it was illegal for him, if not the sovereign, to do business with Papists. James, in the euphoria of the moment, overlooked the insubordination. Catholics were appointed, on the King's initiative, to key positions in the University of Oxford. Obadiah Walker was made Master of University College and was told that he could use whichever room he chose for the exclusive practice of his devotions. John Massey was promoted Dean of Christ Church and was freed from the obligation to attend Church of England services.

James' policy in Ireland was the same mixture of caution and the sudden exercise of arbitrary power in support of individual Catholics and the increase of Catholic influence. His first appointment as Lord Lieutenant was the Protestant Earl of Clarendon. Less than a year after he took office, Clarendon questioned the right of the Earl of Tyrconnell – Commander-in-Chief in Ireland – to remove all Protestant officers from one regiment under his command. Tyrconnell complained to the King, who (encouraged by Archbishop Russell of Dublin) made him Lord Lieutenant in Clarendon's place. Clarendon wrote in his diary, with ironic understatement, 'Sometimes I think it may be possible that the king may have altered his measures so as to bring Roman Catholics into his employment.'[19] He might have added that James should have known that the recruitment of Catholic army officers enabled his enemies to claim that he was planning to impose his religion on the country by military force. If James did realise the dangers of the path he followed, he still saw no reason to change route. He proposed to appoint the Catholic Earl of Carlingford Commander-in-Chief of English troops in the Netherlands, but William, Prince of Orange – James' son-in-law, nephew and husband of the heir presumptive – rejected the proposal. It was an unheeded warning of trouble that lay ahead.

Before he became King, James had been confident that he could rely on the Prince of Orange and at the beginning of his reign he had written to his son-in-law in language which made clear that he certainly wanted his sympathy and might, one day, need his help. 'As for things here, they do not mend but every day grow worse ... All things look as they did at the beginning of the rebellion.'[20] But by 1687 William gratuitously condemned James' determination to repeal the Test Acts. Caspar Fagel, Holland's First Minister, published an open letter which explained that William and Mary 'freely consented to covering of papists from the severities of the laws against them on account of their religion and also that they might have free exercise of it in private ... But they could not consent to the repeal of those laws that tended only to the security of the Protestant religion.'[21] The importance of the pronouncement was that it represented the view of the heir presumptive to the throne of England.

William, prematurely concerned with the laws of the land that his wife expected to rule, sent Everard van Dykvelt as Ambassador

Extraordinary to London with the task of encouraging support for the continuation of the Test Acts. James, not unreasonably, refused to see him, but instructed his temporary friend, John Churchill, to remind the Dutchman that, despite there being no penal laws in the Netherlands, Protestantism remained secure in Holland. It was a good debating point. But it did not reduce the damage done by Prince William's categorical rejection of repeal or his confidence that, one day, he would be in a position to determine the laws of England. Van Dykvelt took home a message that, in 1688, gave William confidence that his coup would succeed. The Princess Anne, the Ambassador reported, 'was resolved by the assistance of God to suffer all extremities, even death itself, rather than be brought to change her religion'.[22] The next in line to the throne after Mary would not stand in the way of a Protestant revolt. All that was needed to set it in train was more provocation. James could be relied upon to provide it.

Part of the pressure on James came from the knowledge that piecemeal promotion of Catholic interests usually served to antagonise Protestant opinion without satisfying Catholic aspirations. Nowhere was that more true than in Ireland, where the King – wanting to maintain English domination – maintained the land settlement which was the economic manifestation of the Reformation. Charles Kelly, High Sheriff of County Roscommon, spoke for the whole Irish peasantry when he complained that by 'failing to restore their estates' James had flouted 'the hereditary rights of the [Catholic] natives'.[23] Land hunger and Catholic suppression remained inseparable and related grievances in seventeenth-century Ireland and were to remain so for two hundred years.

Catholic hopes in Scotland had inevitably been over-excited by the accession of James VII to the throne that had been occupied – some people would argue with more grace than distinction – by Mary, Queen of Scots, his great-grandmother. However, the new King gave them the uncharacteristic (and dispiriting) advice that they should 'do their business quietly at the beginning otherwise they may undo all'.[24] No doubt they were relieved to discover that James' idea of quiet calm included an order that all Scottish priests abroad must return home and prepare for the reconversion of their native land. To facilitate that process, in May 1686 he had asked the Scottish Parliament to repeal the laws which penalised his 'innocent subjects, those of the Roman Catholic religion'.[25] Reluctant to rely on Scottish tolerance alone, he offered, in return, the inducement of free trade with England and the promise to guarantee the rights of the Kirk in law. The Scots agreed – but only if the King further enhanced the status of the Protestant religion by making the Kirk the established Church in Scotland by law. Displeased by the reception of his proposal, the King prorogued Parliament, opened the Chapel Royal in Holyrood House for Catholic worship, established a Jesuit school in the same palace and instructed the Scottish Privy Council to rescind the penal laws. The Privy Council refused and was replaced with Catholic members. In February 1687 – nine months after he had begun what he regarded as an exercise in reasonable compromise – he lost patience with even his highly attenuated form of due process and, using the powers that the courts had ruled were vested in him, acted alone.

On February 12th 1687, James issued his *Declaration of Indulgence to Tender Consciences* in Scotland. Seven weeks later he published an identical *Declaration* for England. Both proclamations promised 'free exercise of their religion for Roman Catholics and of our indulgence to Dissenters', though they still prohibited 'field conventicles'; for some reason James – like his grandfather – feared that open-air services would encourage subversion. Although the 'indulgences' were granted under the royal prerogative, James claimed 'to have no doubt of the concurrence of our two Houses of Parliament when we shall think it convenient for them to meet'. That was a lie. He had canvassed parliamentary opinion and found it overwhelmingly opposed to relaxation of the penal laws.

The most elegant argument employed in the furious debate which followed was advanced by the Marquess of Halifax in his *Letter to a Dissenter upon Occasion of His Majesty's late gracious Declaration of Indulgence*. That polemic asserted that 'The alliance between Liberty and Infallibility is bringing together the most contrary things that are in the world.'[26] Within James' own family, the objection to his policy was less philosophical. Anne had no doubt that the 'desire to take off the Test [Act] and all other laws against Catholics is only a pretence to bring in Popery'[27] and wrote to her sister, 'I believe, in a little while no Protestant will be able to live here.' As a result of what he regarded as his daughters' disloyalty, the King forbade the sisters to correspond with each other.

James recalled that his father had twice drafted Declarations of Indulgence and twice been told by Parliament and the judges that, in doing so, he exceeded his powers. He did, however, undoubtedly possess the power to prorogue Parliament. So, following what had become a family tradition, he suspended sittings for eight months while he prepared the ground for what he intended to be the complete repeal of the Test Acts – 'having been ever against persecuting any for conscience sake'.[28] Protestants were offered the reassurance that members of the Church of England would be 'free to exercise their religion as by the law established', but the Declaration ended with an assertion which was necessary both to salve the King's conscience and to confirm the sincerity of the whole Declaration. 'We cannot but heartily wish, as will easily be believed, that all people of our dominions were members of the Catholic Church.'

The Declaration was greeted with an orgy of gratitude – some spontaneous and some (including the responses of half a dozen Church of England bishops) contrived. The chorus of counterfeit support grew so loud that an unknown satirist published *The Humble Address of the Atheists, or sects of Epicureans*. It congratulated the King on freeing 'the nation from the troublesome Bygottries of Religion' and encouraging 'men to conclude that there is nothing sacred and Divine but Trade and Empire'.[29] There were, however, dissenting voices. Among them were the shrill tones of Princess Anne: 'In taking away the Test and penal laws they have taken away our religion and if that be done, farewell to all happiness for once the Papists have everything in their hands, all we poor Protestants have but a dismal time to hope for.'[30] And Anne was as passionately opposed to freedom for Dissenters as she was against the toleration of Catholicism. 'It is a melancholy prospect that we of the Church of England have. Everyone has the free exercise of their religion – on purpose, no doubt, to ruin us.'

Despite his assertion of confidence in the libertarian instincts of his legislators, James remained reluctant to put his judgement to the test. So, instead of recalling Parliament, he pursued his policy of promoting the Catholic cause in whatever way his sovereign powers allowed. On the day of his Declaration of Indulgence he instructed the Fellows of Magdalen College, Oxford, to fill the vacancy – caused by the death of the President – by electing Anthony Farmer, a Roman Catholic. Farmer, an alcoholic libertine, was unacceptable to the college. The Fellows ignored the King's instruction and elected, as President, John Hough, already a Fellow of Magdalen. Hough was confirmed in his office by the Bishop of Winchester, the College Visitor. He took the oaths which, thanks to the Declaration of Indulgence, were no longer obligatory and was installed as President. James referred the election to his Ecclesiastical Commission. It declared the election of John Hough invalid and, on James' instruction, appointed Samuel Parker, the Bishop of Oxford (thought to be a secret Catholic), in his place. The Fellows refused to accept him as they had refused to accept Anthony Farmer.

James played for time. He decided to make 'a progress' through the Midlands and West Country in order to allow his loyal and grateful people to see his royal person. The journey was punctuated with assurances of his good intentions towards Protestant Dissenters, but it began and ended in controversy. After a brief visit to the south coast, he joined his wife at Bath, where she had taken the waters in the hope of encouraging conception, before moving on for the major part of the tour. On the eve of their departure, the royal couple attended a service in the abbey. Despite the presence of the Bishop of Bath and Wells, the sermon was preached – according to the King's wishes – by one of his Roman Catholic chaplains. On August 3rd the progress ended in Oxford.

The Fellows of Magdalen College were summoned to meet James in Christ Church, where they were reprimanded in the majestic language of a king betrayed. 'Ye have been a stubborn turbulent college ... Is this your Church of England loyalty? ... Go home and show yourselves good members of the Church of England ... I will be obeyed.'[31] The Fellows politely refused to act in a way that violated the college statutes. They were dismissed and, in an act more vindictive than judicial, the Ecclesiastical Commission ordered that they should not receive any other Church appointment. Samuel Parker held precarious office for six months and then died. His successor was Bonaventure Giffard, who was to become Vicar Apostolic for London. He died, in office, at the age of ninety-one – probably unaware that Leyburn had advised the King that making him President of Magdalen was a recklessly provocative invitation to rebellion.

Not only did James fail to take Leyburn's good advice about Oxford, but he determined to impose his Catholic will on Cambridge. He instructed the Vice Chancellor to admit a Benedictine monk to the degree of Master of Arts without taking the oath of loyalty and without possessing the necessary academic qualifications. The first concession was his to make. The second, as the Vice Chancellor told him, was not. The Ecclesiastical Commission was, once more, asked to adjudicate between the King and a disloyal subject. To nobody's surprise, it found for the King, and the Vice Chancellor was removed from office. There is no reason to believe that James ever wanted to take over the universities and make them instruments of the Catholic Church. His instinct was to promote the interests of individual Catholics. When he was frustrated in that endeavour, a combination of vanity and inherited belief in the sovereign rights of kings made him use every power at his disposal to get his way. But to Oxford and Cambridge, he appeared to be a tyrant. His pointless acts of petty tyranny were to count heavily against him when England came seriously to consider the sort of monarch it wanted on the throne.

Mounting Protestant concern about the future of their Church was not matched by increasing confidence among the whole Catholic population. Its more prudent members feared that James was moving too fast towards their full emancipation for it to be accepted by what had become a clear majority opinion in favour of the Church of England. And the Catholic grandees who had felt that they owned their Church when, as a fugitive faith, it was practised more in the seclusion of great houses than in the parish churches, felt understandable – if impious – regret that their power was slipping away. But the Vatican realised that the time had come to establish some sort of organisation in a country which, by the time of James' accession, was accepted in Rome as needing the framework of a missionary organisation. The result, in January 1688, was the division of England into four Apostolic regions – Northern, Midland, London and Western (which included Wales) – each with a Vicar of its own.

The four 'bishops' issued a joint pastoral letter, which told their several flocks: 'now you are in Circumstances of letting it [their faith] appear abroad and of edifying your Neighbours by professing it publicly and living up to the Rules prescribed by it'.[32] Leyburn – walking the streets of London 'in a long cassock and cloak, with a golden cross hanging by a black ribbon round his neck' – had hardly hidden his light under a bushel. But by 1688 Catholics were feeling sufficiently confident to celebrate their beliefs more openly than at any time since the reign of Queen Mary. Relief and rejoicing were tempered with charity. 'The memory of past hardships you have suffered from some among them [Protestant bigots] may be apt to create provoking animosities and the Liberty you now enjoy may possibly tempt you to insult those who formerly abridged you of it. But it must be your care to prevent or suppress all such irregular Motions.' Unfortunately, the quality of the organisation, which was available to the Vicars Apostolic, did not match the ebullience of their prose. They supervised the Church in their vast districts with little or no help. Cardinal Wiseman, looking back from the heyday of Victorian formality, complained that the Vicars Apostolic neither kept records nor observed proper procedures. 'The whole episcopal regimen' he wrote, 'seems to have led a sort of nomadic life, wandering about in stage coaches and gigs from place to place.'[33]

Although James possessed both the will and the power to protect and promote individual Catholics and could, by declarations of tolerance made on his royal initiative, overrule the worst excesses of prejudice and bigotry, absolute and lasting security required Parliament to repeal the penal legislation. That would only be possible in a new

House of Commons, from which many (if not all) the general 'Exclu-
sionist' Members had been ejected. James proposed to bring that about
by calling an election – after he had made sure that most of the
successful candidates, many of whom would be returned unopposed,
were sympathetic to his aims. The Lord Lieutenants were to ensure
that reliable men were nominated. But that, in turn, required the
removal of unreliable Lord Lieutenants. Two Catholics – Lord Walde-
grave in Somerset and the Earl of Huntingdon in Leicester – replaced
Protestants, and eleven other changes were made in three months.

In the less loyal counties, Justices, sheriffs and Deputy Lieutenants
were cross-examined about their willingness to support the abolition
of the Test Acts and penal laws. Office-holders who claimed that
conscience prevented their agreement were urged at least to raise no
objection to the King asserting unilaterally that every one of his
subjects enjoyed freedom of worship. The Lord Lieutenants, who
presided at the meetings, emphasised that the liberty would be available to dissenters of every denomination and that even functionaries
who were not sympathetic to reform owed a duty of loyalty to the
King – on whose goodwill their appointments depended. But the
Members of Parliament who were eventually elected were not responsive to the King's wishes. Neither of the appeals – one to the principle
of universal tolerance and the other to the personal protection of
self-interest – had the desired effect. James was eventually forced to
conclude that he could not contrive a Parliament that would bend to
his will. On May 4th 1688, using the royal prerogative, he made an
Order in Council which suspended the penal legislation and the Test
Acts and ordered that this second Declaration of Indulgence should
be read out in parish churches in London on the last two Sundays in
May and in the provinces on the two following Sundays.

Eight days later, William Sancroft, the Archbishop of Canterbury,
was host to a dinner in Lambeth Palace at which the guests were about
a dozen supposedly carefully chosen bishops. The choice was clearly
not as careful as the Archbishop would have wanted, for the bishops
of Chester and St David's left in protest when the discussion had barely
begun. None of those who remained wanted to be party to the dissemination of the King's Declaration, but some of them feared that outright
refusal would amount to disloyalty to the crown and would undermine
the reputation for fidelity that was central to the stability of an Established Church. So it was agreed that a deputation should petition the
King to change his mind. Six bishops, though not Sancroft, met James
on May 18th, reinforced by the news that clergy in the City of London
were unanimous in their refusal to obey the royal bidding. They agreed

that they should make clear that their objection was less due to 'any want of tenderness to dissenters' than reluctance to involve the Church in a constitutional dispute which might end with Parliament ruling that the Declaration of Indulgence was illegal. Princess Anne applauded the refusal to publicise what she called 'the most seditious document I have ever seen'.[34]

The bishops were not given an opportunity to develop their nice point. As soon as the King had read the petition, he accused the signatories of rebellion. The Bishop of Ely's protestation – 'We rebels! Sir, we are prepared to die at your feet'[35] – was rendered slightly less effective by the delegation's obdurate refusal to order that the proclamation be read from the pulpits of their several dioceses. The bishops were dismissed from the royal presence.

Three weeks later they were summoned, together with the Archbishop of Canterbury, to appear before the Privy Council, where they were told that they would be charged with seditious libel. George Jeffreys – elevated from Lord Chief Justice to Lord Chancellor – would agree that they should be released from custody, while waiting to appear before the King's Bench, only if they posted bail. They refused on the grounds that they were members of the House of Lords and therefore should be spared such indignities. They were remanded in custody and sent, by barge, along the Thames to the Tower. John Evelyn wrote, 'Wonderful is the concern of the people for them … Infinite crowds of people on their knees begging their blessing and praying for them as they passed along Tower wharf.'[36] It was further proof that England had become a Protestant nation – a fact that King James II recognised, without fully understanding how determined its people were to defend themselves from what they believed was the threat from Rome.

Few people of any substance wanted the King to persist with the proposed prosecutions. Many Catholics as well as Protestants were outraged by the imprisonment of the old and sick Archbishop of Canterbury, and most Catholics at Court thought it was foolish for the King to promote a fight which he could not possibly win. It was suggested that he might save face and bring the affair to a conclusion by first admonishing and then releasing the seven prisoners. But he insisted – advised, it was suspected, by Father Petre, who was influenced by the Jesuits – that the prosecution go ahead. The trial began in Westminster Hall on June 15th, but was adjourned for two weeks during which the bishops were released on bail. The resumed hearing lasted for a day, at the end of which two of the four judges summed up for the King and two for the bishops. The jury deliberated into the night and returned a verdict of not guilty. The result provided ample evidence of where, when they had to choose between Protestant Church and Catholic King, the English people's sympathy lay. But on the day before the seven bishops were brought before the Privy Council an event occurred which made James' deposition inevitable. Queen Mary gave birth to a son.

During the fifteen years of her marriage Mary's numerous pregnancies had ended with miscarriages, stillbirths or the early death of the baby. It was therefore generally assumed that an heir apparent was out of the question and that the heir presumptive, the staunchly anti-Catholic Princess Mary, would inherit the throne. The unexpected birth undermined the argument that all Protestants had to do was wait because time was not on Rome's side. Catholics exacerbated Protestant fears by declaring that God had worked another miracle.

Princess Anne denied that the Queen had ever given birth. She invented the slander – joyously repeated by rabid Protestants – that the baby was a changeling who had been smuggled into the palace in a warming pan. She claimed 'good reason to suspect trickery ... the principles of that religion being such that they will stop at nothing, be it never so wicked, if it will promote their interests'.[37] Although she claimed there was 'much reason to believe it is a false belly', the best she could do, by way of evidence, was the claim that the Queen 'has always gone into the next room to put on her smock'. The envious gossip had no effect. The Catholic King had a Catholic successor.

It may well be that, even without the birth of the boy who became the Old Pretender, James' undisciplined, haphazard and precipitous promotion of Catholic interests would have proved too much for the Protestant establishment to stomach indefinitely. But it is at least possible that they would have made the best of him, in the knowledge that he was to be succeeded by his unequivocally Protestant daughter and her Dutch consort. The unexpected arrival extinguished all possibility of James living out his reign. William landed at Torbay with enough troops to defeat James, had the King chosen to fight. He did not – a wise choice, in the light of the desertion of his best general, John Churchill (soon to be Duke of Marlborough) and, perhaps more important, the rising up of what had become a Protestant nation in support of a Protestant claimant to the throne. James, his wife and baby son fled to France where the Bishop of Rheims, with more wit than sensitivity, compared him to Henry of Navarre, his maternal grandfather. The French king had famously declared that Paris was 'worth a Mass'. His grandson had thought the Mass more important than the throne of three kingdoms.

There was an exodus of Catholic gentry to France. Those who could do so joined the King and Court at Saint-Germain. Rich widows joined the Convent of Our Lady of Syon in Paris or the Poor Clares in Rouen. It was at Syon that the cult of James the Martyr was born. After his death, a relic of James was displayed in the chapel and he was described in language that owed nothing to Christian charity. 'Holy King James of blessed and glorious memory . . . was by the perfidious and undutiful and unnatural baseness of his son-in-law and nephew . . . dethroned and driven out of the kingdom; that detestable Prince joining with the treacherous defection of the Protestant subjects of England and a malevolent party which were the dregs of Cromwell's Vipers' blood.'[38]

The Catholic émigrés dreamed of a second Restoration and plotted and planned – sometimes with the encouragement of Spain or France – for England and Scotland to become Catholic countries again. But it was too late. A Church of England, with its chauvinistic overtones, appealed to a people who had no instinctive interest in dogma and liturgy, but had come to believe that the island race had little in common with its continental neighbours. James II offered false hope of a return to Rome. After his deposition, not even the dream survived. Catholics gradually came to accept the need to learn how to survive in an irrevocably Protestant nation.

CHAPTER 15

Fidelity and Intire Obedience

William of Orange landed in England on November 5th 1688. News of his arrival stimulated the worst sort of rejoicing. In London, mobs attacked priests and broke into Roman Catholic churches and chapels. In Birmingham, troops who supported William first ransacked and then burned down the Catholic chapel. Mass houses in Cambridge, Hereford, Norwich, York and Bristol were attacked and damaged. At Ulverston in Lancashire, Clement Smith, a Jesuit, 'was beset by a mob of nearly a hundred men ... He passed the night in a little hut and at day-break betook himself to the woods ...' For three months he was 'compelled to lie so loosely hidden that he was unable to pace about his room'.[1] The Catholic governor of Dover Castle was evicted and replaced by a reliable Protestant who was a mercer by trade.

The monastery in Clerkenwell was burned down and the rioting became so severe that the City of London Aldermen – although in sympathy with the rioters' cause – decided it was necessary to disperse the mob. Normally, the job would have been done by the Trained Bands but, since they could not be trusted to obey their orders, the army was called in. During the confrontation that followed, five rioters were killed. The inquest into their deaths concluded that they were respectable citizens who were loyal to the King whose assumption of the throne they had anticipated by several weeks. The verdict was murder.

When it was clear that the 'glorious revolution' had succeeded, attacks on Catholics and Catholic churches were replaced by panic at the prospect of the victims turning on their tormentors. A document – known as *The Third Declaration* and fraudulently published in William's name – was circulated in the London streets. It warned of plans to massacre Protestants and of a Catholic plot again to set fire to London. Magistrates were instructed to disarm all Papists and execute any Catholic who refused to relinquish his weapon. The Lord Mayor of London – either as the result of stupidity or malice – believed the *Declaration* to be authentic and ordered the arrest of all Catholics who were found to be bearing arms within the city.

After James fled to France, the mobs – no longer terrified of a

Catholic resurgence – began a second orgy of destruction and plunder. The house owned by the printer who had produced Catholic tracts for James was attacked. So were the foreign embassies and the lodgings of the Papal Nuncio. The fear of another Great Fire was replaced by the threat to burn down houses that were occupied by Catholics – accompanied by the oath that 'the flames shall not be put out until the Prince of Orange comes to town'.[2] Despite his attempts to demonstrate his support for William, George Jeffreys, the Lord Chancellor, was recognised as the judge who had presided at the Bloody Assizes and had condemned to death or deportation Monmouth's followers after the West Country rebellion. He was committed, in protective custody, to the Tower of London. There was a brief resumption of panic – caused by the rumour that Irish immigrants had burned down Uxbridge and were advancing east. But that soon passed. Protestants felt triumphantly in control.

The Declaration of Rights – presented to William and Mary by Parliament on February 13th 1689 with the offer of the joint crown – was followed by a Bill of Rights, which gave the Declaration legislative effect. The spirit in which both documents were written was exemplified by a clause which prohibited a Catholic, or the spouse of a Catholic, occupying the English throne. The evidence suggests that most Catholics accepted the prohibition calmly. Being of a practical disposition, they were more concerned about the provision that – ironically and inadvertently – prevented even a benevolent monarch providing protection against a hundred and fifty years of legalised discrimination. Parliament had never been persuaded to repeal any of the penal laws. But, from time to time, the penalties had been suspended by the King exercising the royal prerogative. The Bill of Rights deprived the sovereign of that power. So the penal acts remained in force.

Within weeks the bill was augmented by two new statutes, which the new King's fearful advisers were easily able to convince him – with the support of his aggressively Protestant wife – were essential protection against popish plots. The first prohibited Catholics from holding arms or owning a horse worth more than £5 – a provision which caused a sudden reduction in the valuation of the best hunters in Ireland. It also gave Protestants the right to purchase, for the same sum, any horse owned by a Catholic. Lord Arundel was said to have had four horses taken out of the shafts of his carriage, and there were stories of owners shooting their horses rather than selling them for a fraction of their true value.[3] The exclusion of Catholic priests and dissenting ministers from Westminster and London, imposed during the panic of 1665, was confirmed in legislation which made their 'internal exile' permanent.

King William's second act was as vindictive as it was vicious and made nonsense of the (still repeated) claim that the revolution of 1688 was made glorious by the civil liberties that followed. The edict gave notice that anyone who, after March 25th 1700, 'apprehended a Popish bishop, priest or Jesuit' and secured his conviction for 'saying Mass or exercising his functions within the Realm' was to receive £100. 'Every Popish bishop, priest or Jesuit who said Mass should suffer perpetual imprisonment.' Papists were disqualified from purchasing 'land in this Kingdom or [making] a profit out of the same' and a Catholic beneficiary of a family will could be required to sacrifice the legacy in favour of a Protestant with less claim to the inheritance. Catholic education, at home or abroad was prohibited.

Two months before the arrival of the Prince of Orange, the Catholic Church's Northern District – a vast expanse of territory, stretching from the Trent to the Tweed – had acquired its first Vicar Apostolic. James Smith was welcomed to the north by a chorus 'of the Clergy and Regulars who sang *Te Deum* publicly'[4] and by the offer of a trooper from Lord Dumbarton's Regiment to stand guard at the door of his York lodgings, which he humbly declined. A Vicar Apostolic was, by definition, excluded from the implied promise of tolerance towards discreet Catholics. So he went into hiding and ministered to his flock in secret. His reports to Rome were written in language that – even had they been intercepted – would not have revealed their true nature. Parishioners were called 'friends' and confirmations were referred to as 'performances'.

From the comparative security of his constantly changing hiding places, Smith had preached the gospel of local loyalty. Priests, he claimed, had a duty to return after training to the area from which they came – no matter how great the danger and how intense the hardship. The proposal was calculated to help the hard north at the expense of the soft south – where the idea was rejected more because of the offence it would cause to gentry with resident priests than because of the reluctance to serve God in a cold climate. But in the north the number of priests increased – sometimes with a little help from the penal laws, which were operated most severely in and about London. Father John Marsh, evicted from 'good places in the South', responded to Smith's call and 'humbly betook himself to the most desolate and laborious place in the [Northern] district ... To assist a great number of poore on the moores.'[5]

At the time of James' flight and supposed abdication there were no more than 20,000 Catholics (about 25 per cent of the total population) in Scotland, served by twenty lay priests, nine Jesuits and four Benedictines.[6] Despite their small numbers, or because of it, they affected the belief that James' brief visit to Edinburgh would mark the beginning of a Roman revival. They were, therefore, disappointed when he offered his followers the uncharacteristically wise advice that they should 'do their business quietly and calmly at the beginning lest they may be undone'.[7] He then undermined his own admonition by ordering all Scottish priests home, to begin the work of reconversion. A printing press, for the production of Catholic literature, was set up, and sung Mass was celebrated in Holyrood House. In anticipation of a renewal of the Presbyterian persecution that had preceded James' accession, the Pope appointed Scotland's first Vicar Apostolic with power over all theological, devotional and liturgical matters. The Jesuits objected and reacted even more strongly when a Vicar General for the Highlands was appointed with the same powers. They appealed to Propaganda Fide, with disastrous consequences for their cause. The Vicar Apostolic was given complete authority over all Scottish priests, lay and regular.

Protestants – in the south of Scotland as in England – reacted to the forced abdication of James II with violent triumphalism. In Edinburgh, rioters attacked and sacked the Chapel Royal. Thomas Nicholson, the recently appointed head of the Catholic Church in Scotland, witnessed the procession which celebrated the sacrilege. 'One of the [mob] went in front with a great crucifix, surrounded by a crowd of children and women carrying torches and shouting for joy.'[8] The rioting confirmed that James' attempt to pacify the Presbyterians had failed. He had hoped that enshrining the rights of the Kirk in law would develop the tolerance that is often the consequence of security. But south of the Highland line, anti-Catholicism was too bitter an instinct to be assuaged by promises of equal treatment for all denominations. The activities of the Jesuits were, as always, particularly resented. Edinburgh, a rabidly Protestant city, had been infuriated by the opening of several Jesuit schools – one in Holyrood House itself. And there was a 'great noyse' in Glasgow when a Father Leslie 'opened up a kynd of private chapel'. From Galloway, James Bruce, a Benedictine monk, reported that the local citizenry was 'much averse from poperie' and the aversion was not moderated by the arrival of Protestant William. The same could have been said for most of the Scottish Lowlands. Life was different further north where, although there were fewer priests than in the south (four as compared to fifteen), there were six times as many communicants. In the early years of William's reign, the Church was sufficiently hopeful about its prospects in the north-west to set up a seminary in Lochaber. Like so many Highland hopes, it did not survive the Jacobite Rebellion.

The Welsh Catholic Church was in too sharp a decline for its prospects to be further prejudiced by either statutory persecution or mob violence. Even the Jesuits were reduced in number after a Protestant raid on their headquarters in Cwm. The Catholics who remained were mostly of the superstitious sort that was peculiar to the Principality. Skirrid in Monmouthshire became a place of pilgrimage, in the belief that the nearby mountain split open at the moment of Christ's death. King James' fate could, by those who believed in such things, be attributed to the power of Welsh religious magic. In the year before he was deposed, he had travelled to the shrine at Holywell to pray for a son – the unexpected heir and successor whose arrival made his downfall inevitable.

James believed that he could regain the throne. For eighteen months he presided over a court in exile at Saint-Germain on the outskirts of Paris. Then, supported by French troops, he landed in Ireland on the first step of what he hoped would be a second Stuart Restoration. An Irish army – already employed in subduing Protestant resistance in the northern counties – was waiting to welcome him. The Irish Parliament declared James the lawful king. In doing so, it exceeded its powers. Poynings Law, which James had enthusiastically endorsed, made the Dublin Parliament subordinate to the Parliament in Westminster. But the temporary nationalists were not in a mood to respect constitutional propriety. Nor were they inclined towards magnanimity. Protestant churches – beginning with Wexford[9] – were closed and confiscated.

On July 1st 1690 the English forces – under the command of John Churchill – defeated the Irish army at the Battle of the Boyne. Further south the war had still to be won for King William. At Limerick the Irish garrison – besieged, relieved and besieged again – held out until October. After six months more of bloody fighting, both sides were ready to negotiate peace. The Irish leaders' initial demands were for complete toleration of Catholics and Catholicism, and the return of land to the owners from whom it had been stolen during the Commonwealth and the Restoration. William could not, or dared not, deprive his Protestant supporters of the spoils they had won in earlier wars – though he was prepared to sacrifice the land which King James himself had acquired in sixteen Irish counties. In the end, battle fatigue rather than benevolence prompted concession. William agreed to guarantee Catholics 'such privileges as are consistent with the laws of Ireland or as they did enjoy in the reign of King Charles II'[10] and the examination of individual claims for the restitution of land rights. What came to be called the Treaty of Limerick went on to promise that the Westminster Parliament would be assembled at the first opportunity and that the King would 'endeavour to procure [for] the said Roman Catholics such further security ... as may preserve them from any disturbance upon account of the said religion'. The wording of the English offer was deliberately perfidious. Progress towards toleration depended on the will of a partisan Protestant Parliament. But at least the land-claim promise was kept. By 1695, 483 of the 491 aplications, made under the provision of the Treaty, had been resolved in favour of the claimant.[11] During the next four years thousands of Irish peasants were transformed into landowners. In Limerick alone, something approaching 1,200 claims were approved. Combined with the amnesty offered to soldiers who had fought for James, the restitution of land rights succeeded in neutralising the threat of another uprising. Eleven thousand Irishmen left Ireland to serve the King of France, and the legend of the Wild Geese was born. There were too many Catholics in Ireland to allow a general persecution to result in anything but continued revolt. So it was Protestant policy to placate the masses at the same time as their leaders were being persecuted and exiled.

By the time that James' hopes of restoration had been extinguished on the banks of the Liffey, the English Parliament had passed the Toleration Act. Its true purpose was winning for William the unequivocal support of Nonconformists. Only those of its provisions that reduced the effect of the penal laws on Protestant Dissenters justified its name. Indeed, its effect might well have been to increase the likelihood of Catholic prosecutions since, by offering relief to anyone who took the Oath of Allegiance, subscribed to the Thirty-Nine Articles and repudiated the doctrine of transubstantiation, it explicitly denied them the toleration it proclaimed. But despite its limited application, the principle embodied in the Act proved infectious and there followed a period during which the penal laws were theoretically strengthened, but their application was increasingly ignored.

The Irish Protestant commercial classes – motivated more by greed than theology – used the fear of revolution as an excuse to demand the expulsion of Catholic merchants from Dublin. The City Corporation agreed. The unyielding attitude of the Church of England episcopate was typified by Anthony Dopping, the Anglican Bishop of Meath. His sermon, on the Sunday morning that followed the signing of the Limerick Treaty, proposed – in a play on words – renunciation of the agreement. Since the Irish followed what true Christians did not regard as a true faith, there was no need to keep faith with them.[12] The King removed Bishop Dopping from the Privy Council, thus strengthening the argument of those Whig historians who chose to argue that William was more progressive than his Parliament and that he did all he could to moderate his ministers' penal instincts. In fact his attitude towards Catholics in Ireland (too many to be suppressed and too far away to mount a rebellion) was fundamentally different from his attitude towards English Papists – as witness his reaction to the 1692 Bill of Indemnity.

The Bill of Indemnity – introduced into the (by then) Protestant Irish Parliament – began with the assertion of a general rule of toleration. But it went on to list so many exceptions that it became a directory of proscribed organisations and would have resulted in the enforced exodus of most of the Irish priesthood. At the suggestion of the Spanish Ambassador, William refused to sign it into law and, in consequence, provoked so wild a reaction among Irish Protestant MPs that the Lord Lieutenant thought it expedient to dissolve Parliament. At the same time in England the requirement that Catholics pay taxes at double the prescribed rate was extended to land tax.

Protestants were certainly right to warn that the Catholic followers of the Stuart cause still harboured faint hopes of James II and VII returning to the English and Scottish thrones. In Lancashire – a county where, by the standards of the late seventeenth century, Catholicism flourished – an Irish-supported rising, planned for 1694, was discovered before it began and its leaders brought to trial. They were imprisoned rather than executed. But the talk of insurrection was grist to the mill of those Westminster Members of Parliament who regretted the King's refusal to sign into law an Irish Indemnity Bill. So they took up the fight, adopted the bill in Westminster and added a clause of their own which would have nullified the provision to restore sequestrated estates. As always, it was difficult to distinguish between religious bigotry, fear of a new revolution and the inclination of the English gentry to steal Irish land.

Parliament's submission to the King contended that any relaxations of penal laws 'carry in them a very strong encouragement for the Irish papists and an abasement of English interests there'.[13] It was the Imperial Ambassador's turn to persuade the King – who had come to power on a promise to sustain parliamentary government – that Parliament's wishes must be frustrated. William again refused to sign. He was rewarded by the Emperor asking the heads of monastic Orders to warn their followers in England and Ireland against engagement in treasonable activities. Perhaps William saw danger in attracting support from the Holy Roman Emperor. Whatever the reason, his record of modified tolerance was blemished during the following year. In 1697 he was party to the Irish Parliament's Bishops' Banishment Act.

The Act expelled from Ireland all priests who exercised executive authority and all regular clergy. As a result, 153 members of various Orders were transported from Dublin, 170 from Galway, 75 from Cork and 26 from Waterford.[14] Only two bishops left Ireland; six remained in hiding. According to Edward Comerford, Archbishop of Cashel, they hid in 'cellars and cisterns, mountains and caves'. The secular clergy, exempted from the Act, went about their work harassed but not prevented from performing their offices, for the idea was to cut connections with Rome without further offending the common people. The objective was not completely achieved. Local Catholic life went on virtually undisturbed. But everybody knew that the Treaty of Limerick had been 'broke by a Parliament in Ireland summoned by the Prince of Orange' and a law that banished 'in perpetuity Catholick bishops, dignitaryes and regular clergy'. There was no point in telling the Irish that they might have been treated worse. They had been treated badly and they knew it. The Bishops' Banishment Act simply increased their alienation.

Confident that it represented the true faith, the Catholic Church in England never allowed external danger to distract it from struggling for internal improvement. In 1691, when it would have been reasonable for Catholics to think of little else except escaping penalties and punishment, the secular clergy of Hampshire announced that, after much consideration, they had decided that heads of households were morally responsible for the conduct of everyone in their care or employment and that, in consequence, it was sinful for Catholics to serve meat to Protestants on feast days or Fridays[15] – thus causing great inconvenience to Catholic farmers who had Protestant labourers to feed. Their preoccupation with details of conduct was part of the great tradition of self-examination. The inconvenience caused by the profusion of feast days had exercised the ingenuity of the Yorkshire clergy five years earlier at a time when, thanks to the benevolence of James II, priests could afford to indulge a passion for the reinterpretation of God's will. Their ruling had concluded, among other things, that 'St James' day to be easily dispensed with, but not so if it falls on a Wednesday or Thursday unless the season be very hazardous'.[16] The rubric went on to describe the hazard that would justify ignoring St James, even on a Wednesday or Thursday, as 'when there has been in the fore part of the week, rains or showers as are enough to spoil the greater part of a hay-day'. To the unbeliever, rulings of such arcane complexity seem absurd. But the fact that they continued through years of threat to life, as well as liberty, illustrates the strength of the conviction that made the Catholic Church in England invincible.

Those characteristics also helped to give Catholics a self-confidence which Protestant bigots regarded as effrontery. The Reverend Mr Peploe, a Lancashire Low Churchman, was just one of the Church of England ministers who were astonished by the Papists' presumption. 'In 5 or 6 places in this town where the Papists meet ... They have Chappels deck'd out with all the Popish Trinkets. They go as publically to their meetings as we go to Church ... Since I came to Preston I have observed that a Popish Bishop, one Layburn, has kept his regular Visitations and there is not a month passes but I am credibly inform'd there is a great number of Popish Priests who meet in this Town on Market Days.'

Wealthy Catholics – always afforded more tolerance than the poor – worshipped in increasing freedom. 'The laws,' wrote the Marquess of Halifax, 'have made them men of pleasure by excluding them from public business.'[17] Thomas Tyldesley of Myerscough in Lancashire was such a man, as his diary confirms: 'To prayers [Mass] and home to dinner. Afterwards went fowling ... Alday in town [Lancaster] ... spent with Bro Dalton, Cos, Rigby and others at King's Arms 1s 6d ... Went duck hunting with 3 gentlemen ... Spent 2s each, being invited to a pig feast.'

Despite the gradual emergence of a Catholic middle class and industrial proletariat, Rome still relied on the gentry to keep the faith alive in rural England and continued to do so throughout the eighteenth century. The Catholics of Birchley in Lancashire were protected by, and relied on, the Anderton family. At Claughton-on-Brock it was the Heskeths and the Brokeholes who built the church and paid the priest. Ann Fenwick did the same in the Lune Valley. Patronage was most common in Lancashire because that was the county in which Catholicism survived in greatest strength. But in every county there were priests and parishes which depended on the generosity of a local Catholic landowner or aristocrat.

In Yorkshire, a quarter of the major landowners were Catholics, and during the seventeenth century the West Riding alone produced eighty priests and forty-eight nuns. Other counties, with similar records of devotion, were home to families that responded, almost en masse, to the Church's call. John Poulson of Desborough in Northamptonshire had seven sons. Six became priests. Henry Bedingfield of Oxburgh had eleven daughters. Ten became nuns. Of the six Gascoigne siblings, two became Benedictine monks, two became nuns and one became a secular priest. A single generation of Petres – a family that, as well as providing James II with his most controversial adviser, was to play a major part in the campaign for emancipation – included five Jesuits.

In King William's England, although the anti-Catholic laws were constantly renewed or intensified, they were more often ignored than applied. Queen Anne, who succeeded to the throne in 1702, expected the magistrates to do their duty. Her husband had fought the battle against Catholicism in order to win and consolidate power. Anne fought a holy war that would not end until the enemy was wiped out. In 1704 and 1709 she legislated 'to prevent the further growth of popery'. Regular clergy were banished. Parish priests were required to register and were limited to one per parish. Priests who turned Protestant were awarded a pension of £30 a year for life. Those who did not were denied the assistance of a curate and obliged to perform their offices in a chapel, which was clearly distinguishable from a 'real church' because it had no bell to ring and was not allowed to display a cross. Because the new laws imposed restrictions rather than penalties and punishments, it was easy for the Catholic gentry to convince themselves that, as long as they attended Mass on Sundays and feast days – and paid the recusants' fine on the increasingly infrequent occasions when they were required to do so – they were living good Catholic lives. Nicholas Blundell, of Little Crosby in Lancashire, managed the balancing act between recusant and loyalist with extraordinary panache. He was devout enough a Catholic to arrange that, when the time came, he would be sent on his way to meet his Maker with a Requiem Mass conducted by four priests. But he also agreed to being appointed churchwarden of Sefton parish church – although he could not attend its services.

Most of the Catholic gentry accepted the disabilities that were imposed upon them and their faith – though rarely with the ingenuity that Nicholas Blundell displayed. However, an increasing minority grew to reject their second-class status. At the same time, Anglicans – especially in the counties where the Catholic gentry thrived – grew to resent the success of families who were regarded by them as certainly impious and probably treacherous. Greed also played a part. The Reverend Samuel Peploe spoke for envious Protestants. 'The best estates in the country are in the hands of Papists ... and the Romish party is, of late, very uppish.'[18] Whatever the mood of the 'Romish Party', its members were still the victims of gratuitous – almost casual – extensions of discrimination that amounted to persecution. Peploe made his complaint in 1714, the year of the Schism Act: legislation that initially prohibited teaching without a licence from a Church of England bishop, but was amended to exclude tutors to the nobility and those who gave instruction in reading, writing and navigation.

The state-sponsored persecution was never sufficiently extreme to satisfy the bigots. Indeed, it increased rather than diminished their appetite. In 1709, London and the university cities had been convulsed by a bitter dispute over a sermon delivered by Dr Henry Sacheverell in St Paul's Cathedral. The service was arranged to commemorate the deliverance of King James I from the death which the Gunpowder Plotters had intended, and of Britain from the tyranny of his son, King James II. No doubt the city aldermen expected a routine assault on Catholicism. They got the repetition of a sermon that had been delivered in Derby four years earlier – a condemnation of the Church of England, which was accused and convicted of tolerating behaviour and beliefs that amounted to treason as well as heresy. Sacheverell's sentiments were unacceptable to his hosts, who refused to print his sermon. So he printed it himself and sold 100,000 copies. Intolerance breeds intolerance and Sacheverell was prosecuted for sedition. Weeks of riots followed, with the mob – once so anti-Catholic – demanding penal sanctions against both Dissenters and Church of England communicants who deviated from High Church (now called Anglo-Catholic) principles. Sacheverell was found guilty but was given the lightest possible sentence. The whole episode had a much greater effect on the standing of the Tory Party, which profited by endorsing Sacheverell's extremism, than it had on the Church of England. The government introduced the Occasional Conformity Act of 1711. It was based on the false premise that the corruption of which Sacheverell spoke was the work of Catholics and Dissenters who must be dissuaded from continuing their wicked ways. In particular they must be prevented from avoiding the obligations of the Test Acts by occasionally attending an Anglican service. So the Act imposed a £40 fine on anyone who attended a conventicle or meeting house *after* taking Church of England Communion. More supposedly punitive, but generally pointless, legislation followed.

In 1714 the throne of England was handed to Prince George, the Elector of Hanover – not because of his position in the line of succession, but because he was a Protestant. Emboldened by the knowledge that, although supported by the Whigs, he was less than popular with the Tories, James Edward Stuart – the son of James II, whose paternity Queen Anne had doubted, and Stuart pretender to the throne since his father died in 1701 – decided that the time had come to reclaim his kingdom. By 1715 he had convinced himself that his arrival in Britain would inspire the uprising which had not materialised after an attempted coup of 1708. Naturally enough, he expected the whole-hearted support of the Catholics – the men and women for whose religion his father had sacrificed his crown – and he anticipated that the Scottish Highlands were his for the asking. He was wrong. A force of 4,000 or 5,000 Scots had brief success in Lancashire, where they were 'joined by a great many Gentlemen with their tenants, servants and attendants and some very god figures in the county but all of them still Papists'. The invaders – who were less welcomed by most of the local population than they had anticipated – were defeated at the Battle of Preston. The victors were merciful. Only twenty-six of the hundred captured officers were executed, and no more than one in twenty of the rank-and-file were deported to slavery in the West Indies.

What hopes the Jacobites had of support in the Scottish Highlands were based on the belief that a highly organised Church would mobilise the faithful behind a Catholic pretender. But Catholicism in the High-lands was historically almost entirely dependent on the activities of the religious Orders – particularly the Dominicans and the Jesuits. By the time of the 1715 rebellion, the Dominicans (increasingly committed to work in England) had begun to leave the field clear for the Society of Jesus, whose concern was souls and not the succession. They were led in James VII's Scotland by Father Thomas Forsyth, who was encouraged to move to the north by Lewis Farquharson – a disillu-sioned candidate for ministry in the Kirk. The Kirk blamed Forsyth for reductions in the Church's strength which he, no doubt, was proud to acknowledge as his responsibility. Before Forsyth's arrival – the Kirk reported – there was 'hardly a Papist to be found in all the country'.[19] Naturally enough, the Jesuits boasted about Forsyth's success. Scotland was a country 'where the Catholic religion has scarcely been heard of before, since the introduction of heresy, and into which one of our fathers has penetrated as if laying the foundations of a new church'.

The General Assembly of the Kirk consoled itself with the thought that the Papists – 'who are become so impudent' after recruiting 'upward of 200 persons in Braemar and Glengairn' – were 'Ignorant people naturally given to Superstition'.[20] Other priests, lay and regular, built on the Jesuit foundations and, on the eve of the 1715 rebellion, they 'swarme[d] like locust' across the Highlands, generally uncon-cerned with affairs of state in Edinburgh and London. Highland Catholicism was led by men who believed in converting heretics one by one, not by the demonstrably futile attempts of a Catholic king to impose his religion on a reluctant people. Even the Society of Jesus had come to accept that Britain was a Protestant country.

After the 1715 rising failed there was no purge of Catholics or revived recourse to anti-Catholic law. Although some priests were roughly handled by King George's Hanoverian troops, their worst ordeal was to be 'forced to night in the hills on very cold weather'[21] – exactly the treatment meted out to their own tenants by the Catholic clan chieftains during the Highland Clearances. Father Peter McDonald said Mass within sight of the Hanoverian garrison at Fort William 'and publicly Invited the people of that town to hear and joyn him'. Scottish Catholicism – largely because it showed no real enthusiasm for the Stuart claim – escaped 'the 15' largely intact.

The Catholic Church in Scotland gained new members from conversion, but lost many more through the apostasy of the gentry and the emigration of the poor. The number of priests rose and fell between thirty and forty-five. Only one-third of them lived in the Highlands, the home of two-thirds of the Scottish Catholic population. Efforts were made to found a local seminary that would produce priests who were suited to the rough life in the wild north. The need for special training was confirmed by a report from the Vicar Apostolic. Priests returning to Scotland from foreign seminaries were soft. They were the victims of the easy life – the *delizie straniere* – which they had enjoyed before ordination.[22]

In England peace and tranquillity might have followed after 1715. The Act of Occasional Conformity and the Schism Acts were repealed. A modified Oath of Allegiance replaced the repudiation of Catholic doctrine and belief which had been the old test of loyalty. There was no longer any need to deny the Pope's authority or to reject the doctrine of transubstantiation. The new Oath required no more than the promise to live in peace and to reject, or at least ignore, any incitement to treason. 'I do promise to live peaceably and quietly under his majesty King George and the present Government and that I will not disturb the peace and tranquillity of this realm ... and will not make use of any papal dispensation from the said oath.'[23] Some of the great Catholic families – the Howards, Blounts and Stonors – found the words no more or less than a statement of their true position.

The hopes of tranquillity did not last long. Two years after the Hanoverian succession and one after the Old Pretender's attempt to regain the throne there were 350 convictions for recusancy in the North Riding of Yorkshire alone. Antagonism and apprehension had been revived by a series of plots, and the pretence of plots – none of which amounted to much in itself, but all of which could be used by

Protestant zealots as evidence that Catholicism and treachery went hand in hand. Chief among them was the Atterbury Plot, a conspiracy which had to be taken seriously because of its origins inside the Church of England establishment.

A year before her death, Queen Anne had appointed Francis Atterbury Bishop of Rochester, despite his High Church sympathies, which he had illustrated by his defence of Henry Sacheverell during the trial for high treason that followed the Protestant preacher's denunciation of religious tolerance. Atterbury's plan was to seize the Bank of England and then, with an army of 5,000 men, occupy the whole capital. Atterbury was certainly in correspondence with the Old Pretender, though whether or not he was planning, or even hoping for, a Stuart Restoration remains in doubt. However, the letters were enough to be used as justification not so much for new acts of repression as for attempts to insist on the stricter application of the penal laws that were still on the statute book. The revolt collapsed after the French, who were expected to finance the venture, revealed details of Atterbury's plans to the English Government – but not until after the Duke of Norfolk had been arrested on suspicion of complicity.

Most English Catholics were too busy with the business of their daily lives even to think about revolution. Daniel Defoe, during his travels through England and Wales, found Durham 'full of Roman Catholics who live peaceably and disturb no Body and no Body disturbs them',[24] although they went 'publically to Mass'. At St Winifred's Well in Flintshire, priests were 'very numerous' but 'no Body takes notice of it or enquires where one another goes'.[25] Even in Lancashire, Catholic militancy had faded – diminished by the change of leadership which followed the 1715. When the Jacobite grandees retreated to Scotland, leaving behind their local followers to face their fate, Lancashire had decided that Catholicism was about faith, not dynasties.

Throughout England the Catholic gentry who regarded the Church as their property – with some justification, since they employed the only priests in their villages – survived. But they decreased in absolute numbers and at a far faster rate as a percentage of the total Catholic population. Urban Catholicism was becoming a feature of the expanding towns as craftsmen, in the new trades, became as regular communicants as farm labourers and domestic servants. During the following decade, the shift to town from country was accelerated by a 'noble family' defecting from the Church in almost every county – including the Montagus, Gages and Shelleys in Sussex, the Molyneux in Lancashire, the Gascoignes in Yorkshire and the Chillingtons in Northumberland.[26]

Nowhere was that development more pronounced than in and around Birmingham, soon to become 'the workshop of the world'. Bonaventure Giffard – the Vicar Apostolic for the Midland District – rejoiced at the 'daily increasing number of people coming into the Church' and one of his priests boasted of 'the incredible success we have had in bringing proselytes of all ranks into our communion'.[27] The Catholic Church's success in Birmingham was partly the result of the Church of England's neglect of new industrial Britain and partly the reward for realism. There was no immediate prospect of the whole of Britain returning to the faith. Priests gravitated to the West Midlands. Catholics huddled together in enclaves and made converts when and where they could. Father Randolph, a Franciscan, confined his work to isolated Edgbaston and made fifty-seven converts in the three years 1693–6. Catholic education – which had been established first in rural Osmotherley – moved its centre of gravity to Birmingham and the growing towns of the Black Country. The object was less to educate than to prevent lapses from grace. One prosperous Catholic family, the Purcells, recognised that poverty worked for the devil and paid for a priest to say regular Mass 'for all poor Catholicks ... in the neighbourhood'. In the East Midlands the Jesuits still harboured hopes of enough converts to ignite a Counter-Reformation. The public offensive – mounted from Holbeck in Nottingham – was intentionally ambiguous in that it was both an invitation and a challenge to the law. It asserted the 'free liberty of the People of the Neighbourhood of the place to come at any time to their prayers and devotions'.

London was, in one particular, different. There the growth of a Catholic middle class had given the Church both stability and confidence and, in consequence, fearful and furtive worship was increasingly replaced by the open celebration of Mass and public preaching earlier than it was in the provinces. But the capital was typical of the rest of the country in another aspect of the gradual liberalisation. Protestant bigots were just as scandalised in London as they were in the furthest corner of the most remote county. One complained, 'Mr Yates in Southampton Street has Mass said in his house every day. Also has Mr Conquest in the same street. Mr Talbot in Bloomsbury Square – his house swarms with priests. Mrs Ems in Eagle Street has preaching in her house.'[28] Catholic sermons were advertised as inducements to patronise inns and taverns with landlords who were sympathetic to the Church of Rome. At the Sign of the Ship – an inn known as the Royal Anne – Richard Challoner, destined to become Vicar Apostolic of the London District, was said to have been apprenticed to the proprietor.

Challoner was typical of the new sort of Catholic. His father was a prosperous wine cooper (and Dissenter) who lived and worked in Lewes and, had it not been for his early death, his son might have remained true to his Protestant baptism. But when she became a widow, Mrs Challoner found work with a recusant family and it was, we must presume, through them that Richard found both faith and vocation. The story of his apprenticeship in his family's trade is hard to reconcile with his enrolment in Douai two months before his fifteenth birthday – where he lived for twenty-five years as student and teacher. But whenever and wherever they were acquired, his passion was reading and his obsession writing. He was the author of sixty works on theology which, he hoped and believed, were as much part of his ministry as saying Mass or hearing confessions. But when he returned to England in 1730 – fourteen years after his ordination – he combined scholarship with the pastoral care of Catholics in London. He preached in unlikely places – probably in the cockpit in Drury Lane and certainly at the Sign of the Ship in Gate Street.

A biographer – writing three years after Challoner's death – described the Vicar Apostolic's meeting with his 'persecuted flock at a public house in Gate Street'.[29] Whether or not it accounts for the dubious story of the apprenticeship, it gives a vivid, if slightly over-dramatic picture of Catholic life in mid-eighteenth-century London. 'A sturdy Irishman [stood] at the door [with instructions] to admit none but the faithful ... and the venerable prelate, pitifully bowed down by circumstances under cruel penal laws, came in colourful clothes and preached a comfortable exhortation ... with a pint of porter before him which the good Bishop never tasted ... in case the Philistines should break in.'

Challoner had more to fear from the Philistines than from the penal laws. For it was a time when there was more persecution by private enterprise than by the courts. Indeed, by one of his most notable contributions to the work of the Church, Challoner made special provision for new Catholics living in a new, and marginally more tolerant, age. He was a direct liturgical descendant of John Gother who, as early as the end of the seventeenth century, had begun the campaign to encourage Catholics to understand what was going on in the Masses they were required to attend. His object was not, of course, to persuade them to participate. Participation was the preserve of the priest who officiated. Gother's hope was that the congregation would learn to 'accompany' him rather than regard themselves as spectators, 'some saying their Beads ... others their Morning Prayers, others their Offices of the Day ... with little regard for what the Priest does'.[30] In 1705, he published *Instructions and Devotions for Hearing the Mass.* It was reprinted sixteen times before the end of the century. However, after about 1740 – although still popular – it was superseded, as the textbook of good Mass manners, by Richard Challoner's *The Garden of the Soul.* Challoner (by then Vicar Apostolic of the London District) was firm in his support for the teachings of the Council of Trent. His philosophy of education was taken straight from the Council's conclusions: 'Bishops must teach in a manner adapted to the mental ability' of those they instructed and must explain the 'efficacy and use' of the Eucharist.[31] But, although the idea was not new, it was the right approach for a priest in the changing world of the late eighteenth century. So was his support for making the congregation at Mass more than passive spectators. The move had already begun. It took more than two hundred years to complete.

Challoner was a strict moralist who insisted that every Catholic must constantly examine his or her conduct and improve each day on the previous day's performance. But he was also a realist who understood that – although the eternal truths of faith could not, by their nature, be questioned – the way in which the Church went about its business had to move with the times. He was the advance guard of change. His primary responsibility was for London – a city with 20,000 recusants, most of whom were the forerunners of the Industrial Revolution's working class. But it is other aspects of Challoner's life and work that confirm his place in the history of the Catholic Church in England. While teaching the young, he used Anglo-Saxon alternatives to the Latin nouns and adjectives of the liturgy. Perhaps more than any other priest of his era, he appreciated that the Church had to accommodate a new sort of Catholic – more questioning in temperament, as well as less rural in background.

Included among them were English Catholics who were impeccably loyal to the crown and searched for ways of practising their faith without incurring the civil penalties that increasingly replaced legalised persecution, or attracting the social odium that stigmatised Irish Catholics. The campaign for compromise was led by Sir Robert Throckmorton, who hoped to persuade fellow recusants to take the 1715 Oath of Allegiance and, in consequence, avoid the double taxation that was the punishment for refusal. The Duke of Norfolk – absolved, with suitable apologies, after his arrest following the Atterbury Plot – lent his aristocratic weight to a proposal which, had it been accepted, would have saved him a great deal of time and money. Throckmorton hoped that the Duke's endorsement would guarantee that Bonaventure Giffard, the new Vicar Apostolic of the London District, would give the proposal the Church's blessing.

Giffard neither endorsed nor rejected the plan. Loyal Catholics attributed his indecision to his age (he was seventy-four) and the persecution that he had suffered to a greater degree than most of the priests he led. According to a letter he wrote to the Venetian Ambassador, he had been imprisoned three times between April and October 1714. Old and tired, he spent much of his time on visitations to country houses, where he could be 'amongst friends and relations with much ease and comfort'.[32] So the leadership of the campaign to accept the revised oath was taken up by John Talbot Stonor, grandson of the Earl of Shrewsbury and the recently appointed Vicar Apostolic of the Midland District. He was not the ideal advocate of a cause that was essentially a compromise. Nor was his acolyte, Father Thomas Strickland. Both men – scions of noble houses – were regarded by their contemporaries as arrogant, intolerant, ambitious and – worse still – were known to possess Hanoverian sympathies. It was said that, while he was Elector of Hanover, George I had asked the Pope to make Stonor a cardinal.

Stonor was not thought a suitable candidate for the eminence of a red hat, but he was sufficiently influential in Rome to succeed in persuading the Vatican tentatively to accept that English Catholics be allowed to swear 'fidelity and intire Obedience to the present Government'. But the Pope wanted something in exchange for his concession.[33] The English Parliament must repeal the penal legislation. Although the anti-Catholic laws were consistently ignored, the English Parliament insisted that they remain in place. The new oath was abandoned.

Official persecution became increasingly rare and only became a real threat to life and liberty at times when there were rumours of foreign, and therefore Catholic, subversion or when the Catholic powers of Europe acted against the perceived interests of Britain and the British. But private hostility, whether or not it was diminished by the reduction in the exercise of the penal laws, remained. Sometimes it bubbled under the surface of society and sometimes it burst out in an explosion of bigotry. From time to time, the more open practice of Catholicism which followed neglect of the penal laws provoked the more fanatical members of the Protestant clergy to warn the nation about an ever-present danger that, they complained, the government chose to ignore. Sermons were preached against the persecution of Protestants in Spain and France. Forebodings were expressed about the consequences of Irish immigration swelling the Catholic population of London. And in 1738 – after British merchant captains gave evidence to Parliament about the way in which their 'lawful occasions' were interrupted by the Spanish navy, including the removal of Captain

Jenkins' ear – the London mob took diplomacy into its own hands and once again sacked the Spanish Embassy and attacked anyone who was imagined to be of a Spanish appearance. At times of political hysteria, threats – real or imagined – from Spain were inseparable, in the prejudiced mind, from the likely treachery of Catholics. The poisonous combination of religion and chauvinism was said to result in 'almost everybody having the greatest abhorrence of Papists coming to a Protestant country to pick Protestant pockets'. It also produced acts of meaningless violence. At the climax of the 'Jenkins' ear' crisis, the chapel of the Sardinian Embassy was attacked by a mob who 'not only ridiculed the divine service ... but struck several persons who were at their devotions'.[34] Fortunately such explosions of prejudice grew increasingly rare as Robert Walpole, who had scandalously used agitation about the Atterbury Plot to consolidate his position as Britain's 'first Prime Minister', presided over a long and reassuring peace. And other hate-figures were created to meet the needs of unscrupulous politicians. Among the High Tories, who opposed Walpole's Whig ministry, were residual Jacobites who regarded Nonconformists as the real enemies of both the state and true religion.

In Scotland, the years that followed the First Jacobite Rebellion were marked by both spectacular successes and deeply damaging divisions. In Ardnamurchan and Mull, Father Colin Campbell recruited, baptised and confirmed so successfully that the Kirk called upon the army to arrest him. In Inverness-shire, Father Gregor McGregor worked with equal energy and devotion, but by 1724 conceded that 'our trading [code for ministry] was never as low as at present'.[35] He was assailed by an unusually fierce counter-offensive by the Kirk. And at the same time the Catholics within his care were deeply divided between supporters and opponents of Jansenism – a new doctrine which, although condemned by the Papal Bull *Unigenitus*, was inherently attractive to stern, unbending Scots.

Cornelius Otto Jansen believed in predestination. His most important work – based, in part, on what he believed to be the teaching of St Augustine – asserted that only divine grace could save men and women from hell, and that Christ led a small band of the elect to eternal life while 'the mass of perdition' were doomed to damnation, no matter how extensive, continuous and self-sacrificial their good works. It was a variant of Calvinism which claimed to be supported by more theological scholarship than Calvin could boast, and although its Five Propositions were shown to be based on a selective reading of Augustine's work, Jansenism possessed an attraction that far exceeded its theological merits. It enabled Catholics who chose to embrace it to claim that they numbered among the elect and were, therefore, set aside from the prenatally condemned. And it provided a stick with which to beat the Jesuits who, according to Jansen's doctrine, defied God's will by behaving as if all the world could be converted to Catholicism and saved. Christ on the Jansen crucifix does not have his arms spread wide to embrace the world. They are folded, to signify the exclusion of irredeemable sinners.

The division between Jansenists and supporters of the bull *Unigenitus* was social as well as theological. The Lowland priests who were, in effect, chaplains in noble houses opposed the bull. The itinerant Highland priests – Jesuit or not – supported it. The pattern of Scottish devotion was further complicated by the influence of Irish Dominicans in the north and west. In 1731, Gregor McGregor made formal charges of heresy against the Jansenists and, together with Colin Campbell – a priest from Mull – wrote to James Gordon, the Scottish Vicar Apostolic, with the demand that he require all Scottish priests to endorse *Unigenitus* and proposed the expulsion of Jansenists from the Scots College in Rome. Between 1730 and 1740 Propaganda Fide initiated three inconclusive investigations into the conduct of the college. They served, if they had any effect at all, to widen the breach between what came to be known as Parisians and Romans, as well as between north and south Scotland and between Jesuits and secular priests. The disagreement was still passionate and bitter in 1745 when Scottish Catholics were again called upon, and expected by both incumbent and claimant, to rally to the cause of a Catholic monarchy.

PART THREE

A Prospect Tremendous

CHAPTER 16

Think of Them with Kindness

The Catholic Church in Scotland largely survived the Second Jacobite Rebellion – 'the '45' – in the same way that it had survived the first. It chose to play no further part in the Young Pretender's attempt to secure the throne of England for his father than it had played in the Old Pretender's attempt to secure the throne for himself. Individual priests supported Prince Charles Edward Stuart. Father John Tyrie was wounded at the Battle of Culloden and Father Allan MacDonald (known to his comrades-in-arms as Captain Graham) was captured and deported to the Netherlands. But there was no mass Catholic enrolment in the Jacobite army. The vast majority of the recruits – volunteers and pressed men – were either Episcopalians or Protestants who, for one reason or another, would not take the 1715 Oath of Allegiance. And the Catholic clan chieftains who rallied to the Stuart standard were often motivated by considerations that were more secular than religious. Sometimes the decision to oppose King George was more the result of dislike of his friends than of affection for his enemies. In the north-east of Scotland 'the Popish lords naturally threw their weight in with the prelatic party ... who were far more likely to tolerate their presence than the Presbyterians'.[1] And the *Memoirs of the Rebellion in 1745 and 1746 as far as it concerns the counties of Aberdeen and Banff* records 'a very great understanding between ... Seaton, a priest and Law, a Nonjurant minister'. But – although the Stuarts hoped it would be otherwise – 'the '45' was not a Catholic cause.

Charles Edward Stuart swept south towards London through what he believed – in a sense correctly – was the Catholic county of Lancashire. It had been the scene of his father's only success thirty years earlier. In Manchester he was received with rapture – and bonfires. But only three hundred volunteers joined his army. The decision to turn back at Derby – despite rumours of panic and evacuation in London – was in part determined by the disappointment of the reception he had received during the approach march. On the retreat north, the Young Pretender enjoyed an unexpected victory at Preston. But it was won by Scotsmen, not local recruits. Lancashire was, in part, Catholic but not Jacobite. After the long march home, which ended on Culloden Moor, Jacobite officers who were not party to the Act of Indemnity, which absolved from punishment any combatant who swore allegiance to the House of Hanover, roamed, still armed, the mountains and moors. Their numbers, and their determination, were exaggerated by the supporters of both the King and the Pretender.

The English Colleges abroad were centres of Jacobite sympathy. They existed to return England to the 'true faith' and it was only to be expected that the seminarians, who were to be the vanguard of recon-version, should feel a passionate attachment to the Catholic claimant to the British throne. In early 1745 a High Mass in the English College at Douai celebrated 'the happy success of the Prince of Wales [Charles Edward Stuart] in his campaign against George, the Elector of Hanover'.[2] The English College in Rome had a more personal association with the House of Stuart. Henry, Duke of York studied for the priesthood there and went on – largely because of his blood and birth – to hold the honorific title Cardinal Bishop of Frascati. Later, mostly on merit, he became Dean of the Sacred College. But in Scotland itself, the Catholic Church was only a partisan observer of the conflict and the occasional eruptions that followed, not a participant in them. As was often the case, Catholics were engrossed in their own internal disagreements.

In 1732, Propaganda Fide had divided Scotland into two districts – Highland and Lowland. Initially, the Highlands – remote and inaccessible – proved most loyal to Rome. Indeed, it was reported, as late as 1720, that it included 'some places where the Reformation never yet had a footing'.[3] Three years later there were reports of Catholic priests taking up residence all over the region and holding fast to Rome youths who were, according to the Kirk, 'early bypassed and tainted in their principles with the Popish book ... and songs put into their hands by the Priests'. Some of them were said to give 'great encouragement to the revival of the Stuart cause and disaffection in Scotland'. But, if that was true, they were singularly unsuccessful in their attempts to mount another rebellion. And, after 1745, life changed in the Highlands. The 'clearances' combined with voluntary emigration to depopulate vast tracks of land. As the Lowlands moved on to the dawn of the Industrial Revolution, the Highlands, at best, stood still. The result was an alienation that resulted in antagonism between the Church on the two sides of the Highland line, and a reluctance of priests to serve in the north, which was even greater in the middle of the eighteenth century than it had been at the end of the seventeenth.

However, the great divide in mid-eighteenth-century Scottish Catholicism was the bitter rivalry over status, influence and authority, between seculars and regulars. Jesuits occupied their accustomed place in the thick of the battle. In 1755, the Superior of the Society wrote to Propaganda Fide to complain that Alexander Smith, Vicar Apostolic of the Highland District, was doing all he could to obstruct Jesuit initiatives. At the same time, George Hay, the Vicar Apostolic of the Lowlands District, was doing all he could to bring the Society under his control. In his judgement – not upheld by the Vatican – Pope Benedict XIV's encyclical *Apostolicum Ministerium* gave him authority over every priest in his district. He used the powers that he claimed to promote peace with the Protestant majority – including the prohibition of a revival of liturgical music in the order of service, lest it should offend Presbyterian opinion. Worshippers took comfort in beads, and the rosary was again regarded as an essential feature of Catholic worship, though in England progressive Catholics believed it to be a distraction from the Mass itself. The Scottish Parliament condemned the rosary outright and in 1746 ordered the confiscation of a cargo of beads, which it defined as contraband. To add to its difficulties, the Catholic Church, in both Scottish Divisions, was increasingly short of priests. The Scottish College in Rome – disorderly and rebellious from the start – had failed to provide the regular supply of secular clergy and, after the Second Jacobite Rebellion, many priests had migrated to Canada with their parishioners.

At the same time Protestants were continuing their vigorous campaign to bring about both religious conversion and social modernisation. Four years before the Young Pretender landed in England, Alasdair MacDonald, a well-meaning Presbyterian, had compiled a Gaelic–English dictionary. Its objective was 'Reforming of the Highlands and Islands of Scotland', frustrating 'Popish Emissaries' and eradicating 'Customs, Fashions and Superstitions of their Forefathers', and thus making young Highlanders suitable for careers in 'the Navy or Army or in any other service in the Commonwealth'.[4] Twenty years after Prince Charles fled – leaving most of his followers to the mercy of 'Butcher Cumberland' – the Kirk was still sending ministers 'to take up residence' in Catholic strongholds 'and try to lead the faithful people into heresy'.

The Catholic Church in Scotland not only survived that quarter of a century. It sowed the seeds of what its members called a 'second spring'. The revival was, in part, the result of good organisation. Hugh Macdonald – the new Vicar Apostolic for the Highland District and the survivor of a Hanoverian prison – grouped parishes together and moved priests into the areas in which they could best save souls. The seminary, set up on an island in Loch Morar in 1712, had been closed after the First Jacobite Rebellion, but was replaced by three new foundations: Glenlivet, Glenfinnan and Lismore. Thus the shortage of priests was recognised but not yet remedied. The main reason for Catholic success and survival of the eighteenth-century Highland Church was the tenacious devotion of the faithful – and their isolation from the rationalism of the Scottish Enlightenment.

In England the determination to maintain oppressive laws that were increasingly ignored appeared to be giving way to a willingness to accept a formal relaxation of the penal legislation – at least as it affected Dissenters. In 1719 the Schism Act and the Occasional Conformity Acts were repealed. But the relief which that touch of toleration provided for Catholics was trivial as compared to the freedom they increasingly provided for themselves by inventing ways of circumventing the oppressive statutes. The laws that governed births and marriages had long been interpreted in a way which allowed Catholics to respect the obligations of their faith and still avoid future arguments about legitimacy and inheritance. The Marriage Act of 1753 changed the law, but not the practice. It made all marriages illegal, save those which were performed either by a Church of England cler-gyman or according to the practices of the Society of Friends. Richard Challoner, Vicar Apostolic of the London District, simply approved, for use in the capital, a variation on the established procedure. A legal marriage, in the local parish church, was to be followed by its sanc-tification, later the same day, by a Catholic priest. In 1750, Lord Sheffield and Ursula Tyrwhitt were betrothed in a public ceremony which was carried out in the 'great dining room' of the bride's family house. On the following day, a priest performed what the couple regarded as a proper wedding ceremony – a Nuptial Mass – in the privacy of the steward's parlour.[5] The Challoner procedure was adopted everywhere in Catholic England. So there was no practical problem. But the 1753 Marriage Act did confirm the unhappy truth that there was still a body of influential opinion that regarded Catholi-cism and Catholics as heathen and alien.

The Marriage Act was an early indication of a fear that still haunted rabid Protestants for the next quarter of a century. It was widely supposed that, encouraged by a less repressive environment, Catholi-cism was again growing in confidence and numbers. In 1765 Richard Terrick, the Church of England Bishop of London, warned the clergy of his diocese, 'The visible Increase in Papists in the Cities of London and Westminster [is] a matter of serious Reflection to all who wish well to the Happiness of this Protestant Country.'[6] Terrick's foreboding exercised the imagination of less temperate Protestants, and an epidemic of Papist-hunting broke out again.

The 1700 Act for Preventing the Growth of Popery had awarded £100 – a fortune at the beginning of the eighteenth century – to anyone who provided information that contributed to its objective. For half a century it was rarely invoked. But in the years that followed Terrick's warning, its powers were used again. A letter from London to Propaganda Fide reported that 'at least twenty priests have, at different times, been prosecuted for their religion and most of them more than once'.[7] The bounty attracted the interest of men who were, or had been, common criminals. In 1767, William Payne, the 'Protestant Carpenter', indicted John Baptist Maloney for 'exercising the functions of Catholic priest'. The guilty verdict – the sentence of life imprisonment was commuted to exile – emboldened Payne to aim higher. Later that year he accused four priests, a schoolmaster and Richard Challoner of the same offence. The charges were dropped after defence lawyers had proved that the case against the defendants was based on forged evidence. A third case – initiated by Payne in the same year – was dismissed after Lord Mansfield, the Lord Chief Justice, ruled that the prosecution had failed to prove that the accused were both ordained and acting as priests. In 1768, James Talbot – a future Vicar Apostolic – was brought to trial on the charge of saying Mass. He was acquitted on a technicality. So were Richard Dillon and John Fuller, two Moorfield priests who were charged at the same time. The acquittals could be regarded as the triumph of an independent legal system, but: 'Talbot was indicted five times. The proceeding against him taking more than three years. He was last tried at the Old Bailey and the prosecution, failing in its proof, he was found not guilty.'[8] The capricious nature of the prosecutions illustrates the uncertainty which governed the lives of active Catholics as they struggled on, suspended between an increasing inclination to ignore the penal laws and the determination of a substantial Protestant minority to see them enforced. Sometimes the bigots succeeded. 'Mr Maloney, for administering the Sacrament to a sick man was tried in Surrey by Chief Baron Smythe and sentenced to perpetual imprisonment. He was in prison for four years and then suffered to go abroad on promising never to return to England.'

The pressure for enforcement almost always followed evidence of Catholic expansion in activities or in numbers. In March 1775 Talbot received the warning from 'a Friend to the Roman Catholicks' that 'the number of Roman Catholick Schools which of late have been set up in this nation have given cause of complaint'. Talbot was advised to 'take care of yourself not only in the country but in London, where diligent search will soon be made for you'.[9] Protestant tolerance always wore thin when Catholicism showed signs of evolving from a small, furtive minority into a self-confident community which expected to play a full part in the life of the nation.

In 1767, when Payne's activities were at their height, Parliament – prompted more by anxiety than curiosity – decided that it was essential to know the number of Catholics in England and Wales. The exercise was, like all previous calculations, complicated by the difficulties of definition. But the method by which it was carried out – Church of England clergy, who 'recognised a Catholic when they saw one' – counted the numbers, parish by parish, and produced a more accurate figure than any previous survey had provided. The total was precise – 69,376, including children. It was subsequently suggested that the numbers in the rural parishes were underestimated and that the true figure was nearer 80,000.[10] Six years later the four Vicars General organised a survey of their own which, since it was based on congregation numbers, excluded children who were too young to take Communion and men and women who, although they were born Catholics and still claimed to follow the faith of their baptism, did not regularly attend Mass. The total, thus arrived at, was 59,500 – a figure that, given the differences in definition, was wholly consistent with Parliament's own earlier calculation. Catholic numbers had stabilised. There had been no significant decline for over a century.

The census carried out for the Vicars Apostolic in 1773 was also a register of the 392 priests who lived and worked – openly or covertly – in England. Their distribution around the kingdom gives only a crude indication of where Catholicism had taken strongest hold, in terms of communicant numbers. Despite the emergence of urban and proletarian Catholicism, the possibility of employing a priest often still depended on the availability of local patronage. One hundred and thirty-seven priests lived and worked in the Northern District – almost exactly half of them (sixty-nine) in Lancashire. There were forty-four in the Western District, only nine of whom were in Wales. The London District included seventy priests in the metropolis itself and fifty in the Home Counties. In the Midland District, most of the ninety-one priests inhabited rural Warwick, Worcester and Stafford. Only a little more than half the total number of clergy (175) were secular priests. They were distributed in much the same way as the clergy as a whole. The largest number (sixty-seven) were in the Northern District, the smallest (eleven) in the Western. Because of the dependence on patronage, both the regulars and the secular priests were often in the areas that needed them least. But they were rarely employed for the exclusive use of the family to whom they ministered and by whom they were paid.

Patronage became more common and more public. By the middle of the eighteenth century the noble Catholic families were as notable for supporting missions as for employing domestic chaplains – in most cases, openly. The bolder they were, the greater their investment in a permanent Catholic mission. The boldest of them all was the Petre family, who supported six of the eight Catholic missions in Essex as well as employing a Jesuit as their private confessor. It was, at least in part, as the result of such patronage that the Catholic Church in England – despite the forebodings of some of its leaders – was about to expand and prosper.

The Catholic Church in Ireland, although invincible on account of its size, was still beleaguered. The Archbishop of Dublin – no doubt influenced by a reward of £300 being offered for the capture of Nicholas Sheehy, a Tipperary priest who was accused of high treason – only slightly overstated the widely held view when, in 1745, he described his archdiocese as 'grievously afflicted with misfortune and persecutions'.[11] Some of Ireland's problems were the result of its effective status as an English colony, and the attempt by a succession of Lord Lieutenants to make its economy meet the needs of the imperial power. The disputes that followed – Lord Lieutenant versus Dublin Parliament – were, thanks to Catholic disenfranchisement, fought out between Protestant and Protestant, and the battle over London's proposed debasement of the currency was won by Jonathan Swift, the Dean of St Patrick's Cathedral. But in eighteenth-century England, Ireland's economic problems were always associated with the alleged ignorance of its Catholic peasantry, who were accused, sometimes with good cause, of confusing faith with superstition and progress with exploitation.

Arthur Young – author of twenty-five volumes on the state of agriculture in Britain and Europe – had no doubt about the cause of the Irish economic malaise. His *Tour in Ireland* was emphatic that the country would not prosper until its life and work were freed from the 'ignorance of the people', who were 'more bigoted than anything known in the sister kingdom'. Recognising the gradual liberalisation – of attitudes, if not laws – and the gradual growth in the number of Catholic artisans and tradesmen, he proposed that 'all the personal wealth of the Catholic' be devoted to bringing Irish agriculture up to the standard that he had found in 'other parts of Europe'. Young's solution illustrates why he was a more successful commentator than a practical farmer, but he was not alone in believing that superstition was Ireland's curse. Throughout the eighteenth century the Catholic Church struggled, with mixed success, to stamp out the sort of rites and rituals which were pagan in origin and which the Council of Trent had declared heretical and likely to stand in the way of a successful Counter-Reformation.

The Irish Catholic bishops – no less than the civic authorities, who associated every mass gathering with incipient revolution – wanted to prohibit the County Mayo Day of Folly. Each year as many as 10,000 Catholics travelled to Balla to take part in what could loosely be described as a service around what was believed to be a holy well. In some counties the peasantry were 'afraid of cultivating the Danish forts'[12] in case the ghosts of the long-dead Vikings, who had built the encampments, returned to claim their property. County Roscommon followed a funeral ritual that was as inconvenient as it was pagan. 'When a person dies ... The bed is burned on a height ... Burials are not allowed on Mondays, for burial on that day would bring about the immediate death of someone in the neighbourhood.' Sometimes the priesthood itself promoted what amounted to sacrilege. It was known to supply, on demand, 'gospels': talismans that were said, because they had been blessed, to ward off evil. Some priests also prepared – and were known to sell for a few coppers – bottles of holy water to be drunk to prevent or cure the many illnesses which affected the rural poor. But despite the misdemeanours, it was the clergy itself which dragged the Irish Catholic Church some way out of the Gaelic mist. Social and economic changes – the decay of the native language, the opening up of trade with America, even the Great Famine and the depopulation that followed – played a part. So did the relaxation of oppression. But the impetus for change came from the bishops and the parish priests who supported them.

Ireland was not only short of priests. Some of the seculars in the counties were tactfully described as not of the highest quality. It was common practice for them to 'go abroad to finish their studies' – after ordination. Many of them never returned. In consequence there was increasing reliance on the regulars. The Archbishop of Dublin determined, with more immediate success than had been possible with the monks of England, to keep them under episcopal control and out of politics while he regularised and coordinated every aspect of their work. The coordination was organised through a series of diocesan conferences. At Thurles in 1788, the four metropolitan archbishops held the first of what were to become regular meetings.

Some of the diocesan conferences (upgraded to the status of synods) dealt purely with the matters of Church discipline which had been set out, as suitable subjects for discussion, at the Council of Trent and popularised by the (subsequently canonised) Carlo Borromeo in Milan. At Thurles in County Tipperary, the agenda included the propriety of baptising the unborn, choice of the prayers that were to be learned before confirmation, whether or not it was permissible for a priest to say Mass twice in one day, and the necessary qualifications of candidates for ordination. But the bishops were increasingly turning their attention to the day-to-day social behaviour of the laity. The Church in France and the Low Countries had – for two hundred years – felt an obligation to guide its followers along the path of thrift, sobriety and industry and to lead them away from violence and revolution. The Irish Church decided to follow the continental example.

In the Leinster diocese of Ossory, Bishop Thomas Burke took it upon himself to issue an injunction which reflected a concern that has not diminished with the years. 'Whereas Robbing, Riding, Cursing, Swearing, Excessive Drinking and other great Debaucheries are constantly practised at St John's Well near Kilkenny, arising mostly from vagrant Beggars, many whereof feign themselves to be Lame ... to the great Detriment and Terror of the Inhabitants and the Travellers, whereby many reflections are cast upon the Roman Catholick Religion ... all subjects of that religion are strictly forbid to give Alms to any Beggar whatsoever at St John's Well.'[13]

Bishop Nihell in Kilmacduagh condemned the violence which was becoming a feature of the revolt of 'rack-rented' tenant farmers and landless labourers. The object of his censure was Buachailli Bana, the 'Whiteboys' whose campaign of rick-burning, crop destruction and (most significantly) the breaking down of hedges and filling in of ditches that marked the boundaries of recent enclosures had spread from County Limerick into Tipperary, Cork and Waterford. Bishop Nihell, denounced the 'very large body of people under the denomination of Whiteboys' who had forced good Catholics 'to take certain illegal oaths ... contrary to the dictates of conscience, the laws of the land and even their own temporal interest and advantage'.[14] Nihell must have known that – as well as winning support from law-abiding citizens of all political and religious opinions, he was making enemies even among the clergy. The bands that led the Whiteboy parades – as visible and audible demonstrations of power and numbers – always played 'The Lad with the White Cockade', the Jacobite marching song. Despite such overtones of rebellion, there were few rural priests who did not at least sympathise with the incipient revolt. Some only opposed the random violence with which it was eventually put down. Others actively defended suspects – often claiming, sometimes correctly, that they had been arrested and convicted on the evidence of common informers. Father Nicholas Sheehy of Clogheen in County Tipperary opposed the imposition of tithes and collected for a legal defence fund. Sheehy was charged with sedition, but acquitted. The charge and the acquittal became annual events until he was convicted and hanged.

The Highlands clearances and the failure of the Second Jacobite Rebellion turned the far north of Scotland into a country of landless peasants who lived in a landscape which inspired the romantic movement, but which the Vicar Apostolic, Hugh Macdonald, described as inducing 'terror' and 'horror' in all who beheld it. The itinerant priests, 'worn out with toil and advancing age ... [carried] the burdens of the region [and] could not be borne much longer'.[15] It seems that, in a reversal of the usual roles, Protestants evangelised in the 'wild and very mountainous county' with more ingenuity than the Catholics. Their target was those parts of the Highlands where the Catholic Church had survived – often dormant and therefore undisturbed since the beginning of the Reformation. The task was undertaken by the Scottish Society for the Propagation of Christian Knowledge, which began its work by identifying the number of Catholics in the remote north and on the adjacent islands. There were places in which the faithful still worshipped in substantial numbers – 2,300 in Uist, 1,340 in North Morar and Knoydart and 1,250 in Barr. The SSPCK missionary technique was based on providing Protestant education for the young. Schools were set up in all the predominantly Catholic areas. The Catholic Church responded with a reorganisation which – as in Ireland – aimed to ensure that the areas in greatest danger of conversion received the most attention. But, as the eighteenth century moved on, forces too strong for the Church to resist made the decline of Highland – perhaps more appropriately called Gaelic – Catholicism irresistible.

Gaelic life itself was in decline. Missionaries from the south (ironically including Catholics) contributed to the process by denouncing old customs and superstitions. So did the compilation of an English–Gaelic dictionary. But the main causes of decline were the collapse of the clan system and the emigration that followed the Highland clearances. Some of the emigration was to the increasingly industrial towns of the Lowlands. In the second half of the eighteenth century Scottish Catholicism's centre of gravity – reinforced by the expatriate Irish – shifted from the rural Highlands. That created a Catholic renaissance of sorts in Scottish towns and cities, particularly the increasingly popular sea ports. Aberdeen and its neighbourhood were typical: 260

communicants in 1763, 276 in 1780 and 316 in 1798. Familiarity did not inspire affection. Protestants were still not reconciled to the presence of Catholics in their midst. Dundee in 1776 included a 'congregation of Papists or those of the Church of Rome who have a priest ... but keep not open door, these having no toleration although they are winked at'. The Dundee Catholic congregation expanded to a point at which it needed, and could afford, a new chapel house to accommodate the weekly communicants. But the Catholic Church in Scotland would have to withstand many years of persecution before an 'open door' was possible.

The pattern of Catholicism in England during the eighteenth century was, in many ways, identical to the pattern of Catholicism in Scotland. For the first fifty years it seemed, not only to natural pessimists, that in some parts of the country absolute extinction was at least possible. In 1767, the recusant population of Devon was 235 – which made it a hotbed of Papism as compared with neighbouring Cornwall, where there were fifty-six. But like Scotland and Ireland, the decline in rural Catholicism – largely the result of the nascent Industrial Revolution encouraging a drift from the counties into the towns – was made up by an increase in urban Catholicism and the emergence of a Catholic industrial proletariat. By the last decade of the century, the total Catholic population had grown from the 60,000 that had been identified by Parliament and the Vicars Apostolic in 1773 to 70,000. The biggest increases were in Manchester, Liverpool, Preston and Wigan. During the eighteenth century, the number of Catholics in Lancashire increased fivefold, to a total of 32,000. Second to Lancashire came London. In 1780 there were 4,000 Catholics in Wapping alone. In Wales – which the Catholic Church stubbornly refused to distinguish from England and included in its Western District – urban Catholicism was unknown. In the Principality, numbers certainly did not increase during the eighteenth century and probably declined. There were never more than one hundred in Monmouthshire, the most Catholic of Welsh counties. In Wales, Methodism – the Second Reformation – swept all other faiths before it.

Two distinct sects – Calvinist Methodists, who thought of themselves as an independent denomination, and the followers of John Wesley, who insisted that they were a 'connection' in full communion with the Church of England – took their message into the town squares and onto the village greens. By 1750 there were 433 Nonconformist societies in Wales alone.[16] While the beleaguered Catholic Church was preoccupied with holding on to its existing members, the Nonconformists were making new recruits. Although clearly theological heirs of the Reformation, the secret of their success was their enthusiasm for carrying the message of salvation to the people. It was John Wesley, not the Pope, who announced that the world was his parish.

The Nonconformist message took longer to reach what was to become Wesley's northern heartland than it did to penetrate Wales and the west of England. Preston illustrated the gradual emergence of English Catholicism from dependency on patronage to self-reliance. In 1773, the Vicar General for the Northern District, Francis Petre – himself the member of a noble family and a priest who lived the life of a country gentleman – was explicit about worship in that Lancashire town: 'Our oratories, or places set aside for the Mass and prayers are normally part of some mansion.'[17] By 1793 the parish had a permanent chapel of its own. In Leeds, patronage remained, but changed its character. In 1776, the munificence of a succession of Dukes of Norfolk was replaced by the generosity of John Wade, a local merchant and convert. Hand in hand with the changes in the way in which the Catholic Church was financed went changes in the way that Catholics worshipped. And by the nature of the Church of Rome, with change went controversy.

The controversy of 1773 – Pope Clement XIV's suppression of the Jesuits – largely passed Great Britain and Ireland by, even though, as a seminarian breathlessly reported, the climax of the drama took place in the English College in Rome. 'The rooms of the Jesuits were visited and money collected from each one. On the following day, Father Ferdinand Giovannucci, a Roman priest, was given to the college as Rector. Meanwhile ordinary secular dress was prepared for the use of the Fathers ... Father Ricci, the ex-general of the Jesuits was kept in custody by soldiers in the upper part of the college until he was taken to Castle St Angelo.'[18]

The allegations against the Jesuits – set out in the Papal Bull of July 21st – were the complaints of Catholic princes and ambitious cardinals who believed that the Society defied their authority and would, given the opportunity, usurp their power. In Britain and Ireland they often offended by treating those countries as if they were pagan lands which had never heard the word of God and could only be rescued for Rome by the Society of Jesus. But they were not a threat. The Catholic Church had no power for them to usurp. It was, however, soon to be engulfed in a controversy of its own. Where, within its extending boundaries, did real power lie? And, crucially, who had the right to decide what concessions were worth making as the price paid for a relaxation of the penal laws?

The first Irish Relief Act – which, unaccountably, was never known by that name – was said to be the consequence of the Earl of Bristol (who was also the Protestant Bishop of Derry) visiting Toulouse. At dinner with the superiors of the Irish College he was so impressed by his hosts that he determined to campaign for their rehabilitation in the land of their birth. The Act which was said to be the consequence of that apparently convivial meal did no more than 'enable His Majesty's subjects of whatever persuasion to testify their allegiance to him'. But it gave Irishmen who wished to assert their respectability a chance of doing so. By bringing in the Act, the Dublin Parliament made history in three distinct but related ways. The preamble conceded that it was 'on account of their religious tenets', not because of their inclination to treason, that Catholics were suspect. It included an oath of loyalty to the crown, which became the model for all other oaths in all other Relief Acts. And that oath was the first affirmation of loyalty to a secular authority – potentially in conflict with Rome – that the Vatican chose not to denounce.

Tom Moore, poet and patriot, was not impressed. According to him, the Irish Relief Act of 1774 amounted to 'the kind permission of the victim to come and swear eternal fidelity to his tormentor though as insulting a piece of mockery as can well be imagined was received with the warmest gratitude by the Catholics because it at least acknowledged their existence as Catholics'.[19]

English Catholics were further aggrieved by the decision to offer concessions abroad that were denied at home. The British Government, as part of an eventually unsuccessful attempt to satisfy the troubled colonists of Canada, passed the Quebec Act. Its principal purpose was the extension of Canada's southern border to the Ohio River. But it also provided the colony with a legislative council on which – since they made up a majority of the population – Catholics were to be represented. The Act aimed at reconciling French settlers to British rule. So, to make them feel at home, it incorporated French civil law into the Quebec legal system and – claiming that it was because they were part of the communities in which they lived – allowed the largely French Catholic priesthood to own property, receive bequests and collect tithes as they were collected in England by rectors and vicars of the Anglican Church. As a result, Catholic colonists in the parts of North America which were still under English governance enjoyed a freedom that was denied to Catholics at home in England.

The inequity of the distinction between colonists and citizens contributed to the decision of the Catholic Church in England to make direct representations to the government. Richard Challoner, still Vicar

Apostolic of the London District Region, at the age of eighty-seven, drafted an Address to the King. For some reason, after the opening sentence, he referred to his Church in the third person: 'We the Catholics of England humbly petition: First that they may be allowed by Act of Parliament full liberty of conscience for the further exercise of their religion ... Secondly that the penal legislation enacted against them may be repealed. Thirdly that the Test Act ... requiring them to take an oath contrary to their religion shall also be repealed. And fourthly with regard to the Marriage Act, by which they think themselves aggrieved by having to receive nuptial benediction of a minister who is not of the communion, they humbly crave that they may be exempted from this benediction.'[20] The submission was never made. Challoner added a forlorn note to the end of the draft: 'Thus far had I written when I was honoured by a visit from Lord Stourton who objects to our asking for a repeal of all the penal laws which he thinks will not be obtained.' In fact, Stourton was less opposed to the content of the message than to the choice of messenger.

Strourton's reservations were shared by many members of the Catholic aristocracy. Sir John Dalrymple – one of the bolder spirits among the laymen – took it upon himself to press for the relief which Challoner had envisaged. But when he visited the Vicar Apostolic, he found that his mood had changed. The man who had begun to draft a plea for relief was 'old and timid and [cited] twenty difficulties'[21] to justify procrastination. Dalrymple decided there and then that the task was too important to be left to priests and monks. He consulted the Duke of Norfolk, the Earl of Shrewsbury and the heads of other noble Catholic families. The outcome of his consultations was never in doubt. The lay Catholics did not trust their Church adequately to represent the view that relief was essential and that it could be obtained without forswearing an unacceptable degree of dogma. Indeed, they believed that the concessions that might have to be made concerned matters which were none of the Pope's business. So they decided not to make 'any application to clergy in temporal matters, the English Roman Catholic Gentlemen being quite able to judge and act for themselves'. They judged that it was time to petition the King and formed a committee – Lord Petre, Sir John Throckmorton and Mr William Sheldon – to promote it.

On June 4th 1778, a Humble Address of the Roman Catholic Peers and Commoners of Great Britain, signed by more than two hundred laymen, was delivered to George III. It was written in such obsequious language that it could hardly be described as a request, even less an assertion of rights. 'Our exclusion from the constitution has not diminished our reverence for it ... We have patiently submitted to such Restrictions and Discouragements as the Legislature found Expedient, Thankfully received such Relaxations in the Rigours of the Law as Ministers of an Enlightened Age and the Benignity of Your Majesty's Government have gradually produced. We submissively wait, without suggesting either Time or Measure of other Indulgences ... We hold no Opinion adverse to Your Majesty's Government or repugnant to the Duties of a Good Citizen.'[22] The Address ended – as if any further proof of loyalty was needed – with a reiteration of the signatories' 'detestation of the Designs and Views of any Foreign Power against the Dignity of the Crown' and an assurance that they were 'perfectly ready on any occasion to give proof of [their] Fidelit'.

But it was neither the demands of equity nor the protestations of the Catholic laymen which provided the impetus for reform. The English Relief Act of 1778 was the product of military necessity. The American war was going badly and the British army was in desperate need of recruits. There were Catholics – Irishmen – who, had enlistment not required them to forswear their faith, would gladly have joined the colours. The Relief Act was agreed between the parties to make it possible for them to serve King and country.

Edmund Burke wrote a preamble which – since it philosophised about the role of the state – was rejected in favour of a more prosaic summary by John Dunning. Sir George Savile, the owner of large estates in Ireland, was chosen to present the bill, with the task of providing first-hand evidence of labourers and tenant farmers – estimated to number about 55,000 – who had left home in order to enjoy in America the religious freedom they were denied in their native land. It was introduced into the House of Commons on May 15th 1778. By June 5th it had passed all its stages without objection and received Royal Assent. Its effect on recruitment was immense and immediate and was confirmed by a sudden increase in attendances at Mass in Sheerness, Woolwich and Portsea – all of them garrison towns.

The Act – though the product of the army's needs – had other objectives. Its long title described it as being designed to relieve 'His Majesty's subjects, professing the Papist Religion from certain penalties and liabilities' that had been imposed by the Act of 1700, which was passed to 'Prevent the Growth of Popery'. It did not repeal the whole of that Act. It remained an offence to send a child abroad in order to receive a Catholic education. But Catholics were relieved of the obligation to pay double taxation. The right of Protestants to claim inheritances which had been bequeathed to Catholic members of their families was abolished. Limitations on the ownership and leasing of property were removed for all 'Lands, Tenements and Hereditament within the Kingdom of England, the Dominion of Wales and the Town of Berwick upon Tweed'.[23] To take advantage of the various forms of 'relief', Catholics were required to swear allegiance to King and country in what was virtually the oath proposed in 1715. It was embodied in the Act itself and – as well as rejecting the doctrine that excommunicated 'princes' could be legally deposed, and denying that the Pope possessed temporal authority – actually denounced 'the pretender who called himself James III and his son who calls himself the Prince of Wales'.[24] An identical act was passed by the Irish Parliament.

The bill enjoyed a comparatively easy passage through the House of Commons, despite the interventions of a Mr Ambler, who supported Catholics being given permanent title to any property they owned in 1778, but prevented from acquiring more; and a Mr Turner, who asserted that all religion was evil – since it 'reduced men, by nature free, to a state of slavery' – but Roman Catholicism was no worse than the rest.[25] In the House of Lords the bill was passed unanimously but not without opposition. The Bishop of Peterborough voiced the fear of Catholicism that had haunted England since the Reformation: Papists found it difficult to keep their 'religious principles altogether distinct from the political superstructure which has been raised upon them' and feared that 'should the occasion offer, they might still be made too subservient' to Rome.

Vicars Apostolic, who had doubted the wisdom of the whole exercise, responded with admirable ingenuity. On June 4th 1778, 'clergy, both secular and regular, residing in London, Midland and Northern Districts' were reminded that 'The great Apostle Paul writing to his beloved disciple Timothy, and in him instructing all Christian pastors of the soul, desires that supplications, prayers intercessions and thanksgiving be made for all men, kings and all that are in high station and authority.' Prayers must therefore be offered up for the King and Queen.[26] Charles Walmesley, Vicar Apostolic of the Western District, did even better. He wrote that 'the great humanity of the government towards us suggest a propriety of behaviour on our part, in using the present indulgence with caution, prudence and moderation'.

The Relief Act of 1778 achieved at least one of its purposes. Indeed, it exceeded expectations. War with France required the recruitment of soldiers in far greater numbers than had been thought necessary to subdue the American colonies, and the call to the colours received such an enthusiastic response that it was deemed prudent to appoint the army's first Roman Catholic chaplain – Father Alexander Macdonell of the Glengarry Fencibles.

The circumstance in which that particular regiment recruited so many Catholics suggests that not everyone treated the 'great humanity' with the respect that the Vicars Apostolic demanded. If the new recruits were Scotsmen, they were not legally entitled to take the oath that was required before enlistment. Although the authors of the bill had hoped it would encourage the recruitment of large numbers of Scottish soldiers, the bill did not apply to Scotland. A pastoral letter, sent in February 1779 by the 'Bishop of Daulis to his Flock – On the Occasion of a Persecution being raised against them', explained why. The Catholics of Scotland were afraid that more 'relief' would provoke the Protestant majority to renew the persecution. So, although they 'had every reason to expect that the same indulgence as was granted last year to our Brethren in England would be extended this session of parliament to this country', in light of 'feeling the great opposition raised in Scotland against it ... it was judged expedient not to make any application to Parliament for it at this time'.[27]

The Bishop added a postscript to his letter: 'On Tuesday the threats were effectually put into execution. The mob assembled that day with great fury and attacked the houses possessed by our clergymen.' Bishop Hay of the Eastern District of Scotland was in London when the riots began, but his episcopal record described the attacks on persons and property, hour by hour and day by day:

At about noon on Tuesday February 2nd the Mob assembled around the Chapel House in Chalmers' Close and began to pelt the inmates with stones. Mr James Cameron and Mr Matheson, a young priest just arrived from Spain, sat down to dinner at about two o'clock but the shower of stones became so sharp that they could no longer remain with safety in the house. They managed with great difficulty to force their way through the crowd to the old Chapel in Blackfriars' Wynd, taking with them the servants and as much of the altar as they could collect in a few moments and enclose about their person. Their departure was the signal for the Mob to force the doors of the House. It was instantly filled with wild men armed with hatchets and stones under the vigorous strokes of which the interior of the house soon became an utter wreck. The space of open ground around it and all the avenues were now filled with a dense mass of rabble and a general shout – 'Set fire to it immediately – soon decided the fate of the building. Straw and barrels of tar were distributed over several floors and the whole was suddenly on flames which did not subside until ten o'clock that night.[28]

In other parts of Edinburgh the rioters turned on Catholics as well as their chapels – as George Hay discovered on his return to Edinburgh from London. Not having been forewarned of the disturbances and finding a mob surrounding his church, he asked a woman in the crowd to explain the commotion. She replied, 'We are burning the Popish chapel and only wish we had the bishop to throw into the fire.'[29]

Although many Scottish Catholics, perhaps wisely, thought it prudent to bide their time, English Catholics – particularly wealthy laymen – wanted more than what Lord Mansfield, the Lord Chief Justice, described as 'barely toleration', as it 'only took away the penalties of one act out of many'.[30] And the Relief Act's association with Britain's military capability provided them with the opportunity to press for more reform. Four months after the Act was passed, King George III and Queen Charlotte visited Thorndon Hall in Essex to witness a military review. Thorndon Hall was the home of Lord Petre, a typical example of the great Catholic families of England who had, for three hundred years, accepted the penalties of openly professing their faith and employing priests to say Mass for themselves and their neighbours. The mere fact of the King and Queen of England accepting their hospitality – staying in a house which included a 'Papist chapel' – was in itself the sign of more tolerant times. But the whole atmosphere of the occasion gave Petre the increased confidence that was required to press for the full rights of citizenship. After the colonels of the assembled regiments had dined with the King, he wrote in his diary, 'I shall always hold it as the most flattering circumstance of my life that His Majesty gave me the opportunity of showing him, in the ordinary course of life, that respect, loyalty and affection which the laws of my country prevent me from doing in more important circumstance.'[31] Petre wanted the opportunity to serve.

He became the driving force behind the respectful campaign for more relief. He accepted – having satisfied himself that he was not trespassing on the Duke of Norfolk's territory – the chairmanship of the committee that was to take the measure forward. Optimists claimed that the Relief Act had 'struck the general prejudice against [Catholics] at its centre. It disposes their neighbours to think of them with kindness. It led the public to view the pretensions towards further relief with a favourable eye.'[32] But there was much evidence to justify the fear that at least a rabid anti-Catholic minority would think it their duty to rise up in defence of the Protestant faith.

The rumours of impending war with France had given new life to old fears that Papists were waiting impatiently to support an invasion by a Catholic enemy. Stories circulated about a plot to flood London by bursting the banks of the Thames. Twenty thousand Jesuits were said to be hidden in tunnels under the capital, ready to emerge to welcome the victorious French. It was claimed that Benedictine monks, disguised as sedan chairmen, had poisoned Southwark's flour. In Scotland the recently formed Protestant Association issued a pamphlet: 'Let us call to remember the massacre [of the Huguenots] in Paris. Let not the blood of the martyrs be forgotten.'[33] The suggestion that the Relief Act be extended to Scotland had, as the Bishop of Daulis warned his flock, been followed by days of rioting. The government had heeded the warnings, but one Protestant had violently disagreed with that decision. By keeping in place the penal acts, which overrode the Scotsman's legal right to bear arms, the Westminster Parliament had left Scotland 'naked and defenceless'.[34] The man who held those perverse views and believed the people of Scotland to 'think the king a Papist' was Lord George Gordon.

CHAPTER 17

A Species of Fanatical Phrenzy

Lord George Gordon was a pathological malcontent. In modern society his invariably erratic and bellicose behaviour would be attributed to the neglect he undoubtedly suffered after the death of his father, the Duke of Gordon, and his mother's second marriage. He was enlisted in the navy in 1763 without his agreement or even knowledge, and immediately began to display radical – and therefore unacceptable – inclinations. He complained about the treatment received by (often press-gang-recruited) ratings, declared slavery immoral and expressed doubts about the propriety of the war against the American colonists.

After four years' service he decided – motivated more by perversity than political conviction – to stand for Parliament in Inverness-shire. He approached the election with such manic energy that the sitting Member – General Charles Fraser, son of Lord Lovat – feared defeat. After hasty discussions between the fathers of the two candidates, it was agreed that Lord George would withdraw from the Inverness-shire contest and would be bought a seat elsewhere. At the age of twenty-two he therefore became the Member of Parliament for Ludgershall in Wiltshire. Despite his election, he retained his naval commission. After nine years' service, and still only a lieutenant, he asked for promotion. When his request was refused, Lord George resigned with the explanation that resignation had always been his intention. He was opposed to the war in North America and would not 'imbrue his hands with the blood of men struggling for freedom'.[1] It was then that he concluded that Scotland's exclusion from the Relief Act – and the consequent prohibition on Scotsmen bearing arms – was an insult to a nation and a people, and would leave the country defenceless against the long-expected Catholic uprising.

Perversely, in light of its opposition to all things Catholic, the Edinburgh Protestant Association was attracted to Gordon's strong views on the extension of the Relief Act to Scotland. At its invitation, he visited the city and made a series of provocative speeches. These, in turn, caught the attention of James Fisher, the secretary of the Protestant Association in London. Gordon – fanatic and nobleman –

seemed an ideal figurehead for the organisation. His letter accepting Fisher's invitation to become president mixed aristocratic hauteur with vulgar populism. Gordon's views on the Relief Act had changed diametrically. The bill had been 'introduced in a thin House at the end of the session and passed without public debate'. He did not want to 'raise the apprehensions of the lower classes of people', but it was necessary to make the threat known. 'Popery, when encouraged by Government, has always been dangerous to the liberties of the people.'[2] Gordon was no longer concerned with the Relief Act's application to Scotland. The demand now was for repeal.

Gordon's allegations were reinforced by the increasingly influential John Wesley. In *A Letter to a Roman Catholic*, published in 1749, Wesley had denounced Popery as sinful. His opposition to 'the purple power of Rome advancing by hasty strides to overspeed this unhappy nation' was political rather than theological. In *Popery Properly Considered* he argued that Catholics had, by swearing allegiance to a foreign power, sacrificed all their civil rights. In a letter to the *Public Advertiser*, dated January 1780, he was more categorical, though less philosophical. 'No [Protestant] government ought to tolerate men of a Roman Catholic persuasion.'[3]

Opposition to the Relief Act became so persistent and strong that Lord Petre – who had become the acknowledged leader of the Catholic gentry – thought it expedient to visit George Gordon and suggest to him, as one gentleman to another, that the Protestant Association was 'a mean set of people' and that, rather than follow their lead, Gordon should allow the Act to run, unhindered, for five years to see if his fears about its consequences were justified. Gordon rejected the proposal on the ground that, were he to deny the Association the leadership its members expected, 'there would probably spring up some Wat Tyler' (the leader of the 1381 Peasants' Revolt) with the 'ambition to embroil the country in civil war'.[4] He then, gratuitously, added that he expected that Catholics would take the oath which Petre claimed was the guarantee of their loyalty as well as the requirement of their new liberties – but not respect it. Petre's attempt at reassurance was a disaster. Far from comforting Gordon, the news that the oath had been declared acceptable by a Catholic committee in Paris was greeted with fury. The discussion of British affairs in a foreign, and potentially enemy, capital was an affront to national sovereignty and confirmation that the Papists' first loyalty was not to King George. Gordon was reinforced in the view that the Act must be repealed. The next step would be a petition to Parliament which demonstrated every true Englishman's determination to halt the advance of Popery.

There followed a bizarre series of audiences with the King, which Gordon, the son of a duke, was able to demand as the right of his rank. They certainly took place, but for the details of the proceedings, posterity has to rely on Horace Walpole, an elegant essayist but unreliable historian. In his *Journal of the Reign of George III*, Walpole claimed that, at the first audience, Gordon began, uninvited, to read aloud a pamphlet that he was about to publish. He continued his reading until he received the promise that, if he would stop, the King would finish it himself that evening. The story – true or false – was published in the *Morning Post*. So the second audience was taken up by the King's complaints about Gordon's indiscretions. The third began with Gordon locking the audience chamber doors behind him. Then the captive King was reminded that the last Stuart monarch lost his crown because he was a Papist. Finally, Gordon accused King George of sending Sir John Dalrymple to Edinburgh to strike a bargain with the Scottish Catholics. When George denied the charge, Gordon challenged him to prove the point by instructing his servants to sign a petition calling for the repeal of the Relief Act. The King, at last reacting against Gordon's impertinence, refused. Gordon stormed out, swearing that he would rally the people of Britain against Roman subversion. If the story is half true, the King deserves great credit for his forbearance. And Horace Walpole was justified in declaring Lord George Gordon to be mad.

Mad or not, by the spring of 1780 Gordon was able to tell a meeting at the Crown and Rolls in Chancery Lane that there were 100,000 signatures on his petition and that he proposed to present it to Parliament at once. Alarmed that the campaign was running out of control, James Fisher, the secretary of the Association, proposed a month's pause for calm consideration. Gordon would not contemplate delay. It is at least possible Fisher knew that Lord North, the Prime Minister, intended to offer Lord George Gordon a government sinecure and several thousand pounds in return for a promise to abandon the campaign against the Relief Act. The bribe was offered and instantly rejected. Gordon had become obsessed both with the campaign and with the organisation of a giant petition as a method of promoting it.

In May he told a mass meeting in the Coachmakers' Hall that if the Protestant Association did not accept his battle plan, he would no longer lead the fight. 'The only way to go is in a bold manner and shew that we are to defend Protestantism with our lives.'[5] The meeting – despite the doubts of the campaign's more prudent leaders – accepted Gordon's terms and agreed to organise a mass rally in St George's Field on Friday June 2nd as a prelude to the petition being presented to Parliament. However, Gordon announced that he would only make the presentation if he were accompanied to Westminster by at least 20,000 supporters. The rally attracted more than three times that number. So it was decided, 'for the sake of good order and regularity', that the 50,000 who marched in support of the petition should be divided into four separate columns and should approach Parliament by four different routes. Every marcher was to wear a blue cockade so as to be identified as a supporter of the Protestant cause. The Association's determination to demonstrate its respectability resulted in the composition of a pious statement which set out the way in which the great day was to be organised. The motion 'Resolved that the Magistrates of London, Westminster and Southwark are requested to attend so that their presence may overawe and control any riotous or evil minded persons who may wish to disturb the legal and peaceable deportment of His Majesty's Protestant Subjects'.[6]

Lord George Gordon's arrival at St George's Field was greeted by wild cheering and the only slightly less boisterous singing of Protestant hymns. As he walked towards the rough podium that had been prepared for him, he handed stewards bundles of leaflets for distribution to the crowd. Their message, he explained, was designed to encourage 'inculcation of the same pacific temper' as had inspired the organisers of the petition from the start.[7] But whatever its intention, the brief speech that followed – warning his supporters not to be provoked by Catholic troublemakers in the crowd – excited passions rather than suppressed them. At that moment he was in complete command of his followers. His announcement that he would go at once to the House of Commons in anticipation of the arrival of the petition was greeted by insistent requests to accompany him. But his plan was for the march to follow him an hour later and present the petition to him at Parliament's door. So the requests were rejected, and the rejection was accepted as if Lord George's word was law.

There are a variety of explanations why a disciplined, if angry, march degenerated into a lawless mob. The Protestant Association's explanation exonerated its members, but placed the blame less on Papist agents provocateurs than on other undesirables who infiltrated the columns as they approached Westminster. There is no doubt that a variety of pimps and prostitutes, pickpockets and cut-throats – as well as men and women who had no motive for causing trouble other than the pleasure they found in gratuitous violence – contributed to the mayhem that followed. But the claim that the Protestant Association was blameless is unsustainable. The events of the following week confirm that, from the start, there were Protestants who regarded the march as an opportunity for mounting a Catholic pogrom. Otherwise respectable citizens were caught up in a mood of anti-Catholic hysteria which prevented them from either behaving with discretion or showing respect for the law.

As the four columns converged on the Parliament building, Frederic Reynolds – a fifteen-year-old pupil at Westminster School – abandoned his lessons in order to witness what he described as 'most novel and extraordinary proceedings'. He identified most of the marchers as 'honest Mechanics; the better sort of trades people'.[8] That was not how they behaved. The marchers became a mob and, according to Reynolds, occupied 'every avenue to the House of Commons, the whole of Westminster Bridge and extending to the northern end of Parliament Street' – the greater part of it 'composed of persons decently dressed who appeared to be excited to extravagance by a species of fanatical phrenzy'. Many of the law-abiding and timid citizens, who had joined the march in St George's Field, realised that they had unwittingly become part of a potential riot and returned home. But at the climax of that first day, most of the men and women who remained were members of the Protestant Association and the best that can be said about them is that, although they had started the march with no intention but to express their opinions, they had been carried away by mass hysteria.

From then on, it seemed as if a murderous madness had afflicted previously sane men and women and caused them mindlessly to join with whores and thugs in burning whatever they believed to be the property of Papists and their champions. However, much of the viciousness and violence that followed the march was planned, coldly and calmly, by prosperous artisans. After order was restored, shocked Catholics wrote down what they had heard and seen: 'Macfarlane, who keeps a public house in Church Court in the Strand; Mackenzie, a Taylor; Mackenzie, a cheesemonger; Farquickson, a cabinet maker. On Thursday the 1st or Friday 2nd of June, in company with Mr Bond and Mr Ewen, in the Gallic Language did vow to demolish the Chapels and Houses of Roman Catholics in London and Westminster. Did publically revile His Majesty – saying he was a Papist, had broken his coronation oath, had forfeited his right to the crown.'[9] The veracity of that report to a London priest is only slightly diminished by its bizarre postscript: 'All Highlanders had bagpipes playing.' But if the account of the event – said to have taken place on the day before, or the day of, the march on Parliament – is correct, the informant's not-quite-literate conclusion is wholly justified: 'If this would not amount to treason; and who instigated them but Lord George Gordon?'

Most of the violence, on the first day of what became a riot, was directed at the peers and Members of Parliament who were said to have betrayed the Protestant cause by passing the Relief Act. They were pulled from their carriages and pelted with mud, jostled and threatened with such arcane vengeance as having crosses carved on their foreheads. Attempts were made to invade the chambers of both Houses. Though one of its members, Lord Boston, was held prisoner by the mob, the Lords attempted to continue its noble business in its imperturbable way. The Duke of Richmond, who was in the middle of a long speech in favour of more equal representation in Parliament, refused to give way in order to allow a less composed colleague to ask the government to make a statement on what amounted to a siege. Commons doorkeepers held at bay an invasion by what they claimed to be 14,000 insurgents. So consideration of the Hair Powder Bill and a motion to impose a duty on starch proceeded until Lord George Gordon arrived and immediately moved that he be allowed to present his petition. His proposal was not seconded and he was shouted down.

The confusion continued all day. Magistrates made ineffectual attempts to disperse the crowd. Troops – including Foot and Horse Guards – drew up in front of the mob, as if to charge. But, uncertain of both their powers and their orders, they stood fast and, instead of charging, were charged. Inside the Commons chamber, Members attempted to carry on normal business against the background roar of the mob at the gates of Parliament. From time to time Gordon repeated his proposal that Parliament receive his petition. During the early evening his motion was seconded by Alderman Frederick Bull. The great roll of parchment was dragged into the chamber and Members debated whether or not its contents should be debated. Lord George spoke – or so he claimed – on behalf of the 12,000 of those of His Majesty's subjects who were 'praying for a repeal of the act passed the last session in favour of Roman Catholics'.[10] The opponents of the Act were, he claimed, as 'determined to stand up for their religious rights ... against the pernicious effects of a religion, subversive of all liberty, inimical to all morals, begotten by fraud and superstition and teeming with absurdity, persecution and the most diabolical cruelty'.

From time to time, during the debate that followed, Gordon left the chamber and addressed the milling crowd outside. His speeches usually identified and denounced Members who had spoken against his motion. At one point a voice from the adoring crowd asked him for guidance. Lord George replied that the marchers must decide for themselves. Although he claimed, against the evidence, that Scotland had saved itself from the effects of a Relief Act by remaining 'steady and cool', his description of 'how the matter stands' was an open incitement to occupy Parliament and impose the will of the mob on Members. 'The House is going to divide upon the question whether your petition shall be taken into consideration now or upon Tuesday ... If it is not taken into consideration now it may be lost. Tomorrow the House does not meet. Monday is the King's birthday. Upon Tuesday Parliament may be dissolved.'

The Commons – which had not behaved with great distinction earlier in the day – responded to the threat of mob rule with spirit, if not composure. Colonel Holroyd, asserting that Gordon was bad as well as mad, told him that if he further incited the mob, a resolution would be moved, committing him to the Tower. General Conway – as well as proposing that three Members should defend the narrow entrance to the House, as Horatio and his colleagues defended the bridge across the Tiber – promised that the first fatality in the battle would be the rabble-rouser himself. Others followed Gordon about the chamber, ready physically to prevent him from performing other acts of malice and mischief. After six hours of rancorous argument, the question was put. Lord George Gordon, Alderman Frederick Bull and six other Members voted in favour; 190 Members voted against.

The Guards were recalled to ensure Members a safe passage home, but once again they proved unwilling or unable to disperse the mob. Indeed, they were treated with such good-natured derision that the enterprising Justice Addington, the magistrate who was directing operations, took advantage of the apparent change of mood to make an offer. He would withdraw the troops if the protesters promised, on their honour, voluntarily to disperse. It is not clear how they would have signified their agreement. But Justice Addington, rather than waiting for an answer, immediately instructed the Guards to return to barracks. To Addington's delight, the rest of the mob began to drift away. His pleasure was misplaced. The men who wanted to storm the House of Commons left Westminster because, having failed in their objective of forcing the petition on Parliament, they had decided to express their anti-Catholicism in a different way. Sometime before midnight a group of men, wearing blue cockades and carrying banners of the sort that had festooned the Protestant Association march, were seen marching down Queen's Street towards Lincoln's Inn. They carried pickaxes and spades, hammers and crowbars and flaming torches. They were making for Duke Street and the Sardinian Ambassador's chapel of St Anselm and St Cecilia, 'the Cathedral of London Catholicism'.

The ringleader pushed his crowbar through one of the chapel windows. That was the signal for the destruction to begin. The doors were broken down and hundreds of rioters rushed inside and pulled down the altar. The holy statues were smashed into pieces and thrown, together with the curtains and vestments, into the street, where everything that would burn was made into a giant bonfire. Sampson Rainsforth, the King's Tallow Chandler and an ardent Protestant, attempted to arrest a man he saw carrying off a candlestick. The thief was rescued by his friends and Rainsforth ran to Somerset House Barracks in the hope that the Guards who were stationed there would come to the defence of what was left of the Sardinian Embassy chapel. For the first time that day, military intervention was effective. The chapel itself was on fire and many of the rioters had moved on to find other Catholic premises – as it turned out, houses as well as chapels to destroy. But those who remained were scattered by a bayonet charge. Thirteen men, who loitered rather than ran, were arrested. All of them were in respectable employment and five of them were Roman Catholics.

The destruction of the Sardinian Embassy chapel having been completed to its satisfaction, the mob moved on to the Bavarian Embassy chapel in Golden Square. It was sacked, but not set on fire. Then the cry went up that they should find Richard Challoner – who, in their ignorance, they believed to be one of the authors of the Relief Act – and force him to take part in some sort of sacrilegious ceremony. They found their way to Gloucester Street but could not identify his house. Showing more restraint than they had previously exhibited, the (by now depleted) mixture of hooligans and bigots decided not to burn down the entire road. Exhausted and disappointed, they drifted home. Challoner was sleeping, safe if not at peace, in Finchley under the protection of William Mawhood, a rich woollen merchant.

On Saturday morning a vast crowd waited outside the Savoy Prison in anticipation of eleven of the men, who were arrested at the Sardinian Embassy chapel, being marched to court in Bow Street. When they appeared, the troops who escorted them were greeted with an explosion of booing, but although a few stones were thrown, no serious attempt was made to free the prisoners. After they were remanded in custody, the men and women who watched them being taken to Newgate Prison lined the route in sullen silence. Next day the court concluded that nine of the men were no more than spectators of the arson. They were discharged.

For the whole time that the mayhem continued, Lord George Gordon did not leave his lodging. By early evening it was generally supposed that the riots were over and London could sleep in peace.

The general supposition was wrong. The disturbance that was to grow into a ten-day riot began in Moorfields, a part of London which was the home of hundreds of Irishmen. Most of them were vagrants and casual labourers, but among them lived a handful of rich businessmen. The businessmen's motives for only employing their countrymen were mixed. Some felt a sentimental obligation to fellow Irishmen. Others knew that the immigrants would work longer hours and expect less pay than the native-born Englishmen, who deeply resented the advantage they imagined the Irish enjoyed.

One of the businessmen was a silk merchant named Malo, who was as well known for his ardent Catholicism as for his selective employment policy. And it was probably a combination of both aspects of his reputation that made a restless crowd congregate outside his house on the afternoon of Sunday June 4th. It is because the days of carnage began there that some historians believe the rioting that followed was more about poverty than the Pope. Perhaps. But if that was so, the mob was incited to violence by a handful of fanatics who encouraged the belief that Catholicism – as represented by the Irish – was the cause of their distress. The assaults on Malo's property and person represented a new aspect of anti-Catholic bigotry. As 'Papists' were freed of their legal disabilities and enabled to play a greater part in the economics of the nation, the Irish – whose religion and nationality were always synonymous – came to find work in England in increasing numbers. Catholics, who had always been a threat to England's national security, became a threat to Englishmen's prosperity.

At the first sign of trouble, Malo had asked Alderman Brackley Kennett, the Lord Mayor of London, for protection and was rebuffed during a series of conversations which ended with Kennett displaying his prejudice by asking, 'Surely Sir, you are a Papist?'[11] For most of the day, Kennett's inactivity might have been explained, if not excused, by the crowd around Malo's house behaving in a way that was offensive but not violent. The violence began at about six o'clock when, at what some observers claimed was a pre-arranged signal, the crowd turned into a mob, moved off into Ropemaker's Alley and attacked the Catholic chapel. The marshalmen, who were employed by the ward's alderman to keep order, refused to protect 'any Popish rascals'. Many of them wore blue cockades.

The assault on the chapel was the beginning of Moorfields' two days of terror, during which every Catholic chapel in the area was demolished, houses of identified Catholics were burned down and Catholics – men, women and children – were openly assaulted in the streets. Kennett asked for military assistance and a company of

Coldstream Guards, under the command of a young ensign, was sent to Moorfields. However the magistrates refused permission for them to clear the streets by force, and they returned to barracks. That at least spared the more cerebral soldiers – both officers and men – from wrestling with a dilemma with which some of them had been presented by their Church of England padres. Having taken an oath to defend a Church of England king against his Roman Catholic enemies, were they entitled to take up arms against Protestants whose intention was to suppress potentially rebellious Papists?

The soldiers' retreat left open the way for the climax to the Moorfields riot: the sacking and burning of Malo's house. The family – who had stubbornly refused to leave – escaped over the roof. The furniture, doors and ripped-up floorboards were piled in a heap in the road and set alight. The family's canaries, in their cage, were put on top of the bonfire. One onlooker – displaying, as Englishmen should, greater concern for birds than for the people – offered to buy them and save them from the flames. He was told, 'They are Popish birds and should burn with other Popish goods.'[12]

On the second day, the mob turned its attention to Leicester Fields. Daniel Defoe wrote about the 'ten thousand stout fellows who would spend the last drop of their blood against Popery that do not know whether it be man or horse'. And they were sustained as much by that ignorance as by prejudice in all sorts of diseased imaginings. Charlotte, the sister of Fanny Burney, heard a man justify 'having the Catholic chapel destroyed, for they say it is a shame that the Pope should come here'.[13] And when the riots spread to Bath, one elderly gentleman's life was put at risk when demonstrators decided that 'he must be Pope because he lodges in St James's Parade and has a nightgown with gold flowers on it'.[14] But, obscured by the mindless violence and ingrained ignorance, there was a precise intention to identify and punish the men who had promoted Catholic relief.

Edmund Burke, who had offered to write the preamble to the Act, returned home from Parliament to find that his house had been saved from destruction by soldiers sent, not by the Lord Mayor, but directly by the government. Sir John Savile, who had introduced the bill, was not so lucky. His house was burned to the ground. Sampson Rainsforth, who tried to prevent the destruction of the Sardinian Embassy chapel and had subsequently given evidence that led to the remand of eleven rioters, was unfortunate enough to be described as a hero in some of Saturday's papers. On him, the mob exacted a special vengeance. He was forced to sit in the road outside his house and warehouse and watch the fire, intensified by the tallow that was his stock in trade, consume both buildings. Sir John Fielding, the only magistrate to make a real attempt to disperse the mob, and Mr Justice Hyde, who read the Riot Act in front of Parliament to legitimise troops clearing the way for Members to return to the House of Commons, were spared until Tuesday night. Then their houses were set alight.

When it reassembled, the House of Commons passed four pious resolutions: setting up an inquiry into the causes, calling for the prosecution of the miscreants, providing compensation for the victims and, of course, condemning the invasion of Parliament as a breach of privilege. Each one was passed unanimously. Lord George Gordon not only voted in favour, but issued a statement on behalf of the Protestant Association. It called on 'all true Protestants . . . to show their attachment to their best interests by legal and peaceable deportment'. The sudden conversion to moderation did nothing either to reduce his popularity with the Protestant mob or to limit the vehemence with which it demonstrated its opposition to Popery. When Gordon left the Commons, the horses were taken from the shafts of his carriage and he was pulled home by cheering supporters. No doubt they were less influenced by his conduct in Parliament than by two pamphlets that had been published the previous day and were popularly attributed to Robert Watson, Gordon's secretary. *England in Blood* denounced the 'infernal designs of the ministry' which had allowed the Relief Act to become law. *True Protestants, No Turncoats* called for the continued demonstration of Protestant feeling. So the indiscriminate attacks on Papists and Papist sympathisers continued.

The Duke of Devonshire, certain that his family's history of militant Protestantism would guarantee the safety of Devonshire House, rode out to reinforce the rescue of the besieged Lord Rockingham, whose record was less unequivocal. His coach was stopped in Piccadilly and he was required to step down and cry, 'No Popery.' The mob that had attacked the home of Mr Justice Hyde had been led, in so far as any leadership was possible, by a man riding a carthorse and waving a Protestant Association banner. As the flames began to die, he stood in the stirrups and cried, 'A-hoy for Newgate.' The rioters' next objective was the prison in which four of the men arrested during the assault on the Sardinian Embassy chapel were being held. But as they were to make clear when they arrived at the gates, releasing the arsonists was not their only objective. They were bent on destroying the whole prison – a symbol of the establishment which had always been their enemy and had, in their disturbed minds, betrayed the poor of England by giving succour to the Catholic enemy.

The Keeper of the Prison, acting with commendable courage, refused the mob entry and they set about the methodical destruction of the gatehouse in which he lived. The Justices of the Peace, alarmed at the thought of a mass breakout, raised a hundred constables to charge the crowd. They were ambushed and disarmed. The poet George Crabbe – on one of his occasional visits from Suffolk to London – saw what followed. 'They broke the roof, tore away the rafters and, having got ladders, they descended. Not Orpheus himself had better luck – flames all around them ... About twelve women and eight men ascended from their confinement.' Rather more left through the broken gates. Estimates of the number of prisoners who escaped, some of them still in manacles and chains, vary from 117 to 301. What is certain is that three of them were already condemned to death and awaiting execution at the end of the week.

Drunk with the sense of power that the destruction had created – and with wine and spirits stolen from the Prison Keeper's cellar – the mob moved on. They first attempted to set fire to houses occupied by the Lord Chief Justice, Lord Mansfield, and the Archbishop of Canterbury. The Lord Chief Justice had incurred the wrath of the Protestant Association by acquitting James Talbot of the crimes of being a priest and saying Mass. The second charge had been dismissed because the informant had not heard the words of the Mass spoken – and the crime was *saying* the Mass. The first was thrown out on the grounds that if wearing vestments was proof of a priestly vocation, then every High Court judge was guilty.[15] William Markham, the Archbishop of York, was thought, with some justification, to have sympathy for the Catholic cause. Both attempts at retribution failed. So the rioters relieved their frustration by attacking the Bridewell Prison and the neighbouring New Prison. Then they renewed, with greater success than they had previously enjoyed, their plan to punish Archbishop Markham and Lord Mansfield. Both houses were set alight. Neither burned down.

The mob then discussed – in so far as discussion is possible within a mob – whether or not they should burn the Northampton Chapel in Clerkenwell. Its anti-Papist credentials were impeccable. Charles Wesley appeared there from time to time to celebrate Holy Communion with the Countess of Huntington, its owner and the founder of several Protestant sects. But it had previously belonged to a Mr Maperley, who had sided with Sampson Rainsforth, and there was a strong feeling that it deserved destruction on that account. Eventually they decided to leave the chapel, in favour of another prison. So they marched on to the Fleet.

On Monday the attacks on individually identified Roman Catholics confirmed that, although many – perhaps most – of the rioters were motivated by criminal greed and the love of violence for violence's sake, bigotry still drove on some of the mob. Peter Lyon reported to his priest, 'On Monday morning the rioters came to my house at half past one when I and my family were asleep and we made our escape over the roof and got out backwards. I lost all our furniture and wearing apparel. My loss is to the amount of four hundred and fifty pounds.'[16] By then the riots had lasted four days. On Monday afternoon the King – contemptuous of Parliament's apparent impotence, angered by the army's combination of incompetence and timidity and no doubt disturbed by the rumour that Buckingham Palace had been demolished and that he was dead in the rubble – sent a message to the House of Commons urging Members to 'take such measures as the time requires'. The message was ignored.

A charitable explanation of the army's inactivity was provided by Archbishop Markham. 'A fatal error has prevailed among the military that they could not in any case act without the orders of a civil magistrate which is the case when a great mob has assembled but has not yet proceeded to any acts of violence. But when they have begun to commit felonies, any subject [the military with the rest] is justified in Common Law in using all methods to prevent illegal acts.'[17] The King reacted to the advice that no formal declaration was necessary by issuing a Royal Proclamation offering a £300 reward ('and a pardon if necessary') to anyone who assisted in the prosecution and conviction of 'person or persons ... concerned in pulling down ... the chapel of any Foreign Minister'. Perhaps George was more concerned about diplomatic relations or good order and discipline than the civil rights and safety of his Catholic subjects. Whatever the real reasons for his initiative, the King of England – untainted himself by serious suspicions of Popery – had come to the rescue of Papist property, if not Papist persons.

Not everyone followed the King's lead. On June 7th, the day on which it received the Royal Proclamation, the Common Council of the City of London passed, unanimously, a resolution that called for the repeal of 'the Act of Parliament recently passed in favour of Roman Catholics' as the best way of restoring order. Alderman John Wilkes – claiming that Farringdon Without, his own ward, was at the centre of the riots – proposed that the Royal Proclamation be committed for consideration on another day. His motion was intended to be a calculated insult to the King – a gesture Wilkes regarded as more important than a practical proposal to restore order, protect property and save lives. When no one seconded what amounted to parliamentary games,

Wilkes withdrew his motion and urged immediate action against the rioters.

The army, in the form of the Adjutant General, had already responded to the Royal Proclamation as duty required. Strategic locations – the Bank of England, the Guildhall, the Royal Exchange and the Inns of Court – were all heavily defended. During the next couple of days, Alderman John Wilkes – changed from dissident into City Father – took formal charge of the Buckinghamshire militia and was joined in defence of the Bank by Lord Algernon Percy, who had led the Northumberland militia on a forced march south. They were both surprised by the arrival of an agitated Lord George Gordon, who attempted to harangue the mob. Against the background noise of rapturous cheering which greeted his appearance, it was difficult to make out what he meant to say, but it seems – and he was later explicitly to claim – that he pleaded with them to go home. Whatever his intention, his speech only increased the crowd's frenzy, and a young Guards officer pushed him behind the ranks of the increasingly nervous soldiers. The mob charged, the soldiers opened fire and perhaps as many as a dozen rioters were killed.

The rioters then turned their attention to softer targets. First in line was the brewery owned by Thomas Langdale, a Catholic with twelve children to protect. Initially the mob was more interested in sampling Langdale's produce than in destroying his property but, eventually, the house and the brewery were both set on fire. Several rioters died in the cellar. Some were overcome by the fumes as they tapped the kegs of whisky and gin. Others were too drunk to notice that they were being trapped by the flames. The assault on the Bank was renewed and again repulsed – even though by the time of the attack some of the rioters were armed with stolen muskets. By then the army had belatedly recognised both the size of the threat and its duty to play a part in defeating it. Large contingents of men were stationed on Blackfriars and Westminster Bridges. The rioters were first to be dispersed and then killed, captured or driven back to their hovels.

It is not clear how long it took to clear the streets or whether or not individual acts of arson continued, sporadically, after the riots were generally over. Militant Protestants in Bath, Bristol, Birmingham and Hull heard the news from London and, some days later, felt an obligation to demonstrate their solidarity by behaving in a similarly violent fashion. In Bath, the Catholic community had caused particular offence by acquiring 'a Chapel in Corn Street . . . Well furnished with seats [it] has a gallery with commodious pews, a fine altar with an elegant painting of Our Saviour dying on the Cross over it.'[18] On June 17th, they were punished for their effrontery by both the destruction of the chapel and assaults on those who worshipped within it. The impression the riots made on Henry Stoner – the six-year-old member of a distinguished Catholic family – was so great that, even in old age, he told the story of his escape from the mob: 'In the dead of night I was obliged to get up hastily and was led by my father to York House, where we all passed remainder of the night. Early next morning we all set off for Stonor [the Oxfordshire village to which the family gave its name] leaving the Catholic Chapel in flames.'[19] The Catholics of Bristol acted with greater discretion. A chapel set up in a warehouse in the mid-1770s was taken down, in anticipation of the Bath riots spreading to the coast.

In London the riots lasted for six days. Even when the worst was over, there were still sudden outbursts of violence, including a moment of madness in Fleet Street when a group of men who had broken away from the main mob charged a picket of Horse Guards. Twenty rioters were killed and twice as many wounded. But by the evening of Thursday June 8th patrols of the hastily mustered London Military Association were patrolling the streets, firing on 'any four persons collected together who will not instantly disperse' and searching for the prisoners who had been released from the destroyed gaols. A new rumour – rioters' corpses hanging from hastily constructed gibbets – was joyously received by respectable Londoners. A few libertarians combined with irreconcilable opponents of the government to complain that ministers, who had failed to act when the riot could easily have been put down, acted too severely when the riots were at their height, by sanctioning the troops to open fire on unarmed civilians.

Relief at the return to the rule of law did not incline politicians towards mercy. During the week of the riots and the days that immediately followed, 450 alleged rioters were arrested, 160 of them stood trial, and 75 were found guilty of offences ranging from causing an affray to murder. Twenty-five of the convicted rioters – including a boy of fifteen and a girl a year older – were hanged. Not one of the 450 suspects was found to have signed the Protestant Association petition. The only defendant who confessed to being motivated by strong religious beliefs was Denis Reardon who, when his wife had come home drunk and shouting 'No Popery!', had decapitated her with a carving knife.[20]

On Friday June 9th two King's Messengers arrested Lord George Gordon. He was searched and found to be carrying a pistol and large knife, which he described as 'necessary to defend myself against Roman

Catholics'. He was taken to Westminster where a group of Privy Councillors, including Lord North, the Prime Minister, found he had a case to answer and sent him to the Tower to await a formal trial. Gordon waited there until late December. During the half year he was on remand, he was visited by John Wesley, who recorded in his diary that the 'conversation turned upon Popery and religion'.[21] When the indictment was published, the nearest it got to a mention of either subject was the preamble which described the defendant as 'not having the fear of God before his eyes but being seduced by the instigation of the devil'. The actual charge was purely secular. Among the dubiously judicial description of 'clubs, bludgeons, staves and other warlike weapons' was the allegation that Gordon 'unlawfully, maliciously and traitorously did compass, imagine and intend to raise and levy war against our Lord the King'. Gordon's defence was that the Protestant Association march of June 7th was a peaceful demonstration of support for the Established Church and that the violence on the days that followed was wholly unrelated to the peaceful attempt to deliver a petition to Parliament. Indeed, the Association had published a statement which condemned the riot and called on the rioters to return home. At one point Gordon himself had risked his life by facing, and admonishing, the mob.

The court was occupied for days with accounts of the damage done by the riots, which linked, or claimed to link, the rioters to Gordon and the Protestant Association. Descriptions of burnings, lootings and pillage were interrupted by the Attorney General demanding to know if the perpetrator of the offence was wearing a blue cockade; and Lord Porchester, in answer to the vital question about Lord George himself, attested, 'I certainly saw him with a cockade in the House on Tuesday' – the fourth day of the riots.[22] But not even a court over which Lord Mansfield, a victim of the riots, presided was going to find a man guilty of treason because of the rosette he wore in his hat. It took the jury thirty minutes to conclude, unanimously, that Lord George Gordon was not guilty of the charge which had been laid against him.

English Catholics of a pessimistic disposition were entitled to believe that the acquittal of Gordon confirmed that popular prejudice against Rome remained too strong to allow speedy progress towards full emancipation. To them, it seemed that the Protestant king had called out the troops only when it became clear that more than Catholic lives and property were in danger. But Catholic optimists were justified in insisting that there were signs of a slow change of attitude. The Relief Act was – despite the ravages of the London mob – still in place and it had been complemented by parallel legislation in the Dublin Parliament. Irishmen who had taken the oath of loyalty could lease or own land. Priests were no longer obliged to register with the secular authorities. Catholics could open their own schools and were allowed to own firearms.

It was while London was on fire and half a dozen provincial cities and towns were feeling the heat that John Hornyold, Vicar Apostolic of the Midland District, finally came to a conclusion about how to deal with the reluctance – perhaps in modern times the inability – of his flock to attend Mass on all the feast days in the Church's calendar. Among the rules of conduct that the faithful must respect was the injunction which allowed only one meal on feast days, and rest from menial work. Since days of special obligation included all of Lent, most Fridays and the eve of major feasts, observing the rules of abstinence involved self-discipline of a high order and was out of place and time in a society in which a new industrial proletariat lacked the freedom of the farms and fields. Hornyold solved the dilemma – following consultations with Rome – by relaxing the rule rather than insisting that it be respected. Other Districts followed suit. New 'Directions for the Faithful of the Northern District touching upon the Observance of Holydays' began with a slight misquotation from Chapter 1, Verse 4 of the Lamentations of Jeremiah: 'Sion mourns because there are none that comes to the solemn Feast. The Temple is destroyed.' Matthew Gibson, of the Northern District, then added, 'And we may truly say that, at the present time, there are few that come to the solemn feast, whatever the cause of it.' The remedy to this state of affairs – apparently sanctioned by Pius VI – was not to increase attendance, but to reduce the number of feast days at which attendance was expected, 'thinking it better not to lay any longer a precept of those [less important feast] days on people who are heavy pressed'. One of the reasons for the survival of the Catholic Church in England was its preoccupation with its own affairs – the product not of egocentricity, but of the certainty that, come what may, it would prevail.

CHAPTER 18

A Set of Secular Gentlemen

The Gordon Riots of 1780 – far from unnerving the Catholics of England – gave added impetus to the demands for emancipation. True, the crown had been slow in suppressing the mob and, even when the troops were eventually called out and assured of their legal right to act, the anxiety to preserve public property had seemed greater than the determination to protect Popish lives. But the Church had not only survived. It had retained the 'relief' which the riots had been raised to repeal. The Act of 1778 – which had provided a degree of civil, though not political, emancipation – encouraged influential Catholics to press the government to move further and faster towards granting them full civic rights. The alliance of rich men which chose to call itself the Catholic Committee was reconstituted in 1782, 'for five years to promote and attend to the affairs of the Roman Catholic body in England'. Its status, and therefore its name, were in dispute from the start. John Milner – then a priest in Winchester, but destined to become Vicar Apostolic of the Midland District – always referred to the Committee's foundation as being the work of 'certain Catholics', to emphasise that 'the pretended committee of the Catholics had no commission whatever from anyone except themselves'.[1]

The Committee's membership – Lords Stourton and Petre, Mr (afterwards Sir John) Throckmorton, Mr Thomas Stapleton and Mr Thomas Hornyold – was certainly socially unrepresentative of English Catholics in general. At the beginning of the nineteenth century the Church was still heavily dependent on the patronage of wealthy believers. But they were mostly prosperous country gentry. The petitioners for more relief were rich to a degree that the description 'prosperous' underestimated and, notwithstanding their being Papists, they were influential members of a London elite. They were also men who, personally, had most to gain from political emancipation. When it was eventually achieved, Barons Petre and Stourton immediately took their seats in the House of Lords. The Earl of Surrey, the Duke of Norfolk's son, was the first Roman Catholic MP to sit in the House of Commons after the repeal of the penal laws. Throckmorton's nephew was the second. Charles Butler, the Committee's secretary, was the first

Catholic, under the new dispensation, to be called to the Bar. But the clamour for civil rights was not confined to men of property and status. Humbler Catholics believed passionately in the justice of emancipation – even though, because of the property qualification, many of them would not be entitled to vote even when it was achieved. They saw it as a sign of national respect. But they had different day-to-day concerns and priorities.

At the time when metropolitan leaders of the Catholic laity were preparing to storm the heights of political power, Father Simon Bordley of Aughton wrote to his bishop with a complaint. His neighbour, Father Caton of Fornby, would only hear confessions on a Saturday evening – a time of great inconvenience to his parishioners who were domestic servants or had business in the Liverpool market. He had also increased the expected Mass offering from a shilling to half a crown. Worse still, he did not preach, but read 'a bit out of a book' – a task which 'any old woman' could perform.[2] Father Bordley was seventy-nine and had served his parish for forty continuous years. We have no way of knowing if his complaint was justified. But if Father Caton did neglect both his offices and his parish, he was not typical of a Church that had begun to take advantage of its new freedom – everywhere except in Wales.

Welsh Catholics – perhaps because of neglect – stubbornly refused to put aside their old superstitions. Instead they incorporated them into a hybrid of folklore and Christianity. 'They invoke not the Deity but only the Virgin Mary and other saints: Mair Wen [White Mary]. Jao [James], Tailaw Mawr [Teilo the Great]. Celer, Gelynnogg and others.'[3] Despite that, or because of it, attendance at Mass was sparse. The one cause for rejoicing was Perthir, where Matthew Prichard established a Franciscan outpost. Catholic baptisms increased (on average) from 2.3 a year between 1761 and 1766 to 5.6 between 1799 and 1806.

Members and supporters of the essentially metropolitan Catholic Committee did not concern themselves with such mundane issues as rural baptisms, Mass charges or the times at which it was possible to make confessions without requiring labourers to choose between work and prayer. But – though divided by wealth and class from the gener-ality of Catholics – they espoused an idea which they insisted, without very much evidence, was popular throughout the Catholic Church in England. It was set out in a letter which they sent to the Vicars Apos-tolic on May 24th 1783. The letter offered 'aid and support in taking such measures as may be effectual to constitute them [the Vicars Apostolic] with the full power of ordinaries in order that frequent depositions to Rome for dispensations and other matters might cease'. The Vicars Apostolic, far from welcoming the offer to increase their independence, denounced the proposal as being the first step towards bishops being elected by their peers, acceptance of the notion that priests and people had equal authority, and the creation of what amounted to a national Catholic Church. There was no direct evidence to confirm those fears in either the Committee's message to the Vicars Apostolic or in the 'Letter to the Catholics of England' that it published on the same day. But subsequent events were to prove those fears to be entirely justified.

Monsignor Christopher Stoner, the agent in the Vatican for the English Vicars Apostolic, represented the view of most priests in an angry letter from Rome. It was headed 'The Proceeds of Our Committee as they Call Themselves'. The message was as blunt as the title: 'What displeases me most in all this affair is to see a set of secular gentlemen intermeddling in matters outside their sphere and assuming an air of authority to which they are not entitled.'⁴ The emphasis on the Committee's exclusively secular composition was a criticism too damaging to be ignored. Its members still believed that 'the English Roman Catholic gentlemen, being quite able to act and judge for themselves', no clerical help was needed. But, faced with hostility at once so great and so distinguished, the Committee wisely retreated and three priests were asked to join them. The most senior was James Robert Talbot, the recently appointed Vicar Apostolic of the London District. His colleagues were Joseph Wilkes, a Benedictine priest from Bath, and Charles Berrington, Coadjutor (but soon to become Vicar Apostolic) of the Midland District.

The invitation to Berrington was intended to ensure that at least one clerical member of the Committee supported the lay members' proposals. Berrington had lost his professorship at Douai because of his unorthodox view that the celibacy of the clergy was justified by reference to neither the Bible nor ancient texts, and because of his doubts about papal infallibility. He had become the Catholic Committee's candidate for Vicar Apostolic of the London District and, when John Douglass was nominated, Berrington's admirers had continued to press his claim with an anonymous letter to the clergy which argued that the laity should have been consulted about the appointment and that the Pope's endorsement was unnecessary. Berrington had wisely renounced all claim to London and become chaplain and confessor at Ingatestone Hall, the home of Sir John Throckmorton – the author of the anonymous letter – and was, initially, refused facilities in the London District which he had aspired to lead. All in all, he personified the Committee's view that the Catholic Church in England belonged to them.

It was agreed, at what the Catholic Committee called a General Meeting of the Catholics of England, that the Committee of Five be reconstituted, with the addition of two new lay members and the three priests, as the Committee of Ten. But although it was no longer a purely secular body, it could still not be said to be representative of Catholics at large. Its new members – clerical no less than lay – all had aristocratic connections. The Committee's unorthodox views were not a secret. Father Thomas Weld of Lulworth declined an invitation to become a member with the explanation that his Jesuit education had taught him not to flirt with heresy and that there was only one possible view of the Pope and his powers.

Although its aristocratic composition was the Committee of Ten's greatest weakness, it was also its greatest strength. It could be dismissed as wholly unrepresentative of most Catholics, but its connections enabled it to go where humbler Catholics would not have been admitted. In February 1788, at what it described as a 'meeting of the English Catholics', the Committee had been empowered to draft a 'memorial' for examination by the Prime Minister, William Pitt. It dealt, almost exclusively, with the need for further relief. The time had come for a meeting between the Prime Minister and the Committee's leading members. Pitt wisely asked for 'authentic evidence of the opinion of the Catholic clergy and the Catholic universities with respect to the existence and extent of the Pope's dispensing powers'. It is not clear how the view of the English Catholic clergy was obtained. The Catholic universities of Paris, Louvain, Douai, Alcala and Salamanca were all approached direct. Their answers satisfied the Prime Minister. Pitt was particularly reassured by the unanimous verdict that the doctrine 'faith need not be kept with heretics' had no standing within the Church. Oaths – an essential part of all relief legislation – were as likely to be respected by Catholics as by Protestants. It was time to move on.

Pitt, bound to the Committee by ties of class (though not of religion) and naturally sympathetic to emancipation, accepted that the self-appointed ten emissaries spoke for all English Catholics. In fact they held a view of their Church's proper future which was exclusive to their place in society. The Committee represented those Catholic gentlemen who, during the time of overt persecution, had befriended and defended their local priest – who was often in their employ – and had, in consequence, developed a proprietary feeling towards the Church. They had no wish to interfere with – even less change – what they regarded as theological matters. But they disagreed with more orthodox churchmen about where the boundary between spiritual and secular questions lay. The Committee's view was essentially pragmatic. They believed themselves to be both devoutly Catholic and patriotically British and proposed to reconcile those two positions by rendering unto Caesar the things to which Caesar could reasonably lay claim. They would die (indeed, some of their forebears had died) in defence of the Pope's spiritual supremacy. But they could not accept the Pope's authority over the sovereign Parliament and people of Britain. Their tactic – perfectly consistent with their convictions – was to negotiate a new agreement in which taking an extended oath and accepting a limit on the Pope's authority entitled a Catholic to full civil rights.

Encouraged by Pitt's response, the Committee drafted a new Relief Bill. It proposed that an extension of rights should be granted to every Catholic who had taken, or agreed to take, the oath that was included in the Act of 1778. What progress the bill would have made, given a clear run, is in doubt. Its progress was first impeded and then brought to a halt by an initiative taken by Lord Stanhope, a well-meaning but foolish Protestant who hoped that, by uniting the Established Church, Dissenters and Roman Catholics in the cause of relief, he would make the progress of the bill irresistible. Despite Lord Stanhope's ecumenical hopes, the document he drafted as the basis of agreement was entitled 'The Declaration and Protestation of English Catholics'. Since he was not, himself, a Catholic, the exercise was innately impertinent and it would have come as no surprise if the Catholic members of the Committee had ignored it. None of them had been consulted. Indeed, no Catholic, lay or clerical, had been asked to offer an opinion. Yet the Committee endorsed the Protestation and sent it on to Thomas Talbot, the sympathetic Vicar Apostolic of the Midland District. Talbot signed and urged other priests to do the same. Charles Walmesley, Vicar Apostolic of the Western District, signed and then withdrew his signature. Matthew Gibson of the Northern District gave Talbot permission to add his name if he thought it absolutely essential. Talbot said it was. Largely thanks to his endorsement, 1,523 signatures appeared at the foot of the Protestation.

It was then, and only then, that the Committee decided that a new oath was, after all, necessary. A version was drafted and shown, for approval, to the Archbishop of Canterbury. The Vicars Apostolic were not consulted. Had they been, they would have had no alternative but to reject it. The new oath began, as expected, with a vow of loyalty to the crown. It then went on to reproduce, almost word for word, a passage from James I's 1606 Oath of Allegiance, which required complying Catholics to deny that the Pope possessed 'any spiritual power or jurisdiction ... that can directly or indirectly interfere with the constitution of the kingdom'. They would further be required to denounce as 'impious and heretical' the 'damnable Doctrine and Position that Princes excommunicated by the Pope or by Authority of the See of Rome, may be deposed or murdered by their subjects or any other person whatsoever'.[5] In a phrase intended to echo the Act which had relieved Dissenters of the penalties, Catholics who took the oath were referred to as 'Protesting Catholic Dissenters' as distinct from 'Papists', who did not. That alone was enough to make the bill unacceptable to the clergy, for it implied that the oath-takers hovered uncertainly between the Church of England and Rome. Their antagonism was increased by the discovery that the lay members of the Committee wanted to revive the idea which brought them together: English bishops to be elected by the priesthood, and therefore freed from the authority of the Pope. The Committee was left in the paradoxical position of sponsoring a bill which, although it relieved Catholics of long-resented penalties, was not acceptable to the Catholic Church. The price of liberty was too high to pay.

On October 19th 1789, the Vicars Apostolic met at Hammersmith and, without consulting the Committee, condemned the document out of hand. The Committee pleaded for time to persuade the government to modify the wording of the oath. Talbot agreed and the condemnation was never made public in the London and Midland Districts. But in other parts of England explanations of why the oath was anathema were accompanied by the unequivocal instruction, 'to these determinations we, therefore, require your submission'. Lord Petre, indomitable as well as indefatigable, attempted to convince the censorious Vicars Apostolic that they were in error. His letters to John Douglass, James Talbot's successor in London, show that the task was so unrewarding that even his patience – stretched over nearly ten years of negotiation – was wearing thin. On January 7th 1791 he was conciliatory: 'My Lord, I hope that my explanation of the words which alarmed you will convince your Lordship that there is not the most distant intention of any of the parties concerned, catholic or protestant, to disturb the pope in any of his spiritual right or authority.'[6] On the following day – 'explaining parts of my letter which your Lordship seems simply to have misunderstood' – he exhibited only exasperation: 'Friends of mine to whom I have shown the letter are quite astonished by the interpretation that you have put on my words.'

It was too late. On December 19th 1791 Douglass, Charles

Walmesley of the Western District and Gibson of the Northern published a formal rebuke. 'The Assembly of the Catholic Committee has no right and no authority to determine the lawfulness of Oaths, Declarations or other Instruments whatsoever containing Doctrinal matters. This authority resides in Bishops, they being by Divine institution, the spiritual Governors of the Church of Christ and the Guardians of Religion.'[7] Having rejected the Committee's right to draft the proposed oath, they went on to denounce its contents. 'On October 21st 1789 [we] condemned an Oath proposed at that time to be presented to Parliament ... Some alterations have been made by the Catholic Committee in that condemned oath, but as far as we have learned of no moment. Therefore [the oath] cannot be lawfully or conscientiously taken by any of the Faithful of our Districts.'[8] It took Petre almost a month to reply. His letter was more a rebuttal of the Apostolic Vicars' conduct than a refusal to abandon the campaign. 'We have the greatest respect for Episcopal authority ... But the requisition of submission made by the Apostolic Vicars appears in the present instance not grounded in equity.'

The Committee's formal response was composed in even stronger language. The Vicars Apostolic were, they claimed, 'inculcating principles hostile to society and government, derogatory to the allegiance due to the state'.[9] There was, they believed, no need to search for a compromise. An oath, in the form which they proposed, guaranteed the passing of a new Relief Act. Sir John Mitford, a future Lord Chancellor, agreed to move the bill in the Commons. Almost alone among the Vicars Apostolic, Charles Walmesley remained confident of victory for the Church and defeat for the bill. 'I have,' he wrote, 'asked my Master that this bad oath may not pass and He will grant my prayer.' The drama that followed was enough to convince men of a spiritual disposition that the age of miracles was not dead.

The opponents of the bill were badly in need of a champion. They found one in Winchester. John Milner was a scholar as well as a priest and – significantly in light of the position he was to take up in the oath controversy – neither an aristocrat by birth nor dependent on aristocratic patronage. His views on the governance of the Catholic Church were proclaimed by the titles of his two most famous theological works. One was a simple statement of belief, *The Divine Right of the Episcopacy*. The other was a warning of a dangerous heresy, *Ecclesiastical Democracy Detected*.[10] Milner was a man of energy and ambition, but it is not clear why he suddenly decided to abandon his antiquarian studies and make for London to fight against the Relief Bill. We do, however, know that he thought the call to arms so urgent that, in the coach on the way to London, he drafted a pamphlet denouncing the oath, had it printed immediately upon his arrival and then took a copy to Edmund Burke's lodgings. It seems unlikely that Burke and his associates were moved by Milner's description of the special status enjoyed by the Catholic episcopate. But they were convinced by evidence which he provided that, despite its claims, the Committee did not represent English Catholic opinion and that the bill, as originally drafted, would – because of conscientious objections to the oath – provide relief for only a minority of the Catholic population.

The bill had its First Reading in the House of Commons on March 1st 1790. In his opening speech John Mitford made clear that the Act would only benefit men and women who were prepared to describe themselves as 'Protesting Catholic Dissenters', but suggested that Papists who rejected that description made up a small, and dangerously dissident, group of irreconcilables. According to folklore, the climax of the debate came when the Attorney General, Sir Archibald Macdonald, suddenly rose in his place to announce that, as he entered the chamber, 'a piece of paper had been put into his hand which proved that one of the Catholic parties was as good subjects and as much entitled to favour as the other'.[11] The paper was Milner's pamphlet and, although it almost certainly did not alter the course of the debate in the dramatic fashion the myth-makers claim, it convinced a number of Members that the bill before them was unacceptable to most of the Catholics whom it sought to relieve. In consequence, when the bill reached its committee stage, the objectionable 'Protesting Catholic Dissenters' was replaced by 'Catholic' and it was sent 'as amended' to the House of Lords.

The Vicars General – as opposed to the wording of the oath as to the description of the bill's beneficiaries – campaigned with such effect that when, in June 1790, the bill was debated in the House of Lords, Lord Rawdon (the first speaker) conceded that it would not extend relief to a considerable, perhaps a majority, of Catholics.[12] The Bishop of St David's then made noble flesh creep with the forecast that, if the bill passed into law in the form in which it had reached the Upper House, one set of Catholics would be at the mercy of another, the courts would be swamped by prosecutions initiated by informers, and the prisons would be filled by good citizens whose only crime was the refusal to abjure their faith. When he spoke a second time, he was more constructive. He proposed that the contentious oath be deleted and replaced by the oath that was included in the Irish Relief Act of 1778. The peers wished the Irish oath to be strengthened by the inclusion of an undertaking to support a Protestant succession.

With that slight alteration, the Bishop's amendment was carried. In its new form, the bill passed through both Houses of Parliament without opposition and became the Catholic Relief Act of 1791.

Under its provision, oath-takers could no longer be summonsed for being a 'Papist', for hearing or saying Mass, for being a priest or deacon, for entering or belonging to 'an order affiliated to the church of Rome', for 'performing any right, ceremony, practice or observance of the Popish religion or assisting others therein' or for failing to attend Church of England services. Catholics were freed from the risk of prosecution for organising education in a church. Nor did the law require them to move out of London or register their property. The Act did not relieve Catholics of the obligation to pay double land tax. That penalty was abolished – with little notice and therefore no complaint – by its omission from the annual land-tax bill. Being a practising Catholic or, indeed, a Catholic priest or deacon was no longer illegal. Catholics were allowed to practise law. However, many of the new 'rights' they had acquired were no more than the statutes catching up with what had been common practice for a hundred years. In only one particular were civil rights still denied. Catholics – even if they took the oath of loyalty – were still not allowed to vote or sit in either House of Parliament. The opposition of Protestant bigots was avoided by the imposition, or confirmation, of some petty restrictions on Catholic conduct. Catholic assemblies had to be registered at the quarter sessions. Catholic chapels were to be 'locked, barred and bolted' while services were in progress. No Catholic could become master, provost or warden of an Oxford or Cambridge college or headmaster of a royal foundation grammar school, and no Catholic school could admit Protestant pupils.

One aspect of the movement towards emancipation degenerated into near farce – the usual fate of attempts to impose laws that vary from one part of the United Kingdom to another. The clauses in the 1781 Act, which were intended to give another boost to recruitment and to please the martially inclined Irish gentry, permitted Catholics – previously not allowed to rise above the rank of major – to hold colonelcies. But the Act only applied to Ireland. So, in order to avoid compulsory demotion when an Irish colonel was posted to London, it was proposed that the right be extended to England. The extension required amendment of the Mutiny Act to which initially the King would not agree, but – after many months of argument – he was persuaded to change his mind, and new clauses, which authorised the change in the law, were added to an Appropriations Bill already before the House of Commons. Then the King realised that, as well as agreeing that Irish Catholics could become regimental colonels, he had accepted the possibility of their being awarded staff appointments. He was prepared to allow Catholics to fight for him in the field, but not to plan in which field the fight should take place. Lord Granville, the Prime Minister, was required both to withdraw the offending clauses and to promise never again to introduce a 'Papist bill'. Granville resigned and was succeeded by the Duke of Portland, a vehement opponent of Catholic emancipation.

It was not only Irish colonels serving in England who had to accept the status of second-class citizens. Catholic civilians, as well as being denied the right to vote, still had to face innumerable indignities. Their churches were always officially called 'chapels' to distinguish them from 'proper' places of worship. To drive the point home, the chapels – which had to be built without tower or steeple – were prohibited from ringing bells to summon the faithful to prayer. The wording of the 1791 Relief Act reflected the distaste that Protestant England felt for its Catholic minority. Although the oath which the Act incorporated referred simply to 'Catholics', the long title called its beneficiaries 'Papists or persons professing the Popish religion' – terms known to be offensive to Catholics – and made clear that there were, at best, doubts about their innate right to religious tolerance. Relief was 'thought expedient'. Concessions – reluctantly given – were preferable to resentment, riot and revolution.

The law had changed significantly. But the attitude, and sometimes the conduct, of hard-line Protestants had not. In the northern counties of Ireland – fast becoming the centre of anti-Catholic bigotry – jobs in the emergent heavy industries were denied to Papists. Even in Dublin, where Catholics made up the vast majority of the population, they were still subject to private harassment. At the soup kitchens that, on Fridays, offered meat broth to the starving poor, the recipients of the largesse were harangued on the subject of the Pope's close relationship with the devil. Offers were made, and frequently accepted, to buy the children of pauper Catholic families. The purchase being made, they were assimilated into Protestant families as members or servants.

The Committee of Ten – all of whom would have benefited personally from an extension of the franchise and regarded the Second Relief Act as only a staging post to the achievement of full emancipation – decided to move the process along by calling a general meeting which, they said, would represent the Catholics of England. It was held on June 9th 1791, two days after the Act was passed. Two hundred men – priests and laity – assembled in the Crown and Anchor Tavern in the Strand. The first item on the agenda was a vote of thanks to the Committee. But – as the proposed recipients of the self-generated gratitude should have realised – as many Catholics were as offended by the wording of the original oath as were gratified by the relief. So the vote of thanks was defeated, on the grounds that it 'could not be conscientiously given to persons who had so long and so violently endeavoured to impose a condemned oath of heterodoxy and schism on the Catholics of England'.[13] An amendment which offered congratulations to whoever had persuaded Parliament to accept the orthodox oath was ruled out of order by the chairman. The decision that there should be no vote of thanks to anyone for anything did not augur well for the future of the Committee. Nor did the debate that followed. The outcome of the meeting's main business served only to emphasise the deep division between different groups of Catholics.

There was no discussion of the ways and means by which full emancipation could be achieved. The concern of the Committee was the governance of the Catholic Church in England, not the rights of the English Catholics. They regarded the Church as their property and they wanted to regain the control they had enjoyed during the age of its persecution. The motion, which noted that 'the oath contained in the Bill for the Relief of English Catholics is not expressed in the words of the Protestation' (which the Committee had presented to the government in 1789), and reaffirming the 'Committee's continued adherence to the Protestation as an explanation of their civil and social principles', was carried by 104 votes to 72. The true aims of the Committee – an English Catholic Church which was independent of Rome and governed as much by rich laymen as by its bishops – had been endorsed. But it was no longer possible to argue that emancipation was its only aim, or that it spoke for all of Catholic England. So the Committee of Ten transmogrified itself into the Cisalpine Club – Cisalpine as distinct from (and opposed to) Ultramontane, and because it represented the views of Catholics on the anti-clerical side of the Alps. Its inaugural meeting – held on the appropriately unorthodox premises of the Freemasons' Tavern – confirmed its purpose as organising opposition to papal tyranny. Its members remained vocal, but became ineffectual. The impetus towards emancipation had to come from elsewhere. It came from Ireland.

Most English Protestants who believed in Catholic emancipation as a matter of principle also held the view – and expressed it, to win the support of their more bigoted associates – that improving the status of Catholics was essential to the tranquillity of the kingdom. The need, in terms of stability and security, was greatest in Ireland, which could exert pressure of which England or Scotland was never capable. Political power lay in London. But the power of numbers gave Irish Catholics a strength that the tiny English Catholic minority did not possess.

John Milner – future Vicar Apostolic of the Midland District and hero of the episcopate's battle against the Committee of Ten – believed that, in the last push for full emancipation, Ireland would lead the way. 'The fate of the English Catholics depends on that of our brethren in Ireland. If their claims are overlooked, ours will never be thought worthy of notice. On the other hand, whatever redress of grievances or legal privileges they obtain, we shall not be long deprived of. In a word, they are the stately vessel which catches the breeze and stems the tide. We are the cock-boat which is towed in her wake.'[14] The essentially pragmatic view of emancipation – relief as an expedient – was faithfully expressed by Lord Castlereagh during the debates that ended with the Act of Union and the voluntary dissolution of the Dublin Parliament. 'Until Catholics are admitted into a general participation of rights, which when incorporated with the British Government they cannot abuse, there will be no peace or safety in Ireland.'[15]

It was, therefore, a combination of principle and necessity that produced, in 1793, an Irish Relief Bill with provisions which – in terms of the approach to full emancipation – leapfrogged the English Act of the same name. The Irish Act, as the bill became, abolished the historical penalties imposed on Catholics, but its historic importance lay in the clauses that gave Catholics the right to vote. They were still precluded from sitting in Parliament. So emancipation was far from complete. But it was closer to achievement in Ireland than in England.

The bishops of the Catholic Church in Ireland, with three separate Acts of Indulgence to celebrate (1778, 1782 and 1793), ended the eighteenth century determined to work in harmony (its critics said to ingratiate themselves) with the Protestant establishment. In 1788, before the process of 'relief' was complete, Archbishop Butler had written from Thurles to the priests in his diocese expressing his concern about the health of George III and instructing them to show their gratitude for His Majesty's benevolence by preceding all Masses on both Sundays and holy days with prayers for the royal welfare. His letter was not the product of sudden compassion, but the result of a carefully considered combination of Christian charity and self-interest. In A Justification – a slim volume – he explained that it was the duty of the Irish Catholic Church to give thanks for favours received, and expressed the pious hope that there were more on the way. He did not go into details about the favours for which it should express its gratitude.

Reconciliation was official Church policy. The finest flowering of that aspiration was a message sent by the Irish bishops to the Pope in 1788. They were unanimously in favour of the 'revocation of the censure of excommunication against freemasons as the enforcement of this law involves the denunciation of the very heads of state, of most nobles and military administrators'. The request was not even acknowledged. But the policy achieved some beneficial results. The most important was the decision, taken by the Dublin Parliament in 1795, to make a grant towards the establishment of what became the most influential of all Catholic seminaries. Its full title, the Royal College of St Patrick, Maynooth, County Kildare, was chosen as a gesture of goodwill. But it caused a bitter dispute within the Catholic Church in Ireland which, in some ways, replicated the disagreements in England over the Relief Act oath. It concerned the rights and role of bishops. The episcopacy was in conflict with Rome, not the laity. Of course, Rome won.

The Catholic Church in Ireland had already embarked on a programme of self-improvement. Even as Archbishop Butler was instructing his priests to have a mind for the welfare of the King, he was also holding meetings – as the Thurles conference and, indeed, the Council of Trent required – to ensure that his clergy understood the rules governing the baptism of an unborn child, the prayers that must be learned before confirmation, the circumstances in which it was permitted to say more than one Mass a day, and the qualification of candidates for ordination. But Maynooth, as it was always known, came to dominate more than Irish clerical education. For the next hundred years all of Irish Catholicism was said to be governed by the stern alternative 'Maynooth or may not'.

During the first thirty years of its existence Maynooth prepared 4,000 Irishmen for the priesthood and became such a force in the recruitment of secular clergy that the Irish seminaries in continental Europe shrank and closed. Maynooth illustrated and represented a new era in Irish Catholicism in which a combination of episcopal reorganisation and the relaxation of penal laws enabled the priesthood to discharge its pastoral duties in a way that made it an integral part of Irish life. So, when the Great Famine came in the mid-nineteenth century and the exodus followed, Irish Catholics took with them their own brand of community Catholicism. But arguments over the constitution of the seminary divided the Catholic Church in Ireland, provoked the bizarre suggestion that it might achieve a status something like 'established' and diverted, into a cul-de-sac, the journey towards full emancipation.

The acceptance of a government grant would have ended three hundred years of financial independence during which the Catholic Church in Britain and Ireland – occasionally helped by gifts from abroad – was uncontaminated by any sort of state endowment. But purity came at a price that was deeply resented by many Irish Catholics. Against their will and wishes, they paid for the upkeep of two Churches. Their tithes and glebe charges supported the alien Church of Ireland, while collections and payments for prayers and services provided a meagre living for their own parish priests. They consoled themselves with the thought that help from the state would, inevitably, be accompanied by state interference. And so it proved in the case of the Maynooth grant.

Early in 1795, Richard O'Reilly, Archbishop of Armagh, John Troy, Archbishop of Dublin, and Patrick Plunkett, Bishop of Meath, were asked by the Governor General to discover what official answer the Irish episcopate would give to two related questions. They were predicated on the assumption that the Dublin government would, in some way, help to meet the cost of the Catholic Church in Ireland. The two questions must have caused even more surprise than the offer. They were repeated in a letter that Troy sent to some, though not all, of his colleagues: 'Could the Government be allowed the appointment of the President and Professors at Maynooth?' and 'What answer are they to make to the proposal of the nomination of Bishops by the King?' The four metropolitans and eighteen bishops assembled in Dublin and agreed their reply to the questions. To the first they responded, '*Negative*. No interference.' Their second answer was not quite so emphatic. 'The proposal [to allow the King to nominate bishops] is to be resisted *in limine*.'[16] They then considered how the Pope should respond if the questions were referred to Rome. Their advice was even more equivocal: 'Not to agree to His Majesty's nomination if it can be avoided.' If agreement was unavoidable, they hoped it would be possible to persuade the King 'to nominate one of three recommended by the respective Provincial Bishops'. For two years neither Church nor state thought the question worth pursuing.

There the matter might have ended had not Wolfe Tone, an Episcopalian Irish nationalist, behaved as Catholics were expected to behave and attempted to facilitate a French invasion of Ireland. In December 1798, three months after the abortive rebellion was crushed, John Troy, the Archbishop of Dublin, was called into the presence of the Chief Secretary to the Lord Lieutenant of Ireland. The Archbishop was asked a variant of the old question: was it within the Pope's power to cede influence over episcopal nominations to a secular authority? Assured that it was, he then – no doubt to Troy's astonishment – asked how the bishops would respond to an offer of an annual state grant which was sufficient to provide support for every priest and bishop in Ireland. Troy answered that the total cost of such a scheme (£200,000) made the idea totally impractical. Then, much to his credit, he added that, were the Catholic Church in Ireland to become the creature of the state, it would wither and die.

On August 17th 1799 Troy wrote to Cardinal Borgia at Propaganda Fide with an explanation of what had prompted the Lord Lieutenant to ask such unexpected questions. 'The government gave me to understand that the guilty conduct of some of our priests, secular and regular, in the recently suppressed rebellion brought suspicion on our clergy.'[17] The government attributed their disloyalty to their 'abject dependence on the people'. The only way to restore the King's confidence in the loyalty of the Irish Catholic Church was agreement by Pope and Church 'that His Majesty should have the privilege, as in Canada, of presenting to the Pope the candidates whom he deems suitable to be Bishops'.

Troy, according to his own account, stood his corner. The rebel priests were relatively few. Salaried priests would be regarded as government mercenaries. The cost of state support would be greater than the government would be prepared to pay. Only the Pope could alter the way in which bishops were selected and appointed. Having assured the Cardinal that he had 'made other difficulties', Troy gave Borgia notice that he proposed to consult 'the three Metropolitans, my Suffragan Bishops and other Prelates'. During the second week in January 1799 they met in Dublin, to 'deliberate on the proposal from government'.

The assembled bishops did not, as might have been supposed, dismiss the proposal out of hand. Instead they replied to the questions that were really a proposal in a paper that amounted to their alternative offer. It began by setting out the normal procedure for the selection of a bishop and confirmed the necessity of respecting the established rules. Then it added two additional steps which might be taken before the appointment took effect: 'The candidates so selected to be presented by the President of the election to the Government which, within one month after such presentation, will transmit the name of the said candidate, if no objection shall be made against him, to the Holy See.' If there were an objection – the proposal did not suggest what objections would be regarded as legitimate – 'the President of the election will be informed ... who in that case will convene the election of another candidate'.[18] The paper ended with the necessary and proper caveat that their proposals could have 'no effect without the sanction of the Holy See', and added that the Irish clergy would 'use their best endeavours to procure' papal agreement. The four arch-bishops and six bishops were offering a Protestant government the power of veto over the appointment to the Roman Catholic episcopate. They were, in fact, proposing a little, local Reformation. Henry VIII's break with Rome had been caused by differences neither over liturgy nor theology. Henry had denied the right of the Pope to interfere in English affairs. The ten bishops proposed to follow his lead and usurp, on behalf of the Westminster government, the Pope's power in Ireland.

King George did not regard the concession as sufficiently significant to warrant his agreement to what he regarded as creeping emancipa-tion. So the negotiations might have ended with the veto being vetoed. But, wisely, the bishops decided to keep the whole discussion secret until the entire Irish episcopate had pronounced on the proposals. A majority of Ireland's thirty bishops, firmly but discreetly, rejected the idea that the government might be given the power to veto the nomin-ation of an Irish bishop. They insisted that the ten of their colleagues who had drawn up the response to the government had no authority to speak or negotiate on behalf of the whole Catholic Church in Ireland. They were merely the episcopal trustees of Maynooth College. That dismissive description was not the worst thing to be said about them. One observer called them a 'terrified little coterie'. A Dublin barrister, who meant to speak up in their defence, said that they dared not defy 'an Administration exercising martial law'.

The allegations of coercion – vigorously denied by the government when the story of the negotiations were made public ten years later – did the ten bishops less than justice. John Milner, their greatest critic, wrote about the negotiations taking place at a time when 'Orangemen and soldiers were demolishing chapels and torturing Catholic peas-ants'.[19] But he added, more accurately, that the negotiators were 'really led to believe that the Church ... would not only be protected and honoured but also that it would, in a sort of subordinate way, become the Established Church of Ireland'. He might have added that – relying on both European and South American precedence – they believed that the proposal was acceptable to the Church and would be endorsed by the Pope. Their error was over-enthusiasm – compounded by the failure to acknowledge that the Church in Ireland was, in effect, a political as well as religious institution. Their memorial was Maynooth. The ruined reputations and frustrated hopes left behind an institution that became crucially important to the progress of Irish Catholicism.

While Catholic Ireland was developing its distinctive form of seminary education, at the expense of the continental institutions on which it had once relied, the Scots College in Rome was struggling to meet the incessant demands of the Church by which it had been created. It had been set up to provide 'a steady and regular supply of secular clergy who would spend their lives working in Scotland amongst Scottish Catholics' and, according to Abbé Paul McPherson, who examined the college after the turn of the century, the ill discipline of the students and incompetence of the staff meant that the college had 'failed and failed lamentably' to fulfil that purpose.[20]

If Scottish Catholic confidence recovered, following the passage of the Scottish Relief Act in 1793, the improvement must be attributed to the behaviour of the nobility. The Huntley family built a chapel, dedicated to St Gregory, which they claimed to be 'bigger than the best Roman Catholic chapel in London', and there they celebrated the first High Mass to be said and sung in Scotland since the Reformation. In 1796, the refugee brother of the executed Louis XVI of France took refuge in Holyrood House. Inevitably the French Revolution left its mark on the Catholics of Britain and of its Irish province.

The Catholic Church in England benefited from the aspects of the revolution that it found most distasteful – the Reign of Terror and the assault on religion, which included the Cathedral of Notre-Dame becoming a Temple of Reason. From 1790 onwards there was a steady flow of refugee priests from across the Channel. Three émigré curés arrived at Whitby, on the Yorkshire coast, in or about 1794. They left after the Bourbons were restored in 1815, but their twenty-year influence on the fishing port was profound. One, Nicholas Alain Gilbert – who published *Methods of Sanctifying the Sabbath in Whitby, Scarborough etc*[21] – left behind him a tradition of service and scholarship that sustained the Church for years. But the most important contribution he and his colleagues made to Catholic life in the East Riding was evangelical, not academic. In 1774 there were fifteen Catholics in Whitby; in 1805 there were three hundred and they celebrated Mass in a new chapel. Reading fared even better. Priests who, after crossing the Channel, had made a temporary home in Winchester, moved on to the Berkshire town, where they took up permanent residence in the King's Arms. At the time of their arrival, Mass was said in a rented room. One of the priests taught French to the locals and used what he earned to build a new chapel that could accommodate five hundred worshippers.

During the 1790s there was a great exodus of English nuns from France and the Low Countries – Carmelites from Antwerp to Cornwall, Benedictines from Dunkirk to Hammersmith in London and from Ghent to Preston. The seminary at Douai was forced to close and some of its staff joined the Old Hall Academy in Hertfordshire and helped it to evolve into St Edmund's College, which it remains today. But most of the Douai staff were relocated to the sites of new English seminaries at Ushaw in County Durham and Oscott in Birmingham – thus helping to drag English Catholicism out of the country and into the new industrial towns. All in all, the one English Catholic casualty (and that resulted in only temporary injury) was the English College in Rome, which was suppressed by Napoleonic edict and its building used as an infantry barracks. Graves were opened and the lead coffin linings were taken for melting down and making into musket balls. Amongst the bodies to be desecrated were the last mortal remains of William Allen.

Fear and hatred first of revolutionary France, then of Napoleonic France and perhaps of France and the French in general, increased English sympathy for followers of the religion that the Republic had persecuted and which remained at odds with the authoritarian state. But the next attempt to move on towards full emancipation was brought about by changes in the parliamentary alliances rather than by shifts in the national mood. William Pitt had steadfastly refused to denounce, though he was unable to endorse, a pamphlet – written by an Undersecretary in his own government – which, as well as anticipating the 1798 Relief Act, proposed that a share of Irish tithes should go to the Catholic Church. Pitt's view was partly principled and partly pragmatic – as represented by the 1798 Act. 'The benefits of a free constitution' increase 'the prosperity and strength of all His Majesty's Dominions'. That view was shared by Henry Grattan, Prime Minister of Ireland and a man of immovable opposition to even the prospect of a Catholic hegemony: 'I shall never assent to any measure tending to shake the security of the Kingdom or subvert the Protestant ascendency.'[22] But he also believed that 'the Irish Protestant can never be free while the Irish Catholic is a slave'.

In the summer of 1794, Pitt had formed his second administration and appointed the Earl Fitzwilliam Lord Lieutenant of Ireland. Fitzwilliam rashly courted Grattan's support and replaced anti-emancipation Tories with Whig Reformers. Believing that what the Whigs called 'a new order' was about to transform Irish politics, Grattan introduced an Emancipation Bill. The King was scandalised that Fitzwilliam had, 'after no longer stay than three weeks in Ireland',[23] flouted 'the wisdom of ages'. He ordered that the bill be withdrawn and announced that emancipation was 'beyond the power of ministers'. Enfranchising Catholics would be a betrayal of his coronation oath. It seemed that emancipation was as far away as ever.

CHAPTER 19

The Most Jacobinical Thing

If a Catholic ploughman, homeward plodding his weary way in any part of Britain, felt passionately engaged in the struggle for complete and unqualified emancipation, his emotions were stirred less by resentment at the denial of his own civil rights than by the affront to his Church faith that the denial embodied. The Relief Acts had guaranteed his legal right freely to follow the religion of Rome. Their extension, to include the full rights of citizenship – would be of no immediate benefit to him. He was doubly disenfranchised: first because he was a Catholic, and second because he did not possess the social and financial status that qualified him to vote. Talk of electoral reform rarely went beyond the hope that the franchise could be extended to the property-owning middle classes of the expanding industrial towns. And when that hope was first realised, in the shape of the (extravagantly named) Great Reform Bill of 1832, it only increased the electorate from 435,000 voters to 652,000. Most Catholics – like other working men and women – remained disenfranchised until 1884. In England, at the start of the nineteenth century, emancipation was the active concern of the Catholic nobility and gentry. A recital of the grievances, felt by Catholics at the beginning of the new century, shows how class-related the campaign for full emancipation was.

In July 1804, John Douglass, Vicar Apostolic of the London District, drew up a list of complaints for a rich Catholic laymen, John Brockholes – undeterred by the knowledge that his great-grandfather had died fighting for the Old Pretender at the Battle of Preston – to pass on to the government. It was astonishingly limited to three grievances. Catholic marriages (being outside the law) deprived 'deserted parties' from receiving relief and redress. Catholics, serving in the army, were obliged to attend Protestant church parades. Monies, collected for the maintenance of priests, was – if 'seized upon by malevolent persons' who claimed it had been intended for 'superstitious purposes' – not recoverable by law.[1]

In his Address to the Protestants of the United Kingdom, Charles Butler of the Catholic Committee composed a more comprehensive list of disabilities. Most of them were penalties which only bore down

321

on the prosperous classes. Catholics were 'excluded from offices in cities and corporations' and from 'civil and military offices'. They were 'prevented from voting at elections ... filling their hereditary seats in Parliament ... sitting in the House of Commons'. The disposal of property by gift to the religious foundation of their choice ('which the law allows even to the Jew') was prohibited to Catholics. 'No provision [was] made for the religious comfort and duty of Roman Catholic soldiers and sailors.' Catholics, who had to 'support their own religious functionaries', were also required to 'contribute to the religious establishment of the country'. Butler added to his list of grievances two complaints that related less to the legal status of Catholics than to the way in which they were treated by their Protestant contemporaries. They were examples of the sort of discrimination which persisted for two hundred years and, to a lesser degree, persists – for all minority religions – today. 'In hospitals, workhouses and other public institutions' poor Catholics were discouraged from performing the rituals of their faith, and the children of the Catholic poor often had little option but to attend Church of England schools.

Supporters of the campaign for civil emancipation were motivated by a variety of emotions. The most avid – mostly men who had much to gain from the campaign's success – saw the demand to extend the suffrage as an opportunity to promote old causes. The 'nobility and gentry' of the Catholic Association certainly hoped that, as a by-product of their exertions, control of the English Church would be returned to them and the power of both Rome and the priesthood would be diminished. Opposition – or tepid support – was also based on considerations that were supplementary to the main issue. Some Catholics were determined not to concede the rights of Rome as the price of a universal franchise. Others feared that victory for the Catholic Association would guarantee its dominance over the rest of the Church.

In Ireland the 1778 Relief Act had already given the vote to Irishmen who passed the property test. As a result, there were a large number of 'forty shilling freeholders' who qualified as the result of gifts from local landowners. The beneficiaries were expected to demonstrate their gratitude by supporting their benefactor's nominees at election time. But in Dublin, complete emancipation – the right to sit in the House of Commons as well as elect it – was regarded by the growing independence movement as an essential step along the road to national liberation. And the leaders of that movement believed, with much justification, that emancipation had been promised to them in return for their support of the 1801 Act of Union. Pitt, it was said, had put the idea to George III. But the King had already made his position clear. At a levee on January 28th 1801 he dismissed the notion as 'the most Jacobinical thing I ever heard of' and, to avoid any doubt about his feelings, added, 'I shall reckon any man my personal enemy who proposes any such measure.'[2] The House of Hanover – conscious in this, if not every particular, of the obligations placed upon them by the coronation oath – was the last barrier on the road to emancipation. Most, though not all, Whig ministers were in favour. George III, and his two sons who succeeded him, were irrevocably against.

The campaign for Catholic emancipation lasted for almost half a century and ended in success because of the determination, dedication and acumen of the men who both believed in it as a principle and expected to benefit by its acceptance. But while their years of labour rolled the boulder to the very edge of the cliff, one man can claim credit for pushing it over. Daniel O'Connell, a Dublin lawyer from a prosperous landowning family, believed that Catholic emancipation and Irish liberty went hand in hand. But unlike most Roman Catholics – perhaps because of a period of agnosticism in early manhood – he advocated a 'new scale of justice which would emancipate the Protestant in Spain and Portugal as well as the Christian in Constantinople'.[3] That was too comprehensive an aspiration to inspire the many Catholics who saw changes in the law exclusively in terms of their effects on the Church of Rome. As a result, progress towards emancipation was hindered, though not directly opposed, by a man who, although less attractive than O'Connell, was certainly as single-minded and courageous. John Milner – the priest from Winchester whose dramatic intervention had made the 1791 Relief Act acceptable to most of the Catholic clergy but, paradoxically, not to him – was not prepared to make the slightest sacrifice of Roman rites or papal authority in return for political freedom.

John Milner became Vicar Apostolic of the Midland District in 1803. It was an appointment that he regarded as unforgivably belated. The delay was an indignity to which he was never reconciled. In October of the previous year he had written to Sir John Coxe Hippisley – a Member of Parliament with an unaccountable interest in Catholic affairs – to complain that he had twice been passed over for promotion, despite 'having a second time been unanimously recommended by the three Catholic Bishops whose business it is to present candidates'.[4] The letter ended with a request for Coxe Hippisley to write to Rome on Milner's behalf – an extraordinary suggestion in itself, which was made all the more extraordinary by the fact that Milner was to spend much of the rest of his life resisting lay influence on what he regarded as purely clerical business, and the added fact that Coxe Hippisley was a Protestant.

No sooner had his promotion been confirmed than Milner began to cause trouble inside and outside his diocese. In 1807, his reflections on his first four years of episcopal office reveal the low esteem in which he held John Douglass, the Vicar Apostolic of the London District. 'I have again and again, in the reports I have made to Rome on the state of religion in England represented those evils under which it groans viz the frequent and notorious publication of heterodox and schismatical doctrine.'[5] He took his examples from the City of London where, according to his accusation, John Douglass exhibited 'constant and systematic opposition . . . to holding a synod or any other meeting of his episcopal brethren for remedying these and other evils'. Milner's dislike of Douglass had many causes, including the re-admission to London services of Charles Berrington – the sceptical priest who had joined the Catholic Society. Milner was obsessed by London, a condition which his critics attributed to the ambition to become a virtual archbishop. So great was his passion to move to the capital that he petitioned, with the support of the Irish bishops, to become Douglass' Coadjutor. A Congregation (held in December 1806) took the official decision that Milner should remain, for the rest of his vocation, Vicar Apostolic of the Midland District. Milner became English agent for the Irish bishops and spent much of his time in London pursuing old enemies and ingrained obsessions.

Milner understood that, since the campaign for independence was indivisible, 'the fate of us English Catholics depends on that of our brethren in Ireland. If their claims are overlooked, ours will never be thought worthy of notice.'[6] But, although the hopes of both Catholic communities were intimately related, they were not always expressed in identical demands by men with related priorities. The first emancipation initiative to follow the Act of Union did come from Ireland. But it was a petition which – among other grievances – complained that Protestant monopolies were restricting trade. It was signed by six peers, three baronets and eighty-nine 'men of property and distinction'.

William Pitt refused to present the petition to Parliament. His friends offered an explanation. During one of his fits of sanity – which coincided with the Act of Union – George III had sent his Prime Minister a message: 'Tell him that I am well. But what he has to answer for [is] who is the cause of my being ill at all.'[7] And Pitt – in a moment of quixotic irresponsibility – had accepted that it was Catholicism that had driven the King mad and promised never to promote Catholic interests again. So Charles James Fox was left to present the petition to the House of Commons, where the motion to endorse and support it was defeated by 336 votes to 124.

Foolishly, the English Catholic Committee chose to ignore the whole emancipation campaign. A pamphlet, published in the name of Sir John Throckmorton, justified the decision by assertions which, in its dismissal of the Irish emancipation movement, were self-evident nonsense. 'They have yielded before us. Many more statutes are still in force against us. Yet our relative position is far preferable to theirs.'[8] The final sentence confirmed the pamphlet's purpose. Throckmorton promised that, at some yet-to-be-determined future date, 'when there will be an English Catholic petition we shall be happy to prove the sincerity of our position'. The English Catholic gentry were preparing to buy emancipation for a price that Irish Catholics would not pay. The full cost was revealed in another Throckmorton pamphlet. The 'government has only to signify that it is their wish that the king in future shall have the nomination of the Catholic Bishops. This will be conceded.'[9] The veto was back on the agenda. For the next twenty years the emancipation debate ranged around the question 'what "securities" was the Catholic Church prepared to provide as guarantees against subversion?' Only the Catholic Association had an immediate answer, and that – the King's involvement in Church business – was unacceptable to most of the clergy.

There was no doubt that an overwhelming majority of Catholics were loyal subjects of King George and, if they thought about it at all, were willing both to swear their allegiance to the crown and to deny the Pope's authority over secular matters. Putting aside the difficulty of deciding where the line between secular and religious authority should lie – a matter for theologians – dignity and self-respect made many Catholics reluctant to provide 'securities' to guarantee their good faith. And most of those who initially accepted the principle became opponents of the idea when presented with practical examples of the form those securities might take. Coxe Hippisley proposed a scheme which would, in his opinion, convince the English government that only loyalists would become Catholic bishops. A short list of four to eight candidates should be presented to ministers, who would then make the final selection. The proposal, another version of the dreaded veto, only intensified the argument, which was to take years to resolve.

The hope of progress – even at a price – was damaged by events outside the control of both obdurate and compliant Catholics. The Pope travelled across Europe to crown Napoleon Emperor of France and, although the crown was snatched from his trembling hand by the impatient Bonaparte, his presence at the ceremony in Notre-Dame seemed to confirm Rome's support for England's greatest enemy. However, the war against France continued to produce small bonuses for the Catholic Church. One of them was the Church of England lapsing into a moment of ecumenical generosity. John Douglass wrote to the Bishop of London on behalf of the Catholic Church to ask if there would be any objection to a group of émigré nuns setting up a school in the capital. Dr Porteus sent what he, no doubt, thought was a generous reply. He was prepared for the initiative to go ahead, 'as long as the unfortunate ladies educate non but the children of Roman Catholics', but he had a further requirement: 'They must conduct themselves quietly and discreetly.'[10]

William Pitt died on January 23rd 1806. That, in itself, dealt the prospects of emancipation a savage blow, and the already minimal hopes of progress were further reduced by the revolt of self-styled 'orthodox' priests against the concordat between Pius VII and the Emperor Napoleon. John Milner denounced the Pope's critics for doing 'scandalous injuries to the lawful successor to St Peter'. He then turned on what he described as a group of 'lay Catholics who, to the exclusion of their clergy, associated together as a literary club' but failed to 'produce any work in support of their learned pretensions' because they were, in truth, 'a new Catholic Committee'[11] bent on emancipation at any price. After a year of not very convincing claims to possess only cultural aspirations, the 'literary club' admitted its true purpose, changed its name to the Catholic Board and resumed its attempts to find a way of convincing fellow Catholics that an ambiguous oath of loyalty was a price worth paying for full emancipation.

The Board opened membership to clergy as well as laity and invited all the Vicars Apostolic to serve on its general committee. Milner's name appeared on the list of the Board's subscribers, but that did not prevent him from dismissing Edward Jerningham, its secretary, as a nonentity and accusing its committee of publishing 'anonymous defamatory pamphlets, mutilated and altered deeds and false reports of parliamentary speeches'.[12] The invective was accompanied by the encouragement of opposition to any suggestion that Catholics provide some sort of assurance of good conduct – the basic requirement of emancipation as set out by Earl Grey, a supporter and parliamentary advocate of the cause.

A general meeting, called for February 1st 1810, had the ostensible purpose of testing Catholic opinion. Lord Clifford and a 'dozen Catholic gentlemen' agreed to dine together at Doran's Hotel in Dover Street and asked John Milner, together with the Vicar Apostolic of the London District and his Coadjutor, to join them. 'The dinner was no sooner removed and the waiters withdrawn'[13] than Milner realised what should have been clear from the start. The dinner was not a social occasion, but an attempt to gain support for the terms of an emancipation agreement.

Edward Jerningham, the Secretary to the Board, read out the proposed message to Parliament. It was drafted in the form of five 'Resolutions'. The first two asserted the urgent need to end 'the state of political degradation' by a reform that was described as 'essential to the preservation of the Empire'.[14] The third and fourth proposed that a new petition should be presented to Parliament and that the presentation should be entrusted to Earl Grey and William Windham. The fifth, as well as confirming the Catholic commitment to the 'common cause ... of freedom and independence', announced that Catholics were 'firmly persuaded that adequate provision for the main-tenance of the civil and religious establishments may be made consistent with the strictest adherence on their part to the tenets and discipline of the Roman Catholic religion'. It also asserted that 'any arrangements founded on this basis of mutual satisfaction and security and extending to [Catholics] the full benefits of the civil constitution of their country will meet with their grateful concurrence'.[15] The Board clearly expected that such an anodyne form of words would win universal approval. But they were rejected out of hand by Milner. He suspected, rightly as it turned out, that 'security', which the Fifth Reso-lution promised, would be ensured by allowing the government a veto over the choice of bishops. In passing, Milner denounced Father James Archer for the sin of attending the theatre on the previous night.

Next day the Five Resolutions were put to a meeting of 'Catholic gentlemen' in the St Alban's Tavern. The first four were carried without dissent and, according to the minutes of the meeting, the fifth 'was, with the single exception of the Vicar Apostolic for the Midland District, agent for the Irish prelates, unanimously adopted'. In fact the position was far more complicated than the minute suggests. Milner was certainly opposed. He regarded the Fifth Resolution as 'expressly calculated to lay our Church, the inheritance of the martyrs, bound and gagged under the feet of a hypocritical Protestant establishment'. In a more moderate moment, he warned against the folly of accepting the notion of securities 'without knowing ... what the Protestant securities would be'[16] and asked – with language and logic on his side – how a good Catholic could be expected to endorse the secure future of the Established Church.

Milner also argued that, the merits of the Fifth Resolution aside, the meeting should adjourn until the views of the Irish bishops – for whom he acted as English agent – were known. His procedural proposal, like his opposition in principle, was swept aside. The three other Vicars Apostolic who were present at the meeting abstained in the final vote, but – after the meeting had closed – were persuaded to sign the document on which the Five Resolutions appeared. The Irish bishops were particularly affronted. Not only had they failed to be consulted, but their English colleagues had accepted limitations on the freedom of the Church which they had explicitly rejected. John Troy, the Archbishop of Dublin, described the authors of the Fifth Resolution in language more offensive than John Milner's most intemperate invective: 'an assemblage of laymen all of whom ... had long been distinguished for an absence of principle'.[17] In his St Patrick Day's sermon in Cork Cathedral, Father John Ryan accused the English of 'striking a treacherous bargain. The veto has been held out to our brethren in a neighbouring country and they have received the advances with servile complacency.'[18] Only one Englishman escaped condemnation. 'A single pillar of this little church stands alone to uphold the shattering fabric and the name Milner has become identified with whatever honour and safety remains.'[19] Milner himself reported to his fellow Vicars Apostolic that 'From Cape Clear to the Giant's Causeway, nothing was heard but that the English Catholics had betrayed them.'[20] The publication of resolutions was the fashion of the time and the Irish bishops passed six of their own. Number four robustly 'disclaimed ... all right in the Pope or any other Foreign Potentate to interfere in the Temporal Concerns of the Kingdom'. But they were adamant that an Oath of Allegiance was sufficient guarantee of their sincerity. Governments could not be given the power to influence the choice of bishops.

There was so much Irish intrusion into the English debate on the government's role in the selection of bishops that the Duke of Norfolk began to fear that the decision would ultimately be taken in the archdiocese of Dublin and Armagh, and Edward Jerningham thought it necessary to issue a statement to calm his, and less noble, nerves. 'I must again declare that the Catholic Bishops of Ireland do not, nor never did, consider the prelates of England subject to them in any respect.'[21]

In May 1810, the House of Commons prepared again to debate a call for Catholic emancipation. Henry Grattan moved the resolution and, as usual, it was defeated. The highlight of the debate was a speech by George Ponsonby – supporting the motion – during which he read from letters in which John Milner accepted the need for a government veto on episcopal appointments. The letter had been written in 1798 at a time when an unrepresentative group of Irish bishops had persuaded their agent to write to English allies in those terms. But the bitter argument that followed, and which resulted in the Catholic Board refusing 'ever to admit Dr Milner to their confidence again', did not concern his apparent inconsistency. It began with the largely unjustified complaint that he had published confidential correspondence, and degenerated into allegations and counter-allegations of perfidy, disloyalty and apostasy. Milner called Douglass and Poynter – Vicar Apostolic and Coadjutor of the London District – 'abettors of the beginnings of schism' who were 'in league with the enemies of religion'.[22] The leadership of the Catholic Church in England approached the final act in the drama of emancipation hopelessly divided.

The evidence suggests that the faith, and therefore the morale, of less elevated Catholics, both priests and laymen, survived the debilitating effects of the civil war between their spiritual leaders. The details of the battles may not have reached all of rural England, but most Catholics knew that a war was raging. Milner was an obsessive pamphleteer, and broadsheets, outlining his passionate opinions, were distributed in London and the Midlands. Priests, representing the rival camps, preached sermons that excoriated their opponents. The 'nobility, gentry and persons of distinction' (who were for emancipation whatever the cost) instructed their tenants, employees and resident priests about the sins of those who stood between them and full civic recognition. Yet the Church prospered. Liberated by the Relief Acts and encouraged by the enthusiasm of French émigré priests, English Catholics opened nine hundred new chapels during the twenty-three years between 1791 and 1814. The most rapid expansion was in Lancashire. In Wigan the Catholic population, though stable for most of the eighteenth century, doubled during the next ten years and totalled more than 2,000 by 1900. By 1801 there were 9,000 Catholics and four chapels in Liverpool; two chapels and 6,000 Catholics in Manchester. By 1819 the Catholic population in Wigan had grown to 3,000 (two chapels and three priests), in Liverpool to 18,000 (four chapels and six priests) and in Manchester to 15,000 (two chapels and four priests).[23]

The least fertile ground was Wales, but Holywell, in Flintshire, was host to a miracle. Winifred White, a young Cheshire woman who suffered from a crippling condition of the spine, was given only a few weeks to live when she hit upon the idea of visiting Holywell, the shrine of her patron saint. She crawled from her lodgings to the well, bathed in its waters and walked back. The efficacy of the cure, and its divine origins, were validated by both John Milner and William Poynter – a 'realist' who wanted the Church to move with the times and accept government influence over its management.

The increase in numbers – combined with the confidence that came with relaxation of the penal laws – encouraged the drive to provide every Catholic boy with a Catholic education. The colleges that were (or were to become) seminaries had mixed fortunes. St Cuthbert's in County Durham – one of Douai's descendants – became Ushaw. Its new building was opened in 1808. Oscott, in the Midlands, was cleared of debt and its syllabus revived when, in the same year, John Milner took direct control in place of the previous management, whose earlier failure he attributed to their Cisalpine tendencies. But St Edmund's in Ware – another Douai legatee – was evolving from a seminary into England's oldest Catholic public school. In 1809, during the transition, it became the scene of the first-recorded student sit-in. Thirty young men occupied an inn in Waltham Cross and issued a list of grievances about food and discipline. An attempt to flee to Scotland failed and the miscreants were persuaded, by a delegation of priests and parents, to return to the college. The ringleaders were expelled.

The Dominican school at Carshalton failed, but three great public schools (in addition to St Edmund's) were established. The Benedictines, from Dieulouard in Lorraine, settled in Ampleforth, twenty miles west of York. The Community of St Gregory moved from Acton in Shropshire to Downside near Bath. The Jesuits were already established at Stonyhurst – and remained there during the years in which, officially, the Society no longer existed in England. For a time they were therefore regarded as secular priests. Jesuits do not give up easily, so they had applied for affiliation to the Russian Society. Father Gruber, the Russian Jesuit General, agreed, subject to a renewal of vows. Rome initially disagreed. The Jesuits waited, prayed and built a new, and bigger, college. It says much for the single-minded devotion of the teaching Orders that they serenely carried on their work against the background of personal animosity, often dressed up to look like theological disputation, which diminished the early-nineteenth-century Catholic Church.

It fell to Henry Grattan, a Protestant and therefore free from the prejudices of the various Catholic factions, to set the emancipation merry-go-round in motion again. As usual the process was preceded by a petition and the preparation of a draft bill, which, it was proposed, should include explicit assurances about the primacy of the Church of England and the security of the Protestant succession. Between February and April 1813, all the complicated flummery necessary for the discussion of a bill was completed. Its supporters believed that it was both conclusive and ingenious. The rights of succession aside, all Catholic disabilities were to be removed, except for the right to be appointed Lord Chancellor or Lord Lieutenant of Ireland. And the 'security' was to be provided in a fashion to which, it was hoped, no Catholic would take offence. A long Oath of Allegiance, included in the bill, contained the promises never 'to concur or consent to the appointment of any Bishop, Dean or Vicar Apostolic but such as be of unimpeachable loyalty and peaceful conduct' or to have any correspondence with Rome that was 'tending directly or indirectly to overthrow or disturb the Protestant Government and Protestant Church' of England.

The bill's progress was briefly interrupted by a proposal from the assiduous Sir John Coxe Hippisley that its consideration should be postponed until a Select Committee had examined the full extent and consequences of Catholic disabilities. That was quickly brushed aside, but another proposal was not so easily disposed of. For one thing, it originated with George Canning – a brilliant orator and progressive Tory who was to become, briefly, Prime Minister. For another, it could be said to be consistent with the spirit and intention of the bill. Canning proposed that two commissions – one for England, one for Ireland, and both chiefly consisting of Catholics – should supervise the working of the bill. They would confirm the loyalty of candidates for preferment and certify the innocence of communication from the Vatican. Supporters of the new clause claimed that they intended to speed the bill's passage, but it was open to two insurmountable objections. It implied that Catholics could not be trusted to keep their word. And although the right to inspect documents was not to apply to communications that related 'wholly and exclusively to spiritual concerns', there was no way that a document could be classified as outside the Commission's jurisdiction without it first being read by the men who were not allowed to read it. Milner – still a doughty opponent of government interference – had a different but equally compelling objection to the inspection clause as originally drafted. The definition of excluded material was so narrow that it allowed interference with correspondence 'on subjects of literature, health, civility etc as well as on all professional business'.[24]

The Irish bishops were adamant. Canning's clauses – even as amended by Castlereagh, the Foreign Secretary since 1812, to guarantee a Catholic majority on the Commissions – were 'utterly incompatible with the discipline of the Roman Catholic Church and the free exercise of our religion ... We cannot, without incurring a heavy load of guilt, accede to such regulations.'[25] William Poynter – never wholly opposed to accepting the need to guarantee Catholic sincerity, and on good terms with Castlereagh – felt unable to oppose the whole bill and hoped he could secure its improvement. He suffered from all the failings of the reasonable man. John Milner did not labour under that handicap. The bill, he wrote, was 'contrived with a heart of malice which none but the spirits of wickedness in high places, mentioned by St Paul, could have suggested to undermine and wither the fair trees of the English and Irish Catholic Churches'.[26]

John Milner set out his objections in a letter written to William Poynter and travelled to London from his home in the Midland District in order to make sure that London's Vicar Apostolic received it on the day it was written. It suggested that – in light of the Canning clauses – they join forces in opposing the bill. Milner received a reply which he described as evasive: unusually for him, an understatement. Poynter said that he neither knew what was contained in the contentious clauses nor whether the Irish bishops opposed them. What was more, he was 'presently labouring under an indisposition' and, in consequence, 'unfit for any exertion'.[27] On the day after the reply was received, Milner visited Mr Keating's Catholic Bookshop where, by chance, he met Peter Collingridge, Vicar Apostolic of the Western District, who had also come to London to discuss the bill with Poynter. Collingridge was invited to join Milner's campaign. He refused. Milner – still fighting the battle – asked for a meeting of Catholic notables to be convened the next day. It assembled under the chairmanship of the Earl of Shrewsbury and considered a paper which Milner might have written with the intention of continuing the argument, rather than negotiating a mutually acceptable compromise. 'Thirdly. Is not an English Vicar Apostolic obliged to speak out openly, so as to be clearly understood by the Catholic public?'[28] The meeting broke up without taking any decision, apart from the agreement not to follow Milner's lead. 'The success of the Bill on its third reading was as confidently anticipated to take place during the next few hours as the rising of the sun next morning.'

It would have done so, had it not been for an extraordinary breach of convention in the House of Commons. While the bill was in committee, James Abercromby, MP, was in the chair. That enabled Charles Abbot, the Speaker, to defy all precedent and make a strongly partisan speech. The bill, he said, had been introduced to avoid civil strife. The behaviour of John Milner and the Irish bishops made clear that it would not have that result. Then he revealed his real objection. Catholics, he argued, could not be trusted with political power or influence since they owed allegiance to the Pope as well as to the King. He moved that the clause of the bill, that gave them the right to vote and sit in Parliament be struck out. Mr Speaker Abbot's motion was carried by 251 votes to 247 and the bill, having been rendered meaningless, was abandoned.

Milner took credit for the collapse of the bill and the Catholic Board agreed that he should take the blame. A special meeting of the Board was convened. The only item on the agenda was a proposal to remove John Milner from the committee of which he had become a member, at his own request, when the bill of 1813 was first discussed. Milner was asked if he would resign in order to avoid the embarrassment – to both him and the Board – of an expulsion. He declined on the grounds that to do so would imply the acceptance of guilt. But he agreed to attend the meeting at which his position was to be discussed. Indeed, he was the first delegate to arrive. The discussion was as much concerned with the offensive language that Milner used in disputation with his colleagues as it was with responsibility for the demise of the bill, and it was clear from the start that the motion to expel him would be carried by a large majority.

It was not until the result was declared that Milner spoke in his own defence. Then he read a seven-point statement which had clearly been prepared in anticipation of defeat. He then left the meeting, pausing only to pronounce a dramatic valediction that became part of nineteenth-century Catholic folklore. Its mythological status is confirmed by a dispute over the actual words he used. In one version Milner paused at the door before saying, 'I hope you will not turn me out of the Catholic Church nor shut me out of the kingdom of heaven'[29] – an unlikely valediction, since it was hardly a moment for irony and Milner certainly did not believe that the Catholic Board had the power to excommunicate him. An alternative – 'You consider me unfit for your company on earth. May God make me fit for your company in heaven' – reads as if it has been composed and polished by faithful disciples. Another version has the plausible ring of aggressive spontaneity. 'You may expel me from this Board, but I thank God that you cannot exclude me from the Kingdom of heaven.'[30] Whatever words he used, they inspired two of the delegates to leave with him – a gesture that Milner must have found almost as gratifying as the encomium issued by the Irish bishops: 'The Right Reverend Dr J Milner, Bishop of Castabala, our vigilant, incorruptible agent, the powerful and unwearied champion of the Catholic religion, continues to possess our esteem, our confidence and our gratitude.'

The English Vicars Apostolic did not echo the Irish bishops' admiration. When they gathered in Durham, at the suggestion of the 'noblemen and gentlemen of the Catholic Board' who wished 'to be guided by their opinion', Milner – accused of offensive conduct and spreading falsehoods – was not invited to attend. In his absence they reaffirmed their support for the Fifth Resolution, without clarifying what intrusion into Church affairs it would permit, and composed a pastoral letter, which called on all good Catholics to do likewise. They knew that their decisions would win favour in Rome. The Vatican had yet to recover from the chaos caused by the invasion of Napoleon's army and the French annexation of the Papal States in 1809. So relations with the Church in England were, to a very large degree, dictated by Father Paul McPherson, Rector of the Scots College and, in those unusual circumstances, agent in Rome for both the English and Scottish Vicars Apostolic. He was known to be in favour of the Fifth Resolution and it was no surprise when, largely due to him, Milner was instructed to remain in his own district, and Archbishop Troy was told that the Church in England was outside his jurisdiction. Both men responded with glorious irrelevancies. Troy expressed disgust that the Fifth Resolution had been agreed in a tavern 'amid the clatter of plates and glasses'. Milner accused John Douglass, Poynter's predecessor, of being in the pay of Catholic nobility. In their headquarters, the Quirinale Palace, the Vatican high command was sufficiently exercised by the state of English Catholicism to issue two formal statements. One – known, because of the official in whose name it was published, as the Quarantotti Rescript – endorsed the bill that had failed to pass through Parliament and suggested minor alterations to the oath it contained, but urged its acceptance even if the amendments were rejected. The second Rescript emphasised the importance of good relations between England and the Holy See.

The English Catholic Board was delighted by Rome's initiative, but anxious for assurance that the Rescripts could not be revoked. McPherson did his best to provide it. But he had underestimated Milner's energy and enterprise. With the explanation that he had work to do on behalf of the Irish bishops, he visited Rome and on May 24th 1814 was received in audience by Pope Pius VII to whom he claimed that, in England 'schismatic measures have been carried on'.[31] At meetings with Cardinal Litta – the Prefect of Propaganda Fide – he described the English Vicars Apostolic as 'all venal and corrupt and sold to [he meant bought by] the Catholic laity' and accused Poynter of fraud. Poynter was summoned to Rome. He too had an audience with the Pope. But before he arrived, Pius VII received a message from the English Catholic Board rejoicing at the restoration of his authority over the Papal States. His reply was not what they expected. The state of Catholicism in England was to be examined by a congregation of cardinals.

Poynter, like Milner, had a meeting with Cardinal Litta. It began badly, with the Cardinal denouncing the Fifth Resolution as indefensible, demanding the dissolution of the Cisalpine Club (under whatever name it operated) and criticising the exclusion of Milner from meetings of the Vicars Apostolic. Litta then turned to the accusation of fraud. Milner had overplayed his hand by claiming that Poynter had retained more than his proper share of the funds that were distributed among the English Districts after the closure of the continental seminaries. Litta knew that the accusation was groundless and, in consequence, changed his whole position, decided that a veto was acceptable in principle and instructed Milner to draft a form of words which satisfied the Catholic Board without eroding the Pope's authority. The drawn-out negotiations were interrupted by receipt of the news that Napoleon had escaped from Elba. Pius VII fled north and so did Poynter and Milner.

While Milner was still in Rome the Society of Jesus was re-established in England during a ceremony that he was invited to witness. It was, by any standards, an important occasion in the life of the Catholic Church. But Milner thought of it – as his obsession caused him to think of everything – in terms of his dispute with the other English Vicars Apostolic. The readmission of the Jesuits was, he wrote, 'considered by some London Catholics as the downfall of the catholic religion; which proves how different their ideas are from those of the Vicar of Jesus Christ'.[32] He was right to anticipate anxiety in England. In December 1813, the English Jesuits had been granted the long-requested permission to renew their vows as affiliates of the Society in Russia – without the Vatican thinking it necessary to notify the English Vicars Apostolic. But the bull *Sollicitudo Omnium Ecclesiarum*, which restored the Order worldwide, could not be kept secret. Milner immediately welcomed the decision. All his colleagues refused to recognise the bull. The usually flexible William Poynter was particularly opposed. The recognition of the Jesuits would, he feared, renew the old tension between the secular and regular clergy. He also suspected that the Jesuits, once again operating as a society, would vigorously oppose any sort of veto and every sort of oath.

When Poynter expressed his fears to Cardinal Litta, he received the reassuring news that the Pope, conscious of the Society's controversial reputation, intended it to be restored only in countries 'in which the government consents to receive and recall them'. Cardinal Consalvi confirmed that 'the Bull of restoration was not to be forced on any', but the individual Jesuits who had remained in England were not prepared to wait for the approval of a Protestant government. There was particular resentment in Wigan, England's most Catholic town, where priests who had been expelled from Stonyhurst and Liège ministered to 1,400 communicants. The Protestant government came to the aid of the anti-Jesuit Vicars Apostolic. Lord Sidmouth, the Home Secretary, supplied a pre-arranged reply to a letter from William Poynter: 'The Prince Regent and the British feel insuperable objections to the establishment of the Society of Jesus in England.' He later found it necessary to clarify government policy. Like ministers before and after him, he had written 'England' when he meant the 'United Kingdom'. There was to be no restoration of the Jesuits in any part of Great Britain or Northern Ireland. The 'Gentlemen of Stonyhurst' declared themselves an exception and lived like the members of the Society that, they believed, God wished them to be.

The Congress of the Cardinals, which was to decide the fate of the Catholic Church in England, was held in Genoa on April 28th 1815. Its conclusions were conveyed to Poynter (with copies for Troy and Milner) by Cardinal Litta, but it was assumed that the ideas, on which they were based, were Cardinal Consalvi's. The 'Genoese Letter' was emphatic that, if emancipation was ever to be granted, agreement to a veto was essential and suggested that if it be in the form of a short list, drawn up by the temporal power 'to expunge the obnoxious', from which the Pope made a final selection, it would be acceptable. Whatever effect the Genoese Letter had on the English Catholic leadership, it did nothing to reduce the parliamentary opposition to emancipation. Debates in both the Lords and Commons ended with far less support for the Catholic cause than it had attracted in 1813. By December 1815 – with Napoleon defeated and the Pope back in Rome – Litta got close to performing the last rites over its corpse. There was 'no hope' of emancipation 'on those conditions which his Holiness could offer and [which] are so opposite to the principles of the civil power'. And, as if to say that the Vatican had grown weary of the prolonged controversy, Litta added, 'The Pope does not, and never did, ask for the emancipation of Catholics.'[33] The letter's final paragraph read like a coded message that Rome was changing sides. 'With sorrow and even annoyance we learn that the Right Reverend Dr Milner, heedless of the admonitions, indeed reprimands, made to him in Rome continues to cause grave disturbance.'

Mixed messages are always interpreted by partisans as confirming their worst fears. And in Ireland, Daniel O'Connell assumed that the Vatican was on the point of capitulating to the English Catholic Board. He justified his assumption with the plausible explanation that Castlereagh – who had certainly visited Rome while the Cardinals'

Congress was sitting – had struck a bargain with Cardinal Consalvi. The two men had sat together at the Congress of Vienna where, O'Connell suspected, Consalvi had promised to 'concede the British Crown [the] effectual supremacy over the Catholic Church in Ireland' in return for 'the restoration of part of the Pope's territories still with-held'.[34] Ireland would have to act alone.

At a public meeting in Dublin in January 1815, O'Connell set out the principles of an essentially national Catholicism. The Irish people must make clear to Rome that they would never accept English authority over their Church. He believed that Rome would support their stand. But if it did not, Ireland should still resist. 'I am,' he said, 'sincerely a Catholic, but I am not a papist ... I deny the doctrine that the Pope has any temporal authority, directly or indirectly in Ireland.'[35] He went on to argue, more contentiously, that even the Pope's spiritual authority was limited. 'He cannot vary our religious doctrine in any respect.' Although many of the men and women in the audience would not have realised it, he was making a distinction between the authority of the Catholic Church and the Pope – a distinction neither party would have accepted. He changed his mind with the years. In 1837 he 'revere[d] in all things the authority of the Holy See ... My submission to the authority of the Church is complete, whole and universal.'[36] In 1815 he was an Irishman first and a Catholic second.

Whatever the niceties of O'Connell's theology, after the Dublin declaration the relationship between the English establishment and Irish Catholicism acquired a new dimension. Irish Catholics had been suspected first of supporting Spain, then France, in those countries' attempts to overthrow the lawful government of England. After January 1815, Irish Catholics were seen as being subversive for Ireland itself. Irish Catholicism and Irish nationalism went hand in hand.

The militancy of the Irish Catholics was in sharp contrast to the complacency of the Catholics in England – many of whom feared that full emancipation would awaken the sleeping Protestant tiger. Even the real enthusiasts for reform were pitifully grateful for every gesture of support (no matter how tentative) that they received. In May 1816, William Poynter reported to Rome: 'A debate took place in the House of Commons ... The object of it was to take consideration [of] the penal clauses next session. The majority against was 31 – the time, it seems, has not yet come – yet it was pleasing to observe that nothing injurious to the Religion or character of Catholics was said by those who opposed it.'[37] However, there were 'some comments on the intemperate behaviour of some among the Irish'. The drive for emancipation in Ireland was holding back support for emancipation in England.

O'Connell's campaign was built around 'aggregate meetings' – mass rallies by another name. So at least a section of the Irish peasantry was associated with the emancipation movement. O'Connell was not, however, a champion of the landless Irish peasantry who rallied behind him, more because he was an orator than because he represented their political, economic or religious interests. His speeches reflected the interests of his class – the moderately prosperous Irish Catholic land-owners. In England, the campaign for emancipation was still largely the preserve of the priesthood and gentry, sometimes working together and sometimes in opposition to each other.

There the case for emancipation was faithfully represented by *The Tablet* – a weekly newspaper, founded in 1840, which initially found it 'hard to speak with moderation on the subject of Irish politics'.[38] It became more Catholic in content with the resignation of its Church of England joint owner in 1843, but maintained its reputation for controversy until Herbert Vaughan (the future Archbishop and Cardinal) became 'sole and absolute proprietor' in 1868. The paper also reflected the growing appetite for 'popular journalism'. One item in an early edition carried the headline 'Horrible Murder in Barnsley'. Sensationalism aside, its early existence confirmed that, in the middle of the nineteenth century, Catholic England included the beginning of a middle class.

The Church itself was starting to edge away from its dependence on wealthy patrons. That was not a conscious policy. It was the result of the growth in the number of tradesmen and artisans who felt able openly to attend Mass and contribute to the upkeep of chapel and parish. In the London District numbers expanded at such a rate that new chapels opened almost every year – Hampstead and Poplar in 1816, Stratford and Moorfields in 1817 and Horsham in 1819. The Poplar chapel was built to accommodate a congregation greatly increased by the arrival of Irish immigrants – an early manifestation of a phenomenon which, later in the century, was to change the char-acter of the Catholic Church in industrial England.

The London District led the way in the provision of Catholic schools for Catholic children, but it still failed to meet the need or the demand. By 1815 there were three schools funded by Catholic charities, and another run and financed by parishioners and patrons of St Patrick's, Soho. The four schools provided about 1,200 places – leaving more than 1,000 Catholic children without the hope or prospect of a Catholic elementary education. Charities that claimed to be Christian, but not denominational, offered places at their schools and – initially, after assurances were given that the Bible and a spelling book would be all that the pupils were allowed to read – they were taken up. But it was later discovered that, although they were protected from heretical texts, the children sometimes sang Protestant hymns. On the principle that ignorance was to be preferred to heresy, the pupils were withdrawn.

The Catholic Church in Scotland either took education more seriously or apostasy less so than was the case in London. By 1822 there were Catholic schools in Dumfries, Greenock, Ayr and Paisley, where two more were opened during the next decade. In Glasgow the employers of Irish labourers founded three schools for the children of their workers. Although they stipulated that 'no formal creed' should influence the religious instruction, the Catholics of Glasgow sent their children to the schismatic institutions without any recorded objection from their priests. By 1825 they had five schools of their own, teaching Catholicism to 1,400 Catholic children.[39]

Naturally enough, the rising enthusiasm for education coincided with an increase in literacy and, equally naturally – in early nineteenth-century Catholic England – the growth of literacy was regarded by the rival factions as a God-given opportunity to defend their beliefs and attack their enemies in print. Until 1801, when the *Catholic Magazine* was published in Liverpool, there had been no Catholic periodical in Britain. A second publication, *The Conciliator*, was launched in 1813, but survived for only a dozen issues, probably because conciliation does not produce compelling journalism. Polemics does. That is why the *Orthodox Journal*, first published in the same year, succeeded. Its proprietor – William Eusebius Andrews, sometime editor of the *Norfolk Chronicle* – could not have been more frank about its purpose. It was created to combat the policy of the Catholic Board. And, because its proprietor was a long-standing admirer of John Milner, it represented his views in language that he might have used. Although Richard Thompson, the mild and insignificant Vicar General of the Northern District, did no more than express doubts about a fellow priest's rejection of a loyalty oath in any form, the *Orthodox Journal* denounced him with invective that was not even original. It reported that 'he bellowed forth the most unjust imputations against some of the most illustrious members of an order of the Church at a Tavern dinner in the midst of the jingling of glasses and the belching of toasts'.[40]

Milner contributed to almost every issue of the *Orthodox Journal* and always in a style that might have been, and probably was, designed to cause offence. He seemed particularly to enjoy name-calling. George Silvertop, an enthusiast for compromise over the oath and veto, became

'Mr Copper Bottom' and, in what must have come very close to libel, was accused of keeping company with 'fox-hunting laymen amidst the orgies of Bacchus'.[41] Milner's attacks on William Poynter were not as vituperative as his assaults on the Catholic Board, but they were sufficiently wounding to provoke a complaint to Rome. Cardinal Litta responded with the reproof that Milner's conduct was unbecoming. Milner changed his byline rather than his style. For a while he wrote under the pseudonym 'Merlin'.

Anonymity did not suit Milner and it was not maintained for very long. When it was abandoned, Poynter complained to Rome again and Litta replied that Milner, although told to mind his manners, had ignored the Vatican's advice – just as the English Vicars Apostolic had ignored the advice to admit Milner to their meetings. A third complaint (this time by Silvertop, among others) evoked a sterner response from Rome: 'His Holiness commands and orders [you] to take no further part henceforward, directly or indirectly, in the said journal.'[42] It was not a command that Milner could ignore. So, protesting that all the complaints against him were the product of malice, he resigned. The sorrow of parting was, to a degree, alleviated by the knowledge that he had already threatened to resign if the editor persisted in publishing letters that criticised his articles. In fact, the *Orthodox Journal* needed him more than he needed it. Without Milner's polemics, it withered and died after struggling on for seven years. Other Catholic periodicals did not last as long. *The Publicist* – also opposing concessions from Church to state – lasted for three years. The *Catholic Gentleman's Magazine* – reflecting the views of the Catholic Board – survived for only one.

The failure of the Catholic periodicals was a reflection of the Church's opposition to theological speculation. Opposition to the publication of vernacular translations of the Bible had been justified by the fear that, in the hands of laymen, the testaments would be misunderstood and their message misinterpreted. The Word of God came to the world courtesy of Rome. So it was only to be expected that, even in the early nineteenth century, the Catholic Church in England was alarmed by the movement to make bibles readily available to all its members. The movement was begun, in England, by the Protestant Bible Society. When a group of Catholics, believing it was the best way to defend their territory, considered setting up a society of their own, Thomas Smith – Coadjutor of the Northern District – wrote to William Poynter in outraged anxiety: 'Distribution of Bibles is founded upon the avowed principle that each one is to form his creed from the Scriptures independently of tradition and the authority of the Church.'[43]

The Catholic Board did not agree and, when the Protestant Bible Society began to distribute Douai and Rheims editions to whoever wanted them, it decided to form a Roman Catholic Bible Society. William Poynter – always anxious to compromise and moderate – cooperated in the enterprise, with the explanation that he intended to ensure its religious respectability. Milner condemned the whole exercise in the language of impeccable orthodoxy. 'It is not the Catholic rule of faith that every individual should [be] judge of the reasonableness of every article of faith, but he is to believe them on the authority of the Catholic Church.'[44]

Whatever differences divided the factions that made up the emancipation movement, they were certainly united by their indomitability. For the first twenty years of the nineteenth century they tried, time after time, to convince Parliament that their cause was just. Time after time they were rebuffed. And time after time they regrouped and tried again. Sometimes – as with Grattan's House of Commons motion in 1817 – they were heavily defeated. Sometimes – as with General Thornton's free-enterprise resolution – the Commons refused even to discuss the subject. Occasionally – as with Grattan's proposal in 1819 – they came close to success in the Lower House of Parliament. His motion was lost by two votes. Usually – as with Earl Grey's attempt, in the same year, to remove all mention of transubstantiation from the test of loyalty – they were heavily defeated in the Upper House. Grey's bill was defeated by 141 votes to 89. Even the strongest supporters of the cause began to view the attempts at progress with weary resignation. John Gradwell, in London, wrote to his brother Robert in Rome, 'The Irish petition will be presented to the House of commons in April by Mr Grattan who will, *as usual*, move for a committee to take the petition into consideration.'[45]

It was not until 1821 – with Grattan dead and William Plunkett, another Protestant, leading the emancipation faction in Parliament – that success seemed possible. A year earlier the Catholic Board had drawn up an address for presentation to George IV, who had been King since his father's death in the first month of 1820. It was signed by seven bishops, seven peers, fourteen baronets and 8,000 'men of substance and position' and was accompanied by numerous petitions from England and Scotland. It was almost a year before its contents were translated into a bill. Parliament was preoccupied by the King's attempt to divorce Queen Caroline. But eventually a drafting committee was formed. Its first draft contained yet another Oath of Allegiance. It promised 'full and undivided loyalty' to 'his Majesty, his Heirs and successors'. The second draft revived the idea of a

commission to examine candidates for the episcopate and, in consequence, open the way to a royal veto by another name.

Plunkett's proposals proved more popular in the Commons than in
the Catholic Church. They were condemned by Milner, questioned by
Poynter and, after first being supported by the Irish bishops, denounced
by Oliver Kelly, Bishop of Tuam, who claimed to speak for a substantial minority within the Irish Church. In the Commons the Second
Reading was carried by 254 votes to 243 and a wrecking amendment,
which proposed the exclusion of Catholics from Parliament, was
defeated – despite another irregular intervention by the Speaker – by
223 votes to 211. The Catholic Board was so certain of victory that
it had prepared an address of gratitude to be presented to Parliament.
It was not needed. In the Lords the bill was opposed by the Duke of
York (the heir presumptive to the throne), who described it as in
conflict with the coronation oath's vow to uphold the Protestant religion. His intervention proved decisive. The bill was lost by 159 votes
to 120. It was said that thirty-nine peers saved the Thirty-Nine Articles.
They also saved the Vicars Apostolic of England from facing the
dilemma of how to deal with an Act of Emancipation of which they
did not approve.

There followed a year in which the forces of emancipation were so
dormant that they seemed dead. It coincided with the visit to Ireland
by George IV. O'Connell, a passionate advocate of Irish freedom from
the English yoke, had always been equally passionate in his allegiance
to the English crown. At a meeting of Dublin citizens, called to prepare
for the royal visit, he predicted that the King would 'allay the dissen-
tion of centuries – a greater moral miracle' than St Patrick's expulsion
of the snakes from Ireland. A second speech – delivered as George IV
was about to board the boat for home – claimed that, thanks to
'Your Majesty, discord ceased and even prejudice fled.'[46] He then
presented the King with a crown of laurels. The poet Tom Moore
paid him a tribute of sorts. All Ireland had welcomed the King in
'servile style', but O'Connell had been 'pre-eminent in blarney and
inconsistency'.

O'Connell would have refuted Moore's claim with the argument
that his loyalty to the crown was genuine, and that its fulsome expression was a necessary demonstration that Irishmen could be both
Catholics and patriots. In 1823 he began his campaign to prove that
they could also change the course of history without recourse to the
violence that he loathed. The (Irish) Catholic Association was founded
with the avowed aims of healing the wounds sustained during disputes
over the veto, uniting the nation in the demand for emancipation and

providing the common people with the power that comes from solidarity. The inaugural meeting was held in Dempsey's Tavern, Sackville Street, Dublin on May 23rd. The Convention Act, which had been passed to suppress the United Irishmen, was still in force. So although the Association had a formal membership, its meeting had to be open to all 'associates' who paid a shilling a year. The 'Catholic Rent', as it was called, was collected at the rate of a penny a month – very often by the priests who held the Association together. More than £200 was collected in September 1823, and within another year the weekly collection had risen to £1,000. That was less than O'Connell had hoped it would be. But it was enough to subsidise the publication of emancipation broadsheets and accumulate a war chest for when the day of reckoning came.

Enlightened opinion was beginning to make itself heard. In the first number of the *Parliamentary Review*, published in 1825, John Stuart Mill demanded the removal of all Catholic 'disabilities'. But it was politics, not philosophy, which secured the eventual victory of the emancipation campaign. It came after four more years of bills presented and defeated, renewed arguments about the oath and veto, and continued animosity between Milner and the other Vicars Apostolic. The Duke of Wellington – an opponent of every proposal for any sort of reform – presided over a Cabinet composed of six supporters and seven opponents of emancipation. It did not represent parliamentary opinion. The pro-emancipation motion – in what had become the annual debate on the subject – was carried. But it was the resignation of four ministers, over the wholly unrelated issue of disenfranchising two rotten boroughs, which set off the chain of events that changed the law. One of the replacements was Vesey FitzGerald, the Member of Parliament for Clare, who was appointed President of the Board of Trade and, in conformity with the rule of the day, resigned his seat and sought re-election.

The Catholic Association had chosen Major William Nugent McNamara – a Protestant and therefore eligible to sit in the House of Commons – as their candidate for Clare. But he refused to fight the by-election. The decision to replace him with O'Connell was a challenge to the established order. A Catholic was entitled to stand for Parliament, but was not allowed to take his seat unless he took the oath that branded him a heretic. In consequence the campaign concerned only one issue. O'Connell invited the 'electors of County Clare to choose between one who abominates that oath and Mr Vesey FitzGerald who has sworn it full twenty times'.[47]

From the start, it was clear that O'Connell would be the people's champion and choice. A crowd of 30,000 men and women attended, or attempted to attend, the hustings in Ennis. But O'Connell did not leave the result to be determined by his popularity. He spent £14,000, much of it in a way that, today, would result in his imprisonment rather than election. The British Catholic Association – though fearful that his campaign would turn into an attack on property – donated £5. Polling lasted for five days. At the first count O'Connell was only six votes ahead. Every Forty-Shilling Freeholder who could not produce a magistrate's certificate confirming that he had sworn the Oath of Allegiance had been turned away. On the third day sympathetic magistrates administered the oath to Freeholders in batches of twenty-five at a time. Because of their efforts, the final result – declared on Thursday July 4th 1828 – was a landslide: O'Connell, 2,057; Fitzgerald, 982. The defeated candidate, reporting the result to Robert Peel – a one-time rabid anti-Catholic, whose change of view contributed to his reputation as the nineteenth-century Tory Party's greatest reformer – chose, inexplicably, to describe the result as a 'tremendous prospect'. Peel ruefully replied, 'a prospect tremendous, indeed!'[48]

O'Connell did not attempt to take his seat, but waited to see how the government would react. Peel's first instinct was to change the law so as to require the Oath of Allegiance to be taken by all candidates for office. The idea was abandoned as impractical. It seemed certain that Catholics would win every seat in Ireland, likely that the Tories would lose a general election and possible that there would be a civil war. Wellington told the Catholic Archbishop of Armagh – a friend from the Peninsular War, when he was rector of the Irish College in Salamanca – that he did not anticipate 'settlement of the Roman Catholic question'. His pessimism became public knowledge when the letter in which it was confessed was passed from the Archbishop to O'Connell, and from O'Connell to the newspapers.

Robert Peel was both more pragmatic and more optimistic about a solution being possible. The by-election had convinced him that, whatever the merits of emancipation, it was irresistible. He was not the only convert for whom Clare could take the credit. The Irish Protestant Association, meeting in the Dublin Rotunda, declared its support for emancipation. The Prime Minister, the Duke of Wellington, asked Peel to consider what concessions might satisfy the Catholics, and Peel replied that 'partial concessions would not be enough' and that the 'ruling principle must be equality of civil privilege'. Peel believed that his conversion had been so sudden and so complete that honour required him to resign and allow his constituents to pass judgement on his volte-face in a by-election. He lost and was forced to find another seat.

Wellington was not yet convinced. But Peel – with all the zeal of a convert – persuaded him at least to discuss the issue in Cabinet. The Prime Minister therefore advised the King, a rabid opponent of emancipation, 'not to grant the Catholic claims ... precipitately' but to agree to them being examined. George IV gave his grudging agreement and, on February 25th 1829, the King's Speech at the opening of Parliament promised a review of 'the whole condition of Ireland ... and the laws which impose disabilities on His Majesty's Roman Catholic subjects'.[49] In the atmosphere of the time, the review could have only one result. But the King was still not reconciled to the inevitable. On Wednesday March 4th 1829 Wellington and Peel were summoned to Windsor where they were harangued for five hours by George and his brother, the Duke of Cumberland. The King swore never to sign an Emancipation Bill. Wellington and Peel resigned.

They were out of office for less than twelve hours. On the evening of their resignation the King – regarding Wellington, if not Peel, as indispensable – asked them to return to office. They agreed on the understanding that they would introduce, and he would sign, an Emancipation Bill. Peel's First Reading speech lasted for four hours. Much of it concerned the new Oath of Allegiance that a Member of Parliament was required to swear before taking his seat. It did not include the rejection of the doctrine of transubstantiation. Nor did it renounce 'the invocation and adoration of the Virgin Mary'. The duty of good Catholics to depose an excommunicated monarch was not mentioned and was only referred to, in passing, by Peel on the grounds that it was not a notion that could be supported by any sane man. There was no suggestion that the government should have any sort of veto over the appointment of Catholic bishops or be entitled to intercept communications from Rome. One possible cause for Catholic complaint was a clause that promised 'never to subvert the present Church establishment'. And there were a number of other irritants. Catholic bishops were prohibited from taking their titles from ancient sees. There were to be no celebrations of Mass outside churches. Religious Orders were to register with a local magistrate. It was confirmed that no Roman Catholic could occupy the throne.

The bill was approved, in both Houses of Parliament, by gratifyingly large majorities. On St Patrick's Day 1829 the Second Reading was agreed in the Commons by 353 votes to 173. The Third Reading improved on that result: 320 to 142. In the Lords, the Archbishop of Canterbury's wrecking amendment was defeated by 217 votes to 112.

It had taken fifty years of argument and four days of a by-election to right the wrong of three centuries. Asked how the Duke of Wellington had convinced the peers to support the bill, Lord Clarendon said that the conversion had been easily accomplished. He simply issued the order: 'My Lords! Attention! Right about face! Quick march!'

The victory of pragmatism and principle was not complete. In order to prevent Daniel O'Connell's Irish Association from occupying a majority of the Irish seats in Parliament, the Forty-Shilling Freeholders were disenfranchised, the qualification to vote fixed at £10 a year and the Lord Lieutenant given the power to suppress or disband dangerous societies. At last Catholics were legally emancipated, but they were still not free and equal citizens. After 1829 they enjoyed full civil rights. But most of them still suffered the social and economic penalties of prejudice – private rather than official discrimination.

CHAPTER 20

A Halo of Brightness

The good news from England was brought to the Pope by Nicholas Wiseman, since 1828 the Rector of the reopened and reinvigorated English College in Rome. Wiseman was a prodigy who had become Rector at the age of twenty-seven. The appointment had confirmed both his academic distinction and possession of the self-confidence that was to sustain him for the rest of his life. After his ordination and the award of his doctorate by the English College he had served as Vice Rector, but ambition swiftly prompted him to apply for the vacant chair of oriental studies in the Gregorian University of Rome. It was an appointment for which Wiseman was undoubtedly qualified, but – in an act of blatant nepotism – the university did not even consider his application. In a breach of its own statutes, it proposed to appoint an internal candidate.

Wiseman neither sulked nor accepted the rebuff with good grace. Instead he applied for a private audience with Leo XII and, his application being granted, asked for pontifical redress of his undoubted grievance. The Pope was impressed – no doubt as much by Wiseman's presumption as by his scholarship. He would be given a chance to compete for the chair if, and when, he produced enough published work to justify him being called Professor. Wiseman returned to his books and completed *Horae Syriacae*, three related monographs which examined previously ignored ancient Syrian manuscripts. Their tone can be detected from the title given to the second and third text: *Philological Contributions to the Syriac Versions of the Old Testament*.[1] Exhausted but triumphant, Wiseman awaited the call from the university. It never came. Despite the Pope's wishes, the internal candidate's appointment had been confirmed. Wiseman applied again and – suspecting that he would be rejected again – asked, once more, for a private audience with Leo XII. The Pope felt unable to overrule the university's decision. But, in order that justice should be done and determination rewarded, he instructed the Gregorian University to appoint two professors of oriental studies – and to invite Nicholas Wiseman to occupy the second chair.

Even without the gratitude that he rightly felt, Wiseman would have become the Pope's man. He was cosmopolitan by nature and upbringing and was entirely insulated from the doubts and suspicions that often prejudiced the long-distance relationship between London and Dublin, on one hand, and Rome on the other. Wiseman was born in Seville, the son of an Irish cloth merchant who was conspicuously pious, even by the standards of Spain at the beginning of the nineteenth century. As a baby, Wiseman had been laid on the altar in Seville Cathedral while his mother, on her knees, promised that he would devote his life to God. Had his father not died when he was three, Wiseman would, almost certainly, have become a Spanish priest. But his widowed mother returned home to Waterford, where young Nicholas learned English as a second language. When, in preparation for his vocation, he entered Ushaw – then a school as well as a seminary – he was still far from fluent. But he was academically precocious. He went to the English College in Rome with a glowing reputation for industry as well as intellect, which he maintained for the rest of his life.

He was not so conscientious in the discharge of his duty to his mother. He had been in Rome for four months before he wrote home. Then he made up for his neglect with a letter of rather more than 5,000 words, which began with a graphic description of his rough sea passage through the Mediterranean and the confidence with which he faced the danger of shipwreck. 'I can say that in the most violent storms, I felt that God would never suffer us to perish in an undertaking for the good of the church and the promoting of our vocations.'[2] The waters of Galilee were not calmed in vain. Storms had become a test of faith. In the winter of 1735, John Wesley – en route for America – had seen the Moravian passengers on the *Simmonds* face a tempest without fear, and interpreted their courage as proof of their closeness to God.

During the winter of 1827, Wiseman accepted the Pope's invitation to deliver a series of public 'English Sermons'. The first – on the subject of repentance – had its audience and success guaranteed by the presence of twelve members of the papal choir, who concluded the evening with a recital that confirmed the Pope's patronage. The sermons were a triumph. But either the labour of their preparation or the anxiety about their delivery induced what was then diagnosed as a near nervous breakdown. Wiseman, with some reluctance, left Rome for a recuperative holiday. While he was away, Robert Gladwell, the Rector of the English College, was appointed Coadjutor to James Bramston, the Vicar Apostolic of the London District of the Catholic Church in England. On his return to Rome, Wiseman was made Rector of the

College in Gladwell's place. He also became the Roman agent for the English bishops. It was in that capacity that he told the Pope that the Emancipation Bill had passed. The appointment included less pleasant duties. One of them was interceding in the increasingly acrimonious arguments between Catholics in England and the Vatican.

The first dispute concerned the historically moribund Western District where Peter Collingridge, the seventy-two-year-old Vicar Apostolic, was assisted – if not always supported – by Peter Baines, a Benedictine monk of fixed opinions. Baines believed that the Western District would be revitalised by the creation of a seminary within its boundaries and concluded that the best way to achieve that end was to establish it in, or in place of, the school at Downside. The monks resisted and Baines suggested that they might exchange buildings with Ampleforth, whose monks might be more receptive to the idea. The Ampleforth Benedictines were no more cooperative than their brothers at Downside, and Baines abandoned the idea – but only temporarily. He knew it would not be long before he became Vicar Apostolic. When his appointment was confirmed, in the year of emancipation, he attempted to achieve his objective by a series of improbable schemes that included the adaptation of Prior Park – a vast and dilapidated mansion – and the approach to several religious Orders, not previously associated with the area, with the invitation to build a Catholic university within its crumbling walls. The Benedictines objected to intrusion into what they regarded as their territories. But Baines (a Benedictine himself) insisted that the Vicar Apostolic had authority over the monks within his district. Inevitably the monks denied his claim. Wiseman's attempts at mediation were immensely complicated by Baines' visit to Rome, where Pius VIII was so impressed by his dynamism that he considered making him a cardinal.

Baines was not interested in an appointment, no matter how lofty, that kept him away from the Western District. But an English cardinal in Rome – partly to celebrate emancipation and partly to improve relations – was regarded in the Vatican as an absolute necessity. Wiseman himself was considered. But it was agreed (particularly among the old and battle-scarred) that he was too young and inexperienced. Despite his disclaimer, Baines remained the Pope's choice. But because he was regarded by the Curia as too controversial a figure to sit among them, he escaped enforced promotion. So the lot fell to Thomas Weld.

Perhaps the Pope chose Weld to emphasise Rome's respect for King George. Weld's father, although a devout Catholic, had been regarded as such a significant member of society that George III and Queen

Charlotte had stayed with him at Lulworth Castle, and the new Cardinal's family personified the compatibility of Catholicism and patriotism. At the height of the Napoleonic Wars, one member had volunteered to fight with his local yeomanry, but the King – knowing his religion – had refused to sign his commission. So he had served as a sergeant. By comparison, the Weld who took Holy Orders – a widower whose late ordination was swiftly followed by appointment as Bishop of a Canadian see, which he was not required to visit – was a colourless figure. He became a colourless cardinal.

Peter Baines, the Pope's preferred candidate, was busily imposing his ideas on the Western District. He confirmed that Prior Park was to become the home of the long-dreamed-of Catholic University, with Nicholas Wiseman as its President. Wiseman was also invited – or thought he was invited – to become Baines' Coadjutor. A year's leave was agreed with the English College and Wiseman made his way to Bath, where the new Catholic 'university' was enjoying a temporary success – largely at the expense of Downside and Ampleforth. No mention was made of his appointment as Coadjutor and, when it became clear that if it had ever been on offer, the offer was withdrawn, Wiseman resigned from Prior Park. He still had almost a full year to occupy before his return to Rome. The first few months were spent touring England – a foreign country of which he knew virtually nothing.

It seems unlikely that his tour taught him much about the country to which he was to devote most of his life. In post-emancipation England the overworked clergy were increasingly spending their time among the new labouring poor in the towns of the Industrial Revolution. That was not the England that Wiseman set out to explore and, if he may have realised that Catholic England was changing, he showed little sign that he recognised the new reality. Before he left, on what he described as his 'progress through England', he outlined his plans to a friend. He had 'made a resolution never to sleep in an inn or hostelry the whole way; to quarter [himself] upon such of the nobility and gentry as can sufficiently appreciate such an honour', and after a brief interlude in 'Birmingham and the other Midland Cyclopean Towns ... proceed to the princely towers and enchanted gardens of the Earl of Shrewsbury's house at Alton'.[3] The tone was flippant, but he was serious about his intention.

Wiseman was, by nature, a Prince of the Church who would inherit his kingdom at a time when English Catholicism was not at peace with itself. The long battle for emancipation had been won. But changes in the composition of society had not yet extinguished the nobility's claim that the Church's destiny must remain within their hands, and its prospects of growing and prospering were further prejudiced by the reluctance, even among some of the priests, to yield control to Rome of what they thought of as an essentially English Church. Those related issues were, for the next fifty years, to dominate the debate about the future of English Catholicism.

Whatever Wiseman expected from the noble families, he found them incapable of leading the English Catholic revival to which he aspired. Despite emancipation, they continued to behave as if Catholicism was still suppressed. 'The shackles had been removed but not the numbness and cramp which they had produced.'[4] One problem was Catholics who remained reluctant to proclaim the glory of their Catholicism but chose instead, humbly, to avoid causing offence to the Protestants who had graciously granted them the freedom of worship. Another was Catholics who had clung to their faith during the years of persecution, but then fell into the error of which James Bramston, while Vicar Apostolic of the London District, had warned: temporal advantage leading to 'forgetfulness of eternal interests'.

The tour of England completed, Wiseman filled the rest of his year of leave from Rome by performing the duties of a parish priest at the Sardinian Embassy chapel in Lincoln's Inn Fields and delivering a series of Lenten Sermons at Moorfields. The theme of the sermons was the revival of the Catholic Church in continental Europe – a subject that engrossed him and was to lead him into a decade of not-always-friendly disputation with John Henry Newman. During his year in London Wiseman was introduced by Thomas Walsh, Vicar Apostolic of the Midland District, to Michael Quinn, a Dublin journalist, and to Daniel O'Connell, who – having first been denied his seat in the House of Commons – had fought a second by-election and become the undisputed Member for Clare. The three men had come together during the foundation of the Reform Club in 1832 and four years later they had renewed their partnership in order to promote another venture – the publication of a Catholic periodical. It was called the *Dublin Review* and was created to be a Catholic rival to the Tory *Quarterly Review* and the Whig *Edinburgh Review*.

Wiseman gladly accepted an invitation to become associated with the periodical and agreed to join Quinn in editing the first two issues. He announced that he saw himself as 'representing the theological and religious element of the journal', as well as ensuring that the periodical voiced 'no extremes in politics'.[5] The *Dublin Review* became a vehicle for promoting the enduring ideas which, he believed, should guide the Catholic Church in England. Involvement with the *Dublin Review* also provided the expatriate Nicholas Wiseman with an opportunity to meet the English Catholic intellectual elite. Prominent among them was the architect Augustus Welby Pugin. A convert to Catholicism, Pugin believed that art and faith were inseparable.

During the year in which Peter Baines offered Wiseman the presidency of Prior Park, Pugin – then an Anglican – wrote to a friend, 'I can assure you after a most close & impartial investigation, I feel perfectly convinced that the roman Catholick church is the only true one ...'[6] More importantly in terms of his vocation, he added, '... and the only one in which the grand & sublime style of church architecture can ever be restored'. Pugin was working with Charles Barry on the design of the new Houses of Parliament when, in 1836, he published *Contrasts* – so polemical a work that, despite its excoriation of the Georgian architects Nash and Soane, the uninitiated took it to be a theological tract rather than a textbook. The contention that a building should exhibit its purpose, and the insistence that an architect should be identified with his work, were its least contentious assertions. The claim that the Reformation and the creation of an Established Church had brought about the 'overthrow of art' caused such offence that Pugin was banned from drawing in Salisbury Cathedral, where it was his habit to sketch details of the work of craftsmen who were inspired by faith and uncorrupted by materialism.

Pugin was in thrall to the 'backward glance' – the notion that the golden age was in the past. The idea inspired many of the nineteenth-century Catholic revivalists, including, for a time. John Henry Newman. But only Pugin – because of his profession – was able to give the pursuit of the past a tangible form. Romantic and rich Catholics stood ready to finance the re-creation, in stone, of the Middle Ages' aesthetic values. Principal among them was John Talbot, the 16th Earl of Shrewsbury. He was supported by a cadre of young men whose vision of Catholicism was coloured by the way in which they had found faith. Ambrose Phillipps – the co-founder, with the Earl of Shrewsbury, of the Mount St Bernard Cistercian Abbey in Leicestershire – was finally converted by the sight and sound of a Paris Mass, although he had not responded, at the age of sixteen, to a dream in which God had reproved him for rejecting true Christianity. He had converted the Honourable George Spencer, a Church of England clergyman and brother to Lord Althorp. Immediately on his admission to the Church, Spencer had launched, with Phillipps' support, the Campaign of Prayer for the Reconversion of England. Shrewsbury shared Pugin's view that reconversion was best encouraged by providing visible evidence of the beauty that faith could inspire. During the next ten years he financed the building of two Catholic cathedrals (Birmingham and Nottingham) and a dozen parish churches. Phillips made a more personal contribution to the Catholic building boom by employing the architect of Nelson's Column to design him a house with its own chapel and an adjoining Cistercian monastery on 227 acres of Charnwood Forest that he had acquired for the purpose.

By then, Nicholas Wiseman had returned to Rome, where the re-establishment of the English Hierarchy was already under discussion. In late 1838, Cardinal Franzoni – Prefect of the Congregation of Propaganda Fide – had written to the four English Vicars Apostolic suggesting an increase in their number. They responded with a *Statuta Proposita*, which accepted the creation of new districts and proposed that the Vicars Apostolic – while not being given the title and status of bishops – should acquire episcopal powers, including the right to confer Holy Orders and the ability to create a Chapter with the power to take corporate decisions.[7] The Vatican rejected the Vicars Apostolics' proposals, but enforced its own plan for increasing the number of districts. Propaganda Fide let it be known that a more comprehensive change to the organisation of the Church in England was certain – but not imminent.

Thomas Walsh and Thomas Griffiths (successive Vicars Apostolic of the London District) were sent to Rome to express the English Church's hope of a new constitution. They discovered that the Pope was as dissatisfied with the stewardship of the Vicars Apostolic as the Vicars Apostolic were with their status. Rome had received complaints about how they performed their duties. The Rosminians – a nineteenth-century religious community with a special interest in education, who were in temporary occupation of Prior Park – had detected a 'lack of spiritual life among the clergy' and the Earl of Shrewsbury had supported Pugin in his expression of disgust at the poor quality of vestments and church furnishings and echoed his demand that the ancient liturgy be restored. The repetition of the criticisms in Rome fed the growing suspicion that Wiseman – the agent of the English Vicars Apostolic – spent more time undermining the English Church than defending it and representing its views to the Vatican, as his appointment required. He had made no secret of his belief that many of the English clergy lacked fervour and he had become convinced that it was his obligation – perhaps even his destiny – to inspire them to greater efforts. On October 18th 1838 he had written to the Ushaw seminary to say that 'it cannot be long before England is my residence'. He then described his plan 'to establish a small community of missionaries who, living in a common home, should go, two by two, from place to place, giving lectures and retreats etc in different dioceses'.[8] Wiseman had to wait. His permanent return was to be delayed until Rome had made its final disposition on the future of its troublesome outpost.

Despite his belief that his vocation lay in England, Wiseman had become (and was increasingly regarded as) part of the Roman establishment. He had become a 'figure' in Catholic society and invariably played host to the distinguished Englishmen who joined the increasing numbers of 'pilgrims' (cultural as well as religious) who made the journey to the Eternal City. He met Lord Macaulay, William Ewart Gladstone and Henry Manning (then the Church of England Rector of Lavington, a village parish in Sussex), and invariably took his visitors into Rome's catacombs, which were being opened up after years of neglect – a process which Wiseman thought symbolised the emergence of the Catholic Church in England from the dark years of persecution. Twenty years later he was to write *Fabiola*, a historical novel which was intended – by use of the catacombs as a metaphor – to emphasise the timeless continuity of the Catholic Church. But at the turn of the decade 1839–40 Wiseman's theological views, if not his literary talent, were best represented by a poem:

> Full in the panting heart of Rome
> Beneath the Apostle's crowning dome,
> From pilgrims' lips that kiss the ground,
> Breathes in all tongues one only sound:
> 'God bless our Pope, the great and the good.'[9]

Wiseman was the Pope's man and, because of his years in the 'capital of Spiritual Christianity', he believed in the self-confident exposition of the Catholic Church triumphant. It became his mission to convince English Catholics that they should share both his loyalty and his unswerving conviction. He became the predominant Ultramontane of mid-nineteenth-century England and the principal exponent of its doctrine that the 'supreme papal authority in matters of faith and discipline'[10] was beyond question.

Perhaps because his formative years had all been spent abroad, Wiseman did not comprehend the depth and extent of hostility that Catholics faced in England. Pugin could have explained how visceral the antipathy was. Travelling by train, the architect had introduced himself to the passenger who sat opposite to him, who responded, 'You are a Catholic, Sir. I must get into another carriage.'[11] Mindless prejudice was less damaging than what passed for an intellectual

justification for an Established Church. The case for official discrimination against all religious denominations other than the Church of
England had been advanced by William Gladstone. In the week before
Christmas 1838 he had published a tract which argued that the state
could not, itself, distinguish between religious truth and religious error
and that the English Government could only recognise where truth lay
(and accept the consequent duty) by giving 'active and exclusive'
support to the Church of England.

The expression of that principle – even after it had been modified –
caused Gladstone one of the crises of conscience that punctuated his
long political career. In 1842, when he was the President of the Board
of Trade in Peel's Tory Cabinet, he brought himself, after much
agonising, to support the renewal of the government's annual grant to
Maynooth seminary – an obligation inherited from the Irish Parliament
on the union of the two kingdoms. But in 1844, when Peel – disturbed
by O'Connell's growing influence – proposed to increase the grant
threefold and make it permanent, Gladstone resigned. It was not clear
whether he opposed the grant or felt unable to vote for a proposition
that he had once opposed. Understanding his overtly conscientious
position was made more complicated by his offer – if Peel decided to
open diplomatic relations with the Vatican – to become envoy to the
Papal State.

While Gladstone and his friends were worrying about the Catholic
resurgence in England, the Vatican was fearful that it was, if not in a
state of decline, at best incapable of growth and development. But,
unlike Wiseman, they believed that the failures of the Roman Catholic
Church in England were best remedied by reorganisation, and that the
re-establishment of the Hierarchy should be a reward for success rather
than a stimulus to improvement. During the summer of 1839, Cardinal
Franzoni, the Prefect of Propaganda, made the public and official
announcement that England was to contain eight rather than four
Apostolic Districts. Wales was to become a district in its own right
and was placed in the care of the English Benedictines. The Northern
District was to be divided into three separate vicarates: Yorkshire,
Lancashire and the remaining counties of the old regime. A new
Eastern District was to be carved out of London and the Midlands.
Four new Vicars Apostolic and four new Coadjutors would have to
be appointed.

Thanks to the enthusiastic patronage of Thomas Walsh, Wiseman
returned to England for a lecture tour under the auspices of Oscott
College and happily contributed to the missionary zeal that Pugin
expressed in stone. Pugin had been recruited to the college staff as

Professor of Ecclesiastical Antiquities, but it was unclear whether he regarded his duties as teaching or building. He certainly felt an obligation to 'improve' the college by the addition of details, which he believed to be medieval in design, and by the completion of the unfinished chapel. Joseph Potter, the architect appointed to advise on rebuilding and extending the college, resigned.

Pugin's definition of medieval can most charitably be described as idiosyncratic. It included art and architecture of the sixteenth century. But he more than compensated for his lack of historical precision by the fervour with which he pursued his belief that God's goodness (not to mention His aesthetic values) should be exemplified in the buildings that were dedicated to His worship. Initially, his overt piety obscured the traits of character which made him an impossible colleague and intolerable employee. In 1835 Thomas Walsh, the Vicar Apostolic of the Midland District, had written from Oscott to tell Nicholas Wiseman (then Rector of the English College in Rome) that 'the new college is proceeding well and is much admired. The celebrated Pugin is delighted with it and is designing the chapel interior free of charge.'[12] A copy of Pugin's *Contrasts* followed in the parcel post. From then on, the relationship between Walsh and 'God's architect' deteriorated, from silent disagreement to vocal hostility.

If Wiseman read *Contrasts*, he could have been left in little doubt that the celebrated Pugin would prove a difficult man with whom to work. But it is not the assertion that the cities of the Industrial Revolution were 'inexhaustable mines of bad taste' that was to cause the Catholic Church in England such problems. Nor was it the claim that for three hundred years church-building had been 'a disgrace on score of their composition'. The conflict – the Church and its benefactors versus Augustus Welby Pugin – was the result of what *Contrasts* identified as the second cause of the architectural degradation. English post-Reformation churches were a disgrace because of 'the inadequate sum allocated for their construction'. His unwillingness to compromise what he believed to be the medieval beauty of his design was an expensive form of integrity. In December 1838 he wrote to John Hardman – a Birmingham button-manufacturer – to express his thanks for the receipt of £909 7s 5d – the last instalment of his bill for the improvements to Oscott College, and to tell Hardman that there would be more to pay before the aesthetic renaissance was complete. The list of outstanding items included 'lace for the green vestments, a silver and ebony reliquary, three purple and gold vestments, velvet, lace and embroidery'.[13] The Catholic Church was about to discover that the architect of genius thought of himself as a liturgical impresario.

The spirit that Pugin represented spread far outside the Midland District. During the lecture tour Wiseman undertook as a way of familiarising himself with his new home, he witnessed a procession in Huddersfield that he described as 'like an Italian more than an English' celebration.[14] The Guild of Confraternity walked 'two by two with their tippets and badges [and] crucifixes canopied over like Roman ones ... acolytes with surplices and priests with copes'. But it was in the Midlands that Pugin's ideas were – thanks to the patronage of the Earl of Shrewsbury and John Hardman – most spectacularly transformed into the actual building of churches which, by their design, rejected what he saw as the vulgarity of the early-nineteenth-century Catholic Church in England. London was regarded by Pugin as particularly guilty of debasing the faith. At the Warwick Street Chapel, Mass was sung by an Italian opera company and had thus descended from sacrament to entertainment.

Nothing of the sort could possibly take place in the rarefied atmosphere found in the new Church of St Mary in Derby. In 1838 Nicholas Wiseman preached the sermon at the inaugural service and, afterwards, described the church as 'without exception, the most magnificent thing the Catholics have done in modern times and quite worthy of ancient days'.[15] But an even greater work was in progress. Pugin was designing, for Birmingham, the first Roman Catholic cathedral in England since the Reformation and the first cathedral of any sort to be built since Christopher Wren's St Paul's. St Chad's, as it was to be called, was clearly being built in anticipation of a hierarchy being re-established. After the foundation stone was laid, Pugin addressed the assembled dignitaries on the debt that he owed to medieval design. 'There is not,' he said, 'a single detail that has not been faithfully imitated.'[16] He combined the evangelical impulse with the spirit of Victorian enterprise by insisting that the creation of the Kingdom of God 'depended on our own individual exertions' and concluded with a passage that not only echoed William Blake, but was, in its way, more eloquent than 'Jerusalem'. 'Never shall I rest satisfied till I see the cross raised high above every chimney in Birmingham and hear the sound of St Chad's bells drowning the steam whistle and the proving of gun barrels.'

Six years later, in 1844, Wiseman – speaking at the consecration of St Barnabas' Cathedral in Nottingham – told the congregation that 'the architectural taste of Mr Pugin has enkindled a light of rays which will cover the present era with a halo of brightness'.[17] He had not always felt so sympathetic towards designs that were meant to embody a precise, but not universally held, view of the Catholic obligation. A few months before the completion of St Chad's, Wiseman had

discovered that a rood screen, across the head of the chancel, separated
the altar from the people. He proposed that the plans be revised,
since – in what now sounds like the anticipation of the 'reforms' initiated at the Second Vatican Congress in 1966 – it was 'of the utmost
importance to throw our ceremonies open to all'. Hardman, who had
donated £500 towards the screen's cost, wrote an angry letter of
complaint and Pugin threatened to resign, telling a friend, 'Wiseman
has shown his real sentiments.'[18] In fact, Wiseman had shown that –
despite his intellect and experience – he did not fully understand either
the intensity or the theological consistency of Pugin's theory of spiritually inspired architecture. Wiseman apologised and withdrew all opposition to the St Chad's rood screen. So they became a regular, and
apparently uncontroversial, feature of Pugin churches. After the inauguration of St Barnabas' Cathedral in Nottingham, the architect –
escorting a group of Protestant visitors – thought it necessary to
explain the rood screen's Catholic significance: 'Behind it is the Holy
of Holies. The people must remain outside. Never is the sanctuary
entered save by those in sacred orders.' At that moment Wiseman
appeared from within the sanctuary in the company of two ladies.
Pugin broke down in tears.

It is doubtful if the Earl of Shrewsbury – who had commissioned
Pugin to design his new house, Alton Towers, and remained the most
generous contributor to the cost of his churches – either supported or
even understood the architect's inflexible views on the superiority of
medieval design and its inseparable connection with the Church of
Rome. He certainly thought of Pugin as an indispensable contributor
to the Roman Catholic revival and said so. After the Mass which
followed the consecration of St Barnabas' Cathedral in 1844 – sixteen
bishops, a hundred priests wearing Pugin-designed vestments and a
choir that had been specially trained in plainsong – Shrewsbury gave
thanks for the resurgence of 'true faith', first to the Almighty and then
to Pugin. 'When we look back on the condition of Catholicity in this
country ten years ago ... and now see that we occupy the reverse of
our once degraded position we never ought, for a moment, to forget
to thank God.' But credit was also due to 'him whose noble views of
church architecture have of late been developed and whose indefatig-
ability is, in my opinion, the very life and soul of the restorative
movement now going on'.[19] Noble views of church architecture,
combined with an indefatigable architect, come at a high price.

In December 1840, Thomas Walsh wrote from the Midland District
to the Earl of Shrewsbury in language which – had the Vicar Apostolic
not been known as a pious man – might have been regarded as

sacrilegious mimicry of the Prayer Book. 'In my distress, my dear Lord, I fly to thee.'[20] The cost of rebuilding Oscott would, if a benefactor could not be found, ruin him. He explained that 'the church at Derby alone cost nearly double the sum' that was originally estimated, and there were problems with income and expenditure. The 'serious distress and great poverty' of the time made priests 'reluctant to call on their people for the pence'. Shrewsbury obliged. But he instructed the unhappy Walsh to tell Pugin that work on St Chad's and St Mary's in nearby Dudley would have to be delayed. The news spread fast and, in London, Thomas Griffiths thought it prudent to protect himself and his building committee against the consequences of architectural extravagance. Pugin was required to certify that he did 'not expect any money whatsoever from the Rt Rev Dr Griffiths on account of St George's Southwark'.

Six months later Shrewsbury – having reduced his subscription to the national Propagation Fund 'for the purpose of concentrating available means nearer home' – thought it necessary to give advice on how the Church could ensure that it received steady income. Writing from Spa ('available means' having made it possible for him to spend the summer taking the waters) he set out a scheme 'to take advantage of our numbers, which thank God, we are daily increasing ... Every Missionary should be required to have a list of his parishioners pasted up on the Church door or in the school room, with the respective sums affixed to their names which they subscribe. He should also preach to his people at least twice a year on the obligation and necessity of Charity.'[21]

It would have taken more than appeals from the pulpit to finance Pugin's insatiable extravagance, and a more determined man than the Earl of Shrewsbury to hold him to the promises to curb his inclination to excess, which he always made and always broke. As early as November 1841 Shrewsbury wrote to Thomas Walsh in near-despair. It had been agreed that St Barnabas' Cathedral in Nottingham would cost £10,000 – £7,000 of which he would provide. 'The church was to be about 90 feet in the nave, 30 in the choir with Our Lady's Chapel behind the High Altar and the choir & the Chapel of the B Sacrament on the left and the Sacristy on the right ... Now Pugin sends me a design for a Church 109 feet in the nave, 40 in the choir, with transepts, with three extra chapels & an extra corridor & a tower in the centre.' The agreement was that 'the shell' should be built for £7,000, but – Shrewsbury insisted – it was 'utterly impossible' to 'construct such a shell for that amount'. His Lordship demonstrated his determination to frustrate Pugin's pretensions with the news that he had

THE CATHOLICS

'written to Pugin to desire him to inform you that it was utterly impossible that I could come forward with a shilling more'. He concluded his letter by challenging Pugin on his own ground. 'Why did he claim that he must include the tower in the design of the basic church. In Italy 9 out of 10 old Gothic churches have the Campanile entirely independent of the church.'[22]

Some influential Catholics took exception to more than the high cost of Pugin's designs. They were opposed to extravagance in itself, and would have remained opposed even if armies of rich donors had competed for the privilege of paying the bills. Most of Pugin's critics took the 'political' view that it was best to build quietly and gradually on gains of emancipation, rather than behave in a fashion which flamboyantly (and, in their view, prematurely) celebrated the victory of Rome. The *Orthodox Journal* – living up to its name – complained that the Methodists built their chapels at far smaller cost than Pugin, even at his most modest, would ever contemplate. The more dangerous opponents of Pugin's aesthetic objected, in principle, to the idea of resuscitating the medieval spirit through the revival of medieval architecture, vestments, church ornaments and, above all, medieval ceremonial. These were the men who were genuinely offended by the funeral of Pugin's second wife, Louisa. The coffin was placed on a catafalque in the chancel of St Chad's Cathedral, draped with black velvet and covered in flowers. Above it was a 'canopy of fire', made up of row after row of burning candles. The medieval illusion was completed by the distribution of the ancient doles – bread for two hundred paupers and a shilling each for thirty-one widows, as a token of thanks for every year of Louisa's life.

Inevitably moral objections were translated into official complaints. Peter Baines of the Western District took exception to the chasuble Pugin had designed, and enlisted the support of the other Vicars Apostolic in declaring its use illegal. Thomas Griffiths had already banned its use in London, and John Briggs, of the new Yorkshire District, described it as being of Grecian appearance – which was what might be expected from the interference in Church business by a 'mere tradesman'. Baines then complained to Rome, not about any one item in the Pugin repertoire but about his whole, allegedly malign, influence on the English Catholic Church. Rome replied without consulting either Pugin or the men who supported him. English Catholics must desist from making 'immoderate changes' on the advice of 'an architect recently converted from heresy'.[23]

The official rebuke was directed at Thomas Walsh. So Pugin, who replied in typically violent language, was able – out of modesty or a

360

desire to spread the blame – to describe the rebuilding of the Midland District as a triumph for Thomas Walsh's devotion rather than the achievement of his own creative genius. 'Dr Walsh found the churches in his District worse than barns. He will leave them sumptuous erections. The greater part of the vestments were filthy rags and he has replaced them with silk and gold. For this he has been censured.' Walsh had always had his doubts about the silk and gold. In December 1839 he had ended a letter to Wiseman with the nervous postscript, 'Pugin's drawings of the new vestments will now, no doubt, have reached Rome.'[24]

Walsh was right to be anxious about Rome's reaction to the proposal of reversion to Pugin's largely fanciful idea of medieval regalia. Propaganda Fide expected the Catholic Church in England, in common with the rest of the Catholic world, to dress its priests at Mass in what it called traditional (and Pugin called modern) vestments. Walsh felt obliged to obey. He had reacted calmly to the rebuke he had received from Rome, as witness his description of the news of his censure, in a letter to the Earl of Shrewsbury, as the receipt of 'very annoying information'. But he feared that Pugin would not react in the same way. His fears were justified. Pugin was in despair. 'If this decision of the Propaganda is carried out, I have done. I shall give up every hope.'[25] His depression was deepened by the news that Shrewsbury, his most distinguished patron, was to spend a year in Italy.

Nicholas Wiseman was about to travel in the opposite direction. As part of the reorganisation of English Districts, he was to become Coadjutor of the Midlands and President of Oscott College. Wiseman believed that a new era was opening for English Catholicism, that he was destined to be one of its leaders and that Oscott would become its intellectual driving force. In the belief that Wiseman was a natural ally, Pugin was willing to forget the mistakes and misunderstandings of Wiseman's occasional visits to his churches. He did not know that the new Coadjutor had told a friend, 'I would rather see all the splendid cathedrals levelled to the ground than a jot or tittle of Catholic truth pass away.'[26] But Pugin could not fail to notice that, as soon as he arrived at Oscott, Wiseman had instructed that all vestments be cut down from the full length of the Pugin design to the size required by Rome. Instinct, intellect and ambition had all stood in the way of the President of Oscott defying the Vatican.

Pugin's achievements were the triumph of youth and industry as well as genius and obsession. By the time he was thirty – although not an architect by training – he had designed three cathedrals, twenty-two churches, a monastery and a weirdly Gothic 'stately home'. He died in 1852, driven to despair by the barbarity of the building that Paxton had designed to house the Great Exhibition, and mortally depressed by his failure to be elected a member of the Royal Academy. His death was as Gothic as his architecture. During a railway journey from Ramsgate to London he was struck down by a seizure, which left him uncomprehending of the world around him. He was taken off to Bedlam – in sight of his Southwark Cathedral – where he remained until he partially recovered his senses. When he died in a private 'retreat', he was barely forty years of age.

For the last two years of his life Pugin had worked in unsuccessful and acrimonious partnership with Joseph Hansom. He could never have worked in harmony with the architect of the Birmingham Town Hall, a replica of the Roman temple of Castor and Pollux – even though, by the time of their association, Hansom was designing the Gothic Revival Church of St Walburge in Preston for the Jesuits. St Walburge's 300-foot spire – the third-tallest in the country – would be regarded as Hansom's memorial, were it not for his greater claim to a footnote in history. He designed the horse-drawn cab that bore his name.

As well as some of the most distinctive architecture of the nineteenth century, Pugin left behind a son who both followed his father's profession and inherited the characteristics which, as much as his controversial designs, made Augustus a divisive figure within the Catholic Church. Edward Pugin was about to be appointed architect for the rebuilding of the Church of St Thomas of Canterbury in Rome – the church of the English College. He initially refused to cooperate with Vitelleschi – a Roman architect of distinction – on the grounds that 'my idea is that the English Church should be in the distinctive marks of our own style of Gothic'.[27] Then he tried to insist on spending more than had been raised by a ten-year appeal: 'I distinctly told you that a building of the size and style you require could not possibly be erected for under £15,000.'[28] When he was relieved of the responsibility Edward Pugin made public his opinion of the consequence of the decision, which was 'disgrace to everyone concerned . . . The design is utterly worthless in every respect.'

CHAPTER 21

From the Flaminian Gate

When the architectural dispute – both aesthetic and financial – was at its height, Nicholas Wiseman was preoccupied with what he undoubtedly regarded as a far more dangerous division of opinion. Two increasingly polarised factions had grown up within the Catholic Church in England: quietists who were satisfied with toleration, and radicals who demanded the end of England's missionary status and its acceptance, by Rome, as a fully participating part of the worldwide communion. Chief among the radicals was Daniel Rock, chaplain to the Earl of Shrewsbury. In May 1842 he had sent a circular to all his fellow clergy – a formidable task, which could not have been accomplished without the support of his employer. Its intention was the revival of the campaign for the restoration of the English Catholic Hierarchy. 'Long has the yearning for such a measure been growing in the minds of several of the secular clergy of this land but . . . none of them would venture on the first step in this.'[1] The circular went on to report that timidity and torpor had been defeated, that the subject was raised at the annual meeting of Midland clergy and that a petition was to be sent to the Pope. The Adelphi Club was formed to campaign for the restoration of the Hierarchy and boasted, as a proof of progress, that attendance at its weekly meetings increased from two dozen to one hundred and twenty. The subject was discussed at a meeting of Vicars Apostolic in 1843, but – because of hostility from Catholics who wanted a quiet life – no decision was taken. It was not until 1847 that the Catholic Church in England decided formally to request a change in its status. Then Nicholas Wiseman, supported by Father James Sharples, was despatched to Rome, deputed by the English Vicars Apostolic to negotiate the creation of a distinct English hierarchy.

The elevation of Vicars Apostolic to the rank of full bishop involved far greater changes in the status of the Catholic Church in England than the improvement in personal esteem that follows a new title being given to an old job. The creation of the Hierarchy meant far more than the autonomous right to ordain priests and the duty to set up Chapters to govern the new dioceses. It even meant more than a change in the relationship with Propaganda Fide, which would no longer regard the English Catholic Church as a religious colony that was governed from Rome. The creation of an English hierarchy was of fundamental importance because of the place that bishops occupy in the Catholic Church. Collectively they stand, if not side by side with the Pope, then only one step behind him in the inheritance of the Apostolic Succession. They too are the heirs of Peter and Timothy and, in consequence, have a role to play in the governance of the Church and the interpretation of doctrine. The application for the restoration of the Hierarchy was the request that English Catholics, by becoming bishops, be empowered to influence the whole future of their native Church.

Wiseman was a controversial choice of spokesman to argue England's case. He was undoubtedly unpopular with his colleagues, who thought of him both as an 'Ultramontane' who regarded Rome's word as law and as an 'enthusiast' who rejoiced in making new converts from the ranks of troubled Protestants. He wanted the Catholic Church to come out of hiding and had something approaching contempt for what he regarded as the timidity of many senior members of the clergy. Because of those attributes, it was assumed that he sided with the Curia in Rome rather than with the independently minded Vicars Apostolic. That suspicion seemed to be confirmed when the Pope made clear that he would want Wiseman to succeed Thomas Walsh as Vicar Apostolic in London. Discreet representations were made to the Vatican. As is usually the case, the Pope's will prevailed, but in a concession to opponents of the appointment, Wiseman was initially to be known as Pro-Vicar Apostolic.

Yet, despite their doubts, the English Vicars Apostolic chose Wiseman to argue for a hierarchy. That was because he knew his way around Rome and could be relied upon to make England's case with clarity and courage and at least the appearance of conviction. The English Vicars Apostolic needed a brave and lucid champion to counterbalance the influence of Charles Acton, the Pope's adviser on English affairs. Acton – a little younger than Wiseman and equally clever – was essentially a Vatican bureaucrat who, working as Auditor of the Rota, was completely remote from parish life in England and, even after his appointment as Cardinal on the death of Thomas Weld, believed that his first obligation was protecting the Pope's interests. Unfortunately he regarded the English priesthood as, in many ways, antagonistic to Rome. That required him to oppose granting England the semi-autonomous status of a separate hierarchy. Wiseman was rightly thought to be his intellectual match. So he became champion of the cause – supported and, if necessary, held in check by John Sharples, Coadjutor of the newly created Lancashire District.

A new Pope, Pius IX, had been elected in June 1846 to succeed Gregory XVI. 'Pio Nono' was a controversial choice. The conclave that elected him – although he had come bottom in the first ballot – was, in the opinion of formally minded Catholics, of dubious provenance. Because of wars and revolution in Europe, only forty-six of the sixty-two cardinals attended. The English emissaries had no clear idea how the new Pope would respond to their application, but assumed that he would regard a re-established hierarchy as no more than a long-term goal. But Wiseman and Sharples – despite the opposition of Cardinal Acton – determined to press for immediate full episcopal status. Then Wiseman became caught up in the politics of the Risorgimento.

The election of Pius IX had produced what Count Metternich (architect of the Treaty of Vienna in 1815) believed to be impossible: a liberal Pope. Austria – opposed to reform within the Papal States and fearful of losing what amounted to her Italian colonies – sent a warning message to 'Pio Nono' in the form of eight hundred soldiers who crossed the River Po into Ferrara. Hapsburg agents were suspected of being complicit in a plot to assassinate him. It was time for the countries that had called for the liberalisation of the Papal States to act in defence of the changes they had demanded. Approaches had to be made to sympathetic governments, but there were no diplomatic relations between the Holy See and London. So the Pope asked Wiseman to return to England as his emissary and plead for moral support, if not actual intervention. In those days diplomacy was a more informal business than it is today. Wiseman called, unheralded, at the Foreign Office, but found Lord Palmerston out. So he left a seven-page memorandum, which politely asked Her Majesty's Government to endorse the introduction of the Roman reforms for which it had already called and to boost the reformers' morale by the appointment of some sort of plenipotentiary to the Papal States. Palmerston obliged, insomuch as he sent Lord Minto to Rome without any title which might suggest that England had recognised the successor to the Bishop of Rome who had once given his blessing to the murder of Queen Elizabeth.

In much of Europe the liberal rising in Italy turned into the Year of Revolution. That was not what the liberal Pope and his allies had either anticipated or wanted. They were enemies of tyranny, not the friends of democracy. For a while, Pius IX – worried less about Austrian assassination than Italian populism – lived in exile. On his return he turned his mind to the English question and decided, after two Masses that were dedicated to his need for heavenly guidance, that God wished the English Hierarchy restored. The Congregation of Propaganda Fide ordered the English Vicars Apostolic to draw up plans for the new regime. The work was done but, for some reason, the result was never sent to Rome. Impatient Vatican officials drew up a scheme that they believed to be acceptable to the Curia. It was never officially promulgated, but a copy was sent to Lord Minto – the British Government's man in the Vatican. He either failed to read it or chose not to report its contents to the Foreign Office. It was an omission that, when the Hierarchy was eventually re-established, was to heighten the tension between London and Rome, and which can only be explained and excused by the possibility that Minto judged that the negotiations – which it was said were to be based on the Vatican's own proposals – would never take place.

Wiseman, on diplomatic business, and John Sharples, mortally sick, were both in London. And Thomas Grant (by then Rector of the English College and Agent of the English Vicars Apostolic in Rome) responded to an invitation to take over the negotiations with a request to resign the agency. Eventually Bernard Ullathorne – a Benedictine monk and a man of selfless integrity who had been transferred, as Vicar Apostolic, from the old Western to the new Central District – agreed to argue England's case. His previous visit to Rome had been in response to an invitation to discuss the past liabilities and future prospects of the always controversial Prior Park. Advocating the creation, and negotiating the details, of a hierarchy probably seemed easy by comparison. That may have been why he 'lost no time in departing' on a journey which took him 'through the revolutionary scenes that agitated Paris'.[2]

Ullathorne's task was complicated by a request from the 'Clergy of England' that he present to the Pope a petition which 'begged that bishops shall not be made titular till the rights of the clergy be settled, lest their last case be worse than their first'.[3] Parish priests feared that they would lose the freedom that 'colonial status' allowed. The existence of the petition was embarrassing enough in itself. Ullathorne, a monk, was naturally anxious that he should not be accused of ignoring the needs of the secular clergy. But the clergy's concerns were elevated into a much more controversial issue by the intervention of Father Thomas McDonnell – late of St Peter's, Birmingham. Father McDonnell was a well-known troublemaker. A passionate opponent of Pugin and all his work, he had fought a long campaign against the building of St Chad's Cathedral. During its construction he had barricaded himself inside his presbytery and, after the completion of the cathedral, he had first organised his parish fete on the day of its opening service, and later burst into the celebration dinner. His conduct – which later included accusing Wiseman of heresy – had provoked a heated correspondence with William Ullathorne, and McDonnell welcomed the opportunity to undermine his old adversary by writing to Propaganda Fide as an advocate for the Clergy of England. McDonnell was a minor irritant. Wiseman – at least according to Ullathorne's biography – created a major problem.

The two men – piety aside – could hardly have been more different. Ullathorne was a blunt Yorkshireman who regarded administrative competence and financial prudence as important virtues. Wiseman exhibited neither quality. In a letter, written after Wiseman's death, Ullathorne clearly struggled, and failed, to be charitable about the colleague who, when he became Archbishop of Westminster, was promoted into a position that many (perhaps most) English Catholics thought the Vicar Apostolic for the Midland District should occupy. 'If there was success, there were also many failures in his career, owing to an utter deficiency of steady, straightforward business habits and a peculiarly sensitive temperament. He was in many respects a child, indeed I have long noticed that this is the character of men of genius. They carry the child through the life of a man with its intuitions and its susceptibilities.'[4]

In Rome, during the Curia's deliberations on the re-establishment of the English Hierarchy, the first accusation against Wiseman was that he attempted to influence the course of the negotiations long after Ullathorne had been given the responsibility for representing England. The second charge – in its way, even more damning – was that his private interventions with his influential friends often concerned decisions about appointments to the several sees that would be created when the Hierarchy was re-established. Ullathorne, who clearly rejoiced in speaking plainly, set out his complaint in writing: 'On the subject of lay interference . . . The most glaring cases have been ascribed to your lordship's friends, to those over whom you have been supposed to have sufficient influence to guide them.' He had reason to believe that 'members of the aristocracy with Lord Shrewsbury at their head had petitioned Rome to place a particular bishop in the archiepiscopal see of Westminster'.[5] The Curia's subsequent decision to conduct what was left of the discussions in secrecy can be attributed to their suspicion of Wiseman's conduct, to a response to Ullathorne's warnings or to a reversion to normal operating procedures.

Alessandro Barnabo – then Secretary of Propaganda Fide – told

Ullathorne that it would be difficult to confirm any plan, no matter how acceptable to the parties, until the seven cardinals, who were examining the options, had decided how to resolve the difficulty of choosing an English archbishop.[6] The related question – would a young man be acceptable? – helped to encourage the myth of Wiseman's insatiable ambition. Ullathorne claimed that Rome was determined that Thomas Walsh (to whom Nicholas Wiseman, after a period as Pro Vicar Apostolic, had become Coadjutor) would become the first Catholic Archbishop since the Reformation and was prepared to shuffle other appointments to bring that about. Age and time had made Walsh's elevation impossible. But the character of Ullathorne's negotiations make it clear that even the Princes of the Catholic Church argued – like ordinary mortals – about standing and status.

There is now little doubt that Wiseman was right to argue that Rome had decided to accept the principle of England's claim to its own hierarchy before Ullathorne's arrival. Long after the deed was done, he published the long memorandum in which he had initially outlined and sought to justify England's claim:

> The only regulation or code of government possessed by the English Catholics [is] the Constitution of Pope Benedict XIV ... which was issued in 1753 ... Now this Constitution has grown obsolete by the very length of time and, more happily, by change of circumstances ... [In 1753] the Catholics were still under the pressure of heavy penal laws ... All their colleges for ecclesiastical education were situated abroad ... Religious orders had no houses in England ... There was nothing approaching a parochial division and most places of worship were private chapels ... Either the Holy See must issue a new and full Constitution ... or the real and complete code of the Church must at once be extended to the Church in England ... In order to adopt this second and more natural expedient one condition is necessary ... the Catholics must have a hierarchy. The Canon Law is inapplicable under Vicars Apostolic ... Many points would have to be synodically adjusted and without a Metropolitan and Suffragans, a Provincial Synod is out of the question.[7]

The argument was so elegantly advanced that it must be assumed that Wiseman – or the colleagues who advised him – intentionally omitted any mention of the most pressing reason for a change in Church governance.

Over a brief decade the character and size of the Catholic community in England had fundamentally changed. Converts from the Church of England – excited by the doctrinal arguments that John Henry Newman had stimulated – had added zest and confidence to its congregations. And during the ten years that began in 1841, the Irish-born population of England, Scotland and Wales increased from 415,000 to 727,000.[8] As a proportion of the whole nation, they were an insignificant minority. But they concentrated in areas to which access from Ireland was easiest and where the chances of survival was greatest. In consequence, by 1851 they made up a substantial percentage of the population: 22.3 per cent in Liverpool and 18.2 per cent in Glasgow (on direct steamship routes) and 18.9 per cent in Dundee and 13.1 per cent in Manchester-Salford, where the growing textile industries offered the hope of work for women and children. More than 90 per cent of the Irish immigrants were Catholics. But they were Catholics of a sort unknown in England. They had been born and bred in a country in which their faith, although bearing the burden of civic disabilities, was dominant. So they took their Church for granted and often ignored its obligations. Their priests they regarded as the leaders – social and often political, as well as religious – of their communities, on whom they relied for help and advice. And most of the Irish Catholics who came to England in the early years of the nineteenth century were paupers, without jobs, homes or any experience of urban life.

Irish immigrants to England were, almost universally, the victims of prejudice and discrimination – sometimes because they were Irish and Catholic, and sometimes because they undercut the wages of the native-born workmen. The 1836 Report on the State of the Irish Poor had identified them as 'an example of a less civilised population spreading themselves, as a kind of substratum, beneath a more civilised community and, without excelling in any branch of industry, obtaining possession of the lowest departments of manual labour'.[9] While the working man accused the Irish immigrants of stealing English jobs, the establishment castigated them for being work-shy. *The Times* asked two rhetorical questions: 'What is an Englishman for but to work? What is an Irishman for but to sit at his cabin door, read O'Connell's speeches and abuse the English?'[10] Disraeli called Irish immigrants 'wild, reckless, indolent, uncertain and superstitious' and, in unconscious irony, listed bigotry among their defining characteristics. His imperial instinct might have prompted him to say that they gladly fought for the Queen Empress. During the first forty years of the nineteenth century 43 per cent of the 'other ranks' in the British Army were Irish-born.[11]

The Church was increasingly worried about not having the numbers of priests to serve the immigrants adequately and sustain their faith. The problems caused by the overall shortage of clergy were compounded by a particular shortage of Irish priests who were familiar with the mores, the accents and dialects of home. Father George Montgomery, of Wednesbury in Staffordshire, told the Rector of the Irish College in Rome 'nineteen twentieths of my flock come from Connacht'.[12] Sometimes the inability to make themselves understood prevented conscientious Catholics from making confessions. More often – particularly in the case of single men – they chose to ignore the obligations of their faith. The colloquial term for their behaviour was 'leakage'.

The size of the problem was, in one sense, overestimated. Half of the Catholic immigrants to Britain were not regular worshippers before they set sail.[13] So the 'leakage' was as much an Irish as an English problem. But although the immigrant Catholics were more likely to attend church than were their Protestant contemporaries, they were less likely to do so than the English-born Catholics. Very few of them repudiated Catholicism or converted to other denominations. They were indifferent to Catholic ritual and its demanding practices, not to Catholicism itself. They identified with the Church and, unhesitatingly, called themselves Catholics. And practising Catholics they became, when they needed the Church to officiate at weddings, baptisms and funerals.

Perhaps it was because the British Catholic immigrants – unlike their American counterparts – were Irish that they never came to dominate the Church in England as it was dominated by first- and second-generation citizens in the USA. But they did change its character. The Irish played a substantial part in completing the process of replacing lay control of the Church by control that amounted to the hegemony of the priesthood. And although English Catholicism never was, or could be, Ultramontane, antagonism towards Rome decreased with the assimilation of Catholics who had been brought up to believe that the Holy See could do no wrong. Perhaps most important of all, the increase in numbers made the Catholic Church a more visible part of British society. At the close of the eighteenth century there was one itinerant priest in Manchester. He said Mass in private houses. By 1846 thirteen priests served five distinct parishes. Although there were still people, inside and outside the Church, who argued that Catholics should give humble and unobtrusive thanks for the liberties they had lately enjoyed, bolder spirits began to break out from, the often self-imposed, isolation. Catholics also became a distinct community. That meant they enjoyed the benefits of solidarity, but also suffered the penalty of being different from the people around them.

The first half of the nineteenth century was notable for the extension and expansion of Catholic good works. The Asylum of the Good Shepherd rescued 'young women from a career of sin and appalling misery ... During their residence' they 'were not allowed to go out at all' as they prepared for 'employment in needlework and similar occupation'. The Benevolent Society for Relief of the Aged offered help to the 'widowed, childless and aged'. The Society of Charitable Sisters provided shelter for 'the poorest of the poor, principally natives of the Sister Isle, driven by necessity from their homes'. The Society of Catholic Butlers proposed to sponsor the creation of an Institute of Catholic Servants. And a Church which not so long ago had itself been regarded as a missionary enterprise applied to administer a proportion of the money that was allocated, by the government, 'for the education of Youths in those British Colonies in which slavery previously existed'. The obligations of faith were not forgotten. The Society of Christian Ladies for Decoration of the House of God supplied 'the poorer chapels of Great Britain and Ireland with vestments and altar linen'.[14]

Wiseman had been able to argue that England deserved, as well as needed, the benefits that a hierarchy would provide, and it was to support the argument (and not, as was later contended, to ensure that he was elevated above all other English Catholics) that he had exploited his personal connections. He had assumed that, when the Hierarchy was created, he would become Bishop, rather than Vicar Apostolic, in a diocese that corresponded to the London District. But in the high summer of 1849 he was instructed by Cardinal Antonelli, the Vatican's Secretary of State, to return to Rome and attend Consistory, at which he would be nominated Cardinal. Denials that the news gave him either pride or pleasure were implausible, but there is no doubt that he regretted what he wrongly believed would be one consequence of his elevation. He assumed that he would become a member of the Pontifical Court and that 'golden fetters' would frustrate his 'life's wish to labour for England'.[15]

No doubt Nicholas Wiseman left England on August 24th 1850 prepared loyally to discharge whatever duties were imposed upon him. But the grace with which he accepted papal authority was never put to the test. He was granted a private audience on September 5th, the day of his arrival, but it was not until September 13th, when he had a formal meeting, that he was told what his future was to be. When he relayed the great news to friends in England, he cautiously described his destiny as 'more than probable'. In fact he knew for certain that, at the Consistory, 'the Hierarchy will be proclaimed and, in the spring, I shall return to London'.[16] To avoid all doubt about what position he would occupy, he added that he would immediately hold the 'first Synod [Provincial] since the Reformation'.

John Henry Newman – not then the figure he was to become – anticipated that the re-creation of the English Hierarchy would be deeply controversial. Although he did not number understanding of the English character among his many talents, he also forecast, with equal prescience, that the most vehement objections would be based on the bogus claim that English sovereignty was under threat. So he wrote to Wiseman, with what turned out to be highly pertinent questions: 'Should his eminence wait a while in Florence until the ferment is over? ... Ought he also to have about him not only a good canonist but some very good English constitutional lawyer?'[17]

Initially, Newman's caution seemed misplaced. The English press reacted to the news from Rome with bored indifference. *The Times* described, at length, the Consistory that gave formal endorsement to the decision and celebrated England's translation from a mission to an archdiocese. Its description of the occasion leaves no doubt about the grandeur and glory of the ceremony. The newspaper was less interested in the liturgy than in 'the grand display of the diamonds of the old Roman families ... the brilliant jewels of the Torlonias and the splendid heirlooms of the Doria, Borghese and others'.[18]

All might have been well had the new Cardinal Wiseman not reacted to the proclamation of the restored Hierarchy with an exuberance that must, in part, have been fuelled by the sin of pride. He immediately issued a pastoral letter, which he named *From the Flaminian Gate* – referring to the passage north, and therefore to England, through the old city wall of Rome. The pastoral began with understandable rejoicing:

> The great work, then, is complete. What you have long desired and prayed for is granted. Your beloved country has been granted a place among the fair Churches which, normally constituted form the splendid aggregate of the Catholic Communion ... Then truly is this day to us a day of joy and exaltation of spirit, the crowning day of long hopes and the opening day of bright prospects.

He then described his role and responsibilities under the new dispensation in words that were not chosen with care:

> His Holiness was further pleased to appoint us, though most unworthy, to the Archiepiscopal See of Westminster ... giving us at the same time the administration of the Episcopal See of Southwark.

So at present, and till such time as the Holy See shall think fit other-wise to provide, we govern and shall continue to govern the counties of Middlesex, Hertford and Essex as Ordinary thereof and those of Surrey, Sussex, Kent, Berkshire and Hampshire (with the islands annexed) as Administrator with Ordinary Jurisdiction.

It took some time for the full text of the pastoral itself to reach England. But news of Wiseman's badly worded description of his elevation travelled fast. *The Times* – which had initially been more interested in ceremonial than in constitution – thundered its defence of English sovereignty and denounced the encyclical as 'an audacious and conspicuous display of pretentions to resume the absolute spiritual domination of this island'. Worse was to come.

Cardinal Archbishop Nicholas Wiseman left Rome for England on October 12th 1850 and stopped to be feted at every capital along the extended route. So London heard of his elevation some weeks before he arrived home. He learned of the reception that the news had received when he reached Vienna and was shown a week-old copy of *The Times*, which had extended its attack from an assault on the Pope's pretensions to a condemnation of both Pius IX for re-creating the Hierarchy and Wiseman for accepting its leadership. Its editorial described the new Cardinal as seeing 'fit to enter the service of a foreign power and accept its spurious dignities' and accused his master of 'one of the grossest acts of folly and impertinence which the Court of Rome has ventured to commit since the Crown and people of England threw off its yoke'.[19]

Much of the ridicule and abuse that were to follow were at the time – and have been since – attributed to Wiseman's folly in publishing the triumphalist pastoral letter. But the English establishment would, under any circumstances, have attacked what they saw as the Pope's presumption. *The Times'* excoriating editorials were published before it knew the full extent of what came to be regarded as Wiseman's blunder. The wording of *From the Flaminian Gate* only increased the outrage that the facts it described had already provoked. And the description of Wiseman's new responsibilities added ridicule to resentment.

Queen Victoria – thirteen years on the throne – was congratulated by her uncle, the Duke of Nemours, on the 'moderation of her response' to what he regarded as a challenge to her authority.[20] He said nothing about the realism of her proposal that diplomats should travel to Rome, in the hope of persuading the Pope to cancel Wiseman's appointment. The initiative was vetoed by Palmerston, the Foreign

Secretary – and, in Victoria's opinion, 'the obstacle to all that is good and right'. Despite her 'sincere Protestant feelings', she was disturbed by the 'anti-Catholic unchristian and intolerant spirit exhibited by many people at public meetings'. But her journal suggests that she was eventually persuaded to take the threat seriously by politicians who hoped to increase their popularity by what they chose to call 'Papal Aggression'. Wiseman 'was doing all he could to Romanize this country – to detach Roman Catholics from their allegiance to me and bring them entirely under the sway of the Pope. This is very dangerous.' Having read the list of counties that Wiseman had announced he 'ruled', the Queen was said to have asked – uncharacteristically amused – whether she still occupied the throne.

Charles Dickens encouraged the growing hysteria with an article in *Household Words* entitled 'A Crisis in the Affairs of Mr John Bull as Related by Mrs John Bull to the Children'. The Duke of Norfolk temporarily left the Church. Disraeli was said to have been so genuinely troubled by the affair that his romantic attachment to Catholicism (as illustrated in *Sybil*) became a violent antipathy to Rome and its English adherents (as demonstrated in *Lothair*).[21] Lord John Russell, the Whig Prime Minister – who did not know that his representative in Rome had been given notice of progress towards the Hierarchy's restoration – took the opportunity to regain some of the friends whom he had lost through his wholehearted support of Catholic emancipation. When the Bishop of Durham wrote to him to complain about the Pope's 'insolent and insidious' assumption of authority, Russell replied that he felt equally indignant and proved his point by denouncing, in manic language, the pastoral which, at worst, was risibly bombastic. However, he was confident that England was 'strong enough to repel any outward attacks ... and resist any foreign attempts to impose a foreign yoke upon our minds and conscience'.[22] That did not excuse 'the assumption of power in all the documents which have come from Rome – a pretension to supremacy over the realm of England and a claim to sole and undecided sway which is inconsistent with the Queen's supremacy'.

The Prime Minister must have known that fears of 'papal aggression' were groundless. Rome had, long ago, lost both the hope and the ability to reconvert England. But Russell, under attack from the reactionary wing of his party because of his support for the 1832 Reform Bill, sought to placate his enemies by releasing a spectre that ignited the bigotry that smouldered under the surface of civilised middle-class England. *The Tablet*, still in its reckless phase, commented that 'the devil is apt to howl when he is hurt'.[23]

Russell published both the Bishop of Durham's letter and his reply. The popular reaction was what he must have known it would be. The Church of England bishops behaved as if they were competing with each other to determine which diocese could take credit for the most mindless abuse. The Bishop of London described the Catholic clergy as 'emissaries of darkness'. The Bishop of Manchester warned that 'Rome clings to her abomination'. The Bishop of Oxford abhorred the pastoral as 'subtle and unclean'. The Bishop of Hereford feared the re-emergence of 'the sorcerer's cup' and the 'crafts of Satan'. The Bishop of Carlisle abandoned metaphor in favour of the simple claim that the pretensions of Rome were 'profane, blasphemous and anti-Christian'.[24] The Bishop of Chichester thought the pastoral was an act of 'audacious aggression' while the Bishop of Exeter regarded it as a 'daring display of Roman ambition'. The Bishop of Gloucester and Bristol complained of a 'revolting and frightful assumption' of unauthorised authority.[25] Fearful that they had not made their position clear, the English Episcopate – with the exceptions of Norwich and Wells – sent a loyal address to Queen Victoria swearing eternal opposition to any attempt to 'subject our people to a spiritual tyranny from which they were freed at the Reformation'. The Queen replied that she 'heartily concurred'. The Lord Chancellor lent his support by ending his speech at the Mansion House Banquet with two verses of doggerel: 'Under our feet we'll stamp the Cardinal's hat / In spite of Pope or dignities of Church.'

The Prime Minister's correspondence with the Bishop of Durham became public knowledge on November 5th 1850. So preparations were already in hand for celebrating the discovery of the Gunpowder Plot. All over the country effigies of Guy Fawkes were swiftly converted into effigies of Pius IX or Nicholas Wiseman. Some cities went even further. In Salisbury torchlights and brass bands headed the procession, which led crude representations of twelve Catholic bishops, as well as Cardinal Wiseman and the Pope, towards the flames. At Ware a donkey was dressed in a cardinal's robes and an effigy of the Pope, wearing ram's horns as well as the triple crown, was hanged as well as burned. A procession, 10,000 strong, marched from Peckham Common to Camberwell, shouting 'No Popery!' and 'God Save the Queen!' Priests were assaulted in the streets and the windows of Catholic churches were smashed. Wiseman's coach was stoned.

The spontaneity, as well as the extent, of the denunciations and demonstrations was depressing proof that England remained an anti-Catholic, as well as a Protestant, nation. Anthony Ashley Cooper, the 7th Earl of Shaftesbury, wrote that 'the ferment abates not a jot;

meeting after meeting in every town and county in the country ... It resembles a storm over the whole ocean; it is a national sentiment, a rising of the land! All sentiments seem for a while have to be submerged into one feeling.'[26] It was generally agreed that England had seen nothing to compare with the commotion since the Reform Bill riots, and that the most vociferous and violent citizens were members of the middle class – 'usually the calmest and most reflecting section of the community'. Their prejudices had moved with the times. Whereas their forefathers had feared Catholic-inspired external aggression from Spain, they warned against internal subversion – what *The Times* called 'the terrible danger of the renegades of our national Church [exploiting] a foreign usurpation over the conscience of men to sow dissension within our political society'. Shaftesbury prayed: 'Lord purge the Church of those men who, while their hearts are in the Vatican, still eat the bread of the Establishment and undermine her.'

Wiseman, when he eventually arrived home in England, took his detractors head-on. Wisely, he chose to defend the meaning, rather than the language, of his pastoral and graciously forbore to mention that a draft of it had been shown to Lord Minto, Lord Palmerston's representative in the Vatican, who – failing either to read it or grasp its importance – had neglected to report its contents to the government that he served. Wiseman's forbearance was rewarded. Lord Lansdowne, the Lord President of the Council, was admirably, if recklessly, frank. Lord Russell, he wrote, had published this letter to the Bishop of Durham without consulting colleagues – some of whom disapproved of its contents. Wiseman was encouraged to give a public explanation of what the restoration of the Hierarchy really meant. His exposition took the form of a sermon preached in St George's, Southall. Thanks to the controversial nature of the subject, several newspapers, including *The Times* with bad grace, published the sermon verbatim. Thirty thousand pamphlets, also reproducing the sermon in full, were distributed within a week. Wiseman was determined to occupy the high ground. So he began:

At this moment of danger to the religious and civil liberties of Englishmen is not from any infringement of them by the Pope in granting to English Catholics what I hope to show you they had every right to obtain from him. It comes from those who are taking advantage of the occurrence to go back a step, if they can, in the legislation of toleration and take away from a large body of Englishmen what is lawful to them in regard to the free exercise of their religion.[27]

What followed was simultaneously apologetic, dismissive and categoric. The Pope could not, would not and did not claim any authority over secular matters and, despite his own new title, the 'duties and occupation of the Dean and Chapter' of Westminster Abbey 'remain undisturbed'.[28] The combination of reason with an appeal for justice worked surprisingly well. The newspapers that had made the wildest allegations of treason and subversion did not, of course, admit they had been wrong. Instead they claimed that Wiseman's undoubtedly florid language had deceived them. *The Times* reduced its criticism to a complaint against 'Empty gasconades and pompous manifestos' and congratulated the new Cardinal on 'his recovery of the use of the English language'. The *London News* accused 'over sanguine priests' of foolishly overstating the consequences of a 'harmless domestic arrangement'.

Newman wrote to Rome to express his fear that Parliament, 'which the Queen wishes to summon for the despatch of business earlier than usual', would not let the subject rest. 'I don't think they can do us any harm,' he told Talbot at the English College, 'but they will insult us (which we must bear) and like mad animals will think that they have triumphed over us when we have the victory.' Despite the strength of the Catholic Church's position, he suggested a compromise over what, with remarkable prescience, he predicted would be the ground on which the establishment mounted its counter-attack, the naming of bishops. If 'Bishop of Birmingham is made illegal, Bishop of the City of Birmingham might be used consistently with Catholic propriety'. He ended with the glad tidings that 'the Cardinal is firm and vigorous' and 'the effect of his pamphlet (explaining the true meaning of *From the Flaminian Gate* had been enormous.'[29]

Despite Wiseman's protestations, Lord Russell persisted – or pretended to persist – in the belief that the Pope had territorial ambitions and was a predator that had to be held back. In 1851, he introduced the Ecclesiastical Titles Bill, which prohibited the Catholic Hierarchy from ascribing bishoprics to sees over which the Church of England presided, and made illegal the circulation of Papal Bulls. The Act, which remained law until 1871, was as pointless as it was vindictive. The Catholic bishops had already decided not to trespass on Church of England territory. Instead they simply created new sees. Southwark rather than London, and Leeds in place of Ripon. Birmingham, then within the diocese of Lichfield, was free for use by Rome.

Russell's revenge contributed to his downfall. The Irish Members – 'The Pope's Brass Band' – under the leadership of John Sadlier, 'the pocket O'Connell', turned on the government. The

subsequent dilemma was summarised by Richard Cobden: 'Any government which perseveres in the anti-papal policy will be opposed by the
Irish Members on every subject and if an Administration were to do
nothing against the Pope, they would be turned out by the English.'[30]

The damage to Whig prospects was even greater than Cobden
supposed. The hope of forming a government in alliance with the
Peelites and radicals was frustrated by prospective partners refusing
to join a government that promoted an Ecclesiastical Titles Bill.
Shaftesbury saw the crisis as confirmation of his worst fears. 'Who
could now assert that the Pope has no power in England? He has put
out one Administration and now prevents the formation of another.'
Russell revived his government by introducing a bill with the same
title, but that did little more than prohibit the use of specific titles to
which the Catholic Church had never aspired and made no mention
of Papal Bulls. It was carried on its second reading by 438 votes to
95. Amendments, passed in committee – making it a criminal offence
to use, as an episcopal title, the name of 'any city, town or place, or
of any territory or district' – produced a far more savage result than
Russell's original bill. It was passed on its third reading by 263 votes
to 46 and was ignored until it was repealed in 1871.

Gladstone, though no friend of the Pope, was disturbed. The Act
would 'destroy the bonds of concord and good will which ought to
unite all classes and persuasions of Her Majesty's subjects'. During the
debate in the House of Commons he had argued that the 'great subject
of religious freedom is not to be dealt with as one of the ordinary
matters which you may, with safety and honour, do today and undo
tomorrow'.[31] Henry Grattan had made a less measured speech during
which he had proposed an amendment that changed the title of the
proposed legislation to 'A Bill to Prevent the Free Exercise of the
Roman Catholic Religion in the United Kingdom'.[32] Neither of them
spoke for England. The national mood was better represented by Lord
Winchelsea, who told the House of Lords that the bill did not go far
enough to redeem 'the wounded honour of our illustrious Queen'.
Charles Schofield, a Birmingham MP, claimed that cells were being
built at Oscott 'for the forcible detention of some of Her Majesty's
subjects'. Charlotte Brontë – the daughter of the Irish Evangelical
'perpetual curate' at Howarth – predicted that 'a new Joshua [would]
command the sun to set, not merely to stand still but to go back six
centuries'.

Protestants, who were genuinely fearful of Wiseman's intentions,
failed to make allowance for a naivety that his admirers regarded as
holy innocence. He was an incompetent administrator, irresponsible

with money and – most disturbing of all, in an archbishop – a bad judge of character. Despite his intellectual brilliance he made pronouncements which, coming from a less revered figure, would have been regarded as proof of a feeble mind. The Earl of Shrewsbury constantly asked for the public correction of his more impractical proposals. Some concerned the life spiritual. 'The Cardinal preaches a doctrine which is quite new to me and I believe to all Catholics – that everyone, even the Pope, is *bound* to have a Spiritual *Director* besides his Confessor ... If this be so, surely the number of Clergy must be quadrupled.'[33] Sometimes they related to sensitive political issues. 'I fear that the Cardinal's permission, if proved true, for a Public Collection in London for the Irish University will grant great offence to the Govt. It is more than the Archbishop would do in Dublin.'

English Catholics drew many different morals from the Flaminian Gate Affair. The Duke of Norfolk, who had always wanted the Catholic aristocracy to run the English Catholic Church, complained of a drift towards Ultramontanism. Fearful that he would be misunderstood, the Earl of Shrewsbury clarified his own position in a letter to Bernard Ullathorne in Birmingham:

> I did not mean to say that the Hierarchy itself as a mistake – but the time and manner of doing it – & here I am glad to find yr L/p agreeing with me. Indeed, whether they be Protestant or Catholic, I have never found but one opinion on that point. The Hierarchy, *per se*, never have been a bad thing: we should have had it long ago or not quite so soon perhaps. But the manner has done, & will I fear still do us a world of mischief.[34]

He wondered why England could not be patient, like Scotland, and allow the passage of time to make the change acceptable. That alternative would have required a quarter century of forbearance. The Scottish Hierarchy was restored in 1878, immediately Leo XIII became Pope. But the Earl of Shrewsbury's analysis of the national mood was accurate. In 1852 – with Wiseman established in his archdiocese and Protestant England apparently at peace with Rome – Lord Aberdeen, on the point of becoming Prime Minister, wrote to Madame de Lieven, wife of the Russian Ambassador, 'There is more intense bigotry in England than in any other country in Europe.'[35] It was intense, but – as was to be expected in Victorian society – it was clothed in the trappings of respectability. As long as Catholics knew their place and acted with humility, they were tolerated. When they emerged from reticence and obscurity, they felt the full force of unmitigated prejudice.

The restoration of the Hierarchy and the increase in numbers – which had, at least in part, brought it about – marked the point in English history at which the Catholic Church emerged from the gloom of the Reformation into the early dawn of security, acceptance and influence. But it did not justify the ornate encomium by which it was celebrated in the sermon that John Henry Newman preached, on July 13th 1852, to the First Provincial Synod of the new era:

The world grows old, but the Church is ever young ... Arise, make haste, my love, my beautiful one for the winter is now past ... Arise Mary and go forth in thy strength into that north country which was once thine own ... A second temple rises on the ruins of the old. Canterbury has gone its way, and York has gone as Durham has gone, and Winchester has gone ... But the Church in England has died and the Church lives again. Westminster and Nottingham, Beverley and Hexham, Northampton and Shrewsbury, if the world lasts shall be names as musical to the ear, stirring to the heart as the glories we have lost and saints shall rise out of them and Doctors once again shall give the law to Israel and Preachers call to penance and to justice as at the beginning.

After the passage that was at least as vainglorious as Wiseman's address to England from north of the Flaminian Gate, Newman went on to describe, in equally extravagant language, the suffering in post-Reformation England. Catholics, like the early Roman martyrs, had lived '... in corners and alleys, and cellars, and the housetops, or in the recesses cut off from the populous world around them, and dimly seen, as if through a mist or in the twilight as ghosts flitting to and fro, by the high Protestants, the lords of the earth'. He then slightly amended his predictions about the future. In a metaphor based on the unpredictability of English weather, he warned that the spring of the revived Catholic Church might 'turn out to be an English spring, an uncertain anxious time of hope and fear, of joy and suffering – of bright promise and budding hopes, yet withal, of keen blasts, and cold showers and sudden storms'.

Apart from unjustified triumphalism – Canterbury, York, Durham and Winchester had survived the restoration of the Hierarchy unscathed – it is not easy to attribute much real meaning to opinions that were charged with so much emotion and expressed in such elaborate images. But the sermon – thereafter known as 'The Second Spring' – certainly had a dramatic effect on the congregation of bishops who heard it. Most of them were in tears and Newman himself was led away, in a state of near-collapse, to recover from his emotional exertions. It confirmed his position as a major figure in the Catholic Church – a status which, at that time, was the result of his role as the most famous convert in English history since Alban, the Roman soldier who, preferring death to forsaking his new religion, became the country's first martyr. But not even St Alban had agonised so publicly about his conversion, or accompanied the ebbing and flowing of the decision to abandon one faith and embrace another with a constant public commentary on each stage of his indecision. Equally important, Newman's decision to join the Church of Rome had been accompanied by a determination to take with him as many Church of England apostates as he could induce to convert. Most important of all, he provided the English Catholic Church with a vernacular justification of its beliefs and behaviour and, by his uninhibited comments on the shortcomings of the denomination which they had left, he reassured converts that they had made the right decision.

Newman – although a man of both faith and learning – was crucially short of emotional reticence. He had moved, with much public as well as private agonising, from abhorrence of the Catholic Church to reverence of what he eventually decided was the one true faith. Although he had, eventually, embraced Catholicism with the certainty with which he had once condemned it, each step of his spiritual journey had been accompanied by the advocacy of notions about the history of Christianity that were unique to him. Few Protestants had been such constant or such strident critics of the Pope and all his works as the young John Henry Newman. Ten years before he forecast an English Spring he had dismissed a rapprochement between the Church of England and the Church of Rome as 'impossible'. There had been some surprise – since it was an idea favoured by few people in either Church – that he had bothered to focus his acclaimed intellect on such a trivial issue, and it was assumed that he had simply created an opportunity to express his view on Papists and the Pope. 'Rome must change her spirit. We must see more sanctity than we do in her at present. Alas I see no marks of sanctity or, if any, they are confined to converts from [the Church of England] ... What Hildebrand did by faith and Holiness, they do by political intrigue. Their object is to pull down the English Church ... Never can I think such ways the footsteps of Christ.'[36] Hildebrand was a strange example of Rome's previous moderation. As Pope Gregory VII, he excommunicated the Holy Roman Emperor (Henry IV) and deposed him.

With a self-confidence that his disciples regarded as divinely inspired, Newman had then offered the whole Catholic Church advice on how to succeed. 'If they want to convert England let them go bare-footed into our manufacturing towns – let them preach to the people like St Francis Xavier – let them be pelted and trampled on and I will confess that they are our betters far ... I can feel nothing but distrust and aversion towards those who offer peace yet carry on war.'[37] The compliment to the Jesuit saint, which illustrated the criticism of the Church that Xavier served, was not the only ironic element in his suggestion for improvement. Newman's own preaching – rarely, if ever, bare-footed – was seldom directed towards the industrial poor.

John Henry Newman – graduate of Trinity College, Fellow of Oriel, curate of St Clement's and Vice Principal of St Alban Hall of residence for undergraduates – was, in youth and early manhood, a thoroughly Oxford (and therefore a thoroughly Church of England) figure. The son of a banker, his background was essentially middle-class, though being a timid boy – frightened of bullying, both real and imaginary, at his preparatory school – he was spared the rigours of Winchester, for which he was originally destined. Newman was, by any standards, precocious. At the age of sixteen, having read and enjoyed Joseph Milner's *Church History*, he described himself as 'nothing short of enamoured of the long extracts from St Augustine, St Ambrose and other Fathers which I found there'.[38] At the same age 'a deep imagination took hold of him'. It convinced him that God 'wished him to live a single life'. That was the obligation of his calling: 'missionary work among the heathen to which I had a great drawing for some years'. The early sense of vocation also encouraged a characteristic which he described with neither pleasure nor regret. 'It strengthened my feeling of separation from the visible world.' Newman was not destined for missionary work, as it was conceived in Victorian England. When the Provost of Oriel was appointed Bishop of Llandaff, his deputy replaced him and resigned as Vicar of St Mary's, Oxford's parish church. Newman, at the age of twenty-seven, was invited to fill the consequent vacancy. He accepted and set out on what it was assumed would be a glittering career, which would end in Canterbury or in York.

By the time of his appointment to St Mary's, Newman had already met Edward Bouverie Pusey (who was to become Oxford's Professor of Hebrew) and two other Oriel Fellows, Richard Hurrell Froude and John Keble, who was to become Professor of Poetry. Each man influenced Newman in a different way. Pusey brought back from Germany work on the Greek and Latin Fathers, which helped to convince him that true Christianity was to be found in its early centuries. Froude encouraged Newman to believe in the significance of the medieval Church, urged him to accept the doctrine of transubstantiation and, perhaps more important, persuaded him that he had been wrong to regard the Pope as an Antichrist.

Newman's first published work, *The Arians of the Fourth Century*, ostensibly an account of doctrinal disputes in the early Church, reflected his own preoccupations. The Arians were 'guilty' of attempting to explain by reason and logic the mysteries, which could be only accepted and understood by faith.[39] St Athanasius embodied the importance of the ancient Fathers who 'after the Apostles [had] been the principal instrument by which the sacred truths of Christianity have been conveyed and secured in the world'.[40] That overtly historical work also contained a nascent statement of what was to become Newman's motivating conviction. 'There was something greater than the Established Church and that was the Church, Catholic and Apostolic, set up from the beginning, of which she [the Established Church] was both the local presence and the organ. She was nothing unless she was this.' At first, Newman believed that his duty and destiny were to revive and reinvigorate the Church of England by reconnecting it to its roots in the early Christian scholars. But, even as he asserted that it had a mystic connection with the Christianity of saints and martyrs, he harboured doubts about what his future allegiance should be. On June 13th 1833 – at sea on one of the regular excursions that reflected his restless spirit – he wrote the poem, 'The Pillar of the Cloud'. Known by its opening line – 'Lead, Kindly Light – it became one of the most famous of all Church of England hymns. The most revealing sentiment comes at the end of the first stanza: 'I do not ask to see / The distant scene – one step enough for me.'

The next step was taken a month later, shortly after his return to England, and was recorded in his diary: 'The following Sunday, July 14th, Mr Keble preached the Assize Sermon in the University Pulpit. It was later published under the title of National Apostasy. I have ever considered and kept that day as the start of the religious movement of 1833.'[14] The sermon warned of the moral degradation that would follow – perhaps had already followed – neglect of the Christianity of the early Church. Utilitarianism and the notion of democracy had eroded belief. The mysterious significance of the sacraments had been forgotten. Most significant and most corrupting, the Apostolic Succession, as set out in the writings of St Clement – the passage of theological authority from Peter to Timothy, from Timothy to Titus, and from Titus to generations of anointed bishops – had been ignored. As a result, the Church had accepted control by a lay Parliament.

Keble was not alone in his concern. A fortnight after the Assize Sermon, a group of anxious clergymen met in a Suffolk rectory to discuss the latest state intrusion into the affairs of the Church of England. The Irish Church (Temporalities) Bill proposed to eliminate ten Irish bishoprics and reduce the number of dioceses by amalgamation. The meeting broke up without coming to any clear conclusion about how the purity of the Church could be restored and maintained. But Froude, who was among the gathering at Hadleigh, retained the strong belief that *something* must be done. Newman's solution was, as usual, based on a combination of mysticism and historical precedence. 'The early Church threw itself upon the people ... Now that the Crown and the aristocracy have deserted us, must we not do that too?'[42] In practical terms, that meant 'writing letters to our friends as if we were canvassing'. To prepare for composing the messages, Newman began what he described as 'picking into the Fathers with the hope of rummaging forth passages of history which may prepare the imaginations of men for a changed state of things'.

The group of clergy who met at Hadleigh first agreed to circulate letters to friends and then evolved into a committee – which, at Newman's insistence, had Keble at its head. The committee became a society and developed additional ambitions, including 'rousing up the clergy'[43] – the aspiration of Church reformers from Wyclif to Wesley. Because of its geographical origins, the society was initially known as the Oxford Movement.

Meetings were organised throughout England. But, believing that 'living movements do not come out of committees, nor are great ideas worked out through the post',[44] Newman urged his colleagues to rely on the strength of their ideas as expressed through an extension of the letters initiative. The result was a series of pamphlets which came to be called *Tracts for the Times*. They were written by a variety of biblical and theological scholars, but always edited by Newman, and they achieved such an importance that the popular description of the organisation which sponsored them changed from the Oxford to the Tractarian Movement. The *Tracts* were published in the 'hope of rousing members of our Church to comprehend her alarming position as a man might be given notice of a fire or inundation to alarm him'.[45] It is easy enough, as Lytton Strachey demonstrated in *Eminent Victorians*, to ridicule the titles and contents of some of the *Tracts*. One pondered the significance of Abraham circumcising 318 of his housemen rather than his whole household. But even Strachey had to admit that they served their purpose, 'for the sensation which they caused among clergymen throughout the country was extreme'.

The wave of excitement washed across the parish of Lavington-with-Graffham in Sussex, where – during the year in which the first *Tracts* were published – the Reverend Henry Edward Manning, a young Fellow of Merton College, Oxford, had been appointed curate with special responsibility for the hamlet of Upwaltham. Two months after the first publication, Manning began to distribute *Tracts* to selected parishioners. And his enthusiasm for the Movement grew. Henry Wilberforce – son of the great reformer and an Oxford contemporary – visited Lavington as a guest at the wedding of Manning to the vicar's daughter. The following week he wrote to Newman with the news 'Manning has revised his opinion and adopts the Apostolic Succession.'[46] Newman and Manning – who were to dominate the Catholic Church in England for more than half a century – had one important characteristic in common. Each man was completely confident that he had been called to God's service and each man was equally sure that he was supremely qualified to fulfil his destiny. They had a fundamental difference of belief about the English Church's relationship with Rome. But it was neither their disagreement about doctrine nor their differences about authority that determined the fractious nature of their relationship. They were separated by conflicting temperaments: a collision of characters which could only have resulted in continual confrontation.

Although Newman wrote four of the original *Tracts* himself, the work was nothing like enough to satisfy his growing passion for committing the Word of God to print. In 1834 he published the first volume of *Parochial Sermons*. Had they been written in a less deferential time by a man who was not a *soi-disant* intellectual mystic, they would have been described as 'blood and thunder'. In *Religion of the Day* Newman denounced what, not altogether accurately, he described as the contemporary view of the Christian faith. 'It has taken the brighter side of the Gospel – its tidings of comfort, its precepts of love; all darker, deeper views of man's condition being forgotten. This is the religion [which is] natural to a civilised age and well has Satan dressed and completed it into the idol of Truth ... The fear of God is the beginning of wisdom ... Our God is a consuming fire. Approach him with reverence and godly fear ... Fear and love must go together.'[47] Newman despised what he believed to be the godless decadence of his age, in the way that Pugin despised the godless decadence of its church architecture. Nineteenth-century English Christians 'identified their vision of Christ's kingdom with the elegance and refinement of modern civilisation'. That, Newman believed, amounted to spiritual decadence.

At more or less the same time, Manning was feeling doubts that were as great as Newman's. However, he expressed them – even in his thoughts – in less metaphysical language. He was no less academically distinguished than Newman. He had graduated from Balliol with a First in Greats and had, immediately, been invited to become a Fellow of Merton. Newman's Oriel Fellowship had been approached by a much more circuitous route. He had been forced to sit a special examination after graduating with Third Class honours rather than the First that everyone had confidently predicted. But Manning was less overtly intellectual than Newman and, as well as wearing his scholarship more lightly, he possessed two characteristics that distinguished him from his contemporary and eventual adversary.

Manning remained, true to his birth, a natural member of the Victorian establishment. His background – son of a Member of Parliament, captain of cricket at Harrow and an Oxford scholar of distinction – might have prepared him to govern one of the Queen's dominions beyond the seas. The belief that the Church of England must contribute to the fulfilment of Britain's imperial destiny informed his decision to take Holy Orders. 'We must answer for the heathenism of India, for the destitution of Canada, for the degradation of West Indian slaves.'[48] His view that the powers spiritual and temporal must work hand in hand was mistaken for the determination to work his way up the Church of England – an institution which, thanks to its reluctance to fill its international obligations, he regarded as 'on trial like Tyre'. Curate, vicar, rural dean and Archdeacon of Chichester – Manning's progress was swift and relentless. A few of his more charitable friends explained his weakness for success as the way in which he sublimated his grief. His wife had died of consumption. But open ambition was an unforgivable sin in the society in which he moved. So he received little or no credit for putting all hope of further preferment behind him when he left the Church, which he could well have gone on to lead. He was simply suspected of aspiring to the leadership of a different faith.

Newman, no less sure of himself, pursued his destiny with a humility that was more apparent than real. Both men – accused from time to time of possessing a sneaking sympathy with Calvin's doctrine of predestination – were suspected of believing themselves to number among the elect. Although Newman changed his mind more often than Manning, he walked more firmly through the fog of doubt – often altering direction, but always proceeding with a certainty that he was in sight of his true destination. Sometimes he wanted the Church of which he was a member to be all-embracing. At others times he defined acceptable Christianity in the narrowest of terns. While still an ordained priest of the Church of England, he refused to officiate at the weddings of parishioners who had not been baptised and wrote to the *British Magazine* complaining about the proposal that, in order to permit Dissenters admission to the universities, subscription to the Thirty-Nine Articles should no longer be an entrance requirement. In truth, he was less in favour of the retention of the Articles than the exclusion of Dissenters.

Convinced of his mission to purify the Church, Newman converted the Adam de Brome chapel in St Mary's into a public lecture theatre. In 1837 he published an edited version of views that, during the previous three years, he had expressed there: *Lectures on the Prophetical Office of the Church viewed relatively to Romanism and Popular Protestantism*. It advocated what Newman perversely diminishes as 'only a theory' rather than the basis for a new denomination. He called it the *Via Media* – the middle way:

> Protestantism and Popery are real religions. No one can doubt about them. They have furnished the mould within which nations have been cast; but the *Via Media* has never existed except on paper, it has never been reduced to practice. It is known, not positively but negatively, in its difference from rival creeds, not in its own properties and can only be described as a third system, neither the one nor the other.[49]

The Middle Way was the wrong metaphor. The *Lectures on the Prophetical Office of the Church* did not trace a careful path between two different theologies. They were the boulder in the stream that made it possible to cross from one bank to the other.

CHAPTER 22

Time is Short, Eternity is Long

For three years Newman sought to resolve insoluble conflicts between his intellect and his emotions and, at the same time, refute the suggestion that he had been corrupted by ancient heresies. First he feared that his singular views would result in him being condemned as a Monophysite – a separatist sect stigmatised by Pope Leo the Great at the Council of Chalcedon in 451. Then he rebutted the accusation that he behaved like a Donatist – the name given to a schismatic North African sect which had been condemned by St Augustine. But his most difficult task was explaining, to himself as well as to the world, how the Church of England – which had not existed for the first fifteen hundred years of the Christian epoch – was part of an unbroken line of belief that stretched from the caves and cells of Ambrose, Gregory Nazianzen and Martin of Tours, into the rectories and vicarages of Victorian England. And there was a second contradiction which – if Newman felt any obligation to intellectual consistency – he had to explain away. He contended that secular control of spiritual matters polluted the Church that endured it. But the Church of England had been created as a creature of the state. Newman resolved the dilemma, at least to his own satisfaction, in 'Tract XC'.

The *Tracts* had already caused such disquiet – particularly to the Bishop of Oxford – that Newman had offered to suspend their publication. But the Bishop had not pressed the point and Newman had not made good his offer. The uneasy peace was shattered on February 27th 1841, the day on which the clergy of England read, in their copies of 'Tract XC', that the Thirty-Nine Articles were not in conflict with the beliefs of Rome. Indeed, according to the tract, they were a reinforcement of orthodox Catholic opinion. In their condemnation of purgatory, the sale of indulgences, the worship of images and the veneration of relics, they had condemned excesses, which had largely been suppressed by the Council of Trent. A careful reading of the text confirmed that – despite the unpleasantly bellicose style in which they were written – the Articles were compatible with true Roman doctrine. They condemned the 'sacrifices of masses' not 'the Sacrifice of the Mass'. And linguistic analysis even mapped out something approaching common ground on the subject of purgatory. It was the 'Romish' doctrine that was anathematised, not the 'Roman' doctrine – a very different dogma. In fact the anonymous author of 'Tract XC' was arguing that, purged of its evangelical sloth and theological indolence, the Church of England would become a new and improved form of the Church of Rome.

Newman became a lightning conductor for controversy – sometimes with far more intellectual justification than could be claimed for the linguistic contortions of 'Tract XC'. He wrote that 'Mr Darwin's theory *need* not be atheistical, be it true or not'; and he told John Walker, the parish priest at Scarborough, that *The Origin of Species* may simply suggest a 'larger idea of Divine Prescience and skill'. Newman substantiated his claim with the same textual devices that he had used to justify his contention that the Thirty-Nine Articles were not incompatible with Catholic teaching. However commentators had interpreted natural selection, Darwin did not '*profess* to oppose Religion'.[1] More difficult to justify – from any view of life eternal – was his contention that damnation did not mean eternal suffering because spirits in an otherworldly state had no conception of time. And he added – more as an indication of his respect for biblical authority than as an intellectual escape route – that the scriptures said very little on the subject.

The heads of Oxford houses were the first to express their outrage at what they regarded as the heresies inherent in 'Tract XC' – an emotion that spread, with increasing virulence, after it was discovered that Newman was the author of the offending document. The Bishop of Oxford changed his suggestion that the *Tracts* should be abandoned, into the instruction that publication must be discontinued. Newman obeyed, but he continued to write and publish lectures and sermons. Their subjects – *The Life and Work of St Athanasius* and *The Nature of Faith in Relation to Reason* – were invariably acceptable to established opinion. The choice of topic was the result of caution rather than an acceptance of more orthodox views. Newman was moving away from the Church and was ready to discuss his spiritual doubts. Keble was chosen as the sounding board. His advice was accepted and Newman, as a first tentative step towards conversion, began quietly to retract his most aggressive anti-Roman Catholic statements.

Newman decided it was necessary to have a retreat into which he could escape from St Mary's and its parsonage. Property was leased in the village of Littlemore. Although the chapel of Sts Mary and Nicholas, which Newman added to the building, was Roman Catholic in design and spirit, it was consecrated by the forgiving Bishop of Oxford, who was so impressed by Newman's inaugural sermon that he took away, for further study, the notes on which it had been based. He might have been less supportive had he realised that Littlemore was to become the home of a religious community with Newman at its head and Newman's ideas as its guiding doctrine. Newman's growing reputation – as a controversialist as well as a theologian – guaranteed a supply of young men who wanted to sit at his feet. Among them was Ambrose St John, from whom he became inseparable for the rest of his life. Newman's feelings can be best illustrated by the letter he wrote in middle age after hearing of St John's death. In that it is as much concerned with Newman as it is with St John, the letter properly illustrates its author's self-obsession. But the depth of his affection is clear: 'I think that my own wound will never close in the time which remains of my life. It has been granted to me most mercifully to prepare me for that which must be soon.'[2] Fifteen years later, on August 19th 1890, St John's grave in Rednal was opened and the mortal remains of John Henry Newman were laid side by side with the body of his old friend.

The construction of a coach house in the Littlemore outbuildings, in anticipation of acquiring some sort of vehicle to carry him to and from his parish, suggests that Newman was sincere in his protestations of a desire to remain vicar of St Mary's. But the Anglican bishops' unanimous and unqualified condemnation of 'Tract XC' made him think again. There were other signs that he was considering making the great leap. He was already in correspondence with Charles Russell, the Professor of Ecclesiastical History at Maynooth, with the ostensible purpose of clearing his mind of admitted confusion about transubstantiation. Later he was to claim that Russell 'had, perhaps more to do with my conversion than anyone else'.[3] Whatever the cause, in the autumn of 1843 Newman took the first positive step towards Rome by resigning his living. He preached his last sermon on September 25th. It was entitled 'The Parting of Friends'. It recalled some of the Bible's great farewells, but it was – like so much of Newman's writing – essentially about himself: 'O loving friends, should you know anyone who [has] ... made you feel that there is a higher life than this daily one ... remember such a one in time to come though you hear him not and pray for him.'[4]

Littlemore became Newman's refuge. He spent most of his time writing, but occasionally sallied forth to preach highly personalised sermons about his spiritual future. Often he confessed his doubts to friends in the hope that they would, in some way, resolve them. Pusey – his greatest source of comfort – received a letter which asked, 'What then is the will of Providence about me? ... Am I in delusion, given

THE GORDON RIOTS
Newgate Prison in flames

DANIEL O'CONNELL
'The Liberator'

CARDINAL NICHOLAS WISEMAN
His 'life's wish to labour for England'

AUGUSTUS WELBY PUGIN
'God's architect'

CARDINAL HENRY NEWMAN
'Conscience first, the Pope afterwards'

CARDINAL HENRY MANNING
God said, 'Put him there'

CARDINAL PAUL CULLEN
'Poverty most dangerous to religion'

Were they Catholic writers…
Or writers who were Catholics?

HILAIRE BELLOC

G K CHESTERTON

GRAHAM GREENE

EVELYN WAUGH

CATHAL MACDOWELL
Converted during the Easter Rising

over to believe a lie? Am I deceiving myself, convinced when I am not?'[5] But events conspired – Newman, no doubt, believed guided by a divine hand – to concentrate his mind. A newspaper wrongly reported that he had been received into the Catholic Church and he was bombarded with messages of condemnation and congratulation, support and disapproval – to none of which he felt able to provide an adequate reply.

Although Newman had made a conspicuous retreat from the 'Tract XC' controversy, the most ardent Oxford critics of the tract and the movement with which it was associated would not let the matter rest. They first tried to persuade Convocation formally to condemn 'Tract XC'. They failed, but they did succeed in carrying a resolution which deprived William Ward – a Tractarian of extreme views – of his degree. Newman remained silent. With the world in turmoil around him, he returned to the study of St Athanasius, one of the early Fathers, whose work he believed to be crucial to the understanding of true faith, and – following naturally on his conclusion that the teaching of the ancient Church was neglected – he wrote *Essays in the Development of Christian Doctrine*. It ended:

> And now, dear Reader, time is short, eternity is long. Put not from what you have here found; regard it not as a mere matter of present controversy; set not out to resolve or refute it, and looking about for the best way of doing so, seduce not yourself with the imagination that it comes from disappointment or disgust or restlessness or wounded feeling or undue sensibility or other weaknesses. Wrap not yourself round in the associations of years past, nor determine that to be truth which you wish to be so, nor make an idol of cherished anticipations.[6]

Rumours of Newman's impending conversion excited mixed feelings in the Catholic Church. Nicholas Wiseman was wholeheartedly in favour of encouraging the Tractarians to continue their theological speculation, but older 'home-grown' Catholics believed that he was wasting his time by interfering with what was no more than a new branch of an old heresy. Wiseman was vindicated. The Tractarian Movement coincided with a significant increase in individual Catholic converts, and the fears that the *Tracts* would provide a reason for dissatisfied Protestants to stay in a Church of England that was showing new signs of life was proved to be diametrically wrong. However, not all Tractarians shared Newman's growing affection for Catholicism and Catholics. William Ward illustrated the abrasive personality which had contributed to Convocation's decision to deprive him of his degree. 'English Catholics don't know what education means. Many of them can't write English. When a Catholic meets a Protestant in conversation, it is like a barbarian meeting a civilised man.'[7]

Wiseman's attitude towards prospective Tractarian converts was based on the belief that they would invigorate the English Catholic Church, which he judged was in a 'low state ... Let us have but even a small number of such men who write in the tracts ... and we shall be speedily reformed and England quickly converted.'[8] Thomas Walsh, the Vicar Apostolic of the Central District to whom Wiseman was then Coadjutor, was just as enthusiastic – though it was widely believed that both men based their hopes on a romantic rather than reasoned assessment of the possibilities. In Ireland, the Hierarchy's opposition to the Tractarians was intensified by the mistaken belief that the 'Oxford men' were sympathetic to Daniel O'Connell's view that the Catholic Church should be in open support of popular movements. In fact, Tractarians were neither concerned with popular movements nor interested in social questions. Newman's disputations were not intended to deepen the faith or widen the understanding of the working men and their wives. Although he sometimes believed that he was speaking to the 'masses', his support – and his opposition – came from intellectuals who had the time (as well as the ability and inclination) to examine esoteric questions about doctrine and belief. Yet in one of the modern mysteries of the Catholic Church, he became a popular hero.

Newman's supporters were further enthused, and the opponents more firmly antagonised, by the publication of the *Essays in the Development of Christian Doctrine*. It amounted to a coded announcement that Newman had made up his mind. Only the Roman Catholic Church – the modern world's direct connection with the ancient Fathers, and the manifestation of the Apostolic Succession – could provide the authority and unity essential to the propagation of true faith. The basis of his conversion was part mystical and part intellectual. But the timing and occasion of the ceremony by which he was received into his new faith was determined by the example set by his friends. One by one, members of the community which had formed around him at Littlemore converted to Catholicism. On October 2nd 1845 his closest friend, Ambrose St John, was received into the Church. The next day Newman resigned his Oriel Fellowship. The Provost, anticipating the event that made the resignation necessary, responded with an example of what the intellectual elite of the Established Church thought Catholicism required. He hoped that Newman would 'at least be saved from some of the worst errors of the Church of Rome, such as praying to human Mediators or falling down before images – because in you, with all the great advantages with which God has blessed and tried you, I must believe such errors to be most deeply sinful'.[9]

The best that can be said of the Provost's conduct was that he had the grace, and the sense, not to attempt to change Newman's mind. The decision was irrevocable. Only the occasion of its implementation was in doubt. Then Newman heard that Father Dominic Barberi, a Passionist monk who had received several of his friends into the Church, was to visit Littlemore on his way to Belgium. Bernard Dalgairns, one of Newman's converts, was sent to meet Barberi when he arrived in Oxford, on the Birmingham coach. As Dalgairns left Littlemore, Newman asked him, 'When you see your friend, will you tell him that I wish him to receive me into the Church of Christ?'[10] It was raining hard and Barberi had travelled on the exposed top of the coach. He was drying himself in front of the Littlemore fire when Newman entered the room and, kneeling, asked Barberi to hear his confession. On the evening of October 9th 1845, John Henry Newman and two of his young followers became Roman Catholics. Next day, Roman Catholic Mass was said in the Littlemore chapel for the first time.

Newman still felt attracted by collegiate life – the exploration, by similarly inclined young men, of ideas that excited them. So it was natural enough that at the end of the month he should visit the seminary at Oscott where Nicholas Wiseman was President. The two men had met, ten years earlier, in Rome, when Wiseman had urged Newman to spend more time in the Eternal City and Newman had replied that there was work for him to do in England. On November 1st 1845, Newman and his little band of followers were all confirmed in the Oscott chapel. Then Wiseman set out his idea of how Newman's English destiny should be fulfilled. Ordination should precede apostolic work in the Midlands – possibly as an Oratorian.

Until then, Newman had not even considered becoming a Catholic priest. But it is clear that the idea immediately appealed to him. The Oratory – not a religious Order, but a group of secular priests who lived together in a life devoted to pastoral care and scholarship – attracted him. So did the offer of Old Oscott (the college's original buildings) as a home and refuge for himself and his followers. Newman agreed and accepted, but he did not move in for three months. Instead he toured England, familiarising himself with Catholic habits and institutions. Then in February 1846, Old Oscott – renamed Maryvale – became his home. Everything of importance that happened to Newman

THE CATHOLICS

during those early days confirmed his conviction that he had taken the right decision. But he had not enjoyed his early months as a Roman Catholic. He had hated being 'the gaze of so many eyes', as if he were 'some wild incomprehensible beast caught by the hunter and a spectacle for Dr Wiseman to exhibit'.[11] Almost as bad was the indignity that awaited his return to the seminary: the obligation to 'stand at Dr Wiseman's door waiting for Confession amid the Oscott boys'.

Newman remained in Oscott until October, when the summons to Rome – which he had expected since April – arrived. The long days during which he prepared for ordination were no more enjoyable than his early months at Oscott, not least because he regarded himself as ordained already. Together with St John, he was enrolled in the College of Propaganda Fide, where he claimed to be embarrassed by being awarded special status – including the provision of English tea every evening. The lectures were undistinguished and he slept through many of them without guilt or embarrassment. The syllabus included neither Aristotle nor Thomas Aquinas. Most of the Jesuits he met were 'plodding, methodical and unromantic'[12] rather than sinister, as he had been taught to believe, and he came to regard their suppression as 'one of the most mysterious matters in the history of the Church'. He was, however, impressed by the Jesuit rector of the college, Padre Bresciani, who led the 'self-denying life' that Newman thought was part of the priestly vocation.

Granted, with other seminarians, an audience with Pius IX, he stumbled while bending to kiss the Pope's foot and hit his head on the pontifical knee. The highlight of his novitiate was a Christmas visit to the Roman Oratory of St Philip Neri. It convinced him, if further conviction were needed, that he should become an Oratorian. He was made a deacon on May 29th 1847, ordained priest – along with Ambrose St John – on the 30th and said his first Mass. There followed a period of training with and by the Oratorians. It was sufficiently eclectic to include instruction on the liquefaction of the blood of Santa Patrizia on her feast day and 'room-sweeping, slop emptying, dinner serving, bed making and shoe cleaning'.[13] He was given notice that plans for the foundation of an English Oratory would not be approved until November, but in October received news that confirmed more than the creation of the English house. He was to be made Superior for Life of the English Oratory.

Back in England by Christmas, Newman received what should, on the face of it, have been welcome news. Frederick William Faber – a young devotee of his Oxford days – wanted to join the Oratory. Since his conversion Faber had created a community of his own, composed of half a dozen converts who had been Church of England clergymen. They called themselves 'Brothers of the Will of God', but – because they lived in St Wilfrid's House at Cheadle in Staffordshire – were known as the 'Wilfridians'. Newman was reluctant to accept the new recruits, but Wiseman (by then Pro-Vicar Apostolic of the London District) persuaded him that their 'surrender' was providential. So on February 12th 1848, ten days after the English College of the Oratory was set up in Maryvale, Newman travelled to Staffordshire, there to accept the oaths of obedience from the novitiates. Obedience, as defined by Faber, did not preclude disagreement or presumption. He immediately proposed that Newman should leave Maryvale and move to Cheadle. Newman was adamant: St Wilfrid's must close. The Earl of Shrewsbury, who had provided the premises occupied by the brotherhood, immediately registered his strong disapproval of Newman's edict.

Whether or not Shrewsbury's opposition made the difference, Newman's determination did not last for long. But his capitulation – and move to Cheadle – did not mark the end of Faber's role as irritant. Faber was writing, and publishing in episodes, the lives of the saints. That was a worthy enough enterprise in itself, but it was being accomplished in such a florid and hagiographical style that Bernard Ullathorne, the Vicar Apostolic of the Central District, found it offensive and believed that Catholics of a traditional disposition would be scandalised by what they would regard as profanity. Ullathorne asked Faber to abandon the project. Newman shared Ullathorne's dislike of Faber's work, but felt a duty to protect a member of his society. His inclination to yield to Faber's demands was to become a feature of the years in which the Oratories were founded and grew.

The Vatican had ordered that one Oratory was to be established in Birmingham and another in London. Interim sites were found – an old gin factory with a classical façade in Alcester Street, Deritend, Birmingham, and a rundown house in King William Street, the Strand, London. Faber wanted to go to London and take some of the best Oratorians with him. Newman agreed. Inevitably Faber came to regard himself as head of the house and therefore justified in challenging the decisions of the Superior for Life.

In Birmingham a permanent site for the Oratory was found on the Hagley Road in the prosperous suburb of Edgbaston. Newman, while establishing the Oratories, fulfilled what he saw as his pastoral duties – preaching, most weeks, at St Chad's Cathedral and, together with Ambrose St John, moving to Bilston to succour the sick during an outbreak of cholera. The epidemic was virtually over by the time they arrived, but there was cause for concern about a greater threat to the inhabitants of the 'labyrinth of lanes, beneath a firmament of smoke'.[14] The two priests were more concerned about their parishioners' spiritual well-being than their health and physical welfare. Newman had convinced himself that two-thirds of the Bilston residents wanted to become Catholics, but 'could not be received for want of instructors and confessors'.

Anxiety about such neglect might have been expected to make Newman welcome the reinvigoration that was expected to follow the restoration of the Hierarchy in 1850. But on hearing the news, he expressed the fear that the Catholic Church in England was 'not ready' – without explaining what 'not ready' meant. He was more specific about the easily predictable consequences of the Flaminian Gate pastoral letter. Provoking the Protestants could, he argued, only lead to disrupting the work of soul-saving. It certainly led to the demonisation of Catholicism's most famous English figureheads. Despite his doubts about the new dispensation, Newman agreed to preach the sermon at the installation of Bernard Ullathorne as Bishop, as distinct from Vicar Apostolic, of the Midland District. It contained the justified complaint that there was 'no calumny [so] gross [and] no imputation on us so monstrous that they will not greedily drink up'.[15] He forbore to say that Cardinal Wiseman must accept some of the blame.

Newman himself became engulfed in a new, albeit more secular than spiritual, controversy. His programme of lectures continued unabated. The fifth lecture, in a series given in the Birmingham Corn Exchange during the summer of 1851, included a gratuitous, though justified, attack on the sexual incontinence of Giacinto Achilli, a lapsed Dominican priest who was employed by the Protestant Evangelical Alliance to 'expose' corruption in Rome. On September 1st 1851 Newman wrote to his solicitor 'on a most anxious matter on which I shall have to act, I may say for the whole Catholic body. You know that Cardinal Wiseman accused in Dublin, I think in a pamphlet, Dr Achilli of fornication. I repeated what the Cardinal said and he is going to bring an action against me.'[16] He appended the names of witnesses who would endorse his description of Achilli. Newman clearly did not believe that God would provide. Three further letters, sent on December 17th and 20th and on January 9th 1852, contained the names of men and women who would swear that his denunciation of Achilli was unrelated to the plaintiff's apostasy. Two Oratorians were despatched to Italy to find evidence of Achilli's misconduct. The results of their labours were inconclusive.

When the hearing was adjourned, there was a moment of unjustified triumphalism. 'Achilli is afraid to come to court ... He has already managed to put off the trial for nine months and will put it off for a year if he can ... We are now contemplating an indictment against him for perjury.'[17] Six months later, on the eve of the hearing, Newman's mood had changed. 'Some say I may be imprisoned for months. Some say fined.'[18] He was fined a notional £100 and regarded the modest punishment as complete vindication of his conduct.

Manning – the Archdeacon of Chichester – was enduring his religious doubts with greater dignity than Newman displayed during his year of spiritual anxiety. Rome – to which he travelled more to visit the antiquities than in the hope of spiritual comfort – held him in thrall. In 1848 the beleaguered Pope, giving benediction 'with a mixture of majesty, love and supplication', was 'a sight beyond words'.[19] It was, Manning wrote home, 'impossible not to love Pius IX'. But then Pio Nono possessed a special virtue. He possessed 'the most truly English countenance' Manning had seen in Rome. On his way home, he stopped in Milan to view the preserved cadaver of St Charles Borromeo. Everything returned his thoughts to the dilemma that he could not resolve. 'I was thinking in prayer, if only I could know that St Charles – who represents the Council of Trent – was right and we wrong.'[20] Newman, more at peace with himself and firmly embedded in the Church of Rome, found time to write, and publish anonymously, a novel entitled *Loss and Gain*, the story of a convert who found peace in the Catholic Church. The most famous convert of them all was about to be joined, in his new spiritual home, by men and women whose exodus from the Church of England was brought about not by the call he had heard or the sign for which Manning longed. The next stage in the reinvigoration of the Catholic Church in England was the consequence of the revival of the question that lay at the heart of the Reformation. Does ultimate authority over religious matters lie with the spiritual or the temporal power?

In November 1847, the Lord Chancellor had assigned the living of Branford in the diocese of Exeter to the Reverend George Cornelius Gorham. The Right Reverend Henry Phillpotts, Bishop of Exeter, had reason to believe that Gorham was theologically unsound, especially on the question of baptismal regeneration. He therefore conducted an examination – thirty-eight hours of verbal interrogation and 149 written questions – from which he concluded that Gorham was unworthy to become Vicar of Branford or anywhere else. Gorham appealed, as was his right, to the Court of the Arches – for six hundred years the final arbiter of disputes within the Canterbury archdiocese.

His appeal was dismissed. He then appealed against the dismissal to the Privy Council, and the Court of the Arches' decision was overturned. The outburst of anger and horror which greeted the imposition of a secular judgement on a decision that concerned the Church alone was genuine. But the cause of offence should not have come as a surprise. The 'supremacy' of the civil authority had been embodied, since 1534, in an Act of Parliament which bore that name, and a bill – presented to Parliament exactly three hundred years later – had, when passed, made the Privy Council the final court of all appeals. All that the Gorham case did was make High Anglicans face the reality of the Reformation.

Manning supported Phillpotts' stand against 'slovenly unbelief'. But before the Privy Council pronounced, he made clear that his real objection was to the process, not its outcome:

> It is indifferent which way the judgement may go. Indeed a judgement in favour of the true doctrine of baptism would deceive many. A judgement right in matter cannot heal a wrong in the principle of the Appeal. And the wrong is this. The appeal removes the final decision of a question involving both doctrine and discipline out of the Church to another centre and that the Civil Court.[21]

Robert Wilberforce suggested a more ingenious but less magisterial response. Fearful that the Gorham case would make a flight to Rome inevitable, he proposed that Tractarians find a sympathetic colonial bishop and, under his leadership, found a new Church. Manning's dismissive reply illustrated the way in which his mind was working. 'Three hundred years ago we left a good ship for a boat. I am not going to leave the boat for a tub.'

Despite Manning's principal objection being to the process, when the decision was announced he was happy to lead the opposition to the judgement itself. On March 9th 1850 he chaired, with a show of reluctance, a meeting of clergy that drafted a declaration which asserted that the Privy Council had no *locus standi* in the matter and that, in any event, it had come to the wrong conclusion. It was published in *The Times* ten days later, over the signature of both clergy and distinguished laymen. Manning's close friend, William Ewart Gladstone, President of the Board of Trade and Colonial Secretary in Robert Peel's late government, was not (to much surprise) among the signatories. Explanations of his absence vary. John Morley – too devoted a follower to write an objective biography – argued that his hero merely wanted a period of reflection before the denunciation was published. Manning himself attributed Gladstone's absence to propriety. The Privy Council could not be publicly excoriated by one of its members. The likelihood is that Gladstone would not endorse a declaration that was bound to be followed by resignations from the Church of England to which he felt such a messianic devotion that, in 1870, he very nearly prevented the introduction of the Forster Education Bill because it trespassed on Church property. Manning knew that apostasy was the inevitable outcome of being a principal party to the declaration. In the summer of 1850, after he renewed the argument by organising a circular which denounced the idea of royal supremacy in matters of Church doctrine, he told Robert Wilberforce, 'I have written myself fairly over the border – or Tiber rather.'[22]

By September Manning's doubts had finally been resolved. After a visit to Lavington, Samuel Wilberforce – Soapy Sam, the third son of the great reformer – wrote to Gladstone with the news that Manning was on the point of leaving the Church of England. But for six months Wilberforce's judgement was not confirmed. Then, motivated more by the obligation of friendship than the demands of doubt, Manning sought out William Gladstone. Their first meeting lasted three hours and ended in mutual bewilderment. There were two more meetings. Both were as unsatisfactory as the first. On March 25th 1851 Manning resigned as Archdeacon of Chichester. There was one more meeting with Gladstone. Manning described it in his diary. It took place 'in the little chapel off the Buckingham Palace Road'. The two men were kneeling, 'side by side ... Just before the Communion Service began Manning turned to Gladstone and said "I can no longer take Communion in the Church of England" ... and laying my hand on Mr Gladstone's shoulder I said "come" ... Mr Gladstone remained and I went my way.'[23] On April 6th 1851 Henry Manning was received into the Roman Catholic Church in the Jesuit church in Farm Street, Mayfair.

The Catholic Church – in the form of its most influential laymen – did not give up all hope of Gladstone's conversion. Six years after the parting of the ways in the Buckingham Palace Road chapel, the ever-cautious Earl of Shrewsbury expressed to Wiseman his doubts about the wisdom of the tactics that were employed by what would now be called celebrity head-hunters. 'Your Lsp says Gladstone is expected. I hope so with all my heart but I doubt it very much and surely the part taken by those who seem most to desire it is, of all others, calculated to prevent it. By the Cath Standard of the 17th of May, I see his name put *publicly* forth for a novena for his conversion. This will rouse all his Protestant relatives and friends and perhaps drive him into denials and repudiations which may go to counteract all the Grace he may receive by means of the Prayers.'

Manning had told himself, on the day before his Farm Street baptism, that his career was over. That gloomy forecast illustrated both his human ambition and his willingness to set it aside when Catholicism called. His pessimism proved to be unjustified. Cardinal Wiseman, still convinced that the best way to reinvigorate the Church of Rome was to attract distinguished converts from the Church of England, regarded the recently resigned archdeacon as a bigger catch than he could reasonably have anticipated. Unlike Newman – who had been required to serve a sometimes humiliating apprenticeship – Manning was, in the modern colloquialism, 'fast-tracked'. One week after his admission to the Church he was confirmed, tonsured, given First Communion, made subdeacon, went into a brief retreat and was made a deacon – all in one day. Two months later, on June 14th 1851, he was ordained priest. He had become, in Wiseman's words, 'one of the first fruits of the restoration'.[24]

It was not only in England that the Catholic Church showed signs of new life. In Ireland, Paul Cullen, Archbishop of Armagh, was planning the creation of a Catholic university. Like so many of the Church's concessions to progress, its initial purpose was defensive. In 1845 Robert Peel had set up the three non-denominational Queen's Colleges and the Irish Hierarchy – far from welcoming an alternative to the aggressively Protestant Trinity College – regarded the new foundation as a 'Godless' threat, which would elevate science above faith. The campaign against the secular colleges had been led by John McHale, Archbishop of Tuam, who, unable to obtain unanimous support from the other Catholic bishops, appealed to Rome for advice. In October 1847 Propaganda had ruled that the Colleges were 'detrimental to faith' and forbade the bishops to cooperate with them in any way. Propaganda repeated the ruling a year later but, despite the papal condemnation, many priests and lay Catholics continued to teach and learn in the colleges.

Shortly after his return to Ireland in 1849, as Archbishop of Armagh and Papal Legate, Paul Cullen convened the Synod of Thurles. Its purpose was to bring some order and discipline into the divided Irish Church. Ending the dispute over secular education was one item on the agenda, and there was no doubt how unity would be restored. During his last weeks in Rome, Cullen had arranged for the Prefect of Propaganda to write to all the Irish bishops with a condemnation of the colleges which they too had described as 'godless institutions'. At the Synod he tabled a resolution which forbade clergy, on pain of expulsion, from cooperating with the colleges in any way. It was carried by fifteen votes to thirteen. The majority would have been even smaller, had Cullen not insisted that the Abbot of Mount Melleray – a known opponent of the colleges, but not a bishop – be given a vote. A second motion, which opposed the creation of a Catholic university – a subject on which Rome had not pronounced – was defeated. Cullen, in deference to the Synod's recorded wishes, took advice about how a genuine seat of learning (on the model of the Belgian University of Louvain) could be set up. He twice travelled to Birmingham to consult John Henry Newman. After his second visit he invited Newman to be the first rector and prepare the way for the new foundation by delivering, in Dublin, a series of lectures on the definition and content of a truly Catholic education. Newman replied that, before he accepted either suggestion, he should 'know something of the state of public opinion on the subject'. Cullen ignored the proviso. He had already set out the purpose of the university – 'to persuade the people that education should be religious'.[25]

The prospect of the university becoming reality was much improved by Cullen's appointment as Archbishop of Dublin, but progress was slow. During the year in which Newman waited for his appointment to be confirmed – and regularly returned to England, including visits to proclaim the Second Spring and to hear the verdict in the Achilli case – he prepared and delivered his *Discourses on the Scope and Nature of Education*. It was in those lectures that *The Idea of a University* was based – a work which, when it was published in 1873, became second only to Newman's *Apologia Pro Vitá Sua* in securing his lasting fame. The message of the lectures – although at times obscured by metaphors about the futility of attempts to 'quarry the granite rock with razors or moor a vessel with a thread of silk' – was clear: 'If the Catholic Faith is true, a university cannot exist externally to the Catholic pale. For it cannot teach Universal knowledge if it does not teach Catholic theology.'[26]

Setting out the theory of Catholic university education proved to be easier, and less controversial, than the practice of creating the institution. Cullen – ignoring Newman's judgement that the undergraduates would work best outside town – bought land on St Stephen's Green. A Vice Rector (of whom Newman disapproved) was appointed without consultation. John McHale, nationalist and Archbishop of Tuam, announced that he would only support the project if membership was limited to Irish students – not open to the Catholic world, as Newman wanted. The fear that Cullen was losing interest in the scheme was fuelled by the Archbishop's failure to reply to letters. The suspicion that he was losing faith in Newman seemed to be confirmed by his opposition to Wiseman's proposal that the Rector's authority should be enhanced by his appointment as a titular bishop.

Back in England, the London Oratory moved to its permanent home in Brompton and the Oratory Church in Birmingham was consecrated. But Newman's eclectic enthusiasm was focusing his attention on Ireland where, he judged, prospects of founding a Catholic university had diminished and must be revived. He decided to 'consult' – by which he meant attempt to convert – the leaders of the Catholic Church in Ireland. The process began badly. Father John Curtis, the Jesuit Provincial, told him that Ireland was too poor to produce young men of the character and breeding expected of undergraduates, and advised that Archbishop Cullen be told to abandon the idea. Father Curtis was not alone in his pessimism. Bishop Delany of Cork, Bishop Ryan of Limerick and Archbishop Slattery of Thurles all echoed his advice. So did Newman's old friend, Charles Russell, the Vice President of Maynooth. But all the episcopal reservations had to be set aside when, on March 20th 1854, the Pope instructed the Irish bishops to meet and take practical steps towards creating a new university. The papal definition of the university's role was less intellectually exacting than Newman wished. But it was sufficiently rigorous to allow him to propose the creation of six faculties – theology, law, medicine, philosophy, letters and natural science – and begin the appointment of staff. The extent of his aspiration was confirmed by his attempt to recruit Johann von Dollinger, the world's foremost authority on the history of the Catholic Church. On May 5th 1854 Newman was able to write to Rome, 'The Holy Father will be gratified to know that the University is now begun ... Zealous priests in England and Ireland are putting their names on our books.'[27]

Dr Dollinger declined the offer. It was not the only setback during the early months of preparation. Although Archbishop Cullen agreed that the staff should include laymen, he wanted to restrict their number and, despite accepting that it was the best way to attract donations, vetoed the appointment of a lay finance committee because it would diminish the clergy's control of university management. The auguries were not all bad. St Laurence House, which was once Dr Quinn's School, was bought and converted into lecture rooms and studies. Number 16 Harcourt Street was leased to become the rector's residence and chapel. The Celia Street Medical School was incorporated into the university. Twenty students – naturally enough, all members of the Catholic middle class – registered on November 3rd 1854.

The opening of the university was marked by the publication of an associated weekly magazine, the *Catholic Gazette*, and the announcement of a series of inaugural lectures – of which Newman was to give the first. But there was a dark cloud on the horizon. As Christmas approached and Newman prepared to return to Oscott for the celebration of Christ's birth, he confided in Ambrose St John that he was finding it increasingly difficult to meet the demands of the English Oratory and the Irish University. Archbishop Cullen had come to the same conclusion and decided that the university needed a full-time rector.

It was not the possible deterioration in academic standards that worried Cullen – a 'castle bishop' who, in the opinion of nationalist John McHale, always sided with the Lord Lieutenant. The Archbishop believed (correctly) that some of the university's staff had been members of O'Connell's Young Ireland movement and claimed (wrongly) that included among them were participants in the abortive Ballingarry uprising against English rule – Ireland's contribution to the 'year of revolution' in 1848. Newman brushed aside Cullen's concern with a piety about keeping politics out of the university, and increased the Archbishop's worries by adding that, in any case, the Young Ireland survivors were 'admirable persons now'.[28] It was, however, the knowledge that the university had been launched successfully – rather than the minor irritants or the trauma of constant travel – that convinced Newman that the time had come to devote more time to the Oratories, which were in need of his full-time care and protection.

Paul Cullen had gone so far as to complain to Rome about the Rector's too-frequent absences from the university. But when, in 1856, Newman's contract was about to expire and he warned that he would not renew it, the Archbishop became more understanding. Realising that Newman's association with the university was essential to its continued success, he travelled to Birmingham to plead with him to change his mind. The result was a compromise. Newman became non-resident Rector for three years. He refused to accept a salary, but agreed to give each year's inaugural lectures.

Newman's lofty aspiration – a great centre of Catholic learning for the whole English-speaking world – was always beyond achievement. But the Irish Catholic University did evolve, through a series of incarnations, into a genuine centre of academic excellence. During its short life, under one title or another, University College Dublin has boasted among its graduates some of Ireland's most exalted Catholics. According to Newman's *Autobiographical Writings*, its birth pangs were so painful and protracted because, at the time of it foundation, Ireland was not ready to encourage scholars and scholarship. 'I was a poor innocent as regards the actual state of things in Ireland when I went there ... I relied on the word of the Pope, but ... I am led to think it not rash to say that I knew as much about Ireland as he did.'

CHAPTER 23

The State of Things in Ireland

Paul Cullen's appointment as Archbishop of Armagh in 1849 was not unanimously welcomed by either priests or people. Indeed, he was chosen only because all the other possible candidates were even more unacceptable to one of the factions into which the Irish episcopate was divided. His strength was that he was neither a 'castle bishop', in the pocket of the Viceroy, nor a Fenian, more interested in politics than prayer. His weakness was that he returned a stranger to his homeland. He had left Ireland when he was eighteen and spent the subsequent thirty years in Rome as seminarian, director of the printing and publishing arm of Propaganda, Rector (at one time simultaneously) of both the Propaganda College and the Irish College in Rome and agent for the Irish bishops.

Cullen's reputation as man of action was enhanced during Rome's occupation by the revolutionaries of the Risorgimento when it seemed that the Irish College would be requisitioned by the insurgents. There were four Americans on the seminary's rolls. So the Rector announced that the college was under the protection of the United States government, flew the Stars and Stripes and continued his duties undisturbed. But neither his ingenuity nor his dynamism was enough to make the Irish press and people welcome his appointment. Because of his long years in Rome, one newspaper described him as an 'unnaturalised Irishman'.[1] Another called him 'an Italian monk'. The claim that he was 'an agent of Ultramontane advance' was meant to be offensive, but Cullen did not find it so. He was, above all else, devoted to the doctrine that the authority of the Pope was absolute. It was his absolutist view – combined with his experiences during the republicans' siege of the Vatican – which made him believe that it was 'better to have famine than revolution'.[2] A man with a more subtle mind might have come to the conclusion that the two catastrophes were related.

Cullen arrived back in Ireland in 1850, three years after the Irish Poor Law had been amended. Until then it had been identical to the English system. Under the act of 1838 'relief' had been almost entirely provided by the workhouses. The destitution that followed the Great Famine was so widespread that the workhouses could no longer provide enough 'indoor relief' to meet the paupers' needs. So the choice was between revising the Act and mass starvation. A limited form of 'outdoor relief' was introduced. Three years later, more than one million Irish paupers – one-sixth of the whole nation – were still receiving the pittance provided by the Poor Law Commissioners. And the workhouses, although no longer so full that they were turning mendicants away, were still grossly overcrowded. They were under scrutiny as well as under strain. The Mayor of Cork was shocked to discover that most of the juvenile inmates in the city's work-houses died before they reached the age of thirteen. In South Dublin, a Catholic workhouse chaplain was dismissed after he supported women who had complained about assaults by members of the staff.

Pressure from reformers, combined with fear of the whole system's collapse, resulted in the setting up of a Select Committee to which Cullen volunteered to give evidence, for reasons that were entirely consistent with his character and calling. He 'knew a good deal about the working of the [present] system and was persuaded that it was most dangerous to religion' and would, 'if not corrected, destroy the poor'.[3] Cullen had sent a questionnaire to all the workhouse chaplains in his diocese. Their response was unanimous and was typified by the comments of the priest who commended 'the heroism of those afflicted creatures who prefer to endure starvation rather than qualify them-selves for relief in the workhouse'. One of his colleagues explained why 'indoor relief' was anathema to the virtuous. It provided 'an encouragement to the evil habits of the male sex and a nursery to female vice'.

Cullen's evidence to the Select Committee dealt with the physical deprivation as well as the moral danger that indoor relief guaranteed. He rejected the proposition that poverty was a condition which deserved punishment – the basis of the Poor Law – and sought to replace it with a theory of relief which distinguished between the deserving and undeserving pauper. He also wanted the system to make special provision for children and to acknowledge the importance of keeping respectable families together. The spiritual needs of the Catholic poor – 80 per cent of workhouse inmates – were not forgotten. Provision must be made for their form of worship, and Catholic chap-lains should be afforded easier access and more respect. All in all, it was an irrefutable statement of Catholic aims. Yet no other bishop endorsed it. Indeed, Cullen's colleagues were opposed to him giving evidence. They all took it for granted that their submissions would be treated with contempt. John Derry, Bishop of Clonfert, spoke for them all: 'The fruitlessness of all our appeals to parliament and to the governments which have been successively in power since I became bishop has for a long time made me despair of correcting, in that way, the evils we have to complain of.' He cited the behaviour of boards of guardians as an example of the prejudice faced by public-spirited Catholics. In most workhouses only a small percentage of the inmates were Protestants. Yet the masters, matrons, clerks, schoolmasters and mistresses almost invariably were. Not one board was chaired by a Catholic.[4] The bishops' pessimism was proved to be justified. The one substantial reform to flow from the Select Committee was the repeal of the law that required every foundling to be registered as a Protestant. Ireland, and its Catholic Church, was left to wrestle with the other consequence of endemic poverty – emigration to what was, usually wrongly, believed to be a better life.

During Paul Cullen's first year as Archbishop of Armagh, 209,000 men, women and children left Ireland for ever. Between his arrival in 1850 and death (as Archbishop of Dublin) in 1878 Irish emigration totalled well over 2.5 million. One perverse consequence of the depopulation – death as well as departures – was a reduction on the pressure on the clergy. Before the Great Famine there was a ratio of one priest to every 2,800 Catholics. By 1860 it had increased to one priest to every 1,500.[5] Emigration was a desperate expedient about which the Catholic Church could not agree. In 1847, eighty-four prominent land-owners had petitioned Lord John Russell with the request that the government initiate a colonisation programme that would resettle three million Irish citizens in North Africa. It was the sort of remedy to hunger and homelessness which the Protestant ascendancy were expected to propose. But the resigned acceptance that Ireland would never be able adequately to feed its own people stretched across sectarian and social divides. In 1849, Father James Maher of Graigue in County Carlow – Cullen's uncle – wrote that it was 'better to be alive in Illinois than rotting in Ireland'.[6] In the following year Father Malachy Duggan, of Moyarta and Kilballyowen in West Clare, argued that emigration was probably the only alternative to 'people flocking to every door, craving something to prolong life if only for a few hours'.

The bishops – Thomas Feeney of Killala, Edmund Maginn of Derry and John McHale of Tuam – took a different view. Their opposition was partly economic (available funds best spent on domestic relief), partly social (the best people leave, while the worst stay), but primarily religious. Emigrants were notorious for, at best, neglecting their observances and, at worst, losing their faith completely. Archbishop Cullen shared the three bishops' concern. During his years of residence in Rome he had regularly visited his brother – a successful

Liverpool businessman – and discovered that no more than 10 per cent of Irish Catholic immigrants to the city regularly attended Mass and that (to him perhaps, even worse) an alarming number entered into mixed marriages. But, when he helped to establish an Irish Relief Committee in Rome, his appeal to the bishop wisely emphasised the social rather than spiritual effects of famine and consequent immigration – particularly the risk of death and disease faced by heroic priests going about their pastoral duties.

Immediately that he became an archbishop, Cullen wrote to Cardinal Allesandro Barnabo of Propaganda Fide to describe the devastating effects emigration was having on Ireland. A second letter had reported that 5,000 people a week were leaving his archdiocese for America, with the result that 'entire areas of the country are left abandoned'.[7] He was later to wonder if the diaspora was providential – God's way of spreading Catholicism throughout a great empire. But in 1850 he was more concerned with the causes than the consequences. His first pastoral letter – February 24th – ended his description of the poverty he saw each day with a plea for immediate relief and a rhetorical question: 'Is there a heart so hard that it is not moved by such misery and desolation?'

Much of the argument in favour of planned emigration was based on the mistaken belief – shared by the emigrants themselves – that to escape from Ireland was to escape from poverty. John Lynch, Bishop of Toronto, published an open letter to the Irish bishops, which warned against wholesale and improvident emigration. Immigrants to his diocese were forced by poverty to live in areas that were 'haunts of vice', with the result that they were 'lost to morality, to society, to religion and finally to God', and he drove his point home in a private letter to Cullen which reported, with shame and regret, that as in Canada, so in Liverpool. Two-thirds of the city's prostitutes were Irish.

It was not only in Canada that the Catholic immigrants lived in squalor. A Mrs Charlton, author of *Recollections of a Northumbrian Lady*, described Bellingham, where iron ore deposits had been found, as 'full of dirty ill-conditioned Irish labourers'.[8] And some of the Catholic clergy were equally censorious. One Kensington priest complained that the expatriate Irish were responsible for 'immovable belts of stink' in his parish church and that, thanks to them, 'bugs walk about in surplices and take possession of gentlemen's hats'.[9] The priest who opened a new Mass centre in Sheffield recalled that, although trade was good and in general the city prospered, 'our poor people, through neglect and disorderly habits and, most of all drink, were in a state of utmost poverty and degradation'.[10]

Cardinal Cullen was at once more sympathetic to the immigrants and more critical of the English clergy. In November 1856 he wrote to Cardinal Barnabo with the complaint that the Catholic Church in England was less interested in meeting the needs of the poor than in building spectacular churches, 'polished, with palatial salons, covered in beautiful carpets'. He cited, as an example of the sinful regard for respectability, the Redemptorists of Clapham who, he claimed, feared that they could not accommodate the poor within their Sunday congregations without them 'dirtying the fine linen and offending the eyes of the great'.[11]

It was true that the Redemptorist chapel in Clapham could only accommodate seven hundred worshippers, and that was far fewer than the number who wanted to attend Mass on Sunday. And the same problem was prejudicing the work of parishes all over England. Throughout the country Catholics were being denied access to the sacraments because their local church was too small to meet the expanding needs of the area it served. By 1851 – largely thanks to the Irish immigration which followed the famine – the Catholic population of England had grown to 700,000. They had to be accommodated in the 586 churches and chapels that had served the country before the Irish came. The weekly attendance at Mass was a little in excess of 250,000. The churches and chapels could seat about 180,000.[12]

Between 1837 and 1845, thirty-five new Catholic churches had been built in England, most of them in the Gothic style, but not all designed by Pugin.[13] Few were in the places in which the immigrants had settled, and Cardinal Wiseman saw it as his duty – as a central feature of his reorganisation of the English Catholic Church – to create new parishes. Each one must, he had no doubt, have a proper church at its centre. That ambition was most easily performed in places where a rich benefactor could be found. Although he rejoiced that a new church in East London had been 'erected by the penny contributions of Irish labourers, bargemen, bricklayers, hodmen and other toilers',[14] he knew that the poor could not meet the need on their own. The 'people's pence' had an emotional, a romantic and perhaps a moral attraction, but did not build churches as quickly as rich men's pounds.

Father William Lockhart, sent by the Cardinal to Kingsland in North London, found Thomas Kelly, a prosperous builder, and persuaded him to allow the first floor of his house to become a Mass centre and presbytery. Inspired by the sacrifice, Father Lockhart used resources of his own to buy a disused pre-Reformation Church in Ely Place, Holborn. Father George Spencer, the son of an earl, said Mass in a temporary chapel in West Bromwich until – having begun the process with £200 of his own money – he had raised enough capital to build a church. In the provinces, donors were more difficult to find. So working men played a bigger part. Although a Mrs Eyre of Bath financed the creation of a new church to replace the temporary chapel on the ground floor of a cottage in Newport, in other parts of Wales, life was particularly hard. In Merthyr Tydfil, Mass was said in a loft over the local abattoir. In Abersychan, services were held in the club room of a public house. The attic which the priest in Swansea rented was used, despite its rotten roof, but was necessarily abandoned when the floor collapsed.

In Liverpool, Bishop Alexander Goss was determined to replace – with something more appropriate to the Glory of God – the wooden hut in St James' Street where the Society of St Vincent de Paul held services. Unfortunately he could not even afford to complete payment for the site. Nevertheless he laid the foundation stone and, during its dedication, invited members of the congregation to contribute. Some of them had come prepared. At the end of the service the Irish ships' carpenters of the parish passed in line, each one laying one day's wages on the newly blessed stone.[15] Other tradesmen, and men with no trades at all, followed suit. More than £100 was collected on the day.

Before the Great Famine, Ireland was similarly short of churches but – since, unlike England, it was a Catholic country – it was able to mitigate, though not solve, the problem in a Catholic way. 'Mass stations' were established in private houses throughout the country. In them the sacraments were administered at Christmas, through Lent, during Holy Week and on other nominated days. They also provided convenient opportunities for parish priests to collect parish subscriptions; but, for all their utility, they did not find favour with Rome. Lofts, kitchens and clubrooms were acceptable as long as they were permanently converted into chapels. The week-by-week switch from sacred to secular purpose was not. Disapproval was expressed and it might well have become prohibition, had not the shortage of premises – like the shortage of priests – been 'solved' by the famine and consequent emigration. As things turned out, the problem was simply exported to Catholic parts of England.

The problem was most serious in Liverpool, where immigrants from Ireland suffered all the poverty and degradation about which the anti-emigration bishops had warned. In November 1855, the *Catholic Institute Magazine* wrote of 'thousands of homeless, moneyless, raimentless, foodless creatures that call the Catholic Church their mother in Liverpool'.[16] The crisis in care was increased by the Great

Famine, but existed long before the potato crop failed. As early as 1832, the Liverpool District Provident Society – in its annual report for the previous year – had replied to critics who complained about 'relieving so many of the Irish poor'. It conceded the fact, but was unyielding in defence of the necessity. 'Out of 11,303 relieved, 8,069 have been from Ireland. Heavy as the burden must be, it appears unavoidable ... As long as the Irish poor are situated as at present this charge upon the funds of the Society cannot, it is feared, be much diminished.' The report was clear that blame for the 'burden' that the Provident Society – and other Liverpool charitable institutions – had to bear must be shared between the Great Famine and the coming of cheap steamboat travel across the Irish Sea. Liverpool was accessible and it was also a staging post to the promised land of America. Indeed, many illiterate Irish peasants were sold tickets to Liverpool in the belief that they were buying their passage to New York or Boston.

Liverpool thus became the paradigm of nineteenth-century attitudes towards the Catholic poor and the example – magnified and concentrated – of the behaviour of poor Catholics and their Church. In the age of carefully modulated compassion, Protestant and non-denominational charities were far more likely than their Catholic counterparts to discriminate between the deserving and undeserving poor. The Liverpool Select Vestry warned – as numbers of immigrants began to rise – that to 'administer relief indiscriminately is only to offer encouragement to others and increase the evil'. The Provident Society – despite an earlier robust defence of providing indiscriminate help – decided to reduce 'the promiscuous and more particularly the pecuniary relief of beggars' by distributing soup tickets rather than cash. The authorities, as represented by Alfred Austin, the Assistant Poor Law Commissioner for the North West, endorsed the view that thoughtless charity – based on sentimentality rather than reason – exacerbated, rather than relieved, the problem:

> The extremely wretched appearance of most of the Irish immigrants strongly excites the compassionate feelings of the Inhabitants of Liverpool and an indiscriminate alms giving has been the consequence. Every street swarms with Irish beggars and their gains is at once an inducement to them to continue the profitable pursuit of Mendacity and an invitation to fresh numbers to come over from Ireland to Liverpool to participate in the profit.[17]

That was not the Catholic way. The Church embraced a variety of views about the Christian obligation to the poor. But the predominant feeling was compassion, and the almost invariable reaction to the poverty of the time was the organisation and sponsorship of good works. The *Catholic Institute Magazine* went so far as publicly to criticise the Protestant view of charity, which, it claimed, 'proceeds with a fixity of system, a calm calculation of practical results and a rigid economy of good works which utterly destroy, to Catholic eyes, all that in Charity is most beautiful and most holy'. The Catholic charities of Liverpool were competitive as well as critical. J Neal-Lomas, at the 1866 annual dinner of Liverpool Catholic Club, actually challenged the Protestant churches to match the charitable record of the Church of Rome. Eleven out of every twenty inmates of the Liverpool workhouses were, he said, Catholics, and raising funds with which to support them was a constant struggle, and only one in ten of Liverpool houses, with a rateable value of £20 or above, was occupied by members of the same faith. But Neal-Lomas 'felt it a glory to belong to a Church which would take care of the destitute'. John Belchem – historian and author of *Irish, Catholic and Scouse* – believes that Liverpool-Irish Catholics came to regard poverty as a badge of identity. Whether or not that was so, they certainly coalesced into a mutually supportive community in which the rank-and-file clergy believed that their vocation was to give material as well as spiritual succour to their followers. Father James Nugent – admittedly a priest with an unusually active and vocal social conscience – had no doubt where his duty lay: 'I want the poor people with me. I want the poorest of the poor in order that I may throw some ray of comfort and consolation across their troubled lives.'

Nugent became the first president of the Liverpool Catholic Reformatory Association and pioneered a series of work schemes, including harvesting in the fields of a Cistercian monastery. He believed that, as well as providing much-needed material comfort, regular employment would help recipients along the road to redemption and rehabilitation. Alexander Goss, the Catholic Bishop of Liverpool, was clearly more concerned with tranquillity in his respectable flock than in the material and spiritual welfare of its lost sheep. He was dismissive about the Cistercian farm scheme and advocated, in its place, compulsory removal to the colonies. Had his idea been adopted, some young men – who had left Ireland as children in the families of voluntary immigrants – would have been required to emigrate a second time.

Father Nugent was the all-purpose reformer, as determined to redeem fallen women as he was to improve the behaviour of violent and dishonest young men and boys. He was handicapped in his work of redemption by the angry refusal of respectable Catholic Liverpool to face the unpleasant fact of female frailty. The truth about male crime – exposed by Nugent after he became the Catholic chaplain to Walton Gaol – was to be regretted, but had to be accepted. A majority of the male prisoners in Walton Gaol were Roman Catholics and, for the thirty years that followed the Great Famine, 60 per cent of the Catholic prisoners were Irish-born. Usually they were convicted of minor offences, which were often related to the high incidence of drunk-and-disorderly conduct amongst immigrant men. Nugent asked respectable Liverpool to show compassion to petty offenders who were not part of the 'well-to-do class or even skilled labourers and mechanics, but the poorest and most destitute class'.[18]

It was, however, more difficult – in some cases, impossible – to accept Nugent's revelation that so many women, born and bred in the pure Catholic air of Ireland, fell from grace in the more fetid atmosphere of the Liverpool slums. The Irish press, and Irish nationalist newspapers in Liverpool, were outraged by Nugent's assertion – in his first annual report of the Reformatory Association – that 'more than 60% of law-breaking prostitutes in Protestant Liverpool' were what the *Irish People* called 'our own countrywomen'. The facts were, however, irrefutable. According to an 1866 inquiry into contagious diseases in the city, there were 1,313 'houses of bad character' in Liverpool, and Irish prostitutes were to be found in the most squalid brothels. The authors did their best to soften truth's blow. 'It is well known that Irish women in their own country are, even amidst very unfavourable surroundings, a most virtuous class.' However, in Liverpool they made up the 'most degraded class of prostitutes, living in brothels in the very worst streets in the borough and resorted to by the numerous negroes always present in Liverpool as ships' cooks, stewards, seamen and labourers'. It was the consequences for the women's health, as much as for their mortal souls, that caused Nugent – in a fit of despair – to consider the wholly impractical idea of sending vulnerable young girls to Canada, where (he seemed to believe) the wide-open spaces would restore health and encourage respectability.

The determination of respectable Liverpool to clear the borough of its brothels brought Nugent out of semi-retirement – not to cooperate with the authorities, but to mitigate some of the suffering that closure caused. He bought a boarding house and turned it into the St Saviour's Refuge and – proclaiming the need to Rescue the Fallen – set out, in the words of the *Catholic Times*, 'to meet the urgent want occasioned by the local police crusade against immoral houses, whereby large numbers of unfortunate women of this class were thrown destitute and homeless into the streets'.[19] Under the supervision of nuns, the women were prepared for transfer to one of the Homes of the Good Shepherd, where they were employed in the laundries on what was described as 'penitential work' – thus raising one of the questions which hangs over descriptions of the Catholic Church in the nineteenth century. Should the laundries and their harsh penitential regimes – early mornings, long working days, poor food, institutional clothing and virtual imprisonment – be judged by the standard of the times, and therefore admired as demonstrations of love and compassion, or should they be regarded by more modern measurements of those virtues as examples of how harsh and unforgiving the Pharisees can be?

At least the Liverpool Catholic Church felt an obligation to provide some sort of succour for its destitute followers. The Protestant City Fathers felt little obligation to meet the material needs of the borough's new Irish citizens, and none at all to respect the demands of their religion. In 1850, James Whitty – a prosperous draper and immigrant from County Wexford – launched a campaign to shame the Liverpool Vestry into acknowledging its duties to the whole community. The *Lancashire Free Press* – the first Catholic newspaper on Merseyside – joined in with the demand that Catholics be allowed to enjoy 'the full and free benefits of the British constitution',[20] which, it went on to claim, with dubious authenticity, was essentially the product of pre-Reformation England. In consequence a room was set aside in the Brownlow Workhouse – where half the resident paupers were Catholics – for Mass to be said on a Sunday. It was not until thirty years later that the Board of Guardians agreed to pay a fee for the services of a priest. Richard Sheil – a merchant who did business with America and was, for many years, the only Catholic on the Liverpool council – paid, out of his own pocket, for a chaplain to be employed by the Kirkdale Industrial School, where pauper children were prepared for low-skilled work. Although there were 451 Catholic pupils in the school – out of a total roll of 795 – the Vestry rejected the proposal that there should always be one Catholic teacher on the staff. The Protestant politicians campaigned against what they called 'Rome on the Rates' and used their commanding positions in the institutions of the poor to prose-lytise among the young (often orphaned) paupers.

Father James Nugent – mid-nineteenth-century Merseyside's most determined pioneer of Catholic elementary education – estimated that more than 23,000 children regularly spent their days 'roaming about the streets and docks'.[21] The police put the figure even higher. They calculated that 48,782 children, between the ages of five and fourteen, did not attend school, and that more than 25,000 of them ran wild each day. Most were the sons and daughters of Liverpool's 150,000 Catholics. Dissatisfied with the level of provision, and bitter about the Protestant bias in what schools there were, Catholic Liverpool responded by setting up schools of its own whenever resources permitted. A redundant hospital was bought from the West Derby Union and turned into St George's Industrial School under the supervision of the Christian Brothers. Father Nugent – who had a weakness for flamboyant slogans and titles – set up the Association of Providence for the Protection of Orphan and Destitute Boys in a disused theatre. A year later he founded a refuge for homeless boys (under the title 'Nobody's Children'), which began as a night shelter and evolved first into a training centre and then into a paper-bag factory and cobblers' shop to employ the trainees.

Liverpool was not the only, or even the first, diocese in which Catholics struggled to provide what the Vestries and Councils either neglected or organised in ways that discriminated against Catholics, by preventing them from fulfilling the obligations of their faith. The first Catholic orphanage was opened in 1847 at North Hyde, in Middlesex; the first Catholic reformatory at Blythe House, in Hammersmith; and the first Catholic Industrial School at Walthamstow in 1870. But it was in Liverpool where the need was the greatest and where the response, by the nature of the city, was most riven by sectarian prejudice.

Father Nugent's achievement would not have been possible without his flair for publicity. But there were complaints that his work publicised the least attractive aspects of the Liverpool Catholic Irish. Despite that, and the occasional complaint from their leaders that they contributed little to the upkeep of their Church, men and women who could be legitimately so described – Irish by birth, Liverpudlian by residence and Catholic by faith – were remarkably cohesive in their loyalty to the old country, the new homeland and the unchanging religion. Unlike in Glasgow, where they were openly rejected, Irish priests – many of them the product of Maynooth's rigorous regime – were welcomed in Liverpool as a continuing connection with 'the old country'. They acted as interpreters for families who spoke only Gaelic, and they identified families in particularly desperate need of help, and they made sure that none of their parishioners misappropriated funds that were intended for the deserving poor. Most important of all, they became the glue that held the Liverpool Irish Catholics together – even though their leaders sometimes quarrelled among themselves.

The Jesuits, true to form, tried to establish a presence in the city while remaining semi-detached from the rest of the Church, which – it must be said, in fairness to the Society – did its best to keep them at arm's length. In 1841, at the first anniversary meeting of the Society of St Francis Xavier, the sympathetic laymen were given an account of the conflicting arguments with which the objections to the establishment of a Jesuit church had been justified. 'First it is alleged that the proposed church is not necessary ... Secondly it is alleged that a church in Salisbury Street will harm St Anthony's and St Nicholas' ... Thirdly it is alleged that the proposed site is out of town and there is no Catholic population around it.'[22] For their part, the Jesuits were unyielding in their insistence that the special rights of regulars to act independently of lay authority must be respected. And they made their point in uncompromising language. 'During the inspection, the inspectors claimed to be received as the bishop's representatives ... The bishop has no right to do in a school what he has no right to do in a church ... He has no right of inspection.'[23]

In the Midland District the question of inspection (its pecuniary advantages and it procedural pitfalls) had obliged Nicholas Wiseman to emphasise a point of principle which echoed the argument about authority that had dominated Henry's Reformation. His circular – which asked 'how many children in your Mission require Education' but do not receive it? – was accompanied by a covering letter which provided useful information about the possibility of obtaining funds from the 'Catholic Poor-Schools Committee' and government assistance with the payment of teachers' salaries. It ended with a stern injunction to preserve the religious integrity of Catholic schools and their staff:

> Opportunities will be given for Catholic schoolmasters to be examined by an inspector ... Such masters who pass through it and obtain a certificate will be entitled to pecuniary assistance and the employment of a Pupil apprentice ... I urge on you the importance of not allowing your School master to submit to examination by any but a Catholic inspector.[24]

Wiseman's instruction was the result of fear that Catholics in a strange land would forget, or at least dilute, the faith of home. Writing in the year of the Great Famine, a Birkenhead priest claimed, much to his obvious distress, the 'deplorable effects which the woes of the last season seem to have had in almost utterly destroying the religious instincts of the Irish in Britain'.[25] In fact – allowing for the need to adjust to the new life, the deprivation from which they suffered and the bitterness that many of them must have felt towards Providence, as well as society – church attendance remained remarkably high. According to the 1851 census, the 'Irish born' population of Liverpool was 83,813, and 38,123 Catholics were recorded as present at Mass on Sunday March 30th. Some of the worshippers were, no doubt, native Liverpudlians. But a number of 'Irish born' citizens must have been Ulster Protestants. So it is reasonable to assume that the ratio (thirty-eight churchgoers out of every eighty-four Irish immigrants) is more or less correct. But it makes no allowance for Irish-born Catholics who were too old, too young, too sick or too indolent to attend church. Include them in the equation and the ratio changes. Half of the Catholics who were able to do so attended Mass on that specific Sunday. And there would have been many others who – claiming that piety did not require them to make a weekly attendance – called themselves 'good Catholics' because of the occasional appearance at Mass, but happened not to choose Sunday March 30th 1851 as one of the days for formal worship.

Native-born Catholics were more assiduous worshippers than were the Catholic immigrants. But the two groups were divided by more than the frequency of church attendance. Many of the native Catholics regarded themselves as different in kind from most of the faith. During a dinner party at Eaton Hall, the Marquess of Westminster reproved one of his guests for expressing his dislike of Catholics when there was 'a Catholic lady present'. He was referring to Mrs Charlton, the author of *The Recollections of a Northumbrian Lady*. Mrs Charlton assured the Marquis that, far from taking offence, she had never thought that the disparaging remarks in any way related to her. Yes, she was a Catholic, 'but an English one, not an Irish one – which is all the difference in the world'.[26] She was right. Culturally and socially she had little in common with the Liverpool immigrants and hers was a very different Church – at the beginnings of Wiseman's leadership, not yet totally freed from the Catholic gentry's belief that it should be governed by them rather than by rules laid down in Rome. But she did not realise that, because of the primitive energy that had come out of Ireland via Liverpool, the Catholic Church was changing – first in the cities into which the Irish initially came and then, as they spread out, throughout the country. Henry Manning was right to give thanks for the consequences of the diaspora. 'The thing which will save us from low views about the Mother of God and the vicar of Our Lord is the million Irish in England.'[27]

While the Catholic Church in England was being changed by the Irish of the diaspora, Cardinal Paul Cullen was making formal changes to the organisation of the Catholic Church in Ireland. Cullen was wrestling with the rebellious 'spirit ... developing here every day, among not only a few priests but a good many of them'. He described the growing mood of insubordination as 'scant respect, not to say contempt for the authority of the Holy See'.[28] The Synod of Thurles, which had met in August 1850, was the battleground that Cullen chose for his opening assault on the traitors within the gate. The opening skirmish had ended in a narrow victory – the reluctant agreement not to cooperate with the secular colleges. The second engagement was a battle fought on two fronts. The proposal that disagreements between the bishops, which could not be resolved between them, should be referred to Rome was agreed unanimously. The proposition that no bishop was to take action or express an opinion on a subject of mutual concern, without consulting the whole episcopate, was bitterly opposed by the Archbishop of Dublin and was only carried by sixteen votes to twelve. The Synod had also passed regulations which unified, throughout Ireland, the liturgy of the sacraments and laid down new rules for the conduct of the clergy. But it was Cullen's battle with the bishops for which it will be remembered – a battle that was only the beginning of a long campaign.

The month before the Synod met, Cullen had – through his influence with Cardinal Franzoni, the Prefect of Propaganda Fide – arranged for the See of Cloyne and Ross to be split and William Keane, a priest 'well disposed to be obedient to the Holy See, to be made Bishop of Ross. Cullen had already decided that the only way in which he could impose his will on an unruly episcopate was to change its composition. That was essential if he was to obtain the right answer to what, he told Rome, was 'the real question to be decided – whether the decisions of the Holy See ought or ought not to be obeyed, whether the Pope should govern the Irish Church through the majority of the Irish bishops or if the English should govern it by means of the Archbishop of Dublin'. He added that the need for change was reinforced by the age and infirmity of some of the incumbents. 'The Bishop of Dublin is eighty-three years of age. The Bishop of Killaloe has dropsy and, it is believed, will hardly survive Christmas. The Bishop of Dromore is totally deaf and is not fit to govern his diocese. The Bishops of Down and Connor and of Kerry are both very ill.' If the Vatican took 'great care in the choice of new bishops, within three years, things [would] be totally changed in Ireland'. The cull took ten. But long before it had been completed, the rebellious clergy of Ireland had been tamed and Paul Cullen, by 1852 Archbishop of Dublin, was imposing his Ultramontane will on the Catholic Church in Ireland.

CHAPTER 24

A Certain Cleavage

The Irish Catholic immigration that left its indelible mark on mid-nineteenth-century Merseyside played a less obvious part in the development of Victorian western Scotland. In Liverpool, Irish Catholics changed the character of that city by weight of permanent numbers. In Lanarkshire, they were scattered throughout the county. Back in 1813, Alex Cameron – the Scottish Vicar Apostolic – had missed the Durham meeting at which the issue of a government veto on the appointment of bishops was discussed. His note of apology illustrates the strain that was imposed on delicate constitutions by the haphazard distribution of souls which it was their duty to save: 'I had been called to Glasgow and Paisley to administer confirmation and, had the state of my health permitted, it was my intention to visit a large district on that coast where a great number of poor Catholics, generally Irish, are dispersed without a priest.'[1] Fifty years on, the problem had not changed. In Lanarkshire, Catholics were scattered throughout the county and, even after the arrival of Irish labour which followed the Great Hunger, the new arrivals were often only temporary immigrants who returned home after harvest was in, a stretch of canal dug or a branch railway line laid.

Immigration into Lanarkshire had begun with an influx of Highland Scots – many of them worshippers in a semi-pagan Church which had hardly been touched by the Reformation. The first major movement had come in 1792 when, at the invitation of cotton manufacturers, six hundred Catholics moved from Glengarry to Glasgow.[2] They outnumbered the local Catholics by a ratio of ten to one. For, according to the Church, the Glasgow Catholic community – which in 1778 had consisted of twenty secret communicants – had only increased to sixty by 1791. By the turn of the century, Catholic harvesters were coming south each autumn and, long before the Great Hunger forced millions of migrants to leave Ireland, the advent of cheap steamboat travel had enabled thousands of Irishmen to look for a better life abroad. In 1820 there were 10,000 Catholics living in Glasgow. By 1831 the number has risen to 27,000. John Murdoch, Coadjutor of the Western District of Scotland, put the figure in Glasgow and its surrounding villages at

44,000 in 1836.[3] The two estimates are inconsistent with each other, but there was agreement about one feature of the increase in the Catholic population: the Irish who brought it about were almost invariably dirt-poor.

Scotland at the beginning of the nineteenth century was home to the gospel of self-help. In consequence the Irish paupers – despite the enterprise they had shown in making the journey east – were often regarded as victims of their own folly. John Murdoch openly regretted that there was 'nothing like a Catholic aristocracy in Glasgow' and estimated, with obvious disdain, that amongst the Irish immigrants there was 'hardly a handful fit to take houses in the west end' of the city.[4] It was already the home to respectable, prosperous and native-born Catholics – so many that St Andrew's Church (now a cathedral) thought it necessary to appoint 'seat minders to segregate the rich from the poor'. Faced with such inconveniences, Murdoch found little consolation in the effort and initiative shown by those Irish Catholics who thought of the Clyde ports as a staging post in their journey to the promised land of America. 'By and by,' he predicted, 'we will be left with a congregation of beggars.'

The transient nature of the new immigrants to Scotland created a special problem for their Church. On Merseyside the immigrants came to stay, and men with families are more likely than men living alone to attend Mass. Unaccompanied men, who came to Lanarkshire because they had heard that there was a pit shaft to be sunk or a canal lock to be cut, returned home when the job was done. So the demand for priests, and the subscriptions that support churches, ebbed and flowed. Barely a year after its construction the Chapelhall Mission in Lanarkshire was on the point of collapse. The recession caused the closure of the Calderbank ironworks in which most of its worshippers worked. At the same time the mission that had been established at Girvan in 1810 lost so many parishioners that it was on the point of closure and was saved only by donations from a new class of wealthy benefactors.[5] Self- made men were beginning to replace the old nobility as the principal patrons of the Catholic Church. But it was not always clear how their generosity could be employed to best advantage. The diaspora that followed the Great Hunger ended the ebb and flow of migrants, and the arrival of the Irish poor – with neither the wish nor the ability to return home – ended the month-by-month fluctuation in the number of Masses that needed to be said on a Sunday. But it created another problem for the West of Scotland Catholic Church. It was overwhelmed by the numbers to which it had to minister.

There is no reliable estimate of how many Irish Catholic immigrants settled in Scotland during the years that followed the famine. But calculations of increases in individual towns leave no doubt that the overall figure was immense. In Dundee the Irish-born population rose from 5,000 in 1841 to 15,000 ten years later.[6] The linen and jute factories were a particular attraction to men who had worked in the same trades at home in South Ulster. But Dundee was not as accessible as Glasgow, where jobs existed, or were thought to exist, for men whose sole skill was in the use of picks and shovels.

In its account of the years in which 'the Catholic population of Scotland, particularly Glasgow, increased very rapidly', Propaganda Fide described the tension between indigenous and incoming worshippers with admirable delicacy: 'A certain cleavage arose between the two elements ... the native Scotch who had remained faithful to their religion through the years of persecution with their own clergy and the Irish immigrants with Irish priests.' And it went on to explain, with commendable sympathy, the reason why the 'cleavage' had occurred. 'Differing so much as they did in background and temperament, it is not surprising that jealousy between the two groups should arise, and this does not imply any serious fault on either side but plenty of misunderstanding.'[7]

The misunderstandings resulted in a series of 'proposals' – which often read like demands – for changes in the governance of the Catholic Church in Scotland. The first step towards securing and maintaining a fragile peace was the installation, as Vicar Apostolic, of Monsignor Charles Eyre, a member of the Derbyshire family who had been loyal, and often dangerously overt, Catholics since the Reformation. Eyre was wealthy and well connected. His father was a director of the London and South Western Railway Company, but the way in which he approached his job was more important than his pedigree. He believed in the obligation of the Church to involve itself in the life of the city. So he encouraged greater Catholic participation in both Glasgow's own social institutions – the St Vincent de Paul Society and the League of the Cross temperance guild – and the numerous good causes that served every denomination, most notably the Society for the Prevention of Cruelty to Children. More important still, he was not only an Englishman – which, in itself, might have made him unacceptable. He was the sort of Englishman who stood above the fray and was therefore assumed to favour neither the Scots nor the Irish.

On March 4th 1878 the recently elected pope, Leo XIII, announced the restoration of the Scottish Hierarchy. The news was greeted with far less triumphalism than had been displayed during the celebration of the 'second English spring' in 1850. But the congregation of the

Glasgow archdiocese marked the occasion with the gift of a landau to the unequivocally English Archbishop Eyre. It was meant as a tribute to the distance he covered in the service of the Church. Far more important than the cost of the gift was the fact that both Irish and native Scots contributed. The lowly laymen were far less conscious than their clergy of the conflict between the two races. Scottish Catholics were happy to receive Communion from Irish priests.

Father Charles Grant, the first priest to be ordained in Glasgow since the Reformation, had taken Holy Orders in 1829 and since then – apart from a couple of Protestant converts – the churches had been staffed largely by elderly Irish priests who had been recruited before the influx of Irish labour. The priests who came, or would have come, with the immigrants were neither welcomed nor trusted by their Scottish counterparts. They were suspected of fomenting rebellion against the episcopate and of spreading the Fenian doctrine that violence against the English oppressors was an essential ingredient of the campaign for Irish independence. John Murdoch, who could be relied upon to reveal what other Vicars Apostolic thought but were wise enough not to say, complained, 'I have a great deal of unqualified and unsteady priests.'[8] Whether or not that was so, Murdoch should have realised how important it was to provide the new Glaswegians with priests who understood them. It had long been accepted in the Scottish Catholic Church that 'the Irish must be treated in a different manner from our Scots people or they will never be helped on the way to salvation'.[9] But that understanding did not lead to the active recruitment of Irish priests.

Even before the Irish exodus was at its height, there were not enough priests in western Scotland to perform even basic pastoral duties for native Scots. In 1836 in Glasgow there were four priests – one to every 9,000 or 10,000 Catholics.[10] Between them they served St Andrew's in the centre of the city, St Mary's in Abercrombie Street south of the Clyde and various temporary Mass stations in the surrounding villages. The consequent neglect was reflected in the attendance at Sunday Mass. John Murdoch calculated that, during the 1840s, there were rather more than 12,000 regular worshippers – 35 per cent of the Catholic population – in the area. Since very few of them attended Mass on every Sunday, the attendance on an average Sunday was about 18 per cent of the possible congregation. In Belfast, the average attendance was 43.1 per cent.

There is no doubt that the Irish abroad – particularly men who had left the sobering effect of wives and children behind – were less conscientious churchgoers than the Irish at home. But the absence of priests, whose mere presence would have reminded miscreants of their religious responsibilities, certainly contributed to the malaise. In the absence of Irish recruits to the priesthood, all that the Church could do was spread its limited resources as widely as possible. So outside Glasgow, St Andrews and Aberdeen, peripatetic priests – who earned £40 a year while Presbyterian ministers earned £100[11] – served Mass stations that were set up in different places at different times. The pennies of the poor could not finance new buildings. But a number of wealthy patrons – inspired, and in some cases converted, by the fervour of the Oxford Movement – contributed to extensions and improvements to existing churches. The restoration at Girvan was made possible by the gift of bricks, land and lime from the Duc de Coigny. Princess Marie of Baden bought a new altar for the church at Hamilton. At Glenfinnan, Father MacDonald – an unusually wealthy priest – paid for Pugin to design one of his neo-Gothic masterpieces.[12] Robert Monteith imported ten tons of religious sculpture into Lanarkshire to decorate aisles and altars. But, apart from the occasional benevolence, Scotland's most densely populated region did not receive the patronage that other areas enjoyed. In 1840 only five Catholic churches served all Lanarkshire. But – thanks to the pennies of the poor – by the turn of the century there were fifty-four churches, eighteen of which had been, or were about to be, extended to meet the increase in the size of congregations. During the intervening sixty years more had happened to the Scottish Catholic Church than simply a titanic growth in number. The Irish immigrants – unwanted and beleaguered – had begun to assert their independent and distinct identity. Crucial to that process was the proud affirmation of their own brand of Catholicism.

The Irish immigrants had changed the Catholic Church in Scotland, and the Catholic Church in Scotland had changed the Irish immigrants. One Ayrshire priest noticed, with a combination of impatience and admiration, that 'the Irish will not come out on Sunday and go to chapel unless they can be clothed like and appear like natives. They will not go in ragged clothes as they went in Ireland.'[13] In part the pride in race and religion was manifest in the espousal – and sometimes even the practice – of the respectable virtues that were more often associated with Scottish Nonconformity than with Irish Catholicism. Sermons argued that respect in this life and salvation in the next required thrift, sobriety and industry. Drinking, gambling and dancing were all discouraged, and sometimes condemned. Father Mathew, a Catholic priest, administered the pledge of total abstinence to an ecumenical rally on Glasgow Green, which the local press estimated was 40,000 strong.

The notion that life for the poor might be made better by political changes in the social order was replaced by the advocacy of self-help as the sure and certain path to prosperity. That led to a new urgency to increase the extent and improve the quality of available education. The Church had always seen Catholic education as a protection against contamination by heretical ideas. In nineteenth-century Scotland it became a way of enabling Catholics to obtain the jobs and houses that had once been the sole preserve of heretics.

Catholic education – limited in both quality and quantity – had been available in Scotland since the beginning of the nineteenth century. In 1830 there were five Catholic day schools in Glasgow attended by 1,400 pupils who paid a fee of a penny a week. But more than twice as many children of school age were enrolled in the city's eleven Sunday Schools.[14] By 1851 the number of Catholic day-school pupils had increased to 3,436. The Sunday School attendance had increased to 4,950. So there were still 1,500 young Catholics who were without a school place. But the increase in the number of places was matched by an improvement in the quality of teaching. Both trends were destined to continue. Much credit was due to religious Orders who had opened schools in the city. First among them were the Sisters of Mercy. They were closely followed by Franciscan nuns.

The religious Orders did not act alone. The records of the tenure of James Gillis – appointed Vicar Apostolic of Scotland's Eastern District in 1857 – listed the variety of benefactors, including Palmerston's government, to which the Catholic Church in Edinburgh was indebted. The official record set out the achievement and gave thanks for the benefactors who had made it possible:

During the summer of 1858 [Gillis] was much occupied in making extensive alterations to the former chapel in Lothian Street which he converted into two schools for the girls of the Congregation of St Patrick's. This he was enabled to effect chiefly by means of a considerable amount of money which he had obtained from the Privy Council Committee on Education. On completion of these alterations the Schools were placed under the care of the Sisters of Our Lady of Mercy, a colony of which order had been invited from Limerick to found a house in Edinburgh. [The Order was indebted] to the large hearted bounty of a charitable Lady in this community [for] the beautiful convent which it now possesses in Lauriston Gardens and which was erected in 1859 under the superintendence of a gentleman to whom she had intrusted the entire management. Some years previously, Bishop Gillis [then Coadjutor of the Eastern

District] had placed the other schools in better locations so as to improve their condition and increase their numbers. They were set out in connection with the system of Primary Education established by Act of Parliament and were made subject to the annual visit of a Catholic Inspector appointed by the Government. He had also, in 1858, secured a property in Potten Row on which to build an Infant School and had received from a benevolent lady a considerable sum to help him in that undertaking.[15]

It was, however, the Jesuits who staffed and ran the first school to provide anything other than the most basic elementary education. Strangely for that Order, rather than leading the charge, it followed on behind the initiative of lay priests. Fathers Forbes and Belaney – both Irish, and one a convert – bought a disused Protestant church and convinced Father James Johnson, the Jesuit Provincial, that it could be used to meet a long-felt need. Glasgow could offer 'no education fitting boys for any employment above those which kept them where their fathers were when they came out of Ireland in a state of starvation. Hence as *a body* the Church here is nothing, while numerically it is a quarter of this great city. The want of clergy lies at the root of all our endeavours, blighting them as soon as they set forth.' John Murdoch – the stern, unbending Coadjuter of Scotland's Western District – was affronted by the impertinence of the proposal and terrified at the thought of Irish labourers' sons being prepared by Jesuits to lead the Catholic Church in Scotland. But the initiative was irresistibly attractive in the parishes.

The notion of a great Jesuit-led drive towards a place in a Catholic school for every Catholic boy enjoyed the support of a number of Scotsmen who were wealthy enough to make the dream a reality. Most of them were motivated by the fear that, without proper teaching, young Catholics would drift away from the Church. But the Monteith family saw the patronage of a teaching community as, at least in part, atoning for the sin that had stigmatised the family for three hundred years. They had grown prosperous on land which had been stolen from the Church during the Reformation. They first gave a house in Lanark to Franciscan nuns. The experiment failed and the nuns moved to Glasgow. Irish Dominicans were asked to take their place, but the invitation was declined. French Dominicans and Rosminians followed suit. Even the Jesuits thought Lanark a hopeless cause, though they did agree to open a mission in Glasgow. Eventually the Irish Vincentians agreed to staff a church in Lanark, on the understanding that the Monteiths met whatever costs were not met by the parishioners' pennies. Even John Murdoch was reconciled to the initiative by the assurance that the community would always include one English-speaking priest. Monteith's welcome to the Rosminians was less than fulsome. 'There can be no field more important or more rewarding than Scotland. But the priests who come should be thoroughly good and well equipped men. Pray observe what the bishop says about national prejudices.'[16] Even the Jesuits at St Aloysius – a new church in Charlotte Street – obeyed the stern injunction to pay careful respect to the Scottishness of Scotland.

So an increasing number of Catholic children received a Catholic education. But the number of potential pupils still exceeded the number of Catholic school places. Therefore a combination of necessity and native pragmatism forced the Church to accept that, for some Scottish Catholic children, the alternative to education in state schools was no education at all. 'Catholics in parts of Scotland were so scattered that attendances at mixed or neutral schools was almost inevitable.'[17] But the acceptance of that inconvenient truth required special vigilance, and special measures, to protect young Catholics from the malign influence of heretics, some of whom were making a great effort to encourage apostasy. In late-nineteenth-century Scotland there were still men of influence who – motivated by the combination of racism and bigotry – did all they could to limit the opportunities of the Irish Catholic poor. As late as 1893 (twenty years after the introduction of theoretically free elementary education) Glasgow schools still charged fees. Then the Glasgow School Board was admonished by the Sheriff's Court and instructed to obey the law.

Growing numbers and increasing confidence encouraged the Catholic Church in Scotland to feel, and behave, like a community with obligations to provide its members with more than Mass on Sundays and feast days. The Church set up a network of clubs and societies. All of them were Catholic in name and constitution, and most of them were part of long-standing national or international organisations. But their establishment and expansion in Scotland gave Catholicism a social dimension that increased its strength and durability.

Some of the foundations were for Catholics who wanted to know more about Catholicism. The Children of Mary, the Christian Doctrine Society and the Society of Our Lady of Mount Carmel gave theologically inclined laymen an opportunity to study and understand doctrine and dogma. Less spiritually inclined Catholics could attend the St John's literary and temperance society or the St Margaret's debating society, where the discussions usually concerned the Catholic social obligation. The League of St Sebastian encouraged the belief that the

Pope should enjoy temporal as well as spiritual authority. Other organisations – the Catholic Commercial Association and the Catholic Teachers' Club – brought together Catholic concerns and encouraged the confidence that comes with numbers. But the most important development was the creation of societies with a social dimension.

St Mary's, Glasgow, had sponsored a society for the care of the poor since the beginning of the nineteenth century, but its work was extended across the city by the St Vincent de Paul Society which, by 1854, had seven branches in western Scotland. A Catholic Orphan Institution was established. So was a reformatory, an industry and a rescue home in the care of the Nuns of the Good Shepherd. The Catholic Young Men's Society provided respectable and uplifting ways of passing leisure time – a reading room for when it rained and country walks in more suitable weather. Recreational outings to the coast were arranged. Bands were assembled. And football clubs were founded. Glasgow Celtic and Edinburgh Hibernians both emerged from the Catholic Young Men's Society, and members of their supporters' clubs were required to join the League of the Cross temperance society. Archbishop Eyre contributed to the appeal that preceded Celtic's foundation and became the club's first patron.

The habit of coming together in groups united by a common interest, and the feeling of security which that provided, was bound to lead to the formation of some sort of Catholic political alignment. The one surprise about its emergence is the time it took for Catholics – still, after emancipation, the victims of prejudice and discrimination – to take a serious interest in politics. An attempt had been made, in 1844, to found an organisation that would defend the interests of the Catholic working class. It evolved – without attracting much support or winning any notable victories – first into the Association of St Margaret, then the Catholic Defence Association and then the Catholic Union. But, by the end of the nineteenth century, the defining feature of religious politics in western Scotland was not the way in which the Catholic habit of forming clubs was extended into the battles between and within the parties. It was the age-old campaign to ensure that Catholic children received a Catholic education.

CHAPTER 25

Put Him There. Put Him There

In England the Catholic obligation to the disadvantaged and dispossessed was to be best exemplified by the unlikely figure of Henry Edward Manning, a child of the establishment. From the day of his birth in 1808 he was brought up in wealth and privilege and he found, throughout life, that the doors to promotion and preferment opened as he approached. Although Manning's journey to the priesthood had been swift, his entry into Holy Orders was regarded by Wiseman as the beginning, rather than the end, of his Catholic education. It was to be continued in Rome. He travelled to the Eternal City in the company of George Talbot – the Eton- and Oxford-educated fifth son of a peer – who, like Manning, had been a Church of England clergyman before his conversion. Talbot had been sent to Rome as Wiseman's representative and had almost immediately been appointed a papal chamberlain and was to prove Manning's invaluable ally. During the desolation of his early days in Rome – when he missed the comforting complacency of life as an Anglican vicar and agonised about his nostalgia being a betrayal of his new faith – Talbot reassured him that he had found his true vocation by prophesying that Manning would have a glittering career in the Church of Rome and by arranging regular audiences with the Pope, who, he wrote, treated him 'as a father treats a son'.[1]

Manning's studies at the Accademia Ecclesiastica were made tolerable by the access it provided to books outside his narrow syllabus, but he longed to return to England. He declined to accept the title 'Monseigneur' and the appointment as papal chamberlain but he agreed, with joy and relief, to become the Pope's representative to the British Government when – at the outbreak of the Crimean War in 1853 – the Vatican expressed fears that the religious interests of Catholics, serving at the front, would be compromised.

The Vatican's real anxiety was more about the Catholic Church's *amour propre* than the immortal souls of its followers in the British army. The proposal that priests who followed the colours should be under the command of the Protestant Chaplain General was intolerable. Manning persuaded the War Office that they should answer, directly, to the Commander-in-Chief – also a Protestant, but unlikely to spend much time interfering with the work of Catholic chaplains. Having 'solved' the problem he was sent to resolve, Manning explored an idea of his own. Catholic nuns, sent as nurses to the Crimea, would meet the desperate need for more help in the field hospitals and at the same time demonstrate that it was possible to be both a Catholic and a patriot. But the scheme had to overcome a challenge to the Orders' integrity, which was parallel to the 'indignity' that Catholic chaplains had been spared, thanks to Manning's negotiating skills. The nuns would be under the direct command of Florence Nightingale – a friend of Manning, who teetered on the brink of conversion without ever jumping in. Manning employed what he knew to be a verbal and legal fiction. The volunteer nuns would be 'sent' to the Crimea by their Orders and instructed, by their superiors, to work under Florence Nightingale's supervision.

Almost everything Manning did increased the esteem in which he was held by Rome. Newman, in contrast, seemed to court displeasure. He could not resist expressing controversial opinions, without pausing to think of the consequences. Usually their full meaning was obscured by the employment of complicated metaphors. While visiting the city, he preached a sermon on the subject of English visitors and asserted, 'Rome is no place for them, but the very place in the whole world where Michael and the Dragon may almost be seen in battle.'[2] The Pope – while not being sure what Newman meant to say – was furious that he had said it.

Many of Newman's difficulties were caused by his habit of spreading himself too thinly over too many endeavours. While struggling to found a Catholic university in Ireland and to fulfil his obligations to the Oratory, he had written and published a second novel, *Callista – A Tale of the Third Century*. By then the religious tests that entrants to Oxford and Cambridge were once obliged to take and pass had been abolished. So Newman could add to his other activities toying with the idea of creating Catholic colleges in the two ancient universities. He also accepted, without any apparent qualm, the commission of the Catholic Episcopate to make a new translation of the Bible, which would replace both the Rheims–Douai version and the Challoner revision. The idea was abandoned when it was discovered that a new colloquial edition was already in production under the auspices of the Catholic Church of North America. Newman was naturally hurt and offended when he only found out by chance that his labours were no longer needed. But at least the cancellation of the project saved him from a task so great and demanding that even his selfless devotion and prodigious energy could not have saved him from the ignominy of failure. His detachment from the affairs of the Oratory – his critics called it neglect – had allowed the ambitious Frederick Faber to propose changes to the rules about which Newman was not consulted, and which he would have rejected had he been asked, as English Superior, to give his formal approval. He was particularly opposed to relaxing the ordinance which prevented Oratorians from hearing nuns' confessions. The prohibition was intended to prevent members from spending time outside the Order's house, which was meant to be the centre of their work and worship. But it was elevated, in both London and Rome, into an argument about the nature of mid-nineteenth-century Catholicism. It was an argument that Newman lost. Made fearful for his life and pontificate by the revolutions of 1848, Pius IX had changed from radical to reactionary, and the Church of which he was head increasingly favoured the authoritarian, rather than liberal, tendency. Faber's Ultramontane views were in fashion. Propaganda Fide decreed that the two English Oratories were to be run independently of each other and Faber was made Provost of the Order. The London Oratorians were allowed to hear nuns' confessions. It was not the only cross Newman had to bear. Manning – Newman's partner in a lifetime of rivalry – was on the point of coming home.

When the Pope at last agreed to release him, Manning found himself back in England without a parish or a real purpose. He had long thought of establishing a new Order of priests and in 1856 – without the slightest intention of pouring salt on Newman's wounds – he told Wiseman that he hoped to create 'a sort of Oratory with external connections'. The new community would be modelled on the Italian Oblates and he hoped to set the process in motion by obtaining bodily relics of St Charles Borromeo, the founder of the Order, whose miraculously preserved body he had seen in Milan years before. He had to make do with a phial of the saint's blood, which liquefied from time to time. But on the strength of that acquisition he bought land in Buckingham Palace Road as the site of the Order's London home.

Wiseman either persuaded or instructed Manning to turn his attention to Bayswater, where there was already a half-built church and potential parishioners – immigrants from Galway who spoke little or no English. Years later Manning described the time he spent with the Oblates as the happiest period of his life and claimed that it was a special pleasure to be as much out of sight as if he had been in Australia. The obscurity, welcome or not, was not as complete as he pretended. Inevitably comparisons were made between the Oblates and the Oratorians of Birmingham. In terms of priests recruited and outposts created, the Oblates were almost always ahead. But the Oratorians always excited the most sympathy and support. That was, in part, because of their founding fathers' widely different reputations. Newman was much loved. Manning was regarded as cold, arrogant and guilty of the sin that the English find hard to forgive – ambition.

The Oblates were also anathema to 'old Catholics', who regarded them as socially suspect and, because they included so many converts, prone to excess piety and undue reverence towards Rome. Because they felt uneasy about those priests who joined the Order after a conversion which followed the death of their wives, they spoke of the Oblate living in Widowers' House.

George Errington – Cardinal Wiseman's Coadjutor, appointed successor at Westminster and (by courtesy) Archbishop of Trebizond – would never have condescended to smile at such a joke. He was an austere expert on canon law who was to become Manning's most bitter enemy in a dispute that transcended personalities and, in the end, amounted to a fundamental disagreement about the nature of English Roman Catholicism.

Wiseman had made the mistake of appointing Errington as his Coadjutor in the belief that they could renew the relationship (happy at the time) they had enjoyed when the two men had served together at Oscott – Wiseman as President and Errington as prefect of studies. Then the two men held identical views about the obligation of English Catholicism to adopt Roman custom. Errington insisted in lecturing in Latin. But by the time Wiseman became Cardinal Archbishop, Errington had become Bishop of Plymouth and only agreed to move to London on the strict understanding that he would be given sole charge of diocesan administration. It was a promise Wiseman never kept and probably never intended to keep. For a time Errington accepted Wiseman's habit of casually reversing his decisions. Then the Archbishop intervened in what his Coadjutor regarded as a matter of principle.

During a visitation to St Edmund's seminary, Errington ordered that W. G. Ward, a lecturer in moral philosophy, should limit his teaching to students who were preparing for life, not the Church. There were two possible explanations for his action. One was that regulations, laid down by the Council of Trent, prohibited laymen from teaching students for the priesthood. The other was that Ward was a widower and that he was disqualified by his previous married state. The Pope certainly accepted the second explanation. Wiseman reinstated Ward. The Vatican endorsed the decision with the gratuitous comment that 'It is a most novel objection to anyone engaged in the work of God that he has received a Sacrament of the Holy Church which neither you nor I could possibly receive.'[3] Errington wrote to Rome asking to be allowed to leave the Westminster diocese. The Vatican responded by instructing him to remain Coadjutor, but giving him temporary charge of the Clifton district. The notion that time – and distance from Wiseman – would heal proved categorically wrong.

In 1857, the year in which Errington returned to London, the Pope appointed Manning Provost of the Westminster Chapter. It was a promotion, over the heads of older and more experienced priests, that Wiseman had wished, but not dared, to make. Although the appointment was deeply resented by most of the Westminster clergy, Manning brushed aside both the antagonism and the difficulty of combining his new authority with his role as Father Superior of the Oblates. As Provost, he had to preside over a Chapter that was predominantly 'English Catholic' in outlook, while his Oblates were one of Wiseman's instruments for 'Romanising' the English Church. At the same time Manning was still at odds with Errington, who remained wedded to the importance of correct procedure and orthodox regulation. Manning had made the Oblates answerable to the Cardinal rather than the bishops. When Errington complained that Manning had exceeded his authority, the Orders' rules were changed to make them conform to standard practice. Errington was not satisfied by gestures. Manning and Wiseman had, he claimed, colluded in wilfully breaking the Bayswater trust deed, in order to give the church to the Oblates.

There were times when Manning seemed to welcome unpopularity. He caused offence to many of the clergy by setting out what he, with much justification, regarded as necessary reforms to the organisation of the English Catholic Church. He was particularly critical of the more senior priests, whom he regarded as suitable for saying Mass in country houses and hearing the confessions of Irish immigrants, but unable to cope with the demands of a normal mid-Victorian parish. His remedy was the improvement in vocational education – progress that he hoped to achieve by taking personal control of St Edmund's, by then the Westminster Diocese seminary. Without consulting the President, he appointed Herbert Vaughan – a twenty-five-year-old Oblate – as Vice President and instructed him to review the work of the college.

Herbert Alfred Henry Vaughan might have been expected to sympathise with the 'Catholic nobility' who had once believed that the Church in England belonged to them. His father – a retired colonel – had assumed that his eldest son would follow him into the army before managing the family's estate at Courtfield in Herefordshire. But Herbert was encouraged by his mother – a late convert with all the ardour of recent conviction – to become a priest. Five of his six brothers followed him into the Church. All of his eight sisters became nuns. Vaughan was to become a pioneer of missionary work in North America among the emancipated slaves of the Confederacy, Bishop of Salford, and Manning's heir and successor as Cardinal Archbishop of Westminster. In 1857 his appointment provided living proof that the provost of the archdiocese was firmly in control of the Chapter.

George Errington retaliated against Vaughan's appointment by demanding the removal of the Oblates from St Edmund's and persuading the Chapter to support him. Wiseman overruled them. But the conflict was becoming a crisis. Manning only slightly overstated its nature and severity when he told Wiseman, 'The question [is] whether England shall be organised and assimilated to the living devotions and spirit of Rome or perpetuate itself under its own insular centre.'[4] His greatest concern was that, as in the case of the Oblates in St Edmund's, the Pope – or at least the Pope's representative in the form of Cardinal Barnabo, the Prefect of Propaganda – might be less 'Roman' than the English Ultramontanes and might find for Errington. That raised the terrible spectre of first the English bishops, then the College of Cardinals and eventually the Pope all accepting that Errington had a right to succeed to the Archdiocese of Westminster when Wiseman died. Wiseman affected concern that his Coadjutor was overtaxing his strength and suggested that he should be made a bishop in his own right in some less demanding see. Errington was offered Trinidad. The *Glasgow Herald* announced that the Scottish Hierarchy was at last to be re-established and that Errington would be at its head. A year before the proposed date, he made clear that he would not, under any circumstances, go to Glasgow. Every offer was refused and every suggestion rejected. He could not 'accept anything below what I was removed from. That would endorse the sentence of removal instead of merely submitting to the supreme power from which there is appeal.'[5]

Rome, in the form of George Talbot, hardened Errington's opposition to a move by telling him that the Pope hoped for a speedy and, above all, discreet conclusion to the dispute about his future. But the position was still unclear when, in September 1859, Wiseman suffered a heart attack. Manning warned Talbot that if the succession was not speedily resolved, some of the best men would leave the Westminster Diocese, and Wiseman declared himself sufficiently recovered to travel to Rome. 'You may be certain,' Talbot told him, 'that the Pope will grant you all you wish and that he will desire your Coadjutor to retire.'[6] There followed a flurry of exculpatory letters. Manning wrote to Wiseman refuting the accusation 'of a love of power' and asking (rhetorically) what evidence there was to support the charge that he had 'crossed any man's path, deprived him of any due, sought honours or promotion'. Wiseman told Cardinal Barnabo not to believe that Manning 'governs my diocese and that I see everything through his eyes', then undermined his disclaimer by insisting that it would be foolish 'to keep at a distance ... a man gifted with so many excellent qualities, prudence, learning, disinterestedness, gravity and piety'. Manning, while in Rome for no known purpose, wrote directly, 'I am grateful that Mgr, the Archbishop of Trebizond has, at length, brought the whole subject [of his future] before your Holiness so that I may now place myself, with an entire submission as I did in 1837, at your sacred feet.'

It was by no means clear that the Archbishop of Trebizond – who still believed that his future lay in Westminster – had 'brought the subject' before the Pope. But the Pope brought the subject before him. In March and again in July 1860, His Holiness implored Errington to resign or accept a transfer to Trinidad. All that he would agree to do was, as duty required, accept the Pope's authority and obey his orders. So on July 22nd 1860 a Special Papal Decree was promulgated to deprive Errington of his appointment as Coadjutor of Westminster and to remove all rights of succession. Manning was made Protonotary Apostolic, with unspecified duties, and (according to Talbot) 'gained the approbation of the whole Sacred College'.[7] But although his status was enhanced, his view on the proper role of the Oblates was rejected. In 1861 Propaganda instructed that they leave St Edmund's.

John Henry Newman had reacted to the Errington affair exactly as his critics expected. On one hand, he regretted that the offer of a Scottish see had not been accepted – thus ending a 'great scandal' – but on the other, he could 'quite understand his asking for tongs, shovel and other implements, if he was expected to take the chestnuts out of the fire'.[8] The metaphor might well have come to mind as the result of Newman's own fingers being burned when he attempted, with a new venture, to reassert his authority over what had once been at the heart of his vocation. He had, for some time, advocated the creation of another Catholic public school. The brief in which Rome set out the duties of the English Oratorians instructed them to pay special heed to the educated classes. So the actual proposal to begin work on the project caused neither surprise nor concern.

John (later Lord) Acton – historian and convert – and the Duke of Norfolk endorsed the proposal, and Faber promised neither to frustrate nor interfere with its creation. The school was opened in temporary premises during May 1859 with seven boys on its register. In less than two years the roll had increased to seventy and the governors felt sufficiently confident of success to commission work on a new building. It was then that Newman discovered that Nicholas Darnell, the headmaster, wanted to make it independent of the Oratories and was planning, without consultation, to move to a new site. How well Newman would have dealt with the insubordination remains in doubt, for his disagreement with Darnell over the governance of the school was suddenly overshadowed by a bitter dispute over internal discipline. It concerned compassion. Darnell dismissed the school's matron for the offence of being over-indulgent towards sick and delicate boys. Newman, who opposed the dismissal and applauded the indulgence, refused either to endorse her removal or accept her resignation. The battle that followed was long and bitter. It ended in the departure of Darnell and staff who were sympathetic to his belief in rigorous discipline, the appointment of a new headmaster and that rare event in the history of Newman's many disputes and disagreements – victory.

Newman's next excursion into educational matters (albeit vicarious) was less successful. Indeed it ended in near-disaster. Newman – together with John Acton – had long been a patron of *The Rambler*, an intellectual periodical which, by its very nature, offended Catholics who regarded theological debate as a temptation to heresy. The periodical's editorial policy – typified by articles that examined the relationship between faith and reason, doubted the merits of the Council of Trent's advice on seminaries and speculated about the likelihood of eternal punishment – seemed to justify the fears of and attracted criticism from *The Tablet* and condemnation from the *Dublin Review*. In February 1858 Richard Simpson, the editor, caused particular offence by correcting, on matters of detail, work by various luminaries including Cardinal Wiseman. In January of the following year, offence was replaced by outrage when Simpson published an attack by Scott Nasmyth Stokes on the Catholic bishops' refusal to cooperate with the Royal Commission on Education. The bishops had said that they feared that a secular commission, closely associated with the Established Church, would reach conclusions that undermined the extension of Catholic schools. Stokes revealed that, in truth, the claim that Catholic interests were in jeopardy was a device to hide the real reason for boycotting the Commission. The Catholic Poor School Committee had failed to nominate a Commission member. During the uproar that followed, Bernard Ullathorne asked Newman to obtain Simpson's resignation and provide some sort of guarantee of *The Rambler*'s future good behaviour. Newman decided that the only way he could fulfil both tasks was to become editor himself.

His troubles began with the first issue, which contained an editorial that defended the right of laymen to express opinions on matters of faith and morals. It cited, in support of that view, the consultations which, in 1854, had preceded the assertion of the Immaculate Conception. The precedent notwithstanding, the editorial was denounced as the advocacy of near-heresy. Newman reacted to the uproar with what must have been a conscious decision to compound the offence. In the issue of July 1859 – Newman's third and last – he published the essay 'On Consulting the Faithful on Matters of Doctrine'. It advocated the 'sensus fidelium', the united testimony of all the faithful. That implied that the 'given truth' – the scriptures and apostolic wisdom – was open to discussion and interpretation. *The Tablet* immediately condemned the doctrine as schismatic. Then the synod of English bishops discussed Newman's conduct, without telling him that he was virtually on trial. They criticised his conduct, without passing a vote of censure, but Bishop Joseph Brown of Newport made a formal complaint to the Vatican with the claim that Newman was 'totally subversive of the authority of the church in matters of faith'.[9] Bernard Ullathorne, in Rome at the time, did his best to defend Newman. Nicholas Wiseman and Henry Manning, also in the Eternal City, did not.

Consistency was not one of Newman's defining characteristics. Indeed, his determination to pick and choose in matters of dogma and liturgy was one of the attributes that endeared him to 'Cisalpine' Catholics who regarded themselves, theologically, as 'on the other side of the alps' from Rome. At the height of the *Rambler* controversy, he wrote to the Earl of Shrewsbury about opinions expressed by Augustus Pugin. The letter – which began with the prayer that his Lordship's 'pious and zealous labours for the advancement of religion ... may receive an abundant answer from the Almighty' – was clearly meant to damage Pugin's prospect of future patronage. It did not have the desired effect, but it revealed a side of Newman's character – petty-minded, pompous and self-loving – that the advocates of his canonisation overlook:

Just now the inclosed letter was brought to me which I think your Lordship ought to see. It was written, as you will observe by Mr Pugin, some six months ago, to one of our novices, Mr Caswell; not an intimate friend of his for he addresses him 'Dear Sir', so it is not confidential but to a friend and subject of ours. He does not scruple to tell our novice, and thinks it 'only honest to tell him' that he 'holds the new system', by which he means the architectural tradition of Rome and Italy, 'in nearly as much horror as the principles of

Voltaire, for an architectural heathen' (such as a whole line of Popes) 'is only one remove from an infidel and in his way more dangerous.' This applies not only to the Popes of at least three centuries, but to St Philip, St Ignatius and a host of Saints.[10]

Although selective in his attitude towards authority, it was Newman's nature to want to be at peace with the Holy See. When Ullathorne told him that the Pope was 'much pained' by his conduct, he at once offered to make amends and wrote to Wiseman, still in Rome, asking what clarifications and corrections were necessary to restore his reputation as a loyal son of the Church. Propaganda Fide prepared a list of errors to be renounced, and Newman was told that Wiseman would supervise the recantations on his return. Wiseman either forgot or judged it unwise to pursue the question. Newman was left in limbo. *The Rambler* attempted to make a fresh start by changing its name to the *Home and Foreign Review*. It continued, under Acton, to be the voice of Liberal Catholicism and, as such, was publicly condemned by Catholics of the 'old school'. Newman openly applauded Acton's rebuttal of Wiseman's general condemnation of the magazine and Acton rejoiced that 'for the first time Newman declared himself completely on my side.'[11] The rejoicing was short-lived. When Ullathorne accused the *Review* of heresy, Newman appeared to betray his friend whose editorial policy he had laid down. His reply to Ullathorne endorsed the accusation on the grounds that the bishop had identified 'certain passages which have been condemned by Rome'. Newman, who was rightly believed to be more sympathetic to the *Review*'s position than to Ullathorne's, then betrayed his earlier betrayal. He explained that his apparent denial of his own beliefs was 'an act of obedience not of approval'. The nice distinction lost some of its force when it was discovered that Ullathorne had shown the first letter to Wiseman, as proof of Newman's redemption, and Wiseman had passed on the good news to Rome.

Both the *Dublin Review* and *The Rambler* were written for the Catholic elite – men and women (mostly men) who were interested in doctrine and dogma. *The Universe* – founded in 1860 in the wake of *The Rambler* crisis – was intended for a wider readership. The end of the newspaper tax, the development of printing machinery and the increasing literacy of the working population had all contributed to a rise in popular journalism. Much of it – reflecting the nation's enthusiasm for the Italian Risorgimento – was critical of the Catholic Church's apparent support for the old regimes in Naples, Sardinia and, of course, the Papal State of Rome. Cardinal Wiseman thought it essential to answer the criticism and took, as his example of how the reply could be made, France's *L'Univers*. The President of the Society of St Vincent de Paul recruited volunteers who worked without pay for more than two years on a paper that never included book reviews – a staple ingredient of *The Rambler* and the *Home and Foreign Review* – but specialised in columns of general Catholic interest. One was called 'The Saint of the Week'. At the height of its popularity, *The Universe* had a weekly circulation of almost a quarter of a million copies and boasted a gallery of celebrity contributors: Hilaire Belloc, G K Chesterton, Ronald Knox and Philip Gibbs.

For three years after the *Home and Foreign Review* controversy, very little was heard of John Henry Newman. There was talk of a mental breakdown and rumours of physical collapse, suspicions that he had come to regret leaving the Church of England and suggestions that he had lost his faith completely. Critics attributed the silence to resentment that his intellectual powers were not adequately acknowledged by Rome. Friends claimed that, fearful of being separated from the Church he had come to love, he had decided that keeping silent was the only way in which he could avoid the malign attentions of Propaganda Fide. So he wrote, but did not publish, and he travelled, always in the company of Ambrose St John. Had Newman remained silent for the rest of his life, he would have been remembered – had he been remembered at all – as an interesting curiosity. But sometime between Christmas 1863 and the New Year an event occurred which changed his life and enabled him to achieve hero status. He was sent a copy of *Macmillan's Magazine* for January 1864.

The magazine contained an anonymous review of *The History of England* by Newman's old friend, James Anthony Froude. When Newman read it, he understandably assumed that it was written by a 'young scribe who is making a cheap reputation by smart hits at safe subjects'.[12] In fact the author was Charles Kingsley, Regius Professor of Modern History at Cambridge University, ordained Church of England priest, author of half a dozen historical novels and early convert to Darwin's theory of evolution, which he aimed to popularise by his story of *The Water Babies*. The eclectic nature of his knowledge and beliefs was illustrated by the ease with which he simultaneously served as a chaplain to Queen Victoria and as a founding member of the Christian Socialist Movement. The nature and extent of his learning make it difficult to understand how he could bring himself to write:

> Truth, for its own sake, has never been a virtue with the Roman clergy. Father Newman informs us that it need not, and on the whole

ought not to be; that cunning is the weapon which Heaven has given to the saints wherewith to withstand the brute male force of the wicked world which marries and is given to marriage.

Newman wrote the publishers a letter which forbore to point out that most of the paragraph was meaningless nonsense, but merely administered a majestic rebuke:

There is no reference at the foot of the page to any words of mine, much less any quotation from my writing which justifies this state-ment. I should not dream of expostulating with the writer of such a passage or with an editor who could insert it without appending evidence ... Nor do I want reparation ... I do but wish to draw your attention, as gentlemen, to a grave and gratuitous slander, with which I feel confident you will be sorry to find associated with a name so eminent as yours.[13]

Kingsley first responded by contending that Newman's Church of England sermons revealed that he was always a crypto-Catholic. He then conceded that he might have misunderstood their meaning. There followed what Newman regarded as, at best, only half an apology and, at worst, a further imputation of bad faith. It included the two ambiguous passages 'No man knows the use of words better than Dr Newman' and 'It only remains for me to express my hearty pleasure in finding him on the side of Truth.'[14] After a couple of weeks' argu-ment, a truncated version of the 'apology' appeared in *Macmillan's Magazine*. But Newman was still not satisfied. So, at his invitation, Longmans published a pamphlet entitled *Mr Kingsley and Dr Newman – A Correspondence*. It contained most of the letters they had exchanged and Newman's satirical commentary upon them. The pamphlet became a bestseller, as did Kingsley's counterblast. Newman, in a moment of unbecoming hubris, told Jesuit priest Thomas Harper that the 'sensation which the affair had caused proved that he was still feared'.[15]

Feared or not, Newman was still not wholly trusted. He was suffering the fate of all apostates. Some of his critics suspected that he had never been a true Anglican. Others doubted that he had ever become a true Catholic. Kingsley's review had made the first of those allegations a topic of dinner-table dispute throughout educated England. Newman – not altogether free of the sin of pride in his own purity – determined to combat the growing 'prejudice that [he] was a Papist while [he] was an Anglican'.[16] He told William Copeland, a

Littlemore curate who had remained a faithful follower for twenty years, 'The only way in which I can destroy this is to give my history, and the history of my mind, from 1822 or earlier, down to 1845.'[17] The result was the *Apologia Pro Vita Sua*.

What Newman himself rightly called 'an egotistical matter from beginning to end'[18] began life as a weekly pamphlet. The first of seven issues was published on Thursday April 21st 1864 and caused an immediate sensation. To meet his deadlines, Newman worked sixteen hours a day for almost two months. As well as defending his own record, he made an eloquent plea for theological speculation: 'It is manifest how a mode of proceeding, such as this, tends not only to the liberty, but to the courage of the individual theologian or controversialist.' The *Apologia* – published as a book six months after the first pamphlet appeared – became the most famous theological work of the nineteenth century. There is no evidence that it produced a spate of converts to the Catholic faith, but there is no doubt that it moved mountains. George Eliot's view of religion was made plain when she was asked to describe her approach to the 'three trumpet calls to men – God, Immortality and Duty'. She answered, 'How inconceivable the first, unbelievable the second and yet how peremptory and absolute the third.' Yet, asked to comment on *Apologia Pro Vita Sua*, she replied, 'The revelation of life – how different from one's own, yet with how close a fellowship in its needs and burdens. I mean spiritual needs and burdens.'[19]

The *Apologia* was not the only historically important Catholic document to be published in 1864. In the *Syllabus Errorum*, Pius IX – no longer a political or theological radical – denounced the idea that 'the Church can or ought to reconcile itself with Progress, Liberalism and Modern Civilisation'. Manning regarded that rejection of the modern world as 'among the greatest acts of the Pontificate'.[20] In a fusillade that offended with every shot, he described England as possessing 'the melancholy and bad pre-eminence of the most anti-Catholic, and therefore most anti-Christian, power in the world', asserted that the Pope possessed temporal authority and illustrated his devotion to the world as it used to be by condemning the annexation of the Papal States by the Kingdom of Piedmont. It was his destiny to grow more progressive with age.

Newman flaunted his support for the Risorgimento so openly that it was rumoured he had sent money to Garibaldi, and his disdain for Rome was far too well documented to be dismissed as malicious gossip. When Monsignor Talbot invited him to preach a sermon to Protestants in Rome, Newman seized on the unfortunate assurance that he could expect a more highly educated congregation than was usual in England as justification for the gratuitously offensive reply with which he declined the invitation: 'Birmingham people have souls; and I have neither taste nor talent which you cut out for me.'[21] Newman and Manning had diametrically different convictions on the powers of the Pope and the relationship of the Catholic Church in England and Rome. In the history of English Catholicism, that disagreement was infinitely more important than the disagreement – or possibly misunderstanding – about whether or not Newman should be made a cardinal.

In the autumn of 1862, Manning found a new way of advancing his Ultramontane views. He took over from Wiseman theological control of the *Dublin Review*. The editor he appointed, W G Ward – a layman and Professor of Theology – shared Manning's position in the Catholic spectrum, 'narrow and strong – very narrow and very strong'.[22] Ward had a penchant for the flamboyant, and therefore often offensive, phrase. He dismissed claims that the Church should take a greater interest in social justice with the assertion that 'these men who would liberalise Catholicism would never Catholicise Liberalism'. The *Via Media* he dismissed as a compromise heresy. The *Dublin Review* argued that papal infallibility should be extended to include all pronouncements by the Holy See.

Because of his robust defence of papal authority, Manning was already a favourite of the ultras in the Vatican. In 1863 Talbot had written to Wiseman, 'Manning has come out nobly this year, in Rome. He has gained immensely in the opinion of the Pope and I may say all the Cardinals. They are open mouthed about him.'[23] Increasingly he became their champion against Henry Newman, the man who seemed to personify – though not to lead in any active way – the Cisalpine rejection of absolute subservience to the Holy See.

Newman was not alone in his Gallican heresies. Cardinal Wiseman was being constantly challenged – on questions of faith and morals as well as organisation – by the bishops of his archdiocese. Arguments at bishops' meetings were, he complained, resolved by determining which faction had a majority. Democracy was replacing authority and scholarship. Wiseman was sick as well as old. To the constant threat of a mortal heart attack was added the constant debilitation of diabetes. The argument for nominating his coadjutor and successor was overwhelming and made more urgent, in the estimation of Rome, by the (as it turned out unjustified) suspicion that Errington was planning some sort of coup. But there was a problem.

Henry Manning, the candidate whom Rome strongly preferred, was so unpopular with the English bishops that there were fears that his appointment would lead to an episcopal civil war. Herbert Vaughan, the Vice President of Oscott, was an Oblate and a Manning satrap, but he thought it necessary to tell Talbot that most of the English bishops dismissed the views held by the Provost of their Chapter as 'extreme, exaggerated and contentious'.[24] Manning's reaction to his critics confirmed the allegation: 'It is necessary for the bishops in England to feel the weight of Rome as it was ten years ago for priests to feel the weight of the hierarchy.' Even Wiseman, who increasingly relied on Manning and would certainly have chosen him as his successor, flinched at the thought of the outrage that Manning's nomination would cause.

Cardinal Barnabo's official candidate was Bernard Ullathorne, Bishop of Birmingham. Talbot wrote to Wiseman that 'he has many faults but with them all, he is a good bishop and will not undo your work'.[25] That was his public position. In private Talbot repeated his respect for Ullathorne, as a bishop, but added that the plain-speaking Yorkshireman 'seems to have all the faults of an uneducated man'[26] and expressed the hope that if a formal offer were made, he would not accept it. Wiseman, who wrongly regarded Ullathorne as ringleader of the rebellious bishops, would not even consider him as successor to the archbishopric. Manning, belying his ambitious reputation, did his best to change the Cardinal's mind. There are, he told Wiseman, 'many reasons why the nomination would ensure union among the bishops and peace for yourself'.[27] Wiseman was immovable, but Manning was resolute. In Rome he canvassed for Ullathorne with a vigour that was taken to be motivated by self-interest. Frederick Neve, President of the English College, said that there would be 'no peace as long as Manning is here. He is always scheming.' And so he was. But in the affair of Wiseman's successor, he was not scheming on his own behalf.

At home in England, Manning faced new problems from an old source. The assumption that it was the success of the *Apologia* that emboldened Newman, once more, to challenge authority was almost certainly mistaken. He did not need a stimulus to rouse him into action on behalf of the issues that he felt deeply, and the establishment of a Catholic college in Oxford was high on his list of worthy causes. Manning shared his concern that Catholics in England, who did not wish to enter the Church, were effectively denied higher education, but Newman dismissed the idea of sending them to the Gregorian University in Rome as wildly impractical. In the hope of ending Newman's agitation, Manning brought the question of a Catholic college – at either Oxford or Cambridge – before a formal meeting of the English bishops. They roundly condemned it, as Manning knew they would, and went on to urge Catholic parents to discourage their sons from entering either university. Undaunted, Newman bought five acres of Oxford land with the ostensible purpose of building an oratory.

The oratory proposal was, in itself, controversial since it was assumed that, once created, it would enjoy a close relationship with the godless university. Cardinal Reisarch had been sent from Rome to examine the idea and had visited Oxford without telling Newman. The Cardinal's decision was communicated to the bishops, who passed it on to Newman together with a codicil from Propaganda. The oratory could be established, but Propaganda ruled – in an edict which was to be kept secret from all but the directly affected parties – that Newman was never to live in Oxford. Sceptical about Newman's motives in buying land for an oratory which he could not control, the bishops met again, confirmed their opposition to a Catholic college at either of the ancient universities and wrote to Propaganda with a request for a formal and binding ruling. Manning, unsure that Cardinal Barnabo was in sufficiently robust opposition, made one of the dashes to Rome which – in the travel conditions of the day – were a remarkably frequent feature of episcopal intrigue. His journey was unnecessary. Newman had changed his mind. A Catholic college would be 'impeded in its free actions by a number of petty semi-monastic regulations' and would be 'regarded with suspicion by influential portions of the Catholic body'.[28]

Manning had been in Rome for less than a week when he received news from England that Cardinal Wiseman was dying. It took him sixty-eight sleepless hours to reach London. Manning kept vigil for the three days of life that were left to Wiseman. The Cardinal recognised him once. Colleagues who expressed their admiration for Manning's devotion were told – in one of the moments of brusque frankness that so damaged his reputation – that it was necessary for him to return home in order to avoid the accusation that he was canvassing the cardinals to make certain that he secured the succession. In London, instead of pleading his cause, he totally uncharacteristically took it for granted that he had no hope of becoming Archbishop and spent his time undermining the chances of the candidates who were, in his opinion, least suited to the job.

When William Clifford, Bishop of Clifton, was called to Rome, Manning was near to despair. It seemed that the Catholic Church in England was to be led by a member of the Catholic nobility who was deeply opposed to the principles and practice of the Church's

Ultramontane wing and, worse still, was a friend of John Henry Newman. Manning wrote to Talbot to warn him that Clifford was heavily supported by the Farm Street Jesuits and would, therefore, feel under an obligation to them, once he was in office. Talbot's reply ignored the Jesuit threat but implied, without being explicit, that Manning should be prepared for the worst. As a result, Manning took it for granted that when the Chapter met on March 25th 1865, it would submit one name to Rome for the Pope's approval. And so it did. But it was not William Clifford. The Chapter recommended George Errington.

Pius IX regarded the nomination as an intentional insult. Errington was told of the papal outrage and the English bishops were warned as to their future conduct. New names were canvassed. Lord Palmerston 'let it be known' that the British Government would be content if either Clifford or Thomas Clark of Southwark got the job. Cardinal Antonelli, the Papal Secretary of State, reminded the Pope that Clifford would at least avoid open rebellion by the English bishops. Propaganda at last recalled the undoubted merit of Bernad Ullathorne. Pio Nono, in mock despair, joked that he would have to appoint Talbot – who took the idea seriously, sent the good news to Manning and received (apparently sincere) congratulations in return. He added that Talbot should take over without fear of the future. It was the Westminster Chapter, not the English Catholic Church, that was in open rebellion.

Faced with such a plethora of conflicting advice, the Pope consulted the one authority on whom he could rely. He ordered a month of Masses and prayers, in the hope that they would induce the Holy Spirit to come to his rescue. The much-needed help from on high came at the end of April when the Pope announced, 'I shall always believe that I heard a voice saying. "Put him there. Put him there."'[29] Henry Manning was, it seemed, God's choice.

Impelled by a combination of gratitude and common sense, the new Archbishop prepared to mend fences and heal old wounds. The task was accomplished with greater ease and less embarrassment than he had expected. The old Catholic families emphasised what pleasure his elevation had given them. The bishops and the Westminster Chapter stressed their determination to cooperate. There was no formal message of congratulation from Newman, though he did welcome the evidence that Rome was not distrustful of, and biased against, converts. Manning's suggestion that his old adversary be made a bishop in *partibus infidelium* was brushed aside with the half joke, 'He wants to put me in the House of Lords and muzzle me.'[30] Newman's letter, accepting the invitation to attend Manning's consecration, provides further evidence of his egocentricity: 'I will willingly attend ... on a condition which I will state presently ... A year or two ago, I heard that you were doing your best to get me made a bishop ... Your kindly feelings towards me make it not unlikely that you attempt the same thing now.' Newman would not attend the consecration without Manning's 'pledge to have nothing to do with such an attempt'.[31]

Newman, who thrived on controversy, turned his attention from rejecting the episcopal appointment, which he was not offered, to attacking views that, at least in part, he had previously supported. In the year that Manning was consecrated Archbishop, Edward Pusey – like Newman, a veteran of the Tractarian Movement – published *Eirenicon*. Pusey's contention that the Church of England was, by its theological nature and history, a part of the Holy Catholic Church, and that it was necessary for both Churches to work towards unity, echoed Newman's long-held view. And it might have been supposed that the frequently unorthodox Newman endorsed the complaint that attempts to unite the two communions were being hindered by the extreme views held by Ultramontane converts. The role of the Virgin Mary, interceding for sinners, was given as an example of irreconcilable items of dogma. Newman's published objections to sections of the text were part theological and part linguistic. As usual, his argument turned on a point which, according to taste, could be described as intellectual precision or logic-chopping. 'It is one thing to say that no one is saved without the intercession of the Virgin Mary (meaning simply that she is the intercessor who prays according to the will of her Son and is, therefore, the channel by which his will is carried out) but quite different to conclude from this that without invocation of Mary, nobody is saved.'[32] But his real complaint, expressed in a later open letter to Pusey, was the implication that Ultramontane converts represented the Church. 'They are,' the letter concluded, 'in no sense spokesmen for English Catholics and they would not stand in the place of those who have title to such an office.'[33]

The Ultramontanes were losing patience. 'Poor man, by living surrounded by inferior men who idolise him,' Talbot wrote. Newman never 'acquired the Catholic instinct'.[34] Manning had to be encouraged to stand firm against the 'old school of Catholics'. He was reassured that Talbot would 'stand by' him as he fought the battles that the insular character of his countrymen made inevitable. 'Every Englishman is naturally anti-Roman. To be Roman is to every Englishman an effort. Dr Newman is more English than the English. His spirit must be crushed.' Manning confirmed the analysis: 'He has become the centre of those who hold a low view of the Holy See.' Hostilities intensified.

The two men often fought their battles through surrogates. Manning fired Frederick Neve, the Newmanite Rector of the English College in Rome, and replaced him with an Oblate. A letter, signed by the heads of two hundred 'noble' Catholic families, made no mention of Manning, Oxford or the authority of Rome, but told Newman of their belief that 'every blow that touches you inflicts a wound upon the Catholic Church in this country'.[35] The Rome correspondent of the *Weekly Register* caused great offence by writing what everybody involved knew to be true: The Oxford initiative had been abandoned because of Rome's doubts about Newman's reliability. The fight became so bitter that even the chief protagonists began to fear it would end in mutual destruction. Manning told George Talbot – who had dismissed the petition of support for Newman as the work of men whose proper activity was hunting and shooting – that it was necessary to tread carefully. 'A word or act of mine towards Dr Newman might divide the bishops and throw some on his side ... the chief aim of the Anglicans has been to set Dr Newman and myself in conflict.'[36]

Talbot forbore to say that the conflicting characters of the two men had already guaranteed that the aim had been achieved. Instead he applauded Manning's decision to make overtures to Newman. The approach – though meant to safeguard the interests of the Church – was made in the language of personal friendship: 'It would give me great consolation to know from you anything in which you have thought me wanting in you.'[37] Newman's reply was as sanctimonious as Manning's invitation was devious: 'I wish I could get myself to believe that the fault was my own, and that your words, your bearing and your implications ought, though they have not served, to prepare me for your acts.' It was clear that neither man wanted to make peace. Whether or not Manning gave up the idea of a reconciliation, there and then, he certainly spent little subsequent time attempting one. He had other pressing obligations.

On June 26th 1869 Pope Pius IX announced that he was to convene a Vatican Council. Five years earlier the Pope had invited thirty-four carefully chosen clerics – Manning among them – to consider, in confidence, what should be on the agenda, were there to be a worldwide congregation of the Catholic Church. They had kept the secret until 1867. Then, at a celebration of St Peter and Paul in Rome, the assembled bishops somehow discovered that the great gathering was to be held before the end of the decade. When the news reached Newman in Birmingham he already knew that, whenever it happened, the

Council would be asked 'to recognise and reaffirm the Immaculate Conception, not as throwing doubt on the previous definition but as normalising the ecclesiastical proceeding'.[38] He welcomed that intention as 'showing that the normal mode of deciding a point of faith is a Council not the Pope speaking *ex cathedra*' and hoped that there would be a discussion of reunion with the Eastern Orthodox Church. However, he was apprehensive about the general outcome. He feared that the Ultramontanes 'would push for the Pope's Infallibility and be unscrupulous in doing so'. His hopes were not realised, but his fears were, at least in part, justified.

Unscrupulous though the Ultramontanes may have been, they were certainly open about their ambition. Manning regarded papal infallibility as an article of faith and an essential Catholic weapon in the 'internecine conflict ... between the army of dogma and the united hosts of heresy, indifference and atheism'.[39] He was, however, a moderate as compared with some of the infallibility lobby. Some wanted the definition to cover the Pope's whole life and entire range of activities – including his private correspondence. *La Civiltà Cattolica* (published by the Jesuits of Rome) declared thàt the Pope's thoughts were infallible since, in truth, they were God thinking in him. The rest of the English bishops, with the exception of Robert Cornthwaite – Bishop of Beverley, and Manning's only ally – were Cisalpine moderates. None of them was, or could be, opposed to the principle of infallibility, but some wanted a definition that severely limited the circumstances in which it could be invoked, and others wanted to maintain the façade of unity by postponing the definition to some unspecified date. The English bishops, who had fought hard against their power being expropriated by Wiseman and Manning, did not propose to capitulate to a new threat – 'a wild enthusiasm on the part of the converts and a disposition among the clergy and even the laity to lower the power of the episcopate and a stronger centralisation leading ultimately to a narrow door presented to those who are seeking the Church'.[40]

The Papal Bull *Aeterni Patris* decreed that the Council would open the first of its four public sessions on December 8th 1869 – each of which was to be preceded by long, private, preparatory discussions. There was no indication of how long it would have lasted, had it not been indefinitely suspended on October 20th 1870, a month after the Sardinian troops occupied Rome. Infallibility was scheduled to be discussed during the last session and the Council might well have ended without the subject being settled, had it not been for a 'monster petition' – in part initiated by Manning and signed by 380 delegates – which called for assurances that infallibility would be examined and a definition, of some sort, agreed. That in itself guaranteed that the debates on the subject would be heated, that the lobbying, on the fringes of the Council, would be intense and that the delegates would, at least in private, treat their opponents with scant respect. After Georges Darboy, the Archbishop of Paris, made a passionate speech opposing any definition that would widen the gulf between Catholics and other Christian faiths, Paul Cullen, Archbishop of Dublin and an uncompromising Ultramontane, rejoiced that 'his French pronunciation and bad voice prevented him from doing any harm'.[41]

The Vatican Council provided Vaughan's *Tablet* with an ideal opportunity to demonstrate its complete commitment to orthodoxy. Special supplements were published describing, and claiming to analyse, the proceedings. But the descriptions and analysis were openly biased against cisalpines (who were dismissed as 'disloyal'), and letters supporting a more limited definition of infallibility and the opening of discussions with other faiths were excluded from the correspondence columns. The ultimate proof of its Ultramontane loyalty came with the Sardinian occupation of Rome. *The Tablet* asked its readers to subscribe to its own version of Peter's Pence. More than £2,000 was collected and sent to the Pope, a refugee from Rome while the future of the Papal States was challenged by the forces of Italian nationalism.[42]

English history books are inclined – whatever the author's view on infallibility – to make Manning the hero of the Ultramontane campaign, even though the final definition of infallibility was less comprehensive than he wished it to be. Perhaps he was the moving force behind the scene – cajoling, persuading and sometimes bullying. But a major part in the actual proceedings (perhaps *the* major part) was played by Cullen. To him the supreme and unquestioned authority of the Pope was an indispensable part of Catholicism. Failure by the Vatican Council explicitly to proclaim his infallibility would 'inflict a great wound on the Pope's authority and give a triumph to the heretics and infidels of this world'. The 'most dangerous speech' in support of postponing endorsing a definition was made by Cardinal Guidi, the Archbishop of Bologna. Cullen refuted his arguments, point by point, and later reported that Pius IX 'said he was much obliged to me for having administered castigation to one who had corresponded so badly to his favours'.

Manning certainly made one speech of great power – though its effect may not have been what he intended. He began by identifying himself as the only convert at the Council and went on to argue that it was the uncompromising certainty of Catholicism which made it attractive to followers of more tentative faiths. 'To hold back from defining [infallibility] would be a sign and source of weakness in the Catholic position.'[43] It much impressed delegates who were already on his side. The undecided were alienated by a speech of such passion that the chairman thought it necessary to rebuke him: 'This is not the way in which this affair should be conducted.' It would be wrong to suggest that Manning had so badly overplayed his hand that he prevented the acceptance of the uncompromising definition that he favoured. The Council was always likely to seek unity around a formula that both extreme views could at least tolerate. So it agreed:

> We define that it is a dogma divinely revealed that the Roman Pontiff, when he speaks *ex cathedra*, that is ... by his supreme Apostolic Authority, he defines a doctrine regarding faith and morals ... by the divine assistance promised to him by the blessed Peter [and] is possessed of that infallibility with which the divine Redeemer willed that His Church should be endowed.

Back in England the Liberal Government, undaunted by previous failures, was making another attempt to establish in Ireland a university that – while having the intellectual freedom essential to such an institution – was acceptable to the Catholic Church. Gladstone's Irish University Bill (which, among other provisions, proposed to federate Trinity and Maynooth) had pleased nobody and, after Archbishop Cullen had condemned it as another attempt to impose secular education on a Catholic people, it was rejected by the House of Commons. The coalition collapsed, leaving its leader more time for theological questions. During the summer of 1874 he drafted a pamphlet, *The Vatican Decrees in their Bearing on Civil Allegiance: A Political Exposition*. After much soul-searching and consultation with colleagues – including Lord Acton, who was summoned to Hawarden for the purpose – Gladstone decided to publish. In November 145,000 copies were printed. They were all sold by Christmas.

The preface included the claim, 'It has been a favourite purpose of my life not to conjure up, but conjure down, public alarm.' The images by which he described the developments in the Vatican did little to support that contention. 'The myrmidons of the apostolic chamber' had disinterred the claims of ancient popes, 'like hideous mummies picked out of Egyptian sarcophagi'. The temporal power of the Pope was to be reasserted, 'even if it could only be re-erected on the ashes of the city and amidst the whitening bones of the people', and it would be supported by converts who described themselves as 'Catholic first and Englishmen afterwards'.[44]

Manning, as was only to be expected, replied. In a letter to *The Times* he asserted, with commendable restraint, that nothing prevented a Catholic from holding 'a civil allegiance as pure, as true and as loyal as is rendered by the distinguished author of the pamphlet or any other subject of the British Empire'.[45] In a letter to the *New York Herald* he added that the disagreement was the first incident to interrupt the friendship of forty-five years, and Gladstone, in his next sally – *Vaticanism: An Answer to Reproofs and Replies* – emphasised his refusal to withdraw or apologise, with the gratuitous and ungracious insistence that reconciliation might be possible in heaven but not on earth. He also drew what he hoped would be a damaging distinction between Newman and Manning.: 'If we had Dr Newman as Pope, we should be tolerably safe, so merciful and genial would be his rule.'[46]

Newman's position on the controversy had been set out in a pamphlet entitled *A Letter to the Duke of Norfolk*. It claimed that the Vatican Council's decisions needed to be interpreted by theologians just as 'lawyers explain Acts of Parliament' and that he was unable to accept that 'the ultimate decision rest with any except the general Catholic intelligence'.[47] It ended with the usual suggestion that Ultramontanes – far from being typical of Catholic opinion – were a minority within the Church. He chose to emphasise his point with a particularly offensive metaphor: 'The Rock of St Peter, on the summit, enjoys a pure and serene atmosphere, but there is a great deal of Roman malaria at the foot of it.'

The whole of the Vatican was outraged. The Prefect of Propaganda wrote to Manning with the demand that Newman be censured, and initially received the reply – strange but true – that the Archbishop had not read the pamphlet. He did so at Rome's request and concluded that the offensive sentiments would only be read by the more intellectual Catholics who, by definition, would dismiss them as simple abuse. And he added, in a moment of not altogether characteristic charity, that 'The reverend Father Newman is as right and as Catholic as it is possible to be.' So Newman was not rebuked. Gladstone, on the other hand, was accused of attempting to instigate rebellion against the authority of the Pope and was advised that 'if he would incline the Catholics of the Empire to accept the ministries of his compassion, he must first purify his style of both writing and thinking'. Whatever the cause and date of the first breach in the two men's close relationship, the public argument that followed the publication of the *Vatican Decrees* ensured that it was not healed for another twenty years.

CHAPTER 26

The Very Salt of Life

One of Manning's strengths was his ability – unlike many obsessives – to be obsessive about several subjects at the same time. So, as he was pursuing his destiny to make the Catholic Church in England accept the authority of the Pope, he was also actively promoting a whole series of social aims which could, in any sense of the word, only be described as political. From time to time he certainly made pronouncements which made him sound like an imperialist. He was said to have told Disraeli, 'Having an empire we must either give it up or keep it up. To give it up would be extinction as a power in the world.'[1] That may have accounted for Disraeli changing his caricature of Manning from the obnoxious Cardinal Grandison in *Lothair* to the much more sympathetic Cardinal Penruddock in *Endymion*. But Manning was certainly a social radical. Indeed, his position on Home Rule, the great divide in Victorian politics, was far more progressive than the policy of most of the Liberal Members of Parliament who supported Gladstone's first administration. And, he always insisted, 'I was a friend of Ireland before Mr Gladstone' himself.[2]

Manning's concern for Ireland was built on a combination of compassion and an instinct for natural justice. He told Gladstone that England 'held Ireland by force, not only against the will of the majority but in violation of all the rights, natural and supernatural'.[3] He was happy to admit that he saw the Irish Question as an opportunity for promoting the Catholic Church as a natural and integral part of British society. He told Archbishop Cullen, 'I have never known a more propitious time for making the Government feel that they cannot do without us.' But he felt a deep sympathy for a people who had been pauperised by the Protestant ascendancy. Together with the Irish bishops, he proposed to Gladstone an answer to the 'land question – a somewhat heartless euphemism for hunger, thirst, nakedness, notice to quit, labour spent in vain and the toil of years seized upon'.[4] Their scheme of agricultural reform was very like the 'Three Fs' provision of the Second Irish Land Act: fixity of tenure, fair rents and freedom of sale. But the proposals were ten years ahead of their time. Gladstone described Manning as advocating 'changes which neither the nation, nor the Parliament, nor the Cabinet could adopt. We might as well propose repeal of the Union.'[5]

A diary entry in 1847 records that a serious illness had made Manning 'realise much more than I otherwise should the state of the famishing in Ireland'.[6] But evidence provided by refugees from 'The Great Hunger', encountered during his early years in the Catholic Church, was certainly the most powerful influence on his courageous – some would say reckless – support for a change in Ireland's status from a virtual colony to a self-governing province of the United Kingdom. The cause attracted a wide spectrum of adherents, which ranged from the gentlest of 'Home Rulers' to the Fenians, who believed that violence – the assassination of politicians, the burning of crops and the maiming of cattle – was the only plausible route to independence. Manning's pastoral letter for Easter 1864 denounced Fenian outrages. But it condemned the method by which the revolutionaries pursued their aims, not the aims themselves. And even his condemnation – limited though it was – seemed to contain both the hint of an excuse and the implication that violence was to be condemned as much because it was counterproductive as because it was wrong in itself. He denounced the bloodshed because it 'prevented the necessary reforms which would remove their spawning grounds of discontent'. In his 1868 pamphlet, *Ireland: A Letter to Earl Grey*, Manning challenged the political establishment head-on. Robert Lowe – soon to become Gladstone's Chancellor of the Exchequer – had observed, 'It has been the pleasure of Ireland to pass upon herself a sentence of perpetual poverty.' Manning retorted with a question: 'Who checked its agriculture, its cattle trade, its fisheries and its manufactures by Act of Parliament?' He concluded, 'if poverty has ever been inflicted on one party by another it has been inflicted on Ireland by England'. Greater offence was to follow. In 1869, he repeated to a group of Fenianists the message of his 1864 pastoral letter: agreement with the objective but rejection of the means. Charles Newdegate, MP, asked the House of Commons, 'Is this not aiding treason?'

Although Manning could claim that he rarely, if ever, deviated from the pursuit of his boldly defined principles, there were wild inconsistencies in the choice of measures by which he advocated they be implemented. His initial opposition to the 1870 Education Act was based on the fear that state intervention in the provision of elementary schools would undermine the essential requirement of Catholic teaching for Catholic children. But he chose to extend his objection to all that he called government 'intrusion' into what, at the time, he chose to define as essentially private responsibilities. 'The English people ought to educate themselves with such state aid as individuals require. The state did not create our commerce or our empire. The intelligence and will of the people did all these things.'[7] Yet, when he became a member of the Royal Commission on the Housing of the Working Class – sitting alongside the Prince of Wales – he advocated public intervention in the private relationship between landlord and tenant: 'Some authority might be provided to decide what is extortionate rent.'[8] And he advocated statutory limitation of the working day: 'If the hours of labour, resulting from the unregulated sale of a man's strength and skill shall lead ... to turning fathers and husbands into creatures of burden ... the domestic life of man exists no longer.'[9] There were times when his convictions were in conflict with each other. Henry George – the American advocate of land reform – was sternly told that 'the law of property is founded on the law of Nature, sanctioned in Revelation, declared in the Christian law and taught by the Catholic Church'.[10] But Manning robustly opposed – eventually with success – the Vatican's attempts to have George's work included in the 'index' of forbidden work.

Although his policy pronouncements lacked a unifying theme, his public assertions of moral obligation – in both sermons and speeches – invariably included the duty of providing succour and support for the labouring poor. Sympathy with the depressed and destitute had been a theme of his Lavington sermons during his days as a Church of England vicar. When Manning achieved the eminence – and could speak with the authority – of a Catholic bishop, he developed the idea into a series of lectures on the Christian attitude towards the working man. His 1874 address to the Leeds Mechanics' Institute on 'The Dignity and Rights of Labour' was explicitly critical of 'the accumulation of wealth in the land, the piling up of wealth like mountains in the possession of classes or individuals'.[11] His lectures, in 1880 on 'The Catholic Church in Modern Society', and in 1891 on 'The Rights and Dignity of Labour', described the conflict in a modern industrialised society and – again abandoning his earlier objection to state interference – called for legislation to remedy the discrepancy between the powers of masters and men. On January 25th 1891, he set out why he regarded it as essential for the Catholic Church to be on the side of labour rather than capital. 'The coming age will belong neither to the capitalists nor to the commercial classes, but to the people. The people are yielding to the guidance of reason, even of religion. If we can gain their confidence, we can counsel them. If we show them blind opposition, they will have the power to destroy all that is good.'[12] It is not necessary to endorse Manning's analysis to accept that, whatever the reason, he was on the side of the masses rather than the classes.

Manning's determination to make Catholic working men and women feel that the Church belonged to them (as well as that they belonged to the Church) made him break new ground on which his predecessors would not have dared or condescended to set foot. One of his more successful initiatives was the foundation of the *Catholic Herald*. It began life, in 1884, with the avowed intention of promoting 'Catholic Industrial Democracy' and, to further that objective, published local editions in all the large industrial towns. It maintained that role and character for more than fifty years before it turned its attention to news – home and foreign – but always reported from a Catholic perspective. Manning would have approved of its extensive correspondence column as a sign of the respect in which it held its readers.

The Catholic churchmen who feared that concern for improving life on earth would sometimes deflect attention from the hope of life hereafter found cause for much anxiety in Manning's criticisms of the condition of the poor in Victorian England. His social conscience – combined with his observation of life in the city slums – made him thoroughly unreliable on the subject of original sin. 'The bloated and brutal man, if he had been nurtured by a loving mother in a house fit for man to live in, if he had grown up in the consciousness of Divine law and presence, if he had lived in honest labour ... would not have become the wreck in body, mind and speech which we may see in our streets every day.'[13] But he was far too rigid a Catholic ever to espouse a cause that was in conflict with his faith. He would have claimed that everything he did was inspired by his religion. The long campaign to save children from life on the streets cannot be separated from the campaign to ensure that young Catholics received a Catholic education.

There were influential laymen in the diocese who did not share the Archbishop's view that the first call on whatever funds the Church was able to raise should be an assault on the parallel evils of child poverty and secular education. Ever since the restoration of the Hierarchy, powerful voices had been raised to demand the creation of a metropolitan cathedral which celebrated and proclaimed the fact of the Catholic Church's status as an established part of English society. On May 25th 1865, Henry Manning – the recently appointed Archbishop of Westminster – told a public meeting, 'The See of Westminster needs a Cathedral proportionate to the chief diocese of the Catholic Church of the British Empire.'[14] Enthusiasts for a great new basilica reinforced their argument with the proposal that it should be dedicated to the memory of Cardinal Wiseman, the man who had presided over the Second Spring. A building fund was set up and within weeks it had raised £16,000. But Manning – despite his earlier protestations – was not prepared to allow building a cathedral to become the Church's first financial priority. 'Could I leave 20,000 children without education and drain my friends and my flock to pile up stones and brick?'[15] He did, however, prepare for the physical manifestation of a reinvigorated Catholic Church by buying the land on which the stones and bricks would one day be piled. Two sites – on either side of Carlisle Place in Victoria – were bought by the Church. They lay fallow for fifteen years. Then they were exchanged for the land in nearby Tothill Fields on which the old Middlesex County Prison had stood. It was another fifteen years before Westminster Cathedral was consecrated. By then, both Manning and his successor were dead, and not one Catholic child remained in a Board of Guardians workhouse.

On June 6th 1866, the first anniversary of his consecration as bishop, Manning issued a pastoral letter devoted to education. It proposed that a Westminster Diocesan Fund be set up to finance the provision of Catholic education for children without schools who had broken the law and were confined in reformatories, and the thousand or more from the Westminster Diocese who were in workhouses or the few 'ragged schools' that existed in the capital. Within a year, £7,855 was raised and twenty new schools opened. But the initiative – ambitious as it was, and as successful as it seemed likely to be – was overtaken by the Education Act of 1870. The Forster Act (so called because of the Vice President of the Council whose work it was) aimed at augmenting rather than replacing the traditional school system. In England elementary schools had, for years, been provided by the Churches, which received small grants from the Privy Council as a contribution towards the education of pauper children.

The idea of state-provided secular education had been considered in 1850 and abandoned because of the Churches' hostility. Forster hoped to disarm the opposition to state provision by leaving untouched the denominational schools that were working well. Where they did not exist – or where they were clearly inefficient or inadequate – school boards were to be created with powers to levy a rate, set up schools and employ teachers. Grants to efficient denominational schools were to be increased. The churches were provided with further reassurance by an amendment to the bill, which forbade the religious instruction provided in so-called board schools to include any 'catechism or religious formulary distinctive of any denomination'. Not all the Churches were persuaded. Bishop Bernard Ullathorne of

Birmingham urged the Catholic Churches of England to boycott the new system.

Ullathorne made his position clear in a pastoral letter in October 1870: 'We are left then to make the choice, whether we will establish and support sufficient schools and teaching of our own for our own Catholic children or whether, through our neglect, we are to leave our children under the compulsion of having to attend schools in which they either learn no religion or a teaching which is in opposition to the catholic religion.'[16] He strongly supported the heroic alternative. But the idea that the Catholics of England could raise the funds adequately to educate all their children was clearly unrealistic. The Act gave denominations six months to provide schools where previously none existed. Then board schools would fill the gaps. Manning argued, simultaneously with the government, for an extension of the period of grace and – with the large majority of English bishops – against ignoring the demands of the Forster Act. His argument in favour of negotiating a more acceptable arrangement – ideally Catholic schools continuing to receive grants direct from the Privy Council – was pragmatic, but also deeply revealing about Catholic educational priorities. If the Church acted as if the Act does not exist, 'the Boards may destroy our lesser schools by reporting them as insufficient or inefficient.'[17] He estimated that half of London's Catholic schools would be forced to close and would be replaced by board schools. What he accepted was that less-than-adequate schools were to be protected and preserved because they were Catholic. T P O'Connor, MP – writing, in 1905, about the Liverpool Catholic Church's attitude to its schools – explained, perhaps even defended, what he called 'the quality deficit':

> Honest religious conviction was the very salt of the life of any nation and it was through such convictions that Catholics preferred their own, poor, and often squalid schools wherein they were taught their own faith, to the well endowed, well equipped schools that they might have used during the past thirty five years.[18]

There was partisan disagreement as to whether the outcome – grants direct from the Privy Council, though less than the school boards would have provided, and the preservation of existing Catholic schools, whatever their quality – was the consequence of the threat of a boycott or the result of a willingness to negotiate. Both sides of the argument – one wishing to praise and the other to blame – agreed that an even more satisfactory outcome would have been obtained, had Manning not been in Rome during the early stages of the bill's discussion.

The passion to guarantee a Catholic education for Catholic children – or, at least, to ensure that they were protected from exposure to the corrupting influence of secular schools – was regarded as admirable by priests and laymen alike. But there was also the feeling, among more traditional Catholics, that Manning wasted his time and risked the Church's credibility by the championing of other, more outré, causes. Amongst the least popular was temperance – not moderation, but total abstinence. In 1868 he had publicly called on William Gladstone, the Prime Minister, to 'control the terrific domination of Brewers, Distillers and publicans'.[19] The failure of the 1871 Licensing Act drove him to the brief conclusion that the only way to defeat the vested interests was legal prohibition. Calmer consideration convinced him that personal example and public exhortation were the better course. In 1872 he 'took the pledge' and founded the League of the Cross. Members swore a holy oath to attend Mass every Sunday and to resist, for ever and completely, the temptations of the demon drink.

Manning never found it easy to follow any of his favoured causes with moderation and discretion, and the zeal with which he campaigned for total abstinence was – obliquely and vicariously – to inflict permanent damage on his reputation. The story was told by Herbert Vaughan after Manning was dead and his Ultramontane protégé had succeeded him as Cardinal Archbishop. Vaughan thought it necessary to explain, to his private secretary, why he had felt obliged to decline an invitation to the Annual Dinner of the Manchester and Salford Licensed Victuallers' Association. He had attended one 'a few years before, much to Cardinal Manning's disgust',[20] and had been the subject of a severe reproof from his mentor:

I could not accept his views and I suppose, on the contrary, strongly maintained my own. I saw he was a bit put out – but what do you think he did? He went upstairs, took out his will and struck out my name as executor. It was a mistake. If I had been his executor, his private papers would never have fallen into the hands of Mr Purcell.

Edmund Sheridan Purcell was the author of the scurrilous biography on which Lytton Strachey based the brilliant but wildly prejudiced first essay in *Eminent Victorians*. In consequence, outside the Catholic Church – and sometimes inside it – Manning is best remembered for the part he played, or failed to play, in John Henry Newman becoming a cardinal.

The story cannot be separated from the continuing dispute about how Catholics should face the challenges of science and scepticism. Although Newman has gone down in history as the theologically more progressive, there were many occasions when their conflicting view of life – hopeful versus pessimistic – made Manning the more radical. Manning argued strongly for the disestablishment of the (Protestant) Church of Ireland as essential to reconciliation of the two religious communities. When it happened, Newman saw it as proof of secularism's irresistible advance. He was, however, undoubtedly less rigid about respect for papal authority. In 1878, Leo XIII's election to succeed Pius IX was greeted by much rejoicing among the Church's 'liberal' tendency, and their optimism about the nature of his pontificate seemed to be confirmed by a letter which he published soon after his election. A statement of papal policy was, in itself, unusual. A declaration of determination to work for reconciliation of Rome and the modern world was unique. Newman described the letter as 'most excellent' and wrote that he had 'followed, with love and sympathy' the newspaper accounts of the new Pope's 'every act'.[21] Herbert Vaughan, by then Bishop of Salford, prepared for the fight against liberalism by acquiring the ownership of the *Dublin Review*.

The new Pope seemed as pleased with Newman as Newman was with the new Pope. In January 1879, Manning received, from the Papal Secretary of State, a letter which asked him to discover how Newman would respond to an invitation to join the College of Cardinals. It more or less crossed in the post with a letter from Bishop Ullathorne to the Vatican which reported that the new Duke of Norfolk – nephew of the man who had left the Church in protest against the Flaminian Gate encyclical – was pressing for Newman's elevation. A second letter – direct from Duke to Pope – confirmed that a group of influential English Catholics supported the idea. 'In the rise and revival of the Catholic Faith in England, there is no one whose name will stand out in history with greater prominence.'[22] There is no doubt that Norfolk and the men on whose behalf he wrote all felt both admiration and affection for Newman. But it is equally certain that they saw the award of a red hat as papal endorsement for a brand of Catholicism that Manning regarded, at best, as unorthodox.

Ullathorne urged Newman to accept. But Newman – knowing that cardinals who were not diocesan bishops were required to live in Rome – chose to reply that he hoped to end his days in the Oratory. He did not mean to reject the offer. Indeed he asked Ullathorne to send his letter to Manning with a covering note which made clear that he would gladly accept the honour if he were allowed to remain in Birmingham. But to other Catholic luminaries he gave the impression – and probably meant to give the impression – that he would decline. He had emphasised his selfless opposition to promotion for years. As early as February 3rd 1851 he had written to Talbot, 'there has been a report [for] some time that my name has been sent to Rome for one of the Sees. We thought nothing of it until it appeared in one of the leading articles in the *Tablet*. We are all of us in a great fright about it.'[23]

After ten years of protestation that Newman wished for nothing but to be left alone and cared nothing for status and rank, Manning can hardly be blamed for taking the refusal letter at its face value and sending it on to the Vatican without the covering note. A flurry of correspondence followed. Manning wrote to Newman to tell him that the proposal was the result of Norfolk's initiative. Newman replied with an explanation of his reservations. A letter from Manning to the Duke informed His Grace that Newman had declined the honour. Bernard Ullathorne, discovering that rumours were circulating about Newman's rejection of the Pope's proposal, sent a copy of the original covering letter direct to the Vatican. *The Times*, source unknown, published the news of Newman's decision to choose Birmingham rather than Rome. Newman rushed to assure the Duke that *The Times* was wrong. But he was still not ready to admit, outright, that what he wanted was elevation on his own terms. 'As to the statement of my refusing a Cardinal's hat which is in the papers, you must not believe for this reason ... If so high an honour were offered me, I should not answer with a blunt refusal.'[24] Linguistic analysis of the sort that Newman employed would have focused attention on the qualifying adjective 'blunt' and would have asked what sort of refusal he would have chosen.

Newman had no doubt that the rumours about his refusal had emanated from Manning but, instead of contradicting them, answered all enquiries with the technically correct but ambiguous statement that, not having received a formal offer, there had been no opportunity to either accept or decline. However, the more he thought about it, the more he wanted to become a cardinal. He was not, he assured himself, motivated by pride or lust for fame and glory. Indeed, such base considerations never influenced his judgement. His only concern was, as he made clear when the furore had died down, the welfare of the Church that he served:

For 20 or 30 years ignorant or hot-headed Catholics had said almost that I was a heretic ... I knew and felt that it was a miserable evil that the One True Apostolic Religion should be slandered as to cause men to suppose that my portrait of it was not true. And I knew that many would become Catholics, as they ought to be, if only I was pronounced by Authority to be a good Catholic.[25]

Another round of letters began with the Duke of Norfolk writing to Manning, by this time once more in Rome. The Duke wanted to know who had told the Pope that Newman did not wish to become a cardinal. He assumed that, knowing the facts, Manning would tell His Holiness of Newman's true position. Manning accepted responsibility for the confusion – which he promised to rectify – but insisted that it had been the genuine mistake of a friend. In March 1889, Newman received a message from the Vatican. The Pope proposed to make him a cardinal and the rule, which required him to live in Rome, would be waived. Of course he accepted. But he still found it necessary to make clear that he did so with some reluctance. His second explanation, unlike the first, revealed that, as was so often the case, self-esteem was a major influence on his behaviour:

A good Providence gave me the opportunity of clearing myself of former calumnies in my Apologia ... And now he gave me a means ... to set myself as regards new calumnies ... How could I neglect such a loving kindness?[26]

Newman's elevation was celebrated in London with ecumenical rejoicing. There were evening receptions at Norfolk House, which began on May 10th and went on – during every weekday evening – until the 16th. As is to be expected, the now faded guest lists contained the names of most of the Catholic aristocracy: the Earl of Gainsborough, Lord Lyons, Lord and Lady Talbot.[27] But the presence of the Dean of St Paul's and the Bishop of London must have come as a surprise to the ardent Protestants in the capital. It can only be attributed to the near-universal esteem in which Newman was held. But it does not explain *why* he was held in such widespread regard.

There are a series of wildly different, and sometimes conflicting possibilities. His conversion – as well as making him a hero to Catholics – combined with his wilful espousal of controversy to give him the aura of celebrity. But there are other, more substantial, reasons for his lasting fame. The Church that he joined was notable for clerics who – notwithstanding their command of Greek and Latin – wrote ugly English. Newman's prose, although florid and convoluted, showed a respect for the language. A graduate seminarian in the English College in Rome believed that Newman's lasting importance lay in his demonstration that it was 'possible to ask questions without being a heretic'. A related and more usual explanation of his theological significance is his conclusion on the subject of conscience.

In *A Letter to the Duke of Norfolk* Newman discussed the relationship of, and possible conflict between, conscience and ecclesiastical authority. Conscience, he wrote, is the will of God as 'apprehended in the minds of men'.[28] It may suffer some 'refraction [i.e. differences of interpretation] as it passes through those minds, but that should cause neither distress nor surprise – as witness arguments between the saints'. In his Epistle to the Galatians (2:11) Paul wrote, 'when Peter was come to Antioch, I withstood him to the face for he was to be blamed'. Peter and Paul – disagreeing about the necessity of the early Christians respecting Judaic law – provided a perfect example of conscience in action. 'Conscience is not a judgement upon any speculative truth, any abstract judgement but bears immediately on something to be done or not to be done' and cannot therefore 'come into direct collision with the Church's or Pope's infallibility'. However, for conscience to justify defiance of authority, it must be guided by 'serious thought, prayer and all available means of arriving at a right judgement'. If those conditions are met, conscience should prevail. Newman expressed his view on the right order of priority in language that excited his devotees, infuriated his critics and ensured his notoriety. 'If I am obliged to bring religion into after-dinner toasts, which indeed does not seem quite the thing, I shall drink – to the Pope if you please – still, to Conscience first and the Pope afterwards.'[29]

Newman's gentle bravura certainly antagonised his theologically more reticent colleagues, but there is no way of knowing if Manning's failure to pass on Ullathorne's covering note was the product of malice, carelessness or the determination that theological deviance should not be publicly rewarded. The idea that it was prompted by malice is reinforced by the knowledge that Manning and Newman were divided by more than their rival views on the authority of the Pope. Manning was precise and direct in thought and speech. Newman was diffuse in both. He was also consciously and overtly unworldly. Manning regarded involvement in the secular controversies of his time as not so much an option as a duty. It was a duty which he discharged with such constant enthusiasm that even *The Tablet* – a consistent supporter of Manning's view on Catholic orthodoxy – admitted that, although it was impossible to separate 'his work for the world from his work for the Church', there was increasing concern about what it described as his 'state socialism'.[30] Even his closest friends – commenting on the subsequently lauded intervention in the London dock strike of 1889 – admitted to the 'uneasy feeling that it would have been better had the peacemaker been another'.[31] It is unlikely that 'another' could have done it.

In the spring of 1889, the recently unionised London dock workers had made a claim for improved wages and terms of employment – an increase in basic pay from four pence to six pence an hour and a guaranteed minimum of four hours' work for casual labour hired on the dockside. The claim was not so much rejected as ignored by the employers, and the union – motivated by pride as well as concern for its members' standard of living – announced that, unless its demands were met, a strike would close the docks from August 14th until whenever the men's legitimate grievances had been remedied. The employers did not respond and the strike began. After a week of paralysis, during which the employers waited for hunger to drive the men back to work, and the union called for a general strike in support and sympathy, Manning decided to intervene – not in the interest of the striking dockers, but to avert the national catastrophe which he feared would follow. If a 'drunkard or madman' had set fire to the warehouses, 'the commercial wealth of London and the merchandise of the world, the banks and wharves of the Thames might have been pillaged'.[32] To avert the 'unimaginable loss', he determined to act as mediator and conciliator.

Ben Tillett, the dockers' leader, was not a religious man. His most famous recorded reference to matters even obliquely concerned with faith was a remark he made during a subsequent dock dispute. Exasperated by the chairman of the London Port Authority, he prayed, 'Oh God strike Viscount Devonport dead.'[33] But he had been in earlier correspondence with Manning about the deprivations suffered by his members, and it was to Tillett that the Cardinal made his first unsolicited approach. Tillett could not be moved towards abandoning the strike or even seeking a compromise. Indeed, he argued his case with such passion that Manning was convinced of the righteousness of his cause. Pressure had to be exerted on the employers.

The President of the London Chamber of Commerce did not reply to Manning's letter. A joint meeting of the dock companies' directors – which Manning attended without invitation – rejected his overtures. The Home Secretary and the Lord Mayor (from whom he hoped to gain support) were both on holiday. So Manning set up his own Conciliation Committee. Its members included William Temple, Bishop of London, and Sydney Buxton, the Labour Member of Parliament for Poplar. They proposed, as a compromise, that the employers should accept the union's proposals but not implement them until March of the following year. Tillett accepted the postponement of the new terms, but insisted that that they must be put in place in January 1890. The employers were persuaded to agree. But the rank-and-file of the union – claiming that some of the smaller companies had already accepted the original demands – refused to countenance anything except immediate and complete capitulation.

Tillett, hotfoot from a rally of his members in Hyde Park, called on Manning with the news that October 1st was the latest date for the new agreement that there was any chance of the dockers accepting. Manning was not ready to admit that he could not reconcile management and men. So he asked Tillett's permission to address the strike committee. Out of respect for the teetotal Cardinal, the meeting took place in Kirby Street Elementary School rather than at Wade's Arms, the strike committee's headquarters. After four hours of argument it was agreed – by twenty-eight votes to fifteen with six abstentions – to accept November 4th as the starting date. It took four more days to convince the employers that the deal served their best interests. But on September 14th 1889 the London dock strike was over. Manning received a message of congratulations from the Pope and the assurance, from the *Daily Telegraph*, that his behaviour had helped to rehabilitate Catholics in the estimation of the British public. The grateful dockers raised £160 to endow a bed in the London Hospital and emblazoned Manning's portrait on one of the banners which they paraded in the May Day march. It swung in the breeze alongside the more traditional representation of Karl Marx.

Manning, growing old, increased his public involvement in political affairs. He first refused to believe that Charles Stewart Parnell was an adulterer and then, when the courts had confirmed that Katharine O'Shea was his mistress, called for Parnell's resignation as leader of the Irish Party. His interference in Irish affairs did not end there. Fearful that William Walsh, the Archbishop of Dublin – a passionate supporter of Home Rule – would rally to Parnell's defence, Manning told him, 'This is the supreme moment to convince Rome that you do not put politics before faith and morals.'[34]

That was the impertinence of an octogenarian who had outlived his days of sober judgement. But even in old age he retained the passion for social justice that was as much the product of a cool appraisal of the interests of the Catholic Church as it was of his instinct for compassion. Manning's concern for the working poor was part of a movement in the worldwide Catholic Church that contributed to its success and survival in the secular and sinful twentieth century. In France, Action

Catholique de la Jeunesse Française argued that Catholicism was the faith of cooperation and community, not individualism. In the United States of America, Cardinal Gibbons of Baltimore gave such determined support to the Knights of Labour – an organisation of Catholic trade unionists which the Vatican' attempted to condemn as heretical – that the plan was abandoned. The instincts of the Church's more radical members had been elevated into a philosophy by Professor Francesco Nitti of Naples University, who had published *Il Socialismo Cattolico*. But the most compelling evidence to support the view that times were changing was the election of Leo XIII. The new Pope had a long history of involvement in the social problems of the diocese of Perugia.

On May 15th 1891, Pope Leo XIII published *Rerum Novarum – Revolutionary Change or The Rights and Duties of Capital and Labour*. It was a proclamation of the Catholic duty to ameliorate 'misery and wretchedness pressing so unjustly on a majority of the working class'. It asserted that 'the interests of all, whether high or low, are equal' and that a fair day's work should be rewarded with a fair day's pay. It had much to say about freedom of worship and freedom from oppression. But its most controversial, and therefore most memorable, paragraphs concerned the rules of free collective bargaining. 'Let the working man and the employer make free agreement and in particular let them agree freely to wages.' But as Adam Smith and Karl Marx both made clear – and as William Gladstone recognised in the Second Irish Land Act – an agreement between parties of unequal strength is rarely free. 'If, through necessity or fear of worse evil, the workman accepts harder conditions [than are fair and just] because his employer or contractor will afford him no better, he is made victim of force and injustice.' *Rerum Novarum* was clear how that injustice should be remedied. It identified within 'civil society . . . private societies' through which men and women organised and managed their daily lives. Some of them would have evil objectives. The Pope did not intend to allow the suspicion that he endorsed Freemasonry. But most of the private societies were both benevolent and beneficial and 'the most important of these,' pronounced *Rerum Novarum*, 'are the workmen's unions, and it is greatly desired that they should become more numerous and more effective'.

Manning's friends insisted that without his influence there would have been no *Rerum Novarum*. That was certainly an exaggeration. There had been discussion about the Catholic Church's obligation to the working man at the Congress of Mainz in 1848 – two years before his conversion. But Manning certainly helped, by example and exhortation, to stir the Church's social conscience. And he demonstrated that to hold an Ultramontane view of papal authority was neither incon-sistent with a social conscience nor incompatible with scepticism about the legitimacy of the authority that comes with secular power and worldly wealth. After his death, the Ultramontane tradition survived at Westminster thanks to Herbert Vaughan, Manning's protégé and successor as both Archbishop and Cardinal. But the social conscience of the diocese faded and almost disappeared. *The Tablet*, outflanking even Vaughan's position, combined denunciation of what it called 'Cisalpine disloyalty' with antagonism to social and political reform. It abandoned its traditional support for Home Rule (thereby acquiring a reputation for being 'anti-Irish'), insisted that maintaining the reli-gious character of existing Catholic schools was more important than an overall expansion in elementary education, and opposed women's suffrage.

Vaughan's unbending nature, as well as his theological orthodoxy, was illustrated by his attitude towards St George Jackson Mivart, a distinguished biologist and Catholic convert. Mivart believed that the Catholic Church was increasingly exposed to advances in all the sciences, which would lead to a loss of faith unless they were accom-modated. In particular he warned against the outright rejection of evolution. He developed his own version of the theory. It endorsed the Old Testament story of creation, but God – having created Adam and Eve – allowed natural selection to influence the physical development of their issue. Mivart's extreme view on social questions (he described proposals to make cruelty grounds for divorce as 'hideous sexual criminality ... unrestrained licentiousness') did not save him. His scientific work was placed on the *Index Expurgatorius* and Herbert Vaughan, by then a cardinal, asked for written assurances that Mivart accepted the Church's teaching in every particular. When Mivart refused to supply them, Vaughan forbade him to take Communion. He died excommunicate.

Manning had done his best to impose his posthumous will on Herbert Vaughan. He had urged his assumed successor to be 'more human and less ecclesiastical', told him that he would be 'a better Christian when his sympathies were capable of being enlisted in causes which had no concern with his work' and urged him 'not to let the Old Testament close over you and bury you in the sacristy'.[35] By 'Old Testament', Manning meant the Catholic gentry from which Vaughan came. Vaughan shared the 'Old Testament' view that building a metro-politan cathedral as 'a symbol of Catholic resurgence, a visible monu-ment to the triumphalism of the ultramontane church', was a duty that outweighed other obligations.

The obligation to provide a Catholic education for Catholic children was fulfilled by Vaughan taking an admirably pragmatic view of the 1902 Education Bill. The extension and improvement of the Forster Act raised the predictable complaint that the government was making yet another attempt to impose Church of England education on the whole nation. David Lloyd George led a nationwide Nonconformist campaign which, he assumed, would make his name and bring down the government. His first ambition was realised, the second was not. Vaughan described the new Act as 'a large and important advance' and rejoiced that it would 'make Christian and Catholic education a part of the law and constitution of England ... Our hope for the future lies in our schools and our schools can never be self supporting. The idea that we in England could ever hope to throw off state aid and maintain effective schools, such as the government would recognise as efficient, out of our private means is pure chimera.'[36] Lloyd George's fury was increased with the discovery that Vaughan had told the Irish Members to stay in London during the summer recess to ensure the passage of the bill.

The Westminster Cathedral foundation stone was laid, with suitable pomp and ceremony, on Saturday June 29th 1895. Even those who supported the project greeted the occasion with as much apprehension as joy. The Catholic Church had chosen to prove that it was strong enough, sufficiently rich and possessed the organising ability to construct a basilica that stood comparison with the great cathedrals of the world – all of which had taken centuries to build. And Vaughan had announced that he hoped to finish the Westminster work in five years and guaranteed that it would take no longer than eight.

Vaughan originally intended that the cathedral's architect should be determined by a competition which only Catholics would be allowed to enter. But the pressure of time, combined with a host of recommendations, induced him to appoint John Francis Bentley without even considering rival candidates. Bentley was already the architect of a dozen London Catholic churches – the Sacred heart in Hammersmith, St Mary's in Cadogan Square and Corpus Christi in Brixton. He was, however, open to suggestions from his employers. During the years in which the site of the old prison lay fallow, it had been assumed that what was needed was a church of 'ancient Basilica style, taking Constantine's Church of St Peter in Rome as the model',[37] and Bentley travelled to Italy to find inspiration. But Vaughan decided it was unwise to invite comparison with the ancient cathedrals of England and insisted on a 'combination of a Roman Basilica with the constructive improvements introduced by the Byzantine architects'.

Most of Vaughan's hopes were unfulfilled. The cathedral was not finished in eight years. Indeed, it is not finished yet. Work was delayed by a bricklayers' strike, and the marble columns, quarried in Thessalonica, were lost or destroyed during the war between Greece and Turkey. The plan for the liturgy to be supervised by Benedictine monks – members of an Order which had been expelled from Westminster during the Reformation – foundered on disagreements about what exactly their role should be and to which authority they should answer. The news that, after many vicissitudes, the bones of St Edmund, King and Martyr, had found their final resting place in the church of St Sernin in Toulouse prompted Vaughan to apply for their repatriation, thus giving Westminster Cathedral a relic to compare with the remains of Edward the Confessor down the road in Westminster Abbey. But the Toulouse bones, on closer inspection, turned out to belong to someone with no English connection.

Progress, although slower than was hoped, was faster than it had been reasonable to expect. Mass was said in the almost-completed Chapter House on May 7th 1902, and on Lady Day, the following year, the local parish mission was given use of what was to become the Lady Chapel. In June 1903 Edward Elgar's oratorio, *The Dream of Gerontius*, was performed in the still-incomplete nave. It was the perfect choice of a work with which to celebrate the creation of the first Catholic metropolitan cathedral in England since the Reformation. Father Bellasis – a Birmingham Oratorian and son of Elgar's closest friend – recorded in his diary how it came about. Walking with Elgar in the Worcester countryside, he mentioned that General Gordon's effects had been recovered from Khartoum and that they included a copy of *The Month*, a paradoxically bimonthly intellectual magazine in which Newman's poem, *The Dream of Gerontius*, was published. During the days before he was murdered by the Mahdi's Dervishes, Gordon had made notes in the margin. Elgar, who had long thought of writing a religious oratorio and had greatly admired the Christian soldier, regarded the news as a message from a source which he could not ignore. The history of the poem might be said to confirm that its role as consolation to the doomed general – 'I am near to death and Thou art calling me' – had been divinely inspired. Newman wrote it and forgot about it and, years afterwards, found it – by chance – among other papers.

Westminster Cathedral was still not complete – or ready for the installation of Eric Gill's sculptured Stations of the Cross – when, on June 19th 1903, Herbert Vaughan died. 'Into the vast space of that still unfinished church, his body was taken ... for the solemn requiem which, unforeseen, was to become the opening ceremony.'[38] On the centenary of his birth, *The Tablet* wisely wrote that Westminster Cathedral was Vaughan's 'great material work'. In 1932 that was a minority view, even among Catholics. A red-brick cathedral was unheard of – hence the jokes about Vaughan's railway station and, thanks to its single tower, the Roman Candle. Today, the fair-minded observer must see it differently. The shops that once hid it from the passing world have been demolished. Opened up and set back at the west of a piazza, its massive proportions symbolise – just as Vaughan intended – the strength that allowed the Catholic Church to withstand the centuries of persecution and retain the ambition which Vaughan, more than most post-Reformation Princes of the Church, was prepared to articulate – the Reunion of Christendom. When, in 1894, he described it in detail it sounded more like the eventual absorption of the Church of England into the Church of Rome. 'The Real Presence, the sacrifice of the Mass offered for the living and the dead, reservation of the Sacrament, regular auricular confession, Extreme Unction, Purgatory, the devotion to our Lady ...' He went on to complete the list of beliefs and practices which he implied were certainly respected and probably coveted by Anglicans.[39] To nervous Protestants it sounded like another vision of England as seen through the Flaminian Gate.

PART FOUR

The Church Knows All the Rules

CHAPTER 27

That Flame Burns Again

For most of the nineteenth century – the age of the Brontës and Jane Austen, George Eliot and Charles Dickens, William Makepeace Thackeray and Mrs Gaskell, Lord Tennyson, Robert Browning and Lord Byron – the Catholic community of Great Britain was a literary desert in which Cardinal Newman's *Apologia Pro Vita Sua* and *The Idea of a University* and the poetry of Gerard Manley Hopkins were the only oases. From time to time hopes were raised by what turned out to be a mirage. James Anthony Froude – a prominent, if somewhat eccentric, Newman disciple – published *The Nemesis of Faith*, a novel that, as well as costing him his Oxford Fellowship, was an overnight sensation. But, as is often the case with such phenomena, it was quickly dismissed by more discerning critics as melodramatic rubbish. It was not until the turn of the century that anything like a Catholic literary revival began.

Catholics – at the end of the First World War something like 5 per cent of the total British population of about thirty-six million – could not have been expected to produce as many literary geniuses as were born and bred in the Protestant communities. The denial of university education may also have contributed to the dearth of Catholic writers of distinction, though it did not hold back either Dickens or Eliot. Whatever the reason for the absence of Catholic poets, essayists and novelists, it was so complete that, in *Catholic Literature in the English Tongue*, Newman wrote that 'English Literature is essentially Protestant Literature'[1] and was forced to take refuge in the notion that Walter Scott, an aggressive Protestant, had contributed to the Catholic cause by turning 'men's eyes in the direction of the Middle Ages'.

The same claim could have been made, with more justification, for the Pre-Raphaelite Brotherhood. Holman Hunt's *Shadow of Death*, *Christ and The Two Marys* and *The Light of the World* would not look out of place on the walls of a Catholic church. But, although Pre-Raphaelites ranged in belief from Tractarian to atheist, there was not a Catholic among them. In the nineteenth century the religion that inspired the Renaissance could do no better than produce the pictures of martyrs and statues of saints which, on display in parish churches, confirmed the piety, if not the aesthetic judgement, of the congregations. There was, however, one spark of light in the literary gloom. Although John Henry Newman did not know it, there was a poet of great distinction among his most devoted followers. Gerard Manley Hopkins – who had begun to write poetry when he was a Highgate schoolboy – went up to Balliol in 1863 and immediately became a devoted member of the Oxford Movement. He continued to write. But in 1868, when he was received into the Catholic Church and determined to become a Jesuit priest, he symbolically burned all his poems as a sign that he had turned his back on the secular world. Fortunately for posterity, he took the precaution of sending copies to his friend, Robert Bridges. Many of them were published after Hopkins' death.

It was eight years before Hopkins' compulsion to write returned. Then he wrote 'The Wreck of the Deutschland'. It was dedicated 'to the happy memory of five Franciscan nuns exiled by the Falk Laws [and] drowned between midnight and morning of Dec. 7th 1875'. Its message was as Catholic as its inspiration. So was 'sprung rhythm', the metric style that Hopkins employed in much of his verse and which, he contended, was used by old English poets in the golden days before the Reformation. The poem was rejected for publication by *The Month*, a Jesuit periodical, because it was thought to be too hard for its readers to understand:

> I did say yes
> O at lightning and lashed rod;
> Thou heardst me truer than tongue confess
> Thy terror, O Christ, O God.

From then on, all Hopkins' verse was inspired by his faith. Even his 'simpler' poems – a small minority of his work – reflected his piety. 'Glory be to God for dappled things / For skies of couple-colour as a brinded cow.' Hopkins died of typhoid fever in March 1889 after unhappy years as a parish priest in Oxford, Chesterfield, Liverpool (where he was horrified by the vice and squalor) and London. Thanks to Bridges, within a couple of years of his death some of his shorter poems appeared in anthologies of contemporary work. But it was not until 1918 that his faithful friend felt able to present the great body of his work to publishers and public. Hopkins died without realising that he was not only a major poet, but also the only genuine Catholic poet that England had produced since the Reformation.

In *The Catholic Revival in English Literature* Ian Ker – a parish priest as well as an academic theologian – identifies a similarity between the rhythm of Hopkins' poetry and the metre of the litany. He also describes some of the later poems as 'pastoral' – not in the sense that they are about country matters, but because they concern a priest's duty of care. While he was working as a parish priest in Oxford in 1879, Hopkins had written to Bridges, 'I find with my professional experience now, a good deal to write on.'[2] In 'Felix Randal' he describes how a priest watches over a dying man. The priest in 'The Handsome Heart' speculates about what gift he should make to a particularly assiduous altar boy. In 'The Wreck of the Deutschland' and in a second 'disaster poem', 'The Loss of the Eurydice', he expresses something approaching guilt that no priest was at hand to hear the dying men's confessions. Hopkins was a priest who wrote poetry about the priestly vocation.

By the early years of the new century there were a number of writers – mostly of the middle rank – who subscribed to the Catholic faith. That does not, in any real sense of the term, make them 'Catholic writers'. Ernest Dowson (like Hopkins, a poet and convert) wrote several 'devotional works', including 'Nuns of the Perpetual Adoration' and 'Carthusians', but he was more at home in the Café Royal than in Westminster Cathedral and the true spirit of his verse is best illustrated by the defining lines of his two most famous poems: 'They are not long, the days of wine and roses' and 'I have been faithful to thee, Cynara! in my fashion'. He was a friend of Aubrey Beardsley, the illustrator of genius, whose aesthetic, and mildly decadent, views he shared. Beardsley too was a Catholic convert. So, was Coventry Patmore, whose work was said, scandalously, to confuse spiritual and pagan love. Had it not been for Presbyterian prejudice – even against a lapsed Papist – Arthur Conan Doyle would have become the Liberal Member of Parliament for Edinburgh. However, Sherlock Holmes – devoted to deduction based on tangible evidence and addiction to morphine – cannot be described as a character who carries any sort of Catholic message. Wilfred Scawen Blunt, whose sonnets were said to be Byronic in spirit and form, was baptised into the Catholic Church when he was a child, as a result of Cardinal Manning's influence over his (originally Anglican) mother. Perhaps, therefore, he should not be regarded as a convert. Most of the turn of the century's notable Catholic authors certainly were – even though many of them were 'Catholics who happened to write', rather than 'Catholic writers' in the full meaning of the term.

Although Lord Acton wrote that Catholicism was 'dearer than life itself', he would have vehemently denied that his interpretation of history was influenced by his faith – even though he described the Reformation as the 'great modern apostasy'.[3] Acton represents the dignified school of Catholic writers. The disreputable school was led by Frederick William Rolfe, alias Baron Corvo. Rolfe converted in 1886 and, shortly afterwards, entered the Scots College in Rome. He was dismissed within a year. Nearly twenty years later he retaliated by publishing *Hadrian the Seventh*, a fictitious autobiography in which the hero is elected Pope but deposed. Ronald Firbank – the Catholic convert author of *Valmouth*, the erotic exploits of a middle-aged masseuse – was no more a 'Catholic writer' in the full sense of the term than Oscar Wilde, who was admitted to the Church shortly before he died. Francis Thompson's 'The Hound of Heaven' is both religious and mystical:

> I fled Him, down the nights and down the days;
> I fled Him, down the arches of the years;
> I fled Him, down the labyrinthine ways
> Of my own mind;

But it is not an intrinsically Catholic poem. Siegfried Sassoon has been claimed for Rome. But he was a poet of the First World War who became a Catholic in 1955. He joined the remarkable number of twentieth-century writers – Catholic by either the loose or strict definition of the term – who were converts. The list includes Edith Sitwell, Compton Mackenzie, Muriel Spark, Christopher Hollis and Ford Maddox Ford. It is headed by Evelyn Waugh, Graham Greene, G K Chesterton and Ronald Knox.

Gilbert Keith Chesterton was a 'Catholic writer' in every sense of the term. He was born in Campden Hill, London in 1874 and educated at St Paul's School and the Slade, but soon turned from fine art to journalism. Thereafter he wrote anything and everything – history, poetry, belles-lettres, fiction (including the *Father Brown* detective stories) and, above all, polemics. He became both loved and admired for the expansive nature of his thought, his personality and his stature. Occasionally his enthusiasm would result in the espousal of absurdity. Chesterton did not care. Nor did his vast army of devotees.

Like so many Catholic intellectuals, he looked back on the Middle Ages with a sentimental reverence that was unrelated to the facts. In his *Short History of England* (published in 1917) he devotes a chapter to 'The Meaning of Merry England'. It contains a justification of torture in that happy land which is breathtaking, not because of its inhumanity, but because of its inanity:

Torture, so far from being medieval, was copied from pagan Rome and its most rationalist political science; and its medieval application to others beside slaves was really part of the slow medieval extinction of slavery. Torture is, indeed, a logical thing common in states innocent of fanaticism as in the great agnostic empire of China.

Chesterton would not, knowingly, have tortured a fly. And the great British public who read his journalism knew it and laughed at his excesses.

As long as they laughed, Chesterton was happy. He believed in what he called 'beatific buffoonery' – an attribute that he claimed was all-pervasive in the Olde England of maypole-dancing, village fayres and universally respected holy days. 'Greek heroes do not grin but gargoyles do – because they are Christian' and reflect 'the deep levity of the Middle Ages'.[4] He believed that humour was God-given and – though it would have been sacrilegious to be certain – probably sanctified by Christ Himself. That is the view with which he concludes *Orthodoxy*:

> There was something that He hid from all men when he went up the mountain to pray. There was something that He covered constantly by abrupt silence or impetuous isolation. There was something that was too great for God to show us when He walked upon our earth; and I have sometimes fancied that it was His mirth.

In his *Autobiography*, published in 1936, Chesterton announced, 'I could not be a novelist because I really like to see ideas or notions wrestling naked, as it were, and not dressed up in a masquerade as men and women.' But he was a novelist. *The Napoleon of Notting Hill* and *The Man Who Was Thursday* do not compare with the work of Dickens, Chesterton's literary idol. They were, nevertheless, examples of workmanlike fiction that is diminished in the author's mind by his preference for the literature of ideas. He completed the self-analysis with the assertion, 'I could be a journalist because I could not help being a controversialist.' It was an enthusiasm that led him into a number of bad habits. They included the construction of aphorisms and paradoxes that, on close examination, are exposed as meaningless. 'All roads lead to Rome; which is one of the reasons why many people do not get there.' But because of his love of reckless controversy, Chesterton has the ability to embed his ideas in readers' minds to a depth that more cautious writers find beyond them:

Christianity is the only religion on earth that has felt that omnipotence made God incomplete ... When the world shook and the sun was wiped out of heaven, it was not at the crucifixion but at the cry from the cross: the cry that confessed that God was forsaken by God ... [There is] only one religion in which God is seen, for a moment, to be an atheist.[5]

Chesterton, who wrote extensively about beef and beer, would not have objected to being called a whole-hogging sort of person. 'As an apologist,' he wrote, 'I am the reverse of apologetic.' He did 'not want to be in a religion in which [he was] *allowed* to have a crucifix', but although the Catholic Church was disappointingly feeble about crucifixes, it remained 'the only creed that could not be satisfied with a truth but only with the Truth'.[6] The inclination to total commitment, which made him admirable in the eyes of the Church, sounded less admirable when it was deployed in support of less worthy causes, one of which was the defence of his brother Cecil, the editor of an openly anti-Semitic magazine. From time to time, that loyalty caused him to assume the deeply unattractive character of a plain man who speaks his mind, whether or not his views are socially acceptable. 'I said that a particular kind of Jew tended to be a tyrant and another particular kind of Jew happened to be a traitor. I say it again.' That was not the real Chesterton. The real Chesterton was the man who imagined that 'the countries of Europe which are still influenced by priests are exactly the countries where there is still singing and dancing and coloured dresses and art in the open air'. He was the apostle of magnificent nonsense.

George Bernard Shaw wrote, not always complimentarily, of a literary figure called 'Chesterbelloc'. Although G K Chesterton and Hilaire Belloc were not as indistinguishable as the idea of a composite character suggests, the two men had much in common. In particular, they had a mutually eclectic passion for writing in every genre. But Belloc was far more disciplined than Chesterton. He served a term first as a Liberal, then as an Independent, Member of Parliament and was literary editor of the *Morning Post* – occupations which Chesterton would have found irksome. Both men wrote humorous verse, histories, essays, novels and theological polemics. But they were divided by the circumstances of their birth. Belloc was born a French Catholic and became British by naturalisation. Chesterton was converted to Catholicism and was – by birth, upbringing and inclination – quintessentially English.

Hilaire Belloc was born in France but brought up in England – though he was so determined to maintain his dual nationality that he returned to France in order to serve in the army rather than lose his French citizenship. His mother had been admitted into the Catholic Church by Cardinal Manning, who became a lasting influence on her son. Manning's views became his views and, despite three years at Balliol which ended in the award of a First in history, he was profoundly antagonistic to all other intellectual authority. In *Hills and the Sea* – a collection of essays published in 1906 – he was gratuitously offensive about the relationship between religion and formal scholarship: 'When I thought carefully where the nearest Don might be at the moment, I decided that he was at least twenty-three miles away and I was very glad. It permitted me to contemplate ... with common sense and with Faith – which is Common Sense transfigured.'[7] That was how he regarded the 'profound thing' that he had learned from Cardinal Manning. 'All human conflict is ultimately theological.'

Cardinal Manning's *obiter dictum* coloured Belloc's view of the world in general and of Europe in particular. It led him to conclude, in *Survivals and New Arrivals*, that 'religion is at the root of every culture' and that the rise and fall of nations was certainly influenced, and probably determined, by changes in the religion of nationalities. European civilisation, he argued, was the achievement of Christianity: 'The Faith is Europe and Europe is the Faith.' He enlarged on the idea in *Europe and the Faith*. Because of 'the grievous and ugly wound of the Reformation ... the united body of European civilization had been cut asunder'. Britain must take a major share of the blame for the five hundred years of disunity that followed. 'The defection of Britain from the Faith of Europe' made the Reformation permanent, and influenced secular as well as religious life for the next five centuries. The Reformation, he argued, taught that the object of religion was 'the salvation of the individual soul', whereas Catholicism 'had a corporate quality'. Belloc had no doubt that the Reformation promoted the emergence of the nation state. Prussian militarism, and therefore the First Great War, was the result of the Reformation preventing the spread of enlightenment to 'the barbaric, the ill tutored and the isolated places external to the old and deep-rooted Roman civilisation'. Fascism was the consequence of 'making the nation an end in itself'. Protestant princes' insistence 'that their power was not responsible to Christendom or any of it offices, but independent of them', combined with Calvin's doctrine of predestination, encouraged a 'devotion to material success' and was at odds with 'the mystic Catholic doctrine of equality'.

That was the point at which the two interpretations of history – Chesterton and Belloc – converged without quite coinciding. Belloc was not the man to espouse belief in the idealised and entirely fictitious 'Merrie England' of the Middle Ages. But he too imagined that the quality of life had deteriorated since the Reformation. Once upon a time, a fair 'distributive system' was safeguarded by 'the existence of a co-operative system, binding men of the same craft or the same village together [and] guaranteeing the small proprietor against the loss of his independence'. That had been destroyed. So had 'the old safeguards of the small man's property'. Essential values had been swept away by the passion for competition and the toleration of usury. 'Lands and accumulated wealth of the old monasteries were taken out of the hands of their possessor', bringing to an end the happy days when 'poor men might go where they willed' secure in the knowledge that they would be welcome to stay in religious houses with monks who regarded 'nourishing hundreds' as their sacred duty.

At least he was right about the impetus behind the closure of the monasteries, even if he was wrong about the invariable charity of the monks who were evicted from them. Some monasteries were corrupt, but most were closed at the behest of a 'small wealthy class which used the religious excitement of an active minority as an engine to obtain material advantage for themselves'. But Belloc could not resist overstating his case. Like Chesterton, he traded in excess – a more austere excess, but excess nevertheless. 'The Iconoclasts of greed joined hands with the Iconoclasts of blindness and rage and with the Iconoclasts of academic pride' to end the old order. Belloc's history mixed fact with fantasy, but his view of the world was just as idiosyncratic as Chesterton's and, in one particular, it was less progressive than Newman's. Back in 1865, Newman had accepted that Darwin's *Origin of Species* was not, necessarily, at odds with the Christian view of creation. In his very public argument with H G Wells – in which he had expended 100,000 words of polemics, most of which were published in *A Companion to Mr H G Wells's 'Outline of History'* – Belloc argued that the notion of evolution by natural selection was clearly confounded by cold-water mammals' obvious difficulty in mounting ice-floes during the breeding season. He also contended that Wells was guilty of the 'grievous fault of being ignorant that he was ignorant'.

Like Chesterton, Belloc was devoted to food and drink. It was said that Chesterton had soup stains on his waistcoat, while Belloc had fish bones on his lapels. Both men took pleasure in alcohol. Chesterton philosophised about beer; Belloc wrote poems about wine. One, written for Easter Sunday and called 'God the Wine-Giver', began: 'Though Man made wine, I think God made it too.' But he was also an intellectual who wanted to apply his intellect to ideas that are not susceptible to logical or historical examination. That quality made him assert as obvious truths – perhaps even as a higher truth – contentions which he felt no obligation to support with evidence. Often the message they carried was devalued by the verbal tricks with which they were displayed 'The Catholic Church was, from Her origins, a thing not a theory ... She was a society informing individuals, not a mass of individuals forming a society.'[8]

Hilaire Belloc's *The Path to Rome* is part biography and part the story of an expedition across Europe. But unlike most travel books, it is so concerned with religion – the faith of the author and the devotions of the men and women whom he meets along the way – that it is more the account of a pilgrimage than the description of journey. A N Wilson, Belloc's biographer, believes – and justifies his belief from the text – that what he witnessed in the small alpine village of Undervelier had a profound effect on the rest of his life. The sight that so affected Belloc was what seemed to be the whole population of the village turning out to attend vespers. 'Having always thought of the Faith as something fighting odds, and having seen unanimity only in places where some sham religion glossed over our tragedies and excused our sins',[9] he was deeply moved to see that unanimous devotion to a creed was blighted by none of those defects. 'My whole mind was taken up and transfigured by this collective act and I saw for a moment the Catholic Church quite plain and I remembered Europe and the centuries.'[10]

The man who could be so moved by the piety of an alpine village and who believed devoutly in the sanctity of the Catholic Church of the Middle Ages was also the author of books of 'children's verse' which were really written to amuse adults. Sometimes they contained valuable advice: 'And always keep a hold of Nurse / For fear of finding something worse.' Sometimes, as in the case of Lord Finchley, who electrocuted himself while changing a light bulb, they were social satire: 'And serve him right. / It is the business of the wealthy man / To give employment to the artisan.' And sometimes they amused the reader, despite having no real meaning: 'Like many of the upper class / He liked the sound of broken glass.' Belloc's literary reputation, like so many of his aphorisms, is a paradox. It is his ephemera that have lasted and are still read a century after they were written. It is Belloc as a Catholic who was also a writer who is remembered. Belloc the Catholic writer has been overtaken by authors who saw their faith as more demanding and less forgiving.

Belloc's humorous poems, though hardly profound, were far more intellectually sophisticated than Chesterton's 'nonsense verse', which was often meaningless: 'James Hogg / Kept a dog / But, being a shepherd / He did not keep a leopard.' Neither of them had the nerve – solemn Christians would call it the impertinence – to set out a complicated theological theorem in the form of a limerick. That literary exercise was left to Monsignor Ronald Knox, a Catholic convert from the Church of England and a celebrity in the early age of broadcasting and 'popular culture:'

> Oh God, for as much as without Thee
> We are not enabled to doubt Thee,
> Help us all by Thy grace
> To convince the whole race
> It knows nothing whatever about Thee.

Ronald Knox was born into the Church of England. Both his grandfathers were bishops. His father was successively vicar of Aston, in the city of Birmingham, Suffragan Bishop of Worcester – an appointment that gave him episcopal responsibility for the industrial West Midlands – and Bishop of Manchester. Knox's upbringing was impeccably upper-middle-class – Eton and Oxford – and he seemed destined to follow the family tradition and enter Holy Orders. The assumption that he was 'called' to the Anglican ministry was encouraged by the piety of his behaviour when he was an undergraduate. But the services in Balliol College Chapel –'a tradition of "superior" music, indefinite dogma and manly sentiment'[11] – were not to his liking. He preferred the form of worship practised in Pusey House and by the five priests in the community of St Giles. Devotions at Pusey House and the Society of St John the Evangelist – where Knox took Communion twice a week – 'conveyed a feeling . . . of catacombs, oubliettes, Jesuitry and encouraged the atmosphere of mystery that fascinated me'.

In the autumn of 1909, Knox visited the Benedictine community in Caldey Island off the Tenby coast in Wales. He was enthralled by what he believed to be a model of the medieval Church and by the community's leader. He asked his father, a leader of the evangelical movement within the Church of England, for permission to make confession to the High Church priests of Pusey House. His father reluctantly agreed and confession became a regular part of Ronald Knox's week. He had become a thoroughgoing Anglo-Catholic.

Knox's undergraduate years were an unremitting triumph. He won the Hertford Scholarship, the Craven Scholarship, the Gaisford Prize, the Ireland Prize and the Chancellor's Prize, as well as being awarded a First. He was offered a tutorship at Balliol and a Fellowship – together with the college chaplaincy – at Trinity. By then he had decided on his vocation: 'I wanted with all my soul to enter the Anglican ministry.'[12] So he chose Trinity as the direct route to his ordained destination. There was a moment of brief embarrassment during the term's leave before he joined the college. His was discharged as tutor to the young Harold Macmillan for the offence of exposing his charge to the insidious influence of Anglo-Catholicism. But that did not prevent the Bishop of Oxford agreeing that he should take an informal route to ordination and travel at an usually swift speed.

The literary career of Ronald Knox began within months of his taking up the Trinity tutorship. He had become associated with a group of young dons who met together each Friday for theological discussion. Five of them broke ranks and combined in the authorship of a book that advanced a 'progressive' view of the Church of England. It was called *Foundations – A Statement of Christian Belief in Terms of Modern Thought*. Knox's first attack was a poem written in the manner of Dryden and entitled 'Absolute and Abitofhell'. It was followed by a serious argument in favour of traditional values and practices. But Knox could not resist a touch of satire. The response to *Foundations* was called *Some Loose Stones*.

Adult converts have a duty to agonise about their decision, and Ronald Knox had more need to agonise than most. The carnage of the First World War made him long for a faith about which he had no doubts, but the obligation he felt towards his father and family made him hesitate. The result was a pamphlet, *The Essentials of Spiritual Unity*, which he began to write as an Anglican in 1915 and finished, as a Catholic, three years later. He did not apply for the renewal of his Trinity Fellowship. Instead – with the true confidence of the Old Etonian – he sought and obtained an interview with Cardinal Bourne, the Archbishop of Westminster. Bourne, like Wiseman before him, recognised the value of 'celebrity converts'. Knox was told to teach at St Edmund's College while he was 'fast-tracked' towards ordination for the second time in his life.

Knox was a bigger catch than Bourne could possibly have realised. For his restless talents could never be – and never were – satisfied with the duties that the Church required of him. After his appointment as Catholic chaplain to Oxford University he performed his duties assiduously. But still he had time to write. And his writing, and the broadcasting that followed, became his great contribution to the growing acceptance of Catholics and Catholicism in Britain. Despite Knox's undoubted intellectual distinction, Chesterton and Belloc were clearly better writers. Knox's *Spiritual Aeneid*, written shortly after his admission to the Church, is only a poor shadow of Newman's *Apologia Pro Vita Sua* by which it was inspired. But it was his trivial novels about high society, not his serious examination of spiritual awakening, that made him such an asset to the Catholics and Catholicism. An obvious English gentleman, who was also a priest, wrote fiction about the trivial affairs of the upper classes. It all helped to integrate Catholicism into what ordinary people called ordinary life.

In Knox's *Memories of the Future*, Opal, Lady Porstock looked back from 1988 on the events of her long life. *Sanctions: A Frivolity* is the account of a house party given by Sir William and Lady Denham. It does contain the occasional good line. One guest is described as being 'educated out of his prejudices without being educated into any principles'. It also contains a defence of spiritualism which Knox, in effect, repudiated in *Other Eyes than Ours* – another account of a house party that includes another good line: 'If you have been corresponding all this long time with the dead, how is it that the dead have said nothing that is worth saying?' From the 1920s onwards, Knox wrote a novel most years. More often than not they included 'Catholic characters'. He abandoned detective stories in 1937, after he heard that Lady Acton, while cruising in the Mediterranean, had read half of his *Double Cross Purposes* and then thrown it overboard.[13]

The following year Knox wrote what he regarded as incomparably his best work of fiction. *Let Dons Delight* is set in the fictitious Simon Magus College, Oxford, where the narrator falls asleep after dinner and dreams of eight conversations at high table that had taken place at fifty-year intervals between 1588 and 1938. In January 1939, Hilaire Belloc was sent the proofs and judged the work to be 'a masterpiece' by which he was 'quite bowled over'.[14] Despite that, it is not possible to come to a firm conclusion about whether or not Knox's work was Catholic literature. He was certainly a Catholic, but his position in the pantheon of English writers is less secure.

Knox's popularity, and his consequent importance in 'humanising' the Catholic Church, was increased by his aptitude and enthusiasm for performing on the radio – or 'wireless', as it was known in its nascent years. His first broadcast was made from Edinburgh on November 25th 1923, barely a year after the BBC – in process of changing from Company to Corporation – had been created. He wrote his own script and read it in an assumed voice in the manner of an extended news bulletin. The headline announced that a revolutionary mob had occupied Trafalgar Square, sacked the National Gallery and was marching on the Houses of Parliament. Many listeners – not accustomed to 'tuning in' – took the broadcast seriously. John Reith, managing director of the BBC, made a public apology, even though he had received ten times as many compliments as complaints. The *Daily Express*, *Daily Mirror* and *Evening Standard* all denounced Knox. But that did not prevent them from employing him as a columnist. In 1926 he earned about £1,300 from journalism – £15 a week from regular columns in the *Evening Standard* and *The Universe*.[15]

Knox thrived in the era of the 'wireless'. Cardinal Bourne was naturally unwilling to have the Mass broadcast through a medium which, as name of the activity confirmed, might scatter the liturgy on stony ground. But he did agree to the Catholic Church contributing to the series of Sunday sermons. Knox was by far the most popular of the radio preachers – so popular that when the BBC discovered that he was to spend the Easter of 1938 in Dublin, it pioneered a link with the Irish Broadcasting Company rather than have another cleric speak on 'What Happened on Easter Morning'. But most of his broadcasting was about 'current affairs' – alongside, or in debate with, Bernard Shaw, J B Priestley and Beverley Nichols, the fashionable controversialists of the day.

It says much for Knox's energy and self-confidence that, immersed as he was in radio and print journalism, he volunteered to make a new translation of the Bible. English Catholics, who possessed bibles, were still using Richard Challoner's eighteenth-century revision of the Rheims and Douai Testaments, which had been published in 1582 and 1609. Cardinal Hinsley, Cardinal Bourne's successor as Archbishop of Westminster – undeterred by the fate of the proposed Newman version in 1855 – was determined to sponsor an English-language version of the Bible which was the work of an Englishman, and when Knox heard of Hinsley's firm intention, he offered to fulfil the ambition that Newman had been denied. The Cardinal consulted his bishops and in November 1938 wrote to the volunteer, 'We have confidence in you as the one man who can give an English text, readable and understood of the people.'

Knox completed his translation of the New Testament in five years. A limited edition was published in April 1944. At first, for reasons that were never clear, the bishops felt unable to give it their collective backing. But after a year of discussion – and uncharacteristic cries of pain from Knox – yet another new Archbishop, Cardinal Griffin, announced his endorsement and provided a preface that commended Knox's 'masterly command of the English language and limpid style'. Despite those qualities, the 'Knox Bible' was rarely used and is now largely forgotten. So what must have been Knox's hope – that he would have a lasting effect on Catholics and Catholicism – was never realised. But he played a noble part in reconciling the people of Britain to the presence of Catholics among them. And posthumously he was rewarded by a literary accolade: the publication of his biography by one of the great Catholic writers of his era. The author was Evelyn Waugh.

Two of Waugh's novels, *Decline and Fall* and *Vile Bodies*, were written before his conversion to Catholicism in 1932, the year in which he wrote *Black Mischief*. And, insomuch as Catholicism is mentioned at all in that early work, it is portrayed as a sinister and unattractive conspiracy. Father Rothschild, 'a sly Jesuit' in *Vile Bodies*, knows all about intrigue: 'A lock does not prevent a spy from hearing us; but it does hinder us, inside, from catching the spy.' It was not until after the war – in which he, improbably, served in the Royal Marines – that Waugh began to write seriously, though often satirically, about the Church of his adoption. It is not to doubt the sincerity of his belief to say that Waugh, like so many other truly Catholic writers, saw his faith as all that was left of a better age. He makes that claim directly in the *Sword of Honour* trilogy and by implication in *Brideshead Revisited*. The world of Guy Crouchback and Charles Ryder has been corrupted by the changes that were thought necessary to win the war. It is Captain Ryder who, driven to despair by Second Lieutenant Hooper, doubts the wisdom of promoting first-rate NCOs into second-rate officers. Evelyn Waugh, in print and in life, liked the world as it used to be.

Waugh's early manhood was not one long and unmitigated triumph. He came down from Oxford without taking a degree, with the intention of enrolling in art school and becoming a printer of the elevated William Morris kind. He found himself, or was found, unsuited to the occupation. So he became an assistant master in a prep school, where he wrote his first novel. Showing it to his friend, the aesthete Harold Acton, was an error of judgement. Acton was so critical that Waugh burned the manuscript and contemplated suicide. After being sacked from a 'crammer' for harassing the matron during a drunken night out, he joined the *Daily Express* as a gossip columnist. At last he turned to writing – first a biography of Dante Gabriel Rossetti. The novels followed. So did Waugh's reception into the Church by Father Martin D'Arcy, a Farm Street Jesuit. In *Brideshead Revisited*, Rex Mottram (the Canadian adventure) is 'instructed' in preparation for admission by Father Mobray, also of Farm Street:

Then again I asked him; 'supposing the Pope looked up and saw a cloud and said "It's going to rain", would that be bound to happen?'

'Oh, yes Father.' 'But supposing it didn't?' He thought for a moment and said, 'I suppose it would be sort of raining spiritually, only we were too sinful to see it.'

Waugh's Catholicism is obvious enough in his biographies of *Helena* (the Christian convert mother of Constantine the Great) and *Edmund Campion*, the Jesuit martyr. But neither are great works of literature. The 'Catholic novels' undoubtedly are – not least because they concern the sort of unyielding Catholicism in which Waugh believed. To him, the Vatican Council of 1962 was a retrograde step back from the absolute rules laid down by the Council of Trent. His genius lies in the way in which he illustrates the good Catholic's respect for the Church's teaching – often without the reader noticing. In *Unconditional Surrender* – the third volume of the *Sword of Honour* trilogy – Guy Crouchback spends an evening with Virginia Troy, his much-remarried ex-wife. To Virginia's surprise, the highly respectable Guy wants to make love. Then she realises that, in his Catholic eyes, they are still married. The louche Virginia – the Protestant partner in her mixed marriage to Guy – regards the idea as disgusting. But the reader smiles at Guy's naivety and notes that he is a man who respects the rules of his Church. The rules – whatever heretics may think of them – are important to Waugh.

Virginia contemplates arranging the abortion of a baby conceived in a previous liaison but decides against, not because of moral scruples, but because of the bizarre squalor of the premises in which it is to be performed. Her vice is in contrast to Guy's virtue. He agrees to remarry Virginia (a legal and social, if not a religious, necessity) and after her death in an air raid accepts responsibility for her child. In that he is acting in accordance with the obligations of chivalry, not the Rules of Rome. But the two imperatives are related. Guy finds inspiration in the memory of Roger of Waybrooke, a knight who intended to join the Second Crusade but was shipwrecked near Genoa and buried near the Crouchbacks' house in Italy. Antiquity is important to Waugh. So is life's habit – as demonstrated by Waybrooke's failure to reach the Holy Land – of not quite meeting human hopes and expectations.

The thought that some values abide through time is even a comfort to Charles Ryder, the narrator and central character (though hardly the hero) of *Brideshead Revisited*. Back, as a soldier, at Brideshead – where he had loved and lost – Ryder is inspired by the sight of the sanctuary lamp in the dilapidated chapel and the thought that what it signified had survived the years:

A small red flame – a beaten-copper lamp of deplorable design relit before the beaten-copper doors of a tabernacle; the flame which the old Knights saw from their tombs, which they saw put out; that flame burns again for other soldiers far from home, farther in heart than Acre or Jerusalem.

What is it about the small red flame that disturbs Ryder's world-weary cynicism? He is not a Catholic, and as his friend – the doomed Sebastian Flyte – explains, Catholics are not like other people: 'They have an entirely different outlook on life.' The Reserved Sacrament, which the lamp signified, was meant to meet the needs of people like Cordelia, Sebastian's sister. She liked 'popping in [the chapel] at odd times'. There are two possible theological explanations of his experience. Ryder's reaction is either the first stage of the long journey to conversion or evidence that God reaches out and touches even the heathen. Or the passage may appear for the thoroughly laudable literary reason that the author wanted to make his readers finish the book in hope rather than despair. Writers who are Catholics want good reviews on earth as well as in heaven.

The plot of *Brideshead Revisited* turns on a miracle, but the miracle is entirely in the eye of the beholder. Lord Marchmain – a Catholic convert of no strong conviction and the head of the Flyte family – has returned home from Venice to die. His last moments are spent in proper aristocratic fashion with his family and close friends assembled in his house. His wife, a 'bogus saint', is there. So is the mistress for whom he left her. Julia, his daughter – recently divorced from Rex Mottram – is there with Charles Ryder. They have been in love for years and have, at last, decided to marry. The family takes it in turns to discuss whether or not the priest, who is waiting outside the sick-room, should be asked to come in and perform the last rites. Will the shock of seeing a priest kill Lord Marchmain there and then? Is it right to impose the rituals of the Church on a nominal Catholic? Eventually Julia takes the decision. 'Father Mackay, will you please come in and see my father now?' The nurse gives the comforting assurance that he is still alive, but 'past noticing anything', and 'the priest bent over Lord Marchmain and blessed him'. Then Father Mackay says the fateful words, 'I know you are sorry for all the sins of your life, aren't you? Make a sign if you can.'

Lord Marchmain makes the sign and Julia tells Charles, 'I can't marry you. I can't be with you ever again.' She is not moved to obey the rules that forbid remarriage after divorce from a Christian union. By sacrificing earthly happiness, Julia hopes to ingratiate herself with

God. 'If I give up this thing I want so much, however bad I am, he won't quite despair of me in the end.' Julia is not much of a theologian. Even if God possessed human attributes, despair would not be one of them.

The novels of Evelyn Waugh and Graham Greene have in common a preoccupation with despair. Major Scobie, the colonial policeman who is the central character and flawed hero of Greene's *The Heart of the Matter*, remembers that the priests taught him that suicide is 'the unforgivable sin' because it is 'the final expression of unrelenting despair'. It is not surprising that so many of Greene's Catholics lose hope of peace in this world and redemption in the next. They all carry the burden which the priest in *Brighton Rock* describes: 'A Catholic is more capable of sin than anyone ... Because we believe in Him we are more in touch with the Devil than other people.' Belief becomes a burden. As Major Scobie complains, 'The trouble is, we know all the answers. We Catholics are damned by our knowledge.'

To Greene, sin comes in many different shapes and sizes. The 'whisky priest', in *The Power and the Glory* – unfrocked by his Church and indicted as an enemy of an atheist state – is a 'holy sinner'. Although he knows it to be a mortal sin, he continues to act as though he were still in Holy Orders. The men and women whose confessions he hears and to whom he gives Communion take a step nearer to heaven as a result of him turning his back on salvation. It is a reflection of the sacrifice that is celebrated in the opening chant of the Easter Vigil: 'O necessary sin of Adam ... that earned for us so great, so glorious a Redeemer.'

Greene's conversion to Catholicism dated back to 1925. 'I began to believe in heaven because I believed in hell, but for a long time it was only hell that I could picture with any intimacy.' The 'picture' did not do much credit to the power of his imagination. It was of a place in which 'everybody was never quiet at the same time' and the 'lavatories were without locks'. Hell was Berkhamsted School, where he was educated and his father was headmaster. It was his fiancée who persuaded him to become a Catholic. During the instruction that preceded his admission to the Church, Greene 'became convinced of the probability of something we call God', but he was 'not emotionally moved, only intellectually'. Evelyn Waugh was also an 'intellectual' convert who welcomed the fact that Father D'Arcy at Farm Street 'never spoke of experience or feeling', but simply set out the required doctrinal beliefs. Father D'Arcy claimed that it was Waugh himself who rejected the ad hominem route to Rome. 'He was one of the most satisfactory people to talk to about faith whom I have ever known.

He was very different from one or two others I can think of, who kept saying "Yes I think that corresponds to my experience."[16]

In *Ways of Escape*, his second volume of autobiography, Greene wrote that he 'discovered some sort of emotional belief' in 1938 – a date about which he could be precise because of circumstances in which his Catholicism took on a new dimension. The previous year he had begun to contemplate using Catholic characters in his fiction. The changes of heart and mind had the same cause. The Catholic Church was being persecuted by the government in Mexico and the priests were being shot in Spain because of their support for General Franco's 'anti-Communist crusade'. Catholicism was becoming exciting. The immediate result was *The Power and the Glory*, based on Greene's experience as a journalist in Mexico.

Greene always insisted that the ideas expressed by his Catholic characters were not necessarily his ideas – indeed, being true to life, they were not necessarily the true ideas of the characters by whom they are expressed. There is, however, an undeniable similarity between what he said about life and what he wrote in his novels. Shortly before his marriage, Greene – in the mistaken belief that he was an epileptic – asked if it was acceptable to use contraception to avoid the procreation of similarly afflicted children. He was 'repulsed' by the 'hard answer', but impressed by the 'unyielding façade' of the Church. 'Façade' – defined as outward appearance – is an interesting choice or words. But whether or not he meant to imply an element of deception, he was illustrating the conflict between the admiration for strict rules and disgust at their harsh application. He could accept that to 'miss Mass on a Sunday was to be guilty of a mortal sin' and had no doubt that dogma was necessary to avoid Catholicism becoming as 'foggy as Anglicanism'.[17] But he had immense sympathy both for those who break the rules and those who find them incomprehensible. In *The Heart of the Matter*, Helen complains that the Church will forgive Scobie for sleeping with her, but not for marrying her. And Scobie risks his immortal soul – by taking Communion without making the confession that would precede the absolution of his sins – as the price of ensuring the happiness of both his wife and his mistress. Scobie, too, is a holy sinner – a man who, despite his many shortcomings, excites the reader's sympathy rather than contempt because there are moments when his nobility shines through the fog of his flaws.

The constant examination of the conflict between the love of God and the love of man makes it hard to understand how Graham Greene could write, in *Ways of Escape*, 'many times since *Brighton Rock* I have been forced to declare myself not a Catholic writer but a writer who happens to be a Catholic'. *Brighton Rock*, *The Power and the Glory* and *The Heart of the Matter* could not have been written by someone who did not feel for the faith. The same is probably true of *The End the Affair*, though it has some very un-Catholic ingredients. One is a miracle performed by Sarah, the 'heroine'. She touches a child's cheek and the strawberry mark disappears. Another is God's apparent acceptance of an offer that Sarah makes to Him. She promises that if Maurice, her lover, is brought back to life from under the pile of air-raid rubble, their adultery will end. Does God make bargains with sinners? Or was Maurice unconscious rather than dead, and God's reward for Sarah's sacrifice just the product of a convent-educated imagination? Back at Brideshead, Julia Flyte makes God an unconditional offer. The success of her gamble with grace – forgiveness in return for acceptance of the Church's rules – is beyond verification. In *The End of the Affair* the miracle happens – or so the heroine believes. In *Brideshead Revisited* she gambles on God's benevolence.

Both *The End of the Affair* and *Brideshead Revisited* raise a question that rumbles under the surface of many of Greene's, and Waugh's, novels and sometimes seems to need an answer from the Catholic Church itself. Is God really so preoccupied with sex? Although in *The Heart of the Matter* sex is not the fundamental cause of Scobie's destruction, it is the fuse that ignites the explosion. Scobie commits the mortal sin of taking Communion without first making a confession because he cannot promise that he will never sleep with Helen again, even though he longs for the peace that would come with the end of his furtive adultery. Helen needs him. So does his wife. Doing what he sees as his duty requires him to maintain the pretence that he is a loyal and dutiful husband – a loyal and dutiful Catholic husband. That obliges him to accompany his wife to Mass and to kneel next to her to receive the host. The horror with which Scobie awaits what amounts to the approach of damnation is described with painful brilliance. But what Greene regards as the real moral of Scobie's situation is set out during the account of a conversation he has with his parish priest.

Father Rank complains that people in trouble are more likely to go to Scobie for help and comfort than they are to go to him. He then asks, 'If you were in trouble where would you go?' Scobie replies that, 'being dull and middle aged . . . [he] is not the sort of man who gets into trouble'. But he is thinking of the futility of asking the priest to answer the question which tormented him before he decided to take Communion, without the absolution of his sins. 'I know the answer as well as he does. One should look after one's own soul at whatever cost to another and that's what I can't do.' Greene's is a hard, demanding God who is constantly in conflict with the human instinct. That is why so many of Greene's characters – men and women with whom the reader is intended to sympathise – hate their God. In *The End of the Affair*, Maurice, the atheist, first cries into the darkness, 'I hate you, God. I hate you as though you existed.' By the end of the book he is a believer. But the bitterness remains: 'Oh God, you've done enough. You've robbed me of enough ... Leave me alone for ever.'

Broken-hearted lovers cannot be expected to share the Church's view of fate and faith. That is best left to one of Graham Greene's priests. Father Clay, taking Scobie to view a corpse, represents invincible orthodoxy. The man had committed suicide – the ultimate blasphemy, since it results from despair of God's love. 'Mightn't there,' he asks, 'be a hope that it is murder?' Father Rank is a more human figure. After Scobie's death, he reproves his wife for using the phrase 'bad Catholic ... Don't imagine that you – or I – know anything about God's Mercy.' Then he pronounces what reads like Greene's valedictory judgement on Catholicism: 'I know what the Church says. The Church knows all the rules. But it does not know what goes on in a single human heart.' As Greene has reminded his readers, the opinions expressed by his characters should not be thought of as a contribution to Catholic theology. But his novels – fiction though they are – like the novels of Evelyn Waugh, have an effect on the judgements on Catholicism which are made by readers in the real world. Both men were writers of undoubted genius. But theirs is a bleak view of life; and their work, for all its undoubted literary merit, paints an equally bleak picture of the Catholic Church.

CHAPTER 28

Making Catholicism Count

Eamon de Valera – the founding father of the Republic of Ireland –
escaped from British custody courtesy of the Roman Catholic Church.
After several months working as a server at Lincoln Prison's Sunday
Mass he noticed that, during the service, the visiting priest always left
his bunch of keys on the table in the vestry. De Valera made an impression of each one on the wax – the remnants of altar candles – with
which he had filled an old tobacco tin. In December 1919, prisoners
were allowed to make their own Christmas cards. De Valera's was
decorated with a pattern of keys – each one exactly the shape and size
of the impressions in the tobacco-tin wax. The first set of duplicates
that was smuggled into the gaol would not turn in the locks. The
second did. On the moonless night of February 3th 1919 the future
President of Ireland walked out of Lincoln Prison and scrambled
through a hole that had been cut in the fence by which it was
surrounded. As he made his secret way home to Ireland he hid in the
Manchester presbytery of Father Frank O'Mahony. He was back in
Dublin on February 20th, safely hidden by Father Curran, secretary
to Archbishop Walsh, in the gatehouse of the Archbishop's residence.

De Valera, a 'good Catholic', had been in and out of prison ever
since he was captured, commanding the Irish Volunteers in Boland's
Mill. He had initially been condemned to death, but the sentence was
commuted to penal servitude for life because he was a citizen of the
United States. Before the reprieve was granted he had prepared for
death by reading the *Confessions* of Saint Augustine. Despite his piety
he was prepared to confront the Hierarchy in the cause of Irish independence. The need to challenge the bishops' reluctance to 'engage in
politics' arose in April 1918 during one of de Valera's periods of licensed
freedom. The issue on which he demanded their support was the extension of conscription to Ireland. Tim Healy, a veteran of Parnell's Home
Rule campaign, argued that to disagree with the episcopacy was to lack
respect. De Valera told him, 'There's nothing to that.'[1]

The day after the extension of conscription was announced,
Laurence O'Neill, the Lord Mayor of Dublin, convened a protest
meeting in the Mansion House. The idea of mounting some sort of

demonstration may have come from Archbishop Walsh, who certainly approved of its aims and sent a messenger to O'Neill with the news that the Irish bishops were to meet on the same day at Maynooth to discuss, but not necessarily to oppose, the government's decision. The Mansion House meeting swiftly recorded its unanimous agreement to a public declaration of support for 'Defying the right of the British Government to enforce compulsory service on this country, we pledge ourselves solemnly to one another by the most effective means at our disposal.' It was further agreed that the Hierarchy must be invited to endorse the meeting's conclusions, and a delegation, which included O'Neill and de Valera, set out for Maynooth, where it received 'a great ovation' from the seminarians.

The bishops responded more cautiously. But after an hour's discussion – during which they refused to give their blessing to the Mansion House resolution – they agreed to a statement of their own: 'We consider that conscription, forced in this way upon Ireland, is an oppressive and inhuman law which the Irish people have a right to resist by every means consistent with the law of God' – the law of man being more restrictive. In the end, even Cardinal Logue, notorious for his allegiance to the crown, agreed, though he confided to Arch-bishop Walsh that he feared it was 'the worst day's work the bishops ever did'. But, for once, nationalist politicians and the Hierarchy were united. A special anti-conscription Mass was held in Dublin and, on the day that the trade unions held a general strike, Maynooth closed down and sent its seminarians home.

The Catholic Church in Ireland – both its bishops and its priests – had always been divided about the call for Home Rule which evolved into the campaign for independence. However, all but a small and unrepresentative minority of militant priests had been strongly and publicly opposed to the violence that accompanied the nationalist movement. One of the exceptions – identified only by his great age – was with the Volunteers on the roof of the besieged General Post Office on Easter Day 1916. As they waited for the final attack he suggested that, as they were about to die, he should give them conditional abso-lution. 'I shall ask each of you in turn to say that you are sorry ...'[2] They knelt, one by one – still holding their rifles – and asked for forgiveness of their sins.

In Boland's Mill – where the Volunteers were under the command of Eamon de Valera – confessions were made in the privacy of a commandeered baker's van and Cathal MacDowell, one of the small number of Protestants to take part in the Rising, converted to Catholi-cism during the siege and was baptized before the garrison surrendered.

Whether or not Catholics made the Rising, the Rising certainly made Catholics. Three of the sixteen executed leaders – James Connolly, Joseph Plunkett and Thomas MacDonagh – were married to Protestants. The three widows became Catholics.

The Easter Rising was suppressed and there followed six years of sporadic violence – at first Irish republicans against the British, and then Irishmen against Irishmen in a conflict that was sufficiently widespread and organised to amount to civil war. The Catholic Church was virtually unanimous in its condemnation of the often-indiscriminate slaughter. Its attitude was typified by a conversation between a priest and an elderly farmer, overheard by an English journalist, at the end of a by-election meeting in Clare. The Sinn Fein Candidate was Eamon de Valera, on parole from prison. The tone of his speech had been sufficiently incendiary to make the old farmer ask one of the priests in the audience, 'Is there another rising in the air, Father?' The priest replied, 'God forbid, Pat, we want no more bloodshed and we won't have it.'[3]

Nationalism, in its most violent form, proved too strong for even the Church to hold at bay, even though many of the men who committed murder in Ireland's name went to church each Sunday and – having confessed some of their sins – took Communion. The 'outrages' continued and the Church grew increasingly vocal in its condemnation. That did not prevent priests, who believed in Irish independence, supporting Sinn Fein. They were inclined, with dubious authority, to claim that the outrages were not sanctioned by the nationalist leadership. When, in January 1919, two officers of the Royal Irish Constabulary were shot dead in Tipperary, an anonymous priest told the local newspaper, 'Leaders of the popular movement are far too local and God-fearing to countenance such a crime.'[4] The theft of dynamite – which was accompanied by the gratuitous murder of the two policemen – was certainly a local initiative. But there was no reason to believe that the leadership disapproved of the deaths that followed. Public condemnation was left to the Catholic Church.

On the Sunday after the shootings, priests – at Masses throughout County Tipperary – condemned the murders and the murderers, led prayers for the souls of the dead constables and warned that to support the crime, or the criminals, was a mortal sin. In Thurles Cathedral, the Archbishop of Cashel described the killings as a 'Crime against God' and instructed the congregation to 'pray that we may be spared the recurrence of such a deed'.[5] At St Michael's – in the town of Tipperary – Monsignor Ryan ended his sermon, 'God help poor Ireland if she follows this deed of blood.'

Daniel Cohalan, the Bishop of Cork, although a committed and public supporter of Irish independence, went further. Some apologists for nationalist violence tried to justify assaults on officers of the Royal Irish Constabulary with the accusation that they were both willing agents of British oppression and instigators of random acts of violence that exceeded, in brutality, the crimes they were employed to suppress. In March 1920 – after a spate of killings of which the RIC were almost certainly guilty, Bishop Cohalan asked a rhetorical question: 'Who are the Police?' His answer combined naivety with a more under-standable longing for peace. 'They are Irishmen doing their duty. I am satisfied that the National Organisation, which this county accepted and which it supports, has no responsibility for the murders.'[6] The peace for which the bishop hoped was a long time coming.

After the Irish Free State was founded in 1921 and the bloody battle for independence turned into a civil war between supporters of the settlement and irreconcilable opponents of partition, the Catholic Church in Ireland was again required to pronounce on the justice of the rival causes. Opposition to the treaty which partitioned Ireland and created the Irish Free State was led by paramilitary 'Volunteers', who fought their erstwhile colleagues in the independence movement with the ferocity with which they had opposed the British. The violence with which they went about their work was publicly condemned in a statement signed by Cardinal Logue, three archbishops, the entire Hierarchy of bishops and scores of parish priests. But the justice of the campaign against the Six Counties remaining part of the United Kingdom, and the predictions of the anti-partition parties, were both confirmed by the result of dividing Ireland into two nations. For more than half a century after the foundation of the Free State in the south, the Catholic minority in the Protestant north was subject to legalised repression and political discrimination which disqualified it from being described as a free country. Nothing like it had been seen in Britain since the reign of Ulster's hero, William of Orange.

Northern Ireland was created as a Protestant state. The boundary, which divided north from south, was drawn in a way that guaranteed it would so remain for the foreseeable future. Only six of the nine Ulster counties were included. Cavan, Monaghan and Donegal – where Catholics were, or soon would be, in a majority – were excluded on the principle, laid down by the *Belfast Telegraph*, that 'it was better for two thirds to save themselves than all the passengers drown'. Northern Ireland Protestant politicians warned the province of two related dangers. The first was open aggression from the Free State, supported by subversion by Catholics in the North. The second was the prospect of demographic change, brought about by the irresistible force of the Catholic birth rate. Both supposed threats to the integrity of the Protestant province were said to justify keeping the overt suppression of the 'enemy within'.

Anti-Catholic sentiment in the England of the sixteenth, seventeenth and eighteenth centuries had been heightened by the fear – sometimes justified, but more often not – that 'Papists' were standing ready to support an invasion from France or Spain. In twentieth-century Northern Ireland, belief that the Free State was plotting and planning to create a unified Catholic Ireland was increased by the behaviour of Dublin politicians, all of whom came together in their support of a United Ireland. And, when the constitution of the Irish Republic was written, it explicitly refused to recognise the border and formally asserted the South's claim to the Six Counties. The unification clauses were purely symbolic. And the shrewd Protestant politicians of the North must have known that much of the fighting talk was merely posturing. But exaggerating the threat was a convenient way of justifying the suppression of Catholics and the demonisation of Catholicism. The fact that the Protestant politicians often rendered themselves ridiculous did nothing to make their behaviour less sinister. The *Belfast Newsletter* claimed that the beatification of Oliver Plunkett, 'an Irish rebel hanged for treason', was intended to encourage rebellion.[7] On the night that it was announced, Catholics were attacked on the streets of Belfast. The sectarian violence was subsequently attributed, by the Orange extremists, to the malevolent influence of Rome. 'The bigotry of the [Catholic] Church and its constant efforts [open and secret] to increase its powers [had],' the *Belfast Newsletter* asserted, 'brought a large part of Ireland to lawlessness.'

The Catholic Hierarchy – constantly subject to harassment that included Cardinal Logue being stopped and searched at gunpoint and bishops' homes being raided – was said to have justified its pariah status by expressing its formal disapproval of partition. Different bishops expressed their individual opposition in different ways. Cardinal MacRory offered the considered view that Protestants were not real Christians. He was disowned by the rest of the Hierarchy. But when the IRA transmuted from the army of the nascent republic into a secret terrorist society, there was always an episcopal reluctance (and sometimes a refusal) to excommunicate its members, no matter how hideous their crimes. The Bishop of Waterford stood out from the crowd when he described IRA membership as a mortal sin. But the Church, as a whole, was flaccidly 'against all violence', and Bishop Mageean reconciled the conciliatory inclination with the rejection of partition by arguing that the border was created to perpetuate 'those religious animosities that have for so long disgraced the north-east corner of Ireland in the eyes of the civilised world'.[8]

The Protestant majority in the Six Counties never hid its intention of forming what Sir James Craig – the first Prime Minister of Northern Ireland – called 'A Protestant government for a Protestant people'. Craig gloried in being blatantly partisan. 'I have always said that I am an Orangeman first and a politician afterwards.'[9] The prejudices, which he called principles, were the product of the belief that every Catholic was a potential terrorist who was determined to absorb the Protestant, and obsessively British, Six Counties into what became the Catholic Irish republic. That meant guaranteeing an overwhelming Protestant majority in Stormont, the Belfast Parliament, and control of local authorities – if necessary, achieved and secured by manipulation of the voting system and the gerrymandering of boundaries. But that was only the beginning. The security of the state required the administration of Northern Ireland's national and local government to be purged of Catholics who were, by definition, enemies of the state.

The treaty, by which the borderline was drawn and Northern Ireland founded, required a quota of Catholics – previously employed as civil servants in Dublin Castle – to be transferred to Belfast and employed in jobs that were similar to those they had occupied before partition. The quota was never filled. That did not prevent the Ulster Protestant Voters' Defence Association from sending a deputation to Craig with the complaint that Catholics were receiving a greater share of public appointments than was their due. The result was a year-by-year reduction in their already-depleted number. The treaty also stipulated that one-third of the Royal Ulster Constabulary should be recruited from Catholic members of the Royal Irish Constabulary. No attempt was made to meet that requirement. Instead the RUC was made up of Protestants from the Ulster Special Constabulary, members of the violently (and often lawlessly) anti-Catholic Ulster Volunteer Force and the 'Specials' who had played such an ignoble part in the suppression of the rebellion. Within weeks of the supposedly non-sectarian force being founded, its members set up their own Orange Lodge.

Although the creation of a northern state in which Catholics were overwhelmingly outnumbered had guaranteed a Protestant majority in the Stormont Parliament, the Unionist Party felt neither satisfied nor secure. So, in defiance of the treaty which founded the state, it changed the Northern Ireland voting system from proportional representation to the election of single-constituency Members. The Westminster government was complicit in the flagrant breach of the treaty. In 1928, a delegation from the Six Counties minority parties asked the Home

Secretary, William Joynson-Hicks, to insist that the terms of the agreement be respected. He replied that it was purely a matter for James Craig, to whom he wrote with what amounted to the reassurance that Westminster would not stand in the way of continued malpractice. 'I don't know whether you would care, at any time, to discuss the matter with me; of course I am always at your disposal. But beyond that "I know my place" and don't propose to interfere.'[10]

The Catholic minority was permanently under-represented in the Northern Ireland Parliament. In the 1929 general election, Protestant-Unionist candidates won thirty-seven seats and Catholic-Nationalists together with Sinn Fein won fifteen. The Unionist majorities were so entrenched that in twenty-seven seats anti-Unionist candidates did not even contest the election. As a result the Protestant-Unionist Party knew it had won power two weeks before polling day. The situation was tailor-made for exploitation by the IRA, whose members argued that direct action was justified when political representation was denied. That enabled the Ulster Protestants' Defence League to claim that the denial of civil and political rights was justified by the obvious presence of a threat from an enemy within. The official, though unspoken, policy of the Catholic establishment was to work, as best the minority could, within the system. When the Catholic Members of Stormont were on the point of refusing to take their seats, it was their bishops who persuaded them to change their minds.

Protestants were just as determined to take and keep control of local councils as they were to maintain their hegemony in the national Parliament and just as unscrupulous in the pursuit of those objectives. The great municipal prize was Londonderry. In 1920 – against the odds and despite a variety of malpractices – it elected a Catholic mayor. There would have been riots in the city even had he not announced, in a reference to the Prentice Boys who closed the city gates against the advancing army of the Catholic Earl of Antrim, that the 'No Surrender citadel has been conquered after centuries of oppression' and that 'Ireland's right to determine her own destiny will come about whether the Protestants in Ulster like it or not.'[11] The Unionist Party reacted in the only way that could ensure its return to power. It readjusted the Londonderry ward boundaries. And it continued to adjust them, year by year, as demographic changes increased the Catholic vote in previously solid Protestant council seats. By 1930, 10,000 Derry Catholics (voting nationalist) were represented by eight councillors; 7,500 Protestants (voting Unionist) were represented by twelve. But the Protestant Unionists still did not feel safe. As late as 1936, a member of Craig's Cabinet wrote to him in near panic, 'Unless something is done now, it is only a matter of time until Derry passes into the hands of the nationalists for all time. On the other hand, if proper steps are taken now, I believe Derry can be saved for all time.'[12] By 'proper steps' he meant another boundary redistribution that tilted the balance of power further in the Protestant direction. The 'proper steps' were taken.

Ulster Protestants lived in constant dread of eventually being outnumbered because of the high Catholic birth rate and infiltration from the south. What James Craig tastefully described as 'breeding like bloody rabbits' was beyond Unionist control. But it was possible at least to reduce the number of immigrants from the Free State by denying them work in the North. The danger of Catholics from the South taking the jobs of loyal Ulstermen – and in the process acquiring voting rights in the Six Counties – was a constant theme of *Belfast Newsletter* editorials, and the Ulster Unionist Labour Association was particularly exercised by the influx of 'farm boys' who, after a few days' work, could register to vote. 'They have no stake whatever, not owning a blade of grass. Their power at the ballot box is, however, great.'[13] Speaking at a rally of Orangemen, a Major McCormick warned that 'thousands of Roman Catholics have been added to the population. In many places Protestant majorities are now minorities and at that rate of increase twenty years would see the Church of Rome in power.'[14] The Prime Minister himself joined the chorus of demands for discrimination, and the Grand Master of the Orange Lodge was frank about the reason why job applicants should be subject to a religious test: 'Whenever a Roman Catholic is brought into employment, it means one Protestant vote less.'

During the First World War, industries that had only employed Protestants were obliged to widen their recruitment policies. After the armistice and demobilisation, the Unionist Party demanded more than the right and proper reinstatement of returning servicemen. It made clear that it would settle for no less than the re-establishment of exclusively Protestant industries and, when employers were slow to respond to its call, organised riots in protest against what it described as 'pandering to Rome'. Anti-Catholic riots – usually called to protest against imaginary grievances – became a feature of life in Northern Ireland. In 1920 they succeeded in intimidating the dock owners into dismissing 2,000 Catholic workmen and it was estimated that, by the end of the year, 4,000 more were sacked from other Belfast companies. Protestant workers acquired the habit of forcing suspected Catholics to open their shirts to show whether or not they were wearing holy medals. The Prime Minister – in a fine example of his strange use of language – put on record his approval of the campaign to re-create exclusive Protestant companies: 'You boys have taken in the past.'

When the Great Depression of the 1930s brought increased unemployment to both religious communities, riots grew in frequency and violence. There was a brief moment when Protestants and Catholics, united in support of the non-sectarian Unemployed Workers' Committee, joined together to protest about the inadequacy of outdoor relief. But the ecumenical mood did not last. The Ulster Unionist Labour Association was formed with the purpose of insisting that 'it is the duty of our government to find employment for our people'. One of its complaints was that Catholic gravediggers were employed in Protestant cemeteries. The Minister of Labour denied 'scurrilous rumours' that Catholics were employed at Stormont in large numbers. Pressed to be more specific, he 'admitted' that one of the Parliament's thirty-one porters was a Catholic but he was on a short-term contract that would not be renewed. The UULA was superseded in 1931 by the Ulster Protestant League. Although it was created for the specific purpose of 'Safeguarding the employment of Protestants', it also regarded it as its duty to expose defrocked priests and to vilify the Belfast City Corporation for proposing to allow Catholic missionaries to hold a conference in the Ulster Hall.

The demands grew increasingly strident. 'When,' asked the Grand Master of the Orange Lodge, 'will the Protestant employers of Northern Ireland recognise their duty to their Protestant brothers and sisters and employ them to the exclusion of Roman Catholics?' And the official response grew more and more accommodating. Sir Basil Brooke (James Craig's successor as Prime Minister of Northern Ireland) expressed parallel prejudices in a speech that was notable both for the blatant bigotry of its message and for the naivety of the language in which, according to the *Fermanagh Times*, it was expressed:

> There were a great number of Protestants and Orangemen who employed Roman Catholics. He felt he could speak freely on the subject as he had not one Roman Catholic about his place ... He would point out that the Roman Catholics were endeavouring to get in everywhere and were out with all their force and might to destroy the power and constitution of Ulster. There was a definite plot to overpower the vote of Unionists in the north. He would appeal to Loyalists therefore not to employ Catholic lads and lasses.[15]

Brooke, or Lord Brookeborough as he became, maintained the faith. Not once, during all his years in office, did he visit a Catholic school or accept an invitation to a Catholic reception.

One Catholic 'lad' was, however, offered employment by the Ulster

Unionist government. His name was Denis Stanislaus Henry and in August 1921 he was appointed Lord Chief Justice of Northern Ireland – in light of the riots, allegations of treason and accusations of religious persecution, a post of the utmost sensitivity. The incumbent had to be a man who could be trusted neither to feel the slightest sympathy for the nationalist cause nor to be swayed by sentimentality into treating Catholics who broke the law, in the battle against persecution and discrimination, with the slightest leniency. Denis Stanislaus Henry, despite his religious affiliation, was such a man.

Henry was described by T P O'Connor – an Irish Home Rule MP who represented a Liverpool constituency – as 'a somewhat unique type in Irish life ... Entirely at variance with the politics of his co-religionists.'[16] He was the product of his birth and upbringing. The Henrys, landowners in County Derry, had been fierce opponents of the Land League and, although historically Liberals, they had described themselves as 'reluctant to go with Mr Gladstone when he took up Home Rule'. Denis Henry was a pupil at Mount St Mary's, an English boarding school in Derbyshire, and his education continued along an unusual path when he read law at Queen's College, Belfast – an institution of which the Irish Hierarchy thoroughly disapproved. He was a brilliant student and was called to the Irish Bar at the tender age of twenty-one.

Active participation in politics had to wait until his legal reputation had been made and his fortune secured, but he spoke on Unionist platforms during the general election of 1895 and was a delegate to the inaugural meeting of the Ulster Unionist Council, ten years later. He was a defeated candidate in a 1906 by-election – when he was described by the *Irish News* as 'one of that weird class of creature known as an Irish Catholic Unionist' – but had to wait until 1916 before the South Londonderry constituency sent him to Westminster. In the Lloyd George Coalition of 1918 he was appointed Attorney General for Ireland. It was a bad time to be an Irish law officer. A bitter civil war was raging and British troops – together with the para-military auxiliaries – were being accused of murder. Henry, believing that he could defend the indefensible, was a disaster.

He was never at his ease in the House of Commons, but there were a number of occasions when his performance was particularly woeful. In April 1920, when he was challenged about the condition of Sinn Fein hunger strikers in Mountjoy Gaol, it was clear – though not admitted – that Henry barely knew of their existence. The result was the prisoners' release and a confession to the Cabinet that the issue had been 'badly handled'. Later that year he introduced the Restoration of Order Act, which established military-style court martials with the power to impose the death penalty – a measure that, he argued, was warranted by the need to suppress 'rebels' and 'traitors'. It seemed that he saw his duty as defending the police and army, no matter how grave and indisputable the charge against them.

It was in November 1921, when the responsibility for law and order was transferred to Belfast, that Denis Henry became the Lord Chief Justice of Northern Ireland. His four years in office were notable for what might, charitably, be called 'controversial judgements'. Chief among them was his denial of compensation to the relatives and dependants of three Catholic youths who were shot dead by Special Constables. The police claimed that they had returned fire after being ambushed. Sir Denis, as he had become, rejected their evidence. 'My conclusion is that nobody except the police and military even fired at all.'[17] But he dismissed the claim for compensation on the grounds that the youths had been taking part in an unlawful assembly, as defined in the Emergency Powers Act.

During Henry's years as Attorney General for Ireland violence against Protestants had been just as widespread and indiscriminate as violence against Catholics. During the twenty-four months that led up to partition in 1921, 257 Catholics, 157 Protestant civilians and 37 members of the security forces (Protestant to a man) were murdered. After the creation of the Irish Free State and the province of Northern Ireland, the picture changed. South of the border, the Irish Catholic majority was preoccupied by the civil war between the pro- and anti-treaty factions. In the North the Protestants mounted a campaign of lethal violence, which exceeded in calculated brutality the organised savagery of Elizabethan England. During two months in 1922, 232 people – most of them Catholics – were killed, 11,000 Catholic workers lost their jobs, 23,000 Catholic families were evicted from their homes in so-called Protestant districts, and five hundred Catholic shops and businesses were burned and looted.[18]

The burning and looting – though the work of mobs – were an extension of official Orange Lodge policy. The boycott of Catholic shops and public houses began soon after partition, but after 1935 it was coordinated by the Ulster Protestant League. The campaign was nothing if not comprehensive. It required good Orangemen 'neither to talk with, nor walk with, neither to buy nor sell, borrow nor lend, take nor give or to have any dealings with' their natural enemy.[19] Catholic businesses that could not be persuaded to leave the province by bombing and burning were to be forced out by bankruptcy. Commercial assault was to augment street violence. Half-hearted attempts at retaliation by Northern Irish Catholics were condemned by the Church.

From time to time moderate Protestants and Unionists, fearful of the commercial consequences of continued disturbance, spoke out against the anti-Catholic violence and discrimination. Lord London-derry went as far as calling the attacks 'reprehensible'[20] and an alliance of businessmen, from both faiths, warned James Craig of the economic consequences that would follow continued disruption of trade. Prot-estants in the Free State dissociated themselves from the attacks and the all-Irish Protestant Convention denounced attacks on Catholics as 'un-Christian'. The Northern Ireland government made a token gesture of support for the beleaguered minority. A handful of Protestants were interned under the Special Powers Act. Two of them were B-Special police reservists. They were swiftly released and reinstated. The outspoken Bishop MacRory was not impressed by the show of moder-ation. The Protestants, he said, 'talk glibly of civil and religious liberty [but] appear by their actions not to have the most elementary idea of what either means'. The violence was temporarily halted. But the institutional discrimination remained. For Catholics, houses and jobs were in short supply for the next forty years.

Catholics knew they could expect to be protected by neither the law nor the police. Indeed, some of the worst acts of sectarian savagery were committed by police officers and auxiliaries acting, as they claimed, to uphold the peace. The official response to complaints of 'suspects' being shot in their beds and arbitrary executions was an Act of Parliament which provided the police with indemnity against legal action taken against them for conduct that – though outside the law – was certified as necessary to preserve the peace. The Catholic-Police Committee, set up under the provisions of the treaty, was intended to increase confidence in the minority community. It never had that effect. From the start, the Protestant senior officers were reluctant to discuss security with Catholics whose loyalty was automatically suspect. It was disbanded when two of its members were arrested.

The assumption of disloyalty and subversion was not the only – and perhaps not the most damaging – stereotyping that Northern Ireland Catholics had to endure. The ingrained conviction that they were feck-less, work-shy and innately disreputable prejudiced their chances of receiving a fair share of what little help was available to the destitute: the desperate need of men who were denied employment because of their religion. The Belfast Board of Guardians, which was responsible for the distribution of outdoor relief, recorded that 'faced with such sloth, fecklessness and iniquity', it had a duty to 'discourage idleness and create a spirit of enterprise' by withholding payment whenever possible.[21] The respectable well-to-do felt particularly resentful about large Catholic families being subsidised by more provident Protestants. Catholics, said one chairman of a Board of Guardians, do not suffer 'poverty under the blankets'. Professor Corkey, a Presbyterian theologian and former Northern Ireland Education Minister, wrote that parents of large families should be fined for their irresponsibility. His proposal was endorsed by the General Council of the Presbyterian Church.

The education system that was set up in post-treaty Northern Ireland was built on the Protestant myths of Catholic idleness and treachery. The chairman of the Commission which was deputed to draw up the scheme was emphatic about the obstacles that he had to overcome. 'There are two peoples in Ireland, one industrious, law-abiding and God-fearing, the other slothful, murderous and disloyal.'[22] He accommodated the need for protection against disloyalty by including Northern Ireland teachers within the scope of the Promissory Oaths Act, thus requiring them to swear their allegiance to the British crown and Northern Ireland government. The Six Counties reintroduced the Test Acts four hundred years after their first incarnation.

Fortunately, Northern Ireland education was initially saved from further excesses of Protestant zeal by the appointment of Lord Londonderry, a liberal Unionist, as a responsible minister. He attempted the impossible – integrated elementary schools that would demonstrate and protect their non-denominational character by not including religious instruction in their curriculum. To encourage the cooperation of the Catholic Schools board it was announced – more stick than carrot – that the grant they received in support of their own schools was abolished.

The Londonderry proposals were universally condemned. Both Catholics and Protestants *wanted* sectarian education. Some Catholics refused to teach in the new schools. Others refused to accept a salary. The Protestant response was more bellicose and better organised, under the guidance of the United Education Committee of the Protestant Churches. Rallies and protest marches were organised and old slogans were amended to make them appropriate to the new 'threat' from Rome. The battle cry was 'Protestant teachers for Protestant schools' and the awful spectre was raised of Catholic teachers being paid from the rates to indoctrinate the young and innocent with 'Popish' theology. The formal demand of the Orange Lodges was extensive and precise. Protestant denominational schools were to be re-established. Religious instruction was to be reinstated. The schools were to be staffed by teachers who had been appointed by boards of governors which included at least one Protestant minister among its members and which were allowed to ask the religious denomination of applicants. The Stormont government agreed in principle, and Lord Londonderry resigned.

In 1930 a new Northern Ireland Education Act widened and entrenched the sectarian divide. James Craig described it as making state schools 'safe for Protestant children'. The Catholic Church, if it insisted on its own schools, would have to pay part of the running costs. The alternative was Catholic children attending schools in which all children were to receive religious instruction that conformed to the 'fundamental principle of Protestantism'. The attempts to end sectarian education in Northern Ireland foundered, as did all ecumenical initiatives in the province, on the intransigence of both Catholics and Protestants. But because the Catholics made up only a small percentage of the population they were forced to be defiant in defeat, while the Protestants were vainglorious in victory. The result was the brutalising of a whole community – forced to inhabit ghettos, as much by the discrimination in municipal housing policy as by the prejudice of private landlords, and subject to constant humiliation as well as the deprivation that follows long-term unemployment. The bigotry of the Six County Protestants is best illustrated by the refusal of the City Council to honour Belfast's only First World War VC – because he happened to be a Catholic. The riots of the 1960s should not have come as a surprise. Looking back, it is incredible that the Catholics waited so long.

The most depressing aspect of Northern Ireland after the Second World War was its similarity to Northern Ireland before the Second World War. Protestant fears of being absorbed into the Catholic Free State were, irrationally, increased by the Ireland Act, by which the Republic left the Commonwealth, and, rationally, by changes in the demographic pattern of the province. In 1945, Catholics made up 33 per cent of the Northern Ireland population. By the end of the century it was 40 per cent. The Protestant majority reacted to the supposed threat by adding blatantly discriminatory public housing policies to the manipulation of boundaries. 'Loyal' wards and constituencies were kept pure orange.

The boom in post-war council-house building gave the Unionist councils a new opportunity to solidify their support in Protestant areas – a domination that was promoted by the Northern Ireland local government franchise, which limited the vote to ratepayers and their spouses and therefore discriminated against large Catholic families with adult children living at home. The new houses were allocated to tenants on the waiting list by groups of councillors who often identified the applicants by name and religion. Slum clearance of Northern Ireland's mass of condemned properties was concentrated in Protestant districts. The chairman of the Enniskillen housing committee could not have been more frank about the criteria on which the choice of areas was made. 'The Council will decide which wards the houses are to be built in. We are not going to build houses in the South Ward and cut a rod to beat ourselves with later on. We are going to see that the right people are put in those houses and we are not going to apologise for it.'[23] The result was double detriment – votes rigged to prevent Catholic control of councils, and Catholics condemned to remain in slum housing.

The most surprising feature of the 'troubles', which engulfed Northern Ireland in the 1970s and 1980s, is the time they took to begin. By the time that 'power-sharing' reduced, and almost eliminated, the violence, the dissidents' main objective had become 'a united Ireland'. But the civil-rights movement of the late 1960s, and the civil-rights marches it organised, were a response to blatant discrimination, not part of a political campaign. The beginning of the protests and demonstrations can be precisely identified. A house in Caledon, County Tyrone, was allocated to a nineteen-year-old unmarried Protestant woman (the secretary to the council's solicitor, who was a Unionist parliamentary candidate) in preference to two Catholic families who were squatting nearby. The Tyrone Council had refused to build houses in nearby Catholic Dungannon. On June 28th 1968, after the squatters were forcibly evicted by the police, Austin Currie – a Catholic Stormont MP – symbolically 'occupied' the nineteen-year-old woman's house. He too was evicted by the police, one of whom was the young lady's brother and future tenant of the disputed property. That night, Catholic protestors marched from Coalisland to Dungannon, where they were confronted by Ulster Protestant Volunteers. The UPV was the creation of the Reverend Dr Ian Paisley, then pastor of a Belfast church which subscribed to a form of Presbyterianism that Dr Paisley had invented. From then on, the march and counter-march fever reached epidemic proportions. The climax came on October 8th in the city of Londonderry when a giant civil-rights demonstration was first banned by the Stormont government and then, when the ban was ignored, broken up, with unrestrained violence, by the almost exclusively Protestant Royal Ulster Constabulary. As late as 2002, only 8 per cent of Northern Ireland police officers were Catholics.

The Westminster government had little choice but to intervene. Direct Rule, though inevitable, was postponed while Sir Terence

O'Neill – then, by Northern Ireland standards, a progressive Stormont Prime Minister – first initiated and then extended 'bridge-building'. The hard-line Protestant view was promoted by increasingly vocal Protestant workers who feared that 'concessions' to Catholics would threaten their entrenched employment in the industries that they dominated.

As late as March 1992 a survey of Northern Ireland's major companies revealed that only 148 of Harland and Wolff's 2,700 employees were Catholic[24] – a ratio that had been achieved by the expulsion of 500 'Papists' in June 1970, following riots in which four Protestants were killed. But in May 1977 – much to everyone's surprise – Belfast shipyard workers refused to join the strike that had been called by Dr Paisley's United Unionist Action Council in protest against the imposition of Direct Rule. The strike came to an inglorious end when employees at the Ballylumford power station refused to close down the generators.

It took another thirty years for universal human rights and civil peace to be established in Northern Ireland. By then the 'troubles' had regressed to their inter-war form and were principally concerned with the demand for Irish unity. Again, all Catholics were held in suspicion – stigmatisation that was said to be justified by the (undoubted but irrelevant) fact that most members of the IRA and of Sinn Fein (the anti-partition party) were nominal Catholics. The Catholic Hierarchy was open and explicit in its condemnation of the campaign of murder and mayhem. On September 12th 1971, Cardinal Conway and five bishops from his archdiocese denounced the 'small group of people who are trying to secure a united Ireland by use of force ... Who in their right minds wants to bomb 1,000,000 Protestants into a united Ireland?'[25]

In Northern Ireland, Catholic attitudes towards the British Government changed during the second half of the twentieth century. At first there was the fear that the 'imperial parliament' was only interested in preserving the union and that measures, claimed to be necessary to preserve the peace, had the real purpose of suppressing the minority. Sir John Peck, the British Ambassador to Dublin, wrote, with absolute justification, 'Internment attacked the Catholic community as a whole. What was worse, it was directed solely against the Catholics, although there were many Protestants who provided just as strong grounds for internment.'[26] Catholic attitudes changed as the 'peace process' ground on, bringing with it previously unknown levels of social justice and equality of treatment. Yet the Catholic Church, or sections of it, remained magnificently detached from the implementation of the policies that achieved those objectives.

On October 5th 1988 the Westminster government announced its intention of promoting integrated education. Six days later, Monsignor Colm McCaughan, the director of the Catholic Council for Maintained Schools, announced that Catholic parents who sent their children to non-denominational schools would be breaking canon law. It was not only Orangemen who cried 'no surrender' at the suggestion that Northern Ireland's future depended on compromise.

It would be wrong to say that the bitter ancient sectarianism of Northern Ireland was exported to Liverpool. There had been bitter tension between Catholics and Protestants ever since the city had become reluctant host to refugees from the 'Great Hunger' in the 1840s and '50s. But events in the Six Counties intensified the bitterness, and Liverpool Protestant extremists – most of them manual workers or unemployed – took every opportunity to hurt and humiliate the one stratum of society over which they could claim superiority. During the riots that followed the national police strike in 1919, the *Liverpool Catholic Herald* reported that 'Catholic and Irish houses were the first to be attacked' and noted that Peter Murphy's shop had been subject to highly discriminating vandalism. The 'window filled with tobacco and general goods was left untouched', but the 'window stocked with Irish literature, music, statues of Our Lady and other objects of devotion was smashed to atoms'.[27]

The diocese itself had begun the campaign to improve the reputation as well as the living conditions of Catholic Liverpool. Notwithstanding the poverty of many parishes, its status was to be elevated by investment in a prestigious project. Liverpool was to be the home of 'The Cathedral of Our Time', which was to combine half a dozen schools of architecture in a basilica that boasted a higher tower than the Anglican cathedral on the nearby hill. The crypt was constructed, but then the building fund was exhausted. It was forty years before a Catholic cathedral – of totally different design from the original concept – rose above the dashed hopes of the 1920s.

Other areas of activity confirmed that, although the cathedral-building fund dried up between the wars, the Liverpool Catholic Church remained determined to make its civic mark. It had always taken a detached interest in local politics. The nature of its members made tacit – though silent – support for the local (and essentially sentimental) Irish National Party inevitable, but in 1925 it plunged into deeper and more turbulent waters by setting up the Catholic Representation Council. Its founders insisted that it was 'essentially non-political'. Is it, asked the Vicar General, 'politics [for Catholics] to safeguard the Faith of their children? That is all the Council is out for. In the time of the old School Board we got our men in and politics was never dreamed of. If there is any attempt to renew sectarian trouble it will not come from our side.'[28]

The candidates who were defeated by CRC nominees could have found little comfort in the assurance that their victorious opponents had won a non-political battle. The Catholic Representation Council ran essentially Catholic campaigns in predominantly Catholic wards on a manifesto that was built around an unashamed promise to protect Catholic interests. Its candidates undertook, if elected, 'to effectively safeguard the character of Catholic schools and the interests of Catholic children ... [and] to strive for the social betterment of Catholic working men and working women'.[29]

The Catholic candidates were victorious in four seats out of the five which they contested – including the North Scotland ward, where Monsignor George himself won 80 per cent of the votes cast. In the exuberance of victory, they broke the inter-party convention, opposed the re-election of a sitting alderman and replaced him with P J Kelly, who was not even a city councillor. Kelly did, however, possess impeccable Catholic credentials. He was a major figure in the Ancient Order of Hibernians – the self-proclaimed 'only Catholic and national friendly society in the world'.

The Catholic Party did not last long. Within days of the election it was amalgamated with the Irish Party. The policy of the new organisation remained 'that of the Catholic Representation Association ... Being opposed to reactionary Toryism on one side as well as destructive Communism on the other'. The Centre Party, as the new organisation called itself, was dissolved before its successful candidates had the opportunity to stand for re-election. It was infiltrated, overrun and eventually consumed by the Labour Catholics. In 1928, Richard Downey – the recently appointed Archbishop of Liverpool – accepted the inevitable and announced that, in his judgement, Catholic interests would best be served by the pursuit of the Church's interests through the established political parties.

P J Kelly joined the Labour Party. More significant was the death of T P O'Connor, the long-serving Irish nationalist. The seat was inherited by Davie Logan, who had been elected to the council as a Nationalist but had defected to the Labour Party. Among his qualifications to follow the legendary 'Tay Pay' was his prominence in the Knights of St Columba – thought of by fearful Protestants as the 'Catholic Freemasons'. The Knights had been praised by Archbishop Keating (Richard Downey's predecessor) as the 'spear-point for the Catholic movement in Liverpool'[30] and many of the 3,000 men who made up the Order's Merseyside 'province' certainly led the charge in support of Davie Logan during his by-election campaign. He won and became the first of the Liverpool Labour Members of Parliament to express a view of their duties which ran in parallel to the principles proclaimed by the Protestant leaders of the Northern Ireland Unionist Party. They were Catholics first and politicians second. For almost fifty years the Liverpool Labour Party sent a group of MPs to Westminster, who held, and freely expressed, the belief that their first duty was to their faith.

As late as the 1970s, Liverpool was still electing councillors who were candidates of the Protestant Party. It was less interested in promoting its apparent religious affiliation than in exploiting tribal loyalty. Paradoxically, many Labour councillors were more Catholic than socialist. The Church had a special reason for encouraging its members to become involved in local government. Councils were the conduit through which the national government financed schools. Liverpool Catholics faced a problem that was common to every diocese – how to maintain the religious integrity of Catholic schools and still qualify for the government grants which made possible expansion and improvement. Back in Archbishop Keating's day, the Board of Education had condemned the buildings which housed four of Liverpool's Catholic elementary schools and described four others as in urgent need of renovation. Keating had faced the dilemma with which Cardinals Manning and Vaughan had wrestled in London: to build a new cathedral to the glory of God or new schools for the education of His children. Of one thing he was certain. There could be no question of Catholic children being educated in non-denominational schools. In the end the Church was spared the choice between a cathedral and new schools. It could afford neither.

Financing Catholic education had become a problem throughout England as a result of the Fisher Education Act of 1918. The cost of doubling both teachers' pay and pensions was borne by the Board of Education. But the Act raised the mandatory school-leaving age to fourteen, gave local education authorities the right to increase it to fifteen and required provision to be made, for pupils who left at fourteen, to attend 'continuation schools'. In consequence, the school population was dramatically increased and the cost of new buildings, and the extension of old – which the increase required – had to be met by the denominations. A Catholic school place at the time of the 1870 Education Act was twenty-five shillings; this rose to £10 by 1918.[31] Yet the Church built ninety-six new schools during the twelve years that followed the First World War, as well as opening, in

London, St Vincent's – one of the few Day Continuation Schools that prospered. The history of Catholic elementary education between the wars is primarily the story of the Church's continuous struggle to win financial help without losing the independent right to appoint teachers and determine the syllabus.

The Hadow Report of 1931 required even more new buildings – for which the government was prepared to pay if, and only if, it was allowed to be responsible for the appointment of all teachers other than those who gave religious instruction. The Church was not given the chance to discuss the proposed bargain. The clause of the Education Bill, which would have given effect to the arrangement, was deleted – on the initiative of a Catholic MP – during the committee stage in the House of Commons. The support of the whole committee for the amendment was an example of Protestant laymen being more Catholic than the Pope – or, at least, more Catholic than the Archbishop of Westminster. Cardinal Bourne was prepared to consider the government playing some part in appointing teachers of general subjects. Archbishop Hinsley, his successor, was equally – perhaps even more – pragmatic and accepted a building deal which was worse than the one that had been offered to his predecessor.

The more pragmatic and practical the Church's attitude to education became, the more it emphasised in its public statements the importance of not compromising with the secular authorities, national and local. 'It is not,' the Hierarchy thundered, 'the normal function of the state to teach ... The teacher is always acting *in loco parentis*, never *in loco civitatis* ... Whatever authority he may possess to teach and control children, and claim their respect and obedience, comes to him from God through the parents.' Conscience being salved, the Church accepted enough secular funding to allow the number of pupils in full-time Catholic education to increase from one in seventeen to one in fourteen of the total school population.

The Catholic Church in Scotland came to an agreement with the government which was at once tidier in its concept and application, and more satisfactory in terms of ensuring the continued integrity of Catholic education. The contentious issue was identical to the cause of disagreement in England – the guarantee that Catholic children received Catholic religious instruction. The Scottish Office initially proposed that what they called 'administrative dualism' – the Church's right to appoint the teachers in its schools – should be abandoned.

The Bishop of Pella, the Pope's Apostolic Visitor to Scotland, countered with an idea that he called 'religious dualism' – the Church approving the suitability of applicants for teaching posts in Catholic schools and the local education authorities making the actual appointments. Initially rank-and-file Catholics – especially parents with children of school age – were dubious about the merits of what came to be known as the 'concordat'. But the Vatican, in a rare intervention in Scottish affairs, ordered its acceptance. The Catholic schools of Scotland were transferred to secular ownership and were financed directly by the local authorities.

It was one of the few victories in which, between the wars, the Catholics of Scotland could rejoice. In 1923, the General Assembly of the Free Church of Scotland published a pamphlet which, today, would justify prosecution for promoting racial hatred. It was entitled *The Menace of the Irish Race to our Scottish Nationality*. The dire warnings of 'mongrelisation' were given spurious credibility by the work of G R Gair, a luminary of the Scottish Anthropological Society who published a series of articles which 'explained' the cultural and psychological differences between the Irish and the people among whom they had settled. The dangerous Irish characteristics included 'lack of obedience to prescribed ideas'[32] – by which he meant the ideas of the Protestant establishment.

The Irish Catholics of Scotland had ideas of their own. It was because of them that, in the year before the General Assembly, the British Cabinet had to accommodate the selective iconoclasm of John Wheatley, the first radical Catholic (and one of the few Catholics of any political description) to sit at the Cabinet table in Downing Street. While in Liverpool Catholic local politicians were being drawn into the Labour Party, in Glasgow the 'Red Clydesiders' – a political grouping built around the militant socialist trade unionists from the engineering and shipbuilding industries – feared and complained that the Labour Party was being absorbed by the Catholic Church. As with Catholic football clubs, so with Catholic political parties. The same insidious process was being used to spread its influence over other aspects of the city's life.

John Wheatley was an Irish immigrant and self-made businessman who had taken upon himself the task of convincing his fellow Irishmen that Home Rule was no longer their concern and that they should ally themselves to policies related to their new lives in their new country. Fearful that they would be reluctant actually to join Labour, he created a halfway house – the Catholic Socialist Society. At first it was the leadership of the Glasgow Catholic community who attempted to frustrate his plans. Sunday sermons were preached against the 'godless doctrine', and marches – often ending with noisy mass meetings outside his house – aimed to show that there was no support for the contradiction in terms called Catholic socialism. The turning point came as the result of the announcement that Hilaire Belloc was to visit Glasgow as part of his campaign to promote the growth of small businesses owned and run by sturdily independent craftsmen. Wheatley challenged him to a debate. It was held in the packed Pavilion Theatre. Belloc gave the more accomplished performance. Indeed, according to the criteria by which debating skills are normally judged, he won. But Wheatley – talking about colliery wages and working conditions in the dockyards – spoke a language the audience understood. There was a sudden surge in membership of the Catholic Socialist Society. As a result, it had a new enemy to combat: the Labour Party itself. The accusation was that Wheatley had introduced sectarian prejudice into a party which represented every faith and none. The fear was that he was building a power base which would enable him to become a Member of Parliament free from the shackles of the 'Red Clydesiders' who dominated Glasgow Labour politics. Wheatley became Minister of Health in the first Labour Government. His great achievement was a house-building programme which was more ambitious than anything that had gone before. He was certainly the success of the 1922 administration and arguably the most successful Catholic politician of the modern era. He was left out of the second Labour Government. As well as being 'too left-wing', he was said to be too Catholic. It was a time when family planning was becoming fashionable. John Wheatley would not support his Ministry of Health giving advice about contraception. The Catholic Church in Scotland regarded his exclusion as a new sort of martyrdom.

Catholics in Britain were never numerous enough to influence the course of parliamentary politics in the way that early-twentieth-century Nonconformists imposed their principles and prejudices on governments. The Catholics of the Irish Party can, however, take some credit for the invention of the parliamentary guillotine, since they were involved in the persistent obstruction of House of Commons business which, in 1887, led to the invention of a procedure by which debates can be curtailed. And in 1897 Catholic MPs – on the instruction of Cardinal Vaughan – ensured the passage of a contentious Education Bill, which, the Church hoped, would increase government subsidy of Catholic schools. But Catholic influence on Westminster politics has been more notable for the strength of its convictions than strength of numbers. In 2015, Jacob Rees-Mogg, MP, commenting on the proposal to legalise same-sex marriages, announced, 'I take my whip from the hierarchy of the Roman Catholic Church.'

CHAPTER 29

The Needs of Our Age

An institution that is inspired by Providence cannot easily set out on a programme of reform and modernisation. Changes in dogma and discipline carry with them the implication that God's mistakes must be corrected or that divine judgements differ with, and therefore are a consequence of, changes in the temporal world. For more than three hundred years the leadership of the Roman Catholic Church – conscious of that obvious truth – increased its strength (and the confidence of its members) by at least appearing to be impervious to attacks on its beliefs or its behaviour. It was not the habit of popes or bishops ever to give an indication that that they found the slightest merit in the arguments advanced by their critics, and most of the proposals for change and 'improvement' that came from inside the Church advocated tightening of the bonds that held lay Catholics close to Rome. Attack was always the preferred form of defence.

In response to the Reformation, the bull *Exsurge Domine* (published in 1520) identified forty-one errors in Martin Luther's theology. In 1864, the *Syllabus of Errors* – published by Pius IX – condemned eighty flaws and fallacies in the arguments advanced by sceptics, secularists and schismatics. It confirmed and reiterated the principle that Pope Gregory XVI had laid down in 1832. His encyclical, *Mirari Vos*, was a guide to the Church's response to innovation. Now and for ever there was only one way for the Catholic Church to fight the 'conspiracy of impious men'.[1] It would not yield one inch of its territory. 'Nothing of the things appointed ought to be diminished, nothing changed.'

The encyclical went on to denounce the modern heresies which the Church must, and would, combat and defeat. They included the 'abominable conspiracy against the celibacy of the clergy'. But rather more significant, given the mood of the time, was the rejection of 'the absurd and erroneous proposition that claims of freedom of conscience must be maintained for everyone'. Gregory XVI went on to denounce 'immoderate freedom of speech' as demanded by 'shameless lovers of liberty'. The denunciation concluded with the assertion that 'both divine and human law cry out against those who strive by treason and sedition to drive from people confidence in their princes'. Those sentiments were the Church's reaction to the wave of revolutions that swept through mid-nineteenth-century Europe. Their endorsement in the *Syllabus of Errors* was the Church's timeless response to the social and political liberalism which was manifest in the revolutions of 1848 and took root thereafter – movements which not even the Church of Rome was strong enough to brush aside.

The Vatican was less concerned with the health of the Church in Britain than with its condition in continental Europe, where secular political movements were fast gaining ground. But even in England – where the social hierarchy seemed unchanged and unchangeable, political stability was assured and the oppressive anti-Catholic laws had been repealed – there were still voices raised to proclaim that the Church must respond to the new demands of modern society. The complaint usually concluded that the choice lay between change and decay. Thinking Catholics worried about the Church's refusal to see itself as part of an increasingly complex world of scientific and political emancipation and its apparent inability to regard men and women of different faiths as anything other than heretics whose sins must be identified and denounced. Perhaps even more damaging was the reluctance to consider the feelings and convictions of those of its own members who were moving with the times, and at least realise that the Church must respond to economic and social changes in an uncertain world.

There were, from time to time, indications that the Church was looking beyond its own boundaries. In the encyclical *Rerum Novarum*, Pope Leo XIII had proclaimed the moral necessity of decent working conditions, a fair wage and protection of the workers' right to organise themselves in trade unions – highly progressive opinions, when it was published in 1891. But its actual provisions were less important, as an indication of the Church's changing attitude, than the spirit in which the encyclical was written. It conceded that, sometimes, power should be exercised by the meek and lowly, and it demonstrated that the Roman Catholic Church was beginning to take an interest in the world outside its theological boundaries. Pope Leo confirmed that welcome fact with the publication of *Diuturnum*, a disquisition on civil power. But since it concluded that 'it behoves all citizens to submit themselves and to be as obedient to rulers as to God',[2] the growing army of liberal Catholics were not convinced that the Pope's acknowledgement that Catholicism could not survive in a vacuum had made him an advocate of liberty, equality or fraternity.

Some tentative – perhaps even unintended – gestures of sympathy sustained the liberals' hope of real change. *Inter Sollicitudines* encouraged the use of Gregorian chant and, in consequence, the congregations' vocal participation in the Mass. But in 1907, the Vatican decided to challenge head-on what it called the Modernists Movement, which it defined by identifying the sixty-five heresies to which its members subscribed. They included the denial that the Bible, being inspired, was completely free of error and the proposition that marriage was a sacrament that had only become an article of faith during the Middle Ages. The Modernists' mistake was, the Vatican concluded, the belief that dogma is not only able but ought to evolve and to be changed. Its fear was that 'at the head of what the modernists teach is evolution' and the consequent conclusion that 'the state, to which learning has progressed, demands a reform of Christian teaching about God, creation, revelation, the person of the Word Incarnate and of redemption'.[3] The Church twice denounced such modernist heresies – first in *Lamentability* and then in *Pascendi Dominici Gregis*. The second condemnation admitted an important truth. There were 'partisans of error in the very heart and bosom of the Church'. Only one response was possible. Modernists were to be confronted with the unyielding certainty which had been the strength of the Church in its darkest days. When the First World War broke out, the Church was unchanged and apparently unchangeable.

During the twenty years of peace that separated the two World Wars, the pace of social change accelerated. Middle-class women were beginning to assert their rights, and women of all classes discovered that it was possible – easily, safely and cheaply – to avoid annual pregnancies. Sex – its purpose and its consequences – was to involve the Church in a long rearguard action that it is still fighting today. And while its social attitudes at home were forcing the otherwise faithful into disobedience, its attitude towards international affairs was causing a disquiet among liberal Catholics which went to the very heart of what they saw as the fundamental flaw in the Roman philosophy of survival. In 1929, a concordat with Mussolini established the Vatican City as an independent state. And Pius XII – elected Pope in March 1939 – notably failed to condemn the Holocaust. The complaint was not that the Catholic Church was inherently sympathetic to fascism – though it certainly initially welcomed the emergence of Mussolini, who had endeared himself to the Vatican by suppressing the anti-clerical Freemasons' Lodges. The objectionable feature of all the responses to dictatorship was the apparent reluctance to condemn (and even less a willingness to undermine) regimes that preserved and protected the interests of the Catholic Church. The existence of a small violently anti-clerical faction within the generally agnostic Spanish republican movement – not to mention the murder of priests and the rape of nuns – goes some way towards explaining the Vatican's sympathetic attitude towards General Franco's insurrection against the lawfully elected government in Spain. But the moral propriety of its attitude aside, Rome's response to the events that led up to the outbreak of war in 1939 did create the impression that the Catholic Church was turning in on itself rather than facing the problems of the world.

Opponents of Catholicism believed their criticisms to be justified and reinforced by the creation in 1928 of Opus Dei – an organisation which, while bizarrely unrepresentative of the twentieth-century Church, confirms, by its existence, the need – among at least a small percentage of Catholics – for an uncompromising faith that demands the extreme manifestation of an absolute commitment. Although Opus Dei is not, as its enemies claim, a secret society, it certainly works hard to keep secret some of its beliefs. Among them is the importance of mortifying the flesh – sometimes by fasting or sleeping on a hard mattress without a pillow, sometimes by self-flagellation and wearing a hair shirt (*cilice*) and a spiked ring worn round the leg to suppresses sexual desire.[4] In that particular it can claim to act in a tradition that was sanctified, if not popularised, by Thomas More.

The overt purpose of Opus Dei is to enable its members (93,000 worldwide in 2014, 2,000 of whom were priests) 'to find God in daily life'. That objective is said to be achieved by regarding work as a sacrament and by observing strict religious disciplines. There are various categories of membership. The largest (70 per cent) has the ambiguous title of Supernumeraries. They devote part of their lives to prayer and much of their income to Opus Dei. Numeraries (20 per cent) follow the same discipline, but are celibate and live in Opus Dei centres. The civilised hostility that Opus Dei attracts was revealed in 'guidelines' which, in 1982, Cardinal Hume helpfully suggested should govern its conduct – and which were made available to newspapers. No one under the age of eighteen should be allowed to make 'a long-term commitment' to Opus Dei. Young recruits should not be enrolled before they 'discuss the matter' with their parents or guardians. The 'freedom to leave' must be respected.

It would be wrong to imagine that Opus Dei has any connection with events that feature in *The Da Vinci Code*. The most often-heard complaint against it is that – at a time when Catholics should be looking to the world beyond Rome – everything about Opus Dei encourages introspection. Yet the existence of the society was endorsed by Pope Pius XII in 1950, and in 1982 Pope John Paul II made it a 'personal prelature' under the exclusive jurisdiction of its own bishop. At almost exactly the midpoint between those two dates the Second Vatican Council met to consider how best to face the challenges that Opus Dei chose to ignore.

For some years there had been indications that Rome was preparing to move with the times. Throughout the Second World War and the twenty years of troubled peace that followed, the Vatican gave out encouraging signals about its attitude towards the spirit of the age. In his 1943 Christmas message Pius XII announced, with apparent approval, that 'the future belongs to democracy' – a judgement which would have been too liberal for Pio Nono at his most progressive. During the same year *Divino Afflante Spiritu* gave papal approval to the historical and philosophical method of biblical study replacing the traditional 'allegorical' exegesis. *Mystici Corporis Christi* conceded that non-Catholics could be saved if they had lived virtuous lives and would have been baptised into the Church of Rome, had they known of its existence. Liberal Catholicism seemed to be gaining ground. Then on August 4th 1950 *Humani Generis* was published.

In that encyclical Pius XII denounced theologians who, 'desirous of novelty', minimised the distinction between Catholics and subscribers to 'dissident' faiths. The result of their philosophic ecumenisms was, he claimed, a modification of the central doctrine of transubstantiation, an interpretation of Genesis that allowed for the possibility that Adam was not the solitary begetter of the whole human race – a view with which John Henry Newman had compromised one hundred years earlier – and the denial of the doctrine that 'the Mystical Body of Christ and Roman Catholic Church are one and the same thing'. That definition of the Church was to prove crucial to the historic debate on the nature and future of Roman Catholicism which came to be called the Second Vatican Council.

On October 28th 1958, Angelo Giuseppe Roncalli was elected Pope in succession to Pius XII. Fourteen weeks later, having consulted no one and forewarned only Cardinal Domenico Tardini, his Secretary of State, John XXIII, as he had become, announced his intention of calling a Council of the Catholic Church. Councils in the past had most often been called to respond to an external threat or to plan the defeat of persistent heresy. The Council of Trent (1545–61) had been summoned to coordinate opposition to the Reformation, and the First Vatican Council (1869–70) had been assembled to reassert the authority of the Pope in the face of a threat so severe that the assembly had to be abandoned when Italian troops occupied Rome. Vatican I was never officially closed and both Pius XI (in the 1920s) and Pius

XII (in the 1950s) had seriously, and secretly, considered completing its work. It was abandoned unfinished. Vatican II was a new Council with a new purpose.

Pope John XXIII had already established his 'progressive' credentials with three encyclicals: *Princeps Pastorum* (an increased role for the laity), *Mater et Magistra* (the Church's social obligation) and *Pacem in Terris* (the hope of peace). His early indication of the Council's purpose emphasised, as was required of him, the need to reaffirm doctrine and discipline. But he added a more novel objective to his list of intentions. The Council was to promote 'the enlightenment, edification and joy of the entire Christian people' and to offer a 'cordial invitation to the faithful of separated communities to participate with us in this quest for unity and grace, for which so many souls long in all parts of the world'. The Catholic Church – or at least its Pope – was reaching out to the world.

Vatican II, like every Council before it, was called to overcome a crisis in the life of the Church. But, unlike its predecessors, the threat it faced came not from some external enemy or internal subversion. It came from the refusal of its leadership to change with the times – particularly in its attitude towards other faiths. The old certainties had been shaken by the new realities: the risk of nuclear annihilation as much as the determination of free people to take control of their own lives. Pope John XXIII declared himself to be a gardener rather than a museum-keeper.[5]

That homely image was either misunderstood or ignored by most of the bishops and clergy who were invited to nominate items for the Council agenda. They responded without thinking it necessary to consult either parish priests or their parishioners. A majority of the 1,998 replies to the 2,598 invitations proposed the denunciation of modern evils, the confirmation of established values and the reaffirmation of accepted doctrine. The most frequent request was for a renewed emphasis on the intercessory powers of the Virgin Mary. Only a small minority asked for the opportunity to promote the introduction of the vernacular Mass and the greater involvement of the laity in the affairs of the Church; and a dozen or so letters, all from outside Europe and the Americas, wanted to discuss, and possibly relax, the clergy's obligation to celibacy.

The Preparatory Commission 'summarised' the possible subjects for debate in a document of 2,060 pages. Despite its length, it was highly selective in its choice of potential topics. All the preparatory work was based on the same cautious principle. The initial agenda, and the documents on which the discussions were to be based, were drawn up by members of the Curia, the Vatican bureaucracy, and, in consequence, ignored – in both style and substance – anything that might be called modern. But the output of the Council was very different from the input of the men who prepared the schemata on which the discussions were eventually based. Rome did not speak for the Catholic world. It was estimated that 85–90 per cent of the bishops who took part in the Council held opinions that could reasonably be called 'transalpine' rather than 'ultramontane'. They believed that Rome was not the one reliable source of all that was true and holy. They also knew that, historically, they too were inheritors of the Apostolic Succession – a role which had been diminished by Pius IX's claims to infallibility. They were, therefore, entirely justified in rejecting the accusation that they were 'modernists'. In their methodology, they pre-dated the traditionalists. Much of their argument rested on the need to relate dogma to the scholarship of the early Christian Fathers rather than to variations imposed upon it by medieval popes. Naturally enough, the arguments were fiercest when they involved the two extremes of opinion. Cardinal Bea (a Professor of Scripture before his elevation) was happy to be linked with Pope John XXIII by their mutual description – 'the old ones'. In his case the name was meant as a comment on his ideas as well as his age. Cardinal Alfrink, the Archbishop of Utrecht, described himself as 'the wild man' of the Council. He did not expect that much notice would be taken of his progressive view.

The mere fact of the Catholic Church coming together to consider its place in the world gave an immense boost to Rome's reputation – as witness the choice of John XXIII as *Time* magazine's 1962 'Man of the Year'. The size of the gathering was calculated to inspire awe, as was the cost of the enterprise: £100,000 a week.[6] The number of actual participants – that is to say, excluding official observers – made it the biggest deliberative meeting in the history of the world. Its membership included 85 cardinals, 8 patriarchs, 533 archbishops, 2,131 bishops, 26 abbots and 68 superiors of religious Orders. Not surprisingly, for a gathering with an average age of over sixty, 253 members of the Council died during its 168 working sessions; 296 new delegates were added to its number.

The Pope addressed the assembled delegates twice during the first two days that the Council met. His sermon to the inaugural Mass – known by his opening words '*Gaudet Mater Ecclesia*' (Mother Church Rejoices) – included the hope that the Church would 'face the future without fear'. He condemned misanthropists who 'could see nothing but prevarication and ruin in modern times, the prophets of doom who are forever forecasting calamity', rejoiced in the 'marvellous progress of the discoveries of human genius', and committed the Church to making progress by 'demonstrating the validity of her teaching rather than condemnation'. The coded message was not easily deciphered. *L'Osservatore Romano*'s headline announced, 'Chief aim of the Council: To Defend and Promote Doctrine'. *Le Monde* chose a more obscure interpretation of the sermon's message: 'Pope Approves Research Methods in Modern Thought.' Journalists searching for a simple exposition of the Council's purpose should have quoted the first sentence of the first document that it discussed. The delegates' task was 'to adapt to the needs of our age those institutions that are subject to change'.[7] Or they could, with a little imagination, have interpreted the message in the Pope's own words: 'Today Providence is guiding us toward a new order of human relationship which, thanks to human effort and yet far surpassing human hopes, will bring us to the realization of still higher undreamed of experiences.' Two words revealed how revolutionary John XXIII's initial message was meant to be. Popes were not in the habit of demanding something 'new'. And they usually built their hopes of progress on more spiritual forces than 'human' effort.

Pope John XXIII did not live to see the Council's work concluded. But it was continued – to some surprise, in much the same spirit – by his successor, Paul VI. The closing session was held on December 8th 1965. Three years of spasmodic deliberation had produced a series of documents which, in total, amounted to three hundred pages and contained twice as many words as were thought necessary to challenge the Reformation at the Council of Trent. There were sixteen documents in all. Many of them prefaced their title with the forbidding adjective 'Dogmatic' – not as pejorative a description in Rome as it has become in more secular society. To critics of the outcome of Vatican II, its conclusions were nothing like dogmatic enough.

Long after Vatican II was over, Cardinal Heenan told a meeting in his Westminster archdiocese that he had not expected it to amount to much. 'I must confess that I am never over-confident about hearing God's voice at conferences.' He regarded them as little more than opportunities for 'discussion – putting words before and often instead of deeds'. Cardinal Heenan was a member of the triumphantly orthodox school of Catholic prelates. When he was Bishop of Leeds his reputation for discouraging mixed marriages, by requiring the non-Catholic participant to undergo a period of strict 'instruction' and then denying the couple the full ceremonial of the wedding service, had won his see the sobriquet 'The Cruel See'. The reputation for inflexible application of Church rules probably did him less than justice – as his subsequent conduct suggested. But, at the time, it was no great surprise that he passionately opposed 'the rising number of sociology students', which was only likely to 'bring forth the request for fresh surveys' into the state of the Church – a dangerous exercise which was also pointless since the answer to the question was 'known only to God'.[8] In any event, the greatest danger facing the Church was obvious enough. 'The chief heresy,' Heenan said, 'is modernism.'

It was assumed that Cardinal Heenan must have felt particularly offended by the one document that was produced during, and by, the Council itself without any preparation by officers of the Curia. *Gaudium et Spes* was subtitled *Pastoral Constitution on the Church in the Modern World*. It was prepared as a result of an intervention in the scheduled proceedings by Cardinal Leo-Joseph Suenens, who complained – to loud applause – that too much time and energy was being spent on internal affairs of the Church and too little on the great moral issues which faced the world: the pursuit of peace, the alleviation of poverty and the campaign for social justice. The Church, he argued, should enter into triple dialogue – consultations with its own members, with other Christians and with 'the modern world'. The next day, Cardinal Giovanni Battista Montini – who was to become Pope Paul VI – endorsed the proposal on behalf of the Council as a whole. There is no way of knowing the strength and nature of the opposition to the paper being prepared. But the opposition to endorsing its conclusions was passionate and wholly predictable. *Schema 13*, the rearguard claimed, ignored or contradicted much that, up to its publication, had been undisputed Catholic teaching.

The main text dealt more with the nature of the debate that must follow than with the topics which it proposed should be debated. But that in itself was profoundly significant, since it argued for dialogue rather than the didactic assertion that the Church, being divinely inspired, had no need even to consider the views of the heretics outside its theological walls or the 'Modernists' within. The substance of the schema was to be found in five appendices: the human in society, marriage and the family, culture, economic issues and peace. Two of the appendices dominated the time allowed for discussion. One dealt with the hopes of world peace. (The Council met in the shadow of the Cuban missile crisis.) The other was marriage and the family. The discussion of sex, in one form or another, always stimulated the Catholic Church's enthusiasm for denouncing pleasures of the flesh. The Council disposed of both topics by agreeing to compromise.

There was a disposition to abandon the ancient concept of a 'just war' on the grounds that weapons of mass destruction – the use of which invariably caused the death of innocent civilians – made nonsense of the idea. But even bishops feel the pressures of politics and patriotism. Representatives of Britain and the United States, the nuclear powers, argued against outright condemnation of all wars. Instead the Council described the death of non-combatants and the destruction of cities as 'a crime against God and humanity'[9] but defended the right of nations to take up arms in their own defence. When, on October 4th 1965, he addressed the General Assembly of the United Nations, Paul VI provided a more fundamental interpretation of the Vatican Council's conclusion. 'No more war! War never again! It is peace, peace that must guide the people of the world and all humanity.'

Differences over the marriage-and-family appendix were not so easily resolved. Great offence was caused to some delegates by the failure to make the traditional distinction between the primary and secondary purposes of marriage: the procreation of the next generation and the companionship of man and wife. Even greater outrage was caused by the failure of the draft – in a misguided attempt to avoid bitter divisions within the Council – to condemn birth control outright. Statements that are open to several interpretations rarely satisfy either of the parties they are intended to placate. None of the delegates could argue with the assertion that 'there cannot be a contradiction between the divine laws of transmitting life and of promoting genuine married love'. But the anodyne wording was taken, by conservative delegates, as a concession to the claim that decisions about contraception should be determined by personal conscience rather than by obedience to Roman edict. Liberals feared that it signified the Vatican's refusal even to consider a modification of the traditional prohibition. The uproar was so great that the Pope thought it necessary to bring the discussion to a premature end by promising that a special commission would study and report on the true nature of a Catholic marriage. The result was the publication, four years later, of *Humanae Vitae*.

One section of the document that dealt with the Church in the modern world was contested for reasons which, in themselves, made clear how wide was the gulf that separated the modern world from the Church's traditionalists. *Dignitatis Humanae* – the Declaration on Religious Freedom – included the revolutionary proposal that the Church should respect freedom of conscience and the right of men and women who followed other faiths to worship as they chose – even when they chose something other than Catholicism. In AD 313, Constantine the Great had made Christianity the official religion of the Roman Empire, and from then on the Church had assumed that Catholic monarchs would uphold the view that, since other religions were 'in error', they possessed no automatic right to propagate their faith.

Arguments in favour of respecting 'the dignity of conscience' had been aired for a hundred years. But it was not until Vatican II that they received enough support to become a threat to the established order. In 1962, they were advanced in the Council by the Secretariat for Promoting Christian Unity and by Cardinal Spellman of New York, who announced that the bishops of the United States of America were unanimous in their support of the Declaration. The American bishops could have claimed a special interest in *Dignitatis Humanae*. In 1899, the Vatican had condemned what it called 'Americanism', which – because of what they believed was a more casual view of family obligations – they defined as the liberty that becomes licence. Most of the preparatory work on the Declaration on Religious Freedom had been done by John Courtney Murray, a Jesuit who, in 1960, had published *We Hold These Truths*, an exposition of the relationship between the American model of representative democracy and the Catholic Church. Bishops from countries that were occupied by the Soviet Union – some of them, no doubt, envying the freedom enjoyed by their American colleagues – based their support for *Dignitatis Humanae* on the argument that they could not, convincingly, demand their own freedom of worship while they argued that it should be denied to others. The most determined opposition came from the Italian and Spanish bishops and one Frenchman. Archbishop Marcel Lefebvre relied on the undoubtedly true assertion that bedevilled all Church reform. 'If what is being taught is true, then what the Church has taught is false.'[10] Application of that simple logic made him so opposed to the toleration of deviations from the true faith that he set up his own branch of the Roman Catholic Church and demanded that his particular deviation be tolerated.

The debate was so heated and lasted for so long that the American bishops accused the Spaniards of a filibuster. Much concern was expressed about that part of the freedom clause which defended the right of 'like-minded erroneous people to congregate in order to propagate their error'. The anxiety was swept aside by a series of speeches which amounted to apologies for the historic failure to recognise the rights of conscience. Some of them were delivered in such penitential language that Bishop Muldoon of Ireland suggested that the speakers should make their admissions of guilt at confession rather than in the Council.[11] The wrangling went on until the chairman of the last session proposed to bring the discussion to an end without a vote, and appeals to the Pope to overturn his ruling were rejected with the promise to return to the subject before the Council ended. On December 7th 1965 a new document was approved. It asserted that religious freedom was a recognition of the dignity of man and implied – it could do no other – that the Church's teaching on the subject was changing with the times. Rome seemed to be edging its belated way into the twentieth century.

Even though a fleeting reference to Islam appears in the final text, the discussion of *Nostra Aetate* – the Declaration on the Church's Relation to Non-Christian Religions – was essentially a debate about Jews and Judaism. Historically, the Catholic Church had been antipathetic to the Jewish race. *Nostra Aetate*, the medieval denunciation of Jews as 'Christ Killers', had remained part of Catholic doctrine into the second half of the twentieth century. As a result, the only relationship between the two faiths that Rome would allow was a Catholic campaign to convert Jews to Christianity. But the Holocaust – and Pius XII's unheroic response to the rise of Nazi Germany – cast a long shadow over Vatican II. Even so, one delegate argued, 'We don't need to be told to love the Jews. They need to be told to love us.'[12] And the initial draft, considered by the Council, asserted that, although the death of Jesus was the responsibility of the Romans and half a dozen Jewish leaders, his rejection – by the whole Jewish race – prepared the way. The final Declaration agreed unanimously to absolve the Jews from guilt 'before and after' – though, by implication, not at the time of – the Crucifixion. Despite that concession to ancient prejudice, it went further than condemning anti-Semitism and discrimination in all its forms. The Declaration recalled the spiritual ties between Christians and Jews and acknowledged the existence of a covenant between God and the people of Israel. The Council approved *Nostra Aetate* by 2,221 votes to 88.

Many of the delegates who travelled to Rome for Vatican II mistakenly took it for granted that, whatever the Pope's intention, the Council's lasting achievement would be the completion of the work that was begun in Vatican I almost a century earlier. Pius IX had meant to produce a comprehensive statement on no less a subject than the true nature of the Church. Thanks to the outbreak of the Franco-Prussian War, the deliberations had got no further than an assertion and definition of papal infallibility. The Doctrinal Commission's draft – around which the debates were to take place – incorporated some modern (as distinct from modernist) thinking. But it was written in defensive language and therefore reflected the besieged spirit of the nineteenth century – the Church of Christ versus the world.

A new draft was prepared. Its intention was made clear by the revised title of its first chapter. 'On the Mystery of the Church' became 'On the Nature of the Church', and the 'nature' (or 'mystery', if mysteries are capable of definition) was redefined. Pope Pius XII's notion that the Church was 'the mystical body of Christ' remained, but an additional definition broke new ground. The Church was 'the People of God' – that is to say, all its members. For the first time the laity was given a status equal to the clergy and was always expected, rather than sometimes allowed, to play a part in the work of their parishes. What amounted to religious emancipation was accepted without much disagreement. Princes of the Church being human, it was the proposals that touched the life and work of bishops that caused most controversy, particularly the relationship of territorial bishops to the most important bishop of all – the Bishop of Rome, the Pope.

The argument concerned the concept known as 'collegiality' – the notion that the Pope (heir to St Peter) shares power with the bishops (heirs to the Apostles). The disagreement went to the heart of the debate about the source of Church authority. Opponents of the idea claimed that it contradicted the decisions of Vatican I and undermined the power of the Pope. Supporters insisted that they asked no more than a return to the idea of governance laid down by the ancient Church. The Pope came down on the side of 'collegiality' – very largely because he saw it as his duty to support the Council's majority view. But he also felt an obligation to heal the wounded feelings of the minority. So, after *Lumen Gentium* had been approved, with only five dissenting votes, he composed a definition of 'collegiality' which gave the bishops far less power than proponents of the idea believed had been the Council's intention. The definition was written without advice and was published without consultation. The Pope was clearly still in charge. Not all the bishops and clergy who attended Vatican II were scholars. But *Dei Verbum*, the Dogmatic Constitution on Divine Revelation, required them to come to a conclusion on a highly scholarly branch of Christian scholarship: the origins of revelation. The Protestant answer to the question – scripture alone – had been rejected at the Council of Trent. The Catholic alternative was tradition – a word that, in its more common usage, does not do justice to the idea that the truth was revealed to the Apostles and the early Christian Fathers. The draft text, which was presented to the Council, offered a 'two source solution' to the conundrum. It satisfied the proponents of neither alternative. Many of the delegates found the language of *Dei Verbum* suitable only for a document that was prepared for a Church under siege. A motion to reject it out of hand was carried by 1,368 votes to 882. A two-thirds majority was needed for outright rejection. The Council was left to discuss a document with which most of its members disagreed.

It was again time for the Pope to intervene. He ordered the document to be withdrawn and a new text prepared by the Council itself. What amounted to a drafting committee, 2,000 members strong, argued for weeks. It eventually concluded that revelation is God's wish to communicate with the world through two sources – the Bible and apostolic revelation. The resurrection of the old formula was made acceptable to the reformers by the inclusion of the assertion that the scriptures should be made more widely available and that Catholics should be encouraged to read them for themselves. For almost 2,000 years the Church had resisted giving laymen and women direct access to the Testaments. By not so much cancelling as reversing that policy, Vatican II gave life and meaning to the idea that the Church was the whole 'People of God'.

The Council had begun with the discussion of what – on the face of it – seemed a far more esoteric subject than birth control, the power of bishops, the role of the laity or even the origin of revelation. *Sacrosanctum Concilium* concerned the Constitution on the Sacred Liturgy. But although four of the five points that the Liturgical Commission set out for discussion were unlikely to change the nature of Catholic worship, the fifth had a practical and direct bearing on the conduct of the Church that was crucial to its future growth. Point five invited the Council to examine ways in which it was possible to 'promote a more active participation of the faithful in the liturgy'. The Commission made some suggestions of its own. They included the greater use of vernacular liturgy and the right of national bishops' conferences to regulate reforms of the liturgy in the diocese of their episcopates. Point five proved to be as controversial as it was crucial.

Opponents of vernacular liturgy did not underestimate the importance of the proposed changes. The rhetorical question 'What now, are we dealing here with a revolution regarding the whole Mass?' could only be answered with the admission that the upheaval would be greater than even that *cri de coeur* suggested. The Auxiliary Bishop of Cambrai asked, 'How do the people understand what Jesus says if the Gospel is read in incomprehensible language?' Since its foundation the Church had not wanted the people to understand the Gospels without the guidance of their priests. Laymen had never been trusted to read the Bible and interpret its message for themselves. Men had been burned for possessing copies of the scriptures. Even when the printing press and indomitable human curiosity had made the prohibition unworkable, Latin was part of the barrier that divided priests from people. The secretary of the Sacred College of Rites described the acceptance of the vernacular liturgy as a revolution in itself: 'Everything has been ordained by tradition and now you want to change it all.' Yet the Church itself, while proposing its formal retention of the Latin Mass, was, in effect, promoting its actual extinction:

> Latin is to be retained in the liturgies of the Western Church. Since, however, in some rites it is clear that the vernacular has proved very useful for the people, it should be given a wide role in liturgy, especially in reading, announcements, certain prayers and music. Let it be left to episcopal conferences in different parts of the world, in consultation if need be with bishops of nearby regions speaking the same language, to propose to the Holy See the degree and modes of admitting vernacular languages into the liturgy.

Not only was the vernacular to be admitted into the Mass. The principle of liturgical uniformity – which had helped to hold the Church together for 2,000 years – was to be replaced by regional variations.

A last-ditch battle was fought by conservatives who argued that while the use of the vernacular had been approved in principle, it could not apply in practice until a special commission, charged with the revision of biblical texts, had done its work. The French Hierarchy cut the Gordian knot by announcing, as soon as the Council closed, that henceforth epistles and gospels would be read in French, and that French – already used in part during the administration of the sacraments – would, in future, be used throughout the Mass. As the Catholic Church had previously understood, liberalism – once it is allowed to advance a few tentative steps – picks up speed and races away.

Evelyn Waugh – who admired the humble priest as craftsman and claimed to be unimpressed by the ornate ceremonies of the High Mass – nevertheless regretted the popularisation of the liturgy and expressed his regret to Nancy Mitford in pungent language: 'The buggering up of the Church is a great sorrow to me.'[13] Before that expression of grief is dismissed as a typical example of Waugh's attention-seeking linguistic excess, it is important to understand how far, in some places, the 'buggering up' went. George Patrick Dwyer, Archbishop of Birmingham, removed Pugin's rood screen – one of the glories of the Gothic revival – from St Chad's Cathedral as he regarded it as the physical manifestation of the division between priest and people.

The relaxation in discipline for which Vatican II was directly responsible, and the changes in liturgical practice that were its inevitable consequence, did not have the same effect on every Catholic community. The 'opening up' of the Mass – priests facing the people, rather than turning away during the most sacred moments of the service, being at least as important as the abandonment of Latin – had different effects in different countries. In Britain they may not have been entirely benign. Changes in the formality of worship probably had less effect on the Catholic persona than the relaxation of daily obligation. The duty to abstain from eating meat on a Friday had become a proclamation of Catholic identity. Once the fasting was made optional, it was 'a symbol of expiation and atonement no longer' and, as a result, 'English Catholics were like everyone else.'[14] The anthropologist who came to the conclusion that less discipline was followed by loss of identity and lack of confidence thought that the problem would be greatest among 'bog Irish' immigrants and their insecure descendants. But complaints about the liberalisation were not confined to one class or stratum of society.

A study of the effects of the reforms on one Catholic parish suggests that Vatican II and its consequences extended social distinctions within the Church. The working-class congregation of St Dominic's in Newcastle had always believed that they 'participated' in the Mass by witnessing the elevation of the host, and by crossing themselves and kneeling. Once participation was defined as verbal activity, they felt excluded. Charismatic Catholicism – at least in the less unified society of the 1960s – 'did not attract working-class people'.[15] Participation appealed to the educated, the self-confident and the secure. On the evidence of the next two decades, not even their hopes were realised.

In the decade that followed Vatican II, a plethora of committees and commissions examined the role of the laity within the Church. All of them advocated (and some claimed to have initiated) greater participation and continual dialogue. The most practical as well as the most imaginative was the work of the National Pastoral Congress – not an unexpected outcome, as the study was led by Derek Worlock, Archbishop of Liverpool and the most dynamic figure in the post-war Catholic Church. The collection of reports received a neutral interim response – *The Easter People* – from the bishops. It may have been intended to prepare the modernists for the disappointment of the following year. In 1982, *In the House of the Living God* set out the bishops' considered conclusions on the day-to-day management of Church business. There would be three commissions, made up entirely of bishops.

The laity will contribute nationally as experts in the secretariat and Commissions and in the *ad hoc* working parties to be set up by the Commissions. They will have their voices [heard] nationally through the lay liaison groups and the agencies. But like priests and religious the laity are the Church primarily when they are gathered round their bishops.[16]

The idea of 'participation' had been killed stone dead.

That notwithstanding, Vatican II was rightly heralded at the time as the Catholic Church's recognition that the reality of the modern Western world – a more self-confident people enjoying the material benefits of a society in which science seemed often to be at odds with faith – could not be ignored or brushed aside. The proponents of 'reform' argued that, as well as being right in themselves, changes were necessary to prevent, or at least slow down, the haemorrhage of the once-faithful to other Churches or to no Church at all. Opponents feared that 'modernisation' would be the death of the old certainties – the body of doctrine that, since it was unchanging and unchangeable, gave Catholics a confidence in their religion which intellectual doubt and moral compromise could not provide. Whichever view is correct, one thing is certain. In the second half of the twentieth century the world changed so fast that the gap between modern mores and Catholic thinking widened, rather than narrowed as Vatican II had intended.

CHAPTER 30

Love is Love

In most of Britain the 1960s was the decade in which the moral compass pointed in a new direction. It led the way to a society that was described, according to taste, as either 'civilised' or 'permissive' – the second adjective, used in that context, being pejorative. The debate about the consequences of those years of social change continues. One feature of legislation that brought it about is, however, beyond dispute: every item was at odds with Roman Catholic doctrine. The Divorce Reform Act of 1969 made the 'irretrievable breakdown of marriage' the only grounds for divorce, thus removing the stigma of guilt from the proceedings. The Sexual Offences Act belatedly implemented the 1957 Wolfenden Report's recommendation that homosexual acts between consenting adults in private should no longer be a criminal offence. The Medical Termination of Pregnancy Bill legalised abortion during the first twenty-eight weeks of pregnancy, when it was recommended by two doctors. The Catholic Church opposed all three of the proposals, though its opposition was nothing like as strong as the reformers expected. It was in most vociferous disagreement with the Termination of Pregnancy Bill – the one proposal against which lay Catholics were united. A long rearguard action was fought in the House of Commons. The last ditch was occupied by Labour MPs from Merseyside. In the end they were driven back to the expression of the hope that the eventual Act would include a conscience clause, which gave doctors and nurses with a moral objection to abortion the right not to take part in termination procedures. That concession was conceded.

There is no reason to believe that the Vatican was any more concerned about the sexual morality of English Catholics than it was about the beliefs and behaviour of its followers in other countries, or that the Pope felt an obligation to respond to the Termination of Pregnancy Bill. It was no more than a coincidence that the Pope pronounced on birth control, – the most contentious aspect of the marriage ethic, – at the moment when Britain was embracing the notion that men and women had the right to decide for themselves how they should conduct their most intimate relationships. It is far more likely that the decision to pronounce on the subject was prompted by worldwide changes in science and society. Birth control had become easier, cheaper and safer than ever before. And in the words of John F Kennedy – America's first Catholic President – 'a new generation' inhabited the Western world. Its members were not inclined to accept instructions about the conduct, or the conclusion, of their marriages.

John XXIII had established the commission on the subject of marriage in 1963, two years before the outbreak of British liberalism, and it is highly unlikely that he intended to strengthen, or even reiterate, the judgement of the 1930 encyclical *Casti Connubii*. 'The Catholic Church ... standing erect in the midst of the moral ruin which surrounds her ... raises her voice in token of her divine ambassadorship and proclaims anew: any use whatsoever of matrimony exercised in such a way that the act is deliberately frustrated in its natural power to generate life is an offence against God and nature and those who indulge in it are branded with the guilt of a grave sin.'

It is at least possible that Pope John considered a relaxation of the total prohibition of birth control – perhaps in response to the declaration on the dangers of population growth published by the World Health Organisation. He certainly nominated a commission – laity, including women, and clergy in equal numbers – which was unusual by the standards of papal appointments. But by 1968, when the commission had finished, the contraceptive pill made birth control more simple and safe. More important than the changes in science and society was the change of Pope. Paul VI did not accept the commission's majority view that the traditional Catholic teaching on contraception was rationally unsustainable. Instead he published a new encyclical on that and related subjects, *Humanae Vitae*.

Eighteen months elapsed between the rejection of the commission's report and the publication of the encyclical. So – the Vatican being mortal as well as an instrument of Providence – the arguments advanced in the rejected recommendations became public knowledge. The reason for their rejection was starkly set out in the encyclical. 'Certain criteria of solutions had emerged which departed from the moral on marriage proposed with constant firmness by the teaching authority of the Church.' The commission, having been invited to consider if changes in the marriage laws were necessary, had come to the unacceptable conclusion that they were not.

The encyclical was clear that no more than clarification was needed. It acknowledged that 'changes have taken place ... world population growing more rapidly than available resources ... the manner of considering the person of woman and her place in society'. But the basic law governing marriage was immutable. *Humanae Vitae*'s repeated reassertion of the established principles governing marriage reminded the faithful that the laws which governed the 'acts by which husband and wife are united in chaste intimacy' were sanctified by antiquity as well as revelation. 'The Church, calling men back to the observance of the norms of the natural law, as interpreted by their constant doctrine, teaches that each and every marriage act must remain open to the transmission of life.' From there on, the encyclical lived up to its subtitle: 'letter on the Regulation of Birth'.

The Church's objections to birth control were described in obsessive detail. Section 14 of the encyclical dealt with 'Illicit Ways of Regulating Birth'. Section 15, in a step forward from previous pronouncements, sanctioned 'the use of therapeutic means [of birth control which are] truly necessary to cure diseases ... even if an impediment to procreation may result therefrom'. Section 16 described the limited circumstances in which it would be 'licit' to avoid conception by 'taking into account the natural rhythms immanent in the generative functions'. The three paragraphs of Section 17 warned of the Grave (social) Consequences of Methods of Artificial Birth Control. The followers of Marie Stopes spoke long and often about women whose health was shattered, and poverty assured, by a lifetime of annual pregnancies. *Humanae Vitae* countered her argument by enjoining the faithful to remember that men who grow used to 'the employment of anti-conceptive practices, may lose respect for the woman and, no longer caring for her physical or psychological equilibrium, may come to the point of considering her as a mere instrument of selfish enjoyment and no longer his respected and beloved companion'. That sentence alone revealed the inevitable shortcomings of a document about marriage that was written by celibates.

The tone and language of *Humanae Vitae* were less aggressive than the expressions of abhorrence employed to condemn birth control in *Casti Connubii*. But in one crucial sentence it betrayed the hope of Vatican II. The Church – which was 'the people of God' – had been freed from the habit of portraying Catholicism as a life of suffering and sacrifice. Yet paragraph 25 of *Humanae Vitae* – dwelling on 'the sometimes serious difficulties inherent in the life of Christian married persons' – could only offer one consolation: 'For them as for everyone the gate is narrow and the way is hard that leads to life.' Perhaps it was to the Church's timeless credit that it ignored the ethos of the 'swinging sixties'. In any event, the chief cause of alienation was not the reversion to the old forbidding vocabulary, but the substance of the declaration that condemned Catholics either to abandon the use of 'artificial' methods of birth control or sacrifice the right to confession, absolution and Communion. Cardinal Heenan, not the most liberal of prelates but a realist, had no doubt as to how the dilemma would be resolved. 'It does not matter what the Pope says,' he told a colleague. 'The public has made up its mind.'[1]

Most of its members had made up their minds on the basis of clear and consistent moral principles. The post-war generation of young Catholic men and women thought of sex free from the sense of sin and guilt. The more intellectually inclined amongst them could find convincing arguments with which to challenge the Pope on his own terms. Many of them were supplied by *The Tablet*. On August 3rd 1968, it saluted Pope Paul's life 'totally dedicated to the service of God and mankind,' but it continued:

> Every call in his Encyclical for a deepening of dedication in married life will be understood and welcomed ... To many married people however there is a betrayal of their dedication in indiscriminate child bearing on one hand or the alternative of calendar-spaced love-making and total abstinence on the other. These alternatives are more repugnant to a human couple in love than artificial devices. They are less natural in the sense of being less consonant with their continuing close relations.

That was a direct denial of the Catholic Church's established view on the relationship between men and women. The authorised dictum originated with Augustine, who held that the enjoyment of sexual intercourse was sinful unless the intention had been conception rather than pleasure. That evolved into the doctrine that intercourse that deliberately excluded conception was a mortal sin. Then Pope Gregory the Great ruled that, even when conception was intended, taking pleasure in sex was a venal sin, since it encouraged immoderate thoughts and conduct. As the world grew more enlightened, the Catholic Church became more repressive.

Many parish priests found the utmost difficulty in insisting that their parishioners observe what – far from updating the Church's thoughts on marriage – seemed to be a reiteration of the prohibitions set out in *Casti Connubii*. A retired priest, who had served for years in Wigan, expressed surprise that his young colleagues agonised about how they should respond to *Humanae Vitae*'s instruction 'to expound the Church's teaching on marriage without ambiguity'. He, and his contemporaries, had faced a similar dilemma when near-destitute young couples, living in overcrowded slums, had chosen to limit their families 'artificially'. They had ignored the Church's teaching and their priests had invariably granted absolution to the sinners, no matter how regular their offence. His duty was to keep sinners in the bosom of the Church, despite *Casti Connubii* warning that priests who ignored its injunctions 'will have to render to God, the sovereign judge, a strict account of their betrayal of his trust'.[2] The 'whisky priest' in *The Power and the Glory* was not alone in risking his soul in the interests of saving the souls of others.

It took twenty years for the Catholic Church in England to recognise the extent to which it had alienated the young by its confusion over the demands of marriage. But at the 1980 Synod on the Family there was at least acknowledgement of the problem. It came from two men who gave life to the spirit of Vatican II. Cardinal Hume, Archbishop of Westminster, wryly suggested that 'pastors need to learn from married couples who have special authority in matters related to marriage'. Archbishop Worlock of Liverpool told the Synod that, in his experience, divorced and remarried couples 'often long for the restoration of full Eucharistic communion'.[3]

Between the 1960s and the 1980s the decline in the Catholic Church in England and Wales was continuous and comprehensive. The catastrophic reduction in the number of Catholic conversions, baptisms, marriages and ordinations in England and Wales was analysed for the Latin Mass Society by Dr Joseph Shaw. Between 1964 and 1977 the annual number of Catholic baptisms in England and Wales fell from 137,673 to 68,351 and the reduction continues, though at a slower rate. Now, fewer than 10 per cent of the total baptisms are Catholic. Conversions to Catholicism fell from 15,794 in the peak year of 1959 to 5,117 in 1972. Catholic ordinations (233 to 101) and marriages (47,417 to 31,534) declined by similar percentages during similar periods.[4] In Scotland, numbers marginally increased – largely as the result of Polish immigration.

Dr Shaw prefaced his statistics of English decline with a comment that was equally appropriate to Scotland: 'It is not fanciful to connect this catastrophe to the wrenching changes which were taking place at the time when the Second Vatican Council was being prepared, discussed and often erroneously applied.' Pope Benedict XVI endorsed that view:

In many places celebrations were not faithful to the prescription of the new Missal, but the latter was understood as authorising, or even requiring, creativity which frequently led to deformations of the liturgy which were hard to bear. I am speaking from experience since I too lived through the period with all its hopes and its confusion. I too have seen how arbitrary deformation of the liturgy caused deep pain to individuals deeply rooted in the faith of the Church.[5]

The Pope told only a part of the story. 'Erroneous application' was certainly a minor cause of alienation. But correct application – the changes to the traditional liturgy and procedure which were authorised by Vatican II – did much more damage. Nor could the Pope admit that the greatest damage was done, not by innovation, but by the reiteration of old prohibitions. *Humanae Vitae* was greeted with a howl of opposition that was far greater than the cries of disagreement with the conclusions of the Second Vatican Council.

There were far more public protests against the renewed prohibitions on birth control than there were complaints about changes in the liturgy. Fifty-five priests sent a letter of protest to *The Times*.[6] Two days later *The Tablet* published a similar protestation from seventy-five Catholic laymen and women – all of whom numbered among the great and the good. Public meetings were called to demonstrate opposition. Claims were made, with varying degrees of plausibility, that several pastoral letters intentionally implied reservations about the obligation that *Humanae Vitae* laid upon the clergy.

Although it was the renewed prohibition of birth control that caused *Humanae Vitae* to be rejected and openly reviled by so many men and women who regarded themselves as 'good Catholics', it had other consequences which put the Church at odds with the changing world. It was clear, if only by implication, that the renewed emphasis on marriage made pre-marital (and extramarital) sex a sin – even in the unlikely event of the intercourse having the primary purpose of reproducing the species. But heterosexual extramarital sex was, and always had been, a sin that could be confessed, absolved and forgiven. It was more difficult – indeed impossible – to accommodate homosexual relationships, many of which were long-term and therefore amounted to 'living in sin' with a glad heart and no intention of seeking redemption. Priests of an orthodox turn of mind saw the 'gay revolution' in the uncompromising terms that attracted Catholics, who needed certainty, to the faith. The only acceptable form of physical relationship was the marriage of a man and woman – a Catholic marriage, if one of the participants was of that faith. Ergo homosexuality – in Catholic literature, normally treated as a male vice – was a sin. For anyone who accepted the first principle, the logic was impeccable.

In addition to that first principle, provenance for the condemnation of homosexuality is provided by the Old Testament. Genesis records an embarrassing incident at Sodom, and Leviticus demands the death penalty for a 'man [who] lies with a male as with a woman'. St Paul, in his letter to the Romans, attributes gay desires, in both men and women, to the punishment imposed on those who 'do not see fit to acknowledge God'. More modern teaching struggles to meet the obligation of compassion and succeeds in being profoundly patronising and scientifically wrong. In 1975 the Sacred Congregation for the Doctrine of Faith issued *Persona Humana*. It condemned all homosexual acts as intrinsically wrong, but drew a distinction between the result of 'false education [and] a lack of normal sexual development' and a 'pathological' condition. It took the Church almost ten years to realise that 'pathological' was dangerously near to 'natural'. In October 1986, the Congregation of Faith clarified the position. Despite its title, *Homosexualitatis Problema* (The Pastoral Care of Homosexual Persons) was unyielding. Homosexuality, even when endogenous, was, it declared, both morally wrong and 'essentially self-indulgent'. The catechism confirmed the prohibition. Homosexuals, it said, 'are contrary to natural law. They close the sexual act to the gift of life.'

In 1992 changes in the public attitude towards homosexuality required a revision of the statement. *Some Considerations Concerning the Response to Legislative Proposals on the Non-Discrimination of Homosexual Persons* actually specified areas in which discrimination was necessary and right. 'They do not choose their homosexual condition. For most of them it is a trial.' Five years later, someone realised that the 1992 statement had repeated the dangerous ambiguity of 1975 and could be interpreted as conceding that God made homosexuals, too. The wording of the catechism was changed: 'This inclination, which is objectively disordered, constitutes for most of them a trial.'

Cardinal Hume, as always, managed to clothe his basic liberalism and instinct for compassion in the language of Catholic orthodoxy. In a letter to Cardinal Ratzinger – the supposed but not acknowledged author of the *Considerations* and the future Pope Benedict XVI – he made the point with which he sustained his argument that the Catholic Church should treat its divorced and remarried members more sympathetically. Harsh words alienate. 'There are many homosexuals who would never think of acting in a militant manner who feel that the Church has abandoned them ... I do think that we need to find a way of expressing the Church's teaching in a manner that is personally sensitive and in a way that does not threaten the human dignity of homosexuals.'[7]

Although the Vatican issued a statement which condemned violence against homosexuals, the suspicion that there were homophobes in high places persisted, with Cardinal Joseph Ratzinger the victim of most of the rumours. In April 1997 Cardinal Basil Hume made another pronouncement on the subject. Homosexuality was an 'objective disorder', but homosexuals should not be regarded as 'disordered' in general. However, the Church could not 'acknowledge, amongst fundamental human rights, a proposed right to acts which she teaches is fundamentally wrong'. The outcome of the conflicting declarations, clarifications and revisions was the description of homosexuality as a 'deep wound', a call for the end of 'unjust discrimination' and the confirmation that homosexual acts, as distinct from homosexual inclinations, were a sin. Liberal Catholics regarded it as progress of a sort.

The gap between the Catholic Church and public opinion continued to widen. Fifty years after homosexuality was decriminalised, the Civil Partnership Act gave statutory recognition to same-sex unions in Great Britain and prepared the way for the genuine equality that was proclaimed by 'gay marriage' being given the same status in law as marriage between a man and a woman. Both Acts of Parliament were complemented by legislation which prohibited discrimination and were, therefore, said to force Catholic adoption agencies to do business with same-sex couples. If the allegation was justified, five hundred years after the Reformation the law of England was still obliging Catholics to act in conflict with their consciences. The problem was probably overstated. 'The majority of Catholic agencies that had never discriminated in assessing prospective foster carers or adoptive parents were quite happily prepared to comply with the legislation.'[8] So was the claim that, in the promotion of the sinful 'permissive society', Parliament moved faster and further than the people. The opposite was true.

Support for the legislation that legalised stem-cell research was overwhelming, despite the opposition of the Catholic Church. That was only to be expected. The experiment was rightly portrayed as designed to combat and defeat previously fatal diseases. A more significant test of public opinion was provided by a survey into attitudes towards the institution that Catholics regard as the bedrock of personal morality. On the subject of marriage, the people outflanked both the Church and Parliament. Cohabitation has been on the increase for twenty years and one Catholic commentator, sceptical about the likelihood of a marriage tax-break changing young couples' plans, could do no better than describe his remedy in a 'marketing metaphor ... We need to promote marriage much more ... Most products and services tend to be adopted because people close to you have recommended it.'[9]

Whatever the merits of that solution, it is clear that Catholics who battle for their beliefs survive in an increasingly cold climate. Yet such is the moral certainty of Rome that, although it must have realised the problems of a changing world, it chose – during the years that followed the publication of *Humanae Vitae* – to challenge the sexual revolution head-on. Perhaps it had concluded, from the reaction to Vatican II, that a weakening of previous rigid rules is the way to lose support rather than retain it. Certainty has always been the Church's ally. Or perhaps it relied on the all-embracing nature of Catholicism holding fast the faithful by more than the bonds of a common theology.

A survey, carried out among London and Liverpool school students who were the descendants of Irish immigrants, illustrated what 'being a Catholic' has come to mean.[10] The findings suggested that what had been a faith had become a habit which, instead of providing the comfort of resurrection in the next life, offered a reassuring sense of 'belonging' in this. In both cities more than 80 per cent of the students said that their religion was 'meaningful' to them – not because it was the true faith which offered redemption and salvation, but because it defined who they are. In London 73 per cent of the students said that 'their religion was important to them in terms of communal or family identity'. In Liverpool the figure was 56 per cent. The survey – which was so much concerned with family – did not ask the respondents for their views on the Church's doctrine on how family life should be led.

Dr Stephen Bullivant of St Mary's University in Twickenham has spent an academic lifetime examining Catholic attitudes and Catholic opinions. A poll, carried out among a representative sample of Catholics during the spring of 2015, did ask those questions. It revealed that '85% of respondents rejected the Church's position on contraception ... 88% rejected the Church's policy in refusing access to the sacraments for the divorced ... 55% rejected the idea that the Church was right to oppose same-sex marriage.' The general conclusion was that 'love is love'.

CHAPTER 31

Suffer Little Children

The abomination of child abuse is not a new phenomenon. There was a time when it was accepted as a normal feature of civilised society and – difficult though it is now to believe – as late as the mid-twentieth century it was a subject of music-hall jokes about mincing choir masters and lisping cub leaders. It is therefore not surprising that many Roman Catholic dignitaries regarded their Church as, at best, unlucky and, at worst, the victim of prejudice, when it was excoriated both for the existence of pederasts within its ranks and for the failure effectively to exclude them or ensure that they received proper treatment and punishment. Resentment that the Church's failings had been so ruthlessly exposed was unjustified, but understandable. After six hundred years of persecution, followed by two centuries of only slowly diminishing prejudice, many Catholics took it for granted that the Protestant world eagerly seized every opportunity to denigrate their faith and its followers.

The bravest Catholics spoke out, and in October 1994 *The Tablet* was explicit about why the Catholic Church carried an especially heavy burden of guilt:

> The effects of sexual abuse in childhood are so pervasive that they may even reduce the ability of the abused person to experience, consciously, the grace of God mediated through the sacraments. This is especially true when the abuse has been perpetrated by some-one who is said to be the representative of God. In such cases it may seem to victims, and others, that the abuse is 'the will of God'.[1]

And there was a second reason why the Catholic Church was exceptionally culpable. It compounded the original offences – bad enough in themselves – by the way in which a significant minority of senior clergy reacted to the revelations of the rapes and indecent assaults that were being carried out in their midst.

In the worst cases there was a conscious decision to ignore the offence and, therefore, leave the offender free to offend again. Almost as bad were decisions to protect the perpetrators from prosecution by the civil courts and, in place of the punishment prescribed by law, impose some slight inconvenience – temporary exile from the parish over which they presided, or permanent transfer to another part of the diocese. And there were many senior churchmen – genuinely horrified by the revelations, determined to stamp out the evil and conscious, albeit sometimes in retrospect, that criminal priests must face the law – who argued that the incidence of paedophilia was no greater among the celibate Catholic clergy than among priests and ministers of other religions or the male population in general. In 1994, after Scottish Television broadcast a 'special report' on abuse at St Mary's College in Blairs, Keith O'Brien – Archbishop of Glasgow – asked the Scottish public to 'try to keep the present episodes in perspective ... They are inexcusable but we must always remember that only a small percentage of abusers are Catholic priests.'[2] Five years later – after further exposures and allegations that the Church had, at best, been complacent about the incidence of abuse – an angry correspondent complained to *The Tablet* that a conference of concerned priests had failed to make clear that 'Catholic clergy are no more likely to abuse than any other section of society or clergy from other religious denominations.'[3] That claim may be true – the evidence is inconclusive. And there is no doubt that some of the campaigns of exposure contained scarcely disguised anti-Catholic bias. But attempts to spread the guilt always sounded like a calculated diversion from the basic fact that the offences had been committed, that many of the offences had been left unpunished and, in some cases, the offenders had been left free to abuse again.

The underlying assumption of the Church's critics – sometimes expressed and sometimes implied – was that the Catholic authorities cared less for the ruined lives of the victims of abuse than for the reputation of the Church itself. The second charge against the Church was a failure to face hard reality. In its cloistered naivety it did not realise that the only way to minimise the damage to Rome's good name was an unqualified admission of guilt, a clear determination to prevent (as far as prevention was possible) a recurrence of the offences and the establishment of a system which guaranteed that offenders would be appropriately punished.

Some Catholic bishops did react to the exposures with a humble acceptance of guilt and a clear determination to put God's House in order. Crispian Hollis, the Bishop of Portsmouth, told his diocese, 'We are at fault ... The Church is not the victim in all this – the children are.'[4] Kieran Conry, who succeeded Cormac Murphy-O'Connor as Bishop of Arundel and Brighton – and therefore inherited one of the most notorious dioceses – wrote that the Church 'deserved to be scrutinised and castigated'. Vincent Nichols, Archbishop of Birmingham after the retirement of Maurice Couve de Murville in the wake of a West Midland 'cover-up', was more precise and more emphatic in his demands. The Church's first concern should be the creation of safeguards which prevented abuse as far as was possible, and punished abusers whose inclinations had not been detected.

Both the bishops who were robust in their calls for repentance followed by reform and those who seemed to temporise were subject to pressures which it is difficult for the laity – particularly the laity of other faiths or none – to understand. The Catholic Church was their family as well as their faith, and their instinct was to defend it with whatever flimsy arguments were available. History added to the pressures to cause near-panic. The Catholic Church – which by its nature has a long memory – had suffered from the consequences of an errant priesthood before. The declaration that Martin Luther had nailed to the door of the castle church in Wittenberg had included the denunciation of corrupt clergy. Nearer home, the Dissolution of the monasteries had been justified by stories of fornicating nuns and debauched monks. Cardinal Pole, sickened by the corruption in the sixteenth-century Vatican, had warned that sheep would not follow discredited shepherds.

The consequences of disillusion were not the only result of the calls for exposure and punishment that caused profound concern. There was a general, and justified, fear that feelings were so strong against paedophiles that accused priests would be disciplined before they were given an opportunity to prove their innocence. And there was another – to some Catholics insurmountable – obstacle in the way of implementing the only feasible and effective reform. Suspects, the argument ran, should be immediately suspended and reported to the police in order that the processes of the law could begin. But that law was civil law and the conduct of the priesthood was 'properly' regulated by canon law. After five hundred years the question of authority – temporal versus spiritual – had arisen again. Offences committed by previously obscure priests had reawakened the fundamental clash of principle that brought about the Reformation.

The Church's position on the conflict had been reaffirmed in 1864 – almost exactly a century before child abuse became far too great an international scandal for Rome to maintain the exclusive right to discipline paedophiliac priests. The encyclical *Quanta Cura* (On Current Errors) left no room for doubt or flexibility. It anathematised 'wicked, and so often condemned, innovators who dare, with signal impudence, to subject to the will of the civil authority the authority of the Church and of this Apostolic See given her by Christ Himself and to deny all those rights of the same Church and See which concern matters of external order'.[5] Any suggestion that the principle had been eroded by time was confounded by a letter, sent in January 1997 to the Catholic Hierarchy of Ireland by the Pope's envoy to Dublin. It warned the bishops that, if they adopted the policy of automatically reporting pederasts to the police, they would be breaking canon law.

The envoy relied for his ruling on incontrovertible authority. Clarification of canon law in 1917 and in 1983 had condemned the abuse of minors as an offence against 'the sixth commandment of the Decalogue' and prescribed a series of punishments including laicisation. But the directive *Crimen Sollicitationis* had made clear that the discipline must be exercised on the authority of the Church alone and that investigations, indictments, proceedings and sentences must all be kept secret. And those two requirements made it impossible adequately to deal with the growing number of complaints about the conduct of priests in the Catholic Church of nation after nation.

England did not stand condemned alone. The revelations of conduct that was both immoral and illegal engulfed the seminary at Blairs, in Scotland, and Bishop Roddy Wright was caught up in scandal. So was Eamon Casey (the former Bishop of Galway) and the whole Archdiocese of Dublin fell under suspicion. In the United States of America, the National Review Board for the Protection of Children and Young People issued a report which justified its title, *The Crisis in the Catholic Church*. Allegations were also made against priests in Spain, Holland and Austria. The accusations against German priests were substantiated with hard evidence. Cardinal Ratzinger, then Prefect of the Congregation for the Doctrine of Faith, was said to be inundated by complaints from all over the world. He reacted with despair. 'How much filth is there in the Church even among those who, in the priesthood, should belong entirely to God?'[6] He then issued *Sacramentorum Sanctitatis Tutela* – a revision of *Crimen Sollicitationis*. It decreed that the Vatican must deal with all allegations against priests, and that both the charges and the subsequent proceedings must be kept secret. That instruction – effectively preventing civil prosecution – provoked a chorus of calls for Ratzinger, by then Pope, to resign. Asked, on television, if the calls were justified, Vincent Nichols, Archbishop of Westminster, chose his words with care. There was no 'strong reason' for him to do so.[7]

The increase in the number of complaints received from England was not, necessarily, the result of an increase in the number of offences.

Putting aside frivolous, malicious and financially motivated complaints – the frequency of which was much exaggerated by the Church – the apparent growth in the incidence of assaults was not as severe as it seems. There had been abuse for years. The apparent increase was the result of a greater willingness, among victims and their families, to report offences. Accurate figures are difficult to find. At the turn of the century, when demands for reform were at their height, the Catholic Church itself reported that, in England and Wales, twenty-one priests – out of a total of 5,600 – had been *convicted* of offences against children during the previous five years, though more prosecutions were pending.[8] During 1997 there were 250 claims for compensation – made against the Church on the grounds that it had failed to discharge its duty of care. Most of them were 'historic' and turned on the behaviour of two Orders of nuns in two children's homes.[9] The figures for more recent years reflect a willingness to face the fact of regular, if limited, sexual assaults. According to the Chairman of the National Catholic Safeguarding Committee, in 2014 the number of offences (not to be confused with convictions) was at the all-time high of ninety-one.[10]

During the twenty years since the scandals were first exposed, virtually every diocese in the United Kingdom has been revealed to include – or to have included – an active pederast. Some cases that surfaced years after the offence was committed came to be classified as 'historical abuse' – encouraging the suspicion that dozens more cases had been obscured and forgotten. Father Brendan Smyth was gaoled in 1994 for offences committed in Belfast (and reported to the Northern Ireland police) during 1990. In 2004, John Kinsey, OSB – formerly of Belmont Abbey, Herefordshire – was convicted of assaulting schoolboys during the mid-1980s. In 2012 charges that related to assaults which began in 1962 were made against former staff of St Ambrose Christian Brothers' College in Altringham.

The details of those cases, and many more, were lovingly chronicled in tabloid newspaper articles – including one in the now (happily) defunct *News of the World* that was largely invention, against which it had been warned by the solicitor most involved with the campaign to obtain retrospective justice for victims of abuse. Two of the stories need to be told in serious detail because – as well as emphasising that the real significance of each assault is the effect it has on the often-traumatised victim – they chronicle the slow progress towards a radical shift in the Catholic Church's response to allegations of clerical abuse.

The first of the two offences – or, in this case, series of

offences – that led to change was committed by Father Michael Hill. In 1997 he was sentenced to five years' imprisonment for abusing boys over a period of two decades. On May 24th 1993, a programme in the BBC's *Everyman* series examined events in the Birmingham Arch-diocese which, earlier that year, had led to the conviction, for indecent assault on children, of Father Samuel Penney. The court accepted that the offences had been committed over a long period – hence the prison sentence of seven and a half years. The programme also claimed that the archdiocese had been warned about Penney's behaviour as early as 1984, but had responded only by moving him to a new parish. A spokesman for the archdiocese insisted that the Church authorities knew nothing about offences until late 1991 and that they 'immedi-ately arranged an investigation'.[11] He went on to claim that reporting Penney to the police was prevented by the victims' families, who were anxious to avoid the attention of prurient newspapers. If that was so, they soon overcame their reticence. After the broadcast, three families went directly to the police and two sued the diocese for negligence.

Maurice Couve de Murville, the Archbishop of Birmingham, said that he felt 'profoundly concerned for all who had been hurt' and his spokesman conceded that, 'with the benefit of hindsight', the archdio-cese agreed 'that it should have taken legal advice and referred the matter to the police'. In future, when allegations appeared to be 'well founded ... The perpetrator would be placed under custodial care pending charges being made ... there is no question of anyone being sheltered from the due processes of the law.'[12] The Catholic Bishops' Committee of England and Wales responded equally positively by setting up a committee to examine how to deal with allegations of abuse and the needs of victims. It came to nothing. Had positive proposals been swiftly put in place, the Michael Hill scandal would not have arisen.

Michael Hill was ordained in 1960 in the Diocese of Southwark and appointed assistant priest in Folkestone. After a brief second ministry at Hove, he joined the Southwark Diocesan Children's Society and later gained a one-year diploma in childcare from the University of Newcastle. Shortly after the creation of the Diocese of Arundel and Brighton in 1965 he became the parish priest of St Teresa's at Merstham in Surrey. It was there that suspicions about his perverse inclinations were first aroused. One parishioner – hearing and believing stories of bizarre practices – raised her concerns with the then bishop, Michael Bowen. She later reported the conversation to a solicitor who was seeking damages for the abused boys. 'He told me that Michael Hill was a priest. Priests don't behave in that way. As far as the bishop was concerned there was no substance in my complaint.'[13] Despite further accusations, Hill remained at Merstham for five years before, 'as part of a routine transfer procedure', he was moved to St Edmund Church in Godalming and became a frequent visitor to St Dominic's, a nearby residential school that was run by the Sisters of the Sacred Heart. The Godalming boys who were assaulted by Hill claim that their allegations were ignored by the St Dominic's staff. The Church authorities deny that any accusations were ever made, but one complaint undoubtedly reached the authorities. A Godalming parishioner, whose son was one of the priest's casualties, had received a confession of guilt from Father Hill. She showed it to the new Bishop of Arundel and Brighton – Cormac Murphy-O'Connor, the future Cardinal Archbishop of Westminster.

At a Godalming parish meeting, held on Friday October 3rd 1980, the bishop's representative announced that Father Hill was moving to another parish. The move was represented as no more than routine, and unrelated to the unrest that his authoritarian manner was said to have caused among the parishioners. For some unexplained reason he was not inducted in Heathfield until early 1981. It was later assumed to be the result of Heathfield's discovery of his perverse inclinations. Towards the end of his first year in the parish he was sent by the diocese to the Dympna Centre for counselling about his sexual attraction to boys. There is no doubt that the diocese knew about his habits and that the counselling was a failure. He assaulted boys in his new parish.

Hill was removed from Heathfield and spent some months under the supervision of Catholic psychotherapists, who reported to the diocese that he was likely to reoffend. While still receiving treatment, Hill discharged himself and began to seek secular employment. He found a job as an accounts clerk, but in February 1984 wrote to Bishop Murphy-O'Connor, pleading to be allowed to resume what he described as his calling. Murphy-O'Connor agreed to see him. 'He cried with remorse and begged on his knees to be given some work as a priest.'[14] Sentiment triumphed over reason. 'The post at Gatwick Airport was vacant and I decided that he should go there as I believed there would be no prolonged contact with children on their own.' The Bishop was mistaken. During his ministry at Gatwick, Michael Hill regularly assaulted young boys. He was convicted of abuse in 1997 and gaoled for five years and, after confessing further offences, was gaoled again in 2002. Murphy-O'Connor pronounced judgement on his own conduct: 'Of course, I was very wrong.' Several parents of victims – who shared that view – sued Murphy-O'Connor for negligence. Their claims were settled out of court, on condition that the proceedings remained a secret. To general surprise, the seventy-year-old Bishop of Arundel and Brighton was appointed Archbishop of Westminster.

Within weeks of his elevation the BBC's *Today* programme broadcast the results of a long-term investigation into the Hill affair. It included leaked extracts from the previously confidential court documents. It was then that the Archbishop of Westminster was revealed to have admitted that he had allowed a known paedophile licence within his jurisdiction. When the *Today* programme unearthed what it implied was another example of Murphy-O'Connor's indolent indulgence – Father Love, who had moved from Glasgow to Arundel following allegations that the police regarded as too insubstantial to warrant prosecution – *The Tablet* complained of BBC bias, and the Archbishop himself asked priests in the Westminster diocese to read out a personal statement at the end of the following Sunday's morning Mass. 'As you know, not only I personally, but the whole Catholic Church in England and Wales has been under attack from some quarters during these past few days ... For myself I deeply regret any damage that has been done following a mistaken decision in the past ... Failure, of course, has to be acknowledged, but we also recognise the gift of the Lord's forgiveness.'[15] The statement could not have been less felicitously worded. It contained neither a direct personal apology nor an admission of personal guilt. Relatives of the abused boys were particularly offended by the reference to forgiveness. They were not in a mood to forgive.

The uproar that followed cast a deep shadow over Murphy-O'Connor's first months' succession to the much-loved Cardinal Basil Hume, but he seemed quickly to regain his cheerful composure. And what was a temporary catastrophe for him turned out to be a permanent blessing for the Catholic Church. Without the scandal there would have been no decisive action. Because of the weeks of turmoil, Archbishop Murphy-O'Connor set up the Nolan Commission both to examine past errors and to make recommendations on how, in the future, they could be avoided.

It was clear from the start that a Catholic commission, with a majority of non-Catholic members, would not have an easy passage. During the day in which its creation was announced, the Benedictines stated that they would not cooperate. But Lord Nolan – a retired Law Lord who had chaired the inquiry into Standards in Public Life – produced a substantial report, which was unanimously endorsed by the Bishops' Conference. It acknowledged that the autonomous power of bishops made a unified approach difficult to achieve, but stressed the paramount need for:

> a single set of policies, principles and practices ... effective and speedy implementation in the parishes, dioceses and religious orders ... an organised structure in the parish ... a national capability which will advise dioceses and orders, coordinate where necessary and monitor and report on progress ... the provision of adequate resources and support for these arrangements.

In practice that meant the appointment of a lay child-protection representative in every parish and the establishment of a National Child Protection Unit to coordinate the local work. In one particular the priesthood would, therefore, have their conduct monitored by the laity – some of whom would be women. That was bad enough in itself, but the proposal that parishes that failed to follow proper procedure should be reported to the appropriate bishop made it worse. Most controversial of all was the recommendation that all allegations should be reported to the 'statutory authorities straight away without any process of filtering'. That raised the spectre of a priest, who was wrongly accused, facing the ignominy of being assumed guilty until he proved his innocence. All hope of the enquiries being kept secret were dashed by Nolan's contention that 'the person against whom allegations have been made may need to be withdrawn from any contact with the child concerned or any other child'. The attempt to soften the blow – 'It is well understood in professions such as teaching that suspension in these circumstances does not imply guilt' – only caused more offence. Priests do not regard the priesthood as being comparable to other professions and, in a sense, they are right not to do so. The high hopes of Nolan were not realised because of the unacceptability of an essential principle of any effective child-protection policy. When allegations of abuse were made, the committee could 'see no grounds for treating clergy differently from lay people'.

To Nolan, it seemed obvious that claims of 'historic abuse' should be investigated and, where the accusations seemed justified, subject to criminal proceedings. It was 'important to treat such allegations in the same way as current allegations'. In both circumstances conviction should, he recommended, be followed by laicisation when 'right thinking members of the public ... would feel that justice has not been done by any other course'. It was, however, not clear that the higher rank of the Church agreed. A plethora of investigations, most of them carried out by the BBC, unearthed a series of new scandals. Father

Tim Garret, convicted of possessing indecent photographs of boys, was moved from the Portsmouth diocese to Arundel and Brighton, but remained a priest. Archbishop Murphy-O'Connor was notably unrepentant. Father Maxwell Stuart – accused of indecent assault, but acquitted because of lack of evidence – was judged, after a professional assessment, not to be a paedophile, but unsuitable for work with children.[16] Bishop Kieran Conry, Murphy-O'Connor's successor at Arundel and Brighton, attempted to restrict Stuart's activities, but felt unable to enforce the rules of conduct to which the priest had previously agreed. The failure to safeguard vulnerable children from potential harm was certainly against the spirit, and arguably against the letter, of the Nolan Report. The Garret case so increased public concern that Cormac Murphy-O'Connor – realising at last the damage that was being done to the Church's reputation – reacted by arranging for an independent review of the way in which allegations of indecent assault had been dealt with during his time in Arundel and Brighton. It found that ten had been investigated – with a variety of results – and one had been ignored.

The *News of the World*, conscious of its readers' salacious appetites, joined in the pursuit of pederast priests and the Church's alleged inclination to ignore their wrongdoing. The newspaper claimed that, back in 1977, a Father Michael Hollings – a war hero, chaplain to Oxford University and religious adviser to Thames Television – had behaved improperly with a boy put in his care by the probation service. The offences were said to have taken place in the Westminster diocese two years after Cardinal Hume had become Archbishop. So it was possible to implicate Hume by alleging that he either knew and did nothing or that he should have known. Although the newspaper contrived a confrontation between the accused and his accuser, nothing was ever proved and Hollings was given leave of absence, some of which he spent with the Duke of Norfolk in Arundel Castle. It was later discovered that Hollings had been censured by Cardinal Hume – for presiding at a service of blessing for David Frost and Carina Fitzalan-Howard after their registry-office wedding.[17] The fact that some of the multiplicity of charges against the Church were unreasonable was of no consequence. Visible action was necessary.

When Eileen Shearer – who was not a Catholic – was appointed head of the Catholic Office for the Protection of Children and Vulnerable Adults it seemed, in her own words, that the Church had 'listened to Lord Nolan's recommendations and intends to implement them. It has taken these measures extremely seriously.'[18] But what can only be described as institutional obstacles stood in the way of the undoubtedly good intentions. Chief among them was the clergy's obligation to obey canon law. The main barrier to progress was reinforced by the argument that priests were more vulnerable than were members of other professions to malicious and frivolous allegations, and that they had no association to represent them and defend the unjustly accused.

They did, however, have the support of the National Conference of Priests. At its 2003 meeting, a resolution – carried overwhelmingly – called for canon law to be respected in every detail. Canon law does not empower bishops to suspend priests from duty during investigation. The Conference made the point in defence of priests' rights. It was quickly taken up by canon lawyers as an irrefutable doctrine. *Sacramentorum Sanctitatis Tutela* was still in force and must be obeyed. In any case there was no question of implementing Lord Nolan's proposals. They had not received the Vatican's imprimatur. Until they did, the report was advisory, not mandatory.

Critics of the Nolan Report added force to their argument by asserting that canon law, properly followed, would have averted the crisis. They insisted – as traditionalists had claimed for five hundred years – that the Church's problems would be solved by showing respect for established principles and practices, not by inventing new rules and regulations. The opponents of a fresh start argued that sexual abuse of minors is one of the most serious offences in the 1983 Code, one of the gravest *delicta graviora* for which penal standards, up to and including dismissal from the clerical state, are demanded.[19] There was organised opposition to the introduction of a regime that required bishops 'effectively to renounce their responsibilities under canon law' and replaced them with action by 'quasi-judicial bodies'.

There is, however, little doubt that, presented with a straightforward allegation of abuse, most dioceses would – after the new system got under way in 2002 – have reacted in the way that the Nolan Committee had recommended. It was the Church's misfortune that it became involved in the case of Father William Hofton – the implications of which were far from straightforward. In 2004, Hofton had been arrested and charged with offences committed against two teenage brothers in the 1990s. Westminster – the priest's diocese – did not know of the 1990s arrest. However, as a result of the publicity attracted by the case, it became known that Hofton had confessed to another 'historic offence'. Initially the police, who had chosen not to prosecute, had been notified and the priest had been sent for psychiatric assessment. The assessment concluded that there was only a 'low risk' of Hofton reoffending and that he should return, under supervision, to parochial duties.

Hofton became an assistant parish priest in Kentish Town in north London. The local child-protection representative was not told of his record, and what little supervision he was under was provided by the parish priest. The discovery of his record outraged active parishioners who believed, with dubious justification, that they should have been told about his past. It also stimulated the newspapers into searching for other examples of pederasts 'let loose' in unsuspecting parishes. Several were found. Among them was the case of Father Neil Gallanagh, who – after committing offences in Derry – was transferred to the Leeds Diocese, where he became priest at St John's School for the Deaf in Boston Spa. It is not clear whether most offence was caused by his appointment to such an unsuitable post or by the idea that Northern Ireland exported its problems to England. The prominence that was given to cases like Hofton and Gallanagh left the Church with no option other than respond to the renewed call to 'do something'. Since it was not clear what that something should be, Baroness Cumberlege – a Catholic Conservative peer and former junior minister – was asked to report on the effect of the Nolan recommendations on child protection within the Church.

The publication of the Cumberlege Report coincided with the resignation of Eileen Shearer, the head of the Catholic Office for the Protection of Children and Vulnerable Adults. Shearer's carefully worded statement seemed the less critical of the two documents:

> The Catholic Church leaders in England and Wales have undoubtedly risen to the challenge of implementing A Programme For Action. Their serious and consistent commitment to developing sound national structure, policies and practices is very clear and safeguarding vulnerable people is increasingly woven into the fabric of the Church.[20]

But her encomium was directed towards 'Catholic Church leaders' who could take credit for 'substantial progress at national level'. At local level, the work was seriously impeded by lack of resources and, more important, the principles on which the report was based were either rejected or misunderstood. 'The task is far from done. If the tensions that have come to the fore in this review are left unaddressed by those in the Church with the authority to deliver, they risk a serious reversal of some of the important gains made to date.' The problem remained the conflict between the canon-law prescriptions for disciplining priests and the need, under established child-protection policy, to suspend suspects. Baroness Cumberlege suggested that the way to break through the log-jam was the promulgation of an English decree of good practice that was sent to Rome for Vatican *recognito*. But that assumed that the Nolan Report, with all its implications, would be accepted by the Pope. And the Vatican had been notably reluctant to endorse recommendations which included setting aside a thousand years of precedents.

Scotland too had its scandals. The greatest – or at least the most spectacular – was the admission by Cardinal Keith O'Brien, the Archbishop of St Andrews and Edinburgh, that, in the distant past, his 'sexual conduct [had] fallen below the standards expected' of a good Catholic. He resigned as Archbishop on March 3rd 2013, but – as if to confirm that the Vatican's disciplinary wheels grind slowly – it was more than two years before the Pope, following the advice of a specially appointed personal envoy to Scotland, formally accepted it. Cardinal O'Brien was not, it seems, guilty of abuse as gross as that which had scandalised the Church in England. His victims appear to have been seminarians above what is now the age of consent. But he had clearly taken advantage of his status in a relationship that should have been characterised by his 'duty of care', and his offence was compounded by his public pronouncements on sexual morality. Until his exposure, Cardinal O'Brien had been unyielding in his opposition to licence and laxity. That, as much as the fact of his transgression, made his admission and resignation what Tom Devine, Catholic and Professor of History in Edinburgh University, called 'probably the greatest single blow to have hit the Catholic Church in Scotland since the Reformation'.[21]

It was not the O'Brien affair that stirred the Scottish Catholic Church into activity. A series of less spectacular scandals had focused the collective mind of the Bishops' Conference on the need for action. The result was a statement with the comprehensive title *Awareness and Safety*, published in the year that Cardinal O'Brien offered his resignation. Paragraph 5.4.1 was a positive, and unambiguous, instruction to take action, which some authorities argued was in conflict with canon law. 'When a child, young person or an adult is at risk of immediate harm, contact the Police and or Social Work Services, giving full information.' Unfortunately, the hopes of paragraph 5.4.3 – 'following these steps ensures immediate avoidance of further abuse [and] immediate pursuit of the offender' – were not realised. In August 2015 after the Scottish bishops had considered the subject again, the statement that was issued by Philip Tartaglia, Archbishop of Glasgow – far from celebrating the success of their established policy – was a literal apology, offered to 'all those who have been harmed and have suffered in any way as a result of actions by anyone within the Catholic Church. That this abuse should have been carried out within the Church and by priests, takes that abuse to another level.'

There was some suggestion at the time that the bishops had found it easier to condemn past crimes than propose ways of avoiding new ones. But the call for a public apology to victims, which was included in the 2015 report of the McLellan Commission, was its most newsworthy, not its most important, recommendation. The commission – under the chairmanship of the Very Reverend Dr Andrew McLellan, former Moderator of the General Assembly of the Church of Scotland and Her Majesty's Chief Inspector of Prisons – had been set up to examine 'the current safeguarding procedure within the Catholic Church in Scotland'. It proposed that *Awareness and Safety* be completely rewritten to reflect 'best practice' as it had developed in the intervening years. No one could object to that. Two other recommendations were more controversial – not because of what they urged the Scottish Church to do, but because of what they implied had not been done in the past. The revised instructions for combating abuse must be seen to carry the 'full authority of the bishops' conference' and their implementation must be guaranteed by 'external scrutiny'. In the Scottish Catholic Church, as in the English, the potentially most effective procedures for combating abuse only work if they have the full support of the parishes and dioceses.

The Scottish Bishops' Conference gave its unanimous support to the McLellan Report. But that decision, important though it was, should have been overshadowed by the Vatican's announcement, on June 10th 2015, that the Congregation for the Doctrine of Faith – acting on the recommendation of the Council of Cardinals and Pontifical Commission for the Protection of Minors – had assumed powers 'with regard to crimes of abuse of office when connected to the abuse' of children and young people. The Vatican had decided that the time had come to impose sanctions on bishops who chose to ignore their obligations to take swift and decisive action when they were told that priests within their dioceses were guilty – or, indeed, suspected of – sexual assault. And, knowing that good intentions had to go hand in hand with mechanisms that turn hope into reality, the Congregation proposed to set up a new office 'to work as a tribunal in judgment of bishops who fail to act'.[22] Vatican Radio elaborated on the Pope's role in the implementation of the new policy. He would 'continue to have final say on the removal of bishops, but he normally accepts the advice of his offices'. The reference – almost in passing – to the possibility of 'removal' added an unexpected rigour to the announcement.

The Report of the Pontifical Commission for the Protection of Minors was not the only sign that the Catholic Church was increasingly aware of its moral and legal obligation to protect young people against abuse. In England the 2015 report of the National Catholic Safeguarding Committee claimed success in at least part of its work. 'The working party on pastoral support for survivors has made real progress ... We believe we have a model that can be implemented gradually across all our Dioceses and Religious Communities.'

Not 'will be' but 'can be' implemented. The implied doubt is appropriate to all the measures and mechanisms which the Catholic Church has put in place to identify, whenever possible to deter and in all cases swiftly to act against paedophiliac priests. The policies and the procedures have to be implemented. And implementation is held back by misguided loyalty and the mistaken believe that inaction can avoid damage to the Church's reputation. But the most important impediment to decisive action remains the reluctance to yield the rights of the spiritual authority, under canon law, to the temporal power. King Henry would understand.

CHAPTER 32

And You Made Me Welcome

On April 11th 2012, the Reverend Donald Minchew – until earlier in that month vicar of St Michael and All Angels in Croydon – announced that he had left the Church of England and was preparing for baptism as a Roman Catholic. Father Minchew, as he ultimately became, chose the *Daily Mail* as the vehicle for the explanation of his decision. Theological exegesis rarely appears in a tabloid newspaper. But the *Mail* recognises a good story when it sees one and Father Minchew was not only moving a mere fifty yards 'up the road' to St Mary's. He was taking seventy of his parishioners with him. And the language in which he described the reasons for his conversion was unusually trenchant:

> When I was ordained in the Church of England in 1976, there were some things which would never be changed. But now it seems that everything is up for grabs. Those of us who believe in traditional values and opposed the ordination of women and other innovations, who were once an honoured and valued part of the C of E are now just being told to 'sod off'. That's the bottom line. They all talk of being inclusive and being a broad church when what they really mean is bugger off if you don't believe in what we believe.

Father Minchew's complaint of intolerance was slightly undermined by his admission that 'the Anglican bishop and Archdeacon of Croydon were extremely understanding and supportive', but his valediction served the useful purpose of putting the Church of England exodus into perspective. Although the headlines attributed it to the ordination of women, the migration from Canterbury to Rome had deeper causes. The proposal to ordain women was just a symptom of what the converts saw as a general disorder that was diagnosed by the most thoughtful opponents of 'reform' as a rejection – conscious or subconscious – of the movement towards Church unity. They were wrong. The proponents of a 'women's ministry' regarded its creation as a moral imperative in its own right.

The ordination of women as deacons had been agreed in June 1987 and that should have warned supporters of the status quo that it was only a matter of time before full admission to Holy Orders followed. As the day of destiny approached, they claimed to be confident that ecumenicalism would triumph over schism but, nevertheless, thought it wise to demonstrate the strength of their support. The long process that had, as its climax, the General Synod of November 1992 began with meetings of the York and Canterbury convocations in July. Two weeks before they assembled, a religious festival was held in London's Wembley Arena. It began with fifty Catholic bishops and six hundred priests celebrating a two-hour long Eucharist. Then the congregation – estimated to number between 6,000 and 7,000 – heard a variety of distinguished speakers call on the Church of England to break down the old obstacles to Christian unity rather than erect new barriers. The Movement for the Ordination of Women held several regional rallies on the same day. Meanwhile the Church of England Hierarchy behaved as the Church of England was expected to behave. Bishops opposed to the ordination of women asked the Archbishop of Canterbury to set up a new inquiry.

It is not clear why Anglicans who believed in an exclusively male priesthood imagined that the Church of England would be influenced in their favour by the essentially Catholic Wembley rally. Nor was it – at least not enough to save the day for the enemies of innovation. On November 11th 1992 the ordination of women was approved by the General Synod. In the House of Laity, the proposition was endorsed by a single vote. But one was enough. On the following day the *Catholic Herald*, invoking the spirit of John Henry Newman's Tractarianism, pronounced dead 'the hopes and aspirations' of all those who believed that 'corporate reunion [as distinct from individual conversion] was a realistic and possible achievement'. Graham Leonard, the Church of England Bishop of London, writing in *The Times*,[1] retained some hope of a renewed partnership, but he based his guarded optimism on the generosity of Rome. His article ended with a promise that his lineal predecessor – Edmund 'Bloody' Bonner – would have regarded as justifying his burning: 'We come and hope that the Church, the Catholic Church of Rome, will in fact deal with us positively and hopefully. But we come with no prior requirements and with no demands. We come merely as supplicants.' The full meaning of those words became clear on Leonard's retirement. The one-time Anglican Bishop of London converted to Catholicism and was ordained priest.

Within a week of the Synod's decision, Cardinal Hume took advantage of a meeting of the Catholic Bishops' Conference to issue a statement which, it was said, was meant to reassure Church of England clergy that, if they chose Rome, they would receive a generous welcome. Critics thought it sounded like a recruiting initiative:

> We recognise that, in their ministry, they have exercised a call from God. This is the basis of our willingness to assume a continuity of ministry normally leading to ordination to the priesthood in the Catholic Church, depending on a process of mutual discernment.[2]

Even before his formal conversion, Graham Leonard – a close friend of Cardinal Hume – had begun to work on smoothing the path to Rome for other disenchanted Anglicans. Indeed, he played such an early part in the Catholic Church's plans to accommodate them that his conduct raises again the question that was asked of Victorian converts and provoked John Henry Newman into writing *Apologia Pro Vita Sua*. When a man changes sides, can he avoid deceiving – during the transition – either his old or new allegiance? The dilemma did not seem to trouble Graham Leonard. Within a month of the Synod's vote to ordain women, and while still Bishop of London, he attended a meeting that was called to discuss rites of passage from the Anglican to the Catholic Communion.

The meeting – convened by Cardinal Basil Hume, Archbishop of Westminster, and held in his house behind Westminster Cathedral – was held on February 15th 1993. Among the participants were two future cardinals, Murphy-O'Connor and Nichols. According to Murphy-O'Connor, Leonard estimated that 'as many as a third of Anglican clergy might seek to join the church'.[3] The hope of making that risibly inaccurate prediction come true may explain why the three prelates were prepared to discuss a number of alternatives to straightforward conversion. They included the notion that new Catholics might be made to feel at home by the incorporation, into some Catholic services, of items taken from Church of England liturgy, and the creation of a 'personal prelature' through which the new recruits could have enjoyed a degree of collective autonomy. Cardinal Hume expressed some sympathy for the idea, without endorsing it, and the question was left unresolved.

The Church of England, which proposed to pay resigning clergy two-thirds of their salaries for ten years, had relieved Rome of a financial burden that would have made their ordination impossible. But – although their services would effectively be free – there was still some opposition to providing Anglican apostates with a fast track to the diminished ranks of the Catholic priesthood. The north-of-England bishops were strongly against the idea. Indeed, they saw an insuperable obstacle to some of them being admitted at any speed. Married men could not become members of a celibate priesthood. And it was known that the Vatican would not agree to any innovation that was not unanimously approved by the English bishops.

Cardinal Hume was not prepared to settle for half measures. The Church of England clergy must be *welcomed* into the Catholic priesthood. 'I am going to apply to Rome that these people should be allowed to be ordained directly *per saltum* ['hopping over'] and not be required to go through the deaconate. I am going to ask Rome to acknowledge that in certain circumstances they can be allowed to be ordained conditionally.' The opposition of the northern bishops made him temporarily abandon the idea of ordaining married Anglicans. However, he was determined to offer a fast track into the priesthood – a process which he hoped to achieve by obtaining agreement that the English Hierarchy should have sole discretion in selecting candidates for the Catholic priesthood. Hume decided that his best chance of success lay in personal diplomacy. Together with bishops (eventually cardinals) Murphy-O'Connor and Nichols, he would seek an audience with the Pope.

A month after the first meeting of the bridging group, *The Tablet* celebrated Cardinal Hume's seventieth birthday with a long article which included his views on the *Magisterium* – the 'teaching authority' of the Pope:

> He finds a certain irony in that just at the moment when Catholics feel irked by the teaching authority, High Church Anglicans are finding the need of it ... 'This could be the big moment of Grace. It could be the conversion of England for which we have prayed all these years. I am terrified that we are going to turn around and say that we do not want these newcomers.'[4]

For three hundred years the Catholic Mass had ended with prayers for England's conversion. The reproduction of the aspiration in print caused an explosion of resentment that was reminiscent of the outrage which followed the publication of *From the Flaminian Gate*. Ferdinand Mount – then editor of the *Times Literary Supplement* – wondered if the Emancipation Act of 1829 had been a mistake. Murphy-O'Connor wrote that he had persuaded Hume to issue a clarifying statement and send a personal copy to George Carey, the Archbishop of Canterbury. Carey admitted to feeling alarm when he read the newspaper reports of the proposed 'conversion of England', but he accepted that there had been no suggestion of 'absorption by one group'.[5] He must have realised that, had absorption been a possibility, it would have been the moral duty of the 'one group' – usually known as the Catholic Church to – promote it.

Having 'clarified' his position on the possible demise of the Church of England, Cardinal Hume was ready for Rome and the Pope's advice on how to treat the would-be converts. He provided history with a graphic, if idiosyncratic, account of his reception:

> We went to see the Headmaster. We went into his office. There he was, a big bear-like man, standing up, beaming. He called me towards him, put his arm round me and said, 'Basil. Basil. These Anglicans. Be generous. Be generous.' We said at this point we thought we had better go and see the Deputy Headmaster. So we went downstairs to Cardinal Joseph Ratzinger's room and it was all very German. His desk was at the end of a big, long kind of corridor. He was writing away and didn't look up. We crept in and sat in the front row like little schoolboys. And then he looked over his glasses and said, 'Cardinal Hume. Be flexible. Be flexible'. The Pope was saying 'Be generous': Cardinal Ratzinger was saying 'Be flexible.' So we went out and had a Campari.[6]

Formal approval followed. The idea of creating a 'Uniate Church' within the Church itself had, for the time, been abandoned but, in almost every other particular, the prospect offered to dissident Anglicans might have been devised to entice doubters rather than to meet the needs of troubled consciences. Graham Leonard – married with two sons – was ordained a Catholic priest by Basil Hume in the Cardinal's private chapel on April 26th 1994. That was eighteen months before the second ordination. Like Edward Manning in 1851, Leonard was a 'trophy convert' and was – again like Manning – given what other Anglican candidates for the Catholic Holy Orders regarded as indefensibly preferential treatment. Cardinal Hume was entitled to be happy with the outcome. But he must have appreciated the paradox of his own position. He had welcomed into his fold Anglicans who could not, in principle, support the ordination of women. Yet he was not opposed to his own Church making the fundamental change by which the theological refugees had been alienated. On April 6th 1978 he had told a troubled priest, 'My own personal position is that a) there is no theological argument either in favour or against women priests. b) the Roman Catholic depends, therefore, on the authority of the Church. As you will know, the Catholic Church is not in favour of women priests at the present time.'[7] Some weeks later, during a radio interview, he was equally explicit: 'I personally, if the authorities of my Church agreed to the ordination of women, would have no problem about it.'[8]

Hume thus demonstrated that, on the issue of women's ordination, he was 'more progressive' than were traditionalists in the Church of England. Eleven members of the Ecclesiastical Commission – a joint standing committee of both Houses of Parliament – sent an open letter to the Archbishops of Canterbury and York. It called for 'the continuation of the Church of England as a broadly based and national Church'. That, they said, required more protection for the opponents of women's ordination than the appointment of 'flying bishops', to whom clergy – opposed to the new regime – would answer, without reference to the hierarchy in their diocese. The letter asked for assurances about the future, which the two archbishops were clearly unable to provide. The great fear was that some in the future Synod would choose to extend the move towards equality by authorising the appointment of women bishops. The Ecclesiastical Commission had thirty members. So, had they chosen to do so, the eleven opponents of women's ordination could have prevented the Synod's resolution from being sent on for full parliamentary approval, as the 'establishment' of the Church of England required. Respect for convention prevented them from doing so.

There were two more bridges to be crossed. On October 30th 1993, the High Court dismissed the Church Society's claim that the General Synod did not have the power to authorise the ordination of women, and on the following day the House of Commons passed the Priests (Ordination of Women) Measure by 215 votes to 21. In the House of Lords a 'wrecking motion' to postpone discussion was defeated by 135 votes to 25. The most effective speech in the Commons was made by John Selwyn Gummer, a Conservative MP and Minister of Agriculture – speaking from the back benches as a Private Member. Gummer, one of the signatories of the Ecclesiastical Commission letter, had addressed the Wembley Rally and, back in April 1992, had made the intellectual case against the proposed 'reforms:'

The Church of England has always claimed that it has no doctrines or orders of its own but only those of the Universal Church. It was on that basis that it demanded the allegiance of the people of England. It sought both to insist upon Catholic essentials and to uphold the necessity of reform ... Now the Church of England has changed all that. By asserting that it can alter doctrine and order unilaterally, it has relinquished its apostolic claim to the allegiance of the people of England.[9]

His speech in the House of Commons ended with a succinct summary of how traditionalists saw the changes that the ordination of women had brought about: 'When this measure is passed we will have to say that we have been excluded from the Church of England.'

There was an immediate spate of applications for admission to the Catholic Church – a process that purists insisted was not 'conversion' because that term was only properly applied to former heathens, not to recent members of other Christian denominations. Most of the new Catholics quietly accepted instruction and received a private baptism. Some were accompanied into the Church by television cameras and press photographers. A few were helped along the way by a young Franciscan friar on the staff of Westminster Cathedral. He came to be called (and seemed not to mind being called) the 'celebrities' priest'. Tony Blair, three times elected Prime Minister, was said to be among the notables who were led into the Church by his kindly light. Estimates of 'convert' numbers vary, but some figures can be verified. By 2007, 580 one-time Anglicans – 120 of them married – had been ordained Catholic priests.[10]

The Church of England – relieved that the issue of female ordination had been settled and bracing itself for the battle over the appointment of women bishops – accepted the haemorrhage with the grace (sometimes described as complacency) expected of it. However, for some notable Anglican clerics, the creation on January 15th 2011 of the Personal Ordinariate of Our Lady of Walsingham – a semi-autonomous enclave of convert priests – stretched tolerance far past breaking point. John Saxbee, the Bishop of Lincoln, thought the Ordinariate 'did not sit well with all the talk of working towards better relations' and that 'fence mending would need to be done to set conversations back on track'.[11]

Bishop Christopher Hill, the chairman of the Church of England Council for Christian Unity, described the initiative as an 'insensitive act'. Canon Giles Fraser, the Chancellor of St Paul's Cathedral – preaching the sermon in a Westminster Cathedral ecumenical service during a Week of Prayer for Christian Unity – described the announcement of the Ordinariate as 'in corporate terms a little like a takeover bid in some broader power play of Church politics'. He need not have worried. As a recruiting agent, it has been a failure. It has never attracted more than 3,000 members – almost all of whom had (or would have) joined the Roman Catholic Church without the inducement of the Ordinariate. Basing his judgement on that dubious evidence, Monsignor Keith Newton – the former Anglican Bishop of Richborough, who was ordained on the day of its foundation and made its Ordinary – claims that its purpose is ecumenical.

Ordinariates were founded in Canada, Australia and Britain with the object of making Anglican converts feel at home in the Church of Rome. The idea of creating some sort of semi-autonomous enclave had been considered, but left in abeyance, at the meeting at which Basil Hume and Graham Leonard had first discussed how best to respond to Church of England defections. The idea was resurrected, in irresistible form, when – in October 2009 – the Vatican announced that the creation of 'personal ordinariates' was possible under the apostolic constitution *Anglicanorum Coetibus* of Pope Benedict XVI. It seems that Benedict was an enthusiast for the innovation. When the England and Wales Ordinariate was on the point of financial collapse, he arranged for a Vatican subvention of $250,000.

The Personal Ordinariate of Our Lady of Walsingham was described, in its foundation document, as 'within the territory of the Catholic Bishops' Conference of England and Wales'. The words were carefully chosen – even though its writ also ran in Scotland. They were intended to emphasise its semi-autonomous status. Monsignor Newton – who, having been married, could not be made a bishop – answered directly to the Holy See, within but independently of the English episcopate.

For most of the Ordinariate's members – thinly spread over all three British nations – the relationship with their local parish church has not changed. It is there that they go to Mass, to make their confessions, to baptise their children and to bury their dead. Occasionally a priest associated with the Ordinariate – which has no churches of its own – will visit the parish and officiate at a service. Only the best-informed and most perceptive members of the congregation will identify the changes in the normal Catholic liturgy, which were made to comfort homesick Anglicans.

If the well-publicised conversions, which the Ordinariate associates with its creation, really were the result of rising hopes that bridges could be built, many of the new recruits must soon have become disappointed. But, whatever the reason, the autumn and winter of 2010/11 was a fruitful season for Catholics of a missionary disposition. In November 2010, the parish council of St Peter's in Folkestone, Kent, decided to defect en masse. About half the congregation made the move as part of a contingent of six hundred Anglican converts from south-east England. On November 8th 2010, three serving Anglican bishops – Andrew Burnham of Ebbsfleet and John Broadhurst of Fulham, as well as Keith Newton of Richborough – and two retired bishops – Edwin Barnes and David Silk – announced their intention of becoming Catholics. They were received into the Church and made deacons at a private ceremony which preceded their ordination in

Westminster Cathedral on New Year's Day 2011. Their wives were there to witness the great event, together with three erstwhile Anglican nuns from Walsingham. It was the Ordinariate's finest hour. By Easter 2011, nine hundred new Catholics had entered the Church through the door it had opened. More were to enter by a different but even more controversial route.

When, in 1966, the Vatican Council chose to define the Catholic Church as The People of God – thus confirming that it was a community rather than an institution – it reflected both the beginning of a change in attitude from the authoritarian past and an acceptance, as a demographic fact, that the centre of gravity for all of Christendom was shifting away from Europe and towards the emerging nations of Africa, Asia and South America. In 1910, 80 per cent of the world's Christians lived in the northern hemisphere. In 2010, a majority of the world's Christians lived south of the equator. The consequences of the change, even for the timeless Catholic Church, are immense. Rome has at least to take account of the hopes and needs of millions of devout communicants whose habits, mores and life prospects are very different from those of either the richest or the poorest European Catholic family. The half acceptance that contraception is a proper weapon to use in the fight against the Zika virus – the infection that condemns unborn babies to permanent disability – is the response of a Church that has accepted its obligations to South America. The refusal to sanction contraception as a protection against Aids was, and remains, the reaction of a Church which, in its European ignorance, thought of the infection as the 'gay plague'. But Catholicism is no longer a solely European religion.

In 2008, the Catholic Bishops' Conference of England and Wales recognised the new reality in language which made clear that it was to be welcomed: 'The growth of the Church in Africa and Asia over the last thirty years has been phenomenal. When coupled with migration from Africa, Asia, Latin America and Eastern Europe this changes the profile of the Catholic Church throughout the world. Britain is no exception.'[12] It then added for good measure, 'In recent times the Catholic Church has been further strengthened with the arrival of migrants from the new member states of the EU.'

The Catholic Church is most self-confident when it can justify its behaviour by means of the Bible or the works of the early Fathers. So there are few texts on immigration which fail to point out that Joseph, Mary and the infant Jesus were forced to migrate (in what came to be called 'the flight into Egypt') in order to escape Herod's butchery of the firstborn. With that example of the immigrants' claim for help in mind, the Catholic Church consistently championed their cause. Cardinal John Heenan – together with Michael Ramsay, the Archbishop of Canterbury – publicly condemned the 1968 Commonwealth Immigration Act, which was passed explicitly to exclude from Britain Asians who had been expelled from Kenya as part of that country's policy of 'Africanisation'.

For the next twenty years the Catholic Church heroically argued for an immigration policy which it must have known did not represent the view of the British public. In 1988 the Bishops' Conference published *A Statement on the Rights of Migrants and Settlers*. It emphasised the need to protect the dignity and human rights of asylum seekers and foreign workers. So, in 2004, did the Discastery Instruction *Erga Migrantes Caritas Christi* (The Love of Christ Towards Migrants). The Bishops' Conference statement, which was published four years later, was admirably out of step with both public opinion and the policies of the major political parties:

> While most immigrants are in Britain with permission, many are 'undocumented'. Sometimes this is because they have entered the country illegally, but in most cases it is because they have overstayed their visas or where their asylum claims have failed but they cannot return because their countries are still in turmoil or refuse to accept their return. Many of these migrants have been here for several years: some have even set down roots and started families. Without condoning illegal immigration, the Church's position on this, as on other fields of human endeavour, does not allow economic, social and political calculations to prevail over the person. On the contrary the Church argues for the dignity of the human person to be put above everything else and the rest to be conditioned by it. The Church will continue to advocate compassion to allow the 'undocumented' to acquire proper status, so that they can continue to contribute to the common good without the constant fear of discovery and removal.

The Catholic Church in both England and Scotland can claim special authority on the subject of migrant settlement. At the end of the Second World War, 68,000 Polish servicemen – almost all of them Catholics – chose to make their home in Britain. The armed forces of 'Free Poland' had fought against the Axis Powers first under the Polish Government in Exile, then under the Provisional Government of the 'liberated' nation. Liberation had made Poland a Soviet satellite. So one-third of the Polish servicemen chose voluntary exile. They were repatriated to

Britain and formed into a quasi-military unit called the Polish Resettlement Corps, housed in army camps, taught English and prepared for civilian employment. The most fortunate among them were joined by their dependent relatives. The families were the first to think of creating Catholic communities. Missions – social as well as spiritual in purpose – were set up where members of the Corps found employment, usually the centres of heavy industry and manual labour. One of them was in Coventry.

It would be wrong to describe the Coventry experience as typical. The Polish Catholics of Coventry created the sort of community to which Polish Catholics in other parts of Britain aspired but did not always achieve. Their success was a victory for the dogged determination of the thousand or so Poles (two hundred women among them) who, in January 1947, moved from a resettlement camp in Herefordshire to the West Midlands to work on the rebuilding of the blitzed city. Their object – achieved in the end – was the creation of a distinct Polish community with a church at is centre. Progress was slow. It was more than a year before a visiting priest celebrated the first 'Polish Mass'. From then on they became a frequent, though not regular, feature of Catholic life in Coventry. But the Coventry Poles wanted a priest and a church of their own. It was another year before the rector of the Polish Church in Britain was convinced that they could raise enough regular income to make their aspiration a reality, but on May 1st 1949, Father Narcizas Turulski, a former military padre who had ended the war in a Soviet labour camp, became pastor to the Coventry Poles.

On the day after his arrival he distributed the first issue of what was to become a regular Parish Bulletin: 'We cordially [invite] Poles who are living in the Coventry area to take part in our Polish church services ... Attendance at our Polish church services should become the responsibility of every Polish Catholic ... In principle every Pole should be baptised and every Wedding held in the Polish language.' That mission statement revealed why members of a universal Church, which then held its services in a common language, should want acts of worship that were distinct and separate from those that were attended by the members of the same faith amongst whom they lived. Distinct Polish churches were intended to preserve national identity, not religious belief and observance. In consequence they became the subject of some controversy when second- and third-generation Poles – whether or not they were assimilated into British life in general – chose Polish worship in Polish churches.

During the early years of Father Turulski's ministry, the Poles of

Coventry were more or less content for him to celebrate Mass (usually at noon, when the regular services were over) in friendly parish churches. But in February 1956, their patience exhausted, they began to plan for both what they called a temple and for a parish centre. One scheme had to be abandoned because the cost was too great. Another plan was frustrated by Coventry City Council. The Church of St Stanislaus Kostka was consecrated on December 9th 1961 and still thrives. Until 2004 attendances were declining. But after Poland's accession to the European Union, congregations increased year on year. By 2015 there were approaching three hundred worshippers at each of the three Sunday Masses and almost as many at the Saturday Mass. St Stanislaus Kostka's resident priest has no way of knowing how many Polish Catholics worship in the Coventry parishes. The assumption is that a bare majority of Poles choose the Polish church and that some Poles, far from home, have abandoned church completely.

One sad fact is, however, certain. There are very few 'Originals' – the men and women who built the 'mission' – left. Most of what the Catholic Church has said and written about migrants concerned a Christian's duty to the homeless, poor and hungry. The Poles who came to Britain during the early years of the twenty-first century were economic migrants and were, as a result, treated with fear and suspicion by much of the host community. Some influential Catholics were deeply apprehensive about the effect they would have on the Church. If they were to join the Polish parishes in large numbers, there would be a danger of the newcomers – in the words of Cardinal Murphy-O'Connor – 'creating a separate church in Britain'.

The Cardinal's friends argued, with some justification, that – far from regretting the arrival of the Poles – their only wish was for the migrants to play an invigorating part in the life of the Church of their adopted land. He 'clarified' his earlier statements. 'I would want them to be part of the catholic life of this country. I would hope that those responsible for the Polish Church here, and the Poles themselves, will be aware that they should become a part of local parishes as soon as possible when they learn enough of the language.'[13]

Influential Polish Catholics disagreed. Bishop Ryszard Karpinski, then delegate for Polish Catholics abroad, issued a statement that clearly reflected the hope that expatriate Poles would maintain their national identity: 'It remains our position that Polish Catholics should look for their own priests and parishes. But we have no means of forcing anyone. If people want to come to Polish churches, they come. If they want to go to English speaking churches, they go.'[14] Cardinal Jozef Glemp, the Polish Primate, took a less liberal view. Polish migrants had a duty to 'seek out Polish pastors and find Polish church centres'. Grażyna Sikorska of the Polish Mission in London challenged an assertion that Cardinal Murphy-O'Connor had never made: 'How can he demand that we stop praying in Polish? Is it a sin?'[15] Lest anyone should doubt the strength of her feeling, she added that the call to abandon Polish churches made her 'feel my inner conscience has been violated, leaving her spiritually raped'. Father Tadeusz Kukla, the Vicar-Delegate of Poles in England, got near to accepting the real (and essentially temporal) cause of the outrage: 'If we lose our national identity we lose everything.' Hanna Darowska – the director of a Polish school in Oxford – gave an equally temporal explanation of why expatriate Poles preferred Polish churches. The Polish churches 'had been built up with great difficulty over many years'.[16] The Polish immigrants of the early twenty-first century did not, and could not, create a separate Church. It was in existence before their arrival. Although, unlike the enclave of Anglican converts, the Polish Church in England did not have the formal status of Ordinariate, it was – in its way – more distinct. For it aimed to meet the social, as well as the spiritual, needs of its members.

The new wave of Polish immigrants did not think of the Polish Church in England and Scotland as their founders had thought of it seventy years earlier. All that the immigrants of the twenty-first century asked for was the opportunity to attend Mass and make confession. Although they wanted 'to pray in Polish' – and Bishop Wojciech Polak, the new delegate to Catholics abroad, thought it his duty to 'uphold patriotic values'[17] – they had no wish to be absorbed into a lifestyle that tried to replicate the culture of home and they had no intention of playing a part in 'parish life', whatever language the parishioners spoke. The Polish ex-servicemen and women who came to Britain during the late 1940s were genuine refugees who needed what they called 'Polish Catholic Missions' to make life tolerable in a strange land. The Poles who followed them seventy years later were adventurers with the self-confidence, and more often than not the skill, to make their own successful way. Cardinal Murphy-O'Connor was right to hope that they would employ their talents in the indigenous English Church. Unlike the Irish immigrants of the 1850s, it needed them far more than they needed it.

So did the Scottish Church, and the Scots showed every sign of realising the opportunity for renewal and growth that Polish immigration provided. In February 2006, Peter Moran, the Bishop of Aberdeen, visited Poland for 'meetings with key religious leaders', including Archbishop Stanisław Dziwisz. While he was in Warsaw he told the Catholic radio station that in his diocese 'the percentage of Catholics is 3% of the population, but with the arrival of many people from Poland the Catholic population is increasing rapidly'.[18] He said that in Aberdeen itself, the Catholic population had tripled in two years. The Bishop then echoed the call that had been made by three centuries of his predecessors. The diocese still needed more priests. He suggested a new solution to the old problem: 'I have come to Poland because these Polish Catholics need pastoral care.' He then added – making a distinction that was not wholly consistent with the concept of one worldwide Church – 'I also need priests for my own Catholics. I hear there are some priests from Poland who would be happy to come and work in Scotland.'

The English and Welsh Hierarchy, though none of its members said so, was in equal need of an influx of priests. In 2013, 45 per cent of the priests in the archdiocese were over seventy years old and the percentage was predicted to rise until 2023, when only 1,500 priests would be under threescore years and ten – 1,000 fewer than ten years earlier.[19]

According to *The Scotsman*, it was Polish immigration – increasing church attendance by 50,000 between 2002 and 2006 – that made Scotland 'more Roman Catholic than Protestant with its congregations outnumbering the Kirk for the first time since records began'. A spokesman for the Catholic Church added that, in Scotland, 'there are now more Masses being said in Polish than in Gaelic. At St Mary's Cathedral in Edinburgh, there are two Polish Masses every Sunday.' The arrival of new, Polish blood had, he claimed, reinvigorated the whole Church. 'In terms of vocations to the priesthood, we reached rock bottom a few years ago when we had only about four or five men training to be priests. Now there are 15 or 16.'

The Catholic Church in Britain ought to regard May 1st 2004 as a red-letter day, even though it passed without the martyrdom of a single saint or the manifestation of a solitary miracle. It was the date of Poland's accession to the European Union and of the arrival of the first Polish immigrants which, although it did not increase the size of the Catholic population, appeared to have ended the dramatic year-on-year reduction of the early 1990s. Numbers had stabilised, and stabilisation was an achievement. The Catholic Bishops' Conference for England and Wales celebrated the 2011 census as a triumph. In ten years, the total number of citizens who identified themselves as Christians had fallen from 37.3 million (72 per cent) to 33.2 million (59 per cent). 'While precise figures are difficult to determine polling shows that the Catholic population has remained constant at 9%.'

According to an Ipsos MORI survey, the total number remained unchanged, at five million. The Church in Scotland had even more reason to rejoice. Between 2001 and 2011 the number of Scottish Catholics actually increased by 4 per cent to 841,053. During the same period the number of Scots who identified themselves as Christians fell from 3.3 million to 2.8 million. Professor Thomas Gallagher, 'an expert on Scotland and Christianity', attributed the 'relative and absolute improvement to the large-scale arrival of Poles'.[20]

The Protestant Churches of Scotland remained the dominant Scottish denominations. But, by the time of the 2011 census, it was already possible to argue that in England the Catholic Church occupied first place. Attendance at Sunday services is said to indicate the number of 'practising' Christians. A survey by the Institute of Public Policy Research revealed that between 2000 and 2007 the total Church of England Sunday morning congregation fell by 37,000 to an average of 852,000. The average attendance at Mass was 861,000.[21]

It was not only the Poles who pushed the Catholic Church to the top of the Sunday league. There were other immigrants who added to the number of church attendances – most of them by worshipping at outposts of their homeland Church. But the Syro-Malabar, the Chaldean, the Eritrean, the Ethiopian Churches and many more only contributed individuals or occasional families to the total. The Poles came not singly, but in battalions. Stalin once asked how many divisions were under the Pope's command. During the early years of the twenty-first century the Vatican's depleted, but resolute army in Britain received important reinforcements. Its leaders have now to decide how it fights for Catholicism's future.

CONCLUSION

A Matter of Conscience

The Synod on the Family, which was held in Rome during October 2015, was an admirably harmonious gathering. Most of the 1,350 speeches avoided tedious repetition of either the liberal or conservative position, and every one of the *Relatio Synodi*'s ninety-four paragraphs was passed with a two-thirds majority. Some of the conclusions were risibly trite. Paragraph 18 stated that 'grandparents in a family deserve special attention', and paragraph 21 asserted that 'particular attention needs to be given to families whose members have special needs'. But statements of the obvious are unavoidable in a document that synthesises the views of 279 priests and bishops.

The Synod was convened to travel over dangerous, and well-trodden, ground. For, according to the available evidence, the issues that increasingly alienate the otherwise faithful from their Church are not the items of dogma which Protestants rejected at various stages of the Reformation – papal authority, the intercession of saints and transubstantiation. Nor are they the more recent additions to doctrine – the bodily assumption into heaven of the Virgin Mary and the infallibility of the Pope. The apostates who have lost their faith are massively outnumbered by men and women who accept all the basic tenets of Catholicism, but reject its interpretation of God's will about how they should conduct the most intimate aspects of their lives – or, with even more corrosive consequences for Catholicism's future, do not believe that the nature of their private relationships is any of the Church's business. Science and self-confidence, affluence and education have turned many western European Catholics into Protestants – in one particular.

The 2015 Synod was one of the many signs that the Catholic Church has recognised the changing character of its members. But in the past recognising the changes did not lead to accommodating them. Some of the delegates argued that the human condition would be better understood if the laity was allowed to speak for itself. Archbishop Blase Cupich of Chicago – an advocate of the admission, into full communion, of gay and remarried couples – wanted the Synod to hear 'the actual voices of the people who feel marginalised, rather than have them filter through other representatives or the bishops'. In England and Wales, a Catholic pressure group, A Call to Action, made sure that Cardinal Vincent Nichols and the Bishop of Northampton – representing England – went fully briefed to Rome by sponsoring a survey of Catholic attitudes towards the crucial social questions. Its findings confirm how difficult it would, or will, be to reconcile lay convictions and Church doctrine.

Eighty-five per cent of respondents to the survey were opposed to the Church's teaching on contraception – 66 per cent 'very strongly so'. The majority in favour of admitting divorced and remarried couples to the sacraments was smaller. So were the majorities that were critical of the Church's opposition to same-sex marriages and its censorious attitude towards what it calls 'irregular relationships'. Only one of the Church's position-papers on 'family life' and related subjects received overall support in the Call to Action survey. There was a substantial majority for the view that abortion is only morally permissible when the mother's life is in danger – a judgement that is shared by many members of other faiths and of none.

The Synod treated each of the contentious subjects with a sensitivity that has not always characterised the Church's attitude. Paragraph 76 of the *Relatio*, which summarised its conclusions, emphasised that 'every person, regardless of sexual orientation, ought to be respected for his or her dignity and received with respect while avoiding every sign of unjust discrimination'. Liberal hopes of further progress towards equality were, however, confounded by the next magisterial judgement: 'There are absolutely no grounds for considering homosexual unions to be in any way similar or even remotely analogous to God's plans for marriage and families.'

Paragraph 84 of the *Relatio* insisted that men and women 'who had been divorced and civilly remarried ... belong to the Church [and] can have a joyful and fruitful experience of it ... Their participation can be expressed in different ecclesial services which necessarily requires discerning which of the various forms of exclusion, currently practised in the liturgical, pastoral, educational and institutional framework, can be surpassed.' The misuse (or mistranslation) of the word 'surpassed' is not the paragraph's only shortcoming. It diagnoses a problem, speculates on the nature of possible solutions, but proposes no practical remedy. The Synod gave no sign that rights to the sacrament would be restored.

To the pathologically optimistic liberal, paragraph 63 of the *Relatio* offered hope of some modification on the prohibition of birth control. The statement that 'the just way for family planning is that of a consensual dialogue between the spouses, respect for the times of fertility and consideration of the dignity of the partner' was a step away from the extreme view that any form of family planning is a denial of marriage's true purpose. The widely unpopular *Humanae Vitae* – although mentioned with necessary respect in paragraph 43 – was no longer the final word on the subject. There was, however, no indication of what would replace it.

On March 19th 2016 the Pope signed and published his response to the Synod's *Final Reports*. The Apostolic Exhortation, *Amoris Laetitia* (On Love in the Family), did not make precise promises of change. But its tone gave reason for hope to those Catholics who believed, or wanted to believe, that the election of Pope Francis heralded a movement towards a more compassionate Church which, instead of condemning human weakness, tried to understand its causes. Optimism had been encouraged by the Pope's almost casual comment to journalists who travelled with him on his flight back to Rome after his visit to Mexico. He had got very near to accepting that contraception might be a morally legitimate way of stopping the spread of the Zika virus.

There was nothing in *Amoris Laetitia* that even the most conservative Catholic could dismiss as revolutionary. But it provided reformers with more reasons to rejoice than the progressive 'tone' that commentators have identified. It argued that the Church must 'make room' for the exercise of individual conscience, without the usual codicil that conscience must be guided by 'given truth'. And it went further than the Synod in identifying, if not opening, one possible way of relaxing the rule that bans remarried divorcees from taking Communion – the cause of anguish for three hundred years.

The Pope's idea about how relaxation might be managed was, perhaps, the most significant element in the whole Exhortation. He proposed – or at least speculated about – extending the use of the 'internal forum', a procedure already in occasional use to deal with applications (of dubious merit) for admission to the sacraments. 'Conversations with the priest in the internal forum contribute to the formation of correct judgments on what hinders the possibility of a fuller participation in the life of the Church.' The implication was clear. Clergy and laity would not discuss the demands of faith on equal terms. But acceptance of any sort of discussion would be a step forward. It will not compensate reformers for the failure of *Amoris Laetitia* to concede that the Church should examine the needs of its gay Catholics. But added to the Pope's declaration that he would invite the Congregation of the Doctrine of Faith to comment on the possibility of ordaining women deacons, the prospect of progress towards a less exclusive view of Communion marks out early 2016 as the time when the Catholic Church shuffled a small but discernible distance towards achieving a concordat with its members.

There were Catholics who were opposed to their Church taking even that small hesitant step. *Amoris Laetitia* describes them as 'those who prefer a more rigorous pastoral care which leaves no room for confusion'. Their immobility is increasingly rejected by both humanists (important in the Church since Erasmus befriended More) and pragmatists who know that, if the rules governing the use of contraception were enforced, very few young women would take Communion. Heretics of one sort and another find the unquestioning acceptance of ancient doctrine lacking in both compassion and logic.

However, there is an important argument in favour of inflexibility which is, in its way, pragmatic. Catholicism survived the long years of persecution and prejudice because the faith of its followers was reinforced by moral certainty – a condition that provides the confidence that reasonable doubt cannot guarantee. Throughout the history of the Church there were arguments about interpretation and, from time to time, the conduct of the Pope (and more often of past popes) was denounced. But the basic doctrines and fundamental dogma endured. So did the authority of the Church. Catholics gained courage and comfort from the knowledge that, no matter how much pressure was put on principle, it would not break. Men and women do not go willingly to the stake or block in defence of common sense, sweet reason and majority opinion. They die for convictions that allow no reservations.

Now the ancient verities have been eroded by a new certainty. Affluence and education have made freedom the new moral imperative – freedom of conscience, freedom of action, freedom of belief. The world is running away from the Catholic Church, and the Church has yet to decide whether the best response is retrenchment or reform. One thing is, however, certain. The Catholic Church still needs members who reject reasonable compromise in favour of what they believe to be the incontrovertible truth. They are the heirs to the heroic years and – intellectually perverse though they may be – it is impossible not to feel an envious admiration for men and women who identify with the noblest statement of English Catholicism: 'The expense is reckoned, the enterprise is begun; it is of God, it cannot be withstood. So the faith was planted: so it must be restored.'

Notes on Sources

Archives are identified as:
AVCAU – Archivum Venerabilis Collegii Anglorum de Urbe (Archives of the Venerable English College, Rome)
DSCN – Birmingham Diocese
PF – Propaganda Fide
WDA – Westminster Diocese

CHAPTER 1

As Far as the Law of God Allows

1 Jasper Ridley, *The Statesman and the Fanatic* (Constable), p.94
2 J J Scarisbrick, *Henry VIII* (Yale University Press), p.112
3 Ibid., p.113
4 Ibid., p.115
5 Ridley, op. cit., p.60
6 Ibid., p.165
7 Christopher Haigh, *The English Reformation* (Clarendon Press), p.67
8 Ibid., p.68
9 Ibid.
10 Ibid.
11 Ibid., p.102
12 Eamon Duffy, *Fires of Faith* (Yale University Press), p.44
13 Haigh, op. cit., p.93
14 Ibid.
15 W Schenk, *Reginald Pole* (Longmans Green), p.24
16 Ibid.
17 Haigh, op. cit., p.109
18 WDA, Vol. I, 13.241
19 A G Dickens, *The English Reformation* (Batsford), p.138
20 Ibid.
21 Haigh, op. cit., p.119
22 E E Reynolds, *Saint John Fisher* (Burns & Oates), p.342
23 Ibid., p.23
24 Ibid., p.25
25 Ibid., p.114
26 Peter Ackroyd, *The Life of Thomas More* (Vintage), p.343
27 Tracy Borman, *Thomas Cromwell* (Hodder and Stoughton), p.160
28 Ridley, op. cit., p.133
29 Ackroyd, op. cit., p.226
30 Dickens, op. cit., p.163
31 Derek Wilson, *The English Reformation* (Constable), p.101
32 Ridley, op. cit., p.264
33 Wilson, op. cit., p.121
34 Ackroyd, op. cit., p.357
35 Ibid.
36 Ibid., p.359
37 Ridley, op. cit., p.283
38 Ibid., p.276
39 Borman, op. cit., p.194
40 Ackroyd, op. cit., p.394
41 Haigh, op. cit., p.13

CHAPTER 2

The Cause Thereof

1 Haigh, op. cit., p.41
2 Ridley, op. cit., p.244
3 Wilson, op. cit., p.110
4 Ibid.
5 Haigh, op. cit., p.51
6 Ibid., p.77
7 Dickens, op. cit., p.76
8 J D Mackie, *The Early Tudors* (Oxford University Press), p.375
9 Ridley, op. cit., p.34
10 Schenk, op. cit., p.143
11 Haigh, op. cit., p.9
12 Schenk, op. cit., p.101
13 Haigh, op. cit., p.143
14 Ibid.
15 Mackie, op. cit., p.373
16 Haigh op. cit., p.130
17 Wilson, op. cit., p.172
18 Mackie, op. cit., p.376
19 Wilson, op. cit., p.168

20 Ibid., p.170
21 Ibid., p.205
22 Ibid.
23 Geoffrey Moorhouse, *The Pilgrimage of Grace* (Weidenfeld & Nicolson), p.34
24 Ibid., p.41
25 Ibid.
26 Wilson, op. cit., p.186
27 Haigh, op. cit., p.148
28 Christopher Haigh (ed.), *The English Reformation Revisited* (Cambridge University Press), D M Palliser, 'Popular Reaction to the Reformation During the Years of Uncertainty'.

22 Haigh, op. cit., p.96
23 Wilson, op. cit., p.192
24 Dickens, op. cit., p.169
25 Moorhouse, op. cit., p.167
26 Ibid., p.172
27 Ibid., p.173
28 Bush, op. cit., p.411
29 Moorhouse, op. cit., p.193
30 David Loades, *Henry VIII, Court and Conflict* (National Archives), p.194
31 Moorhouse, op. cit., p.208
32 Ibid., p.216
33 Ibid.
34 Ibid., p.235
35 Ibid., p.25
36 Ibid., p.299

CHAPTER 3

Forth, Pilgrims! Forth!

1 Borman, op. cit., p.272
2 Wilson, op. cit., p.189
3 Ibid., p.190
4 Scarisbrick, op. cit., p.343
5 M A Tierney, *Dodd's Church History of England*, Vol. I, Appendix, p.432
6 Ethan H Shagan (ed.), *Catholics and the Protestant Nation* (Manchester University Press), Peter Marshall, 'Is the Pope a Catholic?'
7 Thomas F Mayer, *Cardinal Pole in the European Context* (Ashgate), Vol. II, p.307
8 Schenk, op. cit., p.75
9 Moorhouse, op. cit., p.113
10 Scarisbrick, op. cit., p.341
11 Ibid., p.199
12 Ibid., p.122
13 Michael Bush, *The Pilgrimage of Grace* (Manchester University Press), p.119
14 Moorhouse, op. cit., p.133
15 Ibid.
16 Ibid., p.148
17 Ibid., p.153
18 Ibid., p.156
19 Ibid.
20 Wilson, op. cit., p.183
21 Schenk, op. cit., p.38

CHAPTER 4

The Necessity of Doctrine

1 Eamon Duffy, *The Stripping of the Altars* (Yale University Press), p.381
2 Borman, op. cit., p.190
3 Diarmaid MacCulloch, *Thomas Cranmer: A Life* (Yale University Press), p.169
4 Duffy, op. cit., p.99
5 Ibid., p.397
6 Mayer, op. cit., p.191
7 Scarisbrick, op. cit., p.406
8 Ibid., p.408
9 Ibid., p.409
10 Duffy, op. cit., p.404
11 Ibid.
12 Schenk, op. cit., p.67
13 Ibid., p.71
14 Thomas F Mayer, *Reginald Pole* (Cambridge University Press), p.63
15 Schenk, op. cit., p.79
16 Dickens, op. cit., p.201
17 Ibid., p.207
18 Ibid.
19 Scarisbrick, op. cit., p.420
20 Ibid.
21 Ibid.
22 Haigh, op. cit., p.161
23 Shagan, op. cit., p.24
24 Ibid., p.25
25 Ibid.

26 Ibid., p.14
27 Shenck, op. cit., p.54
28 Haigh, op. cit., p.106

CHAPTER 5

Sufficient Sacrifice

1 Jaspar Ridley, *John Knox* (Oxford University Press), p.29
2 Ibid.
3 Ibid.
4 Ibid.
5 Compton Mackenzie, *Catholicism and Scotland* (George Routledge), p.52
6 John Guy, *My Heart is My Own* (Fourth Estate), p.37
7 Mackenzie, op. cit., p.53
8 Ibid., p.37
9 Ridley (*Knox*), op. cit., p.47
10 Ibid., p.59
11 Ibid., p.47
12 Ibid., p.76

CHAPTER 6

Come to Redeem His People

1 Mackie, op. cit., p.512
2 Christopher Skidmore, *The Lost King of England* (Orion), p.162
3 Ibid., p.176
4 Duffy (*Altars*), op. cit., p.499
5 Jonathan North (ed.), *England's Boy King: The Diaries of Edward VI, 1547–1553* (Ravenhall Books), p.76
6 Wilson, op. cit., p.246
7 WDA, Vol. I, 10.213
8 Wilson, op. cit., p.260
9 Duffy (*Altars*), op. cit., p.451
10 Wilson, op. cit., p.162
11 Skidmore, op. cit., p.81
12 Wilson, op. cit., p.268
13 Skidmore, op. cit., p.147
14 Ibid.
15 Ibid., p.131
16 Ibid., p.168
17 Ibid., p.175
18 Haigh, op. cit., p.174

19 Ibid.
20 Wilson, op. cit., p.274
21 Ibid.
22 Mackie, op. cit., p.519
23 Skidmore, op. cit., p.122
24 Ibid., p.275
25 Ridley (*Knox*), op. cit., p.88
26 Ibid., p.89
27 Ibid., p.97
28 Ibid., p.101
29 Mackie, p.522
30 Ridley (*Knox*), op. cit., p.108
31 Ibid., p.111
32 Ibid., p.116
33 Haigh, op. cit., p.180
34 Ibid., p.193
35 Ibid.
36 Mackie, p.520
37 Skidmore, op. cit., p.167
38 Haigh, op. cit., p.183

CHAPTER 7

The Unquenchable Fyre

1 Foxe, *The Acts and Monuments* (1732 edition), 2/2
2 Mackie, op. cit., p.527
3 Ridley (*Knox*), op. cit., p.151
4 Ibid.
5 Duffy (*Fires of Faith*), op. cit., p.85
6 Haigh, op. cit., p.219
7 Duffy (*Fires of Faith*), op. cit., p.227
8 Ibid.
9 Haigh, op. cit., p.190
10 Ibid.
11 Ibid., p.192
12 Ibid., p.230
13 Ibid.
14 Ibid., p.234
15 Foxe, op. cit., 1/232
16 Ibid., 1/120
17 Duffy (*Fires of Faith*), op. cit., p.90
18 Ibid.
19 Foxe, op. cit., 1/825
20 Ibid.
21 Haigh, op. cit., p.21
22 Duffy (*Fires of Faith*), op. cit., p.112
23 Foxe, op. cit., 1/564
24 Ibid., 1/802
25 Duffy (*Fires of Faith*), op. cit., p.108

26 Foxe, op. cit., 1/627
27 Ibid., 1/640
28 Ibid.
29 Schenk, op. cit., p.124
30 WDA, Vol. I, 25.305
31 Schenk, op. cit., p.125
32 Duffy (Fires of Faith), op. cit., p.37
33 Ibid.
34 Mayer (Reginald Pole), op. cit., p.206
35 Duffy (Fires of Faith), op. cit., p.57
36 Schenk, op. cit., p.129
37 Duffy (Fires of Faith), op. cit., p.44
38 Ibid.
39 Mayer (Reginald Pole), op. cit., p.221
40 Roy Hattersley, David Lloyd George (Little, Brown), p.332
41 Schenk, op. cit., p.137
42 Ibid., p.136
43 WDA, Vol. I, 36.383
44 Foxe, op. cit., 3/110
45 Duffy (Fires of Faith), op. cit., p.88
46 Ibid.
47 Foxe, op. cit., 3/785
48 Haigh, op. cit., p.216
49 Duffy (Fires of Faith), op. cit., p.49
50 Ibid., p.87
51 Ibid., p.120
52 Mayer (Reginald Pole), op. cit., p.274
53 Duffy (Fires of Faith), op. cit., p.142
54 Wilson, op. cit., p.315
55 WDA, Vol. I, 37.389

10 Haigh, op. cit., p.257
11 Jenkins, op. cit., p.254
12 Mullett, op. cit., p.44
13 Jane Dunn, Elizabeth and Mary (HarperCollins), p.287
14 Ibid.
15 Ibid., p.36
16 Ibid., p.37
17 Mullett, op. cit., p.56
18 WDA, Vol. I, 2.3
19 John Bossy, The English Catholic Community: 1570–1850 (Darton, Longman & Todd), p.13
20 Ibid., p.18
21 Anne Somerset, Elizabeth I (HarperCollins), p.285
22 Ibid.
23 Ibid., p.386
24 Ibid., p.387
25 WDA, Vol. I, 23.101
26 Ethelred L Taunton, The History of the Jesuits in England (Methuen), p.29
27 Ibid., p.30
28 Ibid., p.43
29 Francis Edwards, The Jesuits in England: From 1580 to the Present (Burns & Oates), p.19
30 Maurice Whitehead, Held in Trust: 2008 Years of Sacred Culture (St Omer Press), p.71
31 Haigh, op. cit., p.263
32 WDA, Vol. I, 34.369

CHAPTER 8

God Gave Us Elizabeth

1 Haigh, op. cit., p.218
2 Elizabeth Jenkins, Elizabeth the Great (Coward-McCann, New York), p.393
3 Ibid., p.158
4 Michael A Mullett, Catholics in Britain and Ireland, 1558–1649 (Macmillan), p.12
5 Haigh, op. cit., p.243
6 Jenkins, op. cit., p.263
7 Haigh, op. cit., p.249
8 Ibid.
9 Jenkins, op. cit., p.157

CHAPTER 9

Touching Our Society

1 WDA, Vol. II, 46.265
2 Alain Woodrow, The Jesuits (Geoffrey Chapman), p.107
3 Evelyn Waugh, Edmund Campion (Penguin), p.153
4 Mullett, op. cit., p.18
5 Haigh, op. cit., p.262
6 WDA, Vol. II, 28.121
7 Woodrow, op. cit., p.107
8 Ibid., p.182
9 Mullett, op. cit., p.18
10 WDA, Vol. II, 28.121
11 Ibid.

12 Waugh, op. cit., p.94
13 Ibid., p.97
14 Ibid.
15 Edwards, op. cit., p.29
16 Waugh, op. cit., p.131
17 Edwards, op. cit., p.21
18 Somerset, op. cit., p.392
19 J B Black, *The Reign of Elizabeth* (Oxford University Press), p.181
20 AVCAU, Scritture (hereafter Scr.) 178/179
21 Ibid., Scr. 180
22 Jenkins, op. cit., p.294
23 Somerset, op. cit., p.388
24 Jenkins, op. cit., p.245
25 Ibid., p.241
26 Ibid.
27 AVCAU, Scr. 2/213
28 Somerset, op. cit., p.285
29 Ibid.
30 Ibid., p.389
31 Ibid., p.391
32 Mullett, op. cit., p.14
33 Ibid., p.18
34 Haigh, op. cit., p.260
35 Ingleby Family Papers
36 Haigh, op. cit., p.263
37 Ibid., p.265
38 Mullett, op. cit., p.25
39 Black, op. cit., p.451
40 Ibid., p.455
41 Bossy, op. cit., p.45
42 Shagan, op. cit., p.164
43 Roy Hattersley, *The Devonshires* (Chatto & Windus), p.26
44 Ibid., p.27
45 Ibid., p.28
46 Ibid., p.44
47 Ibid.

CHAPTER 10

More an Antique Roman?

1 A L Rowse, *Christopher Marlowe* (Macmillan), p.193
2 John Waterfield, *The Heart of His Mystery* (Universe), p.16
3 Constance Brown Kuriyama, *Christopher Marlowe* (Cornell University Press), p.213
4 Shagan, op. cit., p.149
5 Ibid., p.155
6 A D Nuttall, *Shakespeare the Thinker* (Yale University Press), p.12
7 Ibid.
8 Peter Ackroyd, *William Shakespeare: The Biography* (Chatto & Windus), p.23
9 Ibid.
10 Ibid.
11 Nuttall, op. cit., p.15
12 Waterfield, op. cit., p.2
13 Ibid.
14 Nuttall, op. cit., p.17
15 Ackroyd (*Shakespeare*), op. cit., p.416
16 Ibid., p.433
17 Waterfield, op. cit., p.6
18 Ibid.

CHAPTER 11

Defiled with Some Infirmities

1 Bossy, op. cit., p.190
2 Ibid., p.28
3 G P V Akrigg (ed.), *Letters of King James VI & I* (University of California Press), No. 49
4 Ibid., p.91
5 Neil Rhodes (ed.), *King James VI & I: Selected Writings* (Ashgate), p.299
6 Mullett, op. cit.
7 Shagan, op. cit., p.87
8 Ibid., p.88
9 Ibid., p.165
10 Ibid.
11 Arnold Hunt, 'The Lady is a Catholic', in *Recusant History* (The Catholic Record Society), Vol. 31, No. 3, p.416
12 Ibid.
13 Alan Stewart, *The Cradle King* (Chatto & Windus), p.226
14 Ibid.
15 Ibid., p.231
16 Shagan, op. cit., p.172
17 Ibid., p.170
18 Ibid.
19 Mullett, op. cit., p.24

20 *Recusant History*, op. cit., Vol. 3,
    No. 3
21 Mullett, op. cit., p.51
22 Ibid., p.61
23 Ibid.
24 Ibid.
25 Ibid., p.31
26 AVCAU, Scr. 70/3/25
27 Ibid.

CHAPTER 12

Let Loose to Say Masses

1 Stewart, op. cit., p.301
2 Ibid.
3 Ibid.
4 Pauline Gregg, *King Charles I*
   (Dent), p.96
5 Ibid., p.320
6 Ibid., p.321
7 Ibid., p.333
8 Kevin Sharpe, *The Personal Rule
   of Charles I* (Yale University
   Press), p.279
9 Gregg, op. cit., p.102
10 Bossy, op. cit., p.269
11 Sharpe, op. cit., p.280
12 Gregg, op. cit., p.277
13 Ibid., p.278
14 Sharpe, op. cit., p.306
15 Gregg, op. cit., p.278
16 Sharpe, op. cit., p.365
17 Ibid., p.842
18 Ibid., p.301
19 Ibid.
20 Gregg, op. cit., p.280
21 Richard Cust and Elizabeth
   Hughes (eds), *The English Civil
   War* (Arnold Readers in History),
   p.292
22 Mullett, op. cit., p.26
23 Ibid., p.52
24 PF, *Memoria Rerum*, Vol. I,
   Capitolo VI, p.163
25 Ibid., p.164
26 Mullett, op. cit., p.64
27 Ibid., p.67
28 Michael Braddick, *God's Fury,
   England's Fire* (Allen Lane), p.171
29 Mullett, op. cit., p.63

30 Braddick, op. cit., p.168
31 Ibid.
32 Ibid., p.170
33 Ibid., p.172
34 Bossy, op. cit., p.225
35 Ibid., p.233
36 Christopher Hill, *God's
   Englishman* (Weidenfeld &
   Nicolson), p.63
37 Ibid., p.12
38 Ibid., p.121
39 Antonia Fraser, *Cromwell, Our
   Chief of Men* (Weidenfeld &
   Nicolson), p.33
40 Ibid., p.338
41 PF, *Memoria Rerum*, Vol. I,
   Capitolo VI, p.166
42 Hill, op. cit., p.14
43 Bossy, op. cit., p.64
44 Ibid., p.65
45 Ibid., p.66

CHAPTER 13

Liberty to Tender Conscience

1 Ronald Hutton, *Charles II*
   (Clarendon Press), p.69
2 Jenny Uglow, *A Gambling Man:
   Charles II and the Restoration*
   (Faber & Faber), p.196
3 Hutton, op. cit., p.92
4 John Kenyon, *The Popish Plot*
   (Heinemann), p.28
5 Mullett, op. cit., p.76
6 Uglow, op. cit., p.194
7 Ibid., p.195
8 Ibid., p.370
9 Ibid., p.371
10 K D H Haley, *Politics in the Reign
   of Charles II* (Blackwell), p.61
11 Uglow, op. cit., p.375
12 R C Latham and W Matthews
   (eds), *The Diary of Samuel Pepys*
   (Bell and Hyman), Book 7, 5.11.66
13 Uglow, op. cit., p.375
14 Ibid., p.491
15 Ibid., p.492
16 D M Little and G H Kahrl (eds),
   The Letters of David Garrick
   (Belknap Press), Vol. III, p.162

17 Hattersley (*Devonshires*), op. cit., p.163
18 Ibid., p.167
19 Latham and Matthews, op. cit., Book 9, 26/7.5.1669
20 Kenyon, op. cit., p.243
21 Hattersley (*Devonshires*), op. cit., p.168
22 Mullett, op. cit., p.77
23 Kenyon, op. cit., p.247
24 Nicholas Rhea, *Blessed Nicholas Postgate* (Gracewing), p.164
25 Kenyon, op. cit., p.233
26 William Cobbett, *The Complete Collection of State Trials*, (R Bagshaw) p.481
27 Ibid., p.492
28 George Clark, *The Later Stuarts* (Oxford University Press), p.95
29 Mullett, op. cit., p.77
30 Clark, op. cit., p.96
31 Ibid., p.169

20 Ibid., p.110
21 Ibid., p.219
22 Somerset (*Queen Anne*), op. cit., p.75
23 Mullett, op. cit., p.129
24 Ibid., p.103
25 Ashley, op. cit., p.196
26 Ibid., p.219
27 Somerset, op. cit., p.73
28 Ashley, op. cit., p.197
29 Edward Vallance, *The Glorious Revolution* (Little, Brown), p.87
30 Somerset (*Queen Anne*), op. cit., p.76
31 Ashley, op. cit., p.210
32 Nicholas Schofield and Gerard Skinner, *The English Vicars Apostolic* (Family Publications), p.17
33 Bossy, op. cit., p.212
34 Somerset (*Queen Anne*), op. cit., p.88
35 Ashley, op. cit., p.225
36 John Evelyn, *Diaries* (Everyman), Book IV, p.156
37 Somerset (*Queen Anne*), op. cit., p.83
38 Mullett, op. cit., p.83

CHAPTER 14

Disobedience, Schism and Rebellion

1 Latham and Matthews, op. cit., Book 9, 19.2.67
2 Ibid., 15.4.68
3 Maurice Ashley, *James II* (Dent), p.158
4 Clark, op. cit., p.116
5 Mullett, op. cit., p.79
6 Ibid.
7 Ibid., p.17
8 Bossy, op. cit., p.71
9 Mullett, op. cit., p.70
10 Bossy, op. cit., p.128
11 Mullett, op cit., p.93
12 Ibid.
13 Anne Somerset, *Queen Anne: The Politics of Passion* (Harper Press), p.15
14 Ibid., p.62
15 Ashley, op. cit., p.188
16 Somerset (*Queen Anne*), op. cit., p.64
17 Ashley, op. cit., p.191
18 Ibid., p.179
19 Ibid., p.195

CHAPTER 15

Fidelity and Intire Obedience

1 Mullett, op. cit., p.81
2 Ian Gilmour, *Riots, Risings and Revolution* (Hutchinson), p.33
3 W J Amherst, *The History of Catholic Emancipation* (Kegan, Paul and Trench), Vol. I, p.80
4 Schofield and Skinner, op. cit., p.145
5 Bossy, op. cit., p.228
6 PF, *Memoria Rerum*, Vol. III, Capitolo V, p.633
7 Mullett, op. cit., p.104
8 Ibid., p.105
9 Ibid., p.131
10 Clark, op. cit., p.310
11 Mullett, op. cit., p.130
12 Clark, op. cit., p.310
13 Ibid., p.313
14 Mullett, op. cit., p.131
15 Bossy, op. cit., p.113
16 Ibid.
17 Mullett, op. cit., p.84

18 Ibid., p.86
19 Ibid., p.107
20 Ibid.
21 Mullett, op. cit., p.112
22 PF, *Memoria Rerum*, Vol. II, Capitolo IV, p.626
23 Mullett, op. cit., p.88
24 Daniel Defoe, *A Tour Through the Island of Great Britain* (Penguin), Vol. II, p.326
25 Ibid., p.421
26 Bossy, op. cit., p.324
27 Mullett, op. cit., p.91
28 Ibid., p.92
29 Schofield and Skinner, op. cit., p.35
30 Bossy, op. cit., p.131
31 Mullett, op. cit., p.156
32 Schofield and Skinner, op. cit., p.20
33 Mullett, op. cit., p.95
34 Ibid., p.97
35 Ibid., p.112

CHAPTER 16

Think of Them with Kindness

1 M J Pittock, *The Myth of the Jacobite Clans* (Edinburgh University Press), p.48
2 Nicholas Schofield, *History of St Edmund's College* (St Edmund's Association), p.15
3 Mullett, op. cit., p.170
4 Ibid., p.168
5 Bossy, op. cit., p.36
6 Mullett, op. cit., p.145
7 WDA, Series A, Vol. XLI, 232
8 Ibid.
9 Schofield and Skinner, op. cit., p.46
10 Bossy, op. cit., p.185
11 Mullett, op. cit., p.180
12 Ibid., p.184
13 Ibid., p.189
14 Ibid., p.190
15 Ibid., p.174
16 Roy Hattersley, *A Brand from the Burning* (Little, Brown), p.197
17 Mullett, op. cit., p.146

18 AVCAU, Scr. 50/1b
19 Amherst, op. cit., p.63
20 WDA, Series A, Vol. XLI, 170
21 Schofield and Skinner, op. cit., p.40
22 WDA, op. cit., 173
23 Ibid., p.171
24 Ibid.
25 Amherst, op. cit., p.104
26 Ibid., p.109
27 Ibid., p.176
28 James Gordon, *The Catholic Church in Scotland from the Suppression of the Hierarchy to the Present Time* (Nabu Public Domain Reprints), p.590
29 Christopher Hibbert, *King Mob* (Longmans), p.22
30 Gilmour, op. cit., p.345
31 Mark Bence-Jones, *The Catholic Families* (Constable), p.22
32 Ibid., p.25
33 Hibbert, op. cit., p.21
34 Ibid., p.22

CHAPTER 17

A Species of Fanatical Phrenzy

1 Hibbert, op. cit., p.14
2 Ibid., p.23
3 Hattersley (*Brand from the Burning*), op. cit., p.365
4 Hibbert, op. cit., p.26
5 Ibid., p.31
6 Ibid., p.32
7 Ibid., p.24
8 Ibid., p.33
9 WDA, Series A, Vol. XLI, 226
10 Hibbert, op. cit., p.43
11 Ibid., p.58
12 Ibid., p.61
13 Ibid., p.57
14 Mullett, op. cit., p.147
15 Amherst, op. cit., p.89
16 WDA, Series A, Vol. XLI, 225
17 Steven Watson, *The Reign of George III* (Oxford University Press), p.238
18 Mullett, op. cit., p.148

19 Bence-Jones, op. cit., p.460
20 Hibbert, op. cit., p.130
21 Hattersley (*Brand from the Burning*), op. cit., p.360
22 William Blanchard, *The Trial of George Gordon Esq, Compiled from the Shorthand Writing of Mr William Blanchard* (London, 1781)

CHAPTER 18

A Set of Secular Gentlemen

1 Amherst, op. cit., p.151
2 Bossy, op. cit., p.263
3 Mullett, op. cit., p.163
4 WDA, Series A, Vol. XLII, 120
5 Schofield and Skinner, op. cit., p.48
6 WDA, Series A, Vol. XLII, 4
7 Schofield and Skinner, op. cit., p.52
8 WDA, op. cit., 7
9 Amherst, op. cit., p.171
10 Bossy, op. cit., p.334
11 Amherst, op. cit., p.174
12 Ibid., p.177
13 Ibid., p.191
14 Bernard Ward, *The Eve of Catholic Emancipation* (Longmans Green), Book I, p.5
15 Ibid., p.399
16 Ibid., p.50
17 Ibid., p.52
18 Ibid., p.54
19 Ibid., p.57
20 Mullett, op. cit., p.165
21 Ibid., p.150
22 Watson, op. cit., p.392
23 Ibid.

CHAPTER 19

The Most Jacobinical Thing

1 Ward, op. cit., Book I, p.3
2 Watson, op. cit., p.401
3 Maurice R O'Connell, *Daniel O'Connell: The Man and His Politics* (Irish University Press), p.33
4 Ward, op. cit., Book I, p.23
5 Ibid., p.25
6 Ibid., p.5
7 Amherst, op. cit., Vol. I, p.287
8 Ward, op. cit., Book I, p.390
9 Ibid., p.42
10 Ibid., p.191
11 Amherst, op. cit., Vol. II, p.31
12 Ward, op. cit., Book I, p.103
13 Amherst, op. cit., Vol. II, p.34
14 Ward, op. cit., Book I, 112
15 Amherst, op. cit., p.30
16 Ibid., p.131
17 Ibid., p.133
18 AVCAU, Pl. I
19 Ibid.
20 Amherst, op. cit., p.141
21 AVCAU, Pl. I
22 Amherst, op. cit., p.153
23 Bossy, op. cit., p.304
24 Ward, op. cit., Book II, p.31
25 Ibid., p.37
26 Ibid.
27 Ibid., p.43
28 Ibid., p.46
29 Amherst, op. cit., p.118
30 Ward, op. cit., Book II, p.51
31 Ibid., p.100
32 Ibid., p.107
33 Ibid., p.141
34 Ibid., p.143
35 O'Connell, op. cit., p.39
36 Ibid., p.37
37 AVCAU, Scr. 55/6
38 G A Beck (ed.), *The English Catholics 1850–1950* (Burns & Oates), p.482
39 Mullett, op. cit., p.179
40 *Orthodox Journal*, May 1818
41 Ibid., March 1816
42 Ward, op. cit., Book II, p.188
43 Ibid., p.190
44 Ibid., p.238
45 AVCAU, Scr. 59/5/12
46 Michael MacDonagh, *The Life of Daniel O'Connell* (Cassell), p.110
47 Ward, op. cit., Book II, p.220
48 Ibid., p.227
49 MacDonagh, op. cit., p.174

CHAPTER 20

A Halo of Brightness

1 Wilfred Ward, *Cardinal Wiseman* (Longmans Green), p.46
2 AVCAU, Scr. 76/4/14
3 Ward (*Wiseman*), op. cit., p.215
4 Ibid., p.216
5 Beck, op. cit., p.475
6 Rosemary Hill, *God's Architect* (Penguin/Allen Lane), p.121
7 Beck, op. cit., p.87
8 Ward (*Wiseman*), op. cit., p.267
9 Judith Champ, *The English Pilgrimage to Rome* (Gracewing), p.169
10 *Oxford Concise Dictionary*, p.1513
11 Robert Gray, *Cardinal Manning* (Weidenfeld & Nicolson), p.100
12 AVCAU, Scr. 70/1/47
13 DSCN 0566
14 Denis Gwynn, *Cardinal Wiseman* (Brown and Nolan), p.35
15 Ibid., p.55
16 Hill, op. cit., p.221
17 Ibid., p.311
18 Ward (*Wiseman*), op. cit., p.358
19 Hill, op. cit., p.311
20 Ibid., p.223
21 DSCN 0567, 0582
22 Ibid., 0573, 0575
23 Gwynn, op. cit., p.63
24 AVCAU, Scr. 70/1/56
25 Hill, op. cit., p.223
26 Ibid., p.237
27 AVCAU, Scr. 81/4/1
28 Ibid., 81/4/5

CHAPTER 21

From the Flaminian Gate

1 Champ, op. cit., p.138
2 Ward (*Wiseman*), op. cit., p.489
3 Judith Champ, *William Bernard Ullathorne* (Gracewing), p.142
4 Ibid., p.266
5 Ibid., p.145
6 Beck, op. cit., p.90
7 Ward (*Wiseman*), op. cit., p.475

8 Roger Swift, *The Outcast Irish in the British Victorian City* (Irish Historical Studies Publications), p.265
9 Ibid., p.266
10 *The Times*, 21.1.47
11 M A G O'Tuathaigh, *The Irish in Nineteenth-Century Britain* (Cork University Press), p.155
12 Ibid., p.165
13 Swift, op. cit., p.274
14 WDA, Griffiths Papers
15 Ward (*Wiseman*), op. cit., p.521
16 Ibid., p.526
17 AVCAU, Scr. 76/2/3
18 *The Times*, 30.9.50
19 Ibid., 4.10.50
20 A N Wilson, *Queen Victoria* (Atlantic Books), p.150
21 Robert Blake, *Disraeli* (Eyre & Spottiswoode), p.300
22 Gwynn, op. cit., p.118
23 Beck, op. cit., p.483
24 Gwynn, op. cit., p.119
25 Ward (*Wiseman*), op. cit., p.550
26 Asa Briggs, *Victorian People* (Penguin), p.32
27 Gwynn, op. cit., p.124
28 Ibid.
29 AVCAU, Scr. 76/9/4
30 Briggs, op. cit., p.34
31 John Morley, *Life of Gladstone* (Macmillan), Vol. I, p.412
32 Briggs, op. cit., p.35
33 DSCN 0573, 0575
34 Ibid., 0592 0594
35 Morley, op. cit., p.270
36 Gwynn, op. cit., p.76
37 Ibid.
38 Ian Ker, *John Henry Newman* (Oxford University Press), p.5
39 Ibid., p.48
40 Dermot Mansfield, *John Henry Newman* (Veritas), p.26
41 Ker, op. cit., p.80
42 Ibid., p.81
43 Ibid.
44 Mansfield, op. cit., p.31
45 Lytton Strachey, *Eminent Victorians* (Continuum), p.21
46 Gray, op. cit., p.50
47 Ibid., p.34
48 Ibid., p.71

49 Sheridan Gilley, *Newman and his Age* (Darton, Longman & Todd), p.162

CHAPTER 22

Time is Short, Eternity is Long

1 Gilley, op. cit., p.364
2 AVCAU, Scr. 73/11
3 Gilley, op. cit., p.212
4 Ker, op. cit., p.280
5 Mansfield, op. cit., p.64
6 Ker, op. cit., p.313
7 Gwynn, op. cit., p.70
8 Ibid., p.72
9 Gilley, op. cit., p.243
10 Mansfield, op. cit., p.67
11 Ker, op. cit., p.321
12 Mansfield, op. cit., p.77
13 Gilley, op. cit., p.260
14 Ker, op. cit., p.350
15 Ibid., p.360
16 AVCAU, Scr. 76/2/6
17 Ibid., 76/2/9
18 Ibid., 76/2/11
19 Gray, op. cit., p.125
20 Ibid., p.127
21 Ibid., p.132
22 Ibid., p.134
23 Ibid., p.139
24 Ibid., p.149
25 Daire Keogh and Albert McDonnell (eds), *Cardinal Paul Cullen and His World* (Four Courts Press), p.278
26 Ker, op. cit., p.384
27 AVCAU, Scr. 76/9/13
28 Mansfield, op. cit., p.111

CHAPTER 23

The State of Things in Ireland

1 Desmond Bowen, *Cardinal Paul Cullen and the Shaping of Modern Irish Catholicism* (Wilfrid Laurier University Press), p.103
2 Keogh and McDonnell, op. cit., p.147
3 Ibid., p.151
4 Ibid., p.139
5 Ibid., p.28
6 Ibid., p.166
7 Ibid., p.169
8 Ibid.
9 Gray, op. cit., p.147
10 Beck, op. cit., p.268
11 Keogh and McDonnell, op. cit., p.170
12 Gray, op. cit., p.147
13 E I Watkin, *Roman Catholicism in England from the Reformation to 1950* (Oxford University Press), p.177
14 Beck, op. cit., p.273
15 Ibid., p.275
16 John Belchem, *Irish, Catholic and Scouse* (Liverpool University Press), p.72
17 Ibid., p.74
18 Ibid., p.83
19 Ibid., p.86
20 Ibid., p.77
21 Beck, p.275
22 AVCAU, Scr. 76/2/9
23 Ibid., 70/10/6
24 Ibid., 7/2/48
25 Belchem, op. cit., p.77
26 Beck, op. cit., p.270
27 Gray, op. cit., p.217
28 Keogh and McDonnell, op. cit., p.24

CHAPTER 24

A Certain Cleavage

1 AVCAU, Scr. 55/10
2 Callum V Brown, *The Social History of Religion in Scotland Since 1730* (Methuen), p.45
3 John Devlin (ed.), *Irish Immigration and Scottish Society in the Nineteenth Century*, Proceedings of the Scottish Historical Society (John Donald Ltd), p.69
4 Bernard Aspinwall, 'The Formation of a Catholic Community in Western Scotland', *Innes Review*, Vol. 33/35, p.48
5 Ibid., p.44
6 Devlin, op. cit., p.9

7 PF, *Memoria Rerum*, Vol. VII, Capitolo III, p.243
8 Aspinwall, op. cit., p.48
9 Brown, op. cit., p.162
10 Devlin, op. cit., p.69
11 Brown, op. cit., p.46
12 Aspinwall, op. cit., p.44
13 Brown, op. cit., p.162
14 Aspinwall, op. cit., p.48
15 Gordon, op. cit., p.480
16 Aspinwall, op. cit., p.49
17 PF, *Memoria Rerum*, op. cit., p.248

CHAPTER 25
'Put Him There. Put Him There'

1 Gray, op. cit., p.152
2 Ibid., p.156
3 Schofield (*St Edmund's College*), op. cit., p.70
4 Gray, op. cit., p.166
5 Serenhedd James, *Archbishop George Errington and the Battle for Catholic Identity in the Nineteenth Century* (Oxford University Press), p.206
6 Gray, op. cit., p.170
7 Ibid., p.173
8 James, op. cit. p.207
9 Mansfield, op. cit., p.127
10 DSCN 0591
11 Gilley, op. cit., p.326
12 Mansfield, op. cit., p.140
13 Ker, op. cit., p.531
14 Ibid., p.535
15 Ibid., p.517
16 Ibid., p.542
17 Ibid.
18 Ibid., p.543
19 Rosemary Ashton, *George Eliot* (Hamish Hamilton), p.276
20 Gray, op. cit., p.175
21 Ker, op. cit., p.561
22 Beck, op. cit., p.477
23 Gray, op. cit., p.187
24 Ibid., p.185
25 Ibid., p.189
26 Champ, op. cit., p.293
27 Gray, op. cit., p.190
28 Ker, op. cit., p.362
29 Beck, op. cit., p.157
30 Gray, op. cit., p.202
31 WDA, Vol. II, 5.57
32 Ker, op. cit., p.579
33 Gray, op. cit., p.211
34 Strachey, op. cit., p.74
35 Gray, op. cit., p.215
36 Ibid., p.216
37 Ibid.
38 Ker, op. cit., p.610
39 Gray, op. cit., p.226
40 Champ, op. cit., p.368
41 Keogh & McDonnell, op. cit., p.58
42 Beck, op. cit., p.487
43 Gray, op. cit., p.234
44 Morley, op. cit., Vol. II, p.516
45 *The Times*, 7.11.74
46 Gray, op. cit., p.248
47 Ker, op. cit., p.681

CHAPTER 26
The Very Salt of Life

1 Shane Leslie, *Manning: His Life and Labours* (Burns & Oates), p.259
2 Gray, op. cit., p.291
3 Leslie, op. cit., p.204
4 Gray, op. cit., p.224
5 Roy Jenkins, *Gladstone* (Macmillan), p.317
6 Oliver P Rafferty (ed.), *Irish Catholic Identities* (Manchester University Press), p.243
7 Beck, op. cit., p.159
8 Gray, op. cit., p.300
9 Rafferty, op. cit., p.249
10 Gray, op. cit., p.303
11 Ibid., p.243
12 Robert O'Neill, *Cardinal Vaughan* (Burns & Oates), p.332
13 Gray, op. cit., p.296
14 O'Neill, op. cit., p.362
15 Edmund Purcell, *The Life of Cardinal Manning* (Macmillan), p.345
16 Champ, op. cit., p.334
17 Gray, op. cit., p.239
18 Belchem, op. cit., p.90
19 Gray, op. cit., p.240
20 O'Neill, op. cit., p.339
21 Ker, op. cit., p.714

22 Gray, op. cit., p.264
23 AVCAU, Scr. 76/5/9
24 Ibid., 76/1/45
25 Ker, op. cit., p.716
26 Ibid., p.718
27 AVCAU, Scr. 75/9
28 Ker, op. cit., p.688
29 Ibid., p.690
30 The Tablet, 16.1.92
31 O'Neill, op. cit., p.334
32 Gray, op. cit., p.307
33 Hattersley (Lloyd George), op. cit., p.178
34 Gray, op. cit., p.313
35 O'Neill, op. cit., p.336
36 Hattersley (Lloyd George), op. cit., p.254
37 O'Neill, op. cit., p.304
38 The Tablet, 9.4.32
39 Stuart J Reid, Lord John Russell (Sampson Low, Marston and Co.), p.191

CHAPTER 27

That Flame Burns Again

1 Ian Ker, The Catholic Revival in English Literature 1845–1961 (Gracewing), p.2
2 Ibid., p.50
3 Beck, op. cit., p.522
4 Ker (Revival), op. cit., p.94
5 Ibid.
6 Ibid., p.77
7 Ibid., p.65
8 Ibid.
9 A N Wilson, Hilaire Belloc (Mandarin), p.166
10 Ker (Revival), op. cit., p.73
11 Terry Tastard, Ronald Knox and English Catholicism (Gracewing), p.4
12 Ibid., p.51
13 Evelyn Waugh, The Life of the Right Reverend Ronald Knox (Chapman Hall), p.251
14 Ibid., p.261
15 Tastard, op. cit., p.113
16 Christopher Sykes, Evelyn Waugh (Penguin), p.156
17 Ker (Revival), op. cit., p.111

CHAPTER 28

Making Catholicism Count

1 Tim Pat Coogan, Eamon de Valera (Harper Perennial), p.108
2 Max Caulfield, The Easter Rebellion (Gill & Macmillan), p.180
3 Robert Kee, The Green Flag (Weidenfeld & Nicolson), p.602
4 Ibid., p.633
5 Ibid., p.632
6 Ibid., p.672
7 John D Brewer and Gareth I Higgins, Anti-Catholicism in Northern Ireland: 1600–1998 (Macmillan Press), p.90
8 Ibid.
9 Ibid., p.98
10 David McKittrick and David McVea, Making Sense of the Troubles (Penguin Viking), p.11
11 Brewer and Higgins, op. cit., p.91
12 McKittrick and McVea, op. cit., p.9
13 Brewer and Higgins, op. cit., p.92
14 Ibid. (quoting Devlin Report)
15 Ibid., p.98
16 Oliver P Rafferty, Catholic Unionism: A Case Study (Phoenix), p.293
17 Ibid., p.302
18 Brewer and Higgins, op. cit., p.96
19 Ibid.
20 Ibid.
21 Ibid., p.100
22 D Kennedy, The Widening Gulf (Blackstaff Press), p.97
23 McKittrick and McVea, op. cit., p.14
24 Paul Bew and Gordon Gillespie, A Chronology of the Troubles (Gill & Macmillan), p.258
25 Ibid., p.39
26 McKittrick and McVea, op. cit., p.81
27 Belchem, op. cit., p.268
28 Ibid., p.195
29 Ibid., p.295
30 Ibid., p.293
31 Beck, op. cit., p.391
32 Belchem, op. cit., p.303

CHAPTER 29

The Needs of Our Age

1 John O'Malley, *What Happened at Vatican II* (Belknap Press), p.58
2 Ibid., p.64
3 Ibid., p.69
4 *The Observer*, 30.5.10
5 James Carroll and Edward P Hahnenberg, *Vatican II: The Essential Texts* (Image Press), p.190
6 *The Tablet*, 2.11.63
7 O'Malley, op. cit., p.38
8 *The Tablet*, 16.9.72
9 Carroll and Hahnenberg, op. cit., p.191
10 Ibid., p.302
11 *The Tablet*, 7.12.63
12 O'Malley, op. cit., p.321
13 Ker (*Revival*), op. cit., p.202
14 Michael P Hornsby-Smith (ed.), *Catholics in England 1950–2000* (Cassell), p.8
15 Ibid., p.34
16 Ibid., p.93

CHAPTER 30

'Love is Love'

1 Hornsby-Smith, op. cit., p.72
2 Ibid., p.70
3 Ibid.
4 *The Catholic Directory*, 2011
5 Ibid.
6 *The Times*, 2.10.68
7 Anthony Howard, *Basil Hume: The Monk Cardinal* (Hodder Headline), p.262
8 *The Tablet*, 20.2.10
9 Ibid.
10 Hornsby-Smith, op. cit., p.189

CHAPTER 31

Suffer Little Children

1 *The Tablet*, 8.10.94
2 Ibid., 17.12.94

3 Ibid., 27.11.99
4 Richard Scorer, *Betrayed* (Biteback), p.192
5 Ibid., p.43
6 Ibid., p.1
7 *The Tablet*, 13.3.10
8 *The Guardian*, 13.9.00
9 Ibid., 8.11.97
10 *Huffington Post*, 24.7.14
11 *The Tablet*, 29.5.93
12 Ibid.
13 Scorer, op. cit., p.147
14 Cormac Murphy-O'Connor, *An English Spring* (Bloomsbury), p.144
15 Scorer, op. cit., p.188
16 Ibid., p.183
17 Howard, op. cit., p.257
18 Scorer, op. cit., p.192
19 Ibid., p.197
20 Ibid., p.209
21 *Daily Telegraph*, 25.2.13
22 *Catholic Herald*, 10.6.15

CHAPTER 32

And You Made Me Welcome

1 *The Times*, 20.11.92
2 Howard, op. cit., p.217
3 Murphy-O'Connor, op. cit., p.133
4 Howard, op. cit., p.322
5 Ibid., p.224
6 Steven Cavanaugh, *Anglicans and the Roman Catholic Church* (Ignatius), p.56
7 Howard, op. cit., p.232
8 Ibid., p.233
9 *The Tablet*, 24.4.93
10 Cavanaugh, op. cit., p.57
11 *Daily Telegraph*, 23.1.11
12 Mission of the Church to Migrants in England and Wales
13 *Catholic Herald*, 31.12.07
14 *Ekklesia*, 29.1.08
15 *Sunday Telegraph*, 23.12.07
16 *Ekklesia*, op. cit.
17. *The Tablet*, 27.2.10
18. BBC bulletin, 22.02.06
19. *The Tablet*, 12.1.13
20. Ibid., 5.10.13
21. *Daily Telegraph*, 23.12.07

Select Bibliography

ACKROYD, PETER, *The Life of Thomas More*, Vintage

ACKROYD, PETER, *William Shakespeare: The Biography*, Chatto & Windus

AKRIGG, G P V (ed), *Letters of King James VI & I*, University of California Press

AMHERST, W J, *The History of Catholic Emancipation*, Kegan, Paul and Trench

ASHTON, ROSEMARY, *George Eliot*, Hamish Hamilton

ASPINWALL, BERNARD, 'The Formation of a Catholic Community in Western Scotland', *Innes Review*

BECK, G A, *The English Catholics 1850–1950*, Burns & Oates

BELCHEM, JOHN, *Irish, Catholic and Scouse*, Liverpool University Press

BENCE-JONES, MARK, *The Catholic Families*, Constable

BEW, PAUL, AND GILLESPIE, GORDON, *A Chronology of the Troubles*, Gill & Macmillan

BLACK, J B, *The Reign of Elizabeth*, Oxford University Press

BLANCHARD, WILLIAM, *The Trial of George Gordon Esq, Compiled from the Shorthand Writing of Mr William Blanchard*, London, 1781

BORMAN, TRACY, *Thomas Cromwell*, Hodder and Stoughton

BOSSY, JOHN, *The English Catholic Community: 1570-1850*, Darton, Longman & Todd

BOWEN, DESMOND, *Cardinal Paul Cullen and the Shaping of Modern Irish Catholicism*, Wilfrid Laurier University Press

BRADDICK, MICHAEL, *God's Fury, England's Fire*, Allen Lane

BREWER, JOHN D, AND HIGGINS, GARETH I, *Anti-Catholicism in Northern Ireland: 1600 – 1998*, Macmillan Press

BRIGGS, ASA, *Victorian People*, Penguin

BROWN, CALLUM V, *The Social History of Religion in Scotland Since 1730*, Methuen

BUSH, MICHAEL, *The Pilgrimage of Grace*, Manchester University Press

CARROLL, JAMES, AND HAHNENBERG, EDWARD P, *Vatican II: The Essential Texts*, Image Press

CAULFIELD, MAX, *The Easter Rebellion*, Gill & Macmillan

CHAMP, JUDITH, *The English Pilgrimage to Rome*, Gracewing

CHAMP, JUDITH, *William Bernard Ullathorne*, Gracewing
CLARK, GEORGE, *The Later Stuarts*, Oxford University Press
COBBETT, WILLIAM, *The Complete Collection of State Trials*, Penguin
COOGAN, TIM PAT, *Eamon de Valera*, Harper Perennial
CUST, RICHARD, and HUGHES, ELIZABETH (eds), *The English Civil War*, Arnold Readers in History
DAVIE, GRACE, *Religion in Britain Since 1945*, Blackwell
DEFOE, DANIEL, *A Tour Through the Island of Great Britain*, Penguin
DEVLIN, JOHN (ed), *Irish Immigration and Scottish Society in the Nineteenth Century*, John Donald Ltd
DICKENS, A G, *The English Reformation*, Batsford
DUFFY, EAMON, *Fires of Faith*, Yale University Press
DUFFY, EAMON, *The Stripping of the Altars*, Yale University Press
DUNN, JANE, *Elizabeth and Mary*, Harper Collins
EDWARDS, FRANCIS, *The Jesuits in England: From 1580 to the Present*, Burns & Oates
FOXE, JOHN, *The Acts and Monuments*, 1732 edition
FRASER, ANTONIA, *Cromwell, Our Chief of Men*, Weidenfeld & Nicolson
GILLEY, SHERIDAN, *Newman and his Age*, Darton, Longman & Todd
GILMOUR, IAN, *Riots, Risings and Revolution*, Hutchinson
GORDON, JAMES, *The Catholic Church in Scotland from the Suppression of the Hierarchy to the Present Time*, Nabu Public Domain Reprints
GRAY, ROBERT, *Cardinal Manning*, Weidenfeld & Nicolson
GREGG, PAULINE, *King Charles I*, Dent
GUY, JOHN, *My Heart is My Own*, Fourth Estate
GWYNN, DENIS, *Cardinal Wiseman*, Brown and Nolan
HAIGH, CHRISTOPHER, *English Reformations*, Clarendon Press
HAIGH, CHRISTOPHER, *The English Reformation Revised*, Cambridge University Press
HALEY, K D H, *Politics in the Reign of Charles II*, Blackwell
HIBBERT, CHRISTOPHER, *King Mob*, Longmans
HILL, CHRISTOPHER, *God's Englishman*, Weidenfeld & Nicolson
HILL, ROSEMARY, *God's Architect*, Penguin/Allen Lane
HORNSBY-SMITH, MICHAEL P (ed), *Catholics in England 1950–2000*, Cassell
HOWARD, ANTHONY, *Basil Hume: The Monk Cardinal*, Hodder Headline
HUNT, ARNOLD, 'The Lady is a Catholic', in *Recusant History*, The Catholic Record Society
HUTTON, RONALD, *Charles II*, Clarendon Press

JAMES, SERENHEDD, *Archbishop George Errington and the Battle for Catholic Identity in the Nineteenth Century*, Oxford University Press

JENKINS, ELIZABETH, *Elizabeth the Great*, Coward-McCann

JENKINS, ROY, *Gladstone*, Macmillan

KEE, ROBERT, *The Green Flag*, Weidenfeld & Nicolson

KENNEDY, D, *The Widening Gulf*, Blackstaff Press

KENYON, JOHN, *The Popish Plot*, Heinemann

KEOGH, DAIRE, AND MCDONNELL, ALBERT (eds), *Cardinal Paul Cullen and His World*, Four Courts Press

KER, IAN, *The Catholic Revival in English Literature 1845–1961*, Gracewing

KER, IAN, *John Henry Newman*, Oxford University Press

KURIYAMA, CONSTANCE BROWN, *Christopher Marlowe*, Cornell University Press

LAMBERT, W J, *The History of Catholic Emancipation*, Kegan, Paul and Trench

LESLIE, SHANE, *Manning: His Life and Labours*, Burns & Oates

LITTLE, D M, AND KAHRL, G H (eds), *The Letters of David Garrick*, Belknap Press

LOADES, DAVID, *Henry VIII, Court and Conflict*, National Archives

MACCULLOCH, DIARMAID, *Thomas Cranmer: A Life*, Yale University Press

MACDONAGH, MICHAEL, *The Life of Daniel O'Connell*, Cassell

MACKENZIE, COMPTON, *Catholicism and Scotland*, George Routledge

MACKIE, J D, *The Early Tudors*, Oxford University Press

MANSFIELD, DERMOT, *John Henry Newman*, Veritas

MAYER, THOMAS F, *Cardinal Pole in the European Context*, Ashgate

MAYER, THOMAS F, *Reginald Pole*, Cambridge University Press

MCKITTRICK, DAVID, AND MCVEA, DAVID, *Making Sense of the Troubles*, Penguin Viking

MOORHOUSE, GEOFFREY, *The Pilgrimage of Grace*, Weidenfeld & Nicolson

MORLEY, JOHN, *Life of Gladstone*, Macmillan

MULLETT, MICHAEL A, *Catholics in Britain and Ireland, 1558–1649*, Macmillan

MURPHY-O'CONNOR, CORMAC, *An English Spring*, Bloomsbury

NORTH, JONATHAN (ed), *England's Boy King: The Diaries of Edward VI, 1547–1553*, Ravenhall Books

NUTTALL, A D, *Shakespeare the Thinker*, Yale University Press

O'CONNELL, MAURICE R, *Daniel O'Connell: The Man and his Politics*, Irish University Press

O'MALLEY, JOHN, *What Happened at Vatican II*, Belknap Press

O'NEILL, ROBERT, *Cardinal Vaughan*, Burns & Oates

O'TUATHAIGH, M A G, *The Irish in Nineteenth-Century Britain*, Cork University Press

PITTOCK, M J, *The Myth of the Jacobite Clans*, Edinburgh University Press

PURCELL, EDMUND, *The Life of Cardinal Manning*, Macmillan

RAFFERTY, OLIVER P, *Catholic Unionism: A Case Study*, Phoenix

RAFFERTY, OLIVER P (ed), *Irish Catholic Identities*, Manchester University Press

REID STUART, *Lord John Russell*, Sampson, Low Marston and Co

REYNOLDS, E E, *Saint John Fisher*, Burns & Oates

RHEA, NICHOLAS, *Blessed Nicholas Postgate*, Gracewing

RHODES, NEIL (ed), *King James VI & I: Selected Writings*, Ashgate

RIDLEY, JASPAR, *John Knox*, Oxford University Press

RIDLEY, JASPAR, *The Statesman and the Fanatic*, Constable

ROPER, LYNDAL, *Martin Luther*, Chatto

ROWSE, A L, *Christopher Marlowe*, Macmillan

SCARISBRICK, J J, *Henry VIII*, Yale University Press

SCHENK, W, *Reginald Pole*, Longmans Green

SCHOFIELD, NICHOLAS, *History of St Edmund's College*, St Edmund's Association

SCHOFIELD, NICHOLAS, AND SKINNER, GERARD, *The English Vicars Apostolic*, Family Publications

SCORER, RICHARD, *Betrayed*, Biteback

SCORER RICHARD, *Beyond Belief*, Biteback

SHAGAN, ETHAN H (ed), *Catholics and the Protestant Nation*, Manchester University Press

SHAKESPEARE, WILLIAM, *The Complete Works of William Shakespeare*, OUP, W J Craig Edition

SHARPE, KEVIN, *The Personal Rule of Charles I*, Yale University Press

SKIDMORE, CHRISTOPHER, *The Lost King of England*, Orion

SOMERSET, ANNE, *Elizabeth I*, Harper Collins

SOMERSET, ANNE, *Queen Anne: The Politics of Passion*, Harper Press

STEWART, ALAN, *The Cradle King*, Chatto & Windus

STRACHEY, LYTTON, *Eminent Victorians*, Continuum

SWIFT, ROGER, *The Outcast Irish in the British Victorian City*, Irish Historical Studies Publications

SYKES, CHRISTOPHER, *Evelyn Waugh*, Penguin

TASTARD, TERRY, *Ronald Knox and English Catholicism*, Gracewing

TAUNTON, ETHELRED L, *The History of the Jesuits in England*, Methuen

UGLOW, JENNY, *A Gambling Man: Charles II and the Restoration*, Faber & Faber

VALLANCE, EDWARD, *The Glorious Revolution*, Little, Brown

WARD, BERNARD, *The Eve of Catholic Emancipation*, Longmans Green

WARD, WILFRED, *Cardinal Wiseman*, Longmans Green

WATERFIELD, JOHN, *The Heart of His Mystery*, Universe

WATKIN, E I, *Roman Catholicism in England from the Reformation to 1950*, Oxford University Press

WATSON, STEVEN, *The Reign of George III*, Oxford University Press

WAUGH, EVELYN, *Edmund Campion*, Penguin

WAUGH, EVELYN, *The Life of the Right Reverend Ronald Knox*, Chapman Hall

WHITEHEAD, MAURICE, *Held in Trust: 2008 Years of Sacred Culture*, St Omer Press

WILSON, A N, *Hilaire Belloc*, Mandarin

WILSON, A N, *Queen Victoria*, Atlantic Books

WILSON, DEREK, *The English Reformation*, Constable

WOODROW, ALAIN, *The Jesuits*, Geoffrey Chapman

List of Illustrations

Cardinal Wiseman, J R Herbert, *c.* 19th century. By kind permission of the Rector of St Mary's College, Oscott

Augustus Welby Northmore Pugin, John Herbert Rodgers, 1845 (© Parliamentary Art Collection, London)

Cardinal John Henry Newman, Emmeline Dean, 1889 (Photo © Culture Club/Getty Images)

Cardinal Henry Edward Manning, 1889 (Photo © The Print Collector/Getty Images)

Cardinal Paul Cullen, *c.* 1870. By kind permission of the Rector, Pontifical Irish College, Rome

Hilaire Belloc, artist unknown, *c.* 20th century (Photo © Culture Club/Getty Images)

G K Chesterton, artist unknown, 1927 (Photo © Ann Ronan Pictures/Print Collector/Getty Images)

Graham Greene, photographer unknown, 1982 (Photo © AFP/AFP/Getty Images)

Evelyn Waugh, Mark Gerson, 1963 (Private Collection. Photo © Mark Gerson/Bridgeman Images)

Cathal MacDowell, photographer unknown, *c.* 20th century (© National Museum of Ireland, Dublin)

ENDPAPERS

Augustus Pugin's design for the walls of St Barnabas' Cathedral, Nottingham. By kind permission of the Dean (Photo © Peter Milner)

Acknowledgements

The decision to write *The Catholics* was neither inspired nor promoted by the Church of Rome. Had the commission come from the Vatican or one of its constituent hierarchies, it is unlikely that the chosen author would have been the atheist son of a defrocked priest. Although I always made clear that the book was *about* not *for* Catholics, the Church, at every level, willingly provided all the assistance for which I asked.

Cardinal Vincent Nichols, the Archbishop of Westminster, supported my efforts from the start. The opening paragraph of dozens of letters, in which I asked for help, proclaimed his endorsement of my endeavours. Thanks to him, Cardinal Fernado Filioni – Prefect of the Congregation for the Evangelisation of Souls – allowed me access to the *Memoria Rerum*, in which Propaganda Fide recorded events in Britain before the re-establishment of the English and Scottish hierarchies.

I am particularly indebted to three other sources of original material. Monsignor Philip Whitmore, Rector of the English College in Rome, agreed that I could consult the seminary's archives. I was patiently guided through the profusion of documents by Professor Maurice Whitehead (the Schwarzenback Research Fellow) and Dr Orietta Filippini (the College archivist). I received equally essential guidance from Father Nicholas Schofield and William Johnstone, the archivists of the Westminster diocese and the Reverend Dr John Sharp the archivist of the Birmingham diocese. Many of the documents, in each of the three sources, were in Latin. They were translated for me by Father Bruce Burbidge, then Academic Tutor in the English College and now lecturer in philosophy at St Mary's College, Oscott. Working with all of them was a continual pleasure.

David McKie, a friend for many years, read the first draft of the manuscript and made invaluable suggestions for structural changes. Dr Serenhedd James – of St Stephen's House, Oxford – read the second draft and identified errors. Cynthia Shepherd, my invaluable PA read the third, and corrected grammar and spelling as well as making more general proposals for improvement. Mrs Shepherd also found the pictures and with her husband, the Reverend John Shepherd, created order out of the chaos which was my attempt to set out the notes on sources and references.

The offices of the Catholic Bishops' Conference for England and Wales and the Catholic Trust for England and Wales both supplied me with official reports and pointed me in the direction of other valuable sources of information. The National Museum of Ireland provided me with eye witness accounts of confessions and conversions during the Easter Rising of 1916. The London Library was, as always, indefatigable in the provision of infrequently read books – including a 1732 edition of Foxe's *Book of Martyrs*.

Dr Stephen Bullivant, Director of the Benedict XVI Centre at St Mary's University, Twickenham, provided statistics about Catholic numbers and Catholic attitudes. Brendan Walsh, the Literary Editor of *The Tablet,* enabled me to consult pages from the magazine which are not yet available online. So many other individuals provided help of one sort or another that it impossible to name them all. I therefore express my gratitude to representative members of two groups to which I am especially indebted. Caroline Wakefield sent me family papers which described the Ingleby martyrdom. Canon Jonathan Cotton, of St Joseph's church in Shirebrook, searched parish records on my behalf. I was fortunate in that Poppy Hampson, the editorial director of Chatto & Windus, edited *The Catholics* herself. Her comments, though commendably frank, were always constructive and revealed a real understanding of the spirit in which the book was written. Mandy Greenfield was a meticulous copy editor. I owe an immense debt to them both for the improvements which they made to *The Catholics*. The errors and omissions which undoubtedly remain are, of course, my sole responsibility My sincere thanks are also due to Zoe McGregor and Peter Milner who, in Derbyshire and beyond, provided what the military call logistic back-up. I am grateful for their friendship as well as for their exertions.

Maggie – my literary agent as well as my wife – played a part in the writing of *The Catholics* which is easy to describe and impossible to overestimate. Her help, support and encouragement was essential to every stage of its composition. But then, her help, support and encouragement is essential to all that I do. I take this opportunity to express my gratitude not so much for her assistance with the book as for her existence.

Index

bell-ringing, forbidding of 83
Benedict XIV, Pope 269
Benedict XVI, Pope (formerly
  Cardinal Ratzinger) 534, 542,
  558, 561
Benedictines 192, 319, 330
Bennet, Thomas 11
Bentivoglio, Guido 173
Bentley, John Francis 465
Bernini, Gianlorenzo 195
Berrington, Charles, Vicar Apostolic
  305, 324
Berwick-on-Tweed 91
Bess of Hardwick (Elizabeth Talbot,
  Countess of Shrewsbury) 157
Beverley, Yorkshire 45, 55
Bible: belief in divine inspiration of
  32; Douai-Rheims Bible (1582)
  136, 483; English translations of
  8, 9, 33, 63, 65, 76, 81, 85, 115,
  483; Latin Vulgate of St Jerome
  81; reading of 85, 526
Bigod, Sir Francis 56-7
Bill of Rights (1689) 245
Bilney, Thomas 9, 10-11
Birchley, Lancashire 252
Birmingham 258, 353, 357; Oratory
  395, 402
birth control, Church's attitude to
  522, 530-5, 562, 570-1
Bishop, William, Bishop of
  Chalcedon 192, 193
bishops, absentee 81
Bishops' Banishment Act (1697) 251
Bishop's Book, The (1537) 63-4
'black rubric' 96
'Blacklow's Cabal' 205-6
Blackwell, George (Archpriest)
  154-5, 177-8, 181, 192
Blair, Tony 560
'Bloody Assizes' 231, 245
'Bloody Question, The' 132
Blount, Richard (SJ) 176
Blount family 256
Bluet, Thomas (priest) 154

Blundell, Nicholas 253
Blunt, Wilfred Scawen 473
Blythe House, Hammersmith 414
Bocher, Joan 97-8
Boleyn, Anne 12, 13, 15
Boleyn, Sir Thomas 12
Bolton Abbey 42
Bonner, Edmund, Bishop of
  London 78, 96, 101, 102, 105,
  118-19, 125
book burning 6, 8
Book of Common Prayer: (1549)
  86, 87, 93; (1662) 212-13;
  proscribed after Queen Mary's
  accession (1553) 103; reinstated
  under Queen Elizabeth 122, 123
Bordley, Simon (priest) 304
Borgia, Cardinal 317
Borromeo, Carlo, Archbishop of
  Milan 162, 275, 397, 429
Bourne, Francis, Cardinal Archbishop
  of Westminster 481, 483, 510
Bourne, Gilbert, Bishop of Bath and
  Wells 102
Bowen, Michael, Bishop of Arundel
  and Brighton 544
Boxley, Kent 65
Boyne, Battle of the (1690) 248
Braddick, Michael 201
Bradford, John 102
Bramston, James, Vicar Apostolic
  348, 351
Branges, Charles Barrilon
  d'Armoncourt, Marquis de 207
Breakspear, Nicholas 1, 90
Bresciani, Padre (SJ) 394
Bridewell gaol 148, 297
Bridges, Robert 472, 473
Bristol 73, 244, 299, 300
broadcasting, and Catholicism 481,
  482-3
Broadhurst, John (former Bishop of
  Fulham) 561
Brockholes, John 321
Brokehole family 252

Brompton Oratory, London 402
Brontë, Charlotte 378
Brookeborough, Basil Brooke, 1st
　Viscount 499
Brooks, James, Bishop of
　Gloucester 108
Brooksby, Eleanor 202
Brown, Bishop Joseph 434
Brown, Dan, *Da Vinci Code* 516
Browne, John 22
Bruce, James (OSB) 247
Brushford, John (priest) 152–3
Buachailli Bana ('Whiteboys') 275
Bucer, Martin 78, 91
Buckingham, George Villiers, 1st
　Duke of 188–9, 191
Bull, Frederick 291
Bullivant, Stephen 538
Bures, Suffolk 125
Burgh, Thomas, 1st Baron 42, 43
Burghley, William Cecil, 1st Baron
　135, 147, 150
Burke, Edmund 281, 295, 310
Burke, Thomas, Bishop 275
Burney, Charlotte 295
Burnham, Andrew (former Bishop
　of Ebbsfleet) 561
burnings *see* executions
Butler, Archbishop 314–15
Butler, Charles 303, 321–2
Buxton, Sydney 461
Bye Plot, The (1603) 175
Byland Abbey 42
Byrd, Juliana 146–7
Byrd, William 146–7

Caetani di Sermoneta, Cardinal
　Niccolo 74
Caistor, Lincolnshire 41
Call to Action (pressure group) 570
Calvin, John 17
Calvinism 129, 189, 262
Cambridge: attacks in the 'Glorious
　Revolution' 244; closure of
　religious houses 37; Cromwell

raids College plate 202–3; James
　II's interference with 238; and
　John Fisher 22; 'Little Germany'
　group 9–10, 11; Queen Mary
　repulsed in 100
Cameron, Alex, Vicar Apostolic 418
Campaign of Prayer for the
　Reconversion of England 352
Campbell, Colin (priest) 262, 263
Campeggio, Cardinal 14
Campion, Edmund: arrest and
　execution 145–7; brings
　Borromeo's spiritual Testament
　to England 162; and 'Campion's
　Brag' 143–4; in Ireland 183;
　mission to England 138, 139,
　140–2; *Ten Reasons* 144, 145
Canada 269, 407, 412, 561; Quebec
　Act (1774) 279
Canning, George 331
canon law: and Catholic education
　507; and child abuse scandals
　540–1, 549; and the English
　Hierarchy 368; and Henry VIII
　15, 20
Canterbury Convocation 16–17, 19,
　23, 35
Cardinal College, Oxford 10, 37
Carey, George, Archbishop of
　Canterbury 557
Carier, Benjamin 182
Carlingford, Francis Taaffe, 3rd Earl
　of 234
Carlisle 57
Carmelites 319
Caroline of Brunswick, Queen
　Consort 341
Cartmel Priory 47
Casey, Eamon, Bishop of
　Galway 542
Casti Connubii (papal encyclical,
　1930) 531, 532
Castlemaine, Roger Palmer, 1st Earl
　of 233
Castlereagh, Lord 314, 331, 336

holy days, observance of 302
Holy Roman Emperor *see* Charles V
of Spain; Maximilian II
Holyrood Palace, Edinburgh 128,
236, 247, 319
Holywell, Wales 184, 248, 329
Homilies Set Forth (1555) 118
homosexuality, Church's attitude to
535–7, 571
*Honest Godly Instruction for the
Bringing up of Children, An*
(1555) 118
Hooker, Richard 42
Hooper, John, Bishop of Gloucester
and Worcester 78–9, 81, 88, 93,
95, 96, 97, 102, 105
Hopkins, Gerard Manley 471,
472–3
Hornyold, John, Vicar Apostolic 302
Hornyold, Thomas 303
horses, Catholics prohibited from
owning 245
Hoskins, Anthony (SJ) 181
Hough, John 237
Houghton family 164–5
Howard, Cardinal Philip 226
Howard, Henry *see* Surrey, Henry
Howard, Earl of
Howard, Thomas *see* Norfolk,
Thomas Howard, 3rd Duke
Howard family 256
Hubert, Robert 214
Huddersfield 357
Huddleston, John (priest) 207–8
Huguenots 228
Hull 47–8, 103
Humanae Vitae (papal encyclical,
1968) 522, 531–5, 538, 571
Humani Generis (papal encyclical,
1950) 517
*Humble Address of the Roman
Catholic Peers* (1778) 280–1
Hume, Basil, Cardinal Archbishop
of Westminster 516, 534, 536–7,
546, 548, 555–9, 561

Hune, Richard 34
Hunt, Holman 471
Hunt, Simon (SJ) 164
Huntingdon, George Hastings, 1st
Earl 50
Huntingdon, Theophilus Hastings,
7th Earl of 240
Huntley family 319
Hyde, Anne, Duchess of York 224

iconoclasm 82–4, 125
Immaculate Conception 434, 446
immigration: Catholic Church's
support of 562–3 *see also* Irish
immigrants; Polish immigrants
'index' (of forbidden books) 8,
111, 452
indulgences, sale of 5, 32, 81, 115
Industrial Revolution 258, 260, 268,
277, 350
Ingleby, Francis (priest) 152
Injunctions, Royal (1547), on
idolatry 82–3, 122
*Institution of a Christian Man,
The* (1537) 63
intercession of saints 32, 39, 81,
85, 92
IRA (Irish Republican Army) 495,
497, 506
Ireland: 18th century Catholicism in
273–6, 278–9; and Catholic
emancipation 313–18, 342–4; and
the Catholic Relief Act (1778)
302; and the Catholic Relief Act
(1791) 311–12; Catholic uprising
(1533) 18; under Charles I
199–200; under Charles II
211–12; Easter Rising and civil
war 492–4; under Elizabeth I
130; founding of University
College, Dublin 400–3; Great
Famine and emigration 315,
404–7; and Home Rule 450;
Ireland Act (1949) 504;
under James II 232, 234, 235;

Milner, John, Vicar Apostolic:
appointed as Vicar Apostolic of
the Midland District 323–4; on
Bible reading 341; on the
Catholic Committee 303; on
Irish emancipation 314, 318;
opposition to the Catholic Relief
Act 309–10, 326–9, 331–4,
342–3; and the *Orthodox
Journal* 339–40; at Oscott
College 330; on readmission
of Jesuits into England 335
Minchew, Donald (priest) 554
Minto, Gilbert Elliot, 2nd Earl
365–6, 376
missionary priests, sent to England
from Rome 135–9
Mitford, Nancy 527
Mitford, Sir John 309, 310
Mivart, St George Jackson 464
Modernists Movement 515
Molyneux family 257
monasteries: closures of 22, 36–8,
40; corruption and criticism of
34–5
Monck, General 212
Monmouth, James Scott, 1st Duke
of 223; rebellion (1685) 231
Monmouth, Wales 202
Monophysitism 388
Montague, Lady 192
Montague family 257
Monteagle, William Parker, 4th
Baron 176
Monteith, Robert 422
Monteith family 424
Montgomery, George (priest) 370
Month, The (periodical) 472
Montini, Giovanni Battista, Cardinal
see Paul VI, Pope
Moore, Tom 279, 342
Moorfields, and the Gordon Riots
294–5
Moran, Peter, Bishop of Aberdeen
566

More, Thomas: arrest, death and
posthumous reputation 27–30;
and the *Assertio Septem
Sacramentourm* 7; criticism of
the clergy 35; definition of
Catholicism 70; denounces
Martin Luther 8, 25;
enthusiasm for book burning
and executions 10, 25–7; and
the 'Maid of Kent' 21, 24;
resigns as Chancellor 20; on the
state of Catholicism in England
85; *Utopia* 26
Morley, John 398
Morrice, Richard 220
Morton, John, Cardinal 32
mortuary charges 34
Moseley Hall, Worcestershire 208
Mount, Ferdinand 557
Mount St Bernard Cistercian
Abbey 352
Murdoch, John (priest) 418–19,
421, 424, 425
Murphy-O'Connor, Cormac,
Cardinal Archbishop of
Westminster 540, 545–6, 548,
556, 557, 565, 566
Murray, John Courtney (SJ) 523
Mussolini, Benito 515

Nantes, Edict of 228
Napoleon Bonaparte 326, 335, 336
Napoleonic Wars 325, 334, 350
Nash, Thomas 164
National Catholic Safeguarding
Committee 543, 552
National Child Protection
Unit 547
National Conference of Priests 549
National Heresy Commission
(1557) 119
National Pastoral Congress 528
Neale, Richard, Bishop of Durham
190
Neal-Lomas, J 411

Pole, Cardinal Reginald: created
Cardinal by Pope Paul III
45–6; criticism of the clergy
35–6, 541; *De Unitate* 65–6, 71;
death 120; emissary to Paris for
the King's cause 15–16; on the
English Reformation 12;
equivocation of 71; favourite to
replace Paul III as Pope 89–90;
on justification by faith 80;
made Archbishop of Canterbury
(1556) 116; and the Pilgrimage of
Grace 50–1, 52; and the
'reconversion' of England
108–17; on the state of
Catholicism in England 85
Pole, Margaret *see* Salisbury,
Margaret Pole, Countess of
Polish immigrants, and the Catholic
Church in England and Scotland
563–8
Polycarp 107
Ponet, John, Bishop of Winchester 97
Ponsonby, George 328
Pontefract Castle 47, 48, 52, 54
Popery Act (1700) 271
Popham, John 156
Popish Plot (1678) 217–18, 220,
222, 231, 232
Popish Recusancy Act (1605) 176
population: of Catholics in England
(17th century) 173, 210, 225–6;
(18th century) 272, 277; (19th
century) 329, 338–9, 369, 408,
416; (20th century) 471, 534,
567–8; of Catholics in Northern
Ireland (20th century) 504; of
Catholics in Scotland (17th
century) 246; (18th century)
276–7; (19th century) 418–20;
(20th century) 567–8
Porter, Endymion 194
Porteus, Beilby, Bishop of London 326
Portland, Richard Weston, 1st Earl
of 194

Portland, William Cavendish, 3rd
Duke of 312
Postgate, Nicholas (priest) 219–20
Potter, Joseph 356
Poulson family 252
Poynings Law 248
Poynter, William 329, 331–2, 334–6,
337, 340, 340–1, 342
Praemunire *see* Act of Praemunire
(1534)
Prance, Miles 217
Prayer Book *see* Book of Common
Prayer
Prayer Book riots 88
Pre-Raphaelites 471
Presbyterians 182, 206, 212, 247,
267, 269, 505
Prest, Agnes 105
Preston, Battle of (1715) 255, 321
Preston, Lancashire 267, 278, 362
Prichard, Matthew (priest) 304
priest-holes 145, 208
Priestley, J. B. 483
priests *see* clergy
Prior Park, Bath 349, 350, 366
Profitable and Necessarye Doctryne,
A (1554) 118
Promissory Oaths Act 503
Propaganda Fide: and the English
Oratories 429; forbid
cooperation with Protestant
universities in Ireland 400; and
the governance of the Church in
England 353, 355; and John
Henry Newman 394, 436, 442,
449; and mixed marriages 193;
and the Oblates at St Edmund's
432, 433; and Pugin's designs
361; and the restoration of the
Hierarchy 364, 366–8; and
Scottish Catholicism 194, 198–9,
247, 263, 268–9, 420
Protestant Association (Irish) 344
Protestant Association (Scotland)
285–90, 292, 296, 297, 301

penguin.co.uk/vintage